The Reinterpretation of
American History and Culture

The Reinterpretation of American History and Culture

William H. Cartwright and Richard L. Watson, Jr.
Editors

NATIONAL COUNCIL FOR THE SOCIAL STUDIES

A National Affiliate of the National Education Association

1201 Sixteenth Street, N.W.   Washington, D. C. 20036

Price $8.50

NATIONAL COUNCIL FOR THE SOCIAL STUDIES

Officers for 1973

The National Council for the Social Studies is a National Affiliate of the National Education Association of the United States. It is the professional organization of educators at all levels—elementary, secondary, college, and university—who are interested in the teaching of social studies. Membership in the National Council for the Social Studies includes a subscription to the Council's official journal, *Social Education,* and a copy of the Yearbook. In addition, the Council publishes bulletins, curriculum studies, pamphlets, and other materials of practical use for teachers of the social studies. Membership dues are $15.00 a year. Applications for membership and orders for the purchase of publications should be sent to the Executive Secretary, 1201 Sixteenth Street, N.W., Washington, D.C. 20036.

Acknowledgments

The editors are indebted to many people who have cooperated in the production of this book. We are particularly grateful to the authors, all with many other commitments, who have, without remuneration, contributed the chapters. It is remarkable that twenty-five authors, representing eighteen institutions, completed difficult assignments involving bibliography and interpretation within less than two years after accepting the invitation to participate in the project. The biographical section gives a brief academic sketch of each author, but does not try to include the numerous fellowships and other forms of recognition which the authors have been accorded.

Eric Smith, a graduate assistant in the Department of Education, and his wife, Asta, painstakingly checked and assisted in standardizing the hundreds of footnotes. The editorial work was carried out with the help of a grant from the Research Council of Duke University. Daniel Roselle and Willadene Price, of the editorial staff of the National Council for the Social Studies, put the volume through the final stages before publication. We also appreciate the constructive suggestions made by the members of the Publications Board of the National Council.

Although it has been a cooperative project in the fullest sense of the term, the editors must take full responsibility for errors in editorial judgment.

WILLIAM H. CARTWRIGHT AND RICHARD L. WATSON, JR., *Editors*

Foreword

Edward H. Carr has written that history is "a continuous process of interaction between the historian and his facts, an unending dialogue between the present and the past." Modern social studies educators might well contemplate and apply to the present Carr's further statement that: "I hope I am sufficiently up-to-date to recognize that anything written in the 1890's must be nonsense. But I am not yet advanced enough to be committed to the view that anything written in the 1950's necessarily makes sense."

Certainly the best history is that which is interpretative, and history does not need to be mere description, narration, or exposition. In fact, historians have always recognized that their chief purpose has been to interpret the past to their own generation. This is why each generation writes its own history anew. The past must be used to serve the present. Just as the progressive role of the Supreme Court has been to interpret the Constitution to fit the changing conditions of modern times, so can history relate the past to future hopes.

This is the role that history has to play in a contemporary social issues social studies program. Every modern problem has its roots, and history provides the necessary perspective. As has often been said, it is difficult to know where we are without some understanding of how we got there and where we have been. A knowledge of history can also alert one to the logically weak and sometimes dangerous use of historical analogies.

Many understandings related to contemporary society require more than quantitative analysis (although historians today are making use of empirical studies, including psychology and psychiatry), since they deal with man, his motives, his capacity to change, and even the part played by historical accident. The point is often missed that there are various levels of generalizations and that while some may be less definitive than others, they can, nevertheless, provide the student with some meaningful insights.

Alan Griffin, one of the architects of the "new" social studies, often used illustrations from history to put the student in an intellectual jam and to stimulate reflective thinking. Thus, he not only developed a very useful teaching strategy, but the generalizations which finally emerged were those that had a universal application.

Since historical scholarship is continually arriving at new conclusions and since each generation is rewriting history in the light of current emphases, it is necessary to take stock periodically of areas of agreement and disagreement and to be aware of the discoveries of new historical knowledge. Thus, for example, there have been significant new changes in interpretation related to the colonial period, the American Revolution and the Constitution that are the result of meticulous scholarship. Again, the pendulum of revision has swung back and forth in several areas since the end of World War II. In the late forties and fifties the views of the neo-revisionist consensus historians were prominent. Under the impact of the great social upheavals of the sixties their conclusions are being rewritten and more history is being written from the bottom up. Thus, the influence of the Civil Rights movement has taken a more positive view of the work of Radical Reconstruction and the leaders of this period are given credit for the Fourteenth Amendment, which stands as the basis for much of our current struggle for equality.

It might seem that to present to students changing historical interpretations might only confuse them and cause them to lose faith. On the contrary, such teaching of history would probably be the most effective way to learn. By studying various sources and divergent conclusions the student can come to understand that most great issues are complex and that there are no simple causes or solutions.

Furthermore, in many classes the old legends persist. There is often a considerable gap between the most recent historical scholarship and what is found in textbooks and in the classroom. The classical example of a piece of historical research which took years to change the textbooks was that published by A. H. Lybyer in 1914 entitled "The Influence of the Rise of the Ottoman Turks upon the Roots of Oriental Trade." He showed that Italian trade with the Orient did not decrease following the fall of Constantinople in 1453 but only after 1500 when the Portuguese had established an all-water route to the East. Despite Lybyer's conclusion, the old story—that Columbus had sailed west because the Turks had captured Constantinople and had cut off the trade routes—was still to be found in some textbooks and in the thinking of many teachers and students fifty years later. Many more significant illustrations could be given of the need for historical accuracy and the importance for teachers to keep abreast of historical scholarship.

It is for the reasons noted above that the National Council for the Social Studies has periodically issued significant volumes designed primarily to reinterpret United States history. The 17th Yearbook, published in 1946 and edited by Richard E. Thursfield, was entitled *The Study and Teaching of American History*. This was followed by the 31st Yearbook in 1961, *Interpreting and Teaching American History,* co-edited by William H. Cartwright and Richard L. Watson, Jr. The same editors have cooperated again in making this current volume possible. In both the 1961 and the 1973 books the editors have been successful in bringing together a group of distinguished historians to write the various chapters. This latest study not only has chapters dealing with the various periods of American history, but it has added chapters on ethnic and minority groups and on such topics as urban history, war, and intellectual history. Any teacher of the social studies should find the substantive content and the extensive bibliographies provided by the authors to be extremely useful. The National Council for the Social Studies is once again indebted to William H. Cartwright and Richard L. Watson, Jr. and is grateful to the professional historians for their significant contributions.

HARRIS L. DANTE, *President*
National Council for the Social Studies

The Authors

WILLIAM W. ABBOT. A.B., University of Georgia, 1943; M.A. and Ph.D., Duke University, 1949 and 1953. He has taught at the College of William and Mary, Northwestern University, and Rice University. He has been on the faculty at the University of Virginia since 1966 and is presently Chairman of the Corcoran Department of History. He served as editor of the *Journal of Southern History* from 1961 to 1963 and of the *William and Mary Quarterly* from 1963 to 1966. His publications include *The Royal Governors of Georgia, 1754-1777*. Chapel Hill: University of North Carolina Press, 1959.

RODOLFO ACUÑA. He received the Ph.D. degree from the University of Southern California in 1968. He began teaching in the late 1950's and has taught in junior and senior high schools, in adult education courses, as well as on the university level. Convinced of the ignorance in regard to the Mexican experience in the United States, he helped found the Chicano Studies department at San Fernando Valley State College (now California State University, Northridge) in 1969. Among his publications are *The Story of the Mexican Americans: The Men and the Land*. New York: The American Book Company, 1969; *Cultures in Conflict*. Anaheim, Calif.: Charter Text Books, 1970; *A Mexican American Chronicle*, 1971; *Occupied America: The Chicano Struggle Toward Liberation*. New York: Harper & Row, 1972; *Sonoran Caudillo —Ignacio Pesqueira*. Tucson: University of Arizona Press, 1973.

ROBERT F. BERKHOFER, JR. B.A., New York State Teachers College, Albany; M.A. and Ph.D., Cornell University, 1955 and 1960. He has taught at Ohio State University, the University of Minnesota, Minneapolis, the University of Wisconsin, Madison, and, since 1973, at the University of Michigan. He participated in the "Project Social Studies" at the University of Minnesota. His publications include *Salvation and the Savage: An Analysis of Protestant Missions and American Indian Response, 1787-1862*. Lexington: University of Kentucky Press, 1965; *A Behavioral Approach to Historical Analysis*. New York: Free Press,

1969; and he edited *The American Revolution: The Critical Issues.* Boston: Little, Brown and Company, 1971.

JOHN W. BLASSINGAME. B.A., Fort Valley (Ga.) State College, 1960; M.A., Howard University, 1961; M.Phil., and Ph.D., Yale University, 1968 and 1971. He has taught at Howard University, and was assistant editor of the Booker T. Washington Papers and Lecturer, University of Maryland, 1968-1969. He has been on the faculty at Yale since 1970 and served as acting chairman of Afro-American Studies there in 1971-1972. His publications include *The Slave Community: Plantation Life in the Antebellum South.* New York: Oxford University Press, 1972, and *Black New Orleans, 1860-1880.* Chicago: University of Chicago Press, 1973.

WILLIAM H. CARTWRIGHT. B.S., M.A., and Ph.D., University of Minnesota, 1937, 1942, and 1950. He has taught in the public schools of Minnesota, at Boston University, and, since 1951, at Duke University where he was chairman of the Department of Education from 1961 to 1965 and from 1967 to 1970. He served as president of the National Council for the Social Studies in 1957. His publications include (with Edgar B. Wesley) *Teaching Social Studies in Elementary Schools.* Boston: D. C. Heath, 3rd ed., 1968, and *Interpreting and Teaching American History* (edited with Richard L. Watson, Jr.). 31st Yearbook of the National Council for the Social Studies: Washington, D.C.: NCSS, 1961.

PAUL K. CONKIN. B.A., Milligan College (Tennessee), 1951; M.A. and Ph.D., Vanderbilt University, 1953 and 1957. He has taught at the University of Southwestern Louisiana, and the University of Maryland, and has been on the faculty at the University of Wisconsin since 1967. His publications include *Tomorrow a New World: The New Deal Community Program.* Ithaca: Cornell University Press, 1959, and *Puritans and Pragmatists; Eight Eminent American Thinkers.* New York: Dodd, Mead, 1968.

ROGER DANIELS. B. A., University of Houston, 1957; M.A. and Ph.D., University of California, Los Angeles, 1958 and 1961. He has taught at Wisconsin State University at Platteville, UCLA, and the University of Wyoming. He is currently chairman of the Department of History, State University of New York College at Fredonia. He is an elected member of the Executive Board, Organization of American Historians. His publications include *The Politics of Prejudice; The Anti-Japanese Movement in California and the Struggle for Japanese Exclusion.* Berkeley: University of California Press, 1962, and *Concentration Camps, USA: Japanese Americans and World War II.* New York: Holt, Rinehart and Winston, 1971.

ROBERT F. DURDEN. B.A. and M.A., Emory University, 1947 and 1948; M.A. and Ph.D., Princeton University, 1950 and 1952. He has taught at Duke University since 1952 and occupied the James Pinckney Harrison Chair at the College of William and Mary in 1970-71. His publications include *James Shepherd Pike: Republicanism and the American Negro, 1850-1882.* Durham: Duke University Press, 1957; *The Climax of Populism: The Election of 1896.* Lexington: University of Kentucky Press, 1965; and *The Gray and the Black: the Confederate Debate on Emancipation.* Baton Rouge: Louisiana State University Press, 1972.

ROBERT H. FERRELL. B.S. in Ed. and B.A., Bowling Green State University, 1946 and 1947; M.A. and Ph.D., Yale University, 1948 and 1951; LL.D., Bowling Green, 1971. He has taught at Michigan State University, at Yale University, and, since 1953, at Indiana University. His publications include *Peace in Their Time: The Origins of the Kellogg-Briand Pact.* New Haven: Yale University Press, 1952; *American Diplomacy in the Great Depression: Hoover-Stimson Foreign Policy, 1929-1933.* New Haven: Yale University Press, 1957; *The American Secretaries of State and Their Diplomacy,* Vol. XI, *Frank B. Kellogg and Henry L. Stimson.* New York: Cooper Square Publishers, 1963; *The Teaching of American History in High Schools* (with Maurice G. Baxter and John E. Wiltz). Bloomington: Indiana University Press, 1964.

FRANK OTTO GATELL. B.A., The College of the City of New York, 1956; M.A. and Ph.D., Harvard University, 1958 and 1960. He has taught at the University of Maryland, Stanford University, several Latin American universities, and, since 1965, at the University of California, Los Angeles. His publications include *John Gorham Palfrey and the New England Conscience.* Cambridge: Harvard University Press, 1963, and *Democracy and Union; the United States, 1815-1877.* New York: Holt, Rinehart and Winston, 1972 (with Paul Goodman). He is co-editor with Allen Weinstein of *American Negro Slavery: a Modern Reader.* New York: Oxford University Press, 2nd edition, 1973.

OTIS L. GRAHAM, JR. B.A., Yale University, 1957; M.A. and Ph.D., Columbia University, 1961 and 1966. He has taught at Mount Vernon College, California State College at Hayward, and, since 1966, at the University of California, Santa Barbara. His publications include *An Encore for Reform: The Old Progressives and the New Deal.* New York: Oxford, 1967; *The Great Campaigns: Reform and War in America, 1900-1928.* Englewood Cliffs, N.J.: Prentice-Hall, 1971; and (as editor) *The New Deal; The Critical Issues.* Boston: Little, Brown, 1971.

JACK P. GREENE. B.A., University of North Carolina, Chapel Hill, 1951; M.A., Indiana University, 1952; Fulbright Fellow, University of Bristol, 1953-54; Ph.D., Duke University, 1956. He has taught at Michigan State University, Western Reserve University, University of Michigan, and, since 1966, at The Johns Hopkins University. His publications include *The Quest for Power; the Lower Houses of Assembly in the Southern Royal Colonies, 1689-1776.* Chapel Hill: University of North Carolina Press, 1963, and *The Reappraisal of the American Revolution in Recent Historical Writing.* Washington, D.C.: Service Center for Teachers of History of the American Historical Association, 1967.

ROBERT W. JOHANNSEN. B.A., Reed College, 1948; M.A. and Ph.D., University of Washington, 1949 and 1953. He has taught at the University of Washington, at the University of Kansas, and, since 1959, at the University of Illinois, where he was chairman of the Department of History from 1963 to 1967. His publications include *Frontier Politics and the Sectional Conflict; The Pacific Northwest on the Eve of the Civil War.* Seattle: University of Washington Press, 1955; *The Lincoln-Douglas Debates of 1858* (which he edited). New York: Oxford University Press, 1965; and *Stephen A. Douglas.* New York: Oxford University Press, 1973.

RICHARD S. KIRKENDALL. B.A., Gonzaga University, 1950; M.S. and Ph.D., University of Wisconsin, 1953 and 1958. He has taught at Wesleyan University and, from 1958 to 1973, at the University of Missouri, Columbia, where he served a term as chairman of the Department of History from 1968 to 1971. He is now professor of history at Indiana University and executive secretary of the Organization of American Historians. His publications include *Social Scientists and Farm Politics in the Age of Roosevelt.* Columbia: University of Missouri Press, 1966; *The Truman Period as a Research Field.* Columbia: University of Missouri Press, 1967; and *The Global Power: The United States Since 1941.* Boston: Allyn and Bacon, 1973.

SHAW LIVERMORE, JR. B.A., Harvard College, 1948; M.S. and Ph.D., University of Wisconsin, 1951 and 1959. He has taught at Princeton University and, since 1964, at the University of Michigan. His publications include *The Twilight of Federalism*. Princeton: Princeton University Press, 1962.

RAYMOND A. MOHL. B.A., Hamilton College, 1961; M.A.T., Yale University, 1962; M.A. and Ph.D., New York University, 1965 and 1967. He has taught at Valhalla High School, New York, at New York University, at Indiana University Northwest, and, since 1970, at Florida Atlantic University. His publications include *Poverty in New York, 1783-1825*. New York: Oxford University Press, 1971; *Urban America in Historical Perspective* (co-edited with Neil Betten). Weybright and Talley, 1970; and *The Urban Experience* (co-authored with James F. Richardson). California: Wadsworth, 1973.

J. CARROLL MOODY. B.S., University of Corpus Christi, 1956; M.S., Texas A & I University, 1960; Ph.D., University of Oklahoma, 1965. He has taught in the public schools of Corpus Christi in Texas, at the University of Toledo, and, since 1968, at Northern Illinois University. His publications include *The Credit Union Movement: Origins and Development, 1850-1970* (with Gilbert Fite). Lincoln: University of Nebraska Press, 1971.

BURL NOGGLE. B.A., M.A., Ph.D., Duke University, 1950, 1952, 1956. He has taught at New Mexico State University and, since 1960, at Louisiana State University. His publications include *Teapot Dome: Oil and Politics in the 1920's*. Baton Rouge: Louisiana State University Press, 1962, and "The Twenties: A New Historiographical Frontier." *Journal of American History*. LIII, Sept. 1966, No. 2.

WALTER T. K. NUGENT. B.A., St. Benedict's College, 1954; M.A., Georgetown University, 1956; Ph.D., University of Chicago, 1961; D. Litt., St. Benedict's College, 1968. He has taught at Washburn University, at Kansas State University, and, since 1963, at Indiana University. His publications include *The Tolerant Populists: Kansas Populism and Nativism,* Chicago: University of Chicago Press, 1963; *Creative History; An Introduction to Historical Study*. Philadelphia: Lippincott, 1967; *Money and American Society 1865-1880*. New York: The Free Press, 1968; and *Modern America*. Boston: Houghton Mifflin Company, 1973.

THEODORE ROPP. B.A., Oberlin College, 1934; M.A. and Ph.D., Harvard University, 1935 and 1937. He has taught at Harvard University and, since 1938, at Duke University. He has served as the Ernest J. King professor at the Naval War College, and professor, U. S. Army Military Research Collection at Carlisle Barracks, Pennsylvania. His publications include *War in the Modern World*. Durham, N. C.: Duke University Press, rev. ed., 1962, and "Continental Doctrines of Sea Power," Ch. XVIII in Edward Mead Earle, ed. *Makers of Modern Strategy; Military Thought from Machiavelli to Hitler*. Princeton: Princeton University Press, 1943.

EDWARD N. SAVETH. B.S.S., The College of the City of New York, 1935; M.A. and Ph.D., Columbia University, 1937 and 1948. He has taught at New Mexico Highlands University, the New School for Social Research, Texas Lutheran College, Dartmouth College, Kyoto University, and, since 1968, has been Distinguished Professor at the State University of New York College at Fredonia. His publications include *American Historians and European Immigrants, 1875-1925*. New York: Columbia University Press, 1948; *Understanding the American Past: American History and Its Interpretation* (editor). Boston: Little, Brown, 1954; and *American History and the Social Sciences* (editor). New York: Free Press of Glencoe, 1964.

ANNE FIROR SCOTT. B.A., University of Georgia, 1941; M.A., Northwestern University, 1944; Ph.D., Radcliffe University, 1958. She has taught at Haverford College, at the University of North Carolina at Chapel Hill, and, since 1961, at Duke University. She served as chairman of the North Carolina Governor's Commission on the Status of Women in 1964 and was a member of the President's Advisory Council on the Status of Women (appointed by President Johnson, June, 1965). Her publications include *The Southern Lady: From Pedestal to Politics, 1830-1930*. Chicago: University of Chicago Press, 1970; *Women in American Life: Selected Readings*. Boston: Houghton Mifflin, 1970; and *The American Woman: Who Was She?* Prentice-Hall, 1970.

DANIEL M. SMITH. B.A., M.A., and Ph.D., University of California, Berkeley, 1949, 1950, 1954. He has taught at Stanford University and, since 1957, at the University of Colorado, where he has also been chairman of the department of history since 1969. His publications include *Robert Lansing and American Neutrality, 1914-1917*. Berkeley: University of California Press, 1958; *The Great Departure; The United States and World War I, 1914-1920.* New York: John Wiley and Sons, 1965; and *The American Diplomatic Experience.* Boston: Houghton Mifflin, 1972.

GADDIS SMITH. B.A., M.A., Ph.D., Yale University, 1954, 1958, 1961. He has taught at Duke University and, since 1961, at Yale University. His publications include *American Diplomacy During the Second World War, 1941-1945.* New York: Wiley, 1965, and Dean Acheson. New York: Cooper Square, 1972.

RUDOLPH J. VECOLI. B.A., University of Connecticut, 1950; M.A., University of Pennsylvania, 1951; Ph.D., University of Wisconsin, 1963. He was Foreign Affairs Officer, Department of State, 1951-1954, and has taught at Ohio State University, Pennsylvania State University, Rutgers University, and the University of Illinois. He has been Professor and Director of the Center for Immigration Studies at the University of Minnesota since 1967. His publications include *The People of New Jersey.* Princeton, N.J.: D. Van Nostrand, 1965, and "Ethnicity: A Neglected Dimension of American History," in Herbert J. Bass, ed. *The State of American History.* Chicago: Quadrangle, 1970.

RICHARD L. WATSON, JR. B.A., and Ph.D., Yale University, 1935 and 1939. He taught at the University of Sydney in 1971 and has been on the faculty at Duke University since 1939. His publications include *Bishop Cannon's Own Story,* edited with introduction. Durham: Duke University Press, 1955, and *Interpreting and Teaching American History* (edited with William H. Cartwright). 31st Yearbook, National Council for the Social Studies. Washington, D.C.: NCSS, 1961.

ROBERT H. WIEBE. B.A., Carleton College, 1951; Ph.D., University of Rochester, 1957. He has taught at Michigan State University, at Columbia University, and, since 1960, at Northwestern University. His publications include *Businessmen and Reform: A Study of the Progressive Movement.* Cambridge: Harvard University Press, 1962, and *The Search for Order: 1877-1920.* New York: Hill and Wang, 1967.

Contents

PART ONE

The State of
American History

· Introduction ·

Historical Study
in a Changing Curriculum

William H. Cartwright and Richard L. Watson, Jr.

ANALYSIS of representative literature treating the social studies curriculum and of speeches delivered at conferences devoted to the social studies during the 1960's indicates that the study of history was being de-emphasized. Large proportions of the books, articles, and speeches relating to social studies dealt with the contemporary social sciences, with current problems and issues, with processes of contemporary inquiry, and with current value systems. Some pointed to history courses in the schools as an evil force that had perpetuated false and damaging mythology and prevented the learning of matters relevant to contemporary youth and society.[1]

Such developments were not necessarily bad. The contemporary social sciences have much to offer that is necessary to understanding our society and to developing ways of resolving its problems. Most learning will come about through inquiry; therefore the means of inquiry must be learned. And it is past time that the social studies could ignore values and value systems, gloss over either past or present evil, or confuse careful scholarship with neutrality about fundamental values. Both through commission and omission, school history has perpetuated myths, and too much of it has been irrelevant to matters of enduring value, which is a more serious charge than that it has been irrelevant to contemporary youth and society.

All these statements may be granted. And far more must be done to meet their implications for improving the social studies. But none of the criticisms justifies the removal of history from an important place in the curriculum. Too frequently critics have confused the misuse of something with the thing itself and called for the abolition of the substance as a remedy for its misuse. The error can be observed with regard to a host of things, including medicines, religion, government, and formal education as a whole. Further, and incongruously, the critics—even the critics of history—turn to history as their chief aid in sustaining their charges. Yet, such must be the case, for most of what we know or claim to know comes from a study of history.

Before we decide to dispense with history in the curriculum, we might well give serious consideration to the values that have been claimed for it through the generations during which it developed into what was deemed to be an essential school subject. For the most part, the historical profession did not assert itself with regard to these matters during the generation following World War II although both the American Historical Association and the Organization of American Historians established committees to improve the teaching of history in the schools. Under the aegis of these committees, conferences of historians and schoolteachers were held in many parts of the nation and scores of pamphlets were published to provide teachers with fresh interpretations and bibliographies. Beginning in 1969, the History Education Project of the American Historical Association organized teams of historians, social studies educators, and teachers, who worked with varying effectiveness with several school systems to develop materials and methods for the improvement of the teaching of history. However, unlike learned societies in the contemporary social sciences, neither of the historical societies sponsored major curriculum projects for the purpose of developing school programs in history that would have the support of the organized profession. On the contrary, although individual historians supplied many useful essays, addressed many meetings of teachers, and served as consultants to many curriculum projects, the organized historical profession seemed to assume that the values of historical study were well known and its place in the curriculum assured. Of all scholars, historians should have known that people tend to forget that of which they are not frequently reminded.

One of the most recent studies of American history in the curriculum to be sponsored by the organized profession was made in 1944 by the Committee on American History in Schools and Colleges.[2] The Committee reported the status of the subject, set forth a rationale for its study, related it to other subjects and activities both within and without the school, and recommended content for the curriculum. Of the purposes for studying American history, the Committee said,

> Laymen and educators are generally agreed that knowledge of our own history is essential in the making of Americans. The reasons for this belief may be summed up under four main heads. History makes loyal citizens because memories of common experiences and common aspira-

tions are essential ingredients in patriotism. History makes intelligent voters because sound decisions about present problems must be based on knowledge of the past. History makes good neighbors because it teaches tolerance of individual differences and appreciation of varied abilities and interests. History makes stable, well-rounded individuals because it gives them a start toward understanding the pattern of society and toward enjoying the artistic and intellectual productions of the past. It gives long views a perspective, a measure of what is permanent in a nation's life. To a people it is what memory is to the individual; and memory, expressed or unconscious, guides the acts of every sentient being.[3]

The Committee did not rest with these assertions. It said that while history is essential to achieving these purposes, many other subjects also contribute to them. It called for a broad approach to the study of history, emphasizing that all human activities are interrelated. It recognized that the purposes of history could be abused by twisting the data and condemned chauvinism in history teaching. It placed stress on interpretation as well as fact.

In the twentieth century a number of scholars have studied the history of the teaching of the social studies in the schools, and have been particularly interested in the purposes and values of history in the curriculum. Social studies entered the curriculum of American schools almost with the birth of the nation, as geography and history, with considerable attention to government. Economics, psychology, sociology, and anthropology had not yet emerged as subjects for formal study. During most of the national period, most writing on history as a school subject was strongly in its support. Three studies, by William F. Russell, Rolla M. Tryon, and Agnew O. Roorbach, dealt with pre-Civil War conceptions of the purposes of history teaching.

In 1914, Russell wrote,

> In general, history came into the curriculum for the purpose of moral training, to provide for the leisure period, to give religious training, to inspire patriotism, to obviate international prejudice, to train for citizenship, and to provide discipline for the mind.[4]

Twenty years later, Tryon listed the same purposes except that he omitted the obviation of international prejudice.[5] Russell's sole source for asserting that this had been an early purpose was one textbook on the history of New York. Roorbach, writing in 1936, reiterated the same six purposes and added two others, "to prepare for more extensive reading" and "to equip with practical knowledge."[6]

In 1949 and 1950, William H. Cartwright discussed twelve purposes that had been claimed for American history as a subject of instruction in the previous two hundred years. The research was based on analyses of hundreds of textbooks and on the writings of scores of persons concerned with the teaching of history. He classified the purposes into three categories. The first category included five purposes that were set forth very early and had endured. They were to inspire patriotism, to train for citizenship, to develop moral standards, to train for the use of leisure time, and to broaden the cultural background. Two purposes were claimed earlier, but did not endure in public education. One of these was the training of the mind, which disappeared early in the twentieth century as the theory of mental discipline fell into disrepute. The other was religious training, which has continued in sectarian schools. Four purposes were set forth later than the others. These were the achievement of international understanding, the elimination of prejudice, the attainment of certain intellectual skills, and the understanding of society.[7]

In 1969, Richard S. Craddock reported the views of American professional historians on the purposes and values of historical study based on a massive study of writings published since 1880. He grouped the many values which he identified into several categories which included development of citizenship and patriotism, preparation for life, development of historical method and perspective, a guide to action, and development of better persons.[8] He found that the purposes and values asserted by the professional historians included all those asserted also by persons primarily concerned with the teaching of history and other social studies.

Such are the values and purposes that have been ascribed to the study of history in the United States. It may be argued against them that they are unworthy or that they may be achieved better through some means other than history. Let us look at them from these points of view.

Certainly wise use of leisure time and broadening the cultural background are worthy purposes. The study of history can contribute much toward the achievement of both, but it is no more essential for these purposes than are many other activities. One need know nothing of the history of art, music, horticulture, or sports to enjoy passive or active participation in them. Yet the testimony of those who have some knowledge of their history is that such knowledge often brings greater appreciation. Many a boy who is thought by his teacher to be a poor student of history prides himself on being able to identify athletic record-holders. And both history as a body of knowledge and history as method are necessary to sound interpretation of much that comes to us via the communications media and the fields of popular entertainment.

History can be and has been misused, both to teach moral standards and behavior for which there is only a local or provincial standard and to teach that evil people are always punished and good people always rewarded. Careful study of history will not support either purpose. History is not the best vehicle for teaching what are commonly thought of as standards of conduct. Mythology is probably more effective. And yet history can help. In thoughtful study of history, as Henry Johnson said,

> Man will be seen at the lowest and worst, as he is already seen in any serious study of history. The reaction to that, if healthy, may, as the eighteenth century so firmly believed, be intense hatred of the lowest and worst and a stimulus to conduct more becoming to the dignity of human nature. Man will also be seen at his best and highest. There will be examples of heroism, of patience under suffering, of loving service, of eloquence moving men to better things, of passionate pursuit of the good, the beautiful and the true, moments which, if properly presented, will make children at any stage of school instruction feel that they are standing on holy ground. Experience has shown that emotional appeals of any kind, instead of being minified, are greatly enhanced by a sense of historical trueness.[9]

These sentiments should meet with a sympathetic reception from those designers of curriculum who emphasize consideration of values and those who are popularizing the term "the affective domain."

History has been misused to inspire a blind patriotism, even a vicious chauvinism. It has been misused to lead the adherents of national, ethnic, racial, and religious groups to believe that they were the best, and others the worst, of their kind. Thus history has been Americanized, Germanized, Italianized, Japanized, Chinaized, Sovietized, Celticized, Nordicized, Caucasianized, Africanized, Judaized, Christianized, Moslemized, Catholicized, and Protestantized. Mere persons, not all of them good, have been made into heroes and demi-gods. But the fact that loyalty has been perverted does not justify the condemnation of loyalty itself. Nor does the fact that history has been perverted to help develop a vicious loyalty justify the condemnation of history itself.

Enlightened loyalty is an honorable trait. Loyalty is necessary to the survival of any cultural institution or group, be it family, nation, religion, or the totality of humankind. And history is essential to the development of loyalty. One cannot conceive of any organized group of people enduring long without knowledge of a common past. Such knowledge is one of the strongest bonds of social cohesion.

We can recognize the essential unity of humanity, and we can strive toward a history that will contribute to general recognition of that unity.

But even if that history and that general recognition are achieved, group loyalties will continue to exist and will seem desirable. In our own country, both social studies educators and society as a whole have discarded the idea of the "melting pot" and strive to keep alive the identity and pride of the various groups of which the country is comprised. And those groups, Irish and Italian, Afro-American and Chicano, insist that their part in history must be taught and recognized in order for that identity and that pride to exist. The kind of patriotism advocated by most twentieth-century historians and teachers was an *enlightened* patriotism faithful to the *best* traditions of a people. Indeed, international and intercultural understanding have become major purposes of history. Such understanding cannot be brought about without history. The study of history can support both group loyalty and human unity. Some members of various groups will continue to pervert history in the interest of misguided loyalty, but we can strive toward an ideal history. And we can try to make local, state, parochial, ethnic, and national history parts of that ideal history rather than subversive of it.

Citizenship is closely related to loyalty and is subject to similar perversions. It can, and sometimes has, come to mean a blind subservience to the will of the state. And, as has been demonstrated in totalitarian societies, history can be perverted to help bring about such a condition. But that kind of citizenship and that perverted history are not in the best traditions of an enlightened society. Thomas Jefferson, in explaining the statute that he proposed in 1781 and 1782 for establishing public education in Virginia, said,

> But of the views of this law none is more important, none more legitimate, than that of rendering the people the safe, as they are the ultimate, guardians of their own liberty. For this purpose the reading in the first stage, where *they* will receive their whole education, is proposed, as has been said, to be chiefly historical. History by apprising them of the past will enable them to judge of the future; it will avail them of the experience of other times and other nations; it will qualify them as judges of the actions and designs of men; it will enable them to know ambition under every disguise it may assume; and knowing it, to defeat its views.[10]

In our best tradition we want citizens to make up their own minds on issues on the basis of the best information available, to take action and join with others in action designed to bring about the best situations possible and to defend their own rights and those of others. History is not sufficient for the task of developing such citizens, but history is essential to that task. If, as is reported, a large proportion of our population would support action subversive of the Bill of Rights and oppose action supportive of it, a major reason may well be that they did not learn enough history well enough to appreciate the struggles against tyranny that brought that Bill into existence, that brought about its subsequent extension, and that are and ought to be going on for its further extension.

International and intercultural understanding have been alluded to as being among the purposes of history. History is not sufficient for achieving these purposes, but it is essential to them. One cannot understand peoples of other nations and other cultures without some knowledge of their history. He cannot understand them well unless he knows much of their history. These statements are part of the larger generalization that knowledge of history is necessary to an understanding of society.

No social institution, development, or event can be understood without consideration of history. The crises of the Middle East have little meaning unless long-standing associations and values of Arabs, Jews, and great powers are comprehended. The problems of minority groups are not likely to be solved without serious attention to the long history of the oppression of subject peoples by dominant ones.

History offers a means of studying peoples and persons. Through it, the student should see people at work on matters of universal and enduring importance in different times and settings. Thus, he should come to a sympathetic understanding of peoples different from his own and persons different from him. And he should gain an appreciation of the essential unity of humankind.

In its capacity to sift out of the mass of knowledge those elements which have enduring value, history has unique importance in the social studies. In times of troubles, the concept of stability that can come only from history is especially important. The knowledge that people in other times and places have endured similar trials should help establish a sense of stability. As the Committee on American History said, history is for a society like memory for a person, and without it stability cannot be achieved.

If a sense of stability and of continuity is necessary to an understanding of society, a sense of change and of development is also essential. And that sense cannot come except through the study of history. "Education for a Changing World" has long been a slogan of progressive educators. Since the study of such a topic requires the historical approach, it is almost incredible that the slogan has been employed in advocacy of lessening the attention given to history as a school subject. The content of history is the story of change. The substance of history is social development. Properly taught or learned, history tries to tell how things were becoming more than how things were. This feature is unique to history. To the extent that any other subject presents social development in an organized fashion, that subject becomes history. If the concept of social development were the only contribution that history had to offer, the study of history would be justified as being necessary for anyone seeking to understand society.

There remains for consideration as a purpose of history the development of certain intellectual skills. This purpose is shared with many other subjects, but the historical method has much to offer. It is used by scholars in other disciplines, but it was first systematized by historians. It has been employed in an unsystematic way since the beginning of time. The word "history" comes from the Greek word meaning "inquiry." Insofar as anyone makes thoughtful decisions about social issues, it is the historical method he uses, whether or not he is conscious of it. But, unless it is employed consciously, the resultant decisions are not likely to be as sound as would otherwise be the case.

The historical method requires that the available evidence be gathered. It requires a determination as to whether the evidence is what it is claimed to be. If evidence is spurious, it must be rejected. If it is authentic, many tests must be applied to it. If it is an original source, what meaning may be derived from it? How does that meaning hold up when compared with that derived from other original sources? If it consists of firsthand observation, was the observer in a position to know what he observed? Was he in a position to understand and interpret what he observed? How do his observations hold up when compared with those of others and with available original evidence? If the evidence consists of opinions and interpretations of those removed from the scene, what is the degree of their expertness? What purpose did they have in making their study and interpretations? What were their biases and fundamental assumptions? To what extent were they influenced by the biases and fundamental assumptions of the time and place in which they did their study? What generalizations and inferences can be arrived at from these kinds of considerations of the evidence? What meaning can be derived for the time and place from which the evidence comes, for us here and now, for the future?

It is a joy to watch classes in which students are engaged in these kinds of activities. (These classes may well show that one of the purposes of studying history can be pure enjoyment.) Such classes, however, are all too few. When they are found, it usually does not take much investigation to discover that the students' habits of demanding and criticizing evidence, of making and challenging interpretations, of deriving, agreeing, and disagreeing on meaning with regard to assertions of their peers, their teacher, and the media, are traceable to the purposeful and skillful instruction of a teacher, or of teachers, who brought them to realize the importance of these activities.

That too few teachers of history exploit the subject as method does not justify abolishing the subject any more than does the fact that too few teachers teach the substance of history as continuity and change. These conditions only require continued and intense efforts to improve the teaching of history. Perhaps the newly intensified emphasis placed on method by many of the current leaders and projects in the social studies will have the desired effects.

A cry of the critics of school history today is for relevance. And they seem to mean relevance to the present. A study of history would show that this cry is not new. Only the name changes. Henry Johnson, who devoted much study to the history of history teaching, said of the idea a generation ago,

> It was certainly an old idea in the fifth century B.C. when the Father of History discovered it, and he simply took it for granted. It was still old when Jacob Wimpheling wrote the first known textbook in history for schools, and he simply took it for granted. In this book, published in 1505, every page is plainly inspired by the present in which Wimpheling lived. . . . The idea began to be new when Christian Weise discovered it in 1676, became generally new in the eighteenth century, and since then has always been as new as it was to the Committee on Social Studies in 1916 and still is to its youngest discoverer. . . .
>
> How can any idea so old be regarded as new? An explanation is not far to seek. The conditions which educational reformers strive to meet are actually new. There is always an old education to attack. There is always a new education implying a break with the past, inviting us to begin at the beginning as if nothing had ever been begun before, and leaving an impression that any principle called into play by new conditions must be as new as the conditions themselves. With here and there an unnoticed exception, the second generation of history teachers, and their critics and advisers, thus forgot the first, the third generation forgot the second, and the process of forgetting continued down to the present.[11]

The present is important; we live in it. And much of a sound social studies program must be relevant to it. But whole curricula based on it have never worked and will not work. The present is fleeting, and any program based on it will also be fleeting. In fact any such program will be out of date before it can be put into operation. The "new" social studies promulgated by the critics of a decade ago are already under attack by younger critics who seek curricula relevant to a new present.

At the Annual Meeting of the American Historical Association in 1966, one of the editors of this volume presented a paper entitled, "Can History Maintain Its Place in the Curriculum?" His answer was that it could, but only if it was taught in such a way that it seemed significant to society and students. *The New York Times* reported the remarks on the obituary page.[12] The speaker did not mean to be announcing the death of history. A social studies program, to endure, must be relevant to enduring values. In such a program there will be an important place for history.

There are movements to de-emphasize history in the curriculum. They are finding some success, and a relative de-emphasis on history is necessary in order to make room for other social studies that are needed by individuals and society. In part, however, the de-emphasis is the fault of historians who have not come to a vigorous defense of their subject, of teachers who have not developed skills in relating the present to the past and both to the future, and new "new curriculum" makers who have fallen victim to a recurrence of presentism. But the values of history will be maintained by some and will be rediscovered by others. Enduring purposes that have been asserted for history cannot be achieved without it. Its fundamental subject matter of development is necessary to sound social thought. Its method is necessary to sound social action.

Reasons for New Interpretations

It has been twelve years since the publication of *Interpreting and Teaching American History,* the Thirty-First Yearbook of the National Council for the Social Studies. The fact that that volume was kept in print for more than a decade may indicate that many readers found a volume of interpretations of American history to be useful. But the Thirty-First Yearbook is out-of-date in several ways. It is in the nature of historical interpretations that they require frequent revision. Historical interpretations change in part because of the discovery of new evidence. They change also because social development continues, bringing new problems and shifts in the seeming relative importance of old ones. Further, interpretations change because of changes in the fundamental assumptions of historians and the society of which they are a part.

Social change in the United States was dramatic in the 1960's as its society was affected by a remarkable number of developments. These included spectacular refinements in the technology of communication, almost incredible exploration of space, the Vietnam War, struggles of minority groups against oppression and increasing recognition of them, the women's liberation movement, the population explosion, a continued shift of population to the cities with an accompanying intensification of urban problems, a startling growth of the drug problem, increasing fear of pollution of the environment, a dramatic increase in enrollments at institutions of higher learning, an increase in the relative numbers of the young and the aged, the youth movement, tremendous advances in knowledge of medicine and surgery accompanied by great increases in health costs, and continuing inflation along with high rates of unemployment.

Amid the welter of successes and failures, many people saw more decline than advance of the cause of humanity. As a consequence, many assumptions that had been held almost without question were challenged. Once nearly sacred social, political, and economic institutions were called into question.

Historians were not immune to these shifts in thought. On the contrary, they were often leaders in the movements. There had been revisionist historians in earlier generations, but they did not create so great a stir as those of the present generation are creating. The study and writing of history cannot remain unaffected by the course of events. David Potter put the situation well in the Thirty-First Yearbook. Having described the controversial nature of the literature on the background of the Civil War and having emphasized the disagreement among historians on "the interpretation of every link in the chain of sectional clashes which preceded the final crisis," he wrote,

> The irony of this disagreement lies in the fact that it persists in the face of vastly increased factual knowledge and constantly intensified scholarly research. The discrepancy, indeed, is great enough to make apparent a reality about history which is seldom so self-evident as it is here: namely that factual mastery of the data alone does not necessarily lead to agreement upon broad questions of historical truth. It certainly narrows the alternatives between which controversy continues to rage, and this narrowing of alternatives is itself an important proof of objective progress. But within the alternatives the determination of truth depends more perhaps upon basic fundamental assumptions which are applied in interpreting the data, than upon the data themselves. Data, in this sense, are but the raw materials for historical interpretations and not the determinants of the interpretive process.[13]

It often comes as a shock to beginning students of history and it too often comes as a shock to history teachers to discover the truth of Potter's statement. Yet, unless that truth is recognized, the study of history is woefully incomplete and its teaching is likely to be rank indoctrination. The essays in this volume should aid in this recognition.

It should be added that as one means of insuring that this volume would be more than a revision of the Thirty-First Yearbook, the editors turned to a completely different list of authors as contributors.

Only one author contributed to both volumes, and his contributions are on two fundamentally different topics. Only a very few of the historians who were invited to contribute declined, and their refusals without exception were regretfully made on the basis of previous scholarly commitments. Those who accepted did so in spite of heavy commitments and made their contribution without compensation.

Organization of the Volume

The editors hold to the value of a chronological organization as one that lends itself to disclosing continuity and change and to showing that people confront many problems at the same time. Accordingly, two-thirds of the chapters in this book are arranged chronologically.

Recognition of the values of the order of development does not preclude recognition of the tenor of the times in which history is written. It seemed especially important to recognize pressing current problems and developments in a volume written for teachers and designed to help them keep their teaching up-to-date. So much more history had been written since 1960 that the editors asked a distinguished American historian to introduce this work with a chapter on the historiography of the period. They also asked specialists in nine particular topics to contribute chapters on those topics. Those chapters should help teachers to learn about, to "brush up" on, to gain further leads to understanding the background of matters of current importance to Americans growing up in the 1970's.

The combining of topical and chronological chapters necessarily leads to overlapping among the chapters. For example, while a separate chapter is devoted to the history of women in American life, it is recognized that women contributed to social development in all periods, they participated in all cultural groups, they lived in cities, they thought and wrote about matters of deep import, and they were involved in wars. The editors hope that the unavoidable overlapping among chapters will have value in reinforcement rather than bringing redundancy.

The editors and authors also faced the knotty problem of combining interpretive and bibliographical material. The authors were asked to employ both approaches but to emphasize interpretation and writings published since 1961. The chapters vary in relative emphasis on bibliography and interpretation, but both approaches are used in all of them. Many of the references will not be readily available to most teachers, but to give interpretation without evidence would violate principles of scholarship by which both writers and teachers of history should be bound. Moreover the fact that a book may not be readily available does not mean that a teacher will not profit from knowing that the book exists. Indeed, many of the citations should aid teachers in building both institutional and personal libraries.

Purpose of the Volume

The purpose of this book is to make available as authoritative and up-to-date an account of the state of scholarship in American history as the editors and authors were able to present in a volume of reasonable size. This volume was not commissioned as a work on pedagogy. Hence, it does not treat the great changes in the teaching of history that took place in the last decade.

New textbooks and courses of study, and revisions of earlier ones, called into question perspectives of the past that had seemed settled. They gave much more attention to the contributions and abuses of minority groups. A flood of teaching materials in media other than print came into use. Materials and methods previously considered to be in the domain of other social sciences were employed increasingly in the teaching of history. Coverage of the subject through narrative yielded more and more to emphasis on the development of concepts and of skills of inquiry. These changes were hastened by a host of curriculum projects financed in large part by the Federal Government and carried out by consortia of institutions of higher education and schools. Thus, the knowledge and experience of scholars in the social sciences and pedagogy were combined with those of school personnel. The results of many of the projects were on the commercial market in 1972.

Although this book does not deal with the pedagogy of history, readers will see that many of the concerns that affected curriculum makers were shared by professional historians. Thus, this volume reflects new perspectives of past developments and new emphases on minority groups, on conceptual approaches, and on use of the methods of the social sciences. Because the labors of most historians along these lines are of recent origin, it should not be surprising if their results seem less certain and less satisfying than those of the traditional historians once seemed. Curriculum making and scholarship are different enterprises, yet in matters of knowledge and understanding of a subject it is difficult for sound curricula to be very far ahead of sound scholarship. Teachers and other curriculum makers who seek to create new, challenging, and useful school programs should find assistance from the new scholarship reflected in this book. And they will want to follow further developments in that scholarship.

The Reinterpretation of American History and Culture is not expected to serve as a textbook for the instruction of students in the schools. Rather, it is designed as a resource for teachers and students of American history as they struggle with the task of making every person his own historian.

FOOTNOTES

[1] One of the most challenging and widely-cited articles is Edgar B. Wesley. "Let's Abolish History Courses." *Phi Delta Kappan* 49: 3-8; No. 1, September 1967. While Wesley condemned the teaching of separate history courses, the burden of opprobrium fell on the traditional practice of memorization. Far from proposing the removal of historical study from the curriculum, the article contains much praise for history as distinguished from history courses. An early mimeographed version was entitled "The Place of History in the School Program."

[2] Edgar B. Wesley, Director. *American History in Schools and Colleges: The Report of the Committee on American History in Schools and Colleges of the American Historical Association, the Mississippi Valley Historical Association, the National Council for the Social Studies.* New York: Macmillan, 1944.

[3] Wesley. *American History in Schools and College.* p. 14.

[4] William F. Russell. *The Early Teaching of History in the Secondary Schools of New York and Massachusetts.* Philadelphia: McKinley, 1914. p. 13.

[5] Rolla M. Tryon. "One Hundred Years of History in the Secondary Schools of the United States." *School Review* 42: 94-95; No. 2, February 1934.

[6] Agnew O. Roorbach. *The Development of the Social Studies in American Secondary Education Before 1861.* Philadelphia: the author, 1937. p. 71.

[7] William H. Cartwright. "Values Claimed for American History." Unpublished paper presented at the Annual Meeting of the American Historical Association. Boston, December 30, 1949; and "A History of the Teaching of American History." Unpublished doctoral dissertation, University of Minnesota, 1950. pp. 107-230.

[8] Richard S. Craddock. "Why Teach History?" Unpublished paper presented at the Annual Meeting of the National Council for the Social Studies. New York, November 2, 1970; and "The Views of Professional American Historians on the Values and Purposes of Historical Study." Unpublished doctoral dissertation, Duke University, 1969.

[9] Henry Johnson. *Teaching of History in Elementary and Secondary Schools With Applications to Allied Subjects.* Revised Edition. New York: Macmillan, 1940. p. 126.

[10] Thomas Jefferson. *Notes on the State of Virginia.* Boston: Wells and Lilly, 1829. pp. 155-156.

[11] Henry Johnson. *The Other Side of Main Street.* New York: Columbia University Press, 1943. pp. 240-241.

[12] January 20, 1967.

[13] David M. Potter. "The Background of the Civil War," in William H. Cartwright and Richard L. Watson, Jr., editors. *Interpreting and Teaching American History.* Washington: National Council for the Social Studies, 1961. pp. 118-119.

·1·

A Decade
of American Historiography:
The 1960's

Edward N. Saveth

"WHY," asked Sydney E. Ahlstrom, a historian of American religion, "did the fair weather, the complacency, moral composure, national self-confidence, and optimism of the fifties, of the Eisenhower years and even of Kennedy's early New Frontier days become so quickly clouded? . . . Why . . . have so many long-term processes dropped their bomb load on the sixties?" In seeking an explanation, Ahlstrom concludes, "we touch upon an edge of the *mysterium tremendum*."[1]

The historiography of the 1960's reflected some of this awesome crisis but not the full intensity of it. There was, of course, anxiety and despair among historians as there was among everyone else. Historians, however, had the benefit of the long view, which is to say that from the beginnings of American history there had always been anxiety and despair. So the mood of the 1960's represented an extension and intensification of what had been previously. Did intellectuals who were not historians have more fun with the sense of doom that haunted the 1960's?

The historian's long view, too, ameliorated his sense of crisis. In the decade of the 1960's, poverty, racism, and various urban problems were inescapable for the historian as they were for everyone else. While radical historians focused their researches on these and related problems looking toward social change, it was at least possible for conservatives in the historical guild to conclude that the republic, in the past, had survived with these ills and the mere highlighting of them in the 1960's did not mean that radical change was essential to the survival of the nation. What had existed for so long could conceivably go on forever.[2]

17

Nevertheless, the most sensitive historiographic barometer—reported in the *American Historical Review* as well as in the *Wall Street Journal* —was the group of historians clustered under the vague rubric, New Left.[3] To anyone who had lived through the Old Left of the 1930's and was familiar with the New History earlier in the twentieth century—the writings of Frederick Jackson Turner, Charles A. Beard, James Harvey Robinson, Carl L. Becker, Arthur Meier Schlesinger, and Vernon L. Parrington—the New Left was not very new. In his introduction to an uneven collection of historical essays that could pass as a sort of *Summa* of New Left historiography, the editor of the collection, Barton J. Bernstein, acknowledges an indebtedness to the New History. Bernstein quotes Turner saying in 1910 that "a comprehension of the United States today, an understanding of the rise and progress of the forces which have made it what it is, demands that we should rework our history from the new points of view afforded by the present." Bernstein then quotes Arthur Meier Schlesinger who said about the same thing in 1923 and gives less attention than he should to what Beard was trying to do when he published *An Economic Interpretation of the Constitution* in 1913. Vernon L. Parrington's *Main Currents in American Thought* (1927-30) and Charles and Mary Beard's *The Rise of American Civilization* (1927) mark for Bernstein "the triumph of the progressive synthesis. In broad outlines, it viewed much of American history as a struggle between the privileged and the less privileged: sometimes, as in the lingering influence of Turner, between sections; at other times, as in the works of Beard, Schlesinger and Becker, between class or economic interests." This history, according to Bernstein, "was marked by emphasis upon upheaval and 'revolutions,' upon conflicts between rival ideologies."[4]

The New Left borrowed another leaf from the book of the New History: the latter's conception of history's role in pointing the way toward social reform, which was an aspect of the allied themes of relevance and presentism. Many of the issues of presentism and relevance in today's historiography were present in Schlesinger's *New Viewpoints in American History*. On the other hand, Turner and Beard wrote very little about blacks and ethnics—indeed, a case for racism could be made against them. Relevancy, it would seem, is a sometimes thing.[5]

An additional element of continuity between the New History and the New Left is the tendency of both to confuse Marxism, the economic interpretation of history, and economic determinism. Beard was an economic determinist to the extent that Marx never was, and Beard also gave less scope to the force of ideas in history than Marx did. Beard, if he knew and understood Marxist dialectic and the meaning of Marxist historical materialism, was unimpressed by them. Historical materialism, not economic determinism, is central to Marxism. Parrington, too, was no Marxist insofar as his *Main Currents in American Thought* postulated a closer relationship between ideas and economic forces than did Marx. There were in the era of the New History tracts on American history written from the Marxist viewpoint—mindful that it is hard to establish with any degree of definity what precisely is the Marxist viewpoint—by Algie M. Simons, who had been a student of Frederick Jackson Turner, and by Herman Schluter.[6] Between 1917 and 1919, there appeared A. W. Calhoun, *A Social History of the American Family,* vaguely Marxian in orientation and wrongheaded in its assumption of a direct relationship between family structure and stages of capitalist development.[7]

During the depression decade of the 1930's, Beard and Parrington were very popular among left-thinking historians. Again the category is difficult to define, even as there was continued confusion among the latter between Marxism and mere recognition of the significance of economic forces. Around 1935, there was an effort by the Stalinist Communists in America to sway historiography by bending it to the purposes of their slogan that Communism was twentieth-century Americanism— devised after the Party adopted the united front tactic. This envisioned a proletarian view of American history designed to rescue the American heritage from "bourgeois" historians, the word "elitist" being not yet popular. Yet, despite all the talk and ideological ferment caused by the impact of Marxism upon young historians of the 1930's, there was no significant Marxist historiography.

What we today call the "Old Left" produced only two professional historians: Herbert Aptheker and Philip S. Foner. Their doctoral dissertations, Aptheker's *American Negro Slave Revolts* (1943) and Foner's *Business and Slavery* (1941), were not Marxist tracts. Foner was more of a Beardian than a Marxist, and Aptheker, busily counting slave "revolts," tended to confuse "revolt" and minor incident, but without ideological overtones. W.E.B. Du Bois' *Black Reconstruction* appeared in 1935, but its central theme reached back to earlier work by the author around 1900. Where to place this volume in the Marxist spectrum is difficult to say.

Falling more clearly within the Marxist-Stalinist orbit was James S. Allen's tract on the Reconstruction era which was far inferior to Du Bois' work. *Science and Society,* which began publication in 1936 and continues to publish, provided an outlet for Marxist historiography. There was, too, the abortive *Marxist Quarterly* which represented, in its brief career, a dissident Marxist viewpoint. It contained one notable article by Louis M. Hacker, "American Revolution: Economic Aspects," which is still worth reading.[8]

The New Left is heir to the confusions of the Old. There is no little disagreement as to what Marxism is and where Marxism parted company with mere reformism. The Marxism or Marxiodism of Eugene Genovese is different from that of Staughton Lynd, and they had differences with historians of the Old Left, Philip Foner and Herbert Aptheker.[9] Is Lynd a Marxist when he writes: "I believe Marxism is correct in its understanding of where humanity has been and is going. Think of it as a backdrop to the stage on which historical protagonists play their self-determined parts. It is nonetheless an essential element in the drama."? Convinced Communists would want a doctrine more stringent than this blend of "soft" Marxism and existentialism. Moreover, Lynd has a habit of talking ideology one way and writing history another. His historical writing is geared more to Beard than to Marx. Lynd, one feels, would have a rather short life span in the Marxist paradises of Brezhnev and Mao.

Lynd, however, is a man seeking direction and asking that history provide it, which, of course, asks too much. The past, he asserts, is to be ransacked "not for its own sake, but as a source of alternative models of what the future might become."[10] Similarly, Arnold Waskow at the meeting of the American Historical Association in December 1969 demanded that politics and scholarship be brought together and that historians "rebuild themselves; to reconnect body and mind, morals and information; to do that precisely in resistance to a dehumanizing social system." Thus, Waskow concluded, "the urge is no mere idiosyncratic hang-up: it is the most political of events, and the radical historians, like other newly radical intellectuals, are questioning the whole bureau-cratic-'rational' assumption of the split in roles between citizen and scholar."[11] Most of Waskow's hearers did not agree with his point of view and some, recalling the 1930's, had a sense of déjà vu.

Still, the New Left, interacting with the events of the decade, provided direction for historical research. Black history was a key area as were the slave system, slavery, abolitionism and abolitionists who were New Left heroes, foreign policy and expansion, labor history, protest groups like the Populists, the IWW and non-elitist, including inarticulate groups in the American population. Yet, even as all historians who addressed themselves to these themes were not of the New Left, not all New Left historians were agreed as to how these themes should be handled. Staughton Lynd, for example, disagreed with Jesse Lemisch over the possibility and practicability of writing the history of the inarticulate.[12]

Despite the interest in radical historiography, the radicals hardly dominated American historiography. Most historians are not radicals and this is a reflection of a certain amount of conservatism that has always characterized American historians and, more importantly, the profession's indifference to ideology and theory in history generally. There is ample indication that the "consensus" school of historical writing which attracted so much attention in the fifties was not eclipsed during the sixties.[13]

Despite concern with the issues of relevance and reform, the New Left failed to establish a historical background for a major American tradition of political dissent. This failure is a reflection of the relationship between ideology and politics in America which is not a problem of the New Left alone. Late in 1950, Samuel Eliot Morison, in his presidential address to the American Historical Association, spoke of history written in the Jefferson-Jackson-Franklin Delano Roosevelt tradition and the need to formulate an opposing Federalist-Whig-Republican tradition in American historiography. "We need," he said, "a United States history written from a sanely conservative point of view. . . ."[14]

Morison's hope went unfulfilled. One reason was Louis Hartz's argument in 1955 that owing to the absence of a feudal pattern in the United States, it was questionable whether there were separate liberal and conservative traditions. It was all liberalism, Hartz concluded, more or less. Or it was all non-ideological pragmatism, as Daniel Boorstin had claimed in 1953. When Clinton Rossiter tried to put together a conservative synthesis in 1955, it went nowhere.[15]

Moreover, it is questionable whether there was, as Morison said, a liberal synthesis in American historiography except for Arthur Schlesinger, Jr.'s enormously popular *Age of Jackson* and its rather simplistic final chapter which presents American history in terms of capitalism being rescued from its worst tendencies by liberal leaders like Jackson and Franklin Roosevelt. No historian followed through in terms of this perspective. On the other hand, there were many Jacksonian scholars, none with the audience that Schlesinger reached, however, who faulted Schlesinger's scholarship and his conclusions.

As for the fate of liberalism as an ideology in the 1960's, Schlesinger is himself an indicator. He began the decade in the service of President John F. Kennedy and Schlesinger's *Politics of Hope,* which was published in 1962, was strong in the liberal faith. His 1969 volume, *The Crisis of Confidence: Ideas, Power and Violence in America,* manifested less faith in liberal solutions.[16]

There were other efforts, apart from politics, in terms of which attempts were made to forge a core historical tradition. Carl Bridenbaugh, in his presidential address to the American Historical Association in December 1962, spoke of a synthesis separate from the liberal-conservative dichotomy which, in the 1950's, as John Higham said, seemed to be less of a dichotomy than a consensus. Ignoring politics, Bridenbaugh pointed to the loss of a "shared culture." This was caused in part by the fact that "many of the younger practitioners of our craft, and those who are still apprentices, are products of lower middle-class or foreign origins, and their emotions not infrequently get in the way of historical reconstruction." Origins such as these, according to Bridenbaugh, influenced the capacity of historians "to recapture enough of a sense of the past to enable them to feel and understand it and to convey to their readers what the past was even remotely like."

Bridenbaugh's address was entitled, meaningfully, "The Great Mutation," and it raised eyebrows and hackles among his fellow professionals. Bridenbaugh was reflecting a style in terms of which the historical profession had long operated; in which he matured as a scholar; and which was waning in the 1960's. That is, there were significant overtones of WASPishness in the profession which did not really fade until after World War II and about which not much has been said. Moreover, Bridenbaugh's idea of the relationship between the historian's origins and the capacity to feel history, while labelled reactionary and mossbacked when it was advanced, takes on a different coloration in the light of what was said at the end of the decade concerning the relationship between being black and the teaching of black history. Bridenbaugh's stress upon history as identity—and it was a relatively restrained emphasis compared to what was said later in the decade on this theme—was simply a bad idea that was ahead of its time.

In addition, Bridenbaugh did not want the seamlessness of the American past cut into by considerations of relevance and social science analysis especially "that Bitch-goddess, QUANTIFICATION."[17] Since the historiography of the 1960's went in the very directions that Bridenbaugh opposed, he must have been increasingly unhappy as the decade progressed. However, Bridenbaugh did produce in the decade *Mitre and Sceptre*[18] and *Vexed and Troubled Englishmen*,[19] two good books which reflected his conception of the grass-roots history of the English-speaking peoples.

It is ironic that at the end of the decade of the 1960's Oscar Handlin in his article "History: A Discipline in Crisis?" adopted a position very similar to aspects of Bridenbaugh's argument at the beginning of the sixties. Handlin, whose background included elements of urbanism and foreignism to which Bridenbaugh objected, complained about the inroads of quantification and relevance even as he lamented the absence of a community of scholars in a profession grown outsize. There are some remarkable similarities of viewpoint despite the diverse backgrounds of the two historians.[20]

Along with the historians of the New Left, Bridenbaugh and Handlin, in their individual ways, were seeking unity and synthesis in the profession and data of history. So were many other historians during the sixties since an instinct for synthesis seems to be implicit in historical writing. The two previous decades, the 1940's and 1950's, witnessed an assault upon the so-called Progressive synthesis of Turner, Parrington and Beard, the beginnings of which went back to even before the 1940's. During the 1960's, areas of explanation narrowed still further. In the field of Puritan studies, for example, there was a significant attack upon the work of Perry Miller as too "monolithic" and as failing to take into account the "pluralistic" character of Puritan culture.[21]

Instead of synthesis, there was what Professor Rotenstreich has described as "a multiplicity of particular contents, as partial and piecemeal as the particular portion of time to which particular men direct themselves."[22] Synthesis was hard to come by, not alone in the realms of grand theory and covering law but even if sights were lowered to the hazy and indefinite middle level of generalization. A historian of American science complained of the "aggressively atheoretical tradition" in this field leading to "a bland and unquestioning eclecticism. . . ."[23] Professor Harold D. Woodman called for direction and synthesis in American agricultural history, a tentative synthesis even, between grand theory and minute detail. But there was none, Woodman complained. Instead, there were only insights: a rivalry of insights that stood each other off without explaining social change. The latter was an unsighted goal.[24]

The theme of the historian's relationship to public policy provided a focus for attempts at historical synthesis.[25] John F. Fairbank, in his presidential address before the American Historical Association, drew upon the ancient and dubious theme of historical didacticism—the so-called lessons of history. Fairbank admitted that this idea had been frequently voiced in presidential addresses before the American Historical Association since 1885. He nevertheless proposed "a Sinified updating of the familiar theme of history for use, history the handmaiden of statesmanship. . . . I would not deny its applicability here. . . ."

> Our inadvertent war in Vietnam . . . [is] an object lesson in historical nonthinking. . . . Suppose that our leaders in the Congress and the executive branch had all been aware that North Vietnam is a country older than France with a thousand-year history of southward expansion and militant independence maintained by using guerrilla warfare to expel invaders from China, for example, three times in the thirteenth century,

again in the fifteenth century, and again in the late eighteenth century, to say nothing of the French in the 1950's. With this perspective, would we have sent our troops into Vietnam so casually in 1965?[26]

Fairbank expected "no" as an answer to his rhetorical question. Hannah Arendt, instead, replied, in effect, "yes." The Pentagon Papers and other sources, she said, reveal that the history of Southeast Asia was known to the policymakers who, having elected for war, pursued a policy of deliberate defactualization in order to reach a predetermined conclusion.[27]

Further on the subject of the relationship between policy and history, Professor Louis Morton did not deny the value of the historian's training in the shaping of decision and policy but assigned limits to its utility. History is not predictive; it has a limited capacity for generalization and is not repetitive: there are "wrong" as well as "right" lessons that the past can teach us. Writes Morton:

> Whether the historian, *qua* historian, should play a direct role in the formulation of policy is another matter. By instinct and training, the historian avoids the present. . . . It is in dealing with the contemporary world that he is most vulnerable professionally, since it is in precisely this area that the qualities for which he is most valued and from which he draws his strength—perspective, objectivity, accuracy, and completeness—are least evident.[28]

Richard C. Wade has suggested that understanding the urban crisis of of the 1960's required "the patient reconstruction of our entire urban past," even as he warned against "panic history."[29] Robert H. Bremner pointed out that the historical background of the social welfare problem had only limited policy-making utility. "My own feeling," wrote Bremner, "is that what the historian can offer those who contend with current social issues is not historical precedents or information about right or wrong turns in the road map to the present—not knowledge, not solutions—but method, openness, and sensitivity."[30]

The impact of the social sciences upon American historiography, a major development of the 1960's, brought the historian closer to matters of public policy because of the interrelationship between the so-called policy sciences and the social sciences. This was particularly true of the historian's study of voting behavior, economic growth, and the socio-psychological elements of status and motivation, with the social science concepts serving to lock the past into the present.

Among the social science oriented historians, there were quantifiers and non-quantifiers. The latter had their day during the 1950's and on into the following decade with the application of such concepts as career line, intergroup conflict, status anxiety, reference group, class, mobility, social structure, leadership, power, public opinion, image, type, role, conscious and subconscious motivation, microanalysis—and many others, depending upon how one wanted to define concept and, particularly, social science concept as distinguished—if there is a distinction—from the historian's traditional process of conceptualization.[31]

Non-quantitative social science concepts served as a framework for historical generalization and synthesis. Richard Hofstadter's *The Age of Reform,* for example, made the concept of status anxiety a central theme. There were other volumes and articles written along similar lines. Yet, however popular and convincing certain of these volumes were, especially Hofstadter's *The Age of Reform,* critical reviews as distinct from appreciative blurbs steadily eroded the utility of the concept as covering explanation.[32] The closer the scholarly examination, the less the concept explained.[33]

One reason for the inexactitude of non-quantitative social science concepts as covering explanations centers in the problem of defining group structural outlines and relating group structure to behavior.[34] There was need for greater exactitude in establishing group definition. Toward the middle of the 1960's, quantitative social science concepts seemed to offer this possibility. Quantification involved the isolation of variables pertaining to group definition that were capable of being measured statistically. These variables lent themselves to tabulation, machine processing, and evaluation in terms of rather complex statistical procedures which the traditionally-trained historian had difficulty in mastering. The technique offered at least the possibility of concepts being more rigidly defined than were non-quantitative concepts, and capable of statistical illustration in terms other than impressionistic data.

Again, there was talk of a "new" history, this time centered in quantifiable data and quantitative techniques: "new" political history; "new" economic history; and "new" social history. The focus—but not the exclusive focus—was upon group behavior with the group outline defined by the kind of variables that could be quantified or that lent themselves to statistical expression.[35] However, not all group behavior could be expressed statistically.[36] It is impossible, for example, to quantify so significant a variable as motivation. That motivation cannot be quantified, comments Professor Woodman, does not mean that it should be committed to a secondary role in accounting for economic growth. Similarly, Professor Allan Bogue suggests that the emphasis of behavioral historians upon ethno-cultural factors might reflect the visibility of these variables, that they are capable of being measured, rather than their true significance in influencing voting patterns.[37]

There was a considerable range of opinion within the historical profession concerning cliometrics, the name by which quantitative techniques applied to history came to be known. The traditionally-trained historian tended to find quantitative studies microcosmic and limited in scope; tedious to execute and difficult to read. Less and less of the past seemed to be explained by more and more effort, and the historian's fascination with technique and computer hardware had the potential of outstripping love for history. Certain historical themes considered important by the cliometricians were seen as less significant by traditionally-trained historians to whom history conceived as "problem" was less intriguing. Even after prodigious efforts, the results of small-scale inquiry were not always conclusive insofar as there was frequently some variable, either overlooked or incapable of quantification, that put the whole inquiry in doubt.[38]

On the other hand, there were historians who expected a great deal of cliometrics, perhaps more than it was capable of yielding. Lee Benson, for example, expressed the belief that quantification had the potential of making history the kind of science that Henry Buckle envisioned in 1857.[39] Robert F. Berkhofer's book entitled *A Behavioral Approach to Historical Analysis*[40] and an article by Mario S. De Pillis[41] were stronger in developing the theory of the relationship between history and behavioralism than in its actual practice and application. Perhaps cliometrics can be most sensibly evaluated as one of many techniques and methods available to the historian, to be used where relevant and without reference to the extravagant hopes for the method held out by some historians and the equally extravagant dislikes expressed by others.

The social science approach, quantitative and non-quantitative, as it developed in the 1960's, was essentially value neutral. These techniques could have been used by the historians of the New Left, without ideological sacrifice, but were not used by them to any great extent. Why, it is difficult to say. Their suspicions of the technique could conceivably have been aroused by Professor Samuel P. Hays, a leading quantifier, who spoke of the need for social history to develop categories of structure and change as its proper mode of organization; of the dangers of social history being influenced by forces of relevance in American society; of social history absorbing a problem-policy approach and, therefore, a bias. Hays would put aside the reformist orientation of social history—a heritage from the New History which included the use of social science as a tool of social change. Hays warned, for example, the historian against being captured by ideology and urged that the black problem be approached not as a moral issue but as an aspect of the concept of social mobility.[42]

Nor could the New Left, in the light of its commitment, be expected to embrace Professor David Donald's de-emphasis of moral judgments and moral issues in dealing with the issues of Reconstruction, and Donald's assertion that the process whereby Congress passed the Reconstruction Act of 1867 "can best be described in quasimechanical terms as an equilibrium achieved by a resolution of quantitatively measurable forces."[43] Donald's detachment, geared to his method, led to an altogether different historiographic orientation than the late Robert Starobin's insistence upon "the centrality of the Negro, the South and of racism to American development. . . ."[44]

The social science approach to history represented an effort to get at basic units of analysis; to uncover the "grass roots" of history. The search for "grass roots" did not begin with the decade of the sixties. Professor Bridenbaugh was interested in the grass roots of the English people in America; Professor Hays believed that in compiling voting statistics and studying voting behavior he was getting at grass roots.[45] Black history and the history of white ethnic groups were also supposed to reveal grass roots. So, too, was the emphasis in the 1960's upon "organizational" history; the history of organizations and administrative systems by means of which the historians hoped to approach closer to people and their behavior than would have been the case in conventional historiography's concern with the traditional categories of political, social and economic history.[46]

This was part of the search for smaller and, presumably, more viable units of analysis; of the trend from macro-units to micro-units dictated by the assumption that the latter were less complex than the former— an assumption which the late David Potter, for one, questioned. According to Potter, "a microcosm is just as cosmic as a macrocosm. Moreover, relationships between the factors in a microcosm are just as subtle and the generalizations involved in stating these relationships are just as broad as the generalizations concerning the relation between factors in a situation of larger scale."[47]

Potter's reservations did not inhibit the microanalytic trend. This is manifest in the shift in emphasis by some historians from group and class with their numerous variables to the microunit of family. The family, long neglected by historians as an area for research,[48] began to receive attention in the 1960's because there was interest in it for itself and partly because, as John Demos noted, "as the smallest and most intimate of all social environments" it offered the hope of providing insight into behavior in politics, society and economics. In mid-decade, three very capable young historians, Demos, Philip Greven, Jr., and Kenneth Lockridge, enhanced our knowledge of the colonial family. Also, since their research techniques are demographically oriented, they have increased understanding of social structure and social process in colonial America.[49]

Yet, the family microunit as a determinant of behavior has limitations, with Professor Demos saying that what has been done in the area of family research "has not been enough to stake out a definite area of study, with its own boundaries, internal structure, and guiding themes and questions. There is as yet no sense of the major outlines of the story and little agreement even about research procedures, source materials, and terminology."[50] Beyond the colonial period, family history and the use of family as a determinant of behavior is even more of a wilderness for the investigator.

"In the face of so many uncertainties" in family history, continues Professor Demos, "one response, more instinctive than reasoned, has been to descend to the level of local, almost personal history." This involves reductionism beyond the family to the individual and his immediate environment. During the decade of the sixties there was much interest in psychohistory. In 1965 Erik Erikson and Robert Jay Lifton along with Kenneth Keniston, Bruce Mazlish and Philip Rieff formed the Group for the Study of Psychohistorical Process sponsored by the American Academy of Arts and Sciences. Of the founders Erik Erikson loomed particularly large. There was no one of equal prominence among those who applied psychoanalytical methods to the study of American history, although the names of William B. Willcox, who wrote a biography of Sir Henry Clinton, and David Donald, biographer of Charles Sumner, come readily to mind.[51]

Yet, the analysis of the individual in history, the analysis of his motivation, conscious and subconscious—despite some good theory on the subject by Robert Jay Lifton among others—has its own inherent limitations.[52] Far more frequently than not, the historian has an inadequate grasp of personality, especially the role played by early childhood experience. Despite parallels, some of them valid, between biographical and psychoanalytical methods, a major and probably insurmountable difficulty is the absence of personal data available to the historical biographer. No amount of theory, regardless of how original, can transcend the lack of hard data about individual development.

The limitations of analytical history have bred a certain amount of despair among professional historians about their ability to describe what happened in the past. Such despair is not new and not unique to the decade of the sixties. Historians have long pondered whether they are dealing with the absolute and inherent meaning of events or whether, on the other hand, knowledge of them is considered by the "ever-changing frames of reference" of the historian observer.[53] Martin Duberman, for one, was pessimistic concerning the possibility of ascertaining his own motives in writing history and of the motives of those who were participants in the historical process. Early in 1969, Duberman doubted the wisdom of his having selected history as a profession.[54]

Such a feeling of doubt was suggestive of that of Henry Adams who said, after he had completed his great *History of the United States during the Jefferson and Madison Administrations,* that it was pointless to have written it.[55] Adams gave up traditional history and, instead, embarked upon the marvelous head trip into the Middle Ages, *Mont St. Michel and Chartres,* followed by a venture still further divorced from reality, the application of the second law of thermodynamics to history. This, from the historian's point of view, was all wrong but it expressed a mood in terms of which an unfathomable universe was confronted.

In the decade of the 1960's, a period of *Coming Apart* as one cultural historian described it,[56] the Adamsian mood was still with us. Which is to say that history and the universe continued to be unfathomable. Yet, with all of the crises of the decade, amplified by the historian's fear that technology would destroy us and that his work would not live on in the psychic experience of mankind, there were fewer signs of crisis mentality among historians than were apparent in other fields of literary-cultural endeavor. The average historian went about his main business—dredging up the data of the past—relatively unaffected by ideology. As the decade progressed, my impression is that fewer historians contributed to the theoretical publication *History and Theory* which seemed to be more and more taken over by the philosophical guild. The *Journal of Interdisciplinary History* began publication with the Autumn 1970 issue.

One response to the challenge of an unpredictable universe in which the distinction between chaos and order is subjective, in which meaning in life and history is dubious, in which the modern situation is one of non-relation and disrelation, is revival of interest in narrative history, that oldest form of history writing that approximates to storytelling. The English scholar G. R. Elton justified narrative history because, as he said, there is something unnatural about the process of historical analysis which involves taking history apart and putting it together again in a different way from the manner in which it actually happened.

Thus far, the philosophers of history have manifested greater interest in the possibilities of narrative history than has the historical guild, reflecting the traditional dichotomy between the philosophy of history and the writing of history.[57] However, there was this significant development. In 1971, the final volumes of Allan Nevins' monumental narrative history, *Ordeal of the Union,* appeared. The first of the eight big volumes, embracing the history of the United States from the Compromise of 1850 to the end of the American Civil War, were published in 1947, and the twenty-four year publication history of the series represents both a remarkable personal achievement and an accomplishment in the writing of narrative history that is not likely to be duplicated soon.

Narrative history offers the historian proper ground upon which to stand because of its emphasis upon the unique. In addition, it enables the historian to employ multiple approaches to the data of the past, as varied as the past itself, so that he is not committed to a particular approach. In Nevins' work, for example, there were large blocs of analysis within an overall narrative framework. The medium, however, is not easy to handle and Nevins' ability to manage a large-size historical canvas is difficult to match or surpass. Despite Nevins' achievement, the multi-volume narrative history was not a popular form of historical expression in the 1960's.

Nor do certain non-traditional techniques, like the uses of counter-factual data and events, seem to hold out much promise in terms of their integration into the methodology of historiography.[58] Even less can be expected from the suggestion at the 1971 meeting of the American Historical Association that drugs should be taken by "responsible and tough-minded scholars" to enhance the historian's understanding of, say, President James K. Polk.[59]

Most historians and most teachers of history, especially toward the end of the decade, were concerned with declining enrollments in history courses both in the high schools and colleges. The full significance of these figures—whether the decline was relative or absolute, temporary or long-term—cannot be determined. At the 1971 meeting of the American Historical Association, jobs, and not the doings of the radical caucus, were the primary concern.[60]

There was a growing feeling among history teachers that history's place in the curriculum must be justified in terms of meaning, purpose, and utility, especially in comparison with the social sciences with which it was competing for enrollments. On both the high school and college levels attempts were made to make history courses more attractive. Many of the new course designs stressed relevance, the idea of a usable American past, and the use of social science concepts as a basis for the organization of historical data.[61] There was also stress upon brevity and simplicity of presentation because an increasing number of high school and college students experienced reading and comprehension difficulties.

As the decade concluded, historians, history teachers, and the publishers of teaching materials all felt that history had a message for the in-school generation, but no one was certain as to what this message was or how it was to be conveyed.

FOOTNOTES

[1] Herbert J. Bass, editor. *The State of American History.* Chicago: Quadrangle, 1970. pp. 103-4.

[2] Page Smith. "Anxiety and Despair in American History." *William and Mary Quarterly* 26: 416-424; 3rd series, No. 3, July 1969; Michael Walzer. *The Revolution of the Saints.* Cambridge: Harvard University Press, 1965.

[3] Irwin Unger. "The 'New Left' and American History: Some Recent Trends in United States Historiography." *American Historical Review* 72: 1237-1263; No. 4, July 1967; *Wall Street Journal,* October 19, 1971.

[4] *Towards a New Past: Dissenting Essays in American History.* New York: Pantheon, 1967. p. vi.

[5] Charles Crowe. "The Emergence of Progressive History." *Journal of the History of Ideas* 27: 109-124; No. 1, January-March 1966; Jesse Lemisch. "The American Revolution Bicentennial and the Papers of Great White Men." *American Historical Association Newsletter* 9: 7-12; No. 5, November 1971; Edward N. Saveth. *American Historians and European Immigrants, 1875-1925.* New York: Columbia University Press, 1948.

[6] A. M. Simons. *Social Forces in American History.* New York: Macmillan, 1911; Herman Schluter. *Lincoln, Labor and Slavery: A Chapter from the Social History of America.* New York: Socialist Literature Co., 1913.

[7] Cleveland: Arthur W. Clark Co., 1917-1919.

[8] *The Marxist Quarterly* 1: 46-67; No. 1, January-March 1937. p. 46.

[9] D. M. Bluestone. "Marxism Without Marx: The Consensus-Conflict of Eugene Genovese." *Science and Society* 33: 231-243; No. 2, Spring 1969.

[10] "A Profession of History." *The New Journal* I: November 12, 1967.

[11] *American Historical Association Newsletter* 8: 27-28; No. 8, February 1970.

[12] Philip S. Foner. "Some Reflections on Ideology and American Labor History." *Science and Society* 34: 467-478; No. 4, Winter 1970; August Meier. "Black America as a Research Field: Some Comments." *American Historical Association Newsletter* 6: 18-23; No. 4, April 1968; Ernest Kaiser. "Recent Literature on Black Liberation Struggles and the Ghetto Crisis." *Science and Society* 33: 168-196; No. 2, Spring 1969.

For Lynd's critique of Lemisch's proposal for non-elitist history see "The Historian as Participant," in R. A. Skotheim, editor. *The Historian and the Climate of Opinion.* Reading, Mass.: Addison-Wesley, 1969. p. 117.

Swirls of ideology within the loose framework of New Left historiography are treated in Irwin Unger. "The 'New Left' and American History," *op. cit.;* Eugene D. Genovese. "Marxian Interpretations of the Slave South," in Bernstein, editor. *Towards a New Past.* pp. 90-125, especially the footnotes; "Dr. Herbert Aptheker's Retreat from Marxism." *Science and Society* 27: 212-226; No. 2, Spring 1963; review by Staughton Lynd of W. A. Williams. *The Contours of American History.* Cleveland: World Publishing Co., 1961. *ibid.* pp. 227-31.

[13] Paul Goodman. *The Democratic-Republicans of Massachusetts.* Cambridge: Harvard University Press, 1964; Alfred Young. *The Democratic-Republicans of New York.* Chapel Hill: University of North Carolina Press, 1967; Carl E. Prince. *New Jersey's Republicans, 1789-1817.* Chapel Hill: University of North Carolina Press, 1967.

[14] "Faith of a Historian." *American Historical Review* 56: 272-273; No. 2, January 1951.

[15] Hartz. *The Liberal Tradition in America*. . . . New York: Harcourt, Brace, 1955; Boorstin. *The Genius of American Politics*. Chicago: University of Chicago Press, 1953; Rossiter. *Conservatism in America*. New York: Knopf, 1955. For a fuller discussion see my introduction to Edward N. Saveth, editor. *Understanding the American Past*. 2nd edition. Boston: Little, Brown, 1965. pp. 37-42.

[16] *Age of Jackson*. Boston: Little, Brown, 1945; *The Politics of Hope*. Boston: Houghton Mifflin, 1962; *The Crisis of Confidence*. Boston: Houghton Mifflin, 1968.

[17] "The Great Mutation." *American Historical Review* 68: 315-331; No. 2, January 1963. p. 326.

[18] New York: Oxford University Press, 1962.

[19] New York: Oxford University Press, 1967.

[20] *American Scholar* 40: 447-465; No. 3, Summer 1971. This is the text of an address which Handlin delivered at the December 1970 meeting of the American Historical Association.

[21] Michael McGiffert. "American Puritan Studies in the 1960's." *William and Mary Quarterly* 27: 36-67; 3rd series, No. 1, January 1970. An example of the microcosmic approach is Sumner Chilton Powell. *Puritan Village: The Formation of a New England Town*. Middletown, Conn.: Wesleyan University Press, 1963.

[22] Nathan Rotenstreich. "The Idea of Historical Progress and Its Assumptions." *History and Theory* 10: 197-221; No. 2, 1971. p. 220.

[23] Bass. *op. cit.*

[24] Harold D. Woodman. *ibid.* p. 233.

[25] For earlier examples of historical didacticism and the so-called lessons of history applied to public policy see Herman Ausubel. *Historians and Their Craft*. New York: Columbia University Press, 1950. pp. 17-119.

[26] John K. Fairbank. "Assignment for the '70's." *American Historical Review* 74: 861-879; No. 3, February 1969. pp. 869, 873.

[27] "Lying in Politics." *New York Review of Books*. November 18, 1971. For a similar point of view expressed in 1937 see William A. Dunning. "Truth in History," in *Truth in History and Other Essays*. New York: Columbia University Press, 1937. p. 17. George O. Kent. "Clio the Tyrant: Historical Analogies and the Meaning of History." *The Historian* 32: 99-106; No. 1, November 1969.

[28] Louis Morton. "The Historian and the Policy Process." *History Teacher* 4: 23-29; No. 1, November 1970.

[29] Bass. *op. cit.* p. 49.

[30] *Ibid.* p. 96.

[31] Edward N. Saveth. "The Conceptualization of American History," in Saveth, editor. *American History and the Social Sciences*. New York: Free Press, 1964. pp. 3-22.

[32] Richard Hofstadter. *The Age of Reform*. Vintage edition. New York: 1955. pp. 131-73; David Donald. *Lincoln Reconsidered*. Vintage edition. New York: 1961. pp. 19-36; Marvin Meyers. *Jacksonian Persuasion*. Vintage edition. New York: 1960. pp. 33-56; Ari Hoogenboom. *Outlawing the Spoils: A History of the Civil Service Reform Movement, 1865-1883*. Urbana, Ill.: University of Illinois Press, 1961; Rowland Berthoff. "The American Social Order: A Conservative Hypothesis." *American Historical Review* 65: 495-514; No. 3, April 1960; George Mowry. *The California Progressives*. Chicago: Quadrangle, 1963. c. 1951; *Era of Theodore Roosevelt, 1900-1912*. New York: Harper, 1958. Hofstadter qualified his position in "Pseudo-Conservatism Revisited: A Postscript—1962," in Daniel Bell, editor. *The Radical Right*. Garden City: Doubleday, 1963. pp. 81-86.

[33] "Status Revolution and Reference Group Theory," in Edward N. Saveth, editor. *American History and the Social Sciences*. pp. 196-197; Richard B. Sherman. "The Status Revolution and Massachusetts Progressive Leadership." *Political Science Quarterly* 78: 59-65; No. 1, March 1963; Bonnie R. Fox. "The Philadelphia Progressives: A Test of the Hofstadter-Hays Thesis." *Pennsylvania History* 34: 372-394; No. 4, October 1967.

[34] Edward N. Saveth. "American History and Social Science: A Trial Balance." *International Social Science Journal* 20: 319-330; No. 2, 1968.

[35] Allan G. Bogue. "United States: The 'New' Political History." *Journal of Contemporary History* 3: 5-27; No. 1, January 1968; Lance E. Davis. "'And It Will Never Be Literature'—The New Economic History: A Critique." *Explorations in Entrepreneurial History.* Second Series. 6: 75-92; No. 1, Fall 1968; Stephan Thernstrom. "The Dimensions of Occupational Mobility," in Stephan Thernstrom. *Poverty and Progress: Social Mobility in a Nineteenth-Century City.* Cambridge: Harvard University Press, 1964. pp. 80-114, 255-59.

[36] Christopher Lasch and George Frederickson. "Resistance to Slavery." *Civil War History* 13: 315-329; No. 4, December 1967.

[37] "The 'New' Political History." p. 24.

[38] Useful collections of articles in the field of quantitative history include Robert P. Swierenga, editor. *Quantification in American History: Theory and Research.* New York: Atheneum, 1970. For quantitative political history see Joel H. Silbey and Samuel T. McSeveney, editors. *Voters, Parties, and Elections: Quantitative Essays in the History of American Popular Voting Behavior.* Waltham, Mass.: Xerox College Publishing Co., 1972. For quantitative techniques applied to ethnic groups see Robert P. Swierenga. "Ethnocultural Political Analysis: A New Approach to American Ethnic Studies." *Journal of American Studies* 5: 59-79; No. 1, April 1971, and the forthcoming article in the *International Migration Review,* "Ethnic Groups, Ethnic Conflicts, and Recent Quantitative Research in American Political History," by Samuel T. McSeveney.

[39] "Quantification, Scientific History, and Scholarly Innovation." *American Historical Association Newsletter* 4: 11-13; No. 5, June 1966; "Middle Period Historiography: What is to be Done?", in George Athan Billias and Gerald N. Grob, editors. *American History: Retrospect and Prospect.* New York: Free Press, 1971. pp. 154-190.

[40] New York: Free Press, 1969.

[41] "Trends in American Social History and the Possibilities of Behavioral Approaches." *Journal of Social History* 1: 37-60; No. 1, Fall 1967.

[42] "A Systematic Social History," in Billias and Grob, editors. *op. cit.* pp. 315-366.

[43] *The Politics of Reconstruction, 1863-1867.* Baton Rouge: Louisiana State University Press, 1965. p. 82.

[44] Robert Starobin. "The Negro: A Central Theme in American History." *Journal of Contemporary History* 3: 37-53; No. 2, April 1968.

[45] Samuel P. Hays. "History as Human Behavior." *Iowa Journal of History* 58: 193-206; No. 3, July 1960.

[46] Louis Galambos. "The Emerging Organizational Synthesis in Modern American History." *Business History Review* 44: 279-290; No. 3, Autumn 1970.

[47] Quoted in Saveth, editor. *American History and the Social Sciences.* "Microanalysis." p. 370.

[48] Edward N. Saveth. "The Problem of American Family History." *American Quarterly* 21: 311-329; No. 2, Pt. 2, Summer 1969.

[49] Kenneth A. Lockridge. "The Population of Dedham, Massachusetts, 1636-1736." *Economic History Review.* 2nd Series. 19: 318-344; No. 2, August 1966; Philip J. Greven, Jr. "Family Structure in Seventeenth-Century Andover, Massachusetts." *William and Mary Quarterly.* 3rd Series. 23: 234-256; No. 2, April 1966; John Demos. "Notes on Life in Plymouth Colony." *William and Mary Quarterly.* 3rd Series. 22: 264-286; April 1965; Philip Greven, Jr. "Historical Demography and Colonial America." *William and Mary Quarterly.* 3rd Series. 24: 438-454; No. 3, July 1967; J. Potter. "The Growth of Population in America, 1700-1860," in D. V. Glass and D. E. C. Eversley, editors. *Population in History.* Chicago: Aldine Publishing Co., 1965. pp. 636-663; Robert Higgs and H. Louis Stettler, III. "Colonial New England Demography: A Sampling Approach." *William and Mary Quarterly.* 3rd Series. 27: 282-294; No. 2, April 1970.

[50] John Demos. *A Little Commonwealth.* New York: Oxford University Press, 1970; Saveth. "The Problem of American Family History." *op. cit.*

[51] Robert Jay Lifton. *History and Human Survival.* New York: Random House, 1970; *Portrait of a General: Sir Henry Clinton. . . .* New York: Knopf, 1964; *Charles Sumner and the Coming of the Civil War.* New York: Knopf, 1960; *Charles Sumner and the Rights of Man.* New York: Knopf, 1970.

[52] Lifton. *History and Human Survival.* pp. 288-310.

[53] John T. Marcus. "The Changing Consciousness of History." *South Atlantic Quarterly* 60: 217-225; No. 2, Spring 1961; John Huizinga. "The Idea of History," in Fritz Stern, editor. *The Varieties of History.* New York: Meridian Books, 1956.

[54] "On Becoming an Historian" and "History: A Play," in *Evergreen Review* 13: 49-59+; No. 65, April 1969.

[55] Edward N. Saveth, editor. *The Education of Henry Adams. . . .* New York: Washington Square Press, 1963. Later edition from Twayne Publishers, New York.

[56] William L. O'Neill. *Coming Apart.* Chicago: Quadrangle, 1971.

[57] W. H. Dray. "On the Nature and Role of Narrative in Historiography." *History and Theory* 10: 153-171; No. 2, 1971; Louis O. Mink. "History and Fiction as Modes of Comprehension." *New Literary History* 1: 541-548; No. 3, Spring 1970; M. Mandelbaum. "A Note on History as Narrative." *History and Theory* 6: 413-419; No. 3, 1967.

[58] Robert W. Fogel. *Railroads and American Economic Growth: Essays in Econometric History.* Baltimore: Johns Hopkins Press, 1964.

[59] *New York Times,* December 30, 1971.

[60] Charles G. Sellers. "Is History on the Way Out of the Schools and Do Historians Care?" *Social Education* 33: 509-516; No. 5, May 1969. p. 10. See also the poll by Louis Harris and Associates, Inc. of "100 schools in representative cities, suburbs, small towns and rural areas for *Life.*" 66: 23, 31; No. 19, May 16, 1969. pp. 23, 31; J. Anthony Lukas. "Historians' Conference: The Radical Need for Jobs." *New York Times Magazine.* March 12, 1972. pp. 38-40.

[61] On the idea of a usable past see J. R. Pole. "The American Past: Is It Still Usable?" *Journal of American Studies* 1: 63-78; No. 1, April 1967. On relevance see M. M. Postan. "Fact and Relevance in Historical Study." *Historical Studies* 13: 411-425; No. 51, October 1968. Postan also deals with the relationship between relevance and social science oriented history. The relationship is also developed in C. Vann Woodward. "The Future of the Past." *American Historical Review* 75: 711-726; No. 3, February 1970. p. 718.

PART TWO

Race and Nationality in American History

· 2 ·

Native Americans
and United States History

Robert F. Berkhofer, Jr.

Indian Complaints Against Standard American History

To Native Americans and their spokesmen today, whites first stole their lands and later robbed them of their history. They charge that textbooks and classroom materials on general American history rarely mention Indians, and if they do it is frequently in a derogatory fashion. In line with long dominant American assumptions, writers and teachers presume that those few Indians who did not die in war or of disease became assimilated to white views and ways and therefore disappeared into white society. Since United States history is taught in terms of how we got to be what we are, this assumption of disappearance either through extinction or assimilation permits the neglect of Indian influences earlier in American history. Centuries of white-Indian relations, so much the concern of earlier Americans, receive brief if any mention, although European and American diplomacy, land policy, and western expansion during nearly three hundred years were predicated upon the presence and continued resistance of the many Indian tribes. Even if books and courses dealt with Indians earlier, their existence is denied in the present century. Perhaps for those white children near reservations they are treated as indigents upon the welfare rolls or in jail for drunkenness, but in general Indians are not even granted the status of a problem in the pages of most texts dealing with contemporary trends.[1]

According to Indian leaders and scholars, when Indians are not omitted from the story of the American past, they are deprecated or defamed. From the beginning of European contact to the present, Native Americans are usually presented as inferior in some way to the whites, whether in customs, technology, or government. Sometimes the authors bluntly state Indians are degraded, idle, warlike, and simple; other times the writers use words to imply the same moral judgements without saying so explicitly. Indians are "nomadic," while whites "travel." When Indians slew whites a "massacre" resulted, but whites only "fought" or "battled" Indians. Indians are pictured as hunting and gathering peoples; whites farmed. Indian agricultural practices, except for Squanto's aid to the Pilgrims, are neither described nor considered important, although white pioneer life is lovingly detailed. At the same time as these good pioneers are shown protecting their homes and loved ones from the savage "menace" or "peril," authors rarely point out how red men fought for their lives and lands against greedy, genocidal whites. When texts and teachers concentrate on Indians, they more frequently portray their faults than their virtues, and even the latter are treated as inferior to those of white civilization. All in all, red scholars assert, Indian life is depreciated by word and assumption in favor of white ways and views of the past and the present.[2]

So pernicious are these assumptions behind Indian-white relations, that they long held the field as the chief interpretation of American history. Frederick Jackson Turner combined long-standing American myths into an interpretation of the United States' past which accounted for both white American character and American history in terms of a westward-moving frontier. In his view, Indians like mountains, rivers, deserts, and wild animals posed obstacles for the freedom-loving white farmers. In short, Turner pictured the progress of Anglo-American agriculture as the manifest destiny of the United States, and the Indian gave ground inevitably and deservedly to a superior people and culture. Although historians today seriously question Turner's whole interpretation, it still reigns supreme as a synthesis in many texts and classrooms, and, more significantly, its assumptions continue to inform the basic outlook on the subject. If white technology is portrayed as more efficient than Indian ways, if white governments are described as more complex than Indian ones, if white cultures are pictured as more sophisticated than red ones, then the teacher and the textbook lead the student to think in terms of better and worse, of civilization and savagery, in the same way basically as Turner's American history portrayed the past. No wonder white and many red children alike believe white society deserved to triumph over "primitive" people here and abroad.[3]

As Indian leaders and their friends are fond of pointing out, even when Indian life and ways are included in class and text, elements of the various cultures are ripped out of the context of a whole culture. To represent all Indian societies as hunting and gathering is to falsify the place of agriculture in almost all the societies. Even for most peoples who hunted and fished, agriculture was important to subsistence and economy. Perhaps the most blatant disregard for context occurs in the description of red military activities. Seldom are warriors' lives presented in the total context of male role, of religious beliefs, of the political system, or of the cultural values of a particular Indian people. Peaceful Indian tribes and what role militarism played in the other societies are passed over in favor of a generalized, out-of-context description for all Indians according to the old stereotype. Moreover, the economic and military aspects of Indian life are featured to the disregard of the many religious, musical, political, and other phases of Indian cultures. Perhaps the omission is deliberate, for in these realms of culture a decision as to what is sophisticated or primitive is far more difficult than in technology or warfare. In brief, the multiplicity of Native American societies and the variety of aboriginal cultures are homogenized into a stereotypical "Indian": warlike, crude of technology, and devoid of thought and aesthetics.[4]

Lastly, the stereotype makes the Indian as unbending in the face of time as he is popularly supposed to be under torture. Indian societies and cultures are understood only as they once were. Subsequent changes from pre-white contact days are not attributed to dynamic, innovative Indian leadership and adaptive societies but rather seen as loss of Indian ways for white culture. Change, in this perspective, only destroys Indian cultures, never adds to them. Yet historians do not see, for example, English history as a progressive loss of Anglo-Saxon culture over the years. By not applying the same measure to the past of Indian societies that they do to others, scholars and teachers deny versatility and change to Indian histories. They, in fact, deny Indians a life as Indians, for all changes, for better or for worse, are seen to result purely from white influences. Indian leaders and their societies, under this view, never innovate in religion, politics, or economics but merely respond by meek adoption of white ways after at best militant or passive resistance. A tribe's history therefore becomes entirely the story of white stimulus and Indian response. Each tribe is doomed to extinction as Indians because its people must change and that change involves a compromise with white ways. Indian originality, creative adaptation, or even survival in the face of overwhelming odds, receive no credit under the once-was aboriginal view of history. Internal tribal dynamics are overlooked in favor of external white influences and relationships. The latter are assumed to determine the former, so why bother looking for Indian actions? In this perspective, the historian presumes the cause and limits the possibilities of response by the Indians solely according to stereotype.[5]

Passive Object Problem Common to Many Minorities

In light of these charges no wonder Native Americans see history books, television programs, and popular imagery snuffing out their history and present-day existence through denial, defamation, distortion, and stereotype. Too late to undo the wrongs of the past, they feel impelled to correct the story of their past and to convince other Americans of their growing numbers and continued existence. Convinced that omission and detraction of their past is no mere accident but a deliberate use of the Indian stereotype to "whitewash" the nefarious activities of past Anglo-Americans and to forget present-day neglect, Indian activists, scholars, and their white friends seek to resurrect Indian history both to teach the whites what they did and do and to encourage renewed pride among Indians in their own heritage. By reclaiming the Indians' past as they understand it, these leaders hope to use its story for the welfare and cultural identity long denied the original inhabitants and owners of America.

Their search and its use differs little from that of others who see themselves neglected in the American history customarily taught by and for the middle-class whites. In short, Indians share with Blacks, women, lower classes, and others what we can call the "passive object" problem in interpreting American history. That history as traditionally told omits these groups or treats them as passive rather than active in determining their destinies. Blacks, females, and poor people, like Indians, complain that they too are left out of the telling of United States history, or they are portrayed as lacking innovative leaders and merely following the cues of the dominant white, master class. Scholars, for example, question whether the lower classes could provide their own leaders, or whether they must be led by middle-class politicians seeking their own personal ends. Other scholars wonder whether women constitute a separate analytical category, that is, whether they should be analyzed apart from class, color, husband's status, or family background. Perhaps the passive object problem is pinpointed best by the changing interpretation of the Black experience in the United States. So much of recent scholarship on Afro-American history concentrated on discovering Black people in the past where history books omitted them or on recapturing the thoughts and actions of Black leaders and their followers when evidence of such was believed nonexistent. In short, in each case, the complaints of all these minority groups boil down to accusing traditional American history of being a one-sided story as usually told in text, classroom, and scholarly monograph. Spokesmen for all these submerged groups now hope to produce the other side of the story to show how active each group was in creating the history of the nation considered as a whole as well as in directing its own destiny.

Because the general problem of being treated as passive objects is common to Blacks, Indians, women, and the lower classes, many of the historiographic remedies proposed by spokesmen for each group are similar. Thus all seek admission into the mainstream of United States history by tracing their role in the American heritage and detailing their leaders and contributions. On the other hand, each group has a special role and problems unique to understanding its place in American history, and so I will restrict further discussion to Native American solutions to the passive object problem. Overcoming the passive object status for each group, but especially for Indians, is not so easily achieved as many minority spokesmen would lead us to believe. Significant morally and important as rectifying their traditional image in American history is for the future welfare of Indians, the conceptual problems involved in doing so have not been squarely faced by most scholars, red or white.

Indian-Proposed Remedial Approaches

In common with Blacks and European immigrants, Indians utilize the "contributions" approach as one way of rounding out the one-sided story of the American past. Thus in the pages of the *Indian Historian* and in pamphlets and books by Indian scholars, the reader finds long lists of the contributions Native Americans made to the general American way of life: pioneering trails and sites, words in the language, games, medicinal lore and drugs, foods and crops, inventions and artifacts. Without doubt, American geography, language, and life would be far poorer without the vocabulary and items derived directly or inspired indirectly by Indian sources, but Indian and other scholars claim subtler and more significant contributions to American life than names and artifacts. All point out the influence of the Indian on the American imagination from the popular captivity narratives of the eighteenth century to the dime novels of the nineteenth and the movies and television programs of the twentieth century. William Brandon in a reasoned assessment of the Indian contribution to American history raises the question whether whites could have settled the New World without the open, friendly greeting and aid proffered by Indian societies to the invaders. Since Native American allies helped white conquerors defeat other Indian groups when the Europeans were too weak to control the natives, Brandon argued that only Indian help enabled initial white settlement and later conquest of the Americans.[6] Perhaps the most extreme claims for Indian contributions were put forth by the longtime friend and lawyer for Indian groups, Felix Cohen, in an article with the satirical title, "Americanizing the White Man." To the usual list of contributions, he added the American conception of freedom, lack of respect for hierarchical authority, universal female suffrage, and the pattern of United States union and federalism (inspired by the League of the Iroquois).[7] In these days of environmental concern and the prospect for a cultural revolution by the young, new influences and inspiration are seen in the land ethic, ecological philosophies, and communalism practiced by the first Americans. In short, many white and Indian spokesmen argue that only by following traditional Indian respect for land and the sharing presumed common to Indian tribes in the past can Americans as a whole solve the present-day crisis brought on by previous white greed, racism, and cultural imperialism.[8]

In addition to the "contributions" approach to the forgotten or passive object problem, Indians, like Blacks and European immigrants, have stressed the "great man" or "heroes" approach. They have searched their past for those leaders who worked in the interests of Indian peoples against white adversaries. Alvin Josephy provided a good example of this approach in his book, whose title reveals its criterion of selection, *The Patriot Chiefs: A Chronicle of American Indian Leadership.*[9] Not the compromiser or the politician but the tragic hero opposing overwhelming white odds for the sake of a lost cause are the heroes and true patriots in this approach. In the opinion of Josephy and Indian scholars, such men as Popé, Pontiac, Tecumseh, and Chief Joseph deserve the same place of importance in American history texts as Nathan Hale, George Washington, or Robert E. Lee. Not only do such Indian leaders go unhonored in the history books, they claim, but those men who exploited or killed them, individuals like Andrew Jackson, are extolled.

An approach unique to the Indian tale of American History as opposed to that of other passive object groups is the story of the treaties made between Anglo-American governments and various tribes. Although most European nations denied aboriginal inhabitants sovereignty over themselves or their soil, still they treated Indian peoples as foreign powers and as possessors of their lands for sale purposes. From this incongruous situation in European conception and law came the hundreds of negotiations and documents called treaties when first Europeans and then Americans wished allies, peace, or lands from various native societies. To many Native Americans these treaties could be characterized, as Virgil Vogel has those of the Jackson period, as "masterpieces of intimidation, bribery, threats, misrepresentation, force, and fraud." Thus we could label the history of treaty wrongs the "fraud-and-dispossession" approach to American Indian history. The devious side of treaty-making is well known to scholars but seldom finds much of a place in general American history texts. As a result, Indians claim that other Americans rarely realize the full extent of the fraudulent practices and broken promises of their ancestors, although Helen Hunt Jackson as early as the year 1881 detailed these swindles in her *A Century of Dishonor.*[10]

Allied to the "fraud-and-dispossession" approach in its implications for moral judgments on past white actions is the "who-is-more-civilized" approach. In checking the annals of white-Indian relations, the researcher can find as many barbarities committed by whites against Indians as the usual vice-versa image. White atrocities of scalping, skinning victims, torture, and other practices gruesome to modern sensibilities occur as frequently in the record as those done by so-called savages. Certainly for whites to claim all the civilized virtues on their side and all the barbaric vices on the Indian side as they once did in captivity narratives or in yesterday's movies is to falsify the past. We are beginning to see a reversal of victim and villain in recent movies, so that greedy, vicious whites now destroy hapless Indian innocents.[11]

The "who-is-more-civilized" approach embraces also the correction of distortions about Indian cultures of the past. When Indian writers point out that their ancestors farmed or hunted more often than warred, they seek to show how "civilized" their forebears were. Indian claims to systems of irrigation, a complicated calendar, and toy wheels as well as to beautiful arts and dances, a vast treasurehouse of oral literature, and meaningful philosophies of existence are all efforts to weigh the balance more evenly between the New and Old World cultures and thus refute the invidious equation between civilization and savagery with the two hemispheres. In the same way the "contributions" approach can be used to bolster the "who-is-more-civilized" approach. As traditional middle-class values in the dominant American culture become increasingly questioned, Indian ways of thought and living become more "civilized" than previously appreciated. The current ecological crusade and the modern movement for a cultural revolution, for example, transform the Indian land ethic and communal style of life from a primitive counter-model to the previously civilized Euro-American society to an ideal life-way for modern Americans who wish to preserve civilization from the downfall threatened by a continuation of older American values and practices. A new appreciation of Indian wisdom is spreading through the young population. Thus do the "contributions" and "who-is-more-civilized" approaches join and reinforce each other given the trends of the day in the United States.

Another approach well developed in Black history but more implicit in Indian materials so far is the "crushed-personality" and "cultural-theft" emphases. Stanley Elkins' famed *Slavery* put forth the thesis quite explicitly for Afro-American personality and culture.[12] The traumas of the Atlantic voyage added to the removal from native society shocked Blacks out of their cultures. The absolute control and power of coercion held by the southern slaveholder infantilized the Black person and robbed him of his autonomous personality. To prove the latter, Elkins presented his famous concentration camp analogy. Although scholars and others long have noted the similarity between Indian reservation and concentration camp, they have not developed fully the psychological and cultural implications of the notion in the manner of Elkins. Surely anthropologists provide ample materials to prove such a case in their studies of culture-and-personality and revitalization movements.[13] These studies portray vividly the demoralization among Indians, particularly male, in military defeat, removal from familiar lands, and placement upon reservations. Monographs upon the severe psychological problems of the Indian child in school or his parents at home as they try to straddle two cultures supply additional confirmation of the approach. Certainly the outlines of the story are sufficiently known to develop a lengthy indictment of the systematic white destruction of Indian personalities and cultures, and we only await an Elkins for the Indians.

Indian activists and scholars do not end their search for a usable past with the approaches outlined here, but these constitute the chief trends in the new Indian history as preached and produced. Indians are not the first to condemn traditional American history for omitting or distorting their past in it. Nor are they alone in wanting to produce a heritage that they can be proud of at the same time as it offers a refutation of those white racist and imperialist pretentions that masquerade as the standard history of all the American peoples. Indians basically seek their place in the American history books through some approaches, as "heroes" and "contributions," typical of the Black and immigrant searches for a usable past and through emphases peculiar to their past, as the recital of treaty wrongs and "who is more civilized." The destruction of personality and culture is, so far, more employed by white anthropologists and historians than Indian scholars, and perhaps will remain so, because such a view contradicts Native American emphasis upon the persistence of Indian personality and cultural traits into the present. A white Elkins is sure to advance the thesis as an aid to understanding his red friends only to be repudiated as a racist enemy by Indian leaders. Such a result would only show that often the white search for a usable Indian past is not appreciated by Indians in the way the authors intended.

Intellectual and Moral Implications of Proposed Remedies

The gap between white and Indian searches for a usable past suggests the general problem of the purposes of all the approaches. What ends are sought through the transformation of American history by these methods? The main goal would seem to be the upgrading of the Indian image in both Indian and white eyes. Providing heroes, elevating customs and peoples previously assumed inferior, and in general showing the larger role of red men in the American past offer a new cultural identity to the Indian child who can view his forebears with respect, and provide the white child with the sensitivity and wisdom to acknowledge the sins committed by his ancestors and rectify the wrongs of the present. In fact, though, do the approaches really accomplish what the advocates intend? Are the implications of the methods the same in reality as the ends espoused by Indian leaders? At bottom, do the approaches produce a history according to white or Indian views and values? Most of the approaches give only the appearance of denying white values at the expense of submitting to them in the end. The fundamental criterion for selection and emphasis in the approaches is all too often an appeal to white feeling and basically confirms the white way of looking at things.

The "contributions" approach most obviously rests upon white standards of what is important to American life today. Whether contributions to language, geography, medicine, agriculture, clothing, or economy are listed, all are just those elements of native cultures found useful to and therefore adopted by Euro-Americans. Even the new man-in-nature theme and communalism depend upon the fads of ecology and youth culture. Those many aspects of Indian cultures neither desired nor borrowed by whites are forgotten in the lists of contributions. Indian literature, philosophy, art, and religion can be listed as contributions only insofar as they can be made to be understood and appreciated by white people; otherwise the "contributions" approach fails to work. Its very criterion of selection is based on white values and needs, not Indian values and needs.

Moreover, the "contributions" approach negates the criterion of not ripping elements out of cultural context. Whether hailing quinine or peyote, the religious ceremonies surrounding their use are denied or minimized. Whether praising ecological adaptation to the natural environment or the tribal sharing of goods, the various economic systems and cultures in which these were embedded are omitted. Indian leaders and scholars as well as their white supporters do an injustice to the very diversity of Native American societies and cultures by speaking of "Indian" contributions as such. There was no one Indian philosophy, art, or music, any more than there was one Caucasian or Oriental philosophy, art, or music. The toy wheel was Aztec, and the kayak was Eskimo, not Indian. Thus the very listing of "Indian" contributions supports the ancient white stereotype, which called all New World peoples Indians, rather than acknowledging the diverse cultural experiences lived by Native Americans.

The other approaches may not appear as blatant in their dependence upon white values, but they too rest upon similar premises. The "fraud and-dispossession" approach and the recital of treaty wrongs eliminate the problem of cultural context somewhat but still appeal mainly to white guilt and law procedures. Surely the vivid recounting of the grim misdeeds of past white government agents keeps Native American hostilities and mistrust alive, but the primary utility of this method would seem to hinge upon remedy in white men's courts and consciences. The "who-is-more-civilized" approach, whether as a tale of atrocities or as an upgrading of Indian cultural standing in relation to past white cultures, likewise, appeals to white moral and cultural ends. Insofar as it details the horrible deeds committed by white soldiers and frontiersmen against Indian victims, it relies upon white moral standards and a guilty conscience. To the degree the approach demonstrates the sophistication and complexity of Indian cultures, then it uses a white measurement of progress. Even the "great heroes" approach merely reverses the chauvinism of the whites. In brief we have the same values praised by Indians as do the whites, but the traitor to old-time Americans is now portrayed as the hero to his people. More significant, by praising primarily military heroes, and frequently only in regard to white relationships, the plot of the story is dominated in the end by the white history of westward expansion and leaves out the political innovation, creative adaptation, or the internal dynamics of tribal histories. Concentration upon great men may distort Indian history therefore as much as it does white history, for it minimizes the social and historical context of the leaders in relation to their peoples.

Just as the various approaches usually correct the past according to white criteria, so they also depend upon the framework traditional to white American history. Some Indian additions may be made and some moral judgments reversed, but the overall story is still that of white society and values and not Indian societies and cultures. Pontiac and Tecumseh, moccasins and corn, and treaties of Removal are added to Washington and Jackson, the Constitution and automobiles, and the treaties of Paris and Versailles, but the latter series is in the mainstream of the story and the former is obviously side currents of American history in its overall conception. The red additions enhance and change in detail the white story, but do they alter the fundamental outlines of American history? Such details may aid interracial understanding and equality, but the basic nature of American history remains unchanged in outlook and outcome. Not only do the "contributions," "hero," and "fraud-and-dispossession" approaches not alter the basic framework of American history but neither do they provide the native cultural contexts deemed so essential to the proper understanding of the first Americans, for, in the end, the Indians' actions, artifacts, and attitudes are lodged in a white context. Along with the omission of native cultural contexts goes the failure to present Indian lives as dynamic or changing in a way meaningful to the story of Native Americans in the United States. Restricted by the basic white historical framework, the various approaches neglect perforce the internal dynamics of Indian societies and their relations with each other as well as with white societies. The motive power, so to speak, of American history generally rests in white actions and attitudes, and so by grafting on Indian contributions, treaties, and heroes, changes in Indian lives result from white contact and forces rather than from Indian creativity in adaptation, resistance, or innovation.

Each intended correction, therefore, loses its basic goal in achieving its immediate end. In short, the resolution of the passive-object problem through the various approaches is only apparent, for the fundamental problem remains: Indian history is the by-product of the white story rather than a story in its own right. The Indian moon, although clearly visible in the new historiographic sky, still orbits the white sun and derives its luster from reflecting the larger body. The grossest omissions and distortions are thankfully corrected, but the basic Indian complaint about traditional American history as it has been written and taught holds almost as true for the new Indian history as advocated by so many Native Americans.

The Solution: Indian-Centered History

What is clearly needed is a new Indian-centered history, both to accomplish the larger moral ends and to present better history. As the name suggests, Indian-centered history focuses on Indian actors and Indian-Indian relations and relegates white-Indian relations and white actors to the periphery of the main arena of action. Rather than assuming inevitable unilinear progress toward assimilation, Indian-centered history presents Indians as individuals in their cultures and tribes coping with Indian-introduced as well as white innovations to older ways of life. Indian-centered history follows Indian peoples from before white contact to their present lives on reservations, in urban ghettoes, and on rural farms. The older and the newer Indian history, regardless of moral judgment pro and con white policy and actions, portrayed Indians reacting to white stimuli and native societies being extinguished through death or assimilation. Intra-tribal and external relations with other Indian societies were neglected in favor of white relations presumed the main cause of the eventual outcome of the tribal history. On the other hand, Indian-centered history concentrates on the ways Indians and their leaders coped with the course of *their* destinies. Assimilation and extinction are not presumed; white stimuli are not denied; intra- and inter-tribal relations are not omitted.[14]

The advantages of such an approach to Indian history as proposed here are manifest in terms of the argument so far. This kind of Indian history retains the benefits of the various approaches to eliminate neglect and distortion but achieves these ends by placing the story of a tribe in its proper cultural and historical context. The beginnings of such history must be rooted in pre-white contact culture and society.The diversity of cultures, societies, and political units is built into the very foundations of such an approach. Indian actors are not only the heroes of lost causes, but are also the politicians of compromise, the religious leaders, and everyday men and women going about the mundane activities of existence in a dynamic world, whether caused by natural, Indian, or white forces. Neither virtues nor faults, neither contributions nor misdeeds are stressed apart from how they fitted into the specific culture at the particular time. The static quality of Indian cultures and societies as usually described is eliminated in favor of the normal persistence and change evident in any society throughout its history. The actions of past Indians become natural in terms of their cultural context, and the heritage of Indian-Americans becomes understandable in terms of its historical dynamics and continuity from past to present. In short, what Indian-centered history aims to achieve is what is usually done in any good white-centered history of American society.[15]

To specify the qualities of Indian-centered history is easier than to produce it, given the problems of theory and evidence involved. While the writing of all history involves such problems,[16] certain problems peculiar to Indian history exacerbate the situation. First, so much of the documentary evidence derives from white-perceived accounts of white-Indian relations. To extract Indian-centered history from such sources, the historian and teacher must read between the lines. More Indian-produced evidence will be turned up through careful attention to oral sources and tribal records, but in the end, the historian will never possess the fullness of record he would like for overcoming the passive-object problem. Even for Indian-produced sources the historian faces the personal and political biases that gave rise to the materials. Anthropological data and theory aid the teacher and scholar in considering these problems but offer no quick and sure solutions. Ultimately, theory and evidence in Indian-centered history are inextricably bound to past misunderstandings between whites and Indians and the translation of that confusion into the depiction of both parties' histories. Nothing less than the resolution of these problems of theory and evidence will permit the accomplishment of Indian-centered history, and nothing less than Indian-centered history fulfills the larger moral ends Indian leaders and their white friends see as necessary to providing a usable Indian past for red and white peoples alike.[17]

The desirability of Indian-centered history does not demand the neglect or elimination of the many books presenting a white-centered version of white-Indian relations. Rather, it suggests that their partiality of approach be recognized for what it is: only part of the whole story. The continued validity of a white-centered book or article depends upon the claims of the author and the material presented. If the author pretends to and presents nothing more than a partial tale or analysis of one side in the contact situation, then there seems little problem. On the other hand, if the author assumes that a focus on the white side of Indian relations is more than that, then he fools himself, if not his readers. Perhaps the most culpable author is the one who purports to give an "Indian" view by concentrating on a white-centered story of white-Indian relations but reversing the usual moral judgments upon the two sides in contact. Such an approach is naught but the old one falsely dressed in a new ethical guise. Both white-centered approaches to white-Indian relations and Indian-centered histories are legitimate provided the authors and the readers are aware of the province of each type, for both are different but complementary aspects of the total history of the United States.[18]

FOOTNOTES

[1] The American Indian Historical Society issued a comprehensive indictment from the Indian viewpoint of school materials in *Textbooks and the American Indian.* San Francisco: Indian Historian Press. 1970. Also see the brief pamphlet by Virgil J. Vogel. *The Indian in American History.* Chicago: Integrated Education Associates, 1968. Both available in paper from the publishers. Contemporary political currents prompting demands by Native Americans may be followed in Stan Steiner. *The New Indians.* New York: Harper and Row, 1968 (paper). Earlier twentieth-century Indian politics are the subject of Hazel Hertzberg. *The Search for an American Indian Identity: Modern Pan-Indian Movements.* Syracuse: Syracuse University Press, 1971.

This chapter does not pretend to give the usual bibliography of Indian history because the American Historical Association issued in 1972 a revised edition of William T. Hagan. *The Indian in American History.* Washington, D.C.: Service

Center for Teachers of History, 1963. (paper). Many of the general books listed below contain good bibliographies, including in note 14 some references to films and other items particularly valuable to the classroom teacher.

[2] *The Indian Historian* published by the American Indian Historical Society, 1451 Masonic Avenue, San Francisco, Calif. 94117, contains articles presenting "Indian" views on the American past.

[3] For the frontier imagery of white Americans that went into Turner's interpretation, see Henry N. Smith. *Virgin Land: The American West as Symbol and Myth.* Cambridge: Harvard University Press, 1950 (paper). Books on white images of Native Americans are: Roy H. Pearce. *The Savages of America: A Study of the Indian and the Idea of Civilization.* Baltimore: Johns Hopkins Press, 1953 (published in paper as *Savagism and Civilization: A Study of the Indian and the American Mind.* 1965); Lewis Saum. *The Fur Trader and the Indian.* Seattle: University of Washington, 1965 (paper). A comparison of Spanish, Dutch, French, and English perceptions and policies is Howard Peckham and Charles Gibson, editors. *Attitudes of Colonial Powers Toward the American Indians.* Salt Lake City: University of Utah Press, 1969.

[4] Standard anthropological texts on the various cultures of North America are: Robert F. Spencer, Jesse D. Jennings, and others. *The Native American: Prehistory and Ethnology of the North American Indians.* New York: Harper and Row, 1965; Wendell H. Oswalt. *This Land Was Theirs: A Study of the North American Indian.* New York: John Wiley and Sons, 1966; Ruth M. Underhill. *Red Man's America: A History of Indians in the United States.* Revised edition, Chicago: University of Chicago Press, 1971 (paper); Harold E. Driver. *Indians of North America.* Second edition, revised, Chicago: University of Chicago Press, 1969 (paper). The latter volume is arranged according to topic to facilitate comparison. Ruth Underhill provides a good introduction to *Red Man's Religion: Beliefs and Practices of the Indians North of Mexico.* Chicago: University of Chicago Press, 1965. An extensive bibliography, now somewhat out-of-date, classified by tribe is George P. Murdock. *Ethnographic Bibliography of North America.* Third edition, New Haven: Human Relations Area Files, 1960.

[5] Acculturation studies are frequently accused of assimilationist, if not progress, biases. Two standard acculturation monographs supplying a wealth of historical information on many tribes are: Ralph Linton, editor. *Acculturation in Seven American Indian Tribes.* New York: D. Appleton Century Co., 1940; Edward Spicer, editor. *Perspectives in American Indian Culture Change.* Chicago: University of Chicago Press, 1961.

[6] "American Indians and American History." *The American West* 2: 14-25, 91-93; No. 1, Spring 1965. For other lists of contributions, see Vogel. *The Indian in American History;* especially his bibliography published also in *The Indian Historian,* new series, 1: 36-38; No. 1, Summer 1968; Driver. *Indians of North America;* A. Irving Hallowell. "The Backwash of the Frontier: The Impact of the Indian on American Culture," in Clifton Kroeber and Walker Wyman, editors. *The Frontier in Perspective.* Madison: University of Wisconsin Press, 1965 (paper).

[7] *American Scholar.* 21: 177-191; No. 2, Spring 1952.

[8] One of the points, for example, of Vine Deloria, Jr. *Custer Died for Your Sins: An Indian Manifesto.* New York: Macmillan, 1969 (paper); *We Talk, You Listen: New Tribes, New Turf.* New York: Macmillan, 1970 (paper to be available).

[9] New York: Viking Press, 1961 (paper). Compare, however, Thurman Wilkins. *Cherokee Tragedy: The Story of the Ridge Family and the Decimation of a People.* New York: Macmillan, 1970.

[10] The approach is exemplified well in the title of a recent monograph by Georgianna C. Nammack. *Fraud, Politics, and the Dispossession of the Indians: The Iroquois Land Frontier in the Colonial Period.* Norman: University of

Oklahoma Press, 1969. Wilcomb Washburn provides a survey of the historical and present-day legal status of Indian lands and persons in *Red Man's Land/White Man's Law: A Study of the Past and Present Status of the American Indian.* New York: Charles Scribner's Sons, 1971. Overall Anglo-American government policy and its effects is the main subject of William T. Hagan, *American Indians.* Chicago: University of Chicago Press, 1961 (paper). Also see for the beginnings of United States policy: Reginald Horsman. *Expansion and American Indian Policy, 1783-1812.* East Lansing: Michigan State University Press, 1967; and Francis P. Prucha. *American Indian Policy in the Formative Years: The Indian Trade and Intercourse Acts, 1790-1834.* Cambridge: Harvard University Press, 1962 (paper).

[11] The popularity of Dee Brown's *Bury My Heart at Wounded Knee: An Indian History of the American West.* New York: Holt, Rinehart and Winston, 1970 (paper), attests to the efficacy of this approach.

[12] *Slavery: A Problem in American Institutional and Intellectual Life.* Second edition. Chicago: University of Chicago, 1968.

[13] Anthony F. C. Wallace, an outstanding authority on culture-and-personality and revitalization movements, applies his insights in two histories: *King of the Delawares: Teedyuscung 1700-1763.* Philadelphia: University of Pennsylvania Press, 1949; and *The Death and Rebirth of the Seneca: The History and Culture of the Great Iroquois Nation, Their Destruction and Demoralization, and Their Cultural Revival at the Hands of the Indian Visionary, Handsome Lake.* New York: Knopf, 1969 (paper).

[14] A good introduction to the early history of Native Americans is William T. Sanders and Joseph Marino. *New World Prehistory: Archaeology of the American Indian.* Englewood Cliffs, N.J.: Prentice-Hall, 1970 (paper). Present-day life and problems are the subjects of: Jack O. Waddell and Michael Watson, editors. *The American Indian in Urban Society.* Boston: Little, Brown and Co., (paper); Stuart Levine and Nancy O. Lurie, editors. *The American Indian Today.* Paper edition, Baltimore: Penguin Books, 1970; George Simpson and J. Milton Yinger, editors. "American Indians and American Life," an entire issue of *The Annals of the American Academy of Political and Social Science.* 311: May 1957.

Informative efforts and approaches to the total Indian past and present are: Edward Spicer. *Cycles of Conquest: The Impact of Spain, Mexico, and the United States on the Indians of the Southwest, 1533-1960.* Tucson: University of Arizona Press, 1962 (paper); Jack D. Forbes. *Native Americans of California and Nevada.* Healdsburg, Calif.: Naturegraph Publishers, 1969 (paper); Eleanor Leacock and Nancy O. Lurie, editors. *North American Indians in Historical Perspective.* New York: Random House, 1971; Murray L. Wax. *Indian Americans: Unity and Diversity.* Englewood Cliffs, N.J.: Prentice-Hall, 1971 (paper); Deward E. Walker, Jr., editor. *The Emergent Native Americans: A Reader in Culture Contact.* Boston: Little, Brown and Co., 1972.

[15] The possibilities of such history have been exemplified best so far for the native peoples of Mexico and Guatemala in Eric Wolf. *Sons of the Shaking Earth.* Chicago: University of Chicago Press, 1959 (paper).

[16] *A Behavioral Approach to Historical Analysis.* New York: Free Press, 1969 (paper).

[17] The problems of theory and evidence in producing Indian-centered history are treated in my article, "The Political Context of a New Indian History." *Pacific Historical Review.* 40: 357-382, No. 3, August 1971. The even more difficult problems posed by such an approach for a general history of Indians are examined in my new preface for my book, *Salvation and the Savage: An Analysis of Protestant Missions and American Indian Response, 1787-1862.* New York: Atheneum, 1972 (paper). But see the interesting effort to overcome the problems of an overall history in Edward Spicer. *A Short History of the Indians of the United States.* New York: Van Nostrand Reinhold Co., 1969 (paper).

[18] Most books and articles listed in the bibliographies on American Indian history are white-centered treatments of white-Indian relations. A representative selection of articles (abridged) in the field is anthologized by Roger L. Nichols and George R. Adams. *The American Indian: Past and Present.* Waltham, Mass.: Xerox College Publishing, 1971 (paper). Paul Prucha has collected and abridged essays primarily on some white approaches to *The Indian in American History.* New York: Holt, Rinehart and Winston, 1971 (paper).

· 3 ·

The Afro-Americans:
From Mythology to Reality

John W. Blassingame

SPURRED by mass uprisings in the streets and on the campuses, young scholars launched a campaign in the 1960's for a "usable black past"—a dramatic shift from the conspiracy of silence, vituperation, and misrepresentation of historians bent on preserving white supremacy. Columbia's celebrated John W. Burgess spoke for the white supremacists of the late nineteenth century when he asserted: "A black skin means membership in a race of men which has never of itself succeeded in subjecting passion to reason; has never, therefore, created any civilization of any kind."[1] In the mid-twentieth century, Ellis Merton Coulter went so far as to distort the comments of eyewitnesses to prove his allegation that blacks could not subject their passion to reason during the Reconstruction period.[2]

The influence of the Dunnings and Coulters caused such black scholars as Vincent Harding and Sterling Stuckey to demand an end to the distortion, deletion, and denial of black humanity. While the riots in Watts and Newark gave a new urgency to such demands, they have been made continuously by black intellectuals for more than a hundred years. Young scholars insist on stripping away the hypocrisy and myths surrounding the black past. According to Sterling Stuckey,

> Whether writing about Afro-Americans during and since slavery . . . , the historian must challenge the old assumptions about those on the lower depths—establishment homilies . . .—by revealing the internal values and life styles of the supposedly inarticulate. . . . As history has been used in the West to degrade people of color, black history must seek dignity for mankind.[3]

Although some "New Left" historians have applauded the revisions called for by black scholars, Stuckey charges that many white historians

53

"have not been above lecturing blacks on how they should perceive and record their experiences. . . . Of all the people to deliver sermons to blacks, they would be among those least likely to receive a respectful hearing."[4]

One white historian who has received a respectful hearing is C. Vann Woodward. "The legitimate demand for a 'new' Negro history is the result," Woodward claimed, "of white historians' ethnocentric self-flattery, complacency, racial chauvinism, and self-righteousness. But the resulting distortions will not be corrected by imitation of that same philosophy. . . ." Such a fear of black chauvinism was stated in extreme terms by Stanley Elkins. Practically reducing the movement to the level of the absurd, Elkins contended that "If Negroes want the kind of usable past that Parson Weems offered—a black George Washington chopping down a cherry tree and throwing a silver dollar across the Rappahannock—this can be provided. We can trot any number of black heroes across the stage."[5] Rarely have black intellectuals discussed their historiography in such simplistic terms.[6]

Benjamin Quarles has written in great detail about the "new black history." It is obvious, he argued, that "to properly assess the black past we need newer, non-traditional techniques" embracing several disciplines and approaches. This new history has great potential:

> For blacks it is a new way to see themselves. For whites it furnishes a new version of American history, one that easily challenges our national sense of smugness and self-righteousness and our avowal of fair play. Beyond this the new black history summons the entire historical guild—writers, teachers and learners—to higher levels of expectation and performance. . . . A new black history would revitalize education, quickening whatever it touches.[7]

Whether black history stresses the victories, achievements, and heroes demanded by the black masses seeking pride; focuses on the black nationalist's white exploiters and oppressors in order to undergird the ideology of black liberation; emphasizes the objective search for truth of the black scholar or white students' interest in the impact of the black presence on the American past, it adds a new dimension to our traditional outlook on history. For each of these groups, the objectives are perhaps legitimate and certainly intertwined.

The ideological debates have forced teachers in black history courses to take a new approach to the subject. The question for such teachers is not whether to emphasize the "heroic tradition" or the "realistic" story of blacks. Rather, it is whether to make blacks or whites the major actors in the story. Unfortunately, teachers usually place too much emphasis on the role of whites in the black historical drama. This emphasis often leads to weak "Race Relations" courses which could be better taught by sociologists. When the major emphasis is placed on the activities of black individuals and communities, however, teachers are in a better position to answer the difficult questions students are raising about the contemporary actions of blacks and their position in American society. Such an approach also has the virtue of automatically narrowing the focus of black history courses. Then, too, an overwhelming majority of the lightly researched and tangentially related works on blacks are eliminated from consideration. The number of works in this category alone is enough of a recommendation for taking this approach.

Fortunately, there are many guides which can be helpful. Still, no recent bibliographical aid can pretend to be as extensive as Monroe N. Work's classic, *A Bibliography of the Negro in Africa and America.*[8] Dorothy Porter's *The Negro in the United States: A Selected Bibliography* is the most comprehensive short work.[9] Although the format is sometimes idiosyncratic, James McPherson, *et al., Blacks in America: Bibliographical Essays* is an excellent annotated general guide to articles and books.[10] Elizabeth W. Miller and Mary Fisher, comps., *The Negro in America: A Bibliography* contains a relatively comprehensive list of articles and books published between 1954 and 1970.[11]

Textbooks on black history are numerous but vary considerably in quality. John Hope Franklin's *From Slavery to Freedom: A History of Negro Americans* is the most detailed narrative study[12] while Rayford Logan's *The Negro in the United States: A Brief History* has no peer as a short text.[13] Logan teamed with Irving S. Cohen to write the best high school textbook, *The American Negro: Old World Background and New World Experience,* successfully integrating the story of blacks with that of whites and including review questions, documents, maps and illustrations in each chapter.[14] Lerone Bennett combined a journalistic style and hard-hitting generalizations to make his *Before the Mayflower: A History of the Negro in America, 1619-1966* the most readable and enjoyable of the shorter interpretive histories.[15] While weak on urbanization and cultural and intellectual life, *From Plantation to Ghetto* by August Meier and Elliott Rudwick is the only really sophisticated interpretive black history text with a wealth of detail.[16]

The premier collection of primary sources is still Herbert Aptheker's *A Documentary History of the Negro People in the United States.*[17] More comprehensive than Aptheker on recent events is John Hope Franklin and Isidore Starr, eds., *The Negro in Twentieth Century America: A Reader on the Struggle for Civil Rights.*[18] John H. Bracey,

August Meier, and Elliott Rudwick, eds., *The Afro-Americans: Selected Documents* emphasizes a case study approach with many sources rarely found in other collections.[19] The best collections designed for high school students are William L. Katz, ed., *Eyewitness: The Negro in American History* and Milton Meltzer, ed., *In Their Own Words: A History of the American Negro.*[20]

Increasingly, scholars have abandoned the well-nigh impossible task of compiling general collections in favor of documents on specific topics. Illuminating works on civil rights cases include Richard Bardolph, ed., *The Civil Rights Record: Black Americans and the Law, 1849-1970,* Albert P. Blaustein and Robert L. Zangrando, eds., *Civil Rights and the American Negro: A Documentary History,* and Joseph Tussman, ed., *The Supreme Court on Racial Discrimination.*[21] Louis Ruchames' *Racial Thought in America: From the Puritans to Abraham Lincoln* is indispensable for understanding white racism and Herbert J. Storing, ed., *What Country Have I? Political Writings by Black Americans,* August Meier, Elliott Rudwick, and Francis L. Broderick, eds., *Black Protest Thought in the Twentieth Century,* and Floyd Barbour, ed., *The Black Power Revolt: A Collection of Essays* for insights on the black response.[22]

As of 1972, there are only two really comprehensive collections of essays on black history. Of these, the two-volume *The Making of Black America: Essays on Negro Life and History* edited by August Meier and Elliott Rudwick is the most illuminating.[23] Eric Foner's *America's Black Past: A Reader in Afro-American History* is by far the best one-volume collection.[24] The other collections are, by and large, pale reflections of these works, hashed out too quickly by persons unfamiliar with the field and frequently reprinting the same undistinguished essays. Recent exceptions to the general mediocrity of such collections include the original and often provocative essays contributed to Nat Huggins, *et al.,* eds., *Key Issues in the Afro-American Experience* and the multi-volumed *Explorations in the Black Experience* edited by John H. Bracey, August Meier, and Elliott Rudwick.[25] *Explorations,* with several 200-page books on such topics as *Free Negroes* and the *Rise of the Ghetto,* marked a new departure in interpretive collections which promises to be extremely useful to teachers and students interested in a serious examination of the black experience or including specific topics in general American history courses. Drawing on a wide reading in the sources, the authors have chosen the essays in their collections so carefully that they can often replace textbooks.

The poor quality of most collections and textbooks reflects the failure of historians to grapple with the dilemma that W.E.B. Du Bois posed in

1903: the duality of the black experience. According to Du Bois, blacks always felt their twoness: "an American, a Negro; two souls, two thoughts, two unreconciled strivings; two warring ideals in one dark body, whose dogged strength alone keeps it from being torn asunder."[26] The most crippling effect of the refusal to recognize this fundamental principle is the paucity of sophisticated historiographical works on blacks. Earle E. Thorpe in *The Mind of the Negro: an Intellectual History of Afro-Americans; Negro Historians in the United States; Black Historians: A Critique;* and *The Central Theme of Black History* was the pioneer in this area.[27] A number of recent articles, while less comprehensive than the works of Thorpe, are frequently more critical and suggestive of thematic approaches.[28]

Teachers in black history courses must begin with the nature of tribal societies in West Africa, the ancestral home of the American Negro. It is not enough to discuss briefly the ancient African kingdoms of Ghana, Melle, and Songhay since few American blacks actually came from these kingdoms. Even so, they must be examined in order to appreciate Africa's diversity. A most fascinating, profusely illustrated, authoritative, and readable work on the subject is Margaret Shinnie's *Ancient African Kingdoms*.[29] Based on the latest archaeological investigations, Shinnie's volume surpasses most others in its richness of detail. Olivia Vlahos' *African Beginnings* is also an authoritative text suitable for high school students.[30] Henri Labouret's *Africa Before The White Man* places the ancient kingdoms within the context of African tribal societies.[31] The serious reader should also consult John de Graft-Johnson's *African Glory: The Story of Vanished Negro Civilizations,* Roland Oliver, ed., *The Middle Age of African History,* and Basil Davidson's *The Lost Cities of Africa*.[32]

In order to understand the cultural baggage Africans brought with them to the United States it is necessary to examine some of the general features of their life. The best overviews are provided by Jan Vansina's *Kingdoms of the Savanna,* E. G. Parrinder's *African Traditional Religion,* Daryll Forde, ed., *African Worlds: Studies in the Cosmological Ideas and Social Values of African Peoples,* Paul Bohannan's *Africa and Africans,* and J. F. Ade Ajayi and Van Espie, *A Thousand Years of West African History: A Handbook for Teachers and Students*.[33] These general studies should be supplemented by descriptions of specific African societies. The most revealing study is Georges Balandier's *Daily Life in the Kingdom of the Kongo: From the Sixteenth to the Eighteenth Centuries*.[34] Although lacking Balandier's sophistication, Jacob Egharevba's *A Short History of Benin,* M. M. Green's *Ibo Village Affairs,* K. L. Little's *The Mende of Sierra Leone: A West African*

People in Transition, S. O. Biobaku's *The Egba and Their Neighbours, 1842-1872,* and J. F. Ade Ajayi and Robert Smith's *Yoruba Warfare in the Nineteenth Century* can be read with profit.[35]

There are no studies of the slave trade which focus on the hapless Africans. Instead, we learn a great deal about the traders, their profits and the treatment of white sailors. There is, however, some emphasis on the blacks in Daniel Mannix and Malcolm Cowley, *Black Cargoes: A History of the Atlantic Slave Trade, 1518-1865* and Basil Davidson's *Black Mother: The Years of the African Slave Trade,* while Philip D. Curtin's masterful *The Atlantic Slave Trade: A Census* gives the best estimate of the numbers involved.[36] Unfortunately, the weakest section of Curtin's book is that dealing with the United Sates.

If the African has been ignored as an agent in the slave trade, he practically disappears in studies of the colonial period. By focusing almost exclusively on the development of the slave's legal status and "the chicken or the egg" debate over which developed first, slavery or prejudice, historians have neglected to examine the initial efforts of the Africans to cope with a hostile new environment.[37] Gerald Mullin's *Flight and Rebellion: Slave Resistance in Eighteenth Century Virginia* is in many ways the most satisfactory study of the transplanted Africans and the first work to examine systematically the problem of "adjustment."[38] Darold D. Wax's "Negro Resistance to the Early American Slave Trade" also gives some glimpses of the enslavement process.[39] Both Mullin and Wax, however, stressed "resistance" to the virtual exclusion of the other kinds of "adjustments" the Africans made.

Scholarly neglect of blacks in the seventeenth and eighteenth centuries has seriously crippled efforts to deal with the question of African survivals in black culture. Melville J. Herskovits in *The Myth of the Negro Past*[40] argued that there were many survivals while E. Franklin Frazier in *The Negro in the United States* contended that there were few.[41] Neither man did enough research in the sources to support his theory. The prevailing view is that slavery stripped the black of all manifestations of his African culture. Lorenzo D. Turner, *Africanisms in the Gullah Dialect,*[42] Romeo B. Garrett, John F. Szwed, Daniel J. Crowley, Richard A. Waterman, Alan Lomax, and Robert F. Thompson argue persuasively, however, that there were many African survivals.[43] Still, the debate has not advanced far beyond the questions raised by Herskovits in 1941.

The institution of slavery has been studied for more than one hundred years by historians. Only recently, however, are we beginning to learn something about slaves. Forced to deal for generations with the towering figure of U. B. Phillips and the compelling logic of the theories he expounded in *American Negro Slavery* and *Life and Labor in the Old South*, most scholars have taken the easy way out and concentrated almost exclusively on the white planter.[44] Consequently, we have long-standing debates on profitability, large vs. small planters, antebellum racial (white) attitudes, and plantation management with hardly a glance at the life style of slaves. We know much more about how planters tried to recover fugitive slaves than we do about what the slaves did when they ran away. There are massive studies of efforts of Southern churches to convert the slaves but no systematic examination of slave religion.

Events in the quarters are so insignificant in most studies of slavery that they are useless in black history courses. How could it be otherwise when they devote an average of four pages to the slave family, three to slave religion, and a few lines to spirituals, folklore, and leisure-time activities and follow the narrow focus of Phillips on plantation documents? Assuming that because some of the slave narratives were edited by abolitionists, none of them could be considered as evidence, these scholars automatically guaranteed that the slaves would remain silent. Yet, there were many narrators who had no abolitionist amanuenses and countless other former slaves who wrote their autobiographies after the Civil War. While there are numerous problems involved in using such sources, they are no different in character from those which the historian usually encounters.

Beginning in 1963, scholars attempted to make the debate over slavery less one-sided by bringing the slave forward as a witness. Charles H. Nichols' *Many Thousand Gone: The Ex-Slaves' Account of the Bondage and Freedom* was the first of these suggestive works.[45] Stanley Feldstein examined more narratives than Nichols in his *Once A Slave: The Slave's View of Slavery* but limited his analysis to reporting what the slaves said about a limited number of sometimes unconnected topics. Rather than an intense study of the quarters, Feldstein dealt with too many of the usual topics included in institutional studies of slavery (provisions, crops, types of slaves, and slavery as a national issue). When, however, Feldstein looked at plantation life and attitudes he came closer to the slave.[46] Unfortunately, both Nichols and Feldstein treated the narratives as literature, reporting what the narrators said rather than using them to analyze certain subjects. The methodological weaknesses of Nichols and Feldstein contrasted sharply with Norman R. Yetman's critical introduction and careful selection of WPA interviews for inclusion in his *Life Under the "Peculiar Institution": Selections from the Slave Narrative Collection*.[47] In spite of his care, Yetman had the impossible task of sifting through the reminiscences of blacks who were at least seventy years removed from slavery when they were interviewed in the 1930's.

The selective memory of the ex-slaves is such that their reminiscences generally are more valuable as folklore than as eyewitness accounts. The reprinting of many black autobiographies presents the teacher with the best opportunity to study the plantation from the slave's vantage point. The most revealing of the autobiographies are those of Frederick Douglass, Henry Bibb, Josiah Henson, Gustavus Vassa, Austin Steward, Henry Clay Bruce, Louis Hughes, and Elizabeth Keckley. Several anthologies include the best narratives.[48]

Kenneth Stampp made a valiant effort to characterize slave life in *The Peculiar Institution: Slavery in the Ante-Bellum South* but let Phillips set the terms of the debate and was too wedded to viewing the quarters through the eyes of whites to succeed. In spite of the methodological shortcomings, Stampp presented the most accurate portrait of the plantation.[49]

The most provocative study of slavery to appear in the 1960's is Stanley Elkins, *Slavery: A Problem in American Institutional and Intellectual Life*.[50] Arguing persuasively that Southern slavery differed so much from the Latin American institution that a distinctive personality type emerged on American plantations, Elkins theorized that a majority of Southern slaves were Sambos. The child-like docility of the Southern slave was, according to Elkins, analogous to the behavior of the survivors of the German concentration camps and explainable in terms of role psychology and interpersonal theory. Critics of Elkins have proven conclusively that there were more similarities than differences in Southern and Latin American slavery.[51] So far, however, the underlying assumptions of his Sambo thesis have not been challenged. By and large, critics have accepted Elkins' psychological theories, characterization of the German concentration camp, and the pervasiveness of Sambo in "Southern lore." The most serious charge made against Elkins was his failure to support his theory with primary sources.[52]

John W. Blassingame in *The Slave Community: Plantation Life in the Antebellum South* examines a variety of primary sources, analogous institutions, and psychological theories in his look at slaves and masters.[53] Interpersonal theory, analysis of the autobiographies of slaves and masters, and travel accounts lead to a less deterministic and far more complex view of the plantation and slave personality than Elkins' hypothesis. The primary importance of Blassingame's study, however, is that it is the first attempt to study enslavement, family life, rebelliousness, religion, culture, and behavior from the vantage point of the slave quarters. Profusely illustrated, *The Slave Community* tried to show what it was like to be a slave.

An earlier study by Richard Wade, *Slavery in the Cities: The South, 1820-1860* detailed the unique impact of urbanization on slavery.[54] Utilizing unreliable statistics, Wade concluded that urban slavery declined in importance in the 1850's. Apparently, however, the alleged decline in the number of slaves in southern cities was due to a change in the census-taking procedure. In 1850 the slaves belonging to inhabitants of a city had been credited to that city regardless of where the blacks actually resided in the state. The procedure was reversed in 1860: slaves living in a city were credited to that city regardless of where their masters lived.[55]

Practically all studies of slavery mention the problem of resistance. With the exception of Blassingame and Mullins, none of them approach the subject in the systematic fashion of Herbert Aptheker's *American Negro Slave Revolts*.[56] Focusing primarily on conspiracies and white fears rather than actual revolts, Aptheker's book is sadly mistitled. His overenthusiasm and misguided attempt to force black resistance into a Marxian framework have frequently led historians to ridicule the whole idea of rebelliousness. The unkindest cut of all was given by Chase C. Mooney when he described the work as "so subjective and lacking discrimination that the book—in any of its forms—scarcely deserves to be classed as history."[57] Fortunately, most historians have not been so given to hyperbole as Mooney and have admitted that Aptheker's study was more solidly grounded in the sources than most of his predecessors. It stands in sharp contrast, for example, to the undocumented volume of Nicholas Halasz's *The Rattling Chains: Slave Unrest and Revolt in the Antebellum South*.[58] Studies of individual revolts and conspiracies include John Lofton's *Insurrection in South Carolina: The Turbulent World of Denmark Vesey;* Robert S. Starobin, ed., *Denmark Vesey: The Slave Conspiracy of 1822;* Herbert Aptheker's *Nat Turner's Slave Rebellion;* F. Roy Johnson's *The Nat Turner Slave Insurrection;* and Eric Foner, ed., *Nat Turner*.[59] Larry Gara's *The Liberty Line: The Legend of the Underground Railroad* explores the myth and reality of organized escapes.[60]

Fictional treatments of slavery which rise above the banal are infrequent. While most scholars will begin with Harriett B. Stowe's *Uncle Tom's Cabin,* Richard Hildreth's *The Slave; or Memoirs of Archy Moore* is a more accurate portrait of the institution.[61] Several recent treatments by black novelists are extremely perceptive. Alston Anderson's *All God's Children: A Novel* and Margaret Walker's *Jubilee* are especially illuminating.[62] The best fictionalized characterization of slave resistance is Arna Bontemps' account of Gabriel Prosser, Black

Thunder.[63] The strength of Bontemps' novel is a result of his wide reading of the slave narratives.

While Bontemps depended on primary sources as the basis for his novel, William Styron used his imagination and the writings of U. B. Phillips and Stanley Elkins in composing his "meditations on History," the Pulitzer Prize-winning *The Confessions of Nat Turner.*[64] Praised by white scholars for his historical accuracy, Styron was lambasted by black writers for the unbelievable mental gyrations which led to a "rebel" who was a "Sambo." Although the novel itself was born of ignorance, and simply repeated the errors made by Phillips and Elkins, few scholars had done enough research in the sources to evaluate its historical accuracy. The same was true of the black writers. If one concedes (as this writer does) that a novelist has the license to use his imagination to attempt to explain reality, then Styron deserved his Pulitzer Prize. When, however, that novelist claims that he is "meditating on history" or writing a historical novel, he should be held accountable for his deviation from the facts. As a novel *Confessions* is superb, as a historical novel it is absurd.

Having praised the novel, white historians rushed to the barricades to defend their "liberal" credentials when John Henrik Clarke, ed., *William Styron's Nat Turner: Ten Black Writers Respond* appeared.[65] Generally, the historians missed the essential point that the blacks were trying to make. The award of a Pulitzer Prize to Styron for his emasculation of Nat Turner indicated to blacks that the Great American Novel had become a woman-hating glorification of homosexuality which reduced the black man to the only position in which he is accepted in white America: impotence. Understandably, blacks rejected Styron's effort to kill one of their folk heroes. Their anger could be comparable only to the probable reaction of American whites if some English author wrote a fictional account of George Washington with him fawning on Englishmen, hating other American colonists, masturbating at an age when all of his friends were wenching, having Patrick Henry entering his outhouse and searing his anus with a blazing pine knot, looking longingly at Martha but having homosexual relations with Thomas Jefferson, struck dumb with passion at every English woman he sees and ravishing her in his mind or as he masturbates, so paralyzed with fear that he can not even shoot an English soldier, and then vomiting, retching, and heaving his guts out before, during, and after each battle. However much license a novelist has, such a work would be viewed rightly as the murder of a folk hero.

Unlike the slave, the antebellum free Negro has had few novelists or historians to chronicle his story. There is still (as of 1972) no general history of free Negroes in the South and John Hope Franklin's *The Free Negro in North Carolina, 1790-1860* and Luther P. Jackson's *Free*

Negro Labor and Property Holding in Virginia, 1830-1860 stand alone
as comprehensive state studies.[66] Letitia Brown's *Free Negroes in the
District of Columbia, 1790-1846* is a pioneering though limited study
of urban free blacks.[67] The standard monograph on northern free blacks
is Leon Litwack's *North of Slavery: The Negro in the Free States,
1790-1860* but it is so concerned with race relations that it reveals little
about the internal dynamics of the black community.[68] The most essential sources for studying the free Negroes are the autobiographies they
wrote. John Malvin, Daniel Peterson, Samuel Ringgold Ward, John
Mercer Langston, Daniel A. Payne, Mifflin Gibbs, John P. Green,
Jeremiah Asher, and James Still present the most intimate picture of
their communities.[69] Benjamin Quarles has almost singlehandedly reconstructed many important activities of the free Negroes in his justly
acclaimed *Black Abolitionists* and *The Negro in the American Revolution.*[70]

The drama inherent in the Civil War and the central role of blacks
in the conflict has made it one of the most thoroughly examined periods
in black history. Benjamin Quarles' *The Negro in the Civil War,* Dudley
T. Cornish's *The Sable Arm: Negro Troops in the Union Army, 1861-
1865,* and James McPherson, ed., *The Negro's Civil War* are indis-
pensable for the union story[71] while James H. Brewer's *The Confederate
Negro: Virginia's Craftsmen and Military Laborers, 1861-1865* and Bell
I. Wiley's *Southern Negroes, 1861-1865* recount developments in the
confederacy.[72] The movement toward emancipation is explored in John
Hope Franklin's *The Emancipation Proclamation,* Benjamin Quarles'
Lincoln and the Negro, V. Jacque Voegeli's *Free but Not Equal: The
Midwest and the Negro During the Civil War,* Charles L. Wagandt's *The
Mighty Revolution: Negro Emancipation in Maryland, 1862-1864,* and
Forrest G. Wood's *Black Scare: The Racist Response to Emancipation
and Reconstruction.*[73]

The closest rival to the Civil War in scholarly interest is Reconstruction. Recent writings on the period contrast sharply with earlier racist
tracts in viewpoint and, more importantly, in the extent of research.
Robert Cruden's *The Negro in Reconstruction* is an excellent synthesis
of contemporary monographic studies which goes beyond the traditional
fascination with politics.[74] While Lerone Bennett's *Black Power, U.S.A.:
The Human Side of Reconstruction, 1867-1877* is less comprehensive
than Cruden, it is more readable.[75] Theodore Wilson's *The Black Codes
of the South,* Otis A. Singletary's *Negro Militia and Reconstruction,*
Howard A. White's *The Freedmen's Bureau in Louisiana,* and Martin
Abbott's *The Freedmen's Bureau in South Carolina, 1865-1872* treat
some of the essential special topics.[76]

The much maligned black politician is rarely considered seriously in most studies. E. Merton Coulter's *Negro Legislators in Georgia During the Reconstruction Period* is one of the few exceptions, but it is an antediluvian racist diatribe reminiscent of his strictures on blacks in his *The South During Reconstruction, 1865-1877*.[77] A historiographical curiosity, *Negro Legislators* is an indispensable reminder that Reconstruction history has long been and still remains a "Dark and Bloody Ground." W.E.B. Du Bois' *Black Reconstruction . . ., 1860-1880* and James S. Allen's *Reconstruction: The Battle for Democracy, 1865-1876*, though marred by strained Marxist interpretations, are crucial.[78] Of similar vintage, and lightly researched, are Samuel D. Smith's *The Negro in Congress, 1870-1901*, Luther P. Jackson's *Negro Office-holders in Virginia, 1865-1895*, and J. Mason Brewer's *Negro Legislators of Texas*.[79] Okon E. Uya's *From Slavery to Public Service: Robert Smalls, 1839-1915* is an imaginative study of the South Carolina leader but is weakened by the paucity of manuscripts available.[80] The most complete data on black politicians are found in Laurence Bryant's *Negro Lawmakers in the South Carolina Legislature, 1869-1902* and *Negro Senators and Representatives in the South Carolina Legislature, 1868-1902*.[81] Including age, slave or free status, education, wealth, occupations, and offices held, Bryant inexplicably chose not to analyze his data. Even so, the material culled laboriously from wills, manuscript censuses, tax records, and newspapers presents the most comprehensive portrait of black politicians. Eugene A. Feldman's *Black Power in Old Alabama: the Life and Stirring Times of James T. Rapier, Afro-American Congressman from Alabama, 1839-1883*, suffering from all of the weaknesses of Uya's work with few of its strengths, is notable primarily for its brevity.[82] The most reliable information on such black politicos as P.B.S. Pinchback, Francis L. Cardozo, John R. Lynch, and Blanche K. Bruce is found in their autobiographies and a few articles.[83]

Finally, historians are expanding their purview beyond the political controversies of Reconstruction. Joe M. Richardson examined manuscript census returns in an effort to uncover the social and economic outlines of the black community in his *The Negro in the Reconstruction of Florida, 1865-1877* and Joel Williamson utilized an impressive array of sources to determine economic, social, and racial patterns in *After Slavery: The Negro in South Carolina During Reconstruction, 1861-1877*.[84] Eschewing the traditional state approach, Willie Lee Rose produced a perceptive study of blacks during the first years of freedom in *Rehearsal for Reconstruction: The Port Royal Experiment*.[85] W. McKee Evans followed Mrs. Rose's example in *Ballots and Fence Rails: Reconstruction on the Lower Cape Fear*.[86] Narrowing the focus even further,

John Blassingame ignored the staples of politics and agricultural labor in favor of an urban study, *Black New Orleans, 1860-1880.*[87]
The descent of blacks to their nadir at the beginning of the twentieth century has been analyzed by several scholars. Rayford Logan's *The Negro in American Life and Thought: The Nadir, 1877-1901* is a masterful examination of the racism pervading American thought and its role in the disfranchisement and oppression of blacks.[88] Comprehensive state studies focusing primarily on politics include Frenise Logan's *The Negro in North Carolina, 1876-1894*, George B. Tindall's *South Carolina Negroes, 1877-1900*, Lawrence D. Rice's *The Negro in Texas, 1874-1900*, and Helen G. Edmonds' *The Negro and Fusion Politics in North Carolina, 1894-1901.*[89] One of the most influential treatments of the period is C. Vann Woodward's *The Strange Career of Jim Crow.*[90] Arguing that legal segregation was largely a product of the late nineteenth and early twentieth centuries, Woodward's volume has stirred up considerable controversy. While Albert Sanders, John Hammond Moore, Henry C. Dethloff, and Charles Wynes support the thesis, Joel Williamson, Richard Wade, Roger A. Fischer, Barry Crouch, and Meier and Rudwick find strong evidence of segregation during or before Reconstruction.[91] The movement toward segregation (but little else) in Northern cities is described in Seth M. Scheiner's *Negro Mecca: A History of the Negro in New York City, 1865-1920*, Gilbert Osofsky's *Harlem: The Making of a Ghetto; Negro New York, 1890-1930*, and Allan Spear's *Black Chicago: The Making of a Negro Ghetto, 1890-1920.*[92] Carol K. R. Bleser's *The Promised Land: The History of the South Carolina Land Commission, 1869-1890* and Phillip Durham and Everett L. Jones' *The Negro Cowboys* are excellent explorations of the largely neglected field of nineteenth-century black economic developments.[93]
Twentieth-century economic developments are treated perceptively in E. Franklin Frazier's *Black Bourgeoisie*, Morton Rubin's *Plantation County*, F. Ray Marshall's *The Negro and Organized Labor*, Raymond Wolters' *Negroes and the Great Depression: The Problem of Economic Recovery*, and Donald H. Grubbs's *Cry from the Cotton: The Southern Tenant Farmers' Union and the New Deal.*[94] The most useful examinations of twentieth-century black politics appear in James Q. Wilson's *Negro Politics: The Search for Leadership*, Samuel Lubell's *White and Black: Test of a Nation*, Margaret Price's *The Negro Voter in the South*, and Andrew Buni's *The Negro in Virginia Politics, 1902-1965.*[95] Since few historians other than Buni have written book-length studies of black political movements, most works on the subject are quickly outdated and cluttered with the jargon of the political scientist. Detailed informa-

tion on the military service of blacks since the Civil War can be found in John M. Carroll, ed., *The Black Military Experience in the American West,* William H. Leckie's *The Buffalo Soldiers: A Narrative of the Negro Cavalry in the West,* Arlen L. Fowler's *The Black Infantry in the West, 1869-1891,* Richard Dalfiume's *Desegregation of the U.S. Armed Forces: Fighting on Two Fronts, 1939-53,* and Ulysses Lee's *The Employment of Negro Troops: United States Army in World War II.*[96]

The relationship between blacks and the Communist Party has not (as of 1972) been studied adequately but there are several works which deal with the question. The starting point is still Wilson Record's *The Negro and the Communist Party* and *Race and Radicalism: The NAACP and the Communist Party in Conflict.*[97] Harold Cruse's *The Crisis of the Negro Intellectual* gives a sensitive portrait of the struggles between black artists and white communists, Dan T. Carter's *Scottsboro: A Tragedy of the American South* is the definitive account of the fight black leaders waged against the communists to save nine black boys accused of raping two white women, and Benjamin J. Davis's *The Negro People On the March* and Claude M. Lightfoot's *Ghetto Rebellion to Black Liberation* raise anew the perennial animosity between the communists and black nationalists.[98]

The extent of black protests against white proscriptions is revealed in several excellent volumes. Loren Miller's *The Petitioners: The Story of the Supreme Court of the United States and the Negro* is an impressive summary of the legal struggle for rights while Mary Berry's *Black Resistance, White Law: A History of Constitutional Racism in America* describes the federal government's persistent refusal to protect the lives of blacks.[99] Although unimaginatively, Benjamin Muse has outlined the Civil Rights movement since 1954 in *Ten Years of Prelude: The Story of Integration Since the Supreme Court's 1954 Decision* and *The American Negro Revolution: From Non-violence to Black Power, 1963-1967.*[100] Anthony Lewis's *Portrait of a Decade: The Second American Revolution* and Lerone Bennett's *Confrontation: Black and White* are excellent introductions.[101] The major black protest organizations are examined in Howard Zinn's *SNCC: The New Abolitionists,* Langston Hughes' *Fight for Freedom: The Story of the NAACP,* and Arvarh E. Strickland's *History of the Chicago Urban League.*[102] Comprehensive studies of CORE, SCLC, the Urban League, and the NAACP still have not appeared. The ideological positions of recent black leaders are surveyed in Louis Lomax's *The Negro Revolt* and Lerone Bennett's *The Negro Mood.*[103]

Although none of the analyses prepared American whites for the riots which occurred in the 1960's, historians and reporters have described them and their predecessors in great detail. Among the best of these studies are Robert Conot's *Rivers of Blood, Years of Darkness,* Fred C. Shapiro and James W. Sullivan's *Race Riots, New York, 1964,* Tom Hayden's *Rebellion in Newark: Official Violence and Ghetto Response,* Robert Shogan and Tom Craig's *The Detroit Race Riot . . .,* Ben W. Gilbert's *Ten Blocks from the White House,* Elliott M. Rudwick's *Race Riot at East St. Louis, July 2, 1917,* and William M. Tuttle's *Race Riot: Chicago in the Red Summer of 1919.*[104] Several general perspectives are presented in Joseph Boskin's *Urban Racial Violence in the Twentieth Century,* Allen D. Grimshaw, ed., *Racial Violence in the United States,* Arthur I. Waskow's *From Race Riot to Sit-In, 1919 and the 1960's . . .,* Robert H. Connery, ed., *Urban Riots: Violence and Social Change,* and Robert M. Fogelson's *Violence as Protest: A Study of Riots and Ghettos.*[105]

The marchings, sit-ins, and riots of the 1960's heralded a resurgence in black nationalism. Traditionally, nationalists (blacks stressing group or racial solidarity, pride, and loyalty) have received a bad press in the United States. Since the nationalists focus on a common racial and cultural identity, many of their movements are equated with the Ku Klux Klan. Especially when considering separatist and back-to-Africa movements, white scholars treat them as pathological responses to discrimination. Yet, scholars recognize that a majority of all national movements have involved responses to increased frustrations. And, given the fact that blacks have been struggling for more than 350 years to be integrated into American society, there is a great deal of doubt as to whether integration is more realistic than separatism.

Since many of the back-to-Africa movements have arisen during times of apparent increases in economic, social and political deprivation, scholars have dismissed them as signs of the black man's hopelessness and escapist fantasy. They were indeed this, but at the same time they differed in no important way from the large-scale migration of Europeans to the New World and Australia. Unlike the back-to-Africa movements, scholars when treating European migration focus on the dreams the migrants had for future success, rather than the fact that they were giving up on their native land in the face of economic, political, and religious oppression and deprivation. Such attitudes indicate a kind of myopia about the black experience which is frightening. Take, for example, the oft repeated observation that separatist and African colonization movements arise during periods of increased racial discrimination. First of all, this observation implies that there has been a long golden age in race relations broken periodically by riots, Jim Crow, and Ku Kluxism. Just the opposite seems to be true. For the mass of Negroes, economic deprivation and white oppression have been constant realities with much heralded changes in forms (as during Reconstruction or the 1960's) which made little impact on the structure of discrimination.

Martin Delany, antebellum Negro conventions, Alexander Crummell, studies of the American Colonization society, Edwin Redkey's examination of late nineteenth-century back-to-Africa movements, analyses of the rise of Negro towns, Geis and Bittle's imaginative reconstruction of Chief Albert Sam's efforts just before the first world war, E. David Cronon's biography of Marcus Garvey, and Essien-Udom and Lincoln's sensitive portraits of the Black Muslims indicate that emigration and separatism have been constants in black thought.[106]

The most influential general work stressing nationalism as pathology is Theodore Draper's *The Rediscovery of Black Nationalism*.[107] The paucity of research, however, undermines the reliability of Draper's volume. The reader with a serious interest in the subject must consult the excellent documentary collection of John H. Bracey, Jr., August Meier, and Elliott Rudwick, eds., *Black Nationalism in America*.[108]

Pan Africanism, or the belief in the kinship, and solidarity of peoples of African descent, has been a vital force in black nationalism since the antebellum period. The most informative studies of the subject are Harold Isaacs' *The New World of Negro Americans,* Adelaide C. Hill and Martin Kilson, eds., *Apropos of Africa: Sentiments of Negro American Leaders on Africa from the 1800s to the 1950s,* American Society of African Culture, *Pan-Africanism Reconsidered,*[109] several essays, [110] and the voluminous writings of W.E.B. Du Bois.

Social history is the least studied aspect of the black experience. The most important black institution—the family—has been virtually ignored by historians. Consequently, sociologists, with their penchant for unearthing the pathological side of life, have been swimming along in a sea of ignorance. Ignoring E. F. Frazier's impressive and careful research in his masterful *The Negro Family in Chicago* while accepting (or distorting) the undocumented speculations in his *The Negro Family in the United States,* sociologists and historians have perpetuated the myth of the monolithic matriarchal black family.[111] Recent scholarship has almost entirely revised the Frazierian thesis. The best of this growing body of literature is Andrew Billingsley's *Black Families in White America* and Joyce A. Ladner's *Tomorrow's Tomorrow: The Black Woman.*[112]

A general overview of black education is furnished by Henry A. Bullock's *A History of Negro Education in the South from 1619 to the Present* and Earl J. McGrath's *The Predominantly Negro Colleges and Universities in Transition.*[113] The most authoritative and revealing studies of specific colleges include Rayford W. Logan's *Howard University, the First Hundred Years, 1867-1967,* Clarence A. Bacote's *The Story of Atlanta University: A Century of Service, 1865-1965,* Edward A. Jones' *A Candle in the Dark: A History of Morehouse College,* and Florence M. Read's *The Story of Spelman College.*[114] The incomparable Benjamin Mays discussed his years as Morehouse's president in *Born to Rebel: An Autobiography.*[115] If the test of an educational institution is the contributions of its graduates, then black schools have been successful. The occupations and roles of the "talented tenth" are described in G. Franklin Edwards' *The Negro Professional Class* and Herbert M. Morais' *The History of the Negro in Medicine.*[116] The significant contributions of blacks to American intellectual and cultural life are evaluated in a number of works.

The music of black America is treated in great detail in LeRoi Jones' *Blues People: Negro Music in White America.*[117] Although Jones is by far the most comprehensive and readable, he often tries to see too much of black life and history through the prism of music. The best sociocultural study of jazz is Marshall W. Stearns' *The Story of Jazz* while Eileen Southern's *The Music of Black Americans: A History* is a general work based on a wealth of primary sources.[118] The spirituals are treated in Howard Thurman, *Deep River: Reflections on the Religious Insight of Certain of the Negro Spirituals* and Bernard Katz, ed., *The Social Implications of Early Negro Music in the United States.*[119]

Obsessed by the debate over the purpose of fiction, scholars have produced few illuminating critical studies of black literature. There is no sophisticated study of nineteenth-century black novelists and poets and most studies of twentieth-century writers are overly narrow in scope.

One attempt to study the most important intellectual and cultural movement of the twentieth century—the Harlem renaissance—is Nathan Huggins' *Harlem Renaissance.*[120] Huggins' volume is, however, hardly definitive. A remnant of an older genre concerned with racial interaction and the impact of whites on blacks, *Harlem Renaissance* contains questionable assessments of the major renaissance figures and ignores the internal dynamics of the black community which fostered and nurtured the movement. Instead, we get many speculations on Carl Van Vetchten's influence and what whites projected onto the "primitives" in Harlem but no discussion of the "salons" run by blacks, or the literary contests sponsored by *Crisis* and *Opportunity.* Even if Huggins' thesis that there was a symbiotic relationship between black artists and white America has some validity, he has failed to prove it. After postulating his theory, Huggins neglected the manuscripts of black writers, their published memoirs, and, even more important, failed to read the reviews of black novels written by whites. These sources frequently reveal a different kind of renaissance than that which Huggins found.

Unbelievably, no one has yet (as of 1972) written a sophisticated, general survey of black poetry. Anthologies, on the other hand, are abundant.[121] Appreciation of the black novelist is only a little higher than that of the black poet. For the most part, scholars have been intrigued more by the way white novelists have caricatured blacks than by the black novelists' perception of reality. The essential works on black writers are Hugh M. Gloster's *Negro Voices in American Fiction,* Edward Margolies' *Native Sons: A Critical Study of Twentieth Century Negro-American Authors,* and Robert Bone's *The Negro Novel in America.*[122] Gloster was so obsessed with racial consciousness that he ignored the literary form and quality of the works he analyzed. Bone and Margolies took the opposite view. Stressing "art for the sake of art," they were too quick to denigrate black writers who saw their works as weapons to use against racist America. Analyses of the role of blacks in the theatre combine historical and artistic developments on a much higher level than studies of black novelists. Loften Mitchell's *Black Drama: The Story of the American Negro in the Theatre,* Harold Cruse's *The Crisis of the Negro Intellectual,* and Doris E. Abramson's *Negro Playwrights in the American Theatre, 1925-1959* provide comprehensive detailed surveys which are fascinating to read.[123] In contrast to the theatre, studies of blacks in films are paltry. Peter Noble's *The Negro in Films* and V. J. Jerome's *The Negro in Hollywood Films,* though outdated, provide an introduction[124] while two articles by Thomas R. Cripps, "The Death of Rastus: Negroes in American Films since 1945" and "Movies in the Ghetto, B.P. [Before Poitier]" are the most reliable essays on the subject.[125]

Revelations about practically every aspect of the black experience appear in the growing list of biographies. Collective biographies suitable for high school students include Russell L. Adams' *Great Negroes, Past and Present,* Lerone Bennett's *Pioneers in Protest,* Arna Bontemps' *Famous Negro Athletes,* Lavinia G. Dobler and Edgar A. Toppin's *Pioneers and Patriots: the Lives of Six Negroes of the Revolutionary Era,* Langston Hughes' *Famous Negro Heroes of America,* Wilhelmena S. Robinson's *Historical Negro Biographies,* and Charlemae Rollins' *Famous Negro Entertainers of Stage, Screen, and TV.*[126] Popularly written biographies are so numerous that students can easily find one which will illuminate both the "heroic" and "realistic" aspects of black history. Including scientists, frontiersmen, athletes, ministers, scholars, doctors, lawyers, and slaves and free men, these volumes engender more interest in and empathy with black history than most other works.[127]

Scholarly biographies of major black figures are fewer in number than the popular ones because only a limited number of blacks preserved the letters and diaries written during their lifetimes. In spite of this, there are informative studies of Frederick Douglass, Booker T. Washington, W.E.B. Du Bois, Marcus Garvey, and Martin Luther King.[128] Booker Washington is the only black leader whose life has been discussed in any comprehensive fashion. The indispensable works are August Meier's *Negro Thought in America, 1880-1915: Racial Ideologies in the Age of Booker T. Washington* and the first volume of Louis Harlan's detailed and heavily documented study, *Booker T. Washington: The Making of a Black Leader, 1856-1901.*[129] While Meier explores the economic, social, and intellectual developments in the black community and Washington's role in them, Harlan describes, for the first time, all of the forces which made the man into one of the most complex and least understood figures in American history. A decade of research in the Washington papers, an impressive list of other sources, empathy, and considerable literary skill led Harlan to produce the best biography of Washington so far. Data on less famous blacks can be found in Richard Bardolph's *The Negro Vanguard,* William E. Farrison's *William Wells Brown: Author and Reformer,* Stephen R. Fox's *The Guardian of Boston: William Monroe Trotter,* and Emma Lou Thornbrough's *T. Thomas Fortune: Militant Journalist.*[130]

However good biographies are, they rarely allow students to view the world the way blacks have. The best way to gain intimate knowledge of the way blacks think, act, and view themselves, white America, and their community is through autobiographies. The perennial favorites of students are Booker T. Washington's *Up From Slavery,* first published in 1901, W.E.B. Du Bois' *The Autobiography of W.E.B. Du Bois,* and Malcolm X's *The Autobiography of Malcolm X.*[131] The autobiographies of Anne Moody, Paul Robeson, John C. Daney, Horace Cayton, Langston Hughes, Reba Lee, and Ellen Tarry are also perceptive and extremely interesting.[132] These and other autobiographies move blacks to the center stage in their historical drama and forcefully portray what it means to be black in white America.

A review of writings on Afro-Americans is an important corrective to the mythology of the black past. A realistic portrayal of Afro-Americans will contain black and white villains, heroes, and ordinary black men and women struggling against extraordinary odds. Only those who know nothing of the black past or who still insist that history is limited to the mythological exploits of kings and presidents contend that since blacks have been largely powerless their history is necessarily unheroic. The proper view, it seems to me, was presented by the black scholar

C. V. Roman in 1911. Arguing that a dispassionate study of the past would inevitably add many blacks to America's pantheon of heroes, Roman contended that:

> A Negro woman crossing a mad and swollen river on floating pieces of ice, barefooted and with a child in her arms, that she might find liberty for herself and child, presents a picture of magnificent heroism, fit for song and story.
>
> I am not preaching ethnic antagonism nor endeavoring to give a racial tinge to the facts of history, but I do wish to widen sufficiently the field of *taught* history to include Negroes who justly belong there. . . . It is a long way from a log cabin in Kentucky to the Presidency of these United States, but from the slave-pens of Maryland to the marshalship of the District of Columbia is further. While we justly honor Lincoln for the first, we should remember Douglass made the second.[133]

Since white historians have long written about the American past as if blacks did not exist, it is easy to understand the demands of contemporary blacks that they be given some visibility. Few fair-minded men will deny the legitimacy of their claims. Teachers must abandon the mythology of the white supremacists and present the reality of the black experience in America.

FOOTNOTES

[1] Sterling Stuckey. "Twilight of Our Past: Reflections on the Origins of Black History." *Amistad* 2 (1971), 275.

[2] John Hope Franklin. "Whither Reconstruction Historiography?" *Journal of Negro Education* 17: 446-61; No. 4, Fall 1948. Contains a devastating critique of Coulter.

[3] Stuckey. "Twilight of Our Past. . . ." pp. 272, 290.

[4] *Ibid.* p. 291.

[5] John A. Garraty, editor. *Interpreting American History: Conversations with Historians.* New York: Macmillan, 1970. For Woodward, pt. II, 62; for Elkins, pt. I, 199.

[6] Vincent Harding. "Beyond Chaos: Black History and the Search for the New Land." *Amistad* 1: 267-92; C. Vann Woodward. "Clio with Soul." *Journal of American History* 56: 5-20; No. 1, June 1969; John W. Blassingame. "Black Studies and the Role of the Historian," in Blassingame, editor. *New Perspectives on Black Studies.* Urbana: University of Illinois Press, 1971. pp. 207-226; Nathan Hare. "The Teaching of Black History and Culture in the Secondary Schools." *Social Education* 33: 385-88; No. 4, April 1969; John Hope Franklin. "Discovering Black American History," in Joseph S. Roucek and Thomas Kiernan, editors. *The Negro Impact on Western Civilization,* 1970. pp. 23-31; Earl E. Thorpe. *The Old South: A Psychohistory.* Durham, N.C.: privately printed by Seeman Printery, 1972. pp. 262-287.

[7] Benjamin Quarles. *Black History's Diversified Clientele,* 1971. pp. 20-21.

[8] New York: The H. W. Wilson Company, 1929.

[9] Washington: Library of Congress, 1970.

[10] Garden City: Doubleday, 1971.

[11] 2nd ed. Cambridge: Harvard University Press, 1970.

[12] 3rd. ed. New York: Knopf, 1967.

[13] Princeton: Van Nostrand, 1957.

[14] Boston: Houghton Mifflin, 1970.

[15] 3rd ed. Chicago: Johnson Publishing Co., 1966.

[16] Revised edition. New York: Hill and Wang, 1970.

[17] New York: Citadel Press, 1951.

[18] New York: Vintage, 1967.

[19] Boston: Allyn and Bacon, 1972.

[20] *Eyewitness.* New York: Pitman Pub. Corp., 1967; *In Their Own Words.* New York: Crowell, 3 vols., 1964-1967.

[21] *The Civil Rights Record.* New York: Crowell, 1970; *Civil Rights and the American Negro.* New York: Trident Press, 1968; *The Supreme Court on Racial Discrimination.* New York: Oxford University Press, 1963.

[22] *Racial Thought in America.* Amherst: University of Massachusetts Press, 1970; *What Country Have I?* New York: St. Martin's Press, 1970; *Black Protest Thought in the Twentieth Century.* 2nd ed., Indianapolis: Bobbs-Merrill, 1971; *The Black Power Revolt.* Boston: P. Sargent, 1968.

[23] New York: Atheneum, 1969.

[24] New York: Harper and Row, 1970.

[25] *Key Issues in the Afro-American Experience.* 2 vols. New York: Harcourt, 1971; *Explorations in the Black Experience.* Belmont, Calif.; Wadsworth Publishing Company, 1971.

[26] W.E.B. Du Bois. *The Souls of Black Folk: Essays and Sketches.* Chicago: A. C. McClurg & Co., 1903. p. 3.

[27] *The Mind of the Negro.* Baton Rouge: Ortlieb Press, 1961; *Negro Historians in the United States.* Baton Rouge: Fraternal Press, 1958; *Black Historians.* New York: Morrow, c. 1969; *The Central Theme of Black History.* Durham: Seeman Printery, 1969.

[28] Samuel D. Cook. "A Tragic Conception of Negro History." *Journal of Negro History* 45: 219-40; No. 4, Oct. 1960; Howard N. Meyer. "Overcoming the White Man's History." *Massachusetts Review* 7: 569-78; No. 3, Summer 1966; J. H. O'Dell. "Colonialism and the Negro American Experience." *Freedomways* 6: 296-308; No. 4, Fall 1966; Robert Starobin. "The Negro: A Central Theme in American History." *Journal of Contemporary History* 3: 37-53; No. 2, April 1968.

[29] New York: St. Martin's, 1965.

[30] New York: Viking, 1967.

[31] New York: Walker, 1962.

[32] *African Glory.* New York: Praeger, 1954; *The Middle Age of African History.* London: Oxford University Press, 1967; *The Lost Cities of Africa.* Revised ed., Boston: Little, Brown, 1970.

[33] *Kingdoms of the Savanna.* Madison: University of Wisconsin Press, 1966; *African Traditional Religion.* London: Hutchinson's University Library, 1954; *African Worlds.* London: Oxford University Press, 1954; *Africa and Africans.* Garden City: Natural History Press, 1964; *A Thousand Years of West African History.* Revised ed., Ibadan: Ibadan University Press, 1969.

[34] London: Allen and Unwin, 1968.

[35] *A Short History of Benin.* 4th ed., Ibadan: Ibadan University Press, 1968; *Ibo Village Affairs.* 2nd ed., New York: Praeger, 1964; *The Mende of Sierra Leone.* Revised ed., London: Routledge and K. Paul, 1967; *The Egba and Their Neighbors.* Oxford: Clarendon Press, 1957; *Yoruba Warfare in the Nineteenth Century.* Cambridge, Eng.: Cambridge University Press, 1964.

[36] *Black Cargoes.* New York: Viking Press, 1962; *Black Mother.* Boston: Little, Brown, 1961; *The Atlantic Slave Trade.* Madison: University of Wisconsin Press, 1969.

[37] Carl N. Degler. "Slavery and the Genesis of American Racial Prejudice." *Comparative Studies in Society and History* 2: 49-66; No. 1, Oct. 1959; Winthrop D. Jordan. *White Over Black: American Attitudes Toward the Negro, 1550-1812.* Chapel Hill: University of North Carolina Press, 1968; Oscar and Mary Handlin. "Origins of the Southern Labor System." *William and Mary Quarterly* 7: 199-222; No. 2, April 1950.

[38] New York: Oxford University Press, 1972.

[39] *Journal of Negro History* 51: 1-15; No. 1, Jan. 1966.

[40] New York: Harper & Bros., 1941.

[41] Revised ed., New York: Macmillan, 1957.

[42] Chicago: University of Chicago Press, 1949.

[43] For example: Garrett. "African Survivals in American Culture." *The Journal of Negro History* 51: 239-45; No. 4, Oct. 1966; Norman E. Whitten, Jr. and John F. Szwed, editors. *Afro-American Anthropology: Contemporary Perspectives.* New York: Free Press, 1970; Crowley. "Negro Folklore: An Africanist's View." *Texas Quarterly* 5: 65-71; No. 3, Autumn 1962; Waterman. "African Influence on the Music of the Americas," in Sol Tax, editor. *Acculturation in the Americas: Proceedings and Selective Papers, International Congress of Americanists.* 29th ed. New York, 1949. pp. 207-218; Alan Lomax. "The Homogeneity of African-Afro-American Musical Style," in Whitten and Szwed. pp. 181-201; Thompson. "African Influence on the Art of the United States," in Armstead L. Robinson, *et al.,* editors. *Black Studies in the University.* New Haven: Yale University Press, 1969. pp. 122-70.

[44] *American Negro Slavery.* New York: Appleton and Company, 1918; *Life and Labor in the Old South.* Boston: Little, Brown, 1929.

[45] Leiden: Brill, 1963.

[46] New York: Morrow, 1971.

[47] New York: Holt, 1970. The collection is in the Library of Congress.

[48] Frederick Douglass. *The Life and Times of Frederick Douglass.* Hartford, Conn.: Park Publishing Co., 1881 and New York: Macmillan, 1962; Gilbert Osofsky, editor. *Puttin' on Ole Massa: The Slave Narratives of Henry Bibb, William Wells Brown, and Solomon Northrup.* New York: Harper and Row, 1969; Arna Bontemps, editor. *Great Slave Narratives.* Boston: Beacon, 1969; John F. Bayliss, editor. *Black Slave Narratives.* New York: Macmillan, 1970; Julius Lester, editor. *To Be a Slave.* New York: Dial Press, 1968. Each autobiography was originally published separately.

[49] New York: Knopf, 1956.

[50] Chicago: University of Chicago Press, 1959; 2nd ed., 1968.

[51] Laura Foner and Eugene D. Genovese, editors. *Slavery in the New World: A Reader in Comparative History.* Englewood Cliffs, N.J.: Prentice Hall, 1969; David B. Davis. *The Problem of Slavery in Western Culture.* Ithaca: Cornell University Press, 1966; Marvin Harris. *Patterns of Race in the Americas.* New York: Walker, c. 1964; Carl N. Degler. *Neither Black nor White: Slavery and Race Relations in Brazil and the United States.* New York: Macmillan, 1971; Charles R. Boxer. *The Golden Age of Brazil, 1695-1750: Growing Pains of a Colonial Society.* Berkeley: University of California Press, 1962; Stanley J. Stein. *Vassouras: A Brazilian Coffee County, 1850-1900.* Cambridge: Harvard University Press, 1957; Franklin W. Knight. *Slave Society in Cuba During the Nineteenth Century.* Madison: University of Wisconsin Press, 1970.

[52] Ann J. Lane, editor. *The Debate Over Slavery: Stanley Elkins and his Critics.* Urbana: University of Illinois Press, 1971.

[53] New York: Oxford University Press, 1972.

[54] New York: Oxford University Press, 1964.

[55] William L. Richter. "Slavery in Baton Rouge, 1820-1860." *Louisiana History* 10: 125-145; No. 2, Spring 1969; Terry L. Seip. "Slaves and Free Negroes in Alexandria, 1850-1860." *Louisiana History* 10: 147-165; No. 2, Spring 1969.

⁵⁶ New York: Columbia University Press, 1943.

⁵⁷ Quoted in Bennett H. Wall. "African Slavery," in Arthur S. Link and Rembert Patrick, editors. *Writing Southern History: Essays in Historiography in Honor of Fletcher M. Green.* Baton Rouge: Louisiana State University Press, 1965. p. 190.

⁵⁸ New York: McKay, 1966.

⁵⁹ *Insurrection in South Carolina.* Yellow Springs, Ohio: Antioch Press, 1964; *Denmark Vesey.* Englewood Cliffs, N.J.: Prentice Hall, 1970: *Nat Turner's Slave Rebellion.* New York: Humanities Press, 1966; *The Nat Turner Slave Insurrection.* Murfreesboro, N.C.: Johnson Publishing Co., 1966; *Nat Turner.* Englewood Cliffs, N.J.: Prentice Hall, 1971.

⁶⁰ Lexington: University of Kentucky Press, 1961.

⁶¹ *Uncle Tom's Cabin.* Boston: J. P. Jewett and Company, 1852; *The Slave.* Boston: J. H. Eastburn, 1836. Both novels have been reprinted.

⁶² *All God's Children.* Indianapolis: Bobbs-Merrill, 1965; *Jubilee.* Boston: Houghton Mifflin, 1966.

⁶³ New York: Macmillan, 1936.

⁶⁴ New York: Random House, 1967.

⁶⁵ Boston: Beacon Press, 1968.

⁶⁶ *The Free Negro in North Carolina.* Chapel Hill: The University of North Carolina Press, 1943; *Free Negro Labor and Property Holding in Virginia.* New York: D. Appleton Century Company, 1942.

⁶⁷ New York: Oxford University Press, 1972.

⁶⁸ Chicago: University of Chicago Press, 1961.

⁶⁹ John Malvin. *North into Freedom: The Autobiography of John Malvin, Free Negro, 1795-1880.* Cleveland: Press of Case Western Reserve University, 1966; Daniel Peterson. *The Looking-Glass: Being a True Report . . . of the Life . . . of the Rev. Daniel H. Peterson, a Colored Clergyman. . . .* New York: Wright, 1854; *Samuel Ringgold Ward: Autobiography of a Fugitive Negro.* London: J. Snow, 1855; John Mercer Langston. *From the Virginia Plantation . . . , the First and Only Negro Representative in Congress from the Old Dominion.* New York: Arno, 1969; Daniel A. Payne. *Recollections of Seventy Years.* Nashville, Tenn.: Publishing House of the A. M. E. Sunday School Union, 1888; Mifflin Gibbs. *Shadow and Light; an Autobiography. . . .* Washington, D.C., 1902; republished, New York: Arno, 1968; John P Green. *Recollections of the Inhabitants . . . and Kuklux Outrages. . . .* Cleveland, 1880; Jeremiah Asher. *An Autobiography. . . .* Philadelphia: the author, 1862; James Still. *Early Recollections and Life of Dr. James Still.* Philadelphia: J. B. Lippincott, 1877. The Arno Press has reprinted many autobiographies of nineteenth-century blacks.

⁷⁰ *Black Abolitionists.* New York: Oxford University Press, 1969; *The Negro in the American Revolution.* Chapel Hill: University of North Carolina Press, 1961.

⁷¹ *The Negro in the Civil War.* Boston: Little, Brown, 1953; *The Sable Arm.* New York: Longmans, Green, 1956; *The Negro's Civil War.* New York: Pantheon Books, 1965.

⁷² *The Confederate Negro.* Durham: Duke University Press, 1969; *Southern Negroes.* New Haven: Yale University Press, 1938.

⁷³ *The Emancipation Proclamation.* Garden City: Doubleday, 1963; *Lincoln and the Negro.* New York: Oxford University Press, 1962; *Free but Not Equal.* Chicago: University of Chicago Press, 1967; *The Mighty Revolution.* Baltimore: Johns Hopkins Press, 1964; *Black Scare.* Berkeley: University of California Press, 1968.

⁷⁴ Englewood Cliffs, N.J.: Prentice Hall, 1969.

⁷⁵ Chicago: Johnson Publishing Co., 1967.

⁷⁶ *The Black Codes of the South.* University, Ala.: University of Alabama Press, 1965; *Negro Militia and Reconstruction.* Austin: University of Texas Press, 1957; *The Freedman's Bureau in Louisiana.* Baton Rouge: Louisiana State University

Press, 1970; *The Freedman's Bureau in South Carolina.* Chapel Hill: University of North Carolina Press, 1967.
    [77] *Negro Legislators.* Athens: Georgia Historical Quarterly, 1968; *The South During Reconstruction.* Baton Rouge: Louisiana State University Press, 1947.
    [78] *Black Reconstruction.* New York: Harcourt, Brace, and Co., 1935; *Reconstruction.* New York: International Publishers, 1937.
    [79] *The Negro in Congress.* Chapel Hill: University of North Carolina Press, 1946; *Negro Office-holders in Virginia.* Norfolk, Va.: Guide Quality Press. 1946; *Negro Legislators of Texas.* Dallas: Mathis Publishing Co., 1935.
    [80] New York: Oxford University Press, 1971.
    [81] Both edited by Lawrence C. Bryant. Orangeburg: School of Graduate Studies, South Carolina State College, 1968.
    [82] Chicago: Museum of African American History, 1968.
    [83] John Hope Franklin, editor. *Reminiscenses of an Active Life: The Autobiography of John Roy Lynch.* Chicago: University of Chicago Press, 1970; Edward F. Sweat. "Francis L. Cardozo: Profile of Integrity in Reconstruction Politics." *Journal of Negro History* 46: 217-32; No. 4, Oct. 1961; Melvin I. Urofsky. "Blanche K. Bruce: United States Senator, 1875-1881." *Journal of Mississippi History* 29: 118-41; No. 2, May 1967.
    [84] *The Negro in the Reconstruction of Florida.* Tallahassee: Florida State University Press, 1965; *After Slavery.* Chapel Hill: University of North Carolina Press, 1965.
    [85] Indianapolis: Bobbs-Merrill, 1964.
    [86] Chapel Hill: University of North Carolina Press, c. 1967.
    [87] Chicago: University of Chicago Press, 1973.
    [88] New York: Dial Press, 1954.
    [89] *The Negro in North Carolina.* Chapel Hill: University of North Carolina Press, 1964; *South Carolina Negroes.* Columbia: University of South Carolina Press, 1952; *The Negro in Texas.* Baton Rouge: Louisiana State University Press, 1971; *The Negro and Fusion Politics in North Carolina.* Chapel Hill: University of North Carolina Press, 1951.
    [90] 2nd ed. New York: Oxford University Press, 1966.
    [91] Roger A. Fischer. "Racial Segregation in Ante Bellum New Orleans." *American Historical Review* 74: 926-37; No. 3, Feb. 1969; Henry C. Dethloff and Robert Jones. "Race Relations in Louisiana, 1877-1898." *Louisiana History* 9: 301-23; No. 4, Fall 1968; Charles E. Wynes. *Race Relations in Virginia, 1870-1902.* Charlottesville: University of Virginia Press, 1961; John Hammond Moore. "Jim Crow in Georgia." *South Atlantic Quarterly* 66; 554-65; No. 4, Autumn 1967; Barry A. Crouch and L. J. Schultz. "Crisis in Color: Racial Separation in Texas During Reconstruction." *Civil War History* 16: 37-49; No. 1, March 1970.
    [92] *Negro Mecca.* New York: New York University Press, 1965; *Harlem.* 2nd ed. New York: Harper and Row, 1971; *Black Chicago.* Chicago: University of Chicago Press, 1967.
    [93] *The Promised Land.* Columbia: University of South Carolina Press, 1969; *The Negro Cowboys.* New York: Dodd, Mead, 1965.
    [94] *Black Bourgeoise.* New York: Free Press, 1957; *Plantation County.* Revised ed. Chapel Hill: University of North Carolina Press, 1963; *The Negro and Organized Labor.* New York: John Wiley, 1965; *Negroes and the Great Depression.* Westport, Conn.: Greenwood Publishing Corp., 1970; *Cry from the Cotton.* Chapel Hill: University of North Carolina Press, 1971.
    [95] *Negro Politics.* Glencoe, Ill.: Free Press, 1960; *White and Black.* 2nd ed. New York: Harper and Row, 1966; *The Negro Voter in the South.* Atlanta: Southern Regional Council, 1957; *The Negro in Virginia Politics.* Charlottesville: University Press of Virginia, 1967.
    [96] *The Black Military Experience in the West.* New York: Liveright, 1972; *The Buffalo Soldiers.* Norman: University of Oklahoma Press, 1967; *The Black In-*

fantry in the West. Westport, Conn.: Greenwood Publishing Corp., 1971; *Desegregation of the U.S. Armed Forces.* Columbia: University of Missouri Press, 1969; *The Employment of Negro Troops.* Washington: Office of the Chief of Military History, United States, 1966.

[97] *The Negro and the Communist Party.* Chapel Hill: University of North Carolina Press, 1951; *Race and Radicalism.* Ithaca: Cornell University Press, 1964.

[98] *The Crisis of the Negro Intellectual.* New York: Morrow, 1967; *Scottsboro.* Baton Rouge: Louisiana State University Press, 1969; *The Negro People on the March.* New York: New Century Publishers, 1956; *Ghetto Rebellion to Black Liberation.* New York: International Publishers, 1968.

[99] *The Petitioners.* New York: Pantheon Books, 1966; *Black Resistance, White Law.* New York: Appleton-Century-Crofts, 1971.

[100] *Ten Years of Prelude.* New York: Viking Press, 1964; *The American Negro Revolution.* Bloomington: Indiana University Press, 1968.

[101] *Portrait of a Decade.* New York: Random House, 1964; *Confrontation.* Chicago: Johnson Publishing Co., 1965.

[102] *SNCC.* 2nd ed. Boston: Beacon Press, 1965; *Fight for Freedom.* New York: Norton, 1962; *History of the Chicago Urban League.* Urbana: University of Illinois Press, 1966.

[103] *The Negro Revolt.* New York: Harper, 1962; *The Negro Mood.* Chicago: Johnson Publishing Co., 1964.

[104] *Rivers of Blood, Years of Darkness.* New York: Bantam, 1967; *Race Riots, New York.* New York: Crowell, 1964; *Rebellion in Newark.* New York: Random House, 1967; *The Detroit Race Riot.* Philadelphia: Chilton Books, 1964; Gilbert and the Staff of the *Washington Post. Ten Blocks from the White House.* New York: Praeger, 1969; *Race Riot at East St. Louis.* Carbondale: Southern Illinois University Press, 1964; *Race Riot: Chicago.* New York: Atheneum, 1970.

[105] *Urban Racial Violence in the Twentieth Century.* Beverly Hills, Calif.: Glencoe Press, 1969; *Racial Violence in the United States.* Chicago: Aldine Pub. Co., 1969; *From Race Riot to Sit-In.* Garden City: Doubleday, 1966; *Urban Riots.* New York: Vintage, 1968; *Violence as Protest.* Garden City: Doubleday, 1971.

[106] Edwin S. Redkey. *Black Exodus: Black Nationalist and Back-to-Africa Movements, 1890-1910.* New Haven: Yale University Press, 1969; P. J. Staudenraus. *The African Colonization Movement, 1816-1865.* New York: Columbia University Press, 1961; Robert G. Weisbord. "The Back-to-Africa Idea." *History Today* 18: 30-37; No. 1, Jan. 1968; M. R. Delaney and Robert Campbell. *Search for a Place: Black Separatism and Africa, 1860.* Ann Arbor: University of Michigan Press, 1969; E. David Cronon. *Black Moses: The Story of Marcus Garvey and the Universal Negro Improvement Association.* Madison: University of Wisconsin Press, 1955; William E. Bittle and Gilbert Geis. *The Longest Way Home: Chief Alfred C. Sam's Back-to-Africa Movement.* Detroit: Wayne State University Press, 1964; Howard H. Bell. "Negro Nationalism: A Factor in Emigration Projects, 1858-1861." *Journal of Negro History* 47: 42-53; No. 1, Jan. 1962; Easien Udosen Essien-Udom. *Black Nationalism: A Search for an Identity in America.* Chicago: University of Chicago Press, 1962; Eric Lincoln. *The Black Muslims in America.* Boston: Beacon, 1961.

[107] New York: Viking Press, 1970.

[108] Indianapolis: Bobbs-Merrill, 1970.

[109] *The New World of Negro Americans.* New York: John Day Co., 1963; *Apropos of Africa.* New York: Humanities Press, 1969; *Pan-Africanism Reconsidered.* Berkeley: University of California Press, 1962.

[110] Harold Isaacs. "Du Bois and Africa." *Race* 2: 3-23; No. 1, Nov. 1960; George Shepperson. "Notes on Negro American Influences on the Emergence of African Nationalism." *Journal of African History* 1: 299-312; No. 2, 1960; E. U. Essien-Udom. "The Relationship of Afro-Americans to African National-

ism." *Freedomways* 2: 391-407; No. 4, Fall 1962; John H. Clarke, editor. *Harlem: A Community in Transition*. New York: Citadel Press, 1964, pp. 77-96; Okon E. Uya, editor. *Black Brotherhood: Afro-Americans and Africa*. Lexington, Mass.: Heath, 1971.

[111] *The Negro Family in Chicago*. Chicago: University of Chicago Press, 1932; *The Negro Family in the United States*. Chicago: The University of Chicago Press, 1939.

[112] *Black Families in White America*. Englewood Cliffs, N.J.: Prentice Hall, 1968; *Tomorrow's Tomorrow*. Garden City: Doubleday, 1971.

[113] *A History of Negro Education in the South*. Cambridge: Harvard University Press, 1967; *The Predominantly Negro Colleges and Universities in Transition*. New York: Bureau of Publications, Teachers College, Columbia University, 1965.

[114] *Howard University*. New York: New York University Press, c. 1968; *The Story of Atlanta University*. Atlanta: Atlanta University Press, 1969; *A Candle in the Dark*. Valley Forge: Judson Press, 1967; *The Story of Spelman College*. Atlanta: United Negro College Fund, 1961.

[115] New York: Scribner, 1971.

[116] *The Negro Professional Class*. Glencoe, Ill.: Free Press, 1959; *The History of the Negro in Medicine*. 3rd ed. New York: Publishers Co., 1969.

[117] New York: Morrow, 1963.

[118] *The Story of Jazz*. New York: Oxford University Press, 1956; *The Music of Black Americans*. New York: Norton, 1971.

[119] *Deep River*. New York: Harper and Brothers, 1955; *The Social Implications of Early Negro Music in the United States*. New York: Arno, 1969.

[120] New York: Oxford University Press, 1971.

[121] Arnold Adoff, editor. *I Am the Darker Brother: An Anthology of Modern Poems by Negro Americans*. New York: Macmillan, 1968; Robert E. Hayden, editor. *Kaleidoscope: Poems by American Negro Poets*. New York: Harcourt Brace & World, 1967; Rosey Pool, editor. *Beyond the Blues: New Poems by American Negroes*. Lympne, Kent: Hand and Flower Press, 1962; Clarence Major. editor. *The New Black Poetry*. New York: International Publishers, 1969; LeRoi Jones and Larry Neal, editors. *Black Fire: An Anthology of Afro-American Writing*. New York: Morrow, 1968.

[122] *Negro Voices in American Fiction*. Chapel Hill: University of North Carolina Press, 1948; *Native Sons*. Philadelphia: Lippincott, 1968; *The Negro Novel in America*. Revised ed. New Haven: Yale University Press, 1965.

[123] *Black Drama*. New York: Hawthorn Books, 1967; *The Crisis of the Negro Intellectual*. New York: Morrow, 1967; *Negro Playwrights in the American Theater*. New York: Columbia University Press, 1969.

[124] *The Negro in Films*. London: S. Robinson, 1948; *The Negro in Hollywood Films*. New York: Masses and Mainstream, 1950.

[125] "The Death of Rastus." *Phylon* 28: 267-275; No. 3, Fall 1967; "Movies in the Ghetto." *Negro Digest* 18: 21-27; No. 18, Feb. 1969.

[126] *Great Negroes*. Chicago: Afro-American Publishing Co., 1963; *Pioneers in Protest*. Chicago: Johnson Publishing Co., 1968; *Famous Negro Athletes*. New York: Dodd, Mead, 1964; *Pioneers and Patriots*. Garden City: Doubleday, 1965; *Famous Negro Heroes of America*. New York: Dodd, Mead, 1958; *Historical Negro Biographies*. 2nd ed., revised. New York: Publishers Co., 1969; *Famous Negro Entertainers*. New York: Dodd, Mead, 1967.

[127] Arna Bontemps. *Frederick Douglass: Slave-Fighter-Freeman*. New York: Knopf, 1959; Jacqueline Bernard. *Journey Toward Freedom: The Story of Sojourner Truth*. New York: Norton, 1967; Harold W. Felton. *Edward Rose, Negro Trail Blazer*. New York: Dodd, Mead, 1967; Jean Gould. *That Dunbar Boy: The Story of America's Famous Negro Past*. New York: Dodd, Mead, 1958; Shirley Graham. *Booker T. Washington. . . .* New York: Messner, 1966; Harold W. Felton. *Jim Beckwourth, Negro Mountain Man*. New York: Dodd, Mead,

1966; Rackham Holt. *George Washington Carver.* . . . Garden City: Doubleday, 1963; Edwin Hoyt. *Paul Robeson: The American Othello.* Cleveland: World, 1967; Frances T. Humphreville. *Harriet Tubman: Flame of Freedom.* Boston: Houghton Mifflin, 1967; J. Alvin Kugelmass. *Ralph J. Bunche: Fighter For Peace.* New York: J. Messner, 1962; Charles Osborne. *I Have A Dream, The Story of Martin Luther King in Text and Pictures.* New York: Time-Life Books, 1968; Finis Farr. *Black Champion: The Life and Times of Jack Johnson.* New York: Scribner's, 1964.

[128] Philip S. Foner. *Frederick Douglass.* . . . New York: Citadel Press, 1964; Benjamin Quarles. *Frederick Douglass.* Washington: Associated Publishers, 1948, also Englewood Cliffs, N.J.: Prentice Hall, 1968; Samuel R. Spencer. *Booker T. Washington and the Negro's Place in American Life.* Boston: Little Brown, 1955; Hugh Hawkins, editor. *Booker T. Washington and His Critics: The Problem of Negro Leadership.* Boston: Heath, 1962; Emma Lou Thornbrough, editor. *Booker T. Washington.* Englewood Cliffs, N.J.: Prentice Hall, c. 1969; Francis L. Broderick. *W.E.B. Du Bois, Negro Leader in a Time of Crisis.* Stanford: Stanford University Press, 1959; Elliott M. Rudwick. *W.E.B. Du Bois: A Study in Minority Group Leadership.* Philadelphia: University of Pennsylvania Press, 1960; E.D. Cronon. *Black Moses.* Madison: University of Wisconsin Press, 1955; David L. Lewis. *King: A Critical Biography.* New York: Praeger, 1970.

[129] *Negro Thought in America.* Ann Arbor: University of Michigan Press, 1963; *Booker T. Washington.* New York: Oxford, 1972.

[130] *The Negro Vanguard.* New York: Rinehart, 1959; *William Wells Brown.* Chicago: University of Chicago Press, 1969; *The Guardian of Boston.* New York: Atheneum, 1970; *T. Thomas Fortune.* Chicago: University of Chicago Press, 1972.

[131] *Up From Slavery.* New York: Doubleday Page & Co.; *The Autobiography of W.E.B. Du Bois.* Reprinted New York: International Publishers, 1968; *The Autobiography of Malcolm X.* New York: Grove Press, 1965.

[132] John C. Dancy. *Sand Against the Wind.* . . . Detroit: Wayne State University Press, 1966; Langston Hughes. *I Wonder as I Wander.* . . . New York: Rinehart, 1956; Reba Lee. *I Passed for White.* New York: Longmans, Green, 1955; Paul Robeson. *Here I Stand.* New York: Othello Associates, 1958; Ellen Tarry. *The Third Door: The Autobiography of an American Negro Woman.* New York: Guild Press, 1967; Horace R. Cayton. *Long Old Road.* New York: Trident Press, c. 1964; Anne Moody. *Coming of Age in Mississippi.* New York: Dial Press, 1968.

[133] Charles V. Roman. *A Knowledge of History Is Conducive to Racial Solidarity, and Other Writings.* Nashville: Sunday School Union Print, 1911, pp. 31-32.

· 4 ·

European Americans:
From Immigrants to Ethnics

Rudolph J. Vecoli

ETHNICITY has exercised a persistent and pervasive influence upon American history. Americans have traditionally defined themselves and others as members of ethnocultural groups. On the basis of their origins, national, racial, religious, and regional, they have shared with "their own kind" a sense of a common heritage and collective destiny. Ethnic cultures have sustained patterns of values, attitudes, and behaviors which have differentiated various segments of the population. The resulting ethnic pluralism has profoundly affected all aspects of American life. Religion, politics, social mobility, even the conduct of foreign affairs, have reflected this extraordinary diversity of ethnic identities.

A series of migrations, internal as well as external, brought together peoples of various cultural, linguistic, racial, and religious backgrounds. The peopling of this continent by transoceanic migration has gone on for over four hundred years. The original inhabitants, the true native Americans, were gradually displaced and dispossessed by successive waves of immigrants. They came from all over the world, Africans by the millions, brought to this land in chains, Asiatics by the hundreds of thousands, and others from countries to the north and south and from the islands of the Caribbean. But the vast majority came from Europe. In the greatest population movement in human history, some thirty-five million Europeans immigrated to the United States in the century after 1830. This fact determined the basic character of American society; it was to be predominantly Caucasian, Christian, and Western.

The study of immigration history involves not only the processes of physical migration, but the long-range consequences of this mingling of peoples as well. Despite its importance, the European immigration has been relatively neglected by American historians until recent decades.

81

The reason appears to have been the general acceptance of an assimilationist ideology by scholars and laymen alike. The "Melting Pot," it was assumed, would transform the foreigners into indistinguishable Americans in a generation or two at most. Bemused by the alleged uniqueness of the American character and institutions, historians turned to environmental explanations. The frontier, material abundance, or mobility, rather than Old World influences, determined the values and behavior of the American people. In this light, immigration appeared to be an ephemeral episode.[1]

These assimilationist assumptions have been called into question by the "rediscovery of ethnicity" in recent years. White ethnic groups, as well as blacks, Indians, and Hispanic Americans, have demonstrated an unanticipated longevity. This "New Pluralism" has inspired historians and others to explore the ethnic dimension of American life in the past as well as the present. As a consequence we are in the midst of a renaissance of immigration history. A rich and growing literature awaits the student of European American ethnic groups, one which is enlivened by divergent interpretations and differing methodologies.

We Stand on Their Shoulders

The writing of immigration history was initiated by a handful of scholars a half century ago when the field was less fashionable than it is today. Their thorough and scrupulous scholarship rescued the subject from the partisan concerns of the advocates of immigration restriction and the filiopietists.[2] The major works of these historians remain essential reading for the serious student of the European immigration.

Among these pioneers, Marcus Lee Hansen advanced the most comprehensive interpretation of the Atlantic migration considered as a whole.[3] Viewing emigration as a basic force in European history, Hansen emphasized the underlying demographic, economic, and social causes which transcended political boundaries. Although sensitive to the "pull" of the "Common Men's Utopia," Hansen stressed the "push" of European conditions as of equal importance. Hansen also traced the transatlantic routes of commerce which provided ready-made paths for the westward-bound emigrants.

In his volume of essays, *The Immigrant in American History,*[4] Hansen integrated the story of immigration with certain major themes, such as the westward movement, political democracy, and Puritanism. Viewing the immigrants as "carriers of culture," he focused on the interaction between their heritage and the American environment. Rather than a threat to American democracy, Hansen thought the immigrants had exercised a basically conservative and stabilizing influence. Stressing their receptivity to American values, he declared that "they were Americans before they landed." Reflecting his own rural origins as well as the influence of his mentor, Frederick Jackson Turner, Hansen's writings dealt with the midwestern agrarian rather than the eastern urban phase of the immigrant experience.[5]

Hansen's perspective was shared by his contemporaries who contributed solid studies dealing with specific immigrant groups. Theodore C. Blegen wrote extensively on the Norwegians, his major work being a two-volume history which vividly depicts the Old World conditions as well as American experience of the immigrants.[6] Blegen was particularly skillful in locating and exploiting "America letters," emigrant ballads, and other documents in reconstructing the everyday lives of common folk. His colleague, George M. Stephenson, wrote with equal mastery of the Swedish immigration. *The Religious Aspects of the Swedish Immigrations*[7] is a cultural and social as well as institutional history of the Swedish American churches. In 1926, Stephenson published the first general history of American immigration,[8] one which deals with the role of the immigrant in the political development of the United States. Meanwhile Carl Wittke established himself as the historian of the German Americans; among his studies, those of the "Forty-eighters" and the German language press in America are particularly noteworthy.[9] Wittke was also the author of a survey of immigration history, *We Who Built America*.[10] Viewing the central motif of American history as "the impact of successive immigrant tides upon a New World environment," Wittke's history is a descriptive rather than interpretive account of the various nationalities comprising these tides. In the tradition of Turner, these historians like Hansen conceived of immigration as the interaction between European culture and American geography.

Oscar Handlin's *Boston's Immigrants* (1941) marked a new departure in immigration history.[11] Handlin's theme was one of acculturation, the mutual impact of Irish Catholics and Yankee Protestants in a seaboard city. Through adaptation to the stern conditions of urban life, the Irish created their own ethnic community. Unable and unwilling to assimilate the Irish, Boston became a divided city. Wedding immigration history and urban history, *Boston's Immigrants* served as a model for the coming generation of historians. Robert Ernst's study of immigrant groups in New York City was another early example of this new genre of ethnic history.[12] Ernst skillfully delineated the interplay of the various nationalities in the culture, politics, economy, and other aspects of urban life.

Handlin has written prolifically on the subject of immigration and ethnicity. His major work, *The Uprooted*, depicts the effects of migration upon the immigrants themselves.[13] "The history of immigration," he observed, "is a history of alienation and its consequences." Torn from a traditional peasant community, Handlin's immigrant became an estranged individual without meaningful ties to his fellow men. In dramatic prose, Handlin told of the breakup of European rural society, the flight from disaster, the horrors of the voyage, and the anxieties of life in a strange land. Though the newcomer seeks to regain his lost community by creating ethnic institutions, he fails to escape from his alienated condition. This grim interpretation of the immigrant experience has had a profound influence, but the question has been raised whether Handlin's immigrant was indeed typical of the many different groups represented in the European immigration.[14]

In subsequent writings, Handlin portrayed American society as a mosaic of competing ethnic and racial groups.[15] Despite the resulting prejudice and conflict, Handlin judged pluralism to be a positive value. By providing a focus for personal identity as well as a vehicle for collective activity, ethnic groups served as a bulwark of liberty against the centralizing and dehumanizing tendencies of modern technocratic society.

New General Interpretations

Traditionally, Americans viewed immigration as a single-minded flight from the "Old World" to the "Land of Opportunity." Hansen first noted that the immigration to the United States was to be understood as much in terms of European conditions and that it was a part of a much more complex population movement. These insights have been further developed in the writings of Brinley Thomas and Frank Thistlethwaite. In his *Migration and Economic Growth,* Thomas offered a more sophisticated interpretation of the dynamics of nineteenth-century European migration.[16] Rather than being a simple reflex to the American business cycle, he analyzed the flow of labor and capital within the Atlantic economy in response to business fluctuations on both sides of the ocean. Thomas also stressed the push factor of the "Malthusian Devil," the frontier of surplus population which moved from west to east across Europe in the nineteenth century. Rather than being pulled by American opportunity, huge fragments of the European population were expelled by societies which could not absorb their labor. As the European countries industrialized, internal migrations became alternatives to overseas movements. Thomas also noted the changing character of emigration in response to altered technological and labor conditions in the United States.

In a seminal paper, Thistlethwaite declared that the European migrations must be understood in terms of the transformation of European society in the nineteenth century.[17] The impact of the demographic and industrial revolutions dislodged vast numbers of people from their ancestral homes and sent them wandering over the face of the earth. Thistlethwaite elaborated upon the complex patterns of movement within Europe and between Europe and other continents. While the majority of overseas migrants did come to the United States, Argentina, Brazil, and Canada were also receiving heavy immigrations. The high incidence of repatriation, perhaps a third of all immigrants to the United States, was another aspect of the migratory pattern commented upon by Thistlethwaite. Rather than viewing the immigrants as an anonymous, nondescript mass, Thistlethwaite called for the study of the specific characteristics and peculiar migratory patterns of particular occupational and village groupings.

The realization that the United States was not unique as a host society has stimulated interest in the comparative study of immigration history. Louis Hartz's *The Founding of New Societies* is a pioneering work in this field.[18] Its thesis is that the character of the "new societies" created by European migrations was determined by the stage of historical development of the mother country at the time of mass exodus. These "fragments," removed from the stream of European history, thus retained and reinforced their original ideological cast. In a series of essays, the thesis is applied to the United States, French Canada, South Africa, Australia, and Brazil.

The Hartz thesis is utilized by John Higham in his provocative essay which places immigration history in a comparative setting.[19] Rather than being immigrants, the original colonists, Higham contends, constituted a "charter group" which set the initial character of the society and the terms upon which later arrivals were admitted. To this dominant core-culture, newcomers have been progressively assimilated. Higham contrasted the limited impact of the immigration upon American society as compared with Argentina or Brazil. One factor, he suggested, accounting for this difference was the tremendous variety among the immigrants to the United States while the immigration to Latin America was concentrated in a few nationalities. Thus the cultural diversity of American ethnic groups diluted their impact and hastened their assimilation. With Nathan Glazer, Higham viewed the mass immigration as disruptive of the established American culture and contributing to the emergence of a mass culture.[20]

Several general histories of American immigration which incorporate the more recent findings have appeared since 1960. Maldwyn Allen Jones in an admirably concise and literate volume surveyed this "greatest folk-migration in human history."[21] Acknowledging his debt to Hansen, Handlin, Higham, and others, Jones sought "to tell briefly the story of American immigration from the planting of Virginia to the present." Rejecting traditional distinctions between "colonists" and "immigrants" and "old immigrants" and "new immigrants," Jones, while mindful of the changes taking place in both those who came and in the country which received them, stressed the fundamental sameness of the immigrant and his experience. "As a social process," Jones concluded, "(immigration) has shown little variation throughout American history."

A more recent work by Philip Taylor focuses more narrowly upon the century of mass emigration, 1830-1930.[22] Its point of view is primarily that from the European side of the Atlantic. Though acknowledging "the attracting force of America's economic opportunities and of its free institutions," the volume describes in detail the disruptive forces at work in Europe which stimulated the impulse to emigrate. Though drawing upon the work of others, Taylor brings to bear much fresh material in his discussion of the emigration business and its regulation, the conditions of the journey, and the recruitment of emigrants. Briefer discussion is reserved for the working and living conditions of the immigrants in America, nativism, immigration legislation, and the evolution of ethnic communities. The merit of this volume lies not so much in new interpretations as in the richness of its factual rendering of the subject.

Immigration and ethnicity are major themes in Rowland Berthoff's interpretive social history, *An Unsettled People*.[23] Berthoff projects a cycle of historical development, "from adequate order through a period of excessive disorder and back again toward some satisfactory order," as the paradigm of American history. In this scheme, the massive influx of foreigners joined with intense internal mobility contributed to the general social disorder of nineteenth-century America. In a search for community, new social groups were formed, mainly along ethnic lines. Thus ethnic consciousness became a source of identification of self and others, one which was expressed in institutional patterns such as jobs and housing. Reform, including efforts to exclude or Americanize the immigrants, represents for Berthoff an attempt to bring social order out of chaos.

European Backgrounds and Reactions

Since Hansen's general discussion in *The Atlantic Migration,* the European backgrounds of the emigration have been the subject of a number of specialized studies. Wilbur Shepperson's *British Emigration to North America* deals with a variety of colonization projects in the Victorian era.[24] Shepperson traced the issue of emigration, as it is debated in the press and in state councils, among humanitarians and trade unionists. Was it a panacea or a pandora? Shepperson's account of various ill-fated schemes suggests that for many it was a pandora. In a perceptive essay, Charlotte Erickson analyzed the agrarian myth which lured English emigrants, fleeing from the disruptive effects of the industrial revolution, to the American "Garden of the World."[25] Cecil Woodham-Smith has written a vivid account of the Irish potato famine and of the mass exodus it triggered.[26] The impact upon Irish society and culture of the American emigration is the subject of a monograph by Arnold Schrier.[27] The official and press reaction to the population drain, its effects on Irish agriculture, and the cultural-folkloristic reaction (including the development of the "American wake") to the mass exodus are recounted. The "constructive opposition" to the Swedish emigration has been described by Franklin Scott.[28]

Mack Walker has authored a thorough study of the German emigration of the nineteenth century.[29] Rather than being of one piece, the *Auswanderung* affected the various regions of Germany at different times. Walker analyzed the interplay of population growth, land tenure, technical innovations, and state policy in determining the rates and directions of the outward movement. John S. MacDonald has argued that the differential rates of emigration among the various regions of Italy are related to the various patterns of land ownership and to the resulting ethos of the peasantry.[30] In areas where landownership was widely distributed and an individualistic outlook prevailed, emigration rates were highest; while in those areas characterized by large estates and collective forms of action on the part of agricultural laborers, emigration rates were lowest. Depending on the character of the rural social structure then, militant working-class organization and migration were alternative responses of the cultivators to poverty.

Historians have also been interested in the American influences which filtered back to the homeland through the emigration process. In their article on "The Immigrant and the American Image in Europe, 1860-1914," Merle Curti and Kendall Birr emphasized the role of emigration promotional literature, as well as "America letters," as media through which information and misinformation regarding the United States reached the common folk.[31] Ingrid Semmingsen explored similar influences at work, particularly in Norway, finding that the "America letters" and the returned emigrants were often the agents of change, introducing new ideas regarding agricultural methods, politics, and social relationships.[32] However, she observed that, as in the case of the Irish, the conservative milieu in some countries was not receptive to impulses from America. Schrier's study confirmed that the "returned Yank" had little impact upon Ireland; American money, he concluded, was more important than the repatriate in effecting changes in Irish society.[33]

Since perhaps as many as a third of the immigrants returned to their homelands, the phenomenon of repatriation is important in evaluating the significance of the transatlantic migration for both the United States and Europe. Theodore Saloutos was a trailbreaker in this field with his study of returned Greek-Americans.[34] Primarily through interviews, Saloutos studied a group of repatriates, analyzing their motives and attitudes, their readjustment and status in the Old Country. While many were well-to-do, he found an ambivalence in their feelings toward both Greece and America, as well as generally negative attitudes toward the repatriates on the part of other Greeks. Saloutos has also written a useful summary article on the repatriation in the twentieth century.[35] In a volume suggestively entitled *Emigration and Disenchantment,* Shepperson sketched the portraits of some seventy-five English returnees.[36] While he found great diversity among them, his general conclusion was that those Britons who had migrated to escape change were disillusioned by their failure to find stability in America. Another study by Shepperson deals with the return of British working class immigrants.[37] The heavy return migration of the Italians has been the subject of studies by George R. Gilkey[38] and Francesco Cerase.[39] Gilkey found that the *americani* with their new ideas and dollars had a disruptive effect upon their native villages, but did not affect basic changes in the oppressive conditions of southern Italy. A similar conclusion was arrived at by Cerase: "Their reabsorption into the life of the community has had no consequence of innovation on the economic or political patterns of behavior in the community itself." Other studies of repatriation are needed to fill out this dimension of the history of the Atlantic migration.

The Making of Americans

The making of Americans has been a basic theme in the writing of American immigration history. What was to be the significance of this "foreign invasion" for the emerging American nationality? Was America a "Melting Pot" in which all diverse elements would be fused into a new human type or was it a mosaic composed of distinct ethnic groups? These issues have long been debated, and the echoes of these debates resound in the writings of historians and social scientists. The ideologies are themselves a part of the history of immigration, since they shaped attitudes and public policies. Philip Gleason's article, "The Melting Pot: Symbol of Fusion or Confusion?", traced the changing content, use and meaning of this metaphor.[40] In his work, *Assimilation in American Life,* Milton Gordon summarized three contending ideologies of ethnic group relations: Anglo-Conformity; the Melting Pot; and Cultural Pluralism.[41] Gordon then offered his own theory of assimilation, one which envisioned the persistence of structural pluralism, in terms of inter-personal relations, along with a pervasive cultural assimilation in terms of such things as langauge, manners, and values. Seeking to explain the "religious revival" of the 1950's, Will Herberg proposed the concept of the "triple Melting Pot" as an explanatory hypothesis.[42] While rejecting ethnic definitions, the grandchildren of the immigrants were manifesting the phenomenon of "third generation return" by affirming their identities as Protestants, Catholics, or Jews.

Other writers impressed by the persistence of ethnic groups have offered theories to explain the continuing pluralistic character of America. In their influential work, *Beyond the Melting Pot,* Nathan Glazer and Daniel P. Moynihan declared: "The point about the melting pot is that it did not happen."[43] Based on an analysis of five ethnic groups in New York City, the authors found that ethnicity pervaded all spheres of life. The explanation they suggested was that ethnic groups were not only a source of individual identity, they had also become *interest groups* by which persons sought to defend or advance their position in society.

In his groundbreaking study, *Language Loyalty in America,* Joshua Fishman advanced the theme of cultural maintenance as a neglected aspect of ethnic history.[44] Contrary to the notion that the immigrants gladly shed their native heritage, Fishman argued that they made strenuous efforts to sustain their cultures and languages. Detailed studies of the German, French Canadian, Spanish, and Ukrainian groups document their resistance to pressures for total cultural assimilation. Despite the steady inroads of "de-ethnization," Fishman demonstrated that the immigrants' struggles to keep alive their native tongues and cultures are a vital and neglected aspect of American social history.

A contrary view has been advanced by Timothy L. Smith.[45] Rather than being victims of a coercive Americanization policy, Smith has depicted the immigrants as eagerly pursuing assimilation as a means of advancing their fortunes and those of their children. Espousing Hansen's dictum that "they were Americans before they landed," Smith contended that the newcomers shared with the natives basic values of hard work, thrift, and individual ambition. Advocating "new approaches," Smith chose to stress "assimilation, both cultural and structural, rather than ethnic exclusiveness" as the key to understanding immigration history.

Nativism and Immigration Policy

While the response of native Americans to immigrants ranged from cordial to hostile, it has been xenophobia which has attracted the most attention from historians. An early and still useful work in this vein is Ray Allen Billington, *The Protestant Crusade, 1800-1860*.[46] Focusing on the intense anti-Catholic sentiment of the antebellum years, Billington interpreted the antipathy toward the Irish and Germans as stemming primarily from deep-seated religious prejudice. While noting ethnic rivalries over jobs and politics, the volume concentrates on the manifestations of anti-Catholicism ranging from literary slander to physical violence. A psychological interpretation has since been forwarded by David Brion Davis.[47] Viewing nativism as stemming from fear of internal subversion, Davis attributed this conspiratorial mentality to the insecurities engendered by "bewildering social change." In his analysis of anti-Catholic, anti-Mason, and anti-Mormon literature, Davis found that all shared a common rhetoric and view of reality. Richard Hofstadter found this fear of conspiracy, which he styled "the paranoid style of American politics," recurring in times of stress.[48]

The major work on nativism in post-Civil War America, John Higham's *Strangers in the Land,* also espouses a psychological interpretation.[49] Defining nativism as a form of nationalism, Higham identified three major ideologies of xenophobia: anti-Catholicism; anti-radicalism; and racialism. During periods of national well-being, nativist fears declined, but with a crisis of confidence brought on by economic depression or war, hostility toward foreigners welled up again. While the threat was viewed at various times as Popery, anarchism, and racial degeneracy, all of these phobias fueled the ultimately successful drive for immigration restriction. Higham has had the rare satisfaction of being his own revisionist. Taking a second look at nativism, he pointed out that intergroup conflict could profitably be analyzed from a sociological perspective.[50] The "status rivalries" among ethnic groups in their competitive quest for power and place resulted in recurring friction and hostility. E. Digby Baltzell applied Higham's analysis in his interpretation of the emergence of a "Protestant Establishment."[51] Threatened by the rise of new groups, particularly the Jews, the American upper class responded with exclusionary practices based on ethnic and social prejudice. Baltzell details the development of an ideological defense of caste and of institutions to defend caste privileges by the WASP aristocracy.

Nativism has also been the subject of specialized studies dealing with particular facets of the phenomenon. Barbara M. Solomon analyzed the role of New England Brahmins in developing a rationale for immigration restriction based on an ideology of race.[52] Focusing on the history of the Immigration Restriction League, she found its roots in the anxieties caused by the changes which were undermining the New England way of life. A parallel study by Charlotte Erickson contends that the opposition of organized labor to the southern and eastern European immigration was inspired by ethnic prejudice rather than real economic competition.[53] In her definitive study of the contract labor controversy, Erickson demonstrated convincingly that by the 1880's few immigrants were coming to America under formal labor contracts. From the debate on the Foran Act on, ethnic prejudice rather than practical considerations determined the views of American labor leaders on the immigration question.

The resurgence of anti-Catholicism in the 1890's and its primary manifestation, the American Protective Association, have been described by Donald L. Kinzer.[54] Fear of the Roman Catholic Church and of its alleged political ambitions caused Protestants to rally to the APA. Seeking to deprive the Church of new recruits and votes, the APA advocated immigration restriction as well as a stiffening of naturalization requirements. Robert K. Murray's *Red Scare* is a study of the post-World War I hysteria regarding an anticipated radical uprising in the United States.[55] Fears of Bolshevism fed by labor strikes and general social unrest created a mood in which official and vigilante violence directed against radicals and aliens was generally applauded. In a psychological interpretation of the "Red Scare," Stanley Coben located its sources in the insecurity caused by the social and economic dislocations of the postwar years.[56] Seeking to eradicate "foreign" threats to American institutions and values, the nativists raised the standard of "One Hundred Percent Americanism." The federal policies concerning immigrant radicals have been thoroughly examined by William Preston, Jr.[57] His study is severely critical of the federal government because of the frequent violations of civil rights and injuries inflicted upon persons who were often innocent of any wrong.

The development of American immigration policy to the enactment of the restrictive legislation of the 1920's can best be followed in Higham, *Strangers in the Land.* Higham has also written a brief summary essay on the subject.[58] The story of American immigration policy from 1924 to 1952 has been told by Robert A. Divine.[59] A dispassionate legislative history, the study traces Congressional and executive policymaking from the enactment of the national origins statute to the passage of the McCarran Act. While recording lobbying activities and public debate on specific issues, its perspective is that of Capitol Hill and the White House.

The efforts by public and private agencies to facilitate the adjustment and assimilation of the immigrants have been little studied as of 1972. Edward Hartmann, *The Movement to Americanize the Immigrant,* focuses on the governmental and voluntary programs during the period of World War I.[60] Although inspired by the wartime zeal for national unity, not all of the attention paid to the foreign-born was coercive or mean-spirited. The teaching of the English language and "American ideals" was a primary activity, but there were also sympathetic attempts to safeguard the immigrants from economic exploitation and to assist them to achieve a better life. Another perspective on the Americanization movement is provided by Gerd Korman's account of the response of industrial management to its polyglot labor force.[61] Moved by considerations of improved efficiency and productivity, enlightened industrialists introduced welfare and safety programs in their factories. To these were added during the First World War Americanization classes for the immigrant workers. Under this regime of "benevolent paternalism," as Korman describes it, a group of safety and welfare experts emerged as agents of social control. A recent article on the Illinois Immigrants' Protective League by Robert L. Buroker also emphasizes the role of professional social workers animated by a vision of an efficient, harmonious social order.[62]

A particular episode in the history of American immigration policy has been the subject of several books in recent years. The policy pursued by the United States with respect to Jewish refugees from Nazi Germany has been examined critically by Henry L. Feingold[63] and David S. Wyman.[64] Both studies agree that a combination of factors, bureaucratic inertia, congressional opposition, public indifference, and anti-Semitism, prevented any effective response to the plight of the Jews. While critical of Franklin D. Roosevelt for not doing more, the authors recognized that the domestic political climate appears to have made any intercession by the United States impossible.

There were the fortunate few who did escape from the tyranny of Hitler and Mussolini and who found refuge in America. Among them were many of Europe's most brilliant scholars, scientists, and artists. Their story is told with grace and authority by Laura Fermi, herself one of them, in *Illustrious Immigrants.*[65] The impact of this intellectual migration is a subject of *Perspectives in American History.*[66] Chapters by various contributors, some of them participants in the migration, detail the extraordinary influence exerted by this band of *emigrés* upon the arts and sciences in America.

Studies of Particular Ethnic Groups

By its very nature, immigration history lends itself to studies of particular ethnic groups. The "America fever" struck the various countries of Europe at different times; the arriving immigrants sharing a common language, culture, and sometimes religion formed ethnic communities in the United States. The histories of single ethnic groups tend to follow a common pattern; they begin by examining the causes of the emigration in the Old Country; they trace the routes of migration and patterns of settlement; and conclude with a discussion of the social, economic, and cultural adjustments to American conditions. Such single group studies have the merit of permitting the analysis of the migrant experience in depth, but they are open to the criticism that they neglect the common aspects of that experience which transcend ethnic differences.

Although studies of the British in colonial America abound, historians have only recently (as of 1972) taken note of the large emigration from the British Isles in the nineteenth century. Rowland T. Berthoff has written about the English, Scots, Welsh, and Ulstermen who came to man America's burgeoning industries.[67] Their occupational and cultural skills facilitated their economic and social assimilation. Yet Berthoff pointed out the difficulties they sometimes experienced as well as their retention of particular identities and customs. From their hostile encounters with the American Irish emerged a sense of their common British identity. Frank Thistlethwaite has also described the cultural continuity in the communities of British merchants and artisans.[68] The potters who migrated from the Five Towns of Staffordshire carried on their traditional way of life as well as their craft in Trenton, New Jersey and East Liverpool, Ohio. The role of British immigrants in the American labor movement has been traced by Clifton K. Yearley, Jr.[69] Following the careers of some fifty labor leaders of British origins, Yearley found their Chartist and trade union experience an important influence during the formative period of labor organization in America.

The British agrarian immigration has received less attention (as of 1972). Wilbur Shepperson described the establishment of various agricultural settlements,[70] while Charlotte Erickson has studied the expectations of those British immigrants who sought in America a pastoral Utopia.[71] *Prairie Albion* by Charles Boewe tells the story of an early English settlement in Illinois.[72] The migration of British Mormon converts to Utah is the subject of P.A.M. Taylor, *Expectations Westward*.[73] The study concentrates on the Mormon proselytizing, the planned emigration and the journey, rather than on the immigrants' settlements in Utah. Recently the ethnic minorities within the British emigration have found their historians. Edward G. Hartmann celebrated the achievements of the Welsh,[74] while A. L. Rowse performed the same function for the Cornish.[75]

The Catholic Irish immigration has been the subject of a separate and extensive historical scholarship. Carl Wittke's *The Irish in America* is the most thorough treatment of the subject.[76] Individual chapters deal with such topics as the Irish and the Church, politics, and business. More interpretive and provocative are the works by George W. Potter[77] and William V. Shannon.[78] The harsh urban conditions which the Irish encountered and their successful adaptation to these conditions are depicted by Oscar Handlin, Robert Ernst, and Earl F. Niehaus for Boston, New York, and New Orleans respectively.[79] James P. Shannon's *Catholic Colonization on the Western Frontier* recounts the largely unsuccessful efforts of the Church to settle the Irish immigrants on farms in Minnesota.[80]

The Irish reputation for violence was reinforced by the mayhem allegedly committed by the Molly Maguires. Wayne G. Broehl, Jr., has interpreted the patterns of violence in the Pennsylvania anthracite fields as an expression of the heritage of secret societies and terrorist tactics brought over by the Irish miners.[81] The American Irish were also involved in the long struggle to free Erin from British rule. The origins and character of Irish-American nationalism are the subject of an astute study by Thomas N. Brown.[82] The nationalist movement served as a school for the Irish in which they cultivated an appetite and aptitude for politics which made them a force in American public life. Brian Jenkins has reexamined the episode of the Fenian Brotherhood, particularly in terms of its effect upon Anglo-American relations.[83] The policies of Woodrow Wilson with respect to Ireland and the reactions of Irish Americans have been analyzed in articles by William M. Leary, John B. Duff, and Joseph P. O'Grady.[84]

Although the Germans figured as the largest element in the nineteenth-century immigration, the historical literature dealing with them is quite slim. John A. Hawgood's *The Tragedy of German-America* is (as of 1972) the only general overview of the subject.[85] Accounts of the Germans in New York, Chicago, and Milwaukee can be found in the works by Ernst, Bessie Pierce, and Bayrd Still.[86] The Germans of New Orleans are the subject of a monograph by John F. Nau,[87] while the Cincinnati Germans have been studied by G. A. Dobbert.[88] Despite the fact that many Germans entered agriculture, there has been little written (as of 1972) about their rural settlements. Terry G. Jordon has studied the relative success of the Germans as farmers in Texas,[89] and Hildegard Johnson has analyzed the pattern of German settlement in the Midwest.[90]

Carl Wittke's writings are a major contribution to an understanding of various aspects of the German immigration. His study of the German "Forty-Eighters" describes the influence and careers of these political refugees who served as "the cultural leaven and the spiritual yeast for the whole German element."[91] Wittke's history of the German language press in America, a definitive treatment of the subject, concludes that the newspapers served both as instruments of cultural maintenance and as agencies of Americanization.[92] The role of German Americans in the Catholic Church has been assessed by Colman J. Barry.[93] Focusing upon the "Cahenslyism" controversy of the late nineteenth century, Barry dissected the ethnic rivalries between the Irish and the Germans. Another valuable study of the German-American Catholics is Philip Gleason's history of the Central-Verein, a national federation of German-American Catholic societies.[94] Gleason interpreted the involvement of the Central-Verein in social reform as a "creative response to a critical phase of the process of assimilation." Utilizing quantitative methods, Frederick C. Luebke traced the changing patterns of political behavior of German Americans in Nebraska in the closing decades of the nineteenth century.[95] Ethnocultural rather than economic issues had the major impact upon voting patterns, and political behavior reflected the diversity, particularly religious, among the Germans. Of the other Germanic groups, the Dutch immigrants have been the subject of a comprehensive history by Henry S. Lucas.[96]

While reference is commonly made to the Scandinavian immigration, its historiography is compartmentalized within national lines. William Mulder's excellent study of the Mormon migration is an exception in that it encompasses Danes, Norwegians, and Swedes.[97] Some 30,000 Scandinavian converts, the greater part from Denmark, came to Utah between 1850 and 1905. Mulder discussed the factors causing the emigration, as well as the pioneering life of the immigrants in the "New Zion."

The Norwegian Americans have been particularly fortunate in their historians. Blegen's two volumes remain the classic work on the Norwegian immigration.[98] Carlton C. Qualey's analysis of Norwegian settlement patterns is also a study of enduring value.[99] The volume and character of the Norwegian emigration are succinctly summarized in an article by Ingrid Semmingsen.[100] Einar Haugen's linguistic history of the Norwegian Americans is an impressive work of scholarship.[101] Two volumes by Kenneth O. Bjork add yet other dimensions to Norwegian American history. *Saga in Steel and Concrete* is a thorough study of Norwegian immigrant engineers and architects and of their contributions to American technology,[102] while *West of the Great Divide* tells the story of the Norwegians who settled on the Pacific Coast.[103] The history of the Lutheran Church among the Norwegian Americans is fully presented by E. Clifford Nelson and Eugene L. Fevold.[104]

By contrast, the Swedish immigration has been little studied until recent years. Stephenson's work is a notable exception.[105] James I. Dowie has written about Swedish pioneering on the sodhouse frontier.[106] He has also coedited with Ernest M. Espelie a volume of essays which discuss various facets of Swedish-American life.[107] A monograph by Finis Herbert Capps analyzes the attitudes of the Swedish-American press toward the foreign policy of the United States, finding there a propensity for isolationism and conservatism.[108]

Three major works on the Swedish immigration, all by Swedish historians, were published in 1971. Lars Ljungmark's meticulous study of the post-Civil War efforts to promote emigration from Sweden to Minnesota concludes that these schemes were largely unproductive.[109] Breaking with the rural emphasis of previous writings, Ulf Beijbom has written an important study of the Swedes in nineteenth-century Chicago.[110] Beijbom exploited manuscript census records, church lists, and city directories for his analysis of demographic and social patterns. An equally valuable work by Sture Lindmark focuses upon the maintenance phenomenon among Swedes in the Midwest for the years 1914-1932.[111] Analyzing the activities of ethnic churches, organizations, and press, Lindmark concluded that contrary to prevailing opinion the Swedes nourished a strong desire "to preserve their national identity, their cultural heritage, and their institutions."

The Finnish immigration, set apart by cultural and linguistic differences, has had its own distinctive history. The most comprehensive study is A. William Hoglund's *Finnish Immigrants in America, 1880-1920*.[112] Reviewing the development of Finnish American organizations, Hoglund's thesis is that the immigrants sought a better life through collective effort rather than individual enterprise. A history of the Finns in Wisconsin, by John I. Kolehmainen and George W. Hill, supports this conclusion.[113]

Since the emigration from Denmark was the smallest among the Scandinavian countries, it is to be expected that its history should also be the least studied. Paul C. Nyholm, *The Americanization of the Danish Lutheran Churches*, has been (as of 1972) the one substantial work available.[114] A volume by Kristian Hvidt offers a detailed analysis of the emigration from Denmark prior to 1914.[115] Based largely on computer-processed data, the study provides a profile of the socio-economic characteristics of the Danish emigrants. Hvidt also investigated the "international system of emigrant promotion" established by shipping companies which he concluded served as a vital link between the "push" and "pull" factors.

The literature on the Jews in America, while voluminous, tends to be sociological rather than historical. No comprehensive history of the Jewish immigration has been written (as of 1972), although the surveys by Oscar Handlin and Rufus Learsi are useful.[116] Nathan Glazer's *American Judaism* is a brilliant synthesis of religious and ethnic history.[117] Since American Jews have been predominantly urbanites, studies tend to take the form of histories of particular communities. Less attention has been given to the early German immigration, but Bertram Wallace Korn has written about the Jews in antebellum New Orleans.[118] Moses Rischin's *The Promised City* delineates the encounter between New York City and the East European immigration.[119] With their Old World traditions shattered by the brutal conditions of urban life, the Jews created a new consciousness and institutional network to cope with this new environment. The search for community is also the theme of Arthur Goren's history of the Kehillah experiment.[120] Although it ultimately failed, this was a significant attempt to transplant this European communal organization in order to sustain Jewish life on American soil. Allon Schoener's *Portal to America: the Lower East Side, 1870-1925* brings to life the panorama of immigrant life through photographs and documents.[121] Other Jewish communities have been written about by competent historians: Buffalo by Selig Adler and Thomas E. Connolly; Milwaukee by Louis J. Switchkow and Lloyd P. Gartner; Los Angeles by Max Vorspan and Gartner; and Rochester by Stuart E. Rosenberg.[122] A history of agricultural settlements in New Jersey by Joseph Brandes tells the story of the efforts to transform Jewish immigrants into farmers.[123] Brandes traced the evolution of these communities from 1882 to the present.

The role of the Jewish immigrants in the American labor movement has received less attention than it deserves. An important work by Elias Tcherikower and others, *The Early Jewish Labor Movement in the United States,* is particularly valuable for its descriptions of sweatshop conditions and labor organization in the garment industry.[124] A useful introductory work is Melech Epstein's *Jewish Labor in USA, 1882-1952.*[125] Two interpretive articles on the Jewish labor movement have been authored by Hyman Berman and Moses Rischin.[126]

Anti-Semitism, treated in passing by many of the previously mentioned works, has generated considerable scholarly discussion. Historians have debated its sources and causes: was it rooted in Christian theology or racist ideology? was it a rural or urban phenomenon? was it an expression of status rivalries or economic conflict? Charles Herbert Stember's *Jews in the Mind of America* presents essays from a variety of historical and sociological perspectives, as well as an analysis of a quarter century of survey data.[127] In several articles, John Higham has contended that anti-Semitism in America can best be understood as stemming from status rivalries such as those which resulted from the social climbing of newly wealthy Jews in the Gilded Age.[128] Much attention has centered on the issue of the alleged anti-Semitism of the Populists. Richard Hofstadter initiated the controversy by identifying an antisemitic strain in the Populist psyche. Among others, Norman Pollack and Walter T. K. Nugent have taken exception to this interpretation, while Irwin Unger and Leonard Dinnerstein have supported it.[129] Dinnerstein's history of the Leo Frank case provides a full account of this southern outburst of anti-Semitism.[130]

The eastern and southern European groups, those of the so-called "new immigration," have only in recent years begun to be the subject of historical study. The Italians, although second in numbers only to the Germans in the post-colonial immigration, were virtually ignored in earlier writings. In 1971 two general histories of the Italian Americans appeared. That by Luciano J. Iorizzo and Salvatore Mondello is a brief survey which treats various phases of the Italian immigration in knowledgeable fashion.[131] A more ambitious study is Alexander DeConde, *Half-Bitter, Half-Sweet,* which takes as its subject the full sweep of relationships between Italy and the United States from colonial times to the present.[132] Cultural, literary, and diplomatic contacts, as well as migration, are woven skillfully into a synthesis of Italian American history. Both volumes emphasize the intense prejudice which the Italians encountered as well as their efforts to transcend that barrier. A useful collection of articles dealing with various aspects of the Italian experience in America has been edited by Silvano M. Tomasi and Madeline H. Engel.[133]

Though city dwellers like the Jews, the Italians in urban communities have been the subject of few studies. Rudolph J. Vecoli and Humbert S. Nelli have both written about the Italians in Chicago. Vecoli stressed the continuing influence of Old World culture in the lives of the immigrants,[134] while Nelli argued that the Italians achieved rapid assimilation and upward mobility.[135] The successful adjustment of the Italians in the trans-Mississippi West is the theme of Andrew F. Rolle's *The Immigrant Upraised.*[136] Rolle described the agricultural settlements of Italians in the western states; otherwise little attention has been paid (as of 1972) to these immigrants in rural surroundings. An exception is Robert L. Brandfon's study of the employment of Italian labor in the cotton plantations of the Mississippi Delta.[137]

The clash of religio-cultural traditions resulting from the encounter between the Italian immigrants and the American Catholic Church has been described by Vecoli,[138] while Tomasi has emphasized the role of the national parish as a nucleus for the formation of Italian American communities.[139] The coming of age of the Italians in the politics of New York City is a theme of Arthur Mann's splendid biography of Fiorello LaGuardia.[140] The story of LaGuardia's successor, Vito Marcantonio, as the spokesman for the Italians of East Harlem, has been told by Salvatore LaGumina.[141] In his excellent study of the American response to the rise of Mussolini, John P. Diggins interpreted the pro-Fascist attitude of most Italian Americans as an expression of ethnic pride rather than political ideology.[142] Diggins has also written about the Italian-American opposition to *Il Duce.*

The role of the Italians in the American labor movement has been analyzed by Edwin Fenton.[143] Fenton concluded that the Italians were just as susceptible to organization as other nationalities given favorable conditions in their particular occupations. Nonetheless, Italians were often viewed as wagecutters by American workers and their coming sometimes incited a hostile reception. Herbert G. Gutman has written a full account of an early episode of labor violence directed against the Italians.[144] The striking differences in the part played by Italian immigrants in the labor movements of Argentina, Brazil, and the United States have been studied by Samuel L. Baily.[145] In a study of the Italian immigrant family, Virginia Yans McLaughlin noted the manner in which cultural values conditioned the employment patterns of wives and daughters.[146]

Among the stereotypes of the Italian immigrant was that of the violent anarchist. It was vindicated for some by the trial and conviction of Sacco and Vanzetti. Almost a half century after their execution the battle of the books over their guilt or innocence continued. Among recent writers, David Felix[147] argued for the prosecution and Herbert B. Ehrmann[148] for the defense, while Francis Russell[149] contended that Vanzetti was innocent, but Sacco guilty. Another source of prejudice against the Italians has been the enduring belief in their involvement in secret criminal organizations. Long dominated by journalistic writings, the subject has also been dealt with in a solid work of scholarship by Joseph L. Albini.[150] Albini holds that, rather than being an importation from Sicily, the history of organized crime in the United States long antedated the coming of the Italians. The participation of Italian Americans and other ethnic elements in criminal activities was to be understood in terms of the limited opportunities open to such groups for legitimate careers. These are essentially the conclusions of other studies.[151]

Historians have hardly begun to study the Slavic immigration. No general work encompassing this vast subject has (as of 1972) been attempted. Certain aspects of the history of Slavic immigrants have been explored by Victor R. Greene. *The Slavic Community on Strike* emphasizes the militant participation of Polish, Slovak, and Lithuanian miners in the labor struggles in anthracite.[152] Greene has also analyzed the relationship between the origins of ethnic consciousness and religious faith among the Polish immigrants.[153]

Among the few studies dealing with particular Slavic groups, Joseph A. Wytrwal's *America's Polish Heritage* is a general history, most useful for its description of the Polish ethnic organizations.[154] A similar work is Gerald G. Govorchin's *Americans from Yugoslavia,* which describes the causes of the emigration as well as the achievements of the South Slav immigrants.[155] George J. Prpíc's *The Croatian Immigrants in America* is a comprehensive history of this Slavic group.[156] Among the non-Slavic peoples of the Balkans, only the Greeks (as of 1972) have been the subjects of a full-scale history. In a deeply researched work, Theodore Saloutos has written an authoritative account of the Greeks in America.[157] While following the economic and social lot of the immigrants, Saloutos stressed the continuing involvement of the Greeks with developments in their homeland and the resulting controversies which often rent the Greek American communities. The struggle between Hellenism and Americanism subsided as the Greeks overcame early obstacles of poverty and prejudice to achieve respectability and well-being.

Topical Studies

While the bulk of the writings in immigration history deal with specific ethnic groups, a growing literature addresses itself to issues which encompass two or more groups. Surprisingly few efforts have been made (as of 1972) to write the ethnic history of particular states. One of these is Rudolph J. Vecoli, *The People of New Jersey,* which delineates the successive tides of migration into the Garden State and the persistent ethnic influences on religion, politics, and other spheres of life.[158] Wilbur S. Shepperson's *Restless Strangers* portrays the extraordinary mix of Nevada's population during the early years and its reflection in Nevada literature.[159] Other studies have focused upon certain cities. In addition to the works by Handlin and Ernst, Donald B. Cole described the changing ethnic composition of Lawrence, Massachusetts, over the course of three-quarters of a century.[160] The concepts of the "immigrant cycle" and the "immigrants' search for security" are the synthetic themes which unify Cole's account of life and work in this mill town.

The question of social mobility in America has attracted the attention of an increasing number of historians. Armed with the methodology of quantitative analysis, they have attempted to measure mobility in terms of such variables as occupation, property ownership, and education. The populations analyzed invariably include a variety of immigrant groups and the differentials in mobility among them become one of the phenomena noted if not explained.

In *The Making of an American Community,* Merle Curti sought to test the Turner thesis regarding the democratizing influence of the frontier by the intensive study of a Wisconsin county.[161] Changes in property ownership, office holding, intermarriage, and other socioeconomic characteristics were computed over the course of several decades. Curti concluded that in Trempeleau County at least the frontier did make for a diffusion of economic and political power among the various ethnic groups. But the evidence for Turner's assertion that the frontier was a crucible in which "the immigrants were Americanized, liberated, and fused into a mixed race," was at best inconclusive.

Stephan Thernstrom's study of social mobility among Irish unskilled laborers and their sons in Newburyport, Massachusetts, discovered little upward occupational mobility for either generation.[162] Thernstrom, however, noted a significant increase in property ownership which he concluded validated the mobility ideology for these workers. In his later studies of occupational mobility in Boston, Thernstrom found that there were dramatic differences not only between immigrants and natives, but among newcomers of different nationalities as well.[163] While the British and the Jews scored a significant rise in occupational status, the Irish and the Italians tended to lag behind. Such differences among various ethnic groups were also discerned by Clyde Griffen in his study of Poughkeepsie.[164]

A new sensitivity to group differences has also inspired an ethnocultural analysis of American political history. A critical review of this literature is presented in an article by Robert P. Swierenga.[165] Samuel Lubell, *The Future of American Politics,* pioneered the ethnic interpretation in this study of recent political devolpments.[166] In a volume on Massachusetts politics in the 1920's, J. Joseph Huthmacher stressed the role of changing loyalties of immigrant groups in bringing about a political realignment in the Bay State.[167] A leading proponent of the ethnocultural approach, Lee Benson, in his reassessment of "the concept of Jacksonian democracy," concluded that ethnicity was more closely related to party affiliation than was economic class.[168] Benson ventured the proposition that "at least since the 1820's . . . ethnic and religious differences have tended to be relatively more important sources of political differences." Study of ethnic influences upon political behavior has also been called for by Samuel P. Hays.[169]

Students of Benson and Hays as well as others have pursued the ethnocultural analysis of political history in recent years. Several works which exemplify this approach are Michael Holt's study of the formation of the Republican Party in Pittsburgh, Paul Kleppner's analysis of midwestern politics in the second half of the nineteenth century, John M. Allswang's history of ethnic politics in Chicago, and Frederick C. Luebke's investigation of the politics of Nebraska Germans.[170] All employ a social analysis of political behavior and all agree on the importance of ethno-religious identity as a determinant of voting patterns. A specific issue, the influence of the immigrant vote in the election of 1860, has been the subject of numerous articles; these have been compiled in a volume edited by Luebke.[171]

While the impact of Old Country issues on immigrant communities is discussed in many of the studies previously mentioned, the only general treatment of the relationship between ethnic groups and American foreign policy (as of 1972) is Louis L. Gerson, *The Hyphenate in Recent American Politics and Diplomacy*.[172] Focusing on the periods of the world wars and the "Cold War," Gerson described the efforts of immigrant lobbies to influence the conduct of American foreign relations. These activities are more thoroughly examined for the World War I period in Joseph P. O'Grady, editor, *The Immigrant's Influence on Wilson's Peace Policies*.[173] Essays are devoted to the activities of the various nationalities which tried to promote their homeland's cause, but the overall conclusion is that the immigrants had little influence on Wilson's decisions regarding the peace settlement.

As of 1972, little effort has been made to deal with the religious dimension of the immigrant experience in a collective fashion. Will Herberg briefly reviewed the history of the three major immigrant religions as background for his thesis that the religious revival of the 1950's was caused by an affirmation of religious identity on the part of the third generation.[174] Herberg viewed the assimilation process as culminating in a "triple melting pot" of religious communities. Historians of Catholicism in America have by and large accepted this view of the Church as an agency for the assimilation of immigrants into a de-ethnicized Catholic population. The concept of a Catholic "melting pot" was challenged by Harold J. Abramson.[175] Noting the persistence of distinctive ethnic styles of religious behavior among American Catholics, Abramson sought an explanation through a comparative analysis of the backgrounds of six ethnic groups. He concluded that societal competition among different religio-cultural traditions in the country of origin "is a positive correlate of the degree of religio-ethnic activity and consciousness." The concept of societal competition was utilized by Timothy L. Smith to explain the development of sectarianism not only among, but also within, immigrant nationalities.[176] Citing the example of the Finns and other groups, Smith concluded that the immigrant denomination, competing with other religious and non-religious organizations for members, became an ethnic sect. In a more recent article, Smith has argued that the immigrants from central and southern Europe brought with them traditions of lay initiative and responsibility which facilitated their adaptation to the religious voluntarism of America.[177] Further, the national ethno-religious organizations which were formed to unite scattered congregations fit the American pattern of denominational pluralism. Rather than the clash of dissimilar religio-cultural traditions, Smith found in the religious history of the immigrant groups a confirmation "of the social consensus of which the nation's religious institutions are but one facet."

Smith pressed his thesis of a broad social consensus among newcomers and native Americans in his discussion of immigrant social aspirations and American education.[178] The value system of the immigrants, he asserted, centered on their aspirations for money, education, and respectability, goals consonant with the "Protestant Ethic." Education also served the immigrants' need to create a new structure of family and communal life and their search for a new ethnic identity. These aspirations, according to Smith, "account for the immense success of the public school system, particularly at the secondary level, in drawing the mass of working-class children into its embrace."

A quite different assessment of the relationship between the American educational system and the children of the immigrants was advanced by David K. Cohen[179] and Colin Greer.[180] Basing their studies on historical evidence of school performance, both concluded that more important than the differences in educational achievement as between native and immigrant children were the differences among children of various ethnic origins. While Scandinavian, British, German, and Jewish youngsters tended to be as successful in school as those of native parentage, the children of non-Jewish central and southern European immigrants had much higher rates of failure. On every index of educational attainment, children from these nationalities fared much worse than the others. While recognizing the influence of cultural differences on motivation and aptitude, both Cohen and Greer suggest that the problem may have been "the inability of public education to overcome the educational consequences of family poverty, and to recognize the legitimacy of working class and ethnic cultures."

Conclusion

Clearly the historical literature on European Americans is rich in variety and high in quality. Yet as this review has demonstrated, there are many gaps in our knowledge, many questions unanswered, and many issues undecided. This is not the place to itemize these lacunae, but one can mention the most glaring deficiencies as of 1972. The eastern, central, and southern European immigrations with the few exceptions noted are still *terra incognita.* Even for better known groups such as the Germans, further studies of the patterns of adjustment, particularly of the internal development of ethnic communities, are needed. Little is known about the interaction of ethnic and racial groups in various geographical and institutional settings. Community, mobility, and political behavior studies should be extended to medium-sized cities and small towns. The history of the immigrant family and the immigrant woman remain to be written. The impact of mass immigration upon the educational system, the churches, the political system, and popular culture, all deserve further investigation. Aside from the nativist response, the reception of the immigrants, particularly the role of voluntary agencies which sought to assist the newcomers, has been insufficiently studied.

Recent writings have advanced challenging hypotheses regarding the relationship between immigration and societal development in the United States. Additional studies must provide the data for testing these concepts. Much research which addresses itself to these questions is now in progress. The scholarship of this decade will surely yield answers to many of these questions and will undoubtedly raise as many new ones.

FOOTNOTES

[1] For a fuller exposition of this argument see Rudolph J. Vecoli. "Ethnicity: a Neglected Dimension of American History," in Herbert J. Bass, editor. *The State of American History.* Chicago: Quadrangle, 1970. pp. 70-88, and Moses Rischin. "Beyond the Great Divide: Immigration and the Last Frontier." *Journal of American History* 55: 42-53; No. 1, June 1968.

[2] An excellent account of the early period of immigration historiography is Edward N. Saveth. *American Historians and European Immigrants, 1875-1925.* New York: Columbia University Press, 1948.

[3] *The Atlantic Migration, 1607-1860, A History of the Continuing Settlement of the United States.* Edited with a foreword by Arthur M. Schlesinger. Cambridge: Harvard University Press, 1940.

[4] Edited with a foreword by Arthur M. Schlesinger. Cambridge: Harvard University Press, 1940.

[5] On the influences which shaped Hansen's view of American history see Allan H. Spear. "Marcus Lee Hansen and the Historiography of Immigration." *Wisconsin Magazine of History* 44: 258-268; No. 4, Summer, 1961.

[6] *Norwegian Migration to America,* Vol. I *1825-1860;* Vol. II. *The American Transition.* Northfield, Minn.: Norwegian-American Historical Association, 1931-1940.

[7] *The Religious Aspects of Swedish Immigrations; a Study of Immigrant Churches.* Minneapolis: University of Minnesota Press, 1932.

[8] *A History of American Immigration, 1820-1924.* Boston: Ginn, 1926.

[9] *Refugees of Revolution, The German Forty-Eighters in America.* Philadelphia: University of Pennsylvania Press, 1952; *The German-Language Press in America.* Lexington: University of Kentucky Press, 1957.

[10] *We Who Built America: the Saga of the Immigrant.* New York: Prentice-Hall, 1939.

[11] *Boston's Immigrants, 1790-1880: a Study in Acculturation.* Cambridge: Harvard University Press, 1941; rev. and enlarged ed., New York: Atheneum, 1970.

[12] *Immigrant Life in New York City, 1825-1863.* New York: King's Crown Press, 1949. An early essay calling for this approach to ethnic history is Caroline F. Ware. "Cultural Groups in the United States," in Ware, editor. *The Cultural Approach to History.* New York: Columbia University Press, 1940. pp. 62-73.

[13] *The Uprooted: The Epic Story of the Great Migrations That Made the American People.* Boston: Little, Brown, 1951.

[14] Rudolph J. Vecoli. *"Contadini in Chicago; A Critique of The Uprooted." Journal of American History* 51: 407-417; No. 3, December 1964.

[15] *The American People in the Twentieth Century.* Cambridge: Harvard University Press, 1954; "Historical Perspectives on the American Ethnic Group." *Ethnic Groups in American Life, Daedalus* 90: 220-232; No. 2, Spring 1961.

[16] *Migration and Economic Growth; a Study of Great Britain and the Atlantic Economy.* Cambridge, England: University Press, 1954.

[17] "Migration from Europe Overseas in the Nineteenth and Twentieth Centuries." XIe Congrès International des Sciences Historiques, Stockholm 1960, *Rapports, V: Histoire Contemporaine.* Göteborg-Stockholm-Uppsala: Almquist & Wiksell, 1960. pp. 32-60. Reprinted in Herbert Moller, editor. *Population Movements in Modern European History.* New York: Macmillan, 1964. pp. 73-92.

[18] *The Founding of New Societies: Studies in the History of the United States, Latin America, South Africa, Canada, and Australia.* New York: Harcourt, Brace & World, 1964.

[19] "Immigration," in C. Vann Woodward, editor. *The Comparative Approach to American History.* New York: Basic Books, 1968. pp. 91-105.

[20] Nathan Glazer. "The Immigrant Groups and American Culture." *Yale Review* 48: 382-397; No. 3, March 1959.

[21] *American Immigration.* Chicago: University of Chicago Press, 1960.

[22] *The Distant Magnet: European Emigration to the U.S.A.* New York: Harper & Row, 1971.

[23] *An Unsettled People: Social Order and Disorder in American History.* New York: Harper & Row, 1971. See also Berthoff's article, "The American Social Order: A Conservative Hypothesis." *American Historical Review* 65: 495-514; No. 3, April 1960.

[24] *British Emigration to North America; Projects and Opinions in the Early Victorian Period.* Minneapolis: University of Minnesota Press, 1957.

[25] "Agrarian Myths of English Immigrants," in O. Fritiof Ander, editor. *In the Trek of the Immigrants.* Rock Island, Ill.: Augustana College Library, 1964. pp. 59-80.

[26] *The Great Hunger: Ireland 1845-1849.* New York: Harper & Row, 1962. See also Oliver MacDonagh. "Irish Emigration to the United States of America and the British Colonies during the Famine," in Robert Dudley Edwards and T. Desmond Williams, editors. *The Great Famine: Studies in Irish History, 1845-1852.* Dublin: Browne and Nolan, 1956.

[27] *Ireland and the American Emigration, 1850-1900.* Minneapolis: University of Minnesota Press, 1958.

[28] "Sweden's Constructive Opposition to Emigration." *Journal of Modern History* 37: 307-335; No. 3, September 1965.

[29] *Germany and the Emigration, 1816-1885.* Cambridge: Harvard University Press, 1964.

[30] "Agricultural Organization, Migration and Labour Militancy in Rural Italy." *Economic History Review.* 2nd series. 16: 61-75; No. 1, August 1963. "Italy's Rural Social Structure and Emigration." *Occidente* 12: 437-456; No. 5, September-October 1956.

[31] *Mississippi Valley Historical Review* 37: 203-230; No. 2, September 1950.

[32] "Emigration and the Image of America in Europe," in Henry Steele Commager, editor. *Immigration and American History: Essays in Honor of Theodore C. Blegen.* Minneapolis: University of Minnesota Press, 1961. pp. 26-54.

[33] *Ireland and the American Emigration.*

[34] *They Remember America; the Story of the Repatriated Greek-Americans.* Berkeley: University of California Press, 1956.

[35] "Exodus U.S.A.," in Ander. *In the Trek of the Immigrants.* pp. 197-215.

[36] *Emigration and Disenchantment: Portraits of Englishmen Repatriated from the United States.* Norman: University of Oklahoma Press, 1965.

[37] "British Backtrailers: Working-Class Immigrants Return," in Ander. *In the Trek of the Immigrants.* pp. 179-195.

[38] "The United States and Italy: Migration and Repatriation." *Journal of Developing Areas* 2: 23-36; No. 1, October 1967.

[39] "Nostalgia or Disenchantment: Considerations on Return Migration," in Silvano M. Tomasi and Madeline H. Engel, editors. *The Italian Experience in the United States.* Staten Island, N.Y.: Center for Migration Studies, 1970. pp. 217-239.

[40] *American Quarterly.* 16: 20-46; No. 1, Spring 1964. See also Marian C. McKenna. "The Melting Pot: Comparative Observations in the United States and Canada." *Sociology and Social Research* 53: 433-447; No. 4, July 1969.

[41] *Assimilation in American Life: The Role of Race, Religion and National Origins.* New York: Oxford University Press, 1964.

[42] *Protestant, Catholic, Jew: an Essay in American Religious Sociology.* Garden City, N.Y.: Doubleday, 1955.

[43] *Beyond the Melting Pot: The Negroes, Puerto Ricans, Jews, Italians, and Irish of New York City.* Cambridge: M.I.T. Press, 1963.

[44] Fishman, *et al. Language Loyalty in the United States; The Maintenance and Perpetuation of Non-English Mother Tongues by American Ethnic and Religious Groups.* Janua Linguarum, Series Maior, 21. The Hague: Mouton, 1966.

[45] "New Approaches to the History of Immigration in Twentieth-Century America." *American Historical Review* 71: 1265-1279; No. 4, July 1966.

[46] *The Protestant Crusade, 1800-1860: A Study of the Origins of American Nativism.* New York: Macmillan, 1938.

[47] "Some Themes of Counter-Subversion: An Analysis of Anti-Masonic, Anti-Catholic, and Anti-Mormon Literature." *Mississippi Valley Historical Review* 47: 205-224; No. 2, September 1960.

[48] *The Paranoid Style in American Politics and Other Essays.* New York: Knopf, 1965.

[49] *Strangers in the Land: Patterns of American Nativism, 1860-1925.* New Brunswick, N.J.: Rutgers University Press, 1955.

[50] "Another Look at Nativism." *Catholic Historical Review* 44: 147-158; No. 2, July 1958.

[51] *The Protestant Establishment: Aristocracy and Caste in America.* New York: Random House, 1964.

[52] *Ancestors and Immigrants, A Changing New England Tradition.* Cambridge: Harvard University Press, 1956.

[53] *American Industry and the European Immigrant, 1860-1885.* Cambridge: Harvard University Press, 1957.

[54] *An Episode in Anti-Catholicism: The American Protective Association.* Seattle: University of Washington Press, 1964.

[55] *Red Scare: A Study in National Hysteria, 1919-1920.* Minneapolis: University of Minnesota Press, 1955.

[56] "A Study in Nativism: The American Red Scare of 1919-20." *Political Science Quarterly* 79: 52-75; No. 1, March 1964.

[57] *Aliens and Dissenters: Federal Suppression of Radicals, 1903-1933.* Cambridge: Harvard University Press, 1963.

[58] "American Immigration Policy in Historical Perspective." *Law and Contemporary Problems* 21: 213-235; Spring 1956.

[59] *American Immigration Policy, 1924-1952.* New Haven: Yale University Press, 1957. Useful for its detailed summaries of legislation, even though heavily biased in favor of restriction, is Marion T. Bennett. *American Immigration Policies, A History.* Washington: Public Affairs Press, 1963.

[60] New York: Columbia University Press, 1948.

[61] *Industrialization, Immigrants, and Americanizers: The View from Milwaukee, 1866-1921.* Madison: State Historical Society of Wisconsin, 1967. This volume also includes much information regarding economic and social conditions of immigrant groups in Milwaukee.

[62] "From Voluntary Association to Welfare State: The Illinois Immigrants' Protective League, 1906-1926." *Journal of American History* 58: 643-660; No. 3, December 1971.

[63] *The Politics of Rescue: The Roosevelt Administration and the Holocaust, 1938-1945.* New Brunswick, N.J.: Rutgers University Press, 1970.

[64] *Paper Walls: America and the Refugee Crisis, 1938-1941.* Amherst: University of Massachusetts, 1968. Yet another account is Arthur D. Morse. *While Six Million Died.* New York: Random House, 1968.

[65] *Illustrious Immigrants: The Intellectual Migration from Europe, 1930-41.* Chicago: University of Chicago Press, 1968.

[66] Donald Fleming and Bernard Bailyn, editors. *The Intellectual Migration: Europe and America, 1930-1960* [*Perspectives in American History*, Vol. 2; published by the Charles Warren Center for Studies in American History] Cambridge, 1968.

[67] *British Immigrants in Industrial America, 1790-1950.* Cambridge: Harvard University Press, 1953.

[68] *The Anglo-American Connection in the Early Nineteenth Century.* Philadelphia: University of Pennsylvania Press, 1959; "The Atlantic Migration of the Pottery Industry." *Economic History Review,* 2nd Series. 11:264-278; No. 2, December, 1958.

[69] *Britons in American Labor: A History of the Influence of the United Kingdom Immigrants on American Labor, 1820-1914.* Baltimore: Johns Hopkins Press, 1957.

[70] *British Emigration to North America.*

[71] "Agrarian Myths of English Immigrants."

[72] *Prairie Albion: An English Settlement in Pioneer Illinois.* Carbondale: Southern Illinois University Press, 1962.

[73] *Expectations Westward: The Mormons and the Emigration of Their British Converts in the Nineteenth Century.* Ithaca, N.Y.: Cornell University Press, 1966.

[74] *Americans from Wales.* Boston: Christopher Publishing House, 1967. On the Welsh see also Alan Conway, editor. *The Welsh in America: Letters from the Immigrants.* Minneapolis: University of Minnesota Press, 1961.

[75] *The Cornish in America.* London: Macmillan, 1969.

[76] Baton Rouge: Louisiana State University Press, 1956.
[77] *To the Golden Door: The Story of the Irish in Ireland and America.* Boston: Little, Brown, 1960.
[78] *The American Irish.* New York: Macmillan, 1963.
[79] Handlin. *Boston's Immigrants;* Ernst. *Immigrant Life in New York City;* Niehaus. *The Irish in New Orleans, 1800-1860.* Baton Rouge: Louisiana State University Press, 1965.
[80] New Haven: Yale University Press, 1957.
[81] *The Molly Maguires.* Cambridge: Harvard University Press, 1964.
[82] *Irish-American Nationalism, 1870-1890.* Philadelphia: Lippincott, 1966.
[83] *Fenians and Anglo-American Relations During Reconstruction.* Ithaca, N.Y.: Cornell University Press, 1969.
[84] John B. Duff. "The Versailles Treaty and the Irish-Americans." *Journal of American History* 55: 582-598; No. 3, December 1968; William M. Leary, Jr. "Woodrow Wilson, Irish Americans, and the Election of 1916." *Journal of American History* 54: 57-72; No. 1, June 1967; Joseph P. O'Grady. "The Irish," in O'Grady, ed. *The Immigrants' Influence on Wilson's Peace Policies.* Lexington: University of Kentucky Press, 1967. pp. 56-84.
[85] *The Tragedy of German-America; the Germans in the United States of America During the Nineteenth Century—and After.* New York: G. P. Putnam's Sons, 1940.
[86] Ernst. *Immigrant Life in New York City;* Bessie L. Pierce, *A History of Chicago.* 3 vols.; New York: Knopf, 1937-1957; Bayrd Still. *Milwaukee.* Madison: State Historical Society of Wisconsin Press, 1948.
[87] *The German People of New Orleans, 1850-1900.* Leiden: Brill, 1958.
[88] "German-Americans Between New and Old Fatherland, 1870-1914." *American Quarterly* 19: 663-680; No. 4, Winter 1967; "The Cincinnati Germans, 1870-1920; Disintegration of an Immigrant Community." *Bulletin of the Cincinnati Historical Society* 23: 229-242; No. 4, October 1965. "The 'Zinzinnati' in Cincinnati." *idem.* 22: 209-220; No. 4, October 1964.
[89] *German Seed in Texas Soil: Immigrant Farmers in Nineteenth-Century Texas.* Austin: University of Texas Press, 1966.
[90] "The Location of German Immigrants in the Middle West." *Annals of the Association of American Geographers* 41: 1-41; No. 1, March 1951. "The Distribution of the German Pioneer Population in Minnesota." *Rural Sociology* 6: 16-34; No. 1, March 1941; "Factors Influencing the Distribution of the German Pioneer Population in Minnesota." *Agricultural History* 19: 39-57; January 1945.
[91] *Refugees of Revolution.*
[92] *The German-Language Press in America.*
[93] *The Catholic Church and German Americans.* Milwuakee: Bruce, 1953.
[94] *The Conservative Reformers: German-American Catholics and the Social Order.* Notre Dame: University of Notre Dame Press, 1968: "An Immigrant Group's Interest in Progressive Reform: The Case of the German-American Catholics." *American Historical Review* 73: 367-379; No. 2, December 1967.
[95] *Immigrants and Politics: The Germans of Nebraska, 1880-1900.* Lincoln, Neb.: University of Nebraska Press, 1969.
[96] *Netherlanders in America; Dutch Immigration to the United States and Canada, 1789-1950.* Ann Arbor: University of Michigan Press, 1955. Lucas has also edited *Dutch Immigrant Memoirs and Related Writings.* 2 vols.; Assen, Netherlands: Van Gorcum, 1955.
[97] *Homeward to Zion: The Mormon Migration from Scandinavia.* Minneapolis: University of Minnesota Press, 1957.
[98] *Norwegian Migration to America.*
[99] *Norwegian Settlement in the United States.* Northfield, Minn.: Norwegian-American Historical Association, 1938.

[100] "Norwegian Emigration in the Nineteenth Century." *Scandinavian Economic History Review* 8: 150-160; No. 2, 1960.

[101] *The Norwegian Language in America.* 2 vols.; Philadelphia: University of Pennsylvania Press, 1953.

[102] *Saga in Steel and Concrete; Norwegian Engineers in America.* Northfield, Minn.: Norwegian-American Historical Association, 1947.

[103] *West of the Great Divide: Norwegian Migration to the Pacific Coast, 1847-1893.* Northfield, Minn.: Norwegian-American Historical Association, 1958.

[104] *The Lutheran Church among Norwegian-Americans; a History of the Evangelical Lutheran Church.* 2 vols.; Minneapolis: Augsburg Publishing House, 1960.

[105] *The Religious Aspects of Swedish Immigrations.*

[106] *Prairie Grass Dividing.* Rock Island, Ill.: Augustana Historical Society, 1959.

[107] *The Swedish Immigrant Community in Transition: Essays in Honor of Dr. Conrad Bergendoff.* Rock Island, Ill.: Augustana Historical Society, 1963.

[108] *From Isolationism to Involvement: The Swedish Immigrant Press in America, 1914-1945.* Chicago: Swedish Pioneer Historical Society, 1966.

[109] *For Sale—Minnesota: Organized Promotion of Scandinavian Immigration, 1866-1873.* Stockholm: Scandinavian University Books, 1971.

[110] *Swedes in Chicago: a Demographic and Social Study of the 1846-1880 Immigration.* Växjö, Sweden: Scandinavian University Books, 1971.

[111] *Swedish America 1914-1932: Studies in Ethnicity with Emphasis on Illinois and Minnesota.* Uppsala, Sweden: Scandinavian University Books, 1971.

[112] Madison: University of Wisconsin Press, 1960.

[113] *Haven in the Woods: The Story of the Finns in Wisconsin.* Madison: State Historical Society of Wisconsin, 1965.

[114] Minneapolis: Augsburg Publishing House, 1963.

[115] *Flugten til Amerika eller Drivkraefter i masseudvandringen fra Danmark 1868-1914.* Aarhus, Denmark: Universitetsforlaget, 1971. For an English summary see pp. 490-526.

[116] Handlin. *Adventure in Freedom: Three Hundred Years of Jewish Life in America.* New York: McGraw-Hill, 1954; Learsi. *The Jews in America: a History.* Cleveland: World, 1954.

[117] Chicago: University of Chicago Press, 1957.

[118] *The Early Jews of New Orleans.* Waltham, Mass.: American Jewish Historical Society, 1969. See also by Korn. *American Jewry and the Civil War.* Philadelphia: Jewish Publication Society of America, 1951.

[119] *The Promised City: New York's Jews, 1870-1914.* Cambridge: Harvard University Press, 1962.

[120] *New York Jews and the Quest for Community: The Kehillah Experiment, 1908-1922.* New York: Columbia University Press, 1970.

[121] New York: Holt, Rinehart and Winston, 1967.

[122] Adler and Connolly. *From Ararat to Suburbia: The History of the Jewish Community of Buffalo.* Philadelphia: The Jewish Publication Society of America, 1960; Swichkow and Gartner. *The History of the Jews of Milwaukee.* Philadelphia: The Jewish Publication Society of America, 1963; Vorspan and Gartner. *History of the Jews of Los Angeles.* San Marino, Cal.: Huntington Library, 1970; Rosenberg. *The Jewish Community in Rochester, 1843-1925.* New York: Columbia University Press, 1954.

[123] *Immigrants to Freedom: Jewish Communities in Rural New Jersey Since 1882.* Philadelphia: University of Pennsylvania Press, 1971.

[124] Trans. and rev. by Aaron Antonovsky. New York: Yivo Institute for Jewish Research, 1961.

[125] Melech Epstein. *Jewish Labor in U.S.A.: an Industrial, Political and Cultural History of the Jewish Labor Movement.* 2 vols.; New York: Trade Union Sponsoring Committee, 1950-1953.

[126] Berman. "A Cursory View of the Jewish Labor Movement: an Historiographical Survey." *American Jewish Historical Quarterly* 52: 79-97; No. 2, December 1962; Rischin. "The Jewish Labor Movement in America: a Social Interpretation." *Labor History* 4: 227-247; No. 3, Fall 1963.

[127] New York: Basic Books, 1966.

[128] "Anti-Semitism in the Gilded Age: A Reinterpretation." *Mississippi Valley Historical Review* 43: 559-578; No. 4, March 1957; "Social Discrimination Against Jews in America, 1830-1930." *Publications of the American Jewish Historical Society* 47: 1-33; No. 1, September 1957.

[129] Hofstadter. *The Age of Reform; from Bryan to F.D.R.* New York: Knopf, 1955; Unger. *The Greenback Era.* Princeton: University of Princeton Press, 1964; Pollack. "The Myth of Populist Anti-Semitism." *American Historical Review* 68: 76-80; No. 1, October 1962; Nugent. *The Tolerant Populists.* Chicago: University of Chicago Press, 1963.

[130] *The Leo Frank Case.* New York: Columbia University Press, 1966. Dinnerstein has also edited *Antisemitism in the United States.* New York: Holt, Rinehart, and Winston, 1971.

[131] *The Italian-Americans.* New York: Twayne, 1971.

[132] *Half-Bitter, Half-Sweet: An Excursion into Italian American History.* New York: Scribner's, 1971.

[133] *The Italian Experience in the United States.* Staten Island, N.Y.: Center for Migration Studies, 1970.

[134] *"Contadini* in Chicago."

[135] *Italians in Chicago, 1880-1930: a Study in Ethnic Mobility.* New York: Oxford University Press, 1970.

[136] *The Immigrant Upraised: Italian Adventurers and Colonists in an Expanding America.* Norman, Okla.: University of Oklahoma Press, 1968.

[137] *Cotton Kingdom of the New South: A History of the Yazoo Mississippi Delta from Reconstruction to the Twentieth Century.* Cambridge: Harvard University Press, 1967; "The End of Immigration to the Cotton Fields." *Mississippi Valley Historical Review* 50: 591-611; No. 4, March 1964.

[138] "Prelates and Peasants: Italian Immigrants and the Catholic Church." *Journal of Social History* 2: 217-268; No. 3, Spring 1969.

[139] "The Ethnic Church and the Integration of Italian Immigrants in the United States," in Tomasi and Engels, editors. *The Italian Experience.* pp. 163-193.

[140] *La Guardia: A Fighter Against His Times: 1882-1933.* Philadelphia: Lippincott, 1959; *La Guardia Comes to Power, 1933.* Philadelphia: Lippincott, 1965.

[141] *Vito Marcantonio, The People's Politician.* Dubuque, Iowa: Kendall/Hunt, 1969.

[142] *Mussolini and Fascism: The View from America.* Princeton: Princeton University Press, 1972; "The Italo-American Anti-Fascist Opposition." *Journal of American History* 54: 579-598; No. 3, December 1967.

[143] "Italian Immigrants in the Stoneworkers' Union." *Labor History* 3: 188-207; No. 3, Spring 1962; "Italians in the Labor Movement." *Pennsylvania History* 26: 133-148; No. 2, April 1959.

[144] "The Buena Vista Affair, 1874-1875." *Pennsylvania Magazine of History and Biography* 88: 251-293; No. 3, July 1964.

[145] "The Italians and the Development of Organized Labor in Argentina, Brazil, and the United States, 1880-1914." *Journal of Social History* 3: 123-134; No. 2, Winter 1969-70; "Italians and Organized Labor in the United States and Argentina: 1880-1910," in Tomasi and Engels, editors. *The Italian Experience.* pp. 111-123.

[146] "Patterns of Work and Family Organization: Buffalo's Italians." *Journal of Social History* 5: 299-314; No. 1, Fall 1971.

[147] *Protest: Sacco-Vanzetti and the Intellectuals.* Bloomington, Ind.: Indiana University Press, 1965.

[148] *The Case That Will Not Die: Commonwealth vs. Sacco and Vanzetti.* Boston: Little, Brown, 1969.

[149] *Tragedy in Dedham; The Story of the Sacco-Vanzetti Case.* New York: McGraw-Hill, 1962.

[150] *The American Mafia: Genesis of a Legend.* New York: Appleton-Century-Crofts, 1971.

[151] Humbert S. Nelli. "Italians and Crime in Chicago: the Formative Years, 1890-1920." *American Journal of Sociology* 74: 373-391; No. 4, January 1969; Luciano J. Iorizzo, editor. *An Inquiry into Organized Crime.* New York: American Italian Historical Association, Proceedings of the Third Annual Conference, 1970.

[152] *The Slavic Community on Strike: Immigrant Labor in Pennsylvania Anthracite.* Notre Dame: University of Notre Dame Press, 1968.

[153] "For God and Country: The Origins of Slavic Catholic Self-Consciousness in America." *Church History* 35: 446-460; No. 4, December 1966.

[154] *America's Polish Heritage: a Social History of the Poles in America.* Detroit: Endurance Press, 1961. See also by Wytrwal. *Poles in American History and Tradition.* Detroit: Endurance Press, 1969.

[155] Gainesville, Fla.: University of Florida Press, 1961.

[156] New York: Philosophical Library, 1971.

[157] *The Greeks in the United States.* Cambridge: Harvard University Press, 1964.

[158] Princeton: D. Van Nostrand, 1965.

[159] *Restless Strangers: Nevada's Immigrants and Their Interpreters.* Reno, Nev.: University of Nevada Press, 1970.

[160] *Immigrant City: Lawrence, Massachusetts, 1845-1921.* Chapel Hill: University of North Carolina Press, 1963.

[161] *The Making of an American Community; a Case Study of Democracy in a Frontier County.* Stanford, Cal.: Stanford University Press, 1959.

[162] *Poverty and Progress: Social Mobility in a Nineteenth-Century City.* Cambridge: Harvard University Press, 1964.

[163] "Immigrants and WASPs: Ethnic Differences in Occupational Mobility in Boston, 1890-1940," in Stephan Thernstrom and Richard Sennett, editors. *Nineteenth-Century Cities: Essays in the New Urban History.* New Haven: Yale University Press, 1969. pp. 125-164.

[164] "Workers Divided: The Effect of Craft and Ethnic Differences in Poughkeepsie, New York, 1850-1880," in Thernstrom and Sennett, editors. *Nineteenth-Century Cities.* pp. 49-97.

[165] "Ethnocultural Political Analysis: A New Approach to American Ethnic Studies." *Journal of American Studies* 5: 59-79, April 1971.

[166] New York: Harper, 1952.

[167] *Massachusetts People and Politics, 1919-1933.* Cambridge: Harvard University Press, 1959.

[168] *The Concept of Jacksonian Democracy: New York as a Test Case.* Princeton: Princeton University Press, 1961.

[169] "The Social Analysis of American Political History, 1880-1920." *Political Science Quarterly* 80: 373-394; No. 3, September 1965; "History as Human Behavior." *Iowa Journal of History* 58: 193-206; No. 3, July 1960.

[170] Holt. *Forging a Majority: the Formation of the Republican Party in Pittsburgh, 1848-1860.* New Haven: Yale University Press, 1969; Kleppner. *The Cross of Culture: A Social Analysis of Midwestern Politics, 1850-1900.* New York: Free Press, 1970; Allswang. *A House for All People, 1890-1936.* Lexington, Ky.: University of Kentucky Press, 1971; Luebke. *Immigrants and Politics.*

[171] *Ethnic Voters and the Election of Lincoln.* Lincoln, Neb.: University of Nebraska Press, 1971.

[172] Lawrence, Kansas: University of Kansas Press, 1964.

[173] O'Grady, editor. *The Immigrant's Influence.*

[174] *Protestant, Catholic, Jew.*

[175] "Ethnic Diversity within Catholicism: A Comparative Analysis of Contemporary and Historical Religion." *Journal of Social History* 4: 359-388; No. 4, Summer 1971. See also Vecoli. "Prelates and Peasants."

[176] "Religious Denominations as Ethnic Communities: A Regional Case Study." *Church History* 35: 207-226; No. 2, June 1966.

[177] "Lay Initiative in the Religious Life of American Immigrants, 1880-1950," in Tamara K. Hareven, editor. *Anonymous Americans.* Englewood Cliffs, N.J.: Prentice-Hall, 1971. pp. 214-249.

[178] "Immigrant Social Aspirations and American Education, 1880-1930," *American Quarterly* 21: 523-543; No. 3, Fall 1969.

[179] "Immigrants and the Schools." *Review of Educational Research* 40: 13-27; No. 1, February 1970. See also Mary Fabian Matthews. "The Role of the Public Schools in the Assimilation of the Italian Immigrant Child in New York City, 1900-1914," in Tomasi and Engels, editors. *The Italian Experience.* pp. 124-141.

[180] *The Great School Legend: A Revisionist Interpretation of American Public Education.* New York: Basic Books, 1972.

· 5 ·

Freedom in a Cage: The Subjugation of the Chicano in the United States

Rodolfo Acuña

THIS chapter is an overview of the Mexican American's quest for self-determination and cultural pluralism in America. This struggle has been one of the most neglected areas of American history. In fact the outline of the Mexican American's participation in the American story was only faintly emerging in 1972. It was lamentable as well as a reflection on the historian that not one major historical work had been published on this ethnic group. Carey McWilliams' *North from Mexico*[1] was the first attempt to narrate its history. However, the McWilliams work, although a journalistic masterpiece, is obviously outdated. Acuña's monograph, *Occupied America,* published in 1972,[2] is again a preliminary description of the struggle. Its main virtues are that it challenges the consensus historians' view of the Mexican American and that it opens new frontiers for research and analysis. The narrative that follows is a précis of the latter work.

The Mexican Background

Mexican culture in the United States predates that of the Anglo-American. Mesoamerica (middle America, or the interior of Mexico and Guatemala) was one of the six cradles of civilization. The philosophy that developed from the early Mexican civilization continues to influence those of Mexican extraction today. The settlement of Mexico began with the migration of hunters and gatherers to middle America many thousands of years ago when water, vegetation, and wild game

113

were abundant. When the climate changed and game dwindled, Mexicans met the challenge by developing agricultural communities. Farming, and the stability it produced, meant that various tribes could build ceremonial and trade centers, which later evolved into large cities.

Mexican civilization reached its highest level of development during the classical period (about 200 B.C. to 900 A.D.). Indian civilizations which included Mayans, Teothuacanos, and other Indian tribes built on the gains made by the Olmecs during the pre-classical period. They individually made significant discoveries in science, mathematics (the Olmecs discovered the zero), agriculture, literature and song, and architecture and the arts. During the classical period, emphasis on military concerns was minimal, and the Mexican tribes valued learning and the development of agriculture. It was not until the post-classical period, when nomads from the north invaded Mesoamerica, that war began to play a more dominant role in the civilization.[3]

In general, life remained the same during these periods; the central unit was the family, then came the clan, the tribe, and the village. The people did not have domestic animals other than the dog and the turkey. Their diet—consisting mainly of corn, beans, and squash which they raised themselves—was supplemented by other foods obtained through trading, such as tomatoes, chiles, pineapples, and avocados.

Domestic and geographical conditions made the Mexican people vulnerable to the Spanish invasion that began in 1519. Unlike the invaders, they had no horses, and thus they lacked mobility. The mountains of Mexico separated the various tribes and they could not launch a unified defense; as a result, the Spaniards succeeded in conquering one area at a time—dividing and conquering. Furthermore, the Spaniards' experience in the arid, mountainous land of the Iberian peninsula meant that they could acclimate more easily to conditions in Mexico; in fact this adaptability facilitated Spain's colonization of a large portion of the Americas.

The Spaniards found advanced civilizations in Mexico that were rich in metals and other raw materials. They coveted these treasures and determined to take what they needed for the development of their recently unified nation. Mexico's colonial epoch formally began when the Spaniards subdued the Aztec capital of Tenochtitlán in 1521. The colonizers then superimposed their language, religion, and culture, as well as their political and economic system, on the Mexican people. Based on the right of conquest, the Spaniards created a caste society, which perpetuated their privileged status.

Despite its exploitive nature Spain's brand of colonialism was also pragmatic. During the colonial years, many Indians lived apart in communal villages. Although exploited through middle men, they had little individual contact with the colonizers. Moreover, they resisted assimilation into Spanish culture. Thus, the colonizers found that they had to adapt to their subjects' culture and traditions in order to maintain control; they compromised by adding elements of Indian tradition—including food, language, architecture, thought—to that of their own.[4] The conquerors married and mixed with the conquered* (unlike the later Anglo-American colonizers), and a new race gradually emerged—that of the *mestizo*. During the colonial era, the *mestizo* population increased. In spite of their growing numerical importance, the *mestizos* were denied the privileges of the full-blooded Spanish. At the same time the *mestizos* rejected the world of the Indian. They resided primarily in the cities and large villages and slowly forged a separate identity.

By the end of the 18th century distinct societies existed in Mexico. The principal ones were the *peninsulare* (Spaniard born in Spain), the *criollo* (Spaniard born in Mexico), the *mestizo,* and the Indian. During the colonial era Indian resentment toward the colonizers increased; their isolation and localism, however, prevented the unification needed to oust the oppressors. A crack in the system began in the Spaniards' ranks. The *criollo* became increasingly nationalistic and resented the privileged status of the *peninsulares*. Meanwhile, toward the end of the colonial period the *mestizo* became more involved in the economic and political life of the nation. Both the *criollo* and the *mestizo* saw the economic advantages of independence from Spain.[5] The ideals of liberty, equality, and fraternity espoused by the French Revolution of 1789 affected these groups. Both objected to the *peninsulares'* privilege, at their expense. Finally, on September 16, 1810, Father Miguel Hidalgo began the War for Independence. This launched an eleven-year war during which Mexico received relatively little aid from other nations.

Independence in 1821, however, did not secure stability to the Mexican nation; the variety of cultures and Mexico's size worked against it. The new *mestizo* culture clashed with the firmly rooted Spanish and Indian communities. A power struggle erupted that lasted for one hundred years, with *criollo* pitted against *mestizo*. The former championed conservative interests, including the military, the large landowners, and the Church, and the latter advanced the liberal or federalist ideals committed to ending established privilege. In short, the rising middle class wanted to make Mexico into a capitalist nation. The power struggle triggered constant warfare, with the liberals finally gaining power in 1855. Conservatives, however, initiated a counter-insurgency to regain their lost privileged status. They led two costly wars against the reformers—the

* Miscegenation took place mainly in the urban areas in the interior of Mexico. Many of the Indians of northern and southern Mexico until recent times remained unaffected by the Spaniard or *mestizo*.

War of Reform (1858-1861) and the War of the French Intervention (1861-1867). Under Benito Juárez's leadership, the liberals defeated the conservatives, facilitating Mexico's thrust into capitalism. The process was accelerated when Porfirio Díaz seized the presidency in 1876; he remained in power until 1910.[6]

During Díaz's tenure Mexico progressed economically—but at the expense of the peon and the Indian. Financed by foreign capitalists, 15,000 miles of railroad were constructed, linking the plantations and mines within Mexico to trade centers and merging these centers with the main railway trunk lines that ran from the south to the United States. Díaz also encouraged foreign investment in mining, oil, and agriculture. Meanwhile, Mexican *hacendados* (hacienda owners) increased their holdings by confiscating Indian communal lands. Despite the apparent prosperity, Mexico suffered from the capitalist economic cycle, with the poor getting poorer and privilege passing to a handful of Europeanized *mestizos* and *criollos,* as well as foreigners. Before Díaz, Mexico had been economically dependent on England and France but anti-Americanism lessened during the Díaz regime, with United States capital flooding Mexico to the point that by the turn of the century it became an economic fief of Anglo-America.[7]

Resentment centered among the uprooted Indians, city dwellers, and intellectuals. They objected to the "gringos' " economic encroachments, with even Mexican capitalists attributing their economic plight (caused by depressions) to the Anglo-capitalists. Nationalism became more pronounced, and many Mexicans advocated economic independence from the United States. During the first decade of the twentieth century opposition to Díaz's dictatorship crystallized, for to the nationalists it represented Mexico's artificial association with European symbols and foreign economic dependence. The climax of this movement to forge a Mexican society was solidified by the Revolution of 1910; the revolutionaries advocated that the nation be owned by Mexicans, controlled by the people, and that the land be returned to its rightful owners. During the Revolution *los de abajo* (the underdogs) fought for and, for a time, won control of their institutions. The chaos of the Revolution had a significant impact on the history of Mexicans in the United States—not only did it contribute to the mass migration to the north, but it also worked to revitalize nationalism among *Mexicanos* in Anglo-America.[8]

Mexico's Northwest

Historically and geographically, the U. S. Southwest and Mexico are one. Until the middle of the nineteenth century the Southwest, in fact, was Mexico's Northwest. An imperialist war of aggression and conquest

(The Mexican-American War of 1846-48) gave the region to the Anglo-Americans. When this occurred the area was anything but a wild west, for a Mexican civilization had taken root there. As a result of their conquest, Anglo-Americans inherited a long tradition of Indian and Mexican settlement without which their development of the area would have been retarded.[9]

The Southwest is a land of contrasts, marked by mountains, valleys, and vast deserts. The land, like much of Mexico, is arid. (The unpropitious climate initially discouraged many Anglos from settling there; they called it the Great American Desert.)

The first Indians lived in harmony with the land, and they survived by using its limited water and vegetation judiciously. They established the first trails and traded over many thousands of miles, east to west and north to south.[10] They exchanged goods even in times of warfare. The Indians divided themselves into three basic groups: the *nomadic* tribes hunted, gathered and did some farming; the *rancheria* tribes, which lived in thatched huts in villages of about 300 inhabitants, were sedentary people, and although they hunted, they primarily relied on agriculture; the *pueblo* Indians built stone and adobe buildings which housed many hundreds of settlers. The pueblos had ceremonial and trade centers as well as communal farm lands. In addition to corn, beans, and squashes, they cultivated cotton. Like the other Indians of the Americas, none had domestic animals with the exception of dogs and sometimes turkeys.[11]

The Spaniards *via* Mexico explored the Northwest, mapping most of the area by 1542. Even though led by Spaniards, these expeditions were dominated by Mexican Indians and *mestizos*. The actual colonization of the Northwest did not begin until 1598, but by this time, the land between Mexico's interior and the Northwest had been settled. Domestic animals and plants brought from Spain complemented the Mexicans' crops and techniques. The Indian formed the bulk of the labor which made the system function. Life was not idyllic since the conquerors exploited the masses, but miscegenation did take place, and the Indian and the *mestizo* survived.

In 1598 Juan de Oñate led a large party of men, animals, supplies, and tools from what is now northern Mexico to present-day New Mexico. The settlers founded the first Mexican pueblo in the Northwest, San Juan de los Caballeros, which later became the base for the city of Santa Fe in 1609. The settlement of New Mexico was an extension of Mexico's colonization by the Spaniards. Although a system of privileges operated, miscegenation again took place, with the *mestizo* culture evolving in New Mexico.

The Spanish plan was to convert the Indians into loyal subjects of the crown. Over the next two hundred years, the colonial government used the mission, the presidio, the fort, and the pueblo to complete this subjugation. The missions were directed by priests who Christianized the Indians and taught them Spanish language and crafts. The presidio soldiers supported the *padres,* protecting the missions and keeping the Indians "in line." The Spanish imperialist also sent settlers north from Mexico's interior who were settled in pre-planned pueblos which included a *plaza* (village square), *acequits* (water canals), communal pasture, and farmlands. The forests and the water belonged to the pueblos. The population was also augmented by Indians from the area. By the time the Anglo-American arrived in the Southwest, there were hundreds of pueblos, many of which have become centers of population today—San Antonio, Santa Fe, Albuquerque, Tucson, San Diego, Los Angeles, Santa Barbara, Monterey, San José, and San Francisco are but a few of them. Footholds had been made in California, Arizona, New Mexico, and Texas.[12]

The Mexican legacy was deeply rooted when the United States seized the Southwest. The Spaniards had transferred desert animals to the region and had established an extensive livestock industry. They established *ranchos* (ranches). Ranching was a highly developed institution with laws governing its operation. The open range necessitated *rodeos* (roundups), held by mandate annually, when the *rancheros* (ranchers) branded their cattle. The *vaqueros* (cowboys) had a standard uniform which facilitated their daily work routine. The Anglo learned these skills from the Mexicans. The *vaqueros* were master horsemen and ropemen who used the saddle with a horn, developed in Mexico, and *la riata* (lariat) to round up and herd cattle. The animals themselves were uniquely adapted—the *mesteño* (mustang) and the longhorn were hardy breeds that had been brought to Spain from Africa.[13]

The Mexican established a tradition of sheep herding, with millions of sheep roaming the Northwest by the time the Anglo arrived. It became New Mexico's principal industry with hundreds of thousands of sheep being driven annually to Mexico's interior. Mexicans institutionalized this industry, and the *pastores* (shepherds), followed a set routine.[14] Other animals brought to the Northwest included goats, chickens, burros, mules, and oxen.

Mexico's Northwest had a long tradition of agriculture before the United States conquered it. The Indians knew how to use its wildlife and how to cultivate needed crops. The Indians of Arizona were excellent farmers, and they used irrigation to its best advantage. The Mexican contributed tools, techniques, the use of domestic animals, and innumerable new crops, plants, and trees to the development of the area. They laid the foundation for today's agricultural industry. Wheat, rice, apples, pears, plums, peaches, apricots, quinces, mulberries, oranges, lemons, limes, grapefruits, dates, and grapes, among other products, were brought to Mexico from Spain. They mixed with Mexican crops such as beans, squashes, corn, avocados, and tomatoes. In turn, all of these products were taken to the Northwest where, by the 1830's, they flourished.[15]

A transportation system with established trade routes existed. Mule trains and caravans operated daily over *caminos reales.* Many early Anglo traders marvelled at the skill of the muleteers.[16] Moreover, when the present arbitrary border divided Mexico from its Northwest, a pool of experienced miners lived in the conquered territory as well as just across the border. They pioneered mining operations when the big bonanzas were struck.

Mexican laws governed the property rights of the individual and the community. Water laws were adapted to the land, with everyone entitled to use water from communal sources as needed. After the conquest, however, Anglo-American law decreed that water belonged to the person on whose land it originated, and thus it could be monopolized. Out of necessity, Mexican law was reinstated to stop the range wars which marred the Anglo-American "wild west." Community property laws to protect the family and community were also of Mexican origin.[17]

An understanding of the Mexicans' contributions would not be complete without considering the architecture of the region. To this day, it is influenced by the Mexican period; wood was scarce and nature's adobe was common. In addition, certain words from the Mexican vocabulary, such as *arroyo, coyote, cañon, veranda, patio, barbacoa,* have found popular usage today.[18]

It must also be emphasized that the Northwest, today's Southwest, was a political unit of Mexico as the result of Spanish imperialism. Nevertheless, the assimilation of cultures and races that took place during the colonial era resulted in the formation of the modern Mexican race. Moreover, the Indians north and south of today's border cannot be segregated from each other. They were, and are, one people. This Indo-Mexican civilization made possible the Anglo-American settlement of the region. The reader must realize that after 1821 the Northwest was part of the Mexican Republic, legally belonging to Mexico. Culturally and racially it had little in common with the United States; it became part of that nation only through conquest and colonization.

The Subjugation of the Mexican in the United States

Excuses should not be made for the seizure of over half of the Mexican nation by the United States. Many Anglo-Americans simply coveted their neighbor's property and conspired to steal it. The United States committed an act of imperialism in the tradition of England and other Western European nations when they colonized African and Asian countries. The Mexican venture was not a unique nor isolated act of aggression. The story of early Indian wars, and the subsequent removal of the North American Indians from their tribal lands, is well known. Among the goals of those who supported war with England in 1812 were the acquisition of Canada and the establishment of firm control over the Ohio River Valley. Moreover, Anglo-Americans conducted border raids on Florida to force Spain to cede that territory to the United States in 1819. To some Anglo-Americans, Texas became the next target, and settlers flocked there in the 1820's. The Mexican government allowed Anglos to immigrate there on the condition that they become Catholics and respect Mexican laws. Some did honor their pledge, but an increasing number resented the Mexican authorities and actively planned for the day when the area would be joined with the United States.[19] Evidence that they planned to incorporate Texas became apparent during the administrations of James Monroe through those of John Quincy Adams and Andrew Jackson; repeatedly, the United States Government pressured Mexico through diplomatic channels to sell Texas.

By the end of the decade Anglo-Texan sentiment for annexation to the United States had increased greatly. Anglo-Texans openly protested, and later defied, Mexican laws, especially those that abolished slavery in 1829 and prohibited further Anglo-American immigration into Texas in 1830. Anglo-Americans considered it their God-given right to own slaves and to migrate to the area as they pleased. In the early 1830's word spread that there would be trouble in Texas. Anglo-American land speculators and adventurers entered the territory—among them, according to Mexican sources, were the infamous brawlers Sam Houston, William Barrett Travis, James Bowie, and Davey Crockett.[20] By 1832 conventions were convened to present grievances to the Mexican government and to demand separate statehood for Texas. The Mexican government reacted by strictly enforcing many of its laws and by moving troops to the area; they did not want Texas to be a repetition of the Spanish experience in Florida.[21]

Stephen Austin had been in Mexico since 1821 as an "impresario" strengthening his own power and seeking to advance the Texan cause. In 1833 he wrote a letter to the *ayuntamiento* (city council) of San Antonio, urging it to declare statehood for Texas. The letter's contents fell into the hands of Mexican authorities, and they imprisoned Austin; unfortunately, this action played into the hands of the war advocates. Once Austin was released, he returned to Texas, openly encouraging

Anglos in the United States to come to Texas with gun in hand to help their brothers. The Anglo-Texans revolted in 1836, and the Mexican army under the enigmatic Antonio López de Santa Anna, Mexico's president, entered the territory to protect the nation's interests. This encounter has been portrayed as that of a tyrannical Mexican dictator in opposition to freedom-loving, peaceful settlers.[22] Such simplistic stereotyping is far from the truth.

At the first sign of hostilities, soldiers of fortune swarmed into Texas. Many were experienced fighters, whereas the men under Santa Anna were conscripts, many of whom had never fired a gun. Moreover, they had just been marched over thousands of miles of desert and were not prepared for the battles that followed. Nevertheless, they at first dominated the war, winning convincingly at Goliad and the Alamo. The latter was a major undertaking since it had "perhaps the largest collection" of guns "between New Orleans and Mexico City."[23] For artillery, Anglo-Texans at the Alamo had 21 guns versus the Mexicans' 8 or 10.[24] Although there were only about 180 defenders versus some 1800 attackers,[25] the defenders had Kentucky long rifles with a range of about 200 yards; the Mexicans had smooth-bore muskets with a range of about 70 yards. The men inside the Alamo were anything but peaceful settlers. Travis was a fugitive from justice with military experience; James Bowie, an infamous brawler and former slave trader; and the aging Davey Crockett, an experienced fighter who had entered Texas cocked for a fight.[26] The men inside the Alamo fully expected reinforcements and believed that they could defend the fort. In the end, most died in the battle; however, some like Davey Crockett appear to have surrendered and were tried and executed.[27]

The loss of the Alamo humiliated the Anglo-Texans. But it also had the effect of triggering considerable support from the United States, and volunteers, arms, and money poured into Texas.[28] The United States Government did little to stop the flow, and through its citizens, it became very much involved in the eventual takeover of the province. The incompetency of Antonio López de Santa Anna also helped. The battle of San Jacinto was not so much a Texan victory as it was a Mexican mistake. After the Alamo, the Mexicans routed the Anglos at almost every encounter. Santa Anna, however, did not follow up his victories. In April, he had several skirmishes in the vicinity of the San Jacinto River —all successful. On April 20, 1836, Santa Anna camped his army near the river, expecting Sam Houston to attack on the 22nd. Instead, Houston pulled a surprise attack on the 21st during the siesta hours and completely routed the Mexicans. Santa Anna was captured, and he had no choice but to surrender Texas to the Anglos.[29] Even though it could not reinstate its authority, the Mexican government did not recognize Texan independence, and, for the next nine years, boundary disputes created tensions between Mexico and the Republic of Texas. Moreover, the Mexicans were bitter over the mistreatment of their prisoners of war by the Texans.[30]

Many Texans wanted to expand their holdings at the expense of Mexico and to create a strong Republic, but most wanted annexation to the United States. In the meantime, Washington *politicos* conspired to take all of the Southwest. Historians have long differed over what actually took place, but there appear to have been several schemes to manufacture a war. In 1967 Glenn W. Price described persuasively a plot led by Commodore Robert F. Stockton who went to Texas before annexation and tried to convince authorities there to attack Mexico in order to create an incident.[31] Stockton used his own money to finance his scheme, but Texas authorities refused to acquiesce in Stockton's plot even though it was sanctioned by President James Polk. After Stockton's conspiracy failed, Polk ordered Zachary Taylor into the disputed territory between the Nueces River and the Rio Grande. As Polk undoubtedly expected, Mexican troops fired at them. Polk assumed the posture of the injured party and went before the United States Congress and asked for a declaration of war.[32]

Mexico was unprepared for war, for it was undergoing civil strife. Moreover, Mexico was financially bankrupt and in the process of centralizing her vast territories. It had great potential, and if it had had a competent general, it conceivably could have defended its territory successfully. From the beginning, violence dominated the actions of Zachary Taylor's troops. They invaded northern Mexico, bombarded Matamoros, and went on a rampage—raping, plundering, and murdering as they marched to the interior. Later General Winfield Scott literally levelled Vera Cruz with cannon fire from United States naval ships, destroying hospitals, churches, and the civilian sectors of the city.[33] In many instances, although Scott attempted to maintain discipline, the Anglo-soldiers could not be controlled. They repeated acts of violence all the way to Mexico City. Simultaneously, Stephen Watts Kearny led the "Army of the West" into New Mexico and California. Again the Anglo-American subjugation was brutal and Mexicans resisted as best they could.[34]

The United States won the "manufactured" war, but left behind a legacy of violence and hate.[35] Mexicans remaining in the conquered land became a conquered people. Mexico had no intention of abandoning its citizens, however, and attempted to protect their rights. These guarantees were incorporated into the Treaty of Guadalupe Hidalgo of 1848. Articles VIII and IX, as well as a letter of protocol signed by Anglo-

American ministers in May 1848, specifically provided that Mexicans would be first-class citizens, and that their land, religion, and, by inference, their culture would be respected. The Mexican Congress by a narrow vote ratified the treaty.[36] Many Mexican deputies doubted the good faith of the Anglo-American conquerors, but they had little choice except to sign. Their reluctance proved justified since the Treaty of Guadalupe Hidalgo has generally been ignored.[37]

The Anglo-American Occupation of Mexico's Northwest

The first Anglo-Americans who entered the Southwest after the war thought of themselves as the anointed defenders of democracy and the Mexicans as their enemies. Many Anglos had been veterans of the Mexican War and believed that the right of conquest entitled them to special privileges. They resented that so much land belonged to the "greaser" and viewed the brown-skinned half-breeds as social and racial inferiors who should be controlled. Through legal and illegal methods the subjugation began. The result was that the Mexican lost his land and was politically and economically isolated. A master-servant relationship evolved; the Anglo became the master and the Mexican became the servant.[38]

In Texas the Mexican's submergence crystallized in the Rio Grande River Valley where men like Charles Stillman, a merchant, and Richard King, a rancher, seized enormous power through *de facto* and *de jure* means.[39] The Texas Rangers aided and abetted these unscrupulous men in their quest for power. The Rangers have been immortalized by Walter Prescott Webb, a Texas historian and past president of the American Historical Association. To the Mexicans, however, the Rangers (or *los rinches* as they are popularly called) were paid assassins who terrorized the Mexican majority. Américo Paredes, a professor at the University of Texas, in his work *With a Pistol in His Hand,* documents the atrocities of the Rangers and quotes Webb as calling "retaliatory killings of 1915 an 'orgy of bloodshed' [in which] the Texas Rangers played a prominent part." Webb stated that the number of Mexicans killed had been variously estimated at figures from 500 to 5,000.[40] To this day Mexicans in Texas are bitter toward the Rangers; to the conquered, *los rinches* symbolize an alien occupying army.

The submergence of the Mexican throughout the Southwest followed the Texas pattern. Even in New Mexico, where he remained in the majority until the 1940's, the Mexican was manipulated and robbed of his inheritance.[41] One out of ten Anglo-Americans entering New Mexican territory was a lawyer,[42] and these Anglos allied themselves with rich New Mexicans in order to plunder the territory. The United States Government appointed the territorial governor as well as other high-ranking officials. Several of these officials formed a political machine known as the Santa Fe Ring, which operated for over 65 years and which used its influence with the territorial government to defraud small and large landholders of their property.[43] Moreover, the colonial government condoned the use of violence toward Mexicans. The governor tacitly approved of the Lincoln County Wars of the 1870's, in which the cohorts of the Santa Fe Ring waged war on Anglo competitors and in which innocent Mexican sheepmen were killed.[44] In these years the Mexican was defrauded of over four million acres of private and communal land.[45] Statehood was not granted to the territory until 1912, at which time native New Mexicans commented that there was nothing left to steal.[46]

Arizona was originally part of the New Mexico Territory; however, with the addition of the land south of the Gila after the Gadsden Purchase (1853), Anglo-American colonizers moved to separate Arizona from New Mexico. The major economic activity was mining, although ranching and farming soon flourished as well. The relationship between Anglos and Mexicans there resembled that of Texas and New Mexico; the small number of Anglos who entered the territory believed that they were entitled to the bounties of the Conquest. They controlled the territorial government and established a system of privilege that benefited them directly. The most significant difference was that Mexican labor was almost exclusively recruited from the neighboring state of Sonora, Mexico, which Anglo-Americans conspired to seize because of its mineral wealth.[47] Until recently, a double wage standard existed, with Anglo-Americans receiving twice as much as Mexicans for the same work.[48] As in Texas and New Mexico, the Mexican resisted his subjugation, but as with his brothers in other areas, he was overwhelmed. Arizona did not become a state until 1912, largely because it was easier for the privileged Anglo to maintain their control over the large Mexican population in a territorial situation.

The Anglo-American imperialists of 1846 especially coveted California. Under the guise of an exploratory expedition United States authorities sent filibusterers to foment a revolution there before the declaration of war. The filibusterers called themselves the Bear Flaggers and were led by John C. Frémont. They succeeded in alienating *Californios* by intimidating and terrorizing them.[49] After the conquest veterans poured into the territory but found most of the land in the hands of *Californios*. At first the Mexicans and their holdings were safe, mainly because they outnumbered the gringos. But when gold was discovered at Sutter's Mill in 1848, thousands of treasure seekers poured into the territory. By the middle of 1849, the Anglo population had jumped from 13,000 to some

100,000, and the Mexican quickly found himself in the minority.[50] Leonard Pitt graphically narrates the Decline of the *Californios* in his monograph of the same title. In the early 1850's the Anglo-dominated California legislature passed two laws which accelerated the Mexicans' economic and political demise. The Land Act of 1851 cast a shadow over the Mexican Land Grants, making it mandatory for Californians to confirm their land titles. This law opened the door for unscrupulous speculators to confuse land titles. They challenged property titles in the courts, and often prolonged proceedings so long that the cost of litigation became too great for the *Californios* to bear. They encouraged squatters to move onto the Mexicans' property and physically intimidate the owners into selling their land for much less than its actual worth. By 1870 most of the Mexican-owned land had passed to encroachers.[51]

The Foreign Miner's Tax of 1850 drove many Mexicans, as well as other Latinos, from the mines. Those who chose to pay the tax and remain in the area were harassed by Anglo miners. Mexicans became the victims of intense vigilante activity, which many times ended in lynchings.[52] The Mexican population, concentrated in the southern portion of the state, found that it had been relegated to second-class citizenship, even though the Treaty of Guadalupe Hidalgo had guaranteed Mexicans remaining in the conquered area equal rights.

In the face of these onslaughts, the Mexican resisted the Anglo-American occupation and violence. In Texas Juan Cortina led the Mexican resistance from 1859 to 1876. His stated purpose was to bring justice to his people and to cast off the chains of oppression.[53] A graduate of the University of Notre Dame, Juan Patrŏn championed the Mexican cause during the Lincoln County Wars in New Mexico. He was assassinated for his efforts.[54] In Arizona, constant warfare between the colonizers and the colonized raged and in towns like Tombstone the Mexican became the victim of justice via the six-shooter. Men like Francisco Ramírez, publisher of *El Clamor Público,* a Spanish language newspaper, led nonviolent protest from 1855 through 1859, denouncing racism, lynchings, and injustice.[55] As tactics such as Ramírez's failed, some Mexicans, among them Tiburcio Vásquez, became *bandidos.*[56] The Mexican resistance nevertheless was suffocated by Anglo-American technology, law enforcement officials, and the overwhelming number of encroachers who entered the Southwest.[57]

Mexican Labor as a Commodity

The Mexican became a second-class citizen in what was formerly his land. Thousands fled to Mexico, seeking better opportunity. Economic conditions in Mexico and the United States, however, resulted in the migration of over one-eighth of Mexico's population to the United States between 1910 and 1930.[58] Southwestern agribusiness became big business as a result of the transcontinental railroad and the refrigerated car. Later, reclamation and irrigation made large tracts of land available for exploitation. Moreover, mining boomed. At first in California Chinese labor provided the bulk of manual labor, later supplemented by other Asians. Gradually, Anglo-American racism and ethnocentrism excluded Chinese labor and limited the immigration of Asians in general. The need for cheap labor forced capitalists to look to Mexico to fill the vacuum. In Mexico, the 15,000 miles of railroad construction that took place under the Díaz regime linked the interior of Mexico with the Anglo-American lines, making possible the exploitation of minerals and other raw materials by Mexican and foreign capitalists. Many plantations were transformed from semi-feudal to profit-making institutions. In the process many Mexicans were uprooted, and they sought better paying jobs with railroads, processing plants, and service industries in the cities. The railroads also facilitated the transportation of Mexican workers to northern Mexico and the United States, and industrialists and agribusinessmen sent agents and labor contractors into the interior to recruit Mexican labor.[59]

Agribusinessmen intended that the Mexican would be a temporary supplement to Anglo labor and that he would return home once the work was finished.[60] The number of Mexicans migrating to the United States remained relatively small until the end of the first decade of the 1900's. But then, the Mexican Revolution of 1910 and World War I accelerated the migration of Mexicans from their homeland. Meanwhile, Mexican border towns swelled, and they became employment depots for Southwestern and Midwestern industrialists.[61] During the 1920's approximately one million Mexicans entered the United States. Nativists became alarmed at the large number of Mexicans in the United States, and restrictionists wanted to limit their immigration. Attempts were made to include the Mexicans in the quota provisions of the Immigration Acts of 1921 and 1924, which mainly applied to Eastern and Southern Europeans. These efforts failed since Mexican labor was vital to the Southwest, where agribusinessmen and industrialists used their power to keep the free flow of Mexicans unimpeded.[62]

Constant debates over Mexican immigration raged in Congress where Representative John O Box of Jacksonville, Texas, led the fight to place the Mexican on quota. Hearings on limiting the Mexican flow were held throughout the 1920's and 1930's. Anglo-American Labor especially supported this action on the basis that cheap laborers depressed wages and were used as strikebreakers. Public opinion, as well as that of many elected officials, was vehement, reflecting racial and cultural prejudice toward the Mexican. The restrictionists contended that the Mexican could never be assimilated into American culture. In 1930 Roy L. Garis, a professor at Vanderbilt University and an authority on eugenics, reported to the Congressional committee that "The following statement made to the author by an American who lives on the border seems to reflect the general sentiment of those who are deeply concerned with the future welfare of this country:

> Their minds [the Mexicans'] run to nothing higher than animal functions— eat, sleep, and sexual debauchery. In every huddle of Mexican shacks one meets the same idleness, hordes of hungry dogs, and filthy children with faces plastered with flies, disease, lice, human filth, stench, promiscuous fornication, bastardy, lounging, apathetic peons and lazy squaws, beans and dried chili, liquor, general squalor, and envy and hatred of the gringo. These people sleep by day and prowl by night like coyotes, stealing anything they can get their hands on, no matter how useless to them it may be. Nothing left outside is safe unless padlocked or chained down. Yet there are Americans clamoring for more of this human swine to be brought over from Mexico.[63]

The response of the champions of the free admission of Mexicans was that "Mexicans did work that white men would not do and did it cheaply." In this instance, the pressure of the economic royalists won over racism and ethnocentricism.

The Mexican Resists Oppression

Migrancy worked against the Mexican in his organizational attempts to resist exploitation. Since he was continually on the move, he could not muster sufficient power to force his masters to pay him commensurate wages. The Mexican remained at the mercy of economic interests, which used his labor as a commodity. Nonetheless, Mexicans did attempt to work together; one of the earliest organizations was the *mutualista,* which was an insurance group providing burial and other benefits for its members. Such associations also served as social clubs for the Mexican. From the *mutualistas* other groups evolved, among them civic and political organizations that advocated the Mexicans' cause. In many instances the *mutualistas* became the basis for collective bargaining.[64] It is in this field that the struggle of the Mexican was most notable. Early organizational efforts concentrated on agribusiness, which has proven to be the most difficult industry to unionize; even Big Labor has traditionally hesitated from challenging the agriculturalists.[65]

In the Imperial Valley of California Mexicans formed *La Union de Trabajadores del Valle Imperial* in 1928. Cantaloupe workers struggled for more equitable wages in face of bitter repression. Strikers were harassed, jailed, and deported. The year before, other Mexican workers formed *La Confederación de Uniones Obreros Mexicanos,* which eventually included 2000 members in 20 locals, made up of both rural and urban workers.[66] During the depression of the 1930's Mexicans organized countless strikes in the Southwest, but almost all were put down by authorities in collusion with corporate growers.[67] The berry strike at El Monte, California, in 1933 spread the union fervor throughout California and led to the formation of *La Confederación de Uniones de Campesinos y Obreros Mexicanos del Estado de California* which by 1934 numbered 10,000 members.[68] In 1936 Mexicans led the Pecan Sheller's strike in San Antonio, Texas, in which they won union recognition, only to have their workers phased out by automation.[69] Mexicans were also involved in organizing relief organizations during the depression years.[70]

Throughout efforts to acquire a living wage, Mexicans constantly faced deportation or imprisonment. One of the darkest chapters in the history of the Mexican in the United States occurred in the 1930's when local authorities in the Southwest and Midwest repatriated hundreds of thousands of Mexicans to their homeland. Like many other Americans, Mexicans faced unemployment during the depression. But unlike other groups they were considered foreigners, and authorities pressured or "persuaded" many to return to Mexico or have their welfare payments discontinued. Officially between 1931-1938 some 333,000 Mexicans were repatriated; unofficially the number is estimated at over a half a million. Significantly, the majority of the repatriates were offsprings who were born in the United States. Many social scientists and Anglo-Americans condemned the repatriation program and the motives of its proponents.[71]

World War II marked the end of the mass exodus of Mexicans back to their homeland, for they became essential to the war effort as both workers and soldiers. Raúl Morín, in his *Among the Valiant,* documents the contributions of the Mexican during the war. Many Mexicans died fighting for the United States, and, as a group, they won more Medals of Honor than any other ethnic minority.[72] Still, they did not win acceptance as citizens, for most Anglo-Americans still considered them aliens.

The war years also saw racist persecution of Mexican youth, whom the Anglo public called *Pachucos.* Los Angeles was the center of anti-Mexican activity. There the press and local authorities portrayed any

Mexican who wore a zoot suit or belonged to a neighborhood club a *Pachuco*. The term soon became synonymous with hoodlum. In August 1942, members of the 38th Street Club, one of these Mexican groups, were tried for the alleged murder of José Díaz. The incidents surrounding Díaz's death became known as the Sleepy Lagoon Case. Members of the club were beaten by police authorities and convicted by the Los Angeles press before the trial even started. At the mass trial involving twenty-two Mexicans, the youths were convicted on various charges. Later the verdict was reversed because the district court found that the judge had acted in a prejudicial manner; the higher court also stated that there had been no grounds for the convictions since the prosecution had not even proved that Díaz was murdered.[73]

The police and press continued to persecute and libel the Mexican community. Carey McWilliams' *North from Mexico* graphically narrates the so-called *Pachuco* Riots which occurred in 1943. The Los Angeles press manufactured an ambience of violence, harping on the theme of "*Pachuco* crime." They played up altercations between Mexican youth and servicemen, portraying the Mexican as unpatriotic and the servicemen as defenders of the American way. As a result of a relatively minor incident, sailors stationed at San Pedro and San Diego began a reign of terror on June 3, 1943, which lasted through June 7th. During this time, the sailors beat up Mexican youth, broke into movie houses and business establishments, and marched four abreast through the center of Los Angeles in search of *Pachucos*. The Los Angeles press cheered the sailors on. Los Angeles police did not check the violence and naval authorities were forced to intervene. During this time, only a few citizens condemned the racism of the Los Angeles press, police, and elected officials.[74]

The post-war era brought slight improvement for Mexicans in the United States. Some Anglos considered them citizens and called them "Mexican-Americans." Other significant changes took place: the Mexican community had become more stable and became much more involved in organizational efforts to advance the minority's civil rights. However, Mexican Americans enjoyed few political or social successes during these years and also trailed other citizens in terms of income, housing, and educational opportunities.

Efforts to politicize them were frustrated by the continued deportations of Mexican American leaders under the McCarran-Walter Act of 1952. This Act legalized the de-naturalization of naturalized citizens if they had ever belonged to a subversive organization. During the depression many relief agencies as well as labor unions had been placed on the Attorney General's list of subversive organizations. Authorities used the

Act as an excuse to deport Mexican Americans who did not cooperate with their investigations or who were involved in trade union organization. During the fifties, there were also mass roundups of undocumented workers charged with being in the United States illegally. The *barrios* (Mexican urban communities) were terrorized by these massive raids.[75]

In the post-war years, migrant farm laborers had little success in organizing themselves—mainly because of the use of Mexican *braceros*. *Braceros* were Mexican contract workers who were imported to the United States during the war years when there was a labor shortage. The use of *braceros* continued long after the war. They supplied agribusiness with a constant source of workers who could be sent back to Mexico after the harvest season ended. Growers used the *braceros* to supplant Mexican American farm workers and also as strikebreakers. The program was finally allowed to expire in December 1964, due to the mounting pressure by the Mexican American community, liberals, and union leaders.[76]

The Quest for Self-Determination and Cultural Pluralism: The Rise of the Chicano

The year 1960 ushered in a new era for the Mexican American community. In that year the United States Census showed that nearly four million Mexican Americans lived *legally* in the United States. The Census further illustrated that the Mexican American population no longer confined themselves primarily to the Southwest, but that nearly one million had moved to the Midwest.[77] The political importance of Mexican Americans also emerged in 1960 when they played a leading role in the election of John F. Kennedy to the Presidency of the United States. The Mexican American vote swung Texas for Kennedy and almost delivered California to the Democrats.[78] In retrospect, although the Mexican American became more visible, the community in general gained little from this new recognition. Politically, Mexican Americans received a few more appointments, but in turn, they were exploited by Democrats who took their vote for granted and who gerrymandered the election districts to keep themselves in office.[79] Economically, the Mexican American remained far behind the Anglo-American, whereas educationally he trailed both the Anglo and the Black American.

By the time the War on Poverty was launched in late 1964, discontent had spread in the Mexican American community. César Chávez had already organized his union and prepared to challenge the Mexican's oldest enemy and exploiter—agribusiness. Activists took pride when Chávez's Farm Workers Association joined the Filipinos on September

16, 1965, to commence the now-famous *huelga* (strike) at Delano, California.[80] Frustration and anger erupted when the Federal government ignored the plight of Mexican Americans in what was supposed to be a program to uplift all poor people. However, the ferment created by the War on Poverty, the Watts Riots led by the Blacks, and the *huelga* injected new militancy into the Mexican American community, radically changing its direction. At first it remained within the civil rights framework, but a metamorphosis was beginning to take shape. Not only did Mexican Americans want to be treated as first-class citizens, but they also wanted recognition of their identity. Demands for bilingual-bicultural education were translated into a commitment to cultural pluralism as well as political, economic, and social self-determination. In essence, the Mexican American movement was a revolution that went beyond the aspirations of many ethnic and racial groups in Anglo-America.[81]

Old-time activists in the community were caught in 'he middle between civil rights activities and the movement toward cultural pluralism. When Mexican American youth entered the movement in 1967, a new identity began to emerge; a year later the term "Chicano" symbolized the cause. The new activists rejected the label "Mexican-American," for to them it meant assimilation into Anglo society. "Chicano," on the other hand, was what the middle-class Mexican Americans called the grass roots or the poor sector—which formed the majority of Mexicans in the United States. Youth popularized the terms by stating that they were committed "to the poor Mexican, to the *Chicano*."[82]

Chicano youth were attracted by emerging national leaders. Reies López Tijerina, from New Mexico, championed the return of communal lands to the people,[83] Rodolfo "Corky" Gonzales, from Denver, Colorado, advocated a return to the *barrios* and a reinforcement of national identity in order to seize self-determination.[84] In 1968 at St. Mary's College in San Antonio, Texas, the Mexican American Youth Organization (MAYO) was organized under the leadership of José Ángel Gutiérrez.[85] In Los Angeles David Sánchez formed the Brown Berets, which advocated that *barrios* arm themselves in self-defense against police aggression.

Almost simultaneously, other currents emerged. *La Raza* newspaper in Los Angeles became an advocate of *los de abajo* (the underdog), while in Berkeley, California, a group called *Quinto Sol* Publications under the direction of Dr. Octavio Romano published *El Grito*, a scholarly journal which contributed greatly to the forging of a Chicano philosophy.[86] These currents were complemented by the vitality of Luis Valdez's *Teatro Campesino,* a theatre group which dramatized the plight of the farmworker and the Chicano.[87]

The East Los Angeles high school blowouts in 1968 reflected the new Chicano awareness and, in effect, declared to the nation that the community would fight for its rights. Walkouts spread to other Chicano schools throughout the Southwest and Midwest. At the college and university level, students demanded that Chicano Studies Programs be established. They wanted a vehicle that would reinforce Mexican values and traditions and help them to forge their own. They wanted to train technicians to service their communities once self-determination was achieved.[88] In that vein, *La Raza Unida* Party (LRUP), a Chicano political party, won significant victories in the Winter Garden area of Texas in 1969. Under the leadership of José Ángel Gutíerrez the LRUP won a majority of the seats on the Crystal City Council and its Board of Education. Many activists believed that this was the first step in an all-out assault by Chicanos to recapture political and economic control of their own destinies. Although in many regions Chicanos comprised as much as 85 per cent of the population, they were almost without political representation. In places like California, where large numbers of Chicanos lived in compact districts, they were gerrymandered and thus politically emasculated.[89] For example, although in 1970 one out of six Californians was of Mexican extraction, there were no Mexican state senators, only two assemblymen, and no statewide or federal-elected representatives.[90]

The end of the decade witnessed mounting protest by Chicano youth and activists against the war in Vietnam, as well as against the police oppression that victimized Chicanos in the *barrios*. The major event of 1970 was the National Chicano Moratorium held in Los Angeles, California, on August 29, 1970. An estimated thirty thousand Chicanos marched through East Los Angeles, a *barrio* estimated at one million Chicanos, protesting the war in Southeast Asia. As the demonstrators settled down in Laguna Park to enjoy a program planned by the Moratorium Committee, an unrelated incident of alleged shoplifting occurred one block from the area. Los Angeles Sheriff deputies moved into Laguna Park. The deputies shot tear gas into the crowd; the officers later claimed that they did so only after the crowd had failed to obey their orders to disperse. In any case, the crowd panicked. Those who did not move fast enough were beaten and arrested. These actions triggered a riot. The aftermath was that nearly 400 persons were arrested, hundreds of thousands of dollars of property were lost, and three Chicanos died. One of them was the respected journalist Ruben Salazar, who died from the impact of a tear gas projectile shot into the bar where he was sitting. The Chicano community charged that the police knew he was there and that, in effect, they had assassinated him. The investigative record shows that even if it was not murder, the deputies had acted in a highly reckless and irresponsible manner.[91]

Three more demonstrations followed—on September 16, 1970, January 9, 1971, and January 31, 1971. Each ended in violence. At the time of the demonstrations, the press condemned the Chicano community for the violence, but since then many moderates have had second thoughts. There is considerable evidence that local and federal police agents planted provocateurs in the Chicanos' ranks to incite rioting. One such case was that of Frank Martínez, an informer who became co-chairman of the Moratorium Committee. He has testified that federal agents paid him to start trouble.[92]

After the demonstrations in 1970, the Chicano community turned away from large-scale protests and dedicated itself to solidifying *barrio* organizations. Welfare rights, ex-convict rehabilitation, student associations, and even organizations of illegals occupied the activists. Again the thrust was toward cultural pluralism and self-determination. The main issues continued to be inferior education, poor housing, unemployment, the lack of political representation, police brutality, drugs, and the harassment of United States- and Mexico-born Chicanos.

Conclusion

In not concentrating on the historiography of the Chicano, this discussion has deviated from the format of other chapters in this book. This was necessary for, with the exception of Carey McWilliams' *North From Mexico* and Acuña's text *Occupied America: The Chicano Struggle Toward Liberation,* very little that had been published to 1972 represented the Chicano viewpoint. It seemed essential to expose teachers of the social studies to the contemporary currents of the nation's second largest racial and ethnic minority. According to the 1970 Census there were over seven million Chicanos in the United States, with over three million residing in California alone. Projections indicated that by 1980 the country's Chicano population would nearly double, while the population of the Anglo-American would remain relatively stable. Numbers alone made the Chicano a significant factor on the national scene. Awareness was growing in the Chicano community, and, as the battlefield shifted from the streets to the schools, educators needed to be prepared to understand what Chicanos are demanding in terms of their own identity.[93]

FOOTNOTES

[1] Carey McWilliams. *North From Mexico: The Spanish-Speaking People in the United States.* New York: Greenwood Press, 1948. Reprint 1968.

[2] Rodolfo Acuña. *Occupied America: The Chicano Struggle for Liberation.* New York: Harper & Row, 1972.

[3] Ignacio Bernal. *Mexico Before Cortez.* Garden City: Doubleday, 1963; Eric R. Wolf. *Sons of the Shaking Earth.* Chicago: The University of Chicago Press, 1959.

[4] Wolf. *Shaking Earth.* pp. 176-201, 202-232.

[5] Charles C. Cumberland. *Mexico: The Struggle for Modernity.* New York: Oxford University Press, 1968. pp. 106-112.

[6] Charles A. Hale. *Mexican Liberalism in the Age of Mora, 1821-1853.* New Haven: Yale University Press, 1968.

[7] Cumberland. *Mexico;* James D. Cockcroft. *Intellectual Precursors of the Mexican Revolution, 1900-1913.* Austin: The University of Texas Press, 1968.

[8] William Weber Johnson. *Heroic Mexico: The Violent Emergence of a Modern Nation.* Garden City: Doubleday, 1968.

[9] Rodolfo Acuña. *A Mexican American Chronicle.* New York: American Book Company, 1971.

[10] John Upton Terrell. *Traders of the Western Morning: Aboriginal Commerce in Pre-Columbian North America.* Los Angeles: Southwest Museum, 1967.

[11] Edward Spicer. *Cycles of Conquest: The Impact of Spain, Mexico, and the United States on the Indians of the Southwest.* Tucson: University of Arizona Press, 1967.

[12] Dario Fernández Florez. *The Spanish Heritage in the United States.* Madrid, Spain: Publicaciones Españolas, 1965; Harry Bernstein. "Spanish Influences in the United States: Economic Aspects." *Hispanic American Review* 18: 43-65; No. 1, February 1938.

[13] J. Frank Dobie. *The Mustangs.* New York: Bramhall House, 1952; J. Frank Dobie. *The Longhorns.* New York: Bramhall House, 1941.

[14] Edward Norris Wentworth. *America's Sheep Trails.* Ames, Iowa: The Iowa State College Press, 1948.

[15] Fernández Florez. *The Spanish Heritage;* Arthur P. Whitaker. "Spanish Contributions to American Agriculture." *Agricultural History* 3: 1-14; No. 1, January 1929.

[16] Max L. Moorhead. "Spanish Transportation in the Southwest, 1540-1846." *New Mexico Historical Review* 32: 107-122; No. 2, April 1957; Josiah Gregg. *Commerce of the Prairies.* Max L. Moorhead, editor. Norman: University of Oklahoma Press, 1954.

[17] Acuña. *Chronicle.* pp. 92-94.

[18] Harold W. Bentley. *A Dictionary of Spanish Terms in English with Special Reference to the American Southwest.* New York: Columbia University Press, 1932.

[19] T. R. Fehrenbach. *Lone Star: A History of Texas and the Texans.* New York: The Macmillan Company, 1968; Eugene C. Barker. *Mexico and Texas, 1821-1835.* New York: Russell & Russell, Inc., 1965.

[20] Raphael Trujillo Herrera. *Olvidate De El Alamo.* México, D. F.: La Prensa, 1965.

[21] Fehrenbach. *Lone Star.* pp. 180-181.

[22] Nathaniel W. Stephenson. *Texas and the Mexican War.* New York: United States Publishers, 1921.

[23] Walter Lord. "Myths and Realities of the Alamo." *The American West* 5: 18-25; No. 3, May 1968. p. 21.

[24] *Ibid.*

[25] *Ibid.*

[26] Trujillo Herrara. *Alamo.*

[27] Lord. p. 24.

[28] *Ibid.* p. 25.

[29] Fehrenbach. *Lone Star.* pp. 219-233.

[30] *Ibid.* p. 245.

[31] Glenn W. Price. *Origins of the War With Mexico: The Polk-Stockton Intrigue.* Austin: University of Texas Press, 1967. See David M. Pletcher's review in *Journal of American History* 55: 143-145; No. 1, June 1968.

[32] Robert Selph Henry. *The Story of the Mexican War.* New York: Frederick Ungar Publishing Company, 1950; Carl N. Degler. *Out of Our Past: The Forces That Shaped Modern America.* Revised Edition. New York: Harper & Row, 1970.

[33] Albert C. Ramsey, editor and translator. *The Other Side or Spanish Notes for the History of the War Between Mexico and the United States.* New York: Burt Franklin, 1970. Reprint of the 1850 edition; Samuel E. Chamberlain. *My Confession.* New York: Harper, 1956, narrates a brutal portrait of the atrocities committed during the invasion.

[34] Warren A. Beck. *New Mexico: A History of Four Centuries.* Norman: University of Oklahoma Press, 1962; Leonard Pitt. *The Decline of the Californios: A Social History of the Spanish-Speaking Californians, 1846-1890.* Berkeley & Los Angeles: University of California Press, 1966.

[35] Acuña. *Occupied America.* See Chapter 1.

[36] Henry. *Mexican War.*

[37] Lynn I. Perrigo. *The American Southwest: Its People and Cultures.* New York: Holt, Rinehart, and Winston, 1971; Wayne Moquin with Charles Van Doren, editors. *A Documentary History of the Mexican Americans.* New York: Praeger, 1971; Richard Gonzáles. "Commentary on the Treaty of Guadalupe Hidalgo," in Feliciano Rivera. *A Mexican American Source Book.* Menlo Park, California: Education Consulting Associates, 1970. pp. 184-187.

[38] Acuña. *Occupied America.* See Chapters 2-5.

[39] Fehrenbach. *Lone Star;* Charles W. Goldfinch. *Juan Cortina 1824-1892: A Re-Appraisal.* Brownsville, Tex.: The Bishop's Print Shop, 1950; Américo Paredes. *With His Pistol in His Hand.* Austin: The University of Texas Press, 1958.

[40] Paredes. *With a Pistol;* Walter Prescott Webb. *The Texas Rangers.* 2nd edition. Austin: The University of Texas Press, 1965.

[41] Hubert Howe Bancroft. *History of Arizona and New Mexico, 1530-1888.* Albuquerque, N. M.: Horn & Wallace, 1962. Facsimile of 1889 edition. San Francisco: The History Co.; Patricia Bell Blawis. *Tijerina and the Land Grants: Mexican Americans in the Struggle for Their Heritage.* New York: International Publishers, 1971; Nancie L. González. *The Spanish-Americans of New Mexico.* Revised edition. Albuquerque, N. M.: University of New Mexico Press, 1969.

[42] Armando Váldez. "Insurrection In New Mexico—The Land of Enchantment." *El Grito.* Fall 1967. p. 21.

[43] Howard R. Lamar. "The Santa Fe Ring, 1865-1885," in *The Far Southwest, 1846-1912: A Territorial History.* New Haven: Yale University Press, 1966.

[44] Maurice G. Fulton. *History of the Lincoln County War.* Robert N. Mullin, editor. Tucson: The University of Arizona Press, 1968.

[45] González. *The Spanish-Americans.*

[46] Joan Moore. *Mexican Americans.* Englewood Cliffs, N. J.: Prentice-Hall, 1970; Peter Nabokov. *Tijerina and the Courthouse Raid.* Albuquerque: University of New Mexico Press, 1969.

[47] Acuña. *Occupied America;* Joseph F. Park. "The History of Mexican Labor in Arizona During the Territorial Period." M.A. Thesis, Department of History, University of Arizona at Tucson, 1961.

[48] Park. "Mexican Labor in Arizona."

[49] Pitt. *Decline of Californios.*

[50] *Ibid.*

[51] *Ibid.*

[52] Leonard Pitt. "The Foreign Miners' Tax of 1850: A Study of Nativism and . . . in Gold Rush California." M.A. Thesis, University of California at Los Angeles, 1955.

[53] Goldfinch. *Juan Cortina.* Paul Jacobs and Saul Landau, with Eve Pell. *To Serve the Devil.* Vol. 1. New York: Vintage Books, 1971; Lyman Woodman. *Cortina, Rogue of the Rio Grande.* San Antonio, Tex.: The Naylor Company, 1950.

[54] Fulton. *Lincoln County.*

[55] Microfilm copies of *El Clamor Público* are found in the Huntington Library, San Marino, California.

[56] Robert Greenwood. *The California Outlaw: Tiburcio Vasquez.* Los Gatos, Calif.: The Talsman Press, 1960.

[57] See E. J. Hobsbawm. *Primitive Rebels: Studies in Archaic Forms of Social Movement in 19th and 20th Centuries.* New York: W. W. Norton, 1965.

[58] Ronald W. López. "Los Repatriados." Seminar paper, Department of History, University of California at Los Angeles, June 1968.

[59] Max Sylvius Handman. "Economic Reasons for the Coming of the Mexican Immigrant." *The American Journal of Sociology* 35: 601-611; No. 4, January 1930.

[60] Victor S. Clark. *Mexican Labor in the United States. Bulletin of the Bureau of Labor,* No. 78. Washington: Government Printing Office, 1908.

[61] Julian Samora. *Los Mojados: The Wetback Story.* Notre Dame, Ind.: University of Notre Dame Press, 1971.

[62] Acuña. *Occupied America.*

[63] Roy I. Garis. "Mexican Immigration—A Report for the Information of the Members of Congress," in U. S. Congress, *Western Hemisphere Immigration,* Hearing Before the Committee on Immigration and Naturalization, House of Representatives. 71st Congress, 2nd session. December 1929. p. 436.

[64] Miguel Tirado. "Mexican American Political Organization: The Key to Chicano Power." *Aztlán.* University of California at Los Angeles. Spring 1970. pp. 53-78; Acuña. *Occupied America.*

[65] Ernesto Galarza. *Merchants of Labor: The Mexican Bracero Story. . . .* Santa Barbara: McNally and Loftin, 1964; Ernesto Galarza. *Spiders in the House and Workers in the Fields.* Notre Dame: University of Notre Dame Press, 1970.

[66] Charles Wollenberg. "*Huelga,* 1928 Style: The Imperial Valley Cantaloupe Workers' Strike." *Pacific Historical Review* 38: 45-58; No. 1, February 1969.

[67] Joan London and Henry Anderson. *So Shall Ye Reap.* New York: Crowell, 1970.

[68] Charles B. Spaulding. "The Mexican Strike at El Monte, California." *Sociology and Social Research* 18: 571-580; No. 6, July-August 1934; Ronald W. López. "The El Monte Berry Strike of 1933." *Aztlán.* U.C.L.A. Spring 1970.

[69] Kenneth P. Walker. "The Pecan Shellers of San Antonio and Mechanization." *Southwestern Historical Quarterly* 69: 44-58; No. 1, July 1965.

[70] Philip Stevenson. "Deporting Jesús." *The Nation* 143: 67-69; No. 3, July 18, 1936.

[71] Emory S. Bogardus. "Repatriation and Readjustment," in Manuel E. Servin, editor. *The Mexican-Americans: An Awakening Minority.* Beverly Hills: Glencoe Press, 1970. pp. 88-97; Norman D. Humphrey. "Mexican Repatriation from Michigan: Public Assistance in Historical Perceptive." *Social Service Review* 15: 497-513; No. 3, September 1941.

[72] Raúl Morín. *Among the Valiant: Mexican-Americans in World War II and Korea.* Los Angeles: Borden Publishing Co., 1966.

[73] McWilliams. *North From Mexico.*

[74] *Ibid.*

[75] Patricia Morgan. *Shame of a Nation.* Los Angeles: Committee for Protection of Foreign Born, 1954; Carey McWilliams. "California and the Wetback." *Common Ground* 9: 15-20; No. 4, Summer 1949.

[76] Galarza. *Merchants of Labor.*

[77] Leo Grebler, *et al. The Mexican American People: The Nation's Second Largest Minority.* New York: Free Press, 1970.

[78] McWilliams. *North From Mexico.* See the "Introduction" to 1968 edition.

[79] Stanley Levy, Marvin Gelfand, Michael D. Saphier, Stanton L. Stein and Bruce Warner. "Putting Chicanos on the Political Map." *Los Angeles Times,* May 21, 1972.

[80] Eugene Nelson. *Huelga: Delano, California.* New York: Farrar, Straus & Giroux, 1967; Peter Matthiessen. *Sal Si Puedes: César Chávez and the New American Revolution.* New York: Random House, 1969.

[81] The author was a member of various organizations during the 1960's and was an eyewitness to many of the events described.

[82] *El Plan de Santa Barbara, A Chicano Plan For Higher Education.* Chicano Coordinating Council for Higher Education. Oakland: La Causa Publications, 1969.

[83] Richard Gardner. *Grito! Reies Tijerina and the New Mexico Land Grant War of 1967.* Indianapolis: Bobbs-Merrill, 1970.

[84] Stan Steiner. *La Raza: The Mexican Americans.* New York: Harper and Row, 1970. pp. 378-392.

[85] Acuña. *Occupied America.*

[86] See in particular Octavio I Romano. "The Historical and Intellectual Presence of Mexican-Americans." *El Grito.* Winter 1969.

[87] Daniel Jack Chasan. "Actos." *The New Yorker Magazine* 43: 23-25; No. 26, August 19, 1967; Steiner. *La Raza.*

[88] *Plan de Santa Barbara.*

[89] José Ángel Gutíerrez. "Aztlán: Chicano Revolt in the Winter Garden." *La Raza magazine.* Vol. 1, No. 4, 1971.

[90] Stanley Levy, *et al. Los Angeles Times.* May 21, 1972.

[91] Armando Morales. *Ando Sangrando! i am bleeding.* Los Angeles: The Congress of Mexican American Unity, 1971; "Mexican Americans and the Administration of Justice in the Southwest." *United States Commission on Civil Rights.* Washington: Government Printing Office, March 1970.

[92] Frank Del Olmo. "Provoking Trouble for Lawmen, Chicano Informer Claims." *Los Angeles Times.* February 1, 1972.

[93] Thomas P. Carter. *Mexican Americans in School: A History of Educational Neglect.* New York: College Entrance Examination Board, 1970.

· 6 ·

The Asian American Experience

Roger Daniels

FROM a numerical point of view the experience of Asian Americans[1] represents only a tiny fragment of the total experience of immigrants to what is now the United States. Yet, for reasons that I hope this essay makes clear, that experience has been significant far beyond its mere numerical incidence, although most of the historians and analysts of immigration have failed to understand this.[2] Before noting what historians and social scientists have said and are saying about Asian immigrants and their children, it might be well to summarize both the chronology of immigration and the available demographic data and to place them into some kind of meaningful perspective.

The overwhelming majority of immigrants from Asia have come from three nations: China, Japan, and the Philippines. Chinese began to come in the late 1840's, were excluded by the federal Chinese Exclusion Act of 1882, given a token quota of 100 in 1943 which lasted until the end of the quota system in 1965. Relatively large numbers of Japanese began to come in the 1890's; this immigration was inhibited but not stopped by international agreements beginning with the Gentlemen's Agreement of 1907-08, and halted by the National Origins Act of 1924. A token quota of 100 was granted to Japan by the Immigration Act of 1952, which also lasted until 1965. Statistically significant Filipino immigration began only in the 1920's; since they were "nationals" of the United States their migration was not inhibited by the restrictive legislation of the 1920's. After much Congressional debate, Filipinos were given a token quota of 50 per year under a special provision of the Philippine Independence Act which went into effect in 1934. Filipino immigration resumed with the passage of the Immigration Act of 1952 and has increased since the 1965 act.

Of the 45 million immigrants recorded as entering the United States since 1820, only a million and a half have come from Asia.[3] Of these, more than 400,000 have been Chinese, nearly 400,000 have been Japanese, and some 200,000 have been Filipinos. The 1960 census showed that there were nearly half a million Americans of Japanese ancestry, a little over a quarter of a million of Chinese ancestry, and fewer than 200,000 Filipinos.[4] Asians and their descendants thus represented less than one-half of one per cent of the total population.

Historians, social scientists, and most other commentators on ethnicity in contemporary America now almost invariably agree that the various Asian American communities, while not assimilated in the mythical melting pot, have become highly Americanized and have taken on, to a remarkable degree, essentially middle-class characteristics. One scholar has even referred to the Japanese Americans as "our model minority."[5] Such has not always been the case. No immigrant group—save for Africans and their descendants—has been so universally abused by the public, the various levels of government, and by historians. Asians were the first group of immigrants—other than African slaves—to be barred from entering the United States and the last group to be granted the right of naturalization.

Although it is meaningful to speak, as this essay has done, of Asian Americans as a distinct group, there has been and is very little interaction between the national groups within the United States, so that any meaningful treatment must focus, in the main, on the three major ethnic groupings among them.

The Chinese

The major entry of Chinese into American life came in California—and to a lesser degree other western states—at the time of the 1849 gold rush; even in 1960 more than 40 per cent of American Chinese lived there. Their role in California was essentially that of hewers of wood and drawers of water. As long as there was an absolute shortage of unskilled labor, discrimination against them, while never wholly absent, was not oppressive. But, in the years after the Civil War, and especially after the completion of the first transcontinental railroad in 1869 whose construction had employed some 10,000 Chinese, the Chinese became the target of labor-inspired violence, harassment at the municipal and state level, and, finally, national legislative punishment in the form of the Chinese Exclusion Act of 1882. The violence ranged in kind from verbal abuse to mass murder and in geographical scope from southern California to western Massachusetts. The worst outrages were in Los Angeles in 1871 and Rock Springs, Wyoming in 1885. It should also be noted that this kind of racist violence was not confined to the

United States: western Canada and northern Mexico also had fatal
outbreaks of anti-Chinese activity.[6]

This violence and harassment was directed at a small and shrinking
group. There were probably never more than 125,000 Chinese in post-
Civil War America; the census of 1890 found just over 70,000. But
since about nine out of ten Chinese immigrants were male, the Chinese
American community shrank steadily: the census of 1920 found just
over 61,000, of whom fewer than 8,000 were female. From that point
natural increase, plus a trickle of immigration up to 1952, and about
2,000 per year since then, has produced a growing population, the vast
majority of which is American-born. Legal harassment has virtually
ceased, unless one wishes to regard the 1970 integration and bussing
rulings of the San Francisco School Board which ordered the end of
separate schools in Chinatown and was aimed at mixing Chinese with
white and black students as harassment.

The Japanese

Significant numbers of Japanese began to come to the United States
in the 1890's. Between that time and 1924 when Congress, in the process
of passing the nativist National Origins Act, included language which
barred further immigration of Japanese, some 275,000 Japanese came
to the United States. Many of these, as was the case with all immigrants,
were what scholars have called "birds of passage" or "sojourners": in
plain language people who came and went rather than permanent residents. When immigration ceased—for what turned out to be a period
of twenty-eight years—there were about 125,000 Japanese in the country. Unlike the Chinese, however, the immigrant generation included a
large number of women, so that no sizable decline in population took
place.

Although the anti-Japanese movement in the United States (and
Canada!) was clearly a lineal continuation of the anti-Chinese movement, the Japanese occupied a distinctly different socio-economic position in the society of western America where most of them—as well as
other Asians—have lived. Although the Japanese, like the Chinese
before them, entered the labor force at the very bottom, early twentieth-
century California was a very different place from mid-nineteenth-century
California. Rather than directly competing with the largely white labor
force, most Japanese quickly entered agriculture where they created
a special niche for themselves. The anti-Japanese movement in California and the rest of the West—which flourished from the turn of the
century until the end of World War II—was distinctly different from its

anti-Chinese predecessor. The latter was essentially a labor-dominated movement while the former, in both its leadership and appeal, was distinctly middle class and "progressive." The violence against Japanese was sporadic, and, until the outbreak of World War II, apparently non-fatal. The worst excesses of the anti-Chinese movement occurred rather early and were perpetrated by mobs in then relatively obscure places. The worst excess of the anti-Japanese movement—the incarceration of more than 100,000 west coast Japanese—took place at the end of the movement and had as its chief perpetrators the President, the Congress, and the United States Army.

What must be added to the anti-Japanese equation was the simple fact that the Japanese Americans came from a nation which became a real external threat to the United States. There had been, to be sure, a flurry of scare literature in the 1870's and 1880's which depicted China as a potential invader of the United States, but in the late nineteenth century China was so clearly a victim rather than a predator in world politics that this early "yellow peril" propaganda could have convinced few. Twentieth-century Japan, however, was a different case, and when the bombs actually fell at Pearl Harbor, many Americans, perhaps most, were prepared to believe that the "yellow peril" was a peril after all. When, however, we compare what happened to German Americans in two wars with what happened to a much smaller group of Japanese Americans in one, the conclusion inescapably follows that racial prejudice was perhaps the factor which best explains the divergent results.

German Americans, alien and citizen, suffered certain harassments, legal and extra-legal in both wars; in almost all cases, however, for these white immigrants and their descendants, guilt was individual. For Japanese Americans, guilt was collective. Despite the absence of one indictable act of espionage or sabotage by a Japanese American of either the first or second generation—that is alien or citizen—every person of ascertainable Japanese ancestry of any degree in the western United States was rounded up and sent to a concentration camp, although the government insisted that they were being sent to "Relocation Centers."

Despite this extraordinary treatment—similar in type but not in duration to that meted out to the one non-immigrant element in our population, the Indians—the post-World War II assimilation of the still growing Japanese American community has been quicker and more thorough than anyone could have imagined possible. Some of the reasons for this will be explored at the close of this essay, but a less than incidental factor was certainly the significant (and well publicized) exploits of Japanese American military units in World War II.

The Filipinos

In many ways the Filipino American experience replicates that of other Asian Americans; there is one exception to this generalization. Due in part to their relatively late entry into the United States, the Filipino American community can in no way be called middle class. According to 1960 census data, Filipinos are the most disadvantaged identifiable immigrant and immigrant-descended group: they have less formal education, lower income, and are more heavily concentrated as migrant laborers than any other segment of the population.

Since they are the last of the Asian migrant groups of the pre-1965 era, one is tempted to summarize their history in the 1920's and 1930's with an aphorism: "Last imported, least assimilated." Although the Census of 1910 reported only five Filipinos in all of California, there were more than 30,000 in 1930, almost all of them having come since 1924. The peculiar status of the Philippines as an American possession made immigration law an ineffective barrier against their entry and produced, in the early 1930's, the ironic spectacle of some of Congress' most blatant racists becoming "anti-imperialists": that is, advocating Filipino independence so Filipino immigrants could be kept out. Filipino population stayed almost stationary until the immigration law changes of 1952 and 1965 spurred growth.

Apart from its poverty, its relative lack of upward social mobility, and the fact that most of its members are, at least nominally, Roman Catholics, the Filipino American community is hard to categorize. There are probably more trade unionists, per capita, than among any other Asian group. Since the 1930's the Filipinos have been a vital but under-publicized element in almost every struggle for agricultural unionization in California.[7] Still a very small group numerically—just over 100,000 in the continental United States with another 69,000 in Hawaii in 1960 —it is growing, in both absolute and relative numbers, faster than any other ethnic group. In the year ending June 30, 1970, for example, more Filipinos (31,203) entered the United States as immigrants than any other nationality and Filipinos comprised almost 10 per cent of all immigrants.[8]

The Asian American in Contemporary America

As the foregoing accounts should have made clear, Asian Americans have been written about more as victims than as participants in American society. As victims of a peculiar variant of American racism, they were the first to be excluded and the last to be admitted to naturalization. Yet, from a socioeconomic point of view, their material progress has been outstanding and much more rapid than many other more recent immigrant groups which encountered much less tangible prejudice. And, even more important, is the related fact that the prejudice against them has lessened in a very short period of time. The reasons for this almost polar change in social position are not completely clear, but surely among the more important factors are:

1. The relatively high degree of "middle classness" which so many Asian Americans have attained, at least part of which is due to the high level of motivation which so many individuals received from their patriarchal-dominated families.

2. The changing and bewildering shifts in relationship between the United States and various Asian countries which have produced a growing appreciation for the values of Asian civilizations.

3. Perhaps even more important has been a growing sophistication among Americans in ethnic and racial matters combined with the nationalization of the "Negro question" which black migration from the American South since World War I has produced. Just as the presence of significant numbers of non-whites in the American South and West in the nineteenth century tended to promote the status of all whites, the growing black-white polarization in all the United States after World War II has tended to promote all non-blacks. To a significant degree—and it is a hallmark, perhaps, of their Americanization—many contemporary Asian Americans share the anti-black prejudices of other Americans and behave accordingly. Two concrete examples will suffice: the massive resistance in 1971 of the San Francisco Chinese community to bussing for integration and the way in which Los Angeles Japanese Americans have fled from older neighborhoods, like the Crenshaw district, when blacks began to move in, to otherwise all-white suburbs like Gardena.

Yet, having noted this "Americanization," it must be observed that Asian Americans are still non-white and are not at all likely to be absorbed in the mythical melting pot. The recent renaissance of ethnic consciousness, a by-product of the post-1954 black revolution, has not left the Asian American communities, and especially their younger members, unaffected. Nor have these latter remained indifferent to the upheavals in their ancestral homelands, particularly but not exclusively the rise of the People's Republic of China.

The result is a kind of unprecedented turmoil—largely generational within the various ethnic communities. A very few of the younger Asian Americans are members of groups—such as the Third World Liberation Front centered in the San Francisco Bay area—which have a distinctly Maoist caste. Others, in much greater number, are beginning to explore and question their own ethnic identity in movements largely mimetic of blacks. They have demanded—and received—Asian American courses and study centers from college authorities; they speak, half seriously, half in jest, of "Yellow Power," and in rhetoric whose roots are clearly black, dismiss their obviously middle-class elders and fellows as "bananas": that is, "yellow on the outside, but white on the inside."

But although Asian Americans are not white (Harry Kitano and I have called them "the whitest of the non-white") they are not black either. Nor is their economic condition that of an oppressed group; they are distinctly middle class,[9] and, except for the Filipinos, more likely to go to college and earn advanced degrees than is the general white population. How they will react to the continuing stresses of their ambiguous position is, of course, for them and the future to decide. But it is also clear that their recent experience, however heartening it may be to students of ethnicity and racism, can not be taken as a model for blacks or Chicanos or other oppressed groups. Because of their number, their place and time of entry into American society, and the cultural baggage that they brought with them, the Asian American experience can not be repeated.

Bibliographical Notes

Little comparative work has been done on the total Asian American experience, but H. Brett Melendy, *The Oriental Americans,* New York: Twayne, 1972, is a pioneering first attempt; see also Roger Daniels and Harry H. L. Kitano, *American Racism: Exploration of the Nature of Prejudice,* Englewood Cliffs, N.J.: Prentice Hall, 1970. Roger Daniels and Spencer C. Olin, Jr., *Racism in California: A Reader in the History of Oppression,* New York: Macmillan, 1972, is a collection of secondary works and documents while Roger Daniels, "Westerners from the East: Oriental Immigrants Reappraised," *Pacific Historical Review* 35:373-383: No. 4, November 1966, examines the historiographical treatment.

CHINESE

For many years most historians of California and the West, from Hubert Howe Bancroft on, shared and perpetuated the anti-Chinese prejudices of their section. The last nativist-oriented text was Robert G. Cleland, *California in Our Time, 1900-1940,* New York: Knopf, 1947. Many of the early sympathetic treatments of the Chinese, like Mary Roberts Coolidge, *Chinese Immigration,* New York: Holt, 1909, had an orientation of the Protestant missionary and were hostile to other new immigrants. Modern scholarship begins with Elmer C. Sandmeyer, *The Anti-Chinese Movement in California,* Urbana: University of Illinois Press, 1939 (new edition with introduction and supplementary bibliography by Roger Daniels, 1973). Important recent scholarship includes Gunther Barth, *Bitter Strength: A History of the Chinese in the United States, 1850-1870,* Cambridge, Mass.: Harvard University Press, 1964; Alexander Saxton, *The Indispensable Enemy: Labor and the Anti-Chinese Movement in California,* Berkeley and Los Angeles: University of California Press, 1971; and Stuart C. Miller, *The Unwelcome Immigrant: The American Image of the Chinese, 1785-1882,* Berkeley and Los Angeles: University of California Press, 1969. The last clearly establishes the connection between anti-orientalism and American racism generally. Betty Lee Sung, *Mountain of Gold,* New York: Macmillan, 1967 (paperback edition *The Story of the Chinese in America,* New York: Collier Books, 1971) is a narrative history while Rose Hum Lee, *The Chinese in the United States of America,* Hong Kong University Press, 1960, is a treatment by a sociologist. Jade Snow Wong, *Fifth Chinese Daughter,* New York: Harper, 1950, is a charming and insightful memoir.

JAPANESE

From almost the beginning of their American experience, the Japanese found scholars and apologists willing to defend them. Important contemporary polemics, many of them based on research, include Yamato Ichihashi, *Japanese in the United States,* Stanford: Stanford University Press, 1932 and Raymond Leslie Buell, "The Development of the Anti-Japanese Agitation in the United States," *Political Science Quarterly* 37:38: 605-638, 57-81; No. 4, December 1922 and No. 1, March 1923. Two works that cover the whole anti-Japanese experience are Roger Daniels, *The Politics of Prejudice: The Anti Japanese Movement in California and the Struggle for Japanese Exclusion,* Berkeley and Los Angeles: University of California Press, 1962, and *Concentration Camps, USA: Japanese Americans and World War II,* New York: Holt, Rinehart and Winston, 1971. The best treatment of the Japanese American community is Harry H. L. Kitano, *Japanese Americans: The Evolution of a Subculture,* Englewood Cliffs, N.J.: Prentice-Hall, 1969. The wartime evacuation has been the subject of a number of books, scholarly and popular. The most useful of these, in chronological order, are: Carey McWilliams, *Prejudice: Japanese-Americans: Symbol of Racial Intolerance,* Boston: Little, Brown, 1944; Dorothy S. Thomas and Richard S. Nishimoto, *The Spoilage,* Berkeley and Los Angeles: University of California, 1946; Dorothy S. Thomas, *The Salvage,* Berkeley and Los Angeles: University of California Press, 1952; Morton Grodzins, *Americans Betrayed: Politics and the Japanese Evacuation,* Chicago: University of Chicago, 1949; Jacobus ten Broek *et al., Preju-*

dice, War and the Constitution, Berkeley and Los Angeles, 1954; Stetson Conn, "Japanese Evacuation from the West Coast," in Stetson Conn, Rose C. Engleman, and Byron Fairchild, *The United States Army in World War II: The Western Hemisphere: Guarding the United States and Its Outposts,* Washington: Government Printing Office, 1964. pp. 115-149; Allen R. Bosworth, *America's Concentration Camps,* New York: Norton, 1967; Bill Hosokawa, *Nisei: The Quiet Americans,* New York: Morrow, 1969; Audrie Girdner and Anne Loftis, *The Great Betrayal,* New York: Macmillan, 1969; Edward H. Spicer, *et al.,* *Impounded People,* Tucson: University of Arizona Press, 1969; and Dillon S. Myer, *Uprooted Americans: The Japanese Americans and the War Relocation Authority During World War II,* Tucson: University of Arizona Press, 1971. On special aspects of the evacuation, Robert W. O'Brien, *The College Nisei,* Palo Alto: Pacific Books, 1949, tells of the education of the relocated students; Thomas D. Murphy, *Ambassadors in Arms,* Honolulu: University of Hawaii, 1954, tells of the Japanese American combat units. T. A. Larson, *Wyoming's War Years,* Laramie: University of Wyoming, 1954, contains the best study of a state's reaction to the Japanese sent into it while Leonard J. Arrington, *The Price of Prejudice: The Japanese American Relocation Center in Utah during World War II,* Logan: Utah State University, 1962, is the best published study of a single camp. Hilary Conroy and T. Scott Miyakawa, eds., *East Across the Pacific: Historical and Sociological Studies of Japanese Assimilation and Immigration,* Santa Barbara: Clio Books, 1972, contains valuable original essays.

FILIPINOS

The scholarship about Filipino Americans is still very slight. J. M. Saniel, ed., *The Filipino Exclusion Movement, 1927-1935,* Quezon City, Philippines: University of the Philippines, 1967 (Occasional Papers, No. 1, Institute of Asian Studies), is a collection of papers by American scholars. Older treatments which have not been superseded include Bruno Lasker, *Filipino Immigration to Continental United States and to Hawaii,* Chicago: University of Chicago Press, 1931, and John H. Burma, *Spanish-Speaking Groups in the United States,* Durham: Duke University Press, 1954. Two useful memoir accounts are Manuel Buaken, *I Have Lived with the American People,* Caldwell, Idaho: Caxton, 1948, and Dolores S. Feria, editor, *Sound of Falling Light: Letters in Exile,* Quezon City, Philippines, 1960. The best discussion of Congressional treatment of the Filipinos is in Robert A. Divine, *American Immigration Policy, 1924-1952,* New Haven: Yale University Press, 1957, pp. 52-76.

THE CONTEMPORARY SCENE

There has been, since 1967, a relatively profuse flowering of interest in Asian American Studies, especially, but not exclusively, in west coast universities—most notably at the University of California campuses at Davis and Los Angeles, the University of Washington, and the University of Hawaii. In the East, there are centers at Yale and Columbia. All of these sponsor publications for and by the Asian American community. For a useful guide to these publications and to gain insight into the current interests of the student generation, see Amy Tachiki, Eddie Wong, and Franklin Odo, editors, *Roots: An Asian American Reader,* Los Angeles: UCLA Asian American Studies Center, 1971.

FOOTNOTES

[1] For historical reasons, the Asian American experience in Hawaii will *not* be treated here; all immigration and population data prior to 1952 refer to the continental United States only. Ignorance rather than anti-insular prejudice dictates this somewhat false dichotomy. For the Japanese in Hawaii see: Hilary Conroy. *The Japanese Frontier in Hawaii, 1869-1898.* Berkeley and Los Angeles: University of California Press, 1953, 175 pp.; Andrew Lind. *Hawaii's Japanese: An Experiment in Democracy.* Princeton: Princeton University Press, 1946, 264 pp. H. Brett Melendy, *The Oriental Americans,* New York: Twayne, 1972, treats both Hawaii and the mainland.

[2] See, for example, Edith Abbot. *Immigration: Select Documents.* Chicago: University of Chicago Press, 1924. p. ix, and Carl Wittke. *We Who Built America.* New York: Prentice-Hall, 1939. p. 458.

[3] For a convenient statistical recapitulation see U.S. Immigration and Naturalization Service. *Annual Report.* Washington: GPO, 1970. pp. 61-63. Included in the "Asia" category are about 250,000 from Asia Minor.

[4] An excellent analysis of the 1960 data, on which many of the generalizations on socio-economic status are based, is California, Division of Fair Employment Practices. *Californians of Japanese, Chinese, and Filipino Ancestry: Population, Employment, Income, Education.* San Francisco, 1965.

[5] William Peterson. "Success Story: Japanese American Style." *The New York Times Magazine,* Jan. 9, 1966.

[6] For details of the worst violence, see Paul Crane and Alfred Larson. "The Chinese Massacre." *Annals of Wyoming* 12:47-55, 153-161; Nos. 1-2, January, April 1940.

[7] See, for example, Stuart Jamison. *Labor Unionism in American Agriculture.* Washington; G.P.O., 1945. pp. 70-78, 105-115.

[8] Of a total of 373,326 immigrants admitted in the fiscal year ending 30 June 1970, 92,816, almost 25 per cent, were Asians. This unexpected result of the reform of 1965, if it continues, may well result in demands for a renewal of essentially racist quotas. Apart from the Philippines, other major Asian sources include: China (largely Taiwan)—14,093; India—10,114; Korea—9,314; Japan—4,485; and Hong Kong—3,863. U.S. Immigration and Naturalization Service. *op. cit.* p. 40.

[9] This should not be taken as a denial of the existence of significant poverty and deprivation among some Asian Americans, particularly among Filipinos and the Chinese of San Francisco and New York, many of whom are recent immigrants.

PART THREE

New Perspectives in the Study of American History

· 7 ·

Women in American Life

Anne Firor Scott

F EW topics covered in this volume have received less attention from professional historians than the history of American women. To be sure, individual historians, biographers and essayists have long cherished an interest in the subject, and Arthur Schlesinger, Sr. asserted in 1922 that the time had come when women would begin to be included in the history books.[1] It was forty-odd years, however, before more than an occasional historian showed any sign that he was right. By the mid-1960's a resurgent woman's movement began to call attention to the curious invisibility of women in American history, and by the beginning of the 70's an increasing number of scholars were embarking upon research in the field, and organizing courses in women's history.

The long period of inattention to women in the writing of American history presents an interesting study in the sociology of knowledge. Most American historians have been white males. Only recently, under the pressure of a vigorous social movement, have they begun to perceive that black people were part of the warp and woof of the American past. Even more recently, also under the pressure of a contemporary social movement, they have begun to develop the same perception about women. The rising interest in the history of American women coincides with a dramatic increase in the number of women entering the profession, some of whom have been inspired by their own experience to re-examine the record.

In some ideal world there would be no such thing as women's history since social historians would recognize that male *and* female make up the society, create the mores, pattern the culture; economic historians would be aware that women have always been part of the labor force and have contributed to economic choices; legal historians would know that case law and to some degree statute law have been shaped by the needs and demands of women; political historians would be aware of the people who organized the precincts as well as the people who met at the summit.

With a few notable exceptions such awareness has not been evident, and in reaction against this neglect a good many scholars have begun to focus directly upon women in a variety of contexts. As special studies multiply they will begin to broaden the general conception of historical reality and suggest new ways of viewing the past, so that bit by bit "women's history" as such may become integrated into existing fields. In the meantime, the teacher who sets out to organize a course in women's history, or to expand an existing course by including attention to the role of women, is forced to rely upon an assortment of primary as well as secondary materials, ranging from monographs to novels. The state of the field is such that teachers and students must become their own historians—a situation which is pedagogically useful, since the student's sense of discovery can be entirely authentic.

Just as there is no tidy body of monographs to offer the beginning student, there are no agreed-upon categories for organizing materials. It is useful to examine the history of women in the context of, for example, social history and family life; economic history and the nature of work; educational history; legal history; voluntary organizations, clubs and reform movements. It is also possible to follow a chronological path tracing the experience of women in America from the earliest settlement to the present. Whatever plan of organization is used, much of the substance will be tentative and provocative rather than definitive.

General Overview

No one has yet essayed a comprehensive history of women in American life, though two such works are now in progress [1972].[2] The broadest study in print is Eleanor Flexner's *Century of Struggle,* which is concerned primarily with organizations seeking improvement in women's rights, with higher education and the labor movement. The story is told, as it were, from the inside and no effort is made to relate the women's movement to the larger social context and political changes. It is excellent as far as it goes and used in conjunction with a book of readings is probably the best introduction to the subject now available.[3] Two other general works are William L. O'Neill, *Everyone Was Brave,* which is part polemic and must be used with great care, and Andrew Sinclair's scintillating *The Better Half,* hastily researched but well written. Gerda Lerner, *The Woman in American History,* summarizes the history of American women from colonial times to Women's Liberation in less than two hundred pages, and like Flexner includes black women in her analysis. In 1972, Professor Lerner brought out *Black Women in White America,* a book of readings with a bibliographical essay. This was then the only general discussion of the history of black women who are, as Professor Lerner pointed out, treated briefly and peripherally in most black history sources. This book is, therefore, indispensable. Two sources covering many aspects of women's lives are Mary R. Beard, *America Through Women's Eyes,* and three issues of the *Annals of the American Academy of Political and Social Science* which are helpful for the general study of women in the twentieth century.[4]

Social History: Women at Home

A close study of women's experience can broaden considerably our understanding of the social structure and cultural patterns of the past. Since women's experience was nearly always as part of a family, family history is a good place to begin. An older work, Arthur W. Calhoun's *A Social History of the American Family From Colonial Times to the Present,* is erratically documented and difficult to use, but contains much good material. Julia Cherry Spruill, *Women's Life and Work in the Southern Colonies,* is the best monograph on women's history yet published by an American historian. It is useful on many counts, but indispensable for colonial family life. Edmund Morgan, *Virginians at Home,* relies heavily on Mrs. Spruill's work. A mammoth work on the history of children, recently published, is also filled with data which will be useful to the historian of women.[5]

Demographic historians in Europe and America are trying to begin to get hold of the study of family life in new ways. The seminal work is Philippe Aries, *Centuries of Childhood,* which deals with French history. Three American monographs provide useful methodological ideas, though none of the authors is especially interested in the implications of his findings for women's history.[6]

Social and family history may also be studied through documents of individuals. Carl Van Doren's biography of Jane Mecom, and his volume of the letters she exchanged with her brother Benjamin Franklin, provide a case in point. Jane Mecom was no public figure. She was a wife, mother, tradeswoman, often beset by bad luck (not least in the husband she took unto herself at the age of 15), who would often have been in dire poverty but for the generosity of her famous brother. Yet her lively descriptions of her own life and that of her neighbors, her minute reports of the world she lived in and the way she spent her time, enable the reader to form a picture of a society in which men and women married young and had many children. Since many of them also died young, and survivors remarried, kinship ties became very complex and family structure fluid. Children were raised by aunts, uncles, grandmothers or even occasionally great-grandmothers. Such responsibilities seem to have been taken for granted, as a necessary condition of one's humanity. A major concern of the responsible adults was to be sure that each of the surviving young should find a skill by which to maintain himself or herself. Industriousness was a high value—though the hope for religious salvation stood even higher. From such a single probe into the eighteenth century, using ultratraditional materials (letters), but focusing on *women's* lives, the student can begin to develop a complex view of the daily life, the values, the aspirations which shaped a society. The letters of Harriet Beecher Stowe provide the raw material for a similar analysis for the 1840's and 1850's.[7]

For the twentieth century a new kind of source is available—the sociological study. The Lynds' *Middletown,* for example, has long been used by social and economic historians of the 1920's, but its usefulness as a way of gaining insight into the everyday lives of women has yet to be analyzed. Many observers were fascinated with the changing nature of family life in the early decades of the twentieth century. The student can find commentary of varying quality in such works as Floyd Dell, *Studies in Modern Feminism;* Freda Kirchwey, *Our Changing Morality;* Scott and Nellie Nearing, *Woman and Social Progress.*[8]

The examples cited are only samples to suggest the possibilities of using works which are already in print as a means of learning more about women, an enterprise which can yield dividends for social history generally.

Women at Work

The economic historian is somewhat better provided with monographic material, though here, too, there are large gaps. Women have always constituted a significant part of the labor force, whether on the farm or in the preindustrial city—as partners in a family enterprise, or as independent entrepreneurs, of which there were many in the colonial period. In the nineteenth century the number of women in the labor force increased continually as they became workers in factories, clerks in burgeoning bureaucracy, typists, telegraphers, domestic servants, teachers, or sometimes even professionals. For the colonial period the student is fortunate to have not only Mrs. Spruill's book, but also those of Elizabeth Anthony Dexter and Mary S. Benson. The effect of the Civil War upon women's work patterns is detailed in Mary Elizabeth Massey's *Bonnet Brigades.*[9]

For the nineteenth century we have Helen L. Sumner's magnificent *History of Women in Industry in the United States.* Also useful are monographs by Edith Abbott, Robert Smuts, and Elizabeth F. Baker.[10]

An advice book published in 1885, called *What Can A Woman Do,* throws unexpected light upon the work structure of the eighties as it affected women. This can be cross-checked with the report of the United States Commissioner of Labor made at about the same time, called "Working Women in Large Cities." Books inspired by the concern of middle-class reformers for the working conditions of women are also enlightening—for example, Helen S. Campbell, *Prisoners of Poverty* or Bessie Van Vorst, *The Woman Who Toils,* and nearly all the works of Jane Addams.[11] The autobiographies of Mary Anderson and Agnes Nestor provide materials for studying women in the labor movement.[12]

For the early twentieth century the best monograph is the volume by Sophonisba P. Breckinridge, undertaken as part of the massive study of Recent Social Trends commissioned by President Hoover, and covering nearly every aspect of women's lives. For the years since 1920 materials are vast, but largely to be found in primary sources such as the publications of the Women's Bureau and the United States Department of Labor. A work by William Chafe is based on these sources among others.[13] Chafe is primarily interested in the effects of external social and economic change upon women's roles.

Education of Women

Significantly affecting the changing patterns of women's work, and many other aspects of American life as well, was the revolution in educational opportunity which began with the founding of Troy Female Academy under the aegis of Emma Willard in 1821. A survey of these changes may be found in Mabel Newcomer, *A Century of Higher Education for American Women.*[14] Much additional useful material can be extracted from the biographies of the educational pioneers—Emma Willard, Mary Lyon, Catherine Beecher, Lucy Maynard Salmon, and Alice Freeman Palmer, for example.[15] Barbara M. Cross's little book, *The Educated Woman in America,* provides a penetrating essay and selections from the writings of three extraordinarily different "educated women."[16] Once again, since the analytical and interpretive work is yet in the future, the serious student will have to delve into primary materials such as the *Reports* of the Commissioner of Education, beginning in 1867, wherein digests of state reports provide the data for tracing the growth of public and secondary schools open to women, the proliferation of normal schools, and the rapid movement of women into elementary and secondary school teaching.[17] An older book by Willystine Goodsell is still useful for some of its reflections on these developments.[18] A new book by Dorothy McGuigan on the first hundred years of women at the University of Michigan, demonstrating graphically the conflict precipitated by women's demand for education, combines careful scholarship with useful insight, and can be highly recommended. Another recent book is made up of autobiographies of women who took higher degrees at Columbia University after World War II, and provides a variety of examples of the way in which such education has affected women's lives.[19] Careful studies of the interaction of increasing educational opportunity, family life, work and self-images of American women are badly needed.

Voluntary Associations and Reform Movements

The means by which women have gradually widened and changed their spheres of action are various. One of the most important has been voluntary associations, whether religiously oriented as in the case of missionary societies or the Woman's Christian Temperance Union, or secular organizations such as the many varieties of women's clubs which multiplied in the latter half of the nineteenth century. The most detailed attention to the significance of religious groups for women's emancipation is to be found in a work by the present author which also analyzes the role of women's clubs in the South.[20] The evidence suggests that religious societies first, and then women's clubs, provided a milieu in which women could learn to carry out public responsibilities. Since both types of organization were made up entirely of women, all the responsibilities were theirs to carry out: presiding, organizing, handling money, and carrying out programs. The missionary societies broadened their scope considerably in the last half of the nineteenth century, and women's clubs all over the country centered on a very wide variety of problems. O'Neill's book, already cited, pays a good bit of attention to the General Federation of Women's Clubs. The primary source for the early development of clubs is Mrs. J. C. Croly's documentary collection of reports from a great many of them. Another is Rheta Childe Dorr, *What Eight Million Women Want*.[21]

Women's involvement in movements for social reform also helped to change their general role in the society. The lives of the Grimké sisters, Lucretia Mott, Amelia Bloomer, Elizabeth Cady Stanton, Susan B. Anthony and Dorothea Dix provide insight into this phenomenon before the Civil War.[22] For the last half of the nineteenth century a good introduction is found in Ray Ginger's chapter, "The Women at Hull-House," in *Altgeld's America*. Allen Davis' writing on the Social Settlement movement is also relevant. Jane Addams' reflections in *Democracy and Social Ethics,* and in her writings on women's rights, show the relationship in the life and thought of one of the most important reform leaders.[23]

The drive for suffrage and expanded legal rights became, at least in the public eye, the overarching female reform movement. The beginning point is found in Richard B. Morris, *Studies in the History of American Law,* in Mrs. Spruill's book and in a significant article by Sophie H. Drinker.[24] The Flexner book picks up the early advocates of women's rights and carries the movement through the passage of the suffrage amendment. There are numerous primary sources, of which the most accessible is the massive six-volume *History of Woman Suffrage,* which is both a grab bag and a gold mine for the historian of women.[25] Books by Carrie Chapman Catt and Nettie Rogers Shuler, by Inez Hayes Irwin and by Doris Stevens are also important primary sources.[26] Important interpretations appear in Aileen S. Kraditor, *The Ideas of the Woman Suffrage Movement 1890-1920,* and in her excellent documentary collection, *Up From the Pedestal.*[27] Kraditor sees the suffrage movement as becoming somewhat more conservative and single-minded as it moved into the twentieth century.

Biography, Autobiography, Novels, and Advice Books

It has been apparent throughout this chapter that in the present beginning state of the field, historians of women are heavily dependent upon individual biographies. The recent publication of *Notable American Women,* modelled on the *Dictionary of American Biography* and superbly edited by Edward and Janet James, therefore represents a very significant contribution to the field. The three volumes contain more than thirteen hundred biographical sketches, each with bibliographical notes. Many of the essays represent the first appearance of the women in question outside the obscurity of a manuscript archive or a weighty nineteenth-century biographical encyclopedia. Taken together they provide a massive answer to the query of the uninitiated: But do American women *have* any history? These volumes should be in every school and college library, and in public libraries for the use of teachers and students alike.[28]

The bibliographies attached to the entries in the *Notable American Women* provide a comprehensive list of biographies of American women. They vary greatly in quality, and often the most useful are the old-fashioned life and letters which contain much primary material. Autobiographies are also extremely useful when used with care. No American woman has yet been the subject of a biography of the quality, for example, of Cecil Woodham-Smith's *Florence Nightingale,* but the raw material for many such exists.[29]

Another important primary source for the historian of women is the advice books published at different periods, reflecting the preoccupations of their time and delineating the accepted social expectations of women.[30]

Novels by and about women can also be illuminating. An interpretation of the nineteenth-century novel which contributes to our understanding of the female subculture is Helen Papashvily, *All the Happy Endings.*[31]

Ideology

Though it is sometimes argued that American feminism has lacked an ideology, some American women have made significant contributions to the ongoing discussion of "the woman question." One of the earliest of these was Judith Sargent Murray, whose thoughts on the equality of the sexes were first published in the eighteenth century, preceding Mary Wollstonecraft. The next such work was Sarah Grimké's *Letters on the Equality of the Sexes,* which was soon followed by Margaret Fuller, *Woman in the Nineteenth Century.* Charlotte Perkins Gilman's *Women and Economics* came at the end of the nineteenth century, and Mary Beard's *Woman as Force in History* early in the twentieth. An interesting and not well-known work by Jessie Taft, *The Woman Movement from the Point of View of Social Consciousness,* was submitted for a Ph.D. degree in philosophy at the University of Chicago.[32]

The contemporary woman's movement inspired a whole issue of *Daedalus* in 1964 (subsequently expanded into a book) wherein various thinkers were given free rein to speculate on the subject. Books by Betty Friedan, Kate Millett and—possibly—Germaine Greer will prove useful to the historian of the future who seeks to understand the dynamics of the Woman's Liberation Movement.[33]

At this point in time the most interesting aspect of women's history is not its past (wherein women were neglected, though occasional excellent work was done) or its present, which is suffering from the confusion and chaos attendant upon rapid growth, faddishness and other ills common to the twentieth century, but its future. Enough work has now been done to demonstrate beyond peradventure that women have been a significant part of the American scene from the beginning. Plans are afoot for the production of a comprehensive bibliographical guide for scholars, and the influx of able young scholars holds great promise. At a time when the historical profession is in a state of soul-searching, prophecy is dangerous. Hope is less risky, and one hopes for a many-faceted rediscovery of the female past which will make possible a new synthesis of American history, appropriate to the late twentieth century, which encompasses all, not just a selected few, of the human beings who lived in, shaped, and enjoyed or suffered the past.

FOOTNOTES

[1] Arthur M. Schlesinger. *New Viewpoints in American History.* New York: Macmillan, 1922, Chapter VI, "The Role of Women in American History." "It is unthinkable that this neglect [of women] should continue in the new era of historical writing ushered in by the nineteenth amendment," Mr. Schlesinger wrote. Among nineteenth-century American historians, Henry Adams alone paid any attention to the role of women, primarily in *Mt. St. Michel and Chartres* and *The Education of Henry Adams,* and in his novels.

[2] Carl Degler, at Stanford, and Barbara Solomon, at Harvard, are at work on general interpretive histories of American women.

[3] *Century of Struggle: The Woman's Rights Movement in the United States.* Cambridge: Harvard University Press, 1959. Books of readings which complement Flexner include Anne Firor Scott, editor. *Women in American Life: Selected Readings.* Boston: Houghton Mifflin, 1970, and *The American Woman: Who Was She?* Englewood Cliffs, N.J.: Prentice Hall, 1970. Aileen S. Kraditor, editor, *Up From the Pedestal: Selected Writings in the History of American Feminism,* Chicago: Quadrangle, 1968, has excellent long selections from major feminist writers. William L. O'Neill, *The Woman Movement: Feminism in the United States and England,* London: Allen and Unwin, 1969, (paperback edition by Quadrangle), covers both countries. Miriam Schneir, editor, *Feminism,* New York: Random House, 1971, has a large number of very short selections. See also Gerda Lerner. *Black Women in White America: A Documentary History.* New York: Pantheon Books, 1972.

[4] *Everyone Was Brave: The Rise and Fall of Feminism in America.* Chicago: Quadrangle, 1969; *The Better Half; The Emancipation of the American Woman.* New York: Harper and Row, 1965; *Black Women in White America.* New York: Pantheon, 1972; *The Woman in American History.* Menlo Park, California: Addison-Wesley Publishing Co., 1971; *America Through Women's Eyes.* New York: Macmillan, 1933. The relevant issues of the *Annals* are Vol. LVI, Nov. 1914, "Women in Public Life"; Vol. CXLIII, May 1929, "Women and the Modern World"; and Vol. 251, May 1947, "Women's Opportunities and Responsibilities."

[5] 3 vols. Cleveland: The Arthur H. Clark Co., 1917-1919, also New York: Barnes and Noble, 1945. Chapel Hill: University of North Carolina Press, 1938. *Virginians at Home: Family Life in the Eighteenth Century.* Charlottesville: University of Virginia Press, 1952. Robert B. Bremner, editor. *Children and Youth in America: A Documentary History.* Cambridge: Harvard University Press, 1970, 1971.

[6] *Centuries of Childhood: A Social History of Family Life.* New York: A. Knopf, 1962; Stephan Thernstrom. *Poverty and Progress: Social Mobility in a Nineteenth Century City.* Cambridge: Massachusetts Institute of Technology and Harvard University, 1964; John Demos. *A Little Commonwealth: Family Life in Plymouth Colony.* New York: Oxford University Press, 1970; Philip V. Greven, Jr. *Four Generations: Population, Land and Family in Colonial Andover, Massachusetts.* Ithaca: Cornell University Press, 1970.

[7] *Jane Mecom . . . .* New York: Viking Press, 1950; *The Letters of Benjamin Franklin and Jane Mecom.* Princeton: Princeton University Press, 1950; Annie Field, editor. *Life and Letters of Harriet Beecher Stowe.* Boston: Houghton Mifflin, 1897.

[8] Robert S. and Helen Merrill Lynd. *Middletown: A Study in Contemporary American Culture.* New York: Harcourt, Brace, 1929; *Women As World Builders: Studies in Modern Feminism.* Chicago: Forbes and Co., 1913; *Our Changing Morality: A Symposium.* New York: Albert and Charles Boni, 1924; *Women and Social Progress . . . .* New York: Macmillan, 1912.

[9] Elizabeth A. Dexter. *Colonial Women of Affairs . . . .* 2nd edition, revised. Boston: Houghton Mifflin, 1931; and *Career Women of America: 1776-1840.* Francestown, N.H.: M. Jones Co., 1950. Mary Sumner Benson. *Women in Eighteenth Century America.* New York: Columbia University Press, 1935. New

York: A. Knopf, 1966. See also Eugenie A. Leonard. *The Dear-Bought Heritage.* Philadelphia: University of Pennsylvania Press, 1965.

[10] Vol. IX of U. S. Congress, Senate, *Report on Condition of Women and Children Wage-Earners in the United States.* Sen. Doc. 645, 61st Congress 2nd Session, 1910. Washington: Government Printing Office, 1910; Edith Abbott. *Women in Industry* . . . . New York: D. Appleton, 1928; Robert Smuts. *Women and Work in America.* New York: Columbia University Press, 1959; Elizabeth F. Baker. *Technology and Woman's Work.*

[11] St. Louis, Missouri: F. B. Dickerson and Co., 1885; *Fourth Annual Report of the Commissioner of Labor.* Washington: Government Printing Office, 1889; *Prisoners of Poverty: Women Wage-workers, Their Trades and Their Lives.* Boston: Roberts Bros., 1887; Mrs. John Van Vorst [Bessie van Vorst] and Marie Van Vorst. *The Woman Who Toils: Being the Experiences of Two Ladies as Factory Girls.* New York: Doubleday, 1903; Jane Addams. *Twenty Years at Hull-House.* New York: Macmillan, 1910. See John C. Farrell, *Beloved Lady: A History of Jane Addams' Ideas on Reform and Peace,* for conprehensive bibliography including hundreds of articles. See also Annie Nathan Meyer, editor. *Women's Work in America.* New York: Henry Holt, 1891.

[12] *Woman at Work* . . . . Minneapolis: University of Minnesota Press, 1951. *Woman's Labor Leader* . . . . Rockford, Ill.: Bellevue Books, 1954. See also Allen Davis. "The Women's Trade Union League: Origins and Organization." *Labor History* V: 3-17; No. 1, Winter 1964; Alice Henry. *The Trade Union Woman.* New York: D. Appleton, 1915; and Mary Field Parton, editor. *Autobiography of Mother Jones.* Chicago: C. H. Kerr, 1925.

[13] *Women in the Twentieth Century* . . . . New York: McGraw-Hill, 1933. William Chafe. *The American Woman, Her Changing Social, Economic, and Political Roles, 1920-1970.* New York: Oxford University Press, 1972.

[14] New York: Harper and Bros., 1959. See also Thomas Woody. *A History of Women's Education in the United States.* 2 vols. New York: The Science Press, 1929.

[15] Biography and bibliography for these women in Edward T. James, Janet Wilson James, and Paul S. Boyer, editors. *Notable American Women.* Cambridge: Harvard University Press, 1971.

[16] *The Educated Woman in America: Selected Writings of Catharine Beecher, Margaret Fuller, and M. Carey Thomas.* New York: Teachers College Press, Columbia University, 1965.

[17] Washington: Government Printing Office, 1867-1908. Index published 1909.

[18] *The Education of Women: Its Social Background and Its Problems.* New York: Macmillan, 1923.

[19] *A Dangerous Experiment: 100 Years of Women at the University of Michigan.* Ann Arbor: Center for the Continuing Education of Women, 1970; Eli Ginzberg and Alice M. Yohalem. *Educated American Women: Self-Portraits.* New York: Columbia University Press, 1966. See also Arthur C. Cole. *A Hundred Years of Mount Holyoke College* . . . . New Haven: Yale University Press, 1940.

[20] Anne Firor Scott. *The Southern Lady: From Pedestal to Politics, 1830-1930.* Chicago: University of Chicago Press, 1970.

[21] *The History of the Woman's Club Movement in America.* New York: H. G. Allen, 1898. Boston: Small, Maynard and Co., 1910.

[22] Gerda Lerner. *The Grimké Sisters from South Carolina: Rebels Against Slavery.* Boston: Houghton Mifflin, 1967; Otelia Cromwell. *Lucretia Mott.* Cambridge: Harvard University Press, 1958; Alma Lutz. *Created Equal: A Biography of Elizabeth Cady Stanton, 1815-1902.* New York: The John Day Co., 1940; Francis Tiffany. *Life of Dorothea Lynde Dix.* Boston: Houghton Mifflin, 1890; Ida Husted Harper. *The Life and Work of Susan B. Anthony* . . . . 3 vols. Indianapolis: Hollenbeck Press, 1898-1908; D. C. Bloomer. *Life and Writings of Amelia Bloomer.* Boston: Arena Publishing Co., 1895.

[23] *Altgeld's America.* New York: Funk and Wagnalls, 1958; Allen Davis. *Spearheads for Reform: The Social Settlements and the Progressive Movement, 1890-1914.* New York: Oxford University Press, 1967; *Democracy and Social Ethics.* Cambridge: Harvard University Press, 1964.

[24] *Studies in the History of American Law With Special Reference to the Seventeenth and Eighteenth Centuries.* New York: Columbia University Press, 1930. "Women Attorneys of Colonial Times." *Maryland Historical Magazine* 56: 335-351; No. 4, December, 1961.

[25] 6 vols. Susan B. Anthony, Elizabeth Cady Stanton, Ida Husted Harper, and Matilda Joslyn Gage, editors. Rochester, N.Y.: Fowler and Wells, 1881-1922.

[26] *Woman Suffrage and Politics . . . .* New York: Charles Scribner's Sons, 1926. *Up the Hill with Banners Flying . . . .* Penobscot, Me.: Traversity Press, 1964. *Jailed for Freedom.* New York: Boni and Liveright, 1920. See also Emma Goldman, *Anarchism and Other Essays.* 2nd rev. ed., New York: Mother Earth, 1911, for revolutionary view of the suffrage issue and Abigail Scott Duniway, *Pathbreaking . . . .* Portland, Ore.: James, Kerns, and Abbott Co., 1914, for a highly personal view of the movement in Oregon.

[27] *The Ideas of the Woman Suffrage Movement.* New York and London: Columbia University Press, 1965; *Up From the Pedestal.* Chicago: Quadrangle Books, 1968. See also Alan P. Grimes, *The Puritan Ethic and Woman Suffrage.* New York: Oxford University Press, 1967, wherein a political scientist attempts to explain the early adoption of suffrage in Wyoming and Utah.

[28] Edward T. James, Janet Wilson James, and Paul S. Boyer, editors. *Notable American Women, 1607-1950: A Biographical Dictionary.* 3 vols. Cambridge: Harvard University Press, 1971.

[29] A representative sample of useful biographies would include: Stewart Mitchell, editor. *New Letters of Abigail Adams, 1788-1801.* Boston: Houghton Mifflin, 1947; Jane Addams. *Twenty Years at Hull-House . . . .* New York: Macmillan, 1910; Jane Addams. *Second Twenty Years at Hull-House . . . .* New York: Macmillan, 1930; Ida Husted Harper. *The Life and Work of Susan B. Anthony . . . .* Indianapolis: Hollenbeck Press, 1898-1908. 3 vols.; Alma Lutz. *Susan B. Anthony . . . .* Boston: Beacon Press, 1959; Margaret Mead, editor. *Anthropologist at Work: Writings of Ruth Benedict.* Boston: Houghton Mifflin, 1959; L. Minor Blackford. *Mine Eyes Have Seen the Glory . . . .* Cambridge: Harvard Press, 1954; Louise H. de Koven Bowen. *Open Windows . . . .* Chicago: Seymour, 1946; Mary Gray Peck. *Carrie Chapman Catt.* New York: The H. W. Wilson Co., 1944; Rheta Childe Dorr. *A Woman of Fifty.* 2nd ed. New York: Funk & Wagnalls, 1924; Virginia Gildersleeve. *Many a Good Crusade: Memoirs.* New York: Macmillan, 1954; Richard Drinnon. *Rebel in Paradise: A Biography of Emma Goldman.* Chicago: University of Chicago Press, 1961; Charlotte Perkins Gilman. *The Living of Charlotte Perkins Gilman.* New York: B. Appleton, 1935; Alice Hamilton. *Exploring the Dangerous Trades: The Autobiography of Alice Hamilton, M.D.* Boston: Little, Brown, 1943; Julia Ward Howe. *Reminiscences: 1819-1899.* Boston: Houghton Mifflin, 1899; Laura E. Richards and Maud Howe Elliott. *Julia Ward Howe: 1819-1910.* 2 vols. Boston: Houghton Mifflin, 1915; Louise Hall Tharp. *Three Saints and a Sinner: Julia Ward Howe, Louisa, Annie, and Sam Ward.* Boston: Little, Brown, 1956; Josephine Goldmark. *Impatient Crusader: Florence Kelley's Life Story.* Urbana: University of Illinois Press, 1953; William Rhinelander Stewart. *The Philanthropic Work of Josephine Shaw Lowell . . . .* New York: Macmillan, 1911; Howard E. Wilson. *Mary MacDonald, Neighbor.* Chicago: University of Chicago Press, 1928; Phoebe Mitchell Kendall, editor. *Maria Mitchell: Life, Letters and Journal.* Boston: Lee and Shepard, 1896; George Herbert Palmer. *The Life of Alice Freeman Palmer.* Boston: Houghton Mifflin, 1908; Louise Hall Tharp. *The Peabody Sisters of Salem.* Boston: Little, Brown, 1950; Eleanor Roosevelt. *This Is My Story.* New York: Garden City, 1937; *This I Remember.* New York: Harper, 1949; *It Seems To Me.* New York: W. W.

Norton, 1954; *On My Own.* New York: Harper, 1958; *You Learn By Living.* New York: Harper, 1960; Joseph P. Lash. *Eleanor and Franklin: The Story of Their Relationship, Based on Eleanor Roosevelt's Private Papers.* New York: W. W. Norton, 1971; *Eleanor: The Years Alone.* New York: W. W. Norton, 1972; Louise Fargo Brown. *Apostle of Democracy: The Life of Lucy Maynard Salmon.* New York: Harper & Bros., 1943; Margaret Sanger. *An Autobiography.* New York: W. W. Norton, 1938; Vida Dutton Scudder. *On Journey.* New York: E. P. Dutton, 1937; Anna Howard Shaw. *The Story of a Pioneer.* New York: Harper & Bros. 1915; Theodore Stanton and Harriot Stanton Blatch. *Elizabeth Cady Stanton As Revealed in Her Letters, Diary and Reminiscences.* New York: Harper & Bros., 1922. 2 vols.; Alice Stone Blackwell. *Lucy Stone . . . .* Boston: Little, Brown, 1930; Virginia P. Robinson, editor. *Jessie Taft . . . .* Philadelphia: University of Pennsylvania Press, 1962; Edith Finch. *Carey Thomas of Bryn Mawr.* New York: Harper, 1947; Anne G. Pannell and Dorothea Wyatt. *Julia S. Tutwiler and Social Progress in Alabama.* University, Ala.: University of Alabama Press, 1961; Edith Wharton. *A Backward Glance.* New York: Charles Scribner's Sons, 1964; Mary Earhart Dillon. *Frances Willard . . . .* Chicago: University of Chicago Press, 1944; Jeannette Marks. *Life and Letters of Mary E. Woolley.* Washington: Public Affairs Press, 1955; Mary Church Terrell. *A Colored Woman in a White World.* Washington: Ransdell Publishing Co., 1940; Pauli Murray. *Proud Shoes: The Story of an American Family.* New York: Harper & Row, 1956; Alfreda Duster, editor. *Crusade for Justice: The Autobiography of Ida B. Wells.* Chicago: University of Chicago Press, 1970; Ray A. Billington, editor. *The Journal of Charlotte Forten: A Free Negro in the Slave Era.* New York: The Dryden Press, 1953; Sarah Bradford. *Harriet Tubman: The Moses of Her People.* New York: Corinth Books, 1961; Ethel Waters with Charles Samuels. *His Eye Is on the Sparrow; an Autobiography.* New York: Doubleday & Co., 1951.

[30] Perhaps the most widely read of these was one called *The Ladies Calling* which went through many editions in England and America, and can still be found in major libraries. An advice book by Catharine Maria Sedgwick, *Means and Ends or Self-Training,* New York: Harper & Bros., 1839, is very interesting for the insight it provides into the views of an upper-class New England woman in the Age of Jackson. A collection of advice books may be found in the Schlesinger Library at Radcliffe where there is also an excellent Ph.D. dissertation on "Changing Ideas about Women in the United States, 1776-1825" by Janet James (1954) which is based on this collection.

[31] New York: Harper and Bros., 1956.

[32] *Letters on the Equality of the Sexes and the Condition of Women . . . .* Boston: I. Knopf, 1838, and New York: B. Franklin, 1970. S. Margaret Fuller [Ossoli]. *Woman in the Nineteenth Century.* New York: Greeley and McElrath, 1845; and several subsequent editions including a reprint of the 1874 edition. Boston: Roberts Bros., 1968. Charlotte Perkins Stetson [Gilman]. *Women and Economics: A Study of the Economic Relations Between Men and Women as a Factor in Social Evolution.* Boston: Small, Maynard, and Co., 1898; and several subsequent editions including one edited by Carl N. Degler. New York: Harper and Row, 1968. *Woman as Force in History . . . .* New York: Macmillan, 1946; and several subsequent editions including New York: Collier Books, 1962. Chicago: University of Chicago Press, 1916. (The thesis was dated 1913.)

[33] "The Woman in America." *Daedalus* 93: 577-803; No. 2, Spring 1964; *The Feminine Mystique.* New York: W. W. Norton, 1963; *Sexual Politics.* Garden City: Doubleday, 1970; *The Female Eunich.* New York: McGraw-Hill, 1971.

RECENT PUBLICATIONS TO SUPPLEMENT
THE BASIC BIBLIOGRAPHY OF WOMEN'S HISTORY

Nancy L. Cott. *Root of Bitterness.* New York: E. P. Dutton, 1972. A Fine anthology of primary materials.

James L. Cooper and Sheila McIsaac Cooper. *The Roots of American Feminist Thought.* Boston: Allyn and Bacon, Inc. 1973. An excellent collection of primary documents on feminism.

Jean E. Friedman and William G. Shade. *Our American Sisters.* Boston: Allyn and Bacon, Inc. 1973. A collection of articles on women's history.

J. Stanley Lemons. *The Woman Citizen: Social Feminism in the 1920's.* Urbana: University of Illinois Press, 1973. A study of what happened after suffrage which corrects many of the widespread misapprehensions about feminism in the 1920's.

· 8 ·

The History
of the American City

Raymond A. Mohl

HISTORIANS came late to the study of the city. They lagged far behind scholars in other disciplines who, by the turn of the twentieth century, had begun to apply the tools of the social sciences, especially political science and sociology, to the examination of urban America. National politics, diplomacy, and military exploits absorbed the attention of most early historians, while Frederick Jackson Turner's "frontier thesis" focused the attention of others on the West. To be sure, a few of the classic historians, notably John Bach McMaster and Edward Channing, alluded to the importance of the city in their multi-volume treatments of the American past, but their efforts failed to generate further research as had Turner's writing.[1] But by the 1930's, Turner himself had written of the need for an "urban reinterpretation" of American history and began collecting materials for a never completed essay on "The Significance of the City in American History."[2] Achieving academic respectability of a sort with the writings of Arthur M. Schlesinger and Carl Bridenbaugh in the 1930's, urban history developed slowly over the next several decades.[3] But since the early 1960's, reflecting increased awareness of the modern city and its multiple crises, the literature of American urban history has grown enormously. The quality of this writing has varied widely, and the diversity of approaches utilized by urban historians reveals a field in turmoil. Historians do not agree, as Charles N. Glaab has suggested, whether urban history is "the history of cities, the history of urbanization, or the history of anything that takes place in an urban setting."[4] In a similar vein, Stephan Thernstrom has written that "urban history apparently deals with cities, or with city-dwellers, or with events that transpired in cities, or with attitudes toward cities— which makes one wonder what is *not* urban history."[5] Each approach has its practitioners and many excellent studies of each kind have been published. It is not the purpose of this chapter to pick sides in this internal dispute nor to pretend comprehensiveness of coverage; its objective, simply, is to indicate some of the key interpretive works in the field and suggest the richness and variety of American urban history.

Overviews

A number of interpretive surveys of the history of the American city have been published. In 1940, for example, Arthur M. Schlesinger published his influential article, "The City in American History," the first conscious effort to identify the impact of urban civilization on American life.[6] Adopting a causal interpretation, Schlesinger contended that the city played an important role throughout American history: in stimulating the revolutionary spirit in colonial America, in forging an alliance of business interests behind the federal Constitution, in bringing on the Civil War between the urban North and the rural South, in fostering the agrarian protest of the late nineteenth century. An early critic of Schlesinger's causal approach, William Diamond, in an essay "On the Dangers of an Urban Interpretation of History," found difficulties in Schlesinger's methodology and in his ambiguous use of the terms "city" and "urban."[7] Diamond suggested that developments Schlesinger attributed to urbanization might equally be ascribed to other social changes such as industrialization. Despite these criticisms, the Schlesinger article remains important as a summary statement of an earlier generation of urban historians. Other brief essays which similarly probe the meaning of the American urban experience have been written by Bayrd Still, Richard C. Wade, and Blake McKelvey.[8]

The best full-length treatment of American urban history is Charles N. Glaab and A. Theodore Brown, *A History of Urban America,* an interpretive text which synthesizes much available monographic literature and which, with the exception of two chapters, deals mainly with the nineteenth century.[9] A less comprehensive but nevertheless useful survey is Constance McL. Green's *The Rise of Urban America,* which, like Schlesinger's early essay, often fails to distinguish the distinctly urban from the larger story of American history as a whole.[10] More important is her book, *American Cities in the Growth of the Nation,* which contains chapters on various types of cities—seaport cities of the early nineteenth century, river cities of the Ohio and Mississippi valleys, New England manufacturing cities (Holyoke and Naugatuck), and Great Plains cities (Denver and Wichita)—as well as on several important individual cities (Chicago, Seattle, Detroit, and Washington).[11] These cities or groups of cities are used to illustrate various stages of urban development throughout the course of United States history. More narrowly focused, chronologically, but much more comprehensive in depth of treatment are two volumes by Blake McKelvey. In *The Urbanization of America, 1860-1915,* McKelvey took an all-inclusive, almost encyclopedic, approach and included material on economic and demographic developments, urban government and municipal services, social tensions, welfare and reform movements, and urban culture.[12] Among his many conclusions, he found in urbanization the stimulus for a new and expanded industrial society. Increasing population densities fostered intensified urban tensions and problems, which in turn were met in creative and innovative ways by municipal governments and city residents. McKelvey's second volume, *The Emergence of Metropolitan America, 1915-1966,* emphasizes the relationship between metropolitan problems and the federal government, but is less effective as a survey of twentieth-century urban development.[13] Contrasting with the usual concern of urban historians for large cities, Page Smith's *As a City upon a Hill: The Town in American History* focuses on the enduring importance of small towns.[14] These overviews of urban development in the United States are important starting points for teachers and students. At the same time, they provide useful perspectives for examining more detailed urban biographies and the monographic literature of American urban history.

Urban Biographies

During the 1940's and 1950's, the urban biography provided the format for most scholarly writing on the history of American cities. Efforts to come to grips with the entire span of a single city's history, urban biographies usually emphasize the themes of urban progress, evolving city maturity, and economic growth, while focusing at the same time on the unique characteristics of the city in question. Outstanding examples of this kind of urban history can be found in Blake McKelvey's four-volume history of Rochester, New York, in Bessie L. Pierce's three-volume study of Chicago, in Constance McL. Green's two-volume biography of Washington, and in Bayrd Still's one-volume history of Milwaukee.[15] Scholarly urban biographies have also been written of Norfolk, Memphis, Pittsburgh, Detroit, Houston, Los Angeles, Cairo (Illinois), Lubbock (Texas), Everett (Washington), Neenah-Menasha (Wisconsin), Owatonna (Minnesota), and a number of New England cities: New Haven and Naugatuck in Connecticut, Holyoke and Chicopee in Massachusetts, and Harrisville in New Hampshire.[16] Numerous books have covered limited periods in the history of such cities as New York, Brooklyn, Detroit, Fort Wayne, Pittsburgh, Washington, and Kansas City.[17] Additional studies are treated separately in other sections of this chapter. One important line of argument within the urban field contends that only detailed case studies such as those mentioned above can make possible larger generalizations about the processes of urbanization. Some more recent scholars, however, disparage the urban biography approach, advocating comparative analysis or research on the process of city building instead. Nevertheless, the best of city biographies have provided important insight into the urban past. But, in the 1960's, the biographical approach to the city was surpassed by a proliferation of studies focusing on special themes or topics within an urban setting.

The Colonial City and Town

Carl Bridenbaugh's massively researched volumes, *Cities in the Wilderness* and *Cities in Revolt,* remain essential for study of the colonial city.[18] Focusing on the five largest colonial towns—Boston, Philadelphia, New York, Charleston, and Newport—both books exhaustively trace urban commerce and economic expansion, mounting social problems, patterns of municipal government, and evidences of cultural expression in the cities. Bridenbaugh emphasized the gradual development of a mature colonial civilization as reflected in the leading seaports, which by the end of the colonial period had become thriving centers for the collection, production, and distribution of goods. Moreover, city residents continually met common urban problems through collective action, a pattern which carried over into the emerging revolutionary crisis with Great Britain. A number of historians followed up the themes first outlined by Bridenbaugh. Darrett B. Rutman examined Boston's first twenty years in *Winthrop's Boston: Portrait of a Puritan Town, 1630-1649,* while G. B. Warden covered a later period in *Boston, 1689-1776.*[19] Philadelphia is the subject of Carl and Jessica Bridenbaugh's *Rebels and Gentlemen: Philadelphia in the Age of Franklin,* Frederick B. Tolles' *Meeting House and Counting House: The Quaker Merchants of Colonial Philadelphia, 1682-1783,* and Arthur L. Jensen's *The Maritime Commerce of Colonial Philadelphia.*[20] Very little was written before 1970 on urbanism in colonial New York, although two books by Thomas J. Condon and Van Cleaf Bachman probed the Dutch experience in New Amsterdam in the first half of the seventeenth century.[21] In an older but still important essay on "The Economic Causes of the Rise of Baltimore," Clarence P. Gould attributed the growth of a mid-eighteenth century "boom town" to its emergence as a center for middle-colony wheat exportation.[22] Thomas J. Wertenbaker's *The Golden Age of Colonial Culture* portrays colonial New York, Boston, Philadelphia, Charleston, Annapolis, and Williamsburg as "crucibles of culture."[23] The economic and political role of Williamsburg, Virginia's colonial capital, has been analyzed in books by James H. Soltow and Carl Bridenbaugh.[24]

As noted earlier, Page Smith has suggested the importance of the small town in American history. Although few colonial towns had sufficient population to meet modern definitions of an urban area, most nevertheless fulfilled traditional urban functions by serving as centers for the exchange of goods, services, and ideas. One of the important case studies of the colonial town, Charles S. Grant's *Democracy in the Connecticut Frontier Town of Kent* sought to determine the extent of economic, political, and social democracy in a single town.[25] Grant concluded that economic opportunity was extensive, at least in the early stages of settlement; that political participation, while "incomplete," was more widespread than usually suggested, especially at the town-meeting level; and that social structure became increasingly stratified, dominated by an "elite of ability." In *A New England Town: The First Hundred Years,* Kenneth A. Lockridge described the town of Dedham, Massachusetts, as characterized by stability and social harmony, but only in the seventeenth century; by the eighteenth, the pressure of rising population on limited town land resources fostered economic decline, social stratification, political conflict, and popular discord.[26] By contrast, Michael Zuckerman, in *Peaceable Kingdoms: New England Towns in the Eighteenth Century,* found autonomous, "consensual communities" which enforced compliance, conformity, and social harmony.[27] Other studies of Massachusetts towns, often utilizing the insights of historical demography, cultural anthropology, and social psychology, include books by Sumner Chilton Powell on Sudbury, by John Demos on Plymouth, by Darrett B. Rutman on Plymouth, and by Philip J. Greven, Jr. on Andover.[28] In an important article on "The Absence of Towns in Seventeenth-Century Virginia," John C. Rainbolt suggested that, despite continuous governmental efforts to promote town building as a means of social and economic control, geography, impractical legislation, local animosities, and political conflict between the colonial planters and the crown over the purposes of towns inhibited the development of urbanism in colonial Virginia.[29]

The role of the city in the American Revolution has been inadequately explored. Only a few studies offer insight into urban tensions which fostered radical action or stimulated revolutionary politics. Following a theme enunciated a half-century ago by Arthur M. Schlesinger,

Benjamin W. Labaree's *Patriots and Partisans: The Merchants of Newburyport, 1764-1815* examines the motives of a pro-revolutionary mercantile elite.[30] Richard Walsh, in *Charleston's Sons of Liberty: A Study of the Artisans, 1763-1789,* found urban workers at the forefront of the revolutionary movement.[31] Similarly, important articles by Jesse Lemisch and Staughton Lynd identify strong working-class participation in revolutionary activity.[32] Richard D. Brown's *Revolutionary Politics in Massachusetts: The Boston Committee of Correspondence and the Towns, 1772-1774* shows the influence of city leaders in propagating revolutionary attitudes and action throughout the countryside.[33] Both Hiller B. Zobel's *The Boston Massacre* and Pauline Maier's articles on colonial mobs and violence reveal the depth of anti-British hostility in the cities by the 1770's and suggest that urban riots had important political uses.[34] Jackson Turner Main's *The Social Structure of Revolutionary America* contains information on urban class structure and mobility during the late eighteenth century.[35] Aside from these few works, the city in the American Revolution remains an untouched area for historical research.

Economic Growth, Transportation, and Urban Rivalries

Many urban historians have related urbanization to economic development and focused on the urban commerical rivalries which frequently spurred city growth. These ideas form the prevailing theme of *The Growth of the Seaport Cities, 1790-1825,* edited by David T. Gilchrist.[36] A collection of papers and a transcript of discussions at a conference on urban history, the book analyzes the role of population growth, commerce, banking, manufacturing, and transportation in the shaping of New York, Boston, Philadelphia, and Baltimore in the early nineteenth century. Robert G. Albion's older book, *The Rise of the New York Port, 1815-1860,* remains unsurpassed in explaining the economic dominance of New York City.[37] Albion attributed New York's success to aggressive merchant leadership and the introduction of several important business innovations, including regularly scheduled shipping service to Europe, an economically efficient auction system, and the development of banking and insurance services. New Yorkers also won control of disposal of Southern cotton and thus came to dominate the coastal carrying trade as well as overseas commerce. The success of the Erie Canal in tapping the produce of a vast hinterland simply solidified the commercial primacy of New York City. Geographer Jean Gottmann's massive study, *Megalopolis: The Urbanized Northeastern Seaboard of the United States,* contains historical sections elaborating the economic role of the Atlantic seaport cities.[38] Important articles by George Rogers

Taylor, Allen R. Pred, and Jeffrey G. Williamson treat population expansion, manufacturing, and economic growth, respectively, in the preindustrial city of the nineteenth century.[39]

Construction of transportation facilities frequently stimulated city growth and fostered what one historian has called "urban imperialism"—commercial rivalries among cities for economic domination of a hinterland. Many historians have focused on these interrelated themes. The early studies of James W. Livingood on the Baltimore-Philadelphia trade rivalry, by Wyatt W. Belcher on the economic rivalry between Chicago and St. Louis, by Edward C. Kirkland on urbanization and transportation in New England, and by Glenn C. Quiett on railroads and cities in the West, cover important ground and remain useful.[40] More recently, in *Canal or Railroad,* Julius Rubin compared the responses of businessmen in Baltimore, Boston, and Philadelphia to the success of the Erie Canal in New York.[41] Several newer works showed the importance of railroads in promoting urban growth. Charles N. Glaab, in *Kansas City and the Railroads,* described one city's maturation as a regional metropolis as the result of promotional activities by land speculators and city builders who aggressively sought rail transportation for their frontier village.[42] In *New Orleans and the Railroads,* Merl E. Reed analyzed the largely unsuccessful efforts of a well-established, ante-bellum, commercial city to expand its hinterland and its economic base through publicly and privately financed rail systems.[43] Leonard P. Curry, in *Rail Routes South: Louisville's Fight for the Southern Market, 1865-1872,* illustrated the "urban imperialism" theme in discussing Louisville's rivalry with Cincinnati over control of southern trade.[44]

The City in the West

The city in the West has provided another fruitful theme for urban historians. A pioneer study in this field is Richard C. Wade, *The Urban Frontier: The Rise of Western Cities, 1790-1830,* a comparative study of life in Pittsburgh, Cincinnati, Louisville, Lexington, and St. Louis.[45] Countering the Turnerian conception of westward development, Wade found that the western towns "were the spearheads of the frontier." Established well in advance of the agricultural population, the river cities especially became regional market and manufacturing centers and facilitated settlement of surrounding farmlands. Bayrd Still's early article, "Patterns of Mid-Nineteenth-Century Urbanization in the Middle West," similarly focuses on the urban dimension of the frontier experience, revealing comparable trends in economic development and municipal government in five Great Lake cities—Buffalo, Cleveland, Detroit,

Chicago, and Milwaukee.[46] By contrast another older study, Lewis Atherton's *Main Street on the Middle Border,* shows that not all western towns grew into great cities.[47] Treating the cultural and economic history of small midwestern country towns (less than 5,000 population) from Ohio through the Dakotas, and covering the period from 1865 to 1950, Atherton found a central theme in stability fostered by a sense of community notably absent in larger cities. These pre-1960 studies stimulated an awareness among historians of an urban side of the frontier story.

Several more recent works followed in this tradition. Among the best of these, Robert R. Dykstra's book on *The Cattle Towns* interweaves a variety of themes in recounting the social history of five Kansas cattle centers—Abilene, Ellsworth, Wichita, Dodge City, and Caldwell.[48] Situated at the juncture of cattle trails from Texas and railroads to midwestern cities, the cattle towns flourished between 1867 and 1885 but then declined; only Wichita arrived at metropolitan status in the twentieth century. The cattle trade provided the context for "town-building" —efforts by local entrepreneurs to attract population, transportation, and capital investment. Town promotion, local boosterism, and vigorous competition with rival towns revealed urban aspirations on the frontier. Dykstra also contended that social conflict stemming from rural-urban hostilities, local politics, business factionalism, and differing views on social reform and law enforcement typified the cattle towns and supplied the format for community decision-making, and thus change and progress. The comparative approach is also utilized in Kenneth Wheeler's *To Wear a City's Crown,* a study of mid-nineteenth century urban growth in Texas.[49] Wheeler described and analyzed economic, municipal, cultural, and social conditions in San Antonio, Galveston, Houston, and Austin, finding markedly different patterns in each. Much older than its competitors, San Antonio was really a Mexican town, dependent on trade with Mexico, slowly becoming Americanized. Both port cities exporting cotton, sugar, and wool, Houston and Galveston responded differently to economic opportunity; merchants in Houston aggressively drew the produce of the state, while less innovative businessmen in Galveston failed to capitalize upon potentialities offered by railroads. Although a political center, the planned interior capital city of Austin never developed commercially. Like Wade, Wheeler found the towns ante-dating full settlement of the agricultural frontier.

Other useful studies have revealed the diversity of urbanism in the American West. In *Rocky Mountain Mining Camps: The Urban Frontier,* Duane A. Smith systematically described life, work, municipal government, and urban problems in the boom towns of the mining frontier between 1859 and 1890.[50] Although the mining towns often had a transitory existence, some became centers of permanent settlement based on growth in agriculture, industry, and transportation. James B. Allen's *The Company Town in the American West* similarly depicts a unique form of urbanization using materials from nearly two hundred company-owned towns in eleven Far West states.[51] Mostly built by coal, copper, and lumber companies, the towns faced like problems of housing, welfare, and management, and all had a "company store." Allen downplayed evidence of company oppression and paternalism and emphasized "positive" aspects of company towns. In *Urban Populism and Free Silver in Montana,* Thomas A. Clinch examined the urban, trade unionist character of Montana populism.[52] Robert L. Martin, in *The City Moves West,* dealt with six county-seat towns of over 10,000 population in central west Texas which grew primarily after 1930 as a result of oil discoveries.[53] A chapter in Earl Pomeroy's *The Pacific Slope* traces urban development in the Far West, mainly California, Oregon, Washington, and Utah.[54] The growth of Salt Lake City and other Mormon towns forms an integral part of Leonard J. Arrington's *Great Basin Kingdom: An Economic History of the Latter-day Saints, 1830-1900.*[55] In *The Americans: The National Experience,* Daniel J. Boorstin included a segment on "upstart cities" of the West, characterized by the "booster" or promotional spirit.[56]

The City in the South

There are several recent full-length treatments of urbanism in the South. John G. Clark's *New Orleans, 1718-1812: An Economic History* attributes the Mississippi River port's slow growth during the French and Spanish periods to an inadequate economic base and a circumscribed hinterland.[57] By the American Revolution, however, British merchants had recognized the strategic importance of the city in relation to British colonies in Illinois, Florida, and the West Indies. The gradual migration of American farmers to the Ohio and Mississippi valleys solidified the commercial importance of the city by the beginning of the nineteenth century. New Orleans in a later period is the subject of Robert C. Reinders, *End of an Era: New Orleans, 1850-1860,* which contends that the pursuit of commerce by a newly rich business elite provides the key to understanding the city's character and history.[58] George C. Rogers, Jr., in *Charleston in the Age of the Pinckneys,* evoked an image of the South Carolina city between the mid-eighteenth and mid-nineteenth centuries as an economic and cultural center, but increasingly becoming a "closed city" dominated by a pro-slave elite unwilling to countenance change.[59] In *Antebellum Natchez,* D. Clayton James examined the social, economic, and political history of a relatively unimportant Mississippi River town.[60] Emory M. Thomas's *The Confederate State of Richmond* analyzes the history of the Confederate capital during the Civil War years.[61] By contrast, Kenneth Coleman's *Confederate Athens* reveals the pressures of war on a small Georgia town of 4,000 persons.[62] Gerald M. Capers, in *Occupied City: New Orleans under the Federals, 1862-1865,* describes the impact of Federal occupation on the city's government, social institutions, economy, and population—both Black and white.[63] Urbanism in the "New South" is discussed in an article by Durward Long on Tampa, Florida.[64] An earlier but still important book edited by Rupert B. Vance and Nicholas J. Demerath, *The Urban South,* views twentieth-century southern cities from the perspective of the several social sciences and deals with such diverse subjects as mobility, fertility, crime, social class, race relations, politics, and city planning.[65]

Immigrants in the City*

The writings of Oscar Handlin continue to provide a point of reference for the study of immigrants in the city. Handlin's classic work, *The Uprooted: The Epic Story of the Great Migrations that Made the American People,* reveals the intense problems of adjustment and the "shock of alienation" faced by European peasants in the modern American city.[66] His earlier book, *Boston's Immigrants: A Study in Acculturation,* deals primarily with the Irish between 1790 and 1880 and analyzes the process of adjustment, the development of group consciousness, the emergence of nativism, and the gradual integration of the immigrants within the larger society by the Civil War period.[67] Another important older work, Robert Ernst's *Immigrant Life in New York City, 1825-1863,* remains unsurpassed in handling similar themes for the nation's metropolis.[68] Covering the same period, Earl F. Niehaus' *The Irish in New Orleans, 1800-1860* distinguishes between the "old" Irish (pre-1830) and the "famine" Irish (1830-1860) and details ethnic working and voting patterns, the role of the Catholic Church and other immigrant institutions, and Irish conflict with Blacks.[69] In *Immigrant City: Lawrence, Massachusetts, 1845-1921,* Donald B. Cole

---

* For additional treatment of this topic, the reader is referred to the following chapters: Rudolph J. Vecoli, "European Americans: From Immigrants to Ethnics," *passim;* Rodolfo Acuña, "Freedom in a Cage: The Subjugation of the Chicano in the United States," *passim;* and Roger Daniels, "The Asian American Experience," *passim.*

identified the "search for security" as the key to the immigrant experience in a model factory town which quickly became a notorious city of slums and, eventually, the setting for a great I.W.W. textile strike in 1912.[70] Gerd Korman's *Industrialization, Immigrants, and Americanizers: The View from Milwaukee, 1866-1921* is a unique study in immigrant, business, and urban history which discusses labor procurement practices, industrial safety and welfare work, and business-dominated Americanization programs.[71] Similarly important, *Beyond the Melting Pot: The Negroes, Puerto Ricans, Jews, Italians, and Irish of New York City,* by Nathan Glazer and Daniel P. Moynihan, emphasizes ethnicity in the twentieth-century city.[72]

Two recent studies have focused on the ethnic experience in Chicago. In his important study, *The Italians in Chicago, 1880-1930,* Humbert S. Nelli analyzed the impact of immigration and urban living on the newcomers.[73] Primarily from southern Italy and Sicily and with few communal traditions beyond the nuclear family, Chicago's Italians developed a strong sense of community based upon the Church, mutual benefit societies, "colonial" newspapers, and ethnic trade unions. Nelli contended that the immigrant colony and its institutions represented a departure from old-world traditions and thus advanced rather than retarded assimilation. John M. Allswang, in *A House for All Peoples: Ethnic Politics in Chicago, 1890-1936,* used a sophisticated behavioralist methodology and concludes that ethnic identification, more than any other variable, determined voting behavior in Chicago.[74] Allswang argued that ethnocultural issues such as prohibition and immigration restriction catalyzed the immigrant vote and led to a new ethnic alignment with the Democratic party between 1928 and 1931.

Moses Rischin's *The Promised City* is a scholarly study of the Jewish community of New York City between 1870 and 1914 set against the background of urban problems and reform.[75] Migrating in massive numbers from Russia and Eastern Europe during this period, New York's Jews developed a strong group consciousness under pressures of the modern city. The search for "community" expressed in charitable organizations, Yiddish language and literature, trade unions, and socialism, forms a central theme of the book. A similar thesis is elaborated in Arthur A. Goren's *New York Jews and the Quest for Community,* which examines the kehillah, or communal council, movement in New York, 1908-1922—an effort to break down barriers between German and East European Jews and restore a communal tradition.[76] Numerous other studies, some more antiquarian than scholarly, have dealt with Jewish communities in Buffalo, Syracuse, Baltimore, Los Angeles, and New Orleans.[77]

Blacks in the City*

While some historians have studied ethnic groups in an urban locale, others have focused on Blacks in the city. Richard C. Wade's *Slavery in the Cities: The South, 1820-1860* is an important book which counters the traditional conception of slavery as a rural institution.[78] Significantly different from plantation slavery, urban bondage was typified by slaves who hired themselves out, worked in industrial or skilled as well as domestic occupations, lived separate from their masters, and developed their own forms of independent community. In contrast to the static and unchanging nature of slavery on the plantation, slavery in the cities was a dynamic institution. At first, cities registered an increase in the number of slaves, who comprised at least 20 per cent of the population of the major southern cities in 1820. But gradually, Wade contended, the nature of urban living contributed to a general loosening of slave bonds; a relative degree of freedom, association with free Blacks, the activities of liquor sellers, and other "corrosive" influences blurred the distinction between slave and free. Coming to fear unregulated urban slaves, Southern whites sought to retain control through slave codes and segregation ordinances, while numerous male slaves were sold off to plantations, leaving an imbalance of females in the cities. By 1860, according to Wade, urban slavery was "disintegrating." A more recent study, however, Robert S. Starobin's *Industrial Slavery in the Old South,* contradicts the Wade interpretation, arguing that slavery was not dying in the cities, but rather that the use of slaves in industrial occupations was on the increase.[79] Covering free Blacks in the North during the same period, Gilbert Osofsky's article, "The Enduring Ghetto," and Leon Litwack's book, *North of Slavery: The Negro in the Free States, 1790-1860*, reveal general patterns of repression and discrimination against Blacks in northern cities.[80] While not strictly urban history, both the Starobin and Litwack books provide some useful perspectives on Blacks in the ante-bellum city, North and South.

Other works have examined the Black experience in the city in the late nineteenth and early twentieth centuries. One of the best studies of this kind is Gilbert Osofsky, *Harlem: The Making of a Ghetto; Negro New York, 1890-1930.*[81] Seeking better economic opportunities, Blacks migrated to northern cities in substantial numbers after 1890. Almost uniformly they found racial hatred, violence, and segregated patterns of housing and employment. With the exception of some white progressives,

---

* For additional treatment of this topic, the reader is referred to the chapter by John W. Blassingame, "The Afro-Americans: From Mythology to Reality," *passim.*

most New Yorkers responded to the Black influx with intensified racism, typified in the New York race riot of 1900. Harlem's transition from an upper-middle class white area to a Black ghetto, Osofsky contended, was due to the collapse of a real estate and building boom in the early years of the twentieth century. Houses and apartments built in Harlem by speculators went unrented until the Black-owned Afro-American Realty Company began acquiring long-term leases on such properties and renting them to Blacks—a move which soon forced out neighboring whites and drew newcomers from older Black sections (especially the "Tenderloin" and "San Juan Hill" districts on the West Side) as well as from the American South and the West Indies. Intensified Black migration between 1910 and 1930 made Harlem overcrowded, for few Blacks found housing elsewhere in the city. High rents forced families to double up in apartments or take in boarders. Congested housing stimulated health and sanitary problems and contributed to social disorganization among the primarily rural migrants who had difficulty adjusting to urban life. By the 1920's, Harlem had become a slum as well as a ghetto. Using a somewhat larger chronological framework and going beyond housing to discuss labor, politics, and community institutions such as churches, Seth M. Scheiner in *Negro Mecca: A History of the Negro in New York City, 1865-1920* similarly found white racism central to the Black experience in the urban North.[82]

Comparable to the Osofsky and Scheiner books, Allan H. Spear's *Black Chicago: The Making of a Negro Ghetto, 1890-1920* analyzes the emergence of Chicago's South Side ghetto as primarily the product of organized white discrimination and racism, especially in the areas of housing and jobs.[83] Contending that formation of the ghetto predated the great World War I migration of southern Blacks, Spear focused on the institutions and ideologies of Chicago's Black community. In the late nineteenth century, Black leaders fought against the biracial system, resisted discrimination, and sought full integration. Consequently, the development of Black institutions lagged and Blacks in business and politics remained dependent on whites. As white hostility intensified in the early twentieth century, a new Black leadership emerged which challenged old assumptions and found racial solidarity and self-help more important than a direct attack on white racism. Heightened Black race consciousness thus stimulated institutional development (churches, social welfare groups, lodges and women's clubs, businesses, and political organizations) at the same time that white racism closed opportunties in housing and employment. Exacerbated by the great migration of 1915-1920, mounting racial tensions produced the bloody Chicago race riot of 1919, which Spear treats in his last chapter.

A number of other valuable studies have focused on Blacks in the city. Constance McL. Green, in *The Secret City: A History of Race Relations in the Nation's Capital,* examined the interplay between Blacks and whites over issues of education, housing, social welfare, employment, and civil rights over 175 years of Washington's history.[84] In his article on the formation of the Black ghetto of Los Angeles, Lawrence B. De Graaf recounted the familiar pattern of Black migration followed by intensified white discrimination in housing and consequent congestion and deterioration in Black sections.[85] In his *History of the Chicago Urban League,* Arvarh E. Strickland traced the development of an important institution often hampered by dependence upon white financial support and resistance of white Chicagoans to full citizenship for Blacks.[86] Violence caused by heightened interracial tensions over housing, jobs, politics, police tactics, and the use of recreational areas forms the central theme of William M. Tuttle, Jr., *Race Riot: Chicago in the Red Summer of 1919.*[87] Elliott M. Rudwick has written perceptively of a similar outbreak in *Race Riot at East St. Louis, July 2, 1917.*[88]

Municipal Services

Several historians have illuminated the urban dimension of American history with important studies of municipal services. James F. Richardson's *The New York Police: Colonial Times to 1901* illustrates the municipal response to urban crime and violence, at the same time revealing divided views about the role of the police in society.[89] Mid-nineteenth-century libertarians opposed a uniformed force as a kind of standing army; urban reformers faced the dilemma of demanding rigorous law enforcement while simultaneously seeking to limit or divide police authority. Constantly punctuated by police brutality, departmental corruption, political tampering, patronage appointments, administrative inefficiency, and uneven law enforcement, the history of the force is hardly one of which New York's "finest" can be proud. By the twentieth century, the department remained subservient to Tammany, and New York City still did not have a professional police force. Similar themes are handled sensibly in Roger Lane, *Policing the City: Boston, 1822-1885.*[90] In *Water for the Cities,* Nelson M. Blake detailed the history of urban water supply, primarily in nineteenth-century New York, Philadelphia, Boston, and Baltimore.[91] Ironically, municipal leaders at first sought water for fire protection and street cleaning and only secondarily for drinking, although public health considerations soon forced an alteration in priorities. William W. Sorrels' *Memphis' Greatest Debate: A Question of Water* provides a case study of water supply in another nineteenth-century city.[92] Historians have done very little work on urban fire protection, although two recent articles on nineteenth-century New York City by Stephen F. Ginsberg provide useful information on this important city service.[93] Urban transit is the subject of *The Electric Interurban Railways in America* by George W. Hilton and John F. Due, and of important articles by George Rogers Taylor and George M. Smerk.[94] Street lighting is the topic of Frederick M. Bender's useful article, "Gas Light, 1816-1860."[95] Generally ineffective municipal attempts to grapple with urban sanitation problems in the nineteenth century are handled in representative articles by Lawrence H. Larsen and Richard Skolnik.[96]

The history of public health in the cities has attracted several scholars. One of the best examples of this kind of history is John Duffy's *A History of Public Health in New York City, 1625-1866.*[97] Defining public health broadly, Duffy interwove such diverse subjects as municipal health administration, street cleaning and sanitation, market regulations, water supply, sewerage and drainage, epidemic diseases, medical charity and hospitals, and the medical profession. The New York experience was fraught with shortsighted municipal health policies, inefficient and often dishonest administration, bickering within the medical profession, partisan priorities at public expense, and inadequate compromise reforms which usually came after an epidemic or some other crisis generated public demand. Duffy's evidence buttresses R. Richard Wohl's suggestion that American cities have passed through a continuous series of "cycles of obsolescence"—that is, that cities and urban institutions have been shaped by a haphazard succession of expedients and temporary solutions to pressing municipal problems.[98] Duffy's forthcoming second volume will carry the story of public health in New York City down to the present. John B. Blake's *Public Health in the Town of Boston, 1630-1822* also treats public health within the broad context of one major city's social history.[99] Two other works, Charles E. Rosenberg's *The Cholera Years* and John Duffy's *Sword of Pestilence,* focus on the urban impact of epidemic disease. Drawing evidence and example mostly from New York City, Rosenberg's book deals with cholera outbreaks in 1832, 1849, and 1866 and the urban environments that spawned them.[100] Duffy's work analyzes the municipal response to the devastating New Orleans yellow fever epidemic of 1853.[101] James H. Cassedy, in *Charles V. Chapin and the Public Health Movement,* discusses the career of a leading sanitationist in the half century after 1880.[102] Superintendent of Health in Providence, Rhode Island, Chapin attacked outmoded health practices and promoted systematic methods and preventive techniques for maintaining public health in the city.

The history of urban public schooling has formed the subject of several works, most notably *The Irony of Early School Reform: Educational Innovation in Mid-Nineteenth Century Massachusetts,* by Michael B. Katz.[103] The book focuses on three educational controversies in Massachusetts: the conflict over public high schools in Beverly and Groton, the contest among educators over the new "soft-line" pedagogy of reformers like Horace Mann, and disagreement over new and less punitive state reform schools. Katz argued that middle- and upper-class groups imposed educational reforms such as high schools upon the immigrant and industrial working class as a technique of social control. At the same time, he demonstrated that the lower classes rejected educational innovations ostensibly designed for their benefit. Marvin Lazerson's recent work, *Origins of the Urban School,* covers public education in Massachusetts in the late nineteenth and early twentieth centuries.[104] Much of Lawrence A. Cremin's *The Transformation of the School: Progressivism in American Education, 1876-1957* deals with urban education, as does Raymond E. Callahan's *Education and the Cult of Efficiency.*[105] Both books are concerned with the complex of ideas labeled "progressive" education, the social forces shaping those ideas, and the way they were expressed in instructional and administrative practices. A narrower study, Sol Cohen's *Progressives and Urban School Reform,* presents the history of the Public Education Association of New York City, a powerful pressure group which has promoted educational innovation and reform since its origin in 1895.[106]

Bosses and Reformers

Interest in urban history has sparked a new examination of urban political machines, especially the emergence of bossism in the late nineteenth and early twentieth centuries. An essential point of departure is provided by Jerome Mushkat's book, *Tammany: The Evolution of a Political Machine, 1789-1865,* which traces the origins of an important early political institution whose expedient politics and pragmatic appeals to voters kept it at the center of power and paved the way for the bossism of a later period.[107] An important reinterpretation of the boss phenomenon was offered by Seymour J. Mandelbaum in his book, *Boss Tweed's New York.*[108] Unlike the more straightforward scholarly account by Alexander B. Callow, *The Tweed Ring,*[109] the Mandelbaum book utilizes a communications model drawn from the social sciences to explain the success of the boss in achieving and wielding power. Mandelbaum contended that New York City in the late nineteenth century suffered from a primitive communications network, one lacking effective channels for the distribution of information, which hampered municipal decision-making. Facing the massive problems of an expanding metropolis and with authority diffused and fragmented, municipal government remained uncoordinated, decentralized, and ineffective. Only the political boss, who lubricated the wheels of government with a "big pay-off," according to Mandelbaum, was able to overcome the archaic communications barrier and supply the necessary coordination and centralization, though extra-legal and often illegal. Thus, the boss brought needed improvements in streets, docks, sewers, bridges, and parks, although at frightful cost, whereas the reformers who followed cut back on city services in a drive for honesty and economy. Boss Tweed, this argument runs, overcame the disorder of the city and provided positive government.

The boss as provider of positive government also forms the central thesis of Zane L. Miller's *Boss Cox's Cincinnati.*[110] According to Miller's analysis, disorder and conflict accompanied Cincinnati's rapid growth in the late nineteenth century and destroyed the old "walking city" and the sense of community which characterized it. Fashioning a Republican political machine supported by the ethnic poor of the central city and the rich of newly annexed suburbs, Boss Cox supported moderate reforms and supplied order, unity, and stable government which eased the process of urbanization. Similarly, William D. Miller's *Mr. Crump of Memphis* describes the boss as imposing stability upon a disorderly city and supporting progressive reforms.[111] Walton Bean's *Boss Ruef's San Francisco* traces the career of a boss who rose to power through a Union Labor party and cemented a corrupt relationship between businessmen and politicians.[112] In *Boss Cermack of Chicago,* Alex Gottfried analyzed the powerful machine built by an immigrant who capitalized on an ethnic base and aggressively sought and captured citywide political power.[113] Lyle W. Dorsett's *The Pendergast Machine* takes a functional view of the classic machine in Kansas City dominated by Jim and Tom Pendergast between the 1890's and the 1930's, finding substantive urban accomplishments in boss rule.[114] In *The New Deal and the Last Hurrah: Pittsburgh Machine Politics,* Bruce M. Stave contradicted the popular conception that the New Deal destroyed boss-dominated urban machines.[115] Using quantitative data and techniques of social analysis, Stave demonstrated that by facilitating the transfer of urban political power from Republicans to Democrats, New Deal policies, especially federal work relief, actually strengthened the Democratic machine of David L. Lawrence.

Like the boss, the urban reformer has been a perennial subject of investigation. One of the most important recent books in this area of urban history is Melvin G. Holli's *Reform in Detroit: Hazen S. Pingree and Urban Politics,* which examines the career of a reform mayor in the 1890's.[116] Holli used Pingree's mayorality to illustrate two distinctly different reform traditions: structural reform, which stemmed from middle-class values and assumptions and which emphasized businesslike efficiency and honesty in government; and social reform, which displayed concern for immigrant, working-class conditions and which aimed at the root causes of urban problems rather than the symptoms. Pingree began as a typical businessman in politics, but realized by the time of the 1893 depression the need for reforms which would improve the life of most city residents. Thus, Pingree's administrations focused on municipal ownership, lower utility rates and better services, home rule, tax equalization, social welfare programs, improved schools, more parks and public baths, and other social justice reforms. Holli contradicts Richard Hofstadter's "status revolution" interpretation of progressivism, at least as far as Detroit is concerned, by demonstrating Pingree's dependence on labor and immigrant voters. A similar point had been made earlier about progressive reform by J. Joseph Huthmacher in an important article, "Urban Liberalism and the Age of Reform."[117] Important case studies of urban reform in the late nineteenth and early twentieth centuries include books on Boston by Arthur Mann, on Memphis by William D. Miller, on New Orleans by Joy J. Jackson, and on Baltimore by James B. Crooks.[118] Specific studies of urban reformers were made by Gerald Kurland on Seth Low, by Edwin R. Lewinson on John Purroy Mitchel, by Arthur Mann and Charles Garrett on Fiorello LaGuardia, by J. Joseph Huthmacher on Robert F. Wagner, and by Jack Tager on Brand Whitlock.[119]

Social Welfare

The starting place for the history of urban social welfare remains Robert Bremner's *From the Depths: The Discovery of Poverty in the United States.*[120] A broad survey covering the years from the 1830's to the 1930's, Bremner's book analyzes changing ideologies about poverty, the development of voluntary charity and professional social work, and the central concern of twentieth-century progressives for the urban poor. Several more recent studies have elaborated segments of Bremner's larger story. Raymond A. Mohl's *Poverty in New York, 1783-1825,* a volume in the Urban Life in America series, reveals the surprisingly high incidence of urban poverty and pauperism in the preindustrial period.[121] The book traces patterns of public assistance and private humanitarianism, finding evidence of hardening attitudes toward the poor. By 1825, municipal leaders and charity spokesmen had abandoned earlier benevolent precepts and uniformly blamed poverty on the poor. As immigration, industrialization, and urbanization altered the urban environment, and as old institutional forms broke down in the transitional city—disturbing changes typified by the alarming visibility of the poor—benevolence increasingly became a technique of social control, a method of restoring order and stability. A similar thesis was argued by David J. Rothman in *The Discovery of the Asylum: Social Order and Disorder in the New Republic.*[122] Analyzing the role of prisons, poorhouses, and asylums, primarily in Philadelphia, Boston, and New York, Rothman found that institutional discipline took on familial forms and sought to enforce social order at a time when urban disorder and family disorganization seemed prevalent among criminals and the poor.

Other studies in social welfare history have also expanded our knowledge of the urban past. Nathan I. Huggins' *Protestants Against Poverty: Boston's Charities, 1870-1900* analyzes changes in urban philanthropy within the context of the expanding, "fragmented" city and a consequent decline in the sense of community which characterized Boston in earlier years.[123] As Huggins suggested, charity "reformers" attempted to rationalize urban philanthropy, emphasized moral uplift rather than relief for the needy, and urged the poor to adopt middle-class values and behavior as a means of restoring their commitment to "community." The question of youth and juvenile delinquency in relation to the larger urban society is treated in Robert S. Pickett's *House of Refuge: Origins of Juvenile Reform in New York State, 1815-1857,* a study of a single institution and its influence, and in Joseph M. Hawes's *Children in Urban Society: Juvenile Delinquency in Nineteenth Century America,* a wide-ranging and sensitive analysis which finds gradual abandonment of moralistic attitudes toward youth and increasing individualization of treatment as the nineteenth century progressed.[124] Allen F. Davis' *Spearheads for Reform: The Social Settlements and the Progressive Movement, 1890-1914* discusses the primarily immigrant-oriented settlement houses which emerged by the 1890's in industrial cities.[125] The settlements, according to Davis, especially the nondenominational ones, sponsored needed neighborhood programs, tempered nativist demands for Americanization by building ethnic pride and urging preservation of immigrant heritages, and eventually led larger efforts for social and political reform as a means of improving life for immigrants and the poor. Louise C. Wade's *Graham Taylor: Pioneer for Social Justice, 1851-1938* and Daniel Levine's *Jane Addams and the Liberal Tradition* reveal these trends in two important settlements in Chicago.[126]

The Urban Worker

The working class has always formed a large and important component of urban society. Several works which might more properly be called labor history have explored the place of the urban worker and his institutions. Carl Bridenbaugh's *The Colonial Craftsman* describes the life and work patterns of artisans in the colonial city.[127] The trades union movement of the 1820's and 1830's and the role of the urban worker in the Jacksonian era have received considerable attention. In *The Age of Jackson,* Arthur M. Schlesinger, Jr., effectively advocated the "urban labor thesis" as an explanation of Jacksonian democracy.[128] This argument abandoned the sectional interpretation of Jacksonianism, found a class conflict explanation more in accord with the circumstances of the time, and held that crucial support for Jackson came from the urban lower classes. Schlesinger's work touched off an intensive investigation by historians, notably Edward Pessen and William A. Sullivan, into the workingmen's movement in New York, Philadelphia, Boston, and other cities.[129] The position of labor spokesmen and an analysis of proposed social and economic reforms are set forth in Edward Pessen's *Most Uncommon Jacksonians: The Radical Leaders of the Early Labor Movement.*[130] Walter Hugins' *Jacksonian Democracy and the Working Class* is a detailed study of the workingmen's movement in New York City.[131] *Beyond Equality: Labor and the Radical Republicans, 1862-1872,* by David Montgomery, contains important material on urban labor organization in mid-nineteenth century.[132] On a later period, Melvyn Dubofsky's *When Workers Organize: New York City in the Progressive Era* records organizational efforts among unskilled and semi-skilled workers, particularly in the garment trades, climaxed by an unsuccessful general strike in 1916.[133] In addition, urban historians have generally overlooked a number of excellent studies, written primarily by specialists in the field of industrial relations, which detail the history of the labor movement in specific cities. Representative works of this kind have covered Chicago, Milwaukee, Los Angeles, and San Francisco.[134]

The Urban Church

The role of religion in American urban life has been closely examined. An important recent study, Carroll Smith Rosenberg's *Religion and the Rise of the American City* analyzes the urban missionary movement in nineteenth-century New York City and finds the roots of the "social gospel" in the ante-bellum period.[135] Alvin W. Skardon's *Church Leader in the Cities,* which treats the career of mid-nineteenth-century urban churchman William Augustus Muhlenberg, also ties social reform to religious sponsorship.[136] A number of earlier scholars, notably Aaron I. Abell, Charles H. Hopkins, Henry F. May, and Robert D. Cross, traced the emergence of the social gospel in Protestant and Catholic churches from the post-Civil War industrial era into the twentieth century.[137] Robert D. Cross' *The Church and the City, 1865-1910* is a collection of relevant documents distinguished for its brilliant analytical introduction.[138] Cross established four useful typologies to differentiate among urban churches and their varied responses to the modern city: transformations—changes which occurred when old, established churches became "downtown" churches; transplantations—efforts, usually by newcomers, to recreate in the city churches similar to those they had known in town or country; adaptations—churches which made special efforts to deal with some specific urban problem in a special way (such as revivalism, adventism, or Christian Science); reintegrations—attempts to restore the church to a community-wide role, usually in the form of the "institutional church." Documentary selections illustrate the four typologies. Two other recent studies, both biographies, need mentioning. James F. Findlay, Jr. wrote an excellent study of an important urban revivalist preacher, Dwight L. Moody, and Jacob H. Dorn wrote a fine biography of Washington Gladden, one of the leading exponents of liberal theology and the social gospel in the late nineteenth and early twentieth centuries.[139]

Urban Violence and Social Tensions

Two exemplary books published in recent years suggest the intensity of social tension in the history of urban America. The first, Leonard L. Richards' *"Gentlemen of Property and Standing": Anti-Abolition Mobs in Jacksonian America,* focuses on urban violence, primarily in New York, Philadelphia, Cincinnati, and Utica.[140] Urging unwanted social change and condemned as "amalgamators" (that is, advocates of inter-marriage between Blacks and whites), militant abolitionists became the target of urban mobs in the 1830's and 1840's. Richards distinguished between two types of riots: the organized mob, typically premeditated and planned, which had specific limited goals and whose leadership came from the urban elite; and the unorganized mob, usually larger, more spontaneous, more destructive, composed primarily of lower-class whites more interested in terrorizing Blacks than abolitionists. The second book, Kenneth T. Jackson's *The Ku Klux Klan in the City, 1915-1930,* contradicts the traditional assumption of the Klan as primarily a rural institution, finding instead that it had surprising strength in the cities, both north and south; roughly 50 per cent of all Klan members between 1915 and 1944, according to Jackson, resided in metropolitan areas of more than 50,000 persons.[141] Jackson attributed the Klan's urban strength and popularity to the numerous disturbing and threatening changes posed by the metropolis, especially the concern of white Protestants about heavy immigration from southern and eastern Europe and migration of southern Blacks to northern cities.

City Planning, Architecture, and Housing

Several important studies of city planning were published in the 1960's. John W. Reps, *The Making of Urban America: A History of City Planning in the United States,* is a wide-ranging survey of planning up to the twentieth century which emphasizes the interplay between town design and changing American values and perceptions of "civic beauty."[142] The book is lavishly illustrated with city plans, maps, and drawings, further enhancing its value as a teaching and research tool. Reps has also published three additional studies with a more specific focus—the history of planning in colonial Virginia and Maryland, in frontier America, and in Washington, D.C.[143] Another major study, Mel Scott's *American City Planning Since 1890,* emphasizes the ideology of leading planners and their efforts to shape public policy.[144] Critical of "the persistent disposition [in planning] to favor private gain rather than the enlargement of opportunity for the general public," Scott contended that city planners can become strategists for social change in modern urban America. Clarence S. Stein's *Toward New Towns for America* is an historical and pictorial summary of the "new town" movement in the twentieth century by one who participated in that effort.[145] The close connection between zoning and urban planning, physical growth, and spatial development is suggested in Seymour Toll's *Zoned American.*[146]

A key study which integrates the history of city planning and urban architecture is *American Skyline: The Growth and Form of Our Cities and Towns* by Christopher Tunnard and Henry Hope Reed.[147] Tunnard and Reed established seven periods of city growth in the United States, each with distinctively different patterns of architecture and urban forms and each reflecting changed cultural and economic values. In *The Architecture of America: A Social and Cultural History,* John Burchard and Albert Bush-Brown provided a broad survey of American architecture emphasizing city developments.[148] Wayne Andrews' *Architecture, Ambition and Americans* covers similar ground with considerably less detail.[149] Two important books by Carl W. Condit also deal extensively with urban architecture and building.[150]

A number of specialized studies of planning and architecture provide important insights for urban history. Mel Scott wrote a case history of planning and spatial development in San Francisco entitled *The San Francisco Bay Area: A Metropolis in Perspective*.[151] In *Chicago: The Growth of a Metropolis,* Harold M. Mayer and Richard C. Wade used photographic material extensively and combined the skills of geographer and historian in tracing urban growth and physical change.[152] Edmund H. Chapman's *Cleveland: Village to Metropolis* relates planning and architecture to the physical development of the city in the nineteenth century.[153] Walter Muir Whitehill does the same for Boston in *Boston: A Topographical History*.[154] *Bulfinch's Boston, 1787-1817,* by Harold Kirker and James Kirker, interweaves political and social history with the career of Charles Bulfinch, a town selectman and civic leader, but also an influential architect whose numerous public and private buildings over several decades imposed the neo-classical Georgian, or Federal, style on early nineteenth-century Boston.[155] William H. Wilson's *The City Beautiful Movement in Kansas City* discusses an important early example of civic improvement and urban planning, arguing that American influences, primarily the work of Frederick Law Olmsted, were more significant than Roman or Parisian neo-classical styles in giving shape and inspiration to the Kansas City movement.[156] The work of Olmsted is evaluated by Albert Fein and S. B. Sutton in separate collections of the writings of this pioneer city planner, landscape and park designer, and advocate of "organic" urban growth.[157]

Several works have focused on industrial city planning or emphasized the interconnection between urban planning and housing. Stanley Buder's *Pullman: An Experiment in Industrial Order and Community Planning, 1880-1930* presents the history of George Pullman's once heralded model industrial town which quickly earned the opprobrium of workers.[158] Pullman's pervasive paternalism was reflected in the company's effort to impose social order and moral values on industrial workers while simultaneously earning extra profits through high rent and utility charges—policies which contributed directly to the violent and destructive Pullman strike of 1894. Later planned industrial towns, such as U. S. Steel's Gary, Indiana, consciously sought to avoid Pullman-type paternalism, although with notably meager results.[159] The close relationship between planning and housing is noted in two books by Roy Lubove. In *The Progressives and the Slums,* Lubove detailed the various avenues of tenement-house reform in New York City, focusing especially on the career of reformer Lawrence Veiller.[160] Lubove has also written *Community Planning in the 1920's: The Contribution of the Regional Planning Association of America*.[161] A private group headed by architects Henry Wright and Clarence Stein and generalist Lewis Mumford, the RPAA opposed metropolitan centralization, suburban diffusion, and the "dinosaur city." Instead, the group advocated community planning on a regional basis, contending that the automobile, the superhighway, and electrical power systems permitted establishment of regional cities, thus preserving rural advantages, attaining regional balance of population and resources, and achieving desirable community relationships and social goals. Recognizing that the speculative housing industry had inadequately provided for population needs in the cities, the RPAA experimented with a variety of housing types and methods of financing, but failed to convince real estate interests that good housing could be built for moderate and low-income people and still turn a profit. Joseph L. Arnold's *The New Deal in the Suburbs: A History of the Greenbelt Town Program, 1935-1954* has a similar conclusion.[162] An effort to demonstrate the advantages of "new towns" over decaying central cities and economically segregated suburbs, the greenbelt program failed, Arnold suggested, because it threatened entrenched city business interests and established urban growth patterns. Real estate people and the construction industry, for example, remained hostile to the greenbelt concept of low-cost housing as a radical challenge to private enterprise; others objected to cooperative institutions or the intermixture of poor and affluent families in the greenbelt towns.

Attitudes Toward the City

Several studies during the decade of the 1960's probed shifting attitudes toward urban life or analyzed the way Americans have perceived cities. The persistent theme of anti-urbanism in the United States provides the focus of *The Intellectual Versus the City,* by Morton and Lucia White.[163] The Whites traced hostilities to the city from the writings of Benjamin Franklin and Thomas Jefferson to those of John Dewey and Frank Lloyd Wright and found two significant varieties of anti-urban thought: a romantic view, typified by Jefferson, which saw the city as overcivilized and destructive of nature and virtue; and a reformist tradition, reflected in the thought of Jane Addams or Henry James, which saw the city as undercivilized, lacking a proper sense of community, and requiring reform. Buttressing the Whites' basic theme, Robert H. Walker's article, "The Poet and the Rise of the City," reveals an anti-urban bias in late nineteenth-century poetry, which portrays the city as filled with crime, poverty, alcoholism, sexual deviation, anxiety, and materialism—a stark contrast to the claimed virtues of rural life.[164] Similar arguments were made in earlier studies of American fiction by George Dunlap, Blanche H. Gelfant, and Eugene Arden.[165]

Yet, there is also evidence for a pro-urban tradition, as Charles N. Glaab suggests in his article, "The Historian and the American Urban Tradition."[166] Along the same lines, Michael H. Cowan, in *City of the West: Emerson, America, and Urban Metaphor,* disagreed with the Whites' evaluation of Emerson as anti-urban.[167] Cowan argued instead that although Emerson recognized the multiple dangers symbolized by urbanization, he also viewed the modern city as a potential source of great creativity and freedom. In *Back to Nature: The Arcadian Myth in Urban America,* Peter J. Schmitt contended that the "back to nature" movement of the early twentieth century did not reflect anti-city attitudes or nostalgia for a rural past.[168] Rather, nature stories, wilderness novels, movies of the outdoors, summer camps, scouting, birdwatching, and other reflections of popular culture represented an effort to reinvigorate city life on the part of those who had consciously chosen an urban habitat. In *Images of the American City,* sociologist Anslem Strauss drew upon popular writings and "partisan" urban literature to explore Americans' changing and diverse perceptions of cities as reflected in symbolic imagery.[169] Don S. Kirschner, in *City and Country: Rural Responses to Urbanization in the 1920's,* examined rural perceptions of the city, arguing that real economic distress rather than status anxiety fostered an anti-urban bias.[170] Scott Donaldson's *The Suburban Myth* is an extensive history of attitudes toward suburbs and suburbaniza-tion.[171]

New Directions in Urban History

In recent years, new questions and new techniques of analysis applied to new sources stimulated the emergence of what practitioners have called the "new urban history." In their preface to *Nineteenth-Century Cities: Essays in the New Urban History,* Stephan Thernstrom and Richard Sennett identified three characteristics shared by most studies in the new urban history: application of sociological theory to historical materials; use of quantitative techniques; and an interest in broadening the scope of urban history to include the "social experience" of the ordinary and inarticulate people normally omitted from the historian's record of the past.[172] Mostly dealing in quantitative matters, the new urban historians have concentrated on nineteenth-century cities because of the availability of manuscript census schedules (especially for the period 1850-1880); they also make use of city directories, marriage license files, birth certificates, assessors' records, bank accounts, school records, and the like. In a separate article, "Reflections on the New Urban History," Thernstrom catalogued some of the findings of recent researchers: tremendously high rates of urban population turnover; positive correlations between lack of economic success and spatial mobility in the city; and a general fluidity in rates of occupational and social mobility, although the rates varied for different ethnic groups and Blacks had considerably reduced opportunities.[173]

Only a few studies in the new urban history have reached conclusion, although many are in progress. Thernstrom's *Poverty and Progress: Social Mobility in a Nineteenth-Century City* is an important early work.[174] Utilizing samples from manuscript census schedules for Newburyport, Massachusetts, between 1850 and 1880, Thernstrom tested the conception of nineteenth-century America as a land of opportunity for the working class. He found class antagonisms, considerable out-migration of those who failed economically in the city, and generally limited upward mobility for those who remained. Wages were low, necessitating rigorous underconsumption and employment of wives and children if the family was to acquire property. An unskilled laborer often acquired a home by the end of his lifetime, but occupational mobility was usually limited to his children, who might move up to semi-skilled status. In *The Plain People of Boston, 1830-1860: A Study in City Growth,* Peter R. Knights used quantitative techniques to analyze demographic trends and population movements.[175] Among his several conclusions, Knights detected tremendously high rates of population turnover in Boston, amounting to about 40 per cent annually by the 1850's—a finding suggesting the intense flux of urban life and population. Shorter studies using similar techniques have tackled the problem of nineteenth-century mobility in Philadelphia, Paterson (New Jersey), Atlanta, Poughkeepsie (New York), San Antonio, Cairo (Illinois), Birmingham (Alabama), and Roseburg (Oregon).[176]

A few works in the "new" urban history have gone beyond quantitative mobility studies to draw larger conclusions about urban society. For example, Richard Sennett's *Families Against the City: Middle Class Homes of Industrial Chicago, 1872-1890* utilizes sociological and psychological models and applies quantitative techniques to social data in an effort to illuminate the urban and industrial impact on middle-class family life in the Union Park section of Chicago.[177] Analysis of manuscript census data showed that most Union Park residents lived in nuclear family units, that most families had few children, that children left home at a relatively advanced age, that they married late, and that occupational and social mobility between generations was limited. This evidence led Sennett to speculate that the nuclear family provided a retreat from the fearful realities of the industrial city.

A second new direction in the writing of American urban history has emphasized what Roy Lubove has called "the process of city building over time." Much of this new literature has grown from the earlier suggestions of economic historian Eric Lampard, who, in a number of articles, criticized traditional urban history, especially the city biography and the urban problems approaches on the grounds of outmoded methodology and limited vision.[178] Rather, Lampard argued, historians should be studying urbanization as a "societal process"—that is, examining "interacting elements" (such as population, topography, economy, social organization, political process, civic leadership, urban imagery) for distinctive patterns in a city's development. More recently, both Roy Lubove and Sam Bass Warner, Jr. have urged a similar approach. In an important article on "The Urbanization Process: An Approach to Historical Research," Lubove suggested the utility of the "city-building process" as a conceptual framework for analyzing decision-making, social organization, and change in the urban environment.[179] Lubove illustrated this approach in his book *Twentieth-Century Pittsburgh: Government, Business, and Environmental Change.*[180] Concerned about change in the physical environment and the nature of decision-making which effects such change, Lubove concluded that a corporate and business elite shaped the city. The elite dominated early movements for environmental change, but the voluntary character of reform organizations, the failure to use governmental coercion, and conflicting interests within the business community prevented these efforts from succeeding. But in the post-World War II period, a regional economic crisis forced the elite to overcome business factionalism and sponsor a "reverse welfare state," expanding public power to rebuild and revitalize the city's downtown, primarily for private purposes. Yet, the business-inspired Pittsburgh "Renaissance" did little to expand or improve lower-class housing, and neighborhood action groups emerged in the 1960's to challenge elite decision-making.

An important elaboration of Lampard's original suggestions, Warner's article "If All the World Were Philadelphia: A Scaffolding for Urban History, 1774-1930" provides a model for the collection and comparison of information on urban social and economic change.[181] Warner argued that there can be no systematic analysis of the process of urbanization until data for different time periods are collected on population, industrialization, social geography (residential patterns and location of workplaces), and shifts in occupation and the social organization of work. Warner applied this methodology in his book *The Private City: Philadelphia in Three Periods of Its Growth.*[182] Like Lubove, Warner focused on the city-building process. Analyzing social data from three periods in Philadelphia's history (the colonial town of 1770-1780, the big city of 1830-1860, and the industrial metropolis of 1920-1930), Warner concluded that the city has been primarily an arena for private economic opportunity. This tradition of "privatism" shaped urban decision-making and thus the city's environment as well. Philadelphia became "a community of private moneymakers" but never succeeded in creating a humane urban environment.

Warner also used a sophisticated methodology in his earlier book, *Streetcar Suburbs: The Process of Growth in Boston, 1870-1900,* an important illustration of the urbanization process and environmental change.[183] Warner traced suburban growth in Roxbury, West Roxbury, and Dorchester to technological innovations in the form of streetcar lines, which, along with the rural appeal of suburban living, drew Boston residents outward from the central city. An examination of building permits and construction patterns led to the further conclusion that economic class lines determined neighborhood structure, that architectural and housing styles were strikingly similar in such economically differentiated neighborhoods, and that community life had "fragmented" with suburban growth.

Teaching Tools

The rapid expansion of urban history as a teaching and research field has been accompanied by a proliferation of readers and documentary collections aimed at classroom use.[184] Dwight W. Hoover's *A Teacher's Guide to American Urban History* is an important and useful handbook for teachers, containing suggested teaching units and guides to bibliography, films, and other printed and audio-visual aids.[185] Also useful for teachers of urban history are the volumes in the Localized History series published by Teachers College, Columbia University. Individual volumes in the series deal with separate cities, states, regions, and ethnic groups.[186] Additional bibliographical materials can be found in articles by Blake McKelvey, Charles N. Glaab, and Allen F. Davis.[187] The *Urban History Group Newsletter,* published twice yearly by the history department of the University of Wisconsin-Milwaukee, contains up-to-date bibliography in each issue; some of the early issues included suggested course outlines and teaching materials.[188] The past decade has also witnessed publication of a flood of writings, untreated in this chapter, which examine the contemporary urban condition, diagnose the ills of our cities, and prescribe cures for the modern metropolis.

American urban history came alive in the decade of the 1960's. Teachers of American history at every level have virtually limitless opportunities for exploring the urban dimension of the American past. The richness of subject matter, the multitude of new writings, and the diversity of methodology make urban history one of the most challenging and exciting areas of historical endeavor. The problems and the promise of the contemporary city also make it one of the most important.

FOOTNOTES

[1] John Bach McMaster. *A History of the People of the United States, From the Revolution to the Civil War.* 8 vols.; New York: D. Appleton, 1883-1913; Edward Channing. *A History of the United States.* 6 vols.; New York: Macmillan, 1905-1925.

[2] Ray Allen Billington. "Why Some Historians Rarely Write History: A Case Study of Frederick Jackson Turner." *Mississippi Valley Historical Review* 50: 3-27; No. 1, June 1963. p. 16.

[3] Arthur M. Schlesinger. *The Rise of the City, 1878-1898.* New York: Macmillan, 1933; Carl Bridenbaugh. *Cities in the Wilderness: The First Century of Urban Life in America, 1625-1742.* New York: Ronald Press, 1938.

[4] Charles N. Glaab. "The Historian and the American City: A Bibliographic Survey," in Philip M. Hauser and Leo F. Schnore, editors. *The Study of Urbanization.* New York: John Wiley, 1965. p. 55.

[5] Stephan Thernstrom. "Reflections on the New Urban History." *Daedalus* 100: 359-375; No. 2, Spring 1971. p. 359.

[6] Arthur M. Schlesinger. "The City in American History." *Mississippi Valley Historical Review* 27: 43-66; No. 1, June 1940. On a much broader scale, see Lewis Mumford. *The City in History: Its Origins, Its Transformations, and Its Prospects.* New York: Harcourt, Brace and World, 1961. Also suggestive is Oscar Handlin. "The Modern City as a Field of Historical Study," in Oscar Handlin and John Burchard, editors. *The Historian and the City.* Cambridge, Mass.: MIT Press and Harvard University Press, 1963. pp. 1-26.

[7] William Diamond. "On the Dangers of an Urban Interpretation of History," in Eric F. Goldman, editor. *Historiography and Urbanization: Essays in American History in Honor of W. Stull Holt.* Baltimore: Johns Hopkins Press, 1941. pp. 67-108.

[8] Bayrd Still. "The History of the City in American Life." *The American Review,* 2: 20-34; No. 2, May 1962; Richard C. Wade. "The City in History—Some American Perspectives," in Werner Z. Hirsch, editor. *Urban Life and Form.* New York: Holt, Rinehart and Winston, 1963. pp. 59-79; Richard C. Wade. "Urbanization," in C. Vann Woodward, editor. *The Comparative Approach to American History.* New York: Basic Books, 1968. pp. 187-205; Blake McKelvey. "Urban Social and Economic Institutions in North America," in *Recueils de la Société Jean Bodin.* VII, 1955. pp. 653-676. See also Raymond A. Mohl and Neil Betten. "The History of Urban America: An Interpretive Framework." *The History Teacher,* III, 3: 23-34; No. 3, March 1970.

[9] Charles N. Glaab and A. Theodore Brown. *A History of Urban America,* New York: Macmillan, 1967.

[10] Constance McL. Green. *The Rise of Urban America.* New York: Harper and Row, 1965.

[11] Constance McL. Green. *American Cities in the Growth of the Nation.* New York: De Graff, 1957.

¹² Blake McKelvey. *The Urbanization of America, 1860-1915.* New Brunswick, N.J.: Rutgers University Press, 1963.

¹³ Blake McKelvey. *The Emergence of Metropolitan America, 1915-1966.* New Brunswick, N.J.: Rutgers University Press, 1968. On the same period, see also George E. Mowry. *The Urban Nation, 1920-1960.* New York: Hill and Wang, 1965.

¹⁴ Page Smith. *As a City Upon a Hill: The Town in American History.* New York: Knopf, 1966.

¹⁵ Blake McKelvey. *Rochester.* I, *The Water-Power City, 1812-1854;* II, *The Flower City, 1855-1890;* III, *The Quest for Quality, 1890-1925;* IV, *An Emerging Metropolis, 1925-1961.* I-III, Cambridge, Mass.: Harvard University Press, 1945-1956; IV, Rochester, N.Y.: Christopher Press, 1961; Bessie L. Pierce. *A History of Chicago.* I, *The Beginning of a City, 1673-1848;* II, *From Town to City, 1848-1871;* III, *The Rise of a Modern City, 1871-1893.* New York: Knopf, 1937-1957; Constance McL. Green. *Washington: Village and Capital, 1800-1878.* Princeton, N.J.: Princeton University Press, 1962, and *Washington: Capital City, 1879-1950.* Princeton, N.J.: Princeton University Press, 1963; Bayrd Still. *Milwaukee: The History of a City.* rev. ed.; Madison, Wisc.: State Historical Society of Wisconsin, 1965.

¹⁶ Thomas J. Wertenbaker. *Norfolk: Historic Southern Port.* rev. ed.; Durham, N.C.: Duke University Press, 1962; Gerald M. Capers, Jr. *The Biography of a River Town: Memphis, Its Heroic Age.* Chapel Hill, N.C.: University of North Carolina Press, 1939; Leland D. Baldwin. *Pittsburgh: The Story of a City.* Pittsburgh: University of Pittsburgh Press, 1937; Sidney Glazer. *Detroit: A Study in Urban Development.* New York: Bookman Associates, 1965; Marilyn McAdams Sibley. *The Port of Houston: A History.* Austin: University of Texas Press, 1968; David G. McComb. *Houston: The Bayou City.* Austin: University of Texas Press, 1969; Robert M. Fogelson. *The Fragmented Metropolis: Los Angeles, 1850-1930.* Cambridge, Mass.: Harvard University Press, 1967; Herman R. Lantz. *A Community in Search of Itself: A Case History of Cairo, Illinois.* Carbondale, Ill.: Southern Illinois University Press, 1972; Lawrence L. Graves, editor. *A History of Lubbock.* 3 vols.; Lubbock, Tex.: West Texas Museum Association, 1959-1961; Norman H. Clark. *Mill Town: A Social History of Everett, Washington, from Its Earliest Beginnings on the Shores of Puget Sound to the Tragic and Infamous Event Known as the Everett Massacre.* Seattle: University of Washington Press, 1970; Charles N. Glaab and Lawrence H. Larsen. *Factories in the Valley: Neenah-Menasha, 1870-1915.* Madison, Wisc.: State Historical Society of Wisconsin, 1969; Edgar B. Wesley. *Owatonna: The Social Development of a Minnesota Community.* Minneapolis: University of Minnesota Press, 1938; Rollin G. Osterweis. *Three Centuries of New Haven, 1638-1938.* New Haven: Yale University Press, 1953; Constance McL. Green. *History of Naugatuck, Connecticut.* Naugatuck, Conn.: 1948; Constance McL. Green. *Holyoke, Massachusetts: A Case History of the Industrial Revolution in America.* New Haven: Yale University Press, 1939; Vera Shlakman. *Economic History of a Factory Town: A Study of Chicopee, Massachusetts.* Smith College Studies in History, XX, 1934-1935; John Borden Armstrong. *Factory Under the Elms: A History of Harrisville, New Hampshire, 1774-1969.* Cambridge, Mass.: MIT Press, 1969.

¹⁷ Sidney I. Pomerantz. *New York: An American City, 1783-1803.* 2nd ed. Port Washington, N.Y.: Ira J. Friedman, 1965; Ralph Weld. *Brooklyn Village, 1816-1834.* New York: Columbia University Press, 1938; Harold C. Syrett. *The City of Brooklyn, 1865-1898.* New York: Columbia University Press, 1944; Floyd R. Dain. *Every House a Frontier: Detroit's Economic Progress, 1815-1825.* Detroit: Wayne University Press, 1956; Charles R. Poinsatte. *Fort Wayne During the Canal Era, 1828-1855: A Study of a Western Community in the Middle Period of American History.* Indianapolis: Indiana Historical Bureau, 1969; Catherine E. Reiser. *Pittsburgh's Commercial Development, 1800-1850.* Harrisburg: Pennsyl-

vania Historical and Museum Commission, 1951; James Sterling Young. *The Washington Community, 1800-1828.* New York: Columbia University Press, 1966; A. Theodore Brown. *Frontier Community: Kansas City to 1870.* Columbia, Mo.: University of Missouri Press, 1963.

[18] Carl Bridenbaugh. *Cities in the Wilderness* and *Cities in Revolt: Urban Life in America, 1743-1776.* New York: Knopf, 1955.

[19] Darrett B. Rutman. *Winthrop's Boston: Portrait of a Puritan Town, 1630-1649.* Chapel Hill, N.C.: University of North Carolina Press, 1965; G. B. Warden. *Boston, 1689-1776.* Boston: Little, Brown, 1970.

[20] Carl and Jessica Bridenbaugh. *Rebels and Gentlemen: Philadelphia in the Age of Franklin.* New York: Reynal and Hitchcock, 1942; Frederick B. Tolles. *Meeting House and Counting House: The Quaker Merchants of Colonial Philadelphia, 1682-1763.* Chapel Hill, N.C.: University of North Carolina Press, 1948; Arthur L. Jensen. *The Maritime Commerce of Colonial Philadelphia.* Madison, Wisc.: State Historical Society of Wisconsin, 1963.

[21] Thomas J. Condon. *New York Beginnings: The Commercial Origins of New Netherland.* New York: New York University Press, 1968; Van Cleaf Bachman. *Peltries or Plantations: The Economic Policies of the Dutch West India Company in New Netherland, 1623-1639.* Baltimore: The Johns Hopkins Press, 1969.

[22] Clarence P. Gould. "The Economic Causes of the Rise of Baltimore," in Leonard W. Labaree, editor. *Essays in Colonial History Presented to Charles McLean Andrews by His Students.* New Haven: Yale Universi'y Press, 1931. pp. 225-251.

[23] Thomas J. Wertenbaker. *The Golden Age of Colonial Culture.* 2nd edition, rev. New York: New York University Press, 1949.

[24] James H. Soltow. *The Economic Role of Williamsburg.* Williamsburg, Va.: Colonial Williamsburg, 1965; Carl Bridenbaugh. *Seat of Empire: The Political Role of Eighteenth-Century Williamsburg.* rev. ed. Williamsburg, Va.: Colonial Williamsburg, 1958.

[25] Charles S. Grant. *Democracy in the Connecticut Frontier Town of Kent.* New York: Columbia University Press, 1961.

[26] Kenneth A. Lockridge. *A New England Town: The First Hundred Years. Dedham, Massachusetts, 1636-1736.* New York: Norton, 1970.

[27] Michael Zuckerman. *Peaceable Kingdoms: New England Towns in the Eighteenth Century.* New York: Knopf, 1970.

[28] Sumner Chilton Powell. *Puritan Village: The Formation of a New England Town.* Middletown, Conn.: Wesleyan University Press, 1963; John Demos. *A Little Commonwealth: Family Life in Plymouth Colony.* New York: Oxford University Press, 1970; Darrett B. Rutman. *Husbandmen of Plymouth: Farms and Villages in the Old Colony, 1620-1692.* Boston: Beacon Press, 1967; Philip J. Greven, Jr. *Four Generations: Population, Land, and Family in Colonial Andover, Massachusetts.* Ithaca, N.Y.: Cornell University Press, 1970. See also William Haller, Jr. *The Puritan Frontier: Town-Planning in New England Colonial Development, 1630-1660.* New York: Columbia University Press, 1951 and Anthony N. B. Garvan. *Architecture and Town Planning in Colonial Connecticut.* New Haven: Yale University Press, 1951.

[29] John C. Rainbolt. "The Absence of Towns in Colonial Virginia." *Journal of Southern History* 35: 343-360; No. 3, August 1969.

[30] Benjamin W. Labaree. *Patriots and Partisans: The Merchants of Newburyport, 1764-1815.* Cambridge, Mass.: Harvard University Press, 1962. Schlesinger's classic work, *The Colonial Merchants and the American Revolution,* New York: Columbia University Press, 1918, remains useful, along with two other early studies: Virginia D. Harrington. *The New York Merchant on the Eve of the Revolution.* New York: Columbia University Press, 1935; and Leila Sellers. *Charleston Business on the Eve of the American Revolution.* Chapel Hill, N.C.: University of North Carolina Press, 1934.

[31] Richard Walsh. *Charleston's Sons of Liberty: A Study of the Artisans, 1763-1789.* Columbia, S.C.: University of South Carolina Press, 1959.

[32] Jesse Lemisch. "Jack Tar in the Streets: Merchant Seamen in the Politics of Revolutionary America." *William and Mary Quarterly* 3rd series. 25: 371-407; No. 3, July 1968; Jesse Lemisch. "The American Revolution Seen from the Bottom Up," in Barton J. Bernstein, editor. *Towards a New Past: Dissenting Essays in American History.* pp. 3-45; New York: Pantheon, 1968; Staughton Lynd. "The Mechanics in New York Politics, 1774-1788." *Labor History* 5: 225-246; No. 3, Fall 1964.

[33] Richard D. Brown. *Revolutionary Politics in Massachusetts: The Boston Committee of Correspondence and the Towns, 1772-1774.* Cambridge, Mass.: Harvard University Press, 1970.

[34] Hiller B. Zobel. *The Boston Massacre.* New York: Norton, 1970; Pauline Maier. "Popular Uprisings and Civil Authority in Eighteenth-Century America." *William and Mary Quarterly* 3rd series. 27: 3-35; No. 1, January 1970; Pauline Maier. "The Charleston Mob and the Evolution of Popular Politics in Revolutionary South Carolina, 1765-1784." *Perspectives in American History,* IV (1970). pp. 173-196.

[35] Jackson Turner Main. *The Social Structure of Revolutionary America.* Princeton, N.J.: Princeton University Press, 1965.

[36] David T. Gilchrist, editor. *The Growth of the Seaport Cities, 1790-1825.* Charlottesville, Va.: University Press of Virginia, 1967.

[37] Robert G. Albion. *The Rise of the New York Port, 1815-1860.* New York: Scribner's, 1939.

[38] Jean Gottmann. *Megalopolis: The Urbanized Northeastern Seaboard of the United States.* New York: The Twentieth Century Fund, 1961.

[39] George Rogers Taylor. "American Urban Growth Preceding the Railway Age." *Journal of Economic History* 27: 309-339; No. 3, September 1967; Allan R. Pred. "Manufacturing in the American Mercantile City, 1800-1840." *Annals of the Association of American Geographers* 56: 307-338; No. 2, June 1966; Jeffrey G. Williamson. "Antebellum Urbanization in the American Northeast." *Journal of Economic History* 25: 592-608; No. 4, December 1965.

[40] James W. Livingood. *The Philadelphia-Baltimore Trade Rivalry, 1780-1860.* Harrisburg, Pa.: Pennsylvania Historical and Museum Commission, 1947; Wyatt W. Belcher. *The Economic Rivalry Between St. Louis and Chicago, 1850-1880.* New York: Columbia University Press, 1947; Edward C. Kirkland. *Men, Cities, and Transportation: A Study in New England History, 1820-1900.* 2 vols.; Cambridge, Mass.: Harvard University Press, 1948; Glenn C. Quiett. *They Built the West: An Epic of Rails and Cities.* New York: D. Appleton-Century, 1934.

[41] Julius Rubin. *Canal or Railroad? Imitation and Innovation in the Response to the Erie Canal in Philadelphia, Baltimore, and Boston.* Philadelphia: American Philosophical Society, 1961.

[42] Charles N. Glaab. *Kansas City and the Railroads: Community Policy in the Growth of a Regional Metropolis.* Madison, Wisc.: State Historical Society of Wisconsin, 1962.

[43] Merl E. Reed. *New Orleans and the Railroads: The Struggle for Commercial Empire, 1830-1860.* Baton Rouge, La.: Louisiana State University Press, 1966.

[44] Leonard P. Curry. *Rail Routes South: Louisville's Fight for the Southern Market, 1865-1872.* Lexington, Ky.: University of Kentucky Press, 1969.

[45] Richard C. Wade. *The Urban Frontier: The Rise of Western Cities, 1790-1830.* Cambridge, Mass.: Harvard University Press, 1959. See also Wade's article, "Urban Life in Western America, 1790-1830." *American Historical Review* 64: 14-30; No. 1, October 1958.

[46] Bayrd Still. "Patterns of Mid-Nineteenth Century Urbanization in the Middle West." *Mississippi Valley Historical Review* 28: 187-206; No. 2, September 1941.

[47] Lewis Atherton. *Main Street on the Middle Border.* Bloomington, Ind.: Indiana University Press, 1954.

[48] Robert R. Dykstra. *The Cattle Towns: A Social History of the Kansas Cattle Trading Centers.* New York: Knopf, 1968.

[49] Kenneth W. Wheeler. *To Wear a City's Crown: The Beginnings of Urban Growth in Texas, 1836-1865.* Cambridge, Mass.: Harvard University Press, 1968.

[50] Duane A. Smith. *Rocky Mountain Mining Camps: The Urban Frontier.* Bloomington, Ind.: Indiana University Press, 1967.

[51] James B. Allen. *The Company Town in the American West.* Norman, Okla.: University of Oklahoma Press, 1966.

[52] Thomas A. Clinch. *Urban Populism and Free Silver in Montana: A Narrative of Ideology in Political Action.* Missoula, Mont.: University of Montana Press, 1970.

[53] Robert L. Martin. *The City Moves West: Economic and Industrial Growth in Central West Texas.* Austin: University of Texas Press, 1969.

[54] Earl Pomeroy. *The Pacific Slope: A History of California, Oregon, Washington, Idaho, Utah, and Nevada.* New York: Knopf, 1965. pp. 120-164.

[55] Leonard J. Arrington. *Great Basin Kingdom: An Economic History of the Latter-day Saints, 1830-1900.* Cambridge, Mass.: Harvard University Press, 1958.

[56] Daniel J. Boorstin. *The Americans: The National Experience.* New York: Random House, 1965. pp. 113-168.

[57] John G. Clark. *New Orleans, 1718-1812: An Economic History.* Baton Rouge, La.: Louisiana State University Press, 1970.

[58] Robert C. Reinders. *End of an Era: New Orleans, 1850-1860.* New Orleans: Pelican, 1964.

[59] George C. Rogers, Jr. *Charleston in the Age of the Pinckneys.* Norman, Okla.: University of Oklahoma Press, 1969.

[60] D. Clayton James. *Antebellum Natchez.* Baton Rouge, La.: Louisiana State University Press, 1968.

[61] Emory M. Thomas. *The Confederate State of Richmond: A Biography of the Capital.* Austin: University of Texas Press, 1971.

[62] Kenneth Coleman. *Confederate Athens.* Athens, Ga.: University of Georgia Press, 1967.

[63] Gerald M. Capers. *Occupied City: New Orleans Under the Federals, 1862-1865.* Lexington, Ky.: University of Kentucky Press, 1965.

[64] Durward Long. "The Making of Modern Tampa: A City of the New South, 1885-1911." *Florida Historical Quarterly* 49: 333-345; No. 4, April 1971.

[65] Rupert B. Vance and Nicholas J. Demerath, editors. *The Urban South.* Chapel Hill, N.C.: University of North Carolina Press, 1954.

[66] Oscar Handlin. *The Uprooted: The Epic Story of the Great Migrations that Made the American People.* Boston: Little, Brown, 1951.

[67] Oscar Handlin. *Boston's Immigrants: A Study in Acculturation.* rev. ed.; Cambridge, Mass.: Harvard University Press, 1959.

[68] Robert Ernst. *Immigrant Life in New York City, 1825-1863.* New York: King's Crown Press, 1949.

[69] Earl F. Niehaus. *The Irish in New Orleans, 1800-1860.* Baton Rouge, La.: Louisiana State University Press, 1965.

[70] Donald B. Cole. *Immigrant City: Lawrence, Massachusetts, 1845-1921.* Chapel Hill, N.C.: University of North Carolina Press, 1963.

[71] Gerd Korman. *Industrialization, Immigrants, and Americanizers: The View from Milwaukee, 1866-1921.* Madison, Wisc.: State Historical Society of Wisconsin, 1967.

[72] Nathan Glazer and Daniel P. Moynihan. *Beyond the Melting Pot: The Negroes, Puerto Ricans, Jews, Italians, and Irish of New York City.* Cambridge, Mass.: The MIT Press, 1963. See also Oscar Handlin. *The Newcomers: Negroes*

and Puerto Ricans in a Changing Metropolis. Cambridge, Mass.: Harvard University Press, 1959.

[73] Humbert S. Nelli. *Italians in Chicago, 1880-1930: A Study in Ethnic Mobility.* New York: Oxford University Press, 1970.

[74] John M. Allswang. *A House for all Peoples: Ethnic Politics in Chicago, 1890-1936.* Lexington, Ky.: University Press of Kentucky, 1971.

[75] Moses Rischin. *The Promised City: New York's Jews, 1870-1914.* Cambridge, Mass.: Harvard University Press, 1962.

[76] Arthur A. Goren. *New York Jews and the Quest for Community: The Kehillah Experiment, 1908-1922.* New York: Columbia University Press, 1970.

[77] Selig Adler and Thomas E. Connolly. *From Ararat to Suburbia: The History of the Jewish Community of Buffalo.* Philadelphia: Jewish Publication Society of America, 1960; B. G. Rudolph. *From a Minyan to a Community: A History of the Jews of Syracuse.* Syracuse: Syracuse University Press, 1970; Isaac M. Fein. *The Making of an American Jewish Community: The History of Baltimore Jewry from 1773 to 1920.* Philadelphia: Jewish Publication Society of America, 1971; Max Vorspan and Lloyd P. Gartner. *History of the Jews of Los Angeles.* San Marino, Calif.: Huntington Library, 1970; Bertram Wallace Korn. *The Early Jews of New Orleans.* Waltham, Mass.: American Jewish Historical Society, 1969.

[78] Richard C. Wade. *Slavery in the Cities: The South, 1820-1860.* New York: Oxford University Press, 1964.

[79] Robert S. Starobin. *Industrial Slavery in the Old South.* New York: Oxford University Press, 1970.

[80] Gilbert Osofsky. "The Enduring Ghetto." *Journal of American History 55:* 243-255; No. 2, September 1968; Leon Litwack. *North of Slavery: The Negro in the Free States, 1790-1860.* Chicago: University of Chicago Press, 1961.

[81] Gilbert Osofsky. *Harlem: The Making of a Ghetto: Negro New York, 1890-1930.* New York: Harper and Row, 1966.

[82] Seth M. Scheiner. *Negro Mecca: A History of the Negro in New York City, 1865-1920.* New York: New York University Press, 1965.

[83] Allan H. Spear. *Black Chicago: The Making of a Negro Ghetto, 1890-1920.* Chicago: University of Chicago Press, 1967.

[84] Constance McL. Green. *The Secret City: A History of Race Relations in the Nation's Capital.* Princeton, N.J.: Princeton University Press, 1967.

[85] Lawrence B. DeGraaf. "The City of Black Angels: Emergence of the Los Angeles Ghetto, 1890-1930." *Pacific Historical Review* 39: 323-352; No. 3, August 1970.

[86] Arvarh E. Strickland. *History of the Chicago Urban League.* Urbana Ill.: University of Illinois Press, 1966. See also Guichard Parris and Lester Brooks. *Blacks in the City: A History of the National Urban League.* Boston: Little, Brown, 1971.

[87] William M. Tuttle, Jr. *Race Riot: Chicago in the Red Summer of 1919.* New York: Atheneum, 1970.

[88] Elliott M. Rudwick. *Race Riot at East St. Louis, July 2, 1917.* Carbondale, Ill.: Southern Illinois University Press, 1964.

[89] James F. Richardson. *The New York Police: Colonial Times to 1901.* New York: Oxford University Press, 1970.

[90] Roger Lane. *Policing the City: Boston, 1822-1885.* Cambridge, Mass.: Harvard University Press, 1967.

[91] Nelson M. Blake. *Water for the Cities: A History of the Urban Water Supply Problem in the United States.* Syracuse: Syracuse University Press, 1956.

[92] William W. Sorrels. *Memphis' Greatest Debate: A Question of Water.* Memphis: Memphis State University Press, 1970.

[93] Stephen F. Ginsberg. "The Police and Fire Protection in New York City: 1800-1850." *New York History* 52: 133-150; No. 2, April 1971; Stephen F. Gins-

berg. "Above the Law: Volunteer Firemen in New York City, 1836-1837." *ibid.* 50: 165-186; No. 2, April 1969.

[94] George W. Hilton and John F. Due. *The Electric Interurban Railways in America.* Stanford, Calif.: Stanford University Press, 1960; George Rogers Taylor. "The Beginnings of Mass Transportation in Urban America." *Smithsonian Journal of History* 1: 35-50; No. 2, Summer 1966. 31-54; No. 3, Autumn 1966; George M. Smerk. "The Streetcar: Shaper of American Cities." *Traffic Quarterly* 21: 569-584; No. 4, October 1967.

[95] Frederick M. Bender. "Gas Light, 1816-1860." *Pennsylvania History* 22: 359-373; No. 4, October 1955.

[96] Lawrence H. Larsen. "Nineteenth-Century Street Sanitation: A Study of Filth and Frustration." *Wisconsin Magazine of History* 52: 239-247; No. 3, Spring 1969; Richard Skolnik. "George Edwin Waring, Jr.: A Model for Reformers." *New York Historical Society Quarterly* 52: 354-378; No. 4, October 1968, which deals with a leading sanitationist of the late nineteenth century.

[97] John Duffy. *A History of Public Health in New York City, 1625-1866.* New York: Russell Sage Foundation, 1968.

[98] R. Richard Wohl. "Urbanism, Urbanity, and the Historian." *University of Kansas City Review* 22: 53-61; No. 1, October 1955.

[99] John B. Blake. *Public Health in the Town of Boston, 1630-1822.* Cambridge, Mass.: Harvard University Press, 1959.

[100] Charles E. Rosenberg. *The Cholera Years: The United States in 1832, 1849, and 1866.* Chicago: University of Chicago Press, 1962.

[101] John Duffy. *Sword of Pestilence: The New Orleans Yellow Fever Epidemic of 1853.* Baton Rouge, La.: Louisiana State University Press, 1966.

[102] James H. Cassedy. *Charles V. Chapin and the Public Health Movement.* Cambridge, Mass.: Harvard University Press, 1962.

[103] Michael B. Katz. *The Irony of Early School Reform: Educational Innovation in Mid-Nineteenth Century Massachusetts.* Cambridge, Mass.: Harvard University Press, 1968. See also Michael B. Katz. *Class, Bureaucracy, and Schools: The Illusion of Educational Change in America.* New York: Praeger, 1971.

[104] Marvin Lazerson. *Origins of the Urban School: Public Education in Massachusetts, 1870-1915.* Cambridge, Mass.: Harvard University Press, 1971.

[105] Lawrence A. Cremin. *The Transformation of the School: Progressivism in American Education, 1876-1957.* New York: Knopf, 1961; Raymond E. Callahan. *Education and the Cult of Efficiency: A Study of the Social Forces that have Shaped the Administration of the Public Schools.* Chicago: University of Chicago Press, 1962.

[106] Sol Cohen. *Progressives and Urban School Reform: The Public Education Association of New York City, 1895-1954.* New York: Bureau of Publications, Teacher's College, Columbia University, 1964. See also the special issue on "Urban Education" in *History of Education Quarterly* 9: No. 3, Fall 1969.

[107] Jerome Mushkat. *Tammany: The Evolution of a Political Machine, 1789-1865.* Syracuse: Syracuse University Press, 1971. Another important study of nineteenth-century urban politics is Michael F. Holt. *Forging a Majority: The Formation of the Republican Party in Pittsburgh, 1848-1860.* New Haven: Yale University Press, 1969.

[108] Seymour J. Mandelbaum. *Boss Tweed's New York.* New York: John Wiley, 1965.

[109] Alexander B. Callow. *The Tweed Ring.* New York: Oxford University Press, 1966.

[110] Zane L. Miller. *Boss Cox's Cincinnati: Urban Politics in the Progressive Era.* New York: Oxford University Press, 1968.

[111] William D. Miller. *Mr. Crump of Memphis.* Baton Rouge, La.: Louisiana State University Press, 1964.

[112] Walton Bean. *Boss Ruef's San Francisco: The Story of the Union Labor Party, Big Business, and the Graft Prosecution.* Berkeley, Calif.: University of California Press, 1952.
[113] Alex Gottfried. *Boss Cermak of Chicago: A Study of Political Leadership.* Seattle: University of Washington Press, 1962. Joel A. Tarr deals with an earlier Chicago boss in *A Study in Boss Politics: William Lorimer of Chicago.* Urbana, Ill.: University of Illinois Press, 1971.
[114] Lyle W. Dorsett. *The Pendergast Machine.* New York: Oxford University Press, 1968.
[115] Bruce M. Stave. *The New Deal and the Last Hurrah: Pittsburgh Machine Politics.* Pittsburgh: University of Pittsburgh Press, 1970. An older study of bossism which remains useful is Harold Zink. *City Bosses in the United States: A Study of Twenty Municipal Bosses.* Durham, N.C.: Duke University Press, 1930.
[116] Melvin G. Holli. *Reform in Detroit: Hazen S. Pingree and Urban Politics.* New York: Oxford University Press, 1969.
[117] J. Joseph Huthmacher. "Urban Liberalism and the Age of Reform." *Mississippi Valley Historical Review* 49: 231-241; No. 2, September 1962.
[118] Arthur Mann. *Yankee Reformers in the Urban Age: Social Reform in Boston, 1880-1900.* Cambridge, Mass.: Harvard University Press, 1954; William D. Miller. *Memphis During the Progressive Era, 1900-1917.* Madison, Wisc.: American History Research Center, 1957; Joy J. Jackson. *New Orleans in the Gilded Age: Politics and Urban Progress, 1880-1896.* Baton Rouge, La.: Louisiana State University Press, 1969; James B. Crooks. *Politics and Progress: The Rise of Urban Progressivism in Baltimore, 1895 to 1911.* Baton Rouge, La.: Louisiana State University Press, 1968.
[119] Gerald Kurland. *Seth Low: The Reformer in an Urban and Industrial Age.* New York: Twayne, 1971; Edwin R. Lewinson. *John Purroy Mitchel: The Boy Mayor of New York.* New York: Astra Books, 1965; Arthur Mann. *LaGuardia: A Fighter Against His Times, 1882-1933.* Chicago: University of Chicago Press, 1959; Arthur Mann. *LaGuardia Comes to Power, 1933.* Philadelphia: J. B. Lippincott, 1965; Charles Garrett. *The LaGuardia Years: Machine and Reform Politics in New York City.* New Brunswick, N.J.: Rutgers University Press, 1961; J. Joseph Huthmacher. *Senator Robert F. Wagner and the Rise of Urban Liberalism.* New York: Atheneum, 1968; Jack Tager. *The Intellectual as Urban Reformer: Brand Whitlock and the Progressive Movement.* Cleveland: The Press of Case Western Reserve University, 1968. Other studies of bossism and reform include: Eric McKitrick. "The Study of Corruption." *Political Science Quarterly* 72: 502-514; No. 4, December 1967; Samuel P. Hays. "The Politics of Reform in Municipal Government in the Progressive Era." *Pacific Northwest Quarterly* 55: 157-169; No. 4, October 1964; James Weinstein. "Organized Business and the City Commission and Manager Movements." *Journal of Southern History* 28: 166-182; No. 2, May 1962; Mark D. Hirsch. "Reflections on Urban History and Urban Reform, 1865-1915," in Donald Sheehan and Harold C. Syrett, editors. *Essays in American Historiography: Papers Presented in Honor of Allan Nevins.* New York: Columbia University Press, 1960. pp. 109-137.
[120] Robert H. Bremner. *From the Depths: The Discovery of Poverty in the United States.* New York: New York University Press, 1956.
[121] Raymond A. Mohl. *Poverty in New York, 1783-1825.* New York: Oxford University Press, 1971.
[122] David J. Rothman. *The Discovery of the Asylum: Social Order and Disorder in the New Republic.* Boston: Little, Brown, 1971.
[123] Nathan I. Huggins. *Protestants Against Poverty: Boston's Charities, 1870-1900.* Westport, Conn.: Greenwood, 1971.
[124] Robert S. Pickett. *House of Refuge: Origins of Juvenile Reform in New York State, 1815-1857.* Syracuse: Syracuse University Press, 1969; Joseph M. Hawes.

Children in Urban Society: Juvenile Delinquency in Nineteenth-Century America.
New York: Oxford University Press, 1971.
[125] Allen F. Davis. *Spearheads for Reform: The Social Settlements and the Progressive Movement, 1890-1914.* New York: Oxford University Press, 1967.
[126] Louise C. Wade. *Graham Taylor: Pioneer for Social Justice, 1851-1938.* Chicago: University of Chicago Press, 1964; Daniel Levine. *Jane Addams and the Liberal Tradition.* Madison, Wisc.: State Historical Society of Wisconsin, 1971.
[127] Carl Bridenbaugh. *The Colonial Craftsman.* New York: New York University Press, 1950.
[128] Arthur M. Schlesinger, Jr. *The Age of Jackson.* Boston: Little, Brown, 1946.
[129] Edward Pessen. "Did Labor Support Jackson? The Boston Story." *Political Science Quarterly* 64: 262-274; No. 2, June 1949; Edward Pessen. "The Workingmen's Movement of the Jacksonian Era." *Mississippi Valley Historical Review* 43: 428-443; No. 3, December 1956; William A. Sullivan. "Philadelphia Labor During the Jackson Era." *Pennsylvania History* 15: 305-320; No. 4, October 1948; William A. Sullivan. *The Industrial Worker in Pennsylvania, 1800-1840.* Harrisburg, Pa.: Pennsylvania Historical and Museum Commission, 1955.
[130] Edward Pessen. *Most Uncommon Jacksonians: The Radical Leaders of the Early Labor Movement.* Albany: State University of New York Press, 1967.
[131] Walter Hugins. *Jacksonian Democracy and the Working Class: A Study of the New York Workingmen's Movement, 1829-1837.* Stanford, Calif.: Stanford University Press, 1960. On a later period, see the older but still useful study by Norman Ware. *The Industrial Worker, 1840-1860.* Boston: Houghton Mifflin, 1924.
[132] David Montgomery. *Beyond Equality: Labor and the Radical Republicans, 1862-1872.* New York: Knopf, 1967. See also Montgomery's article, "The Working Classes of the Pre-Industrial American City, 1780-1830." *Labor History* 9: 3-22; No. 1, Winter 1968.
[133] Melvyn Dubofsky. *When Workers Organize: New York City in the Progressive Era.* Amherst, Mass.: University of Massachusetts Press, 1968.
[134] Barbara Warne Newell. *Chicago and the Labor Movement: Metropolitan Unionism in the 1930's.* Urbana, Ill.: University of Illinois Press, 1961; Thomas W. Gavett. *Development of the Labor Movement in Milwaukee.* Madison, Wisc.: University of Wisconsin Press, 1965; Grace Heilman Stimson. *Rise of the Labor Movement in Los Angeles.* Berkeley, Calif.: University of California Press, 1955; Louis B. Perry and Richard S. Perry. *A History of the Los Angeles Labor Movement, 1911-1941.* Berkeley, Calif.: University of California Press, 1963; Robert Knight. *Industrial Relations in the San Francisco Bay Area, 1900-1918.* Berkeley, Calif.: University of California Press, 1960.
[135] Carroll Smith Rosenberg. *Religion and the Rise of the American City: The New York City Mission Movement, 1812-1870.* Ithaca, N.Y.: Cornell University Press, 1971.
[136] Alvin W. Skardon. *Church Leader in the Cities: William Augustus Muhlenberg.* Philadelphia: University of Pennsylvania Press, 1971. See also Timothy Smith. *Revivalism and Social Reform in Mid-Nineteenth-Century America.* New York: Abingdon, 1957.
[137] Aaron I. Abell. *The Urban Impact on American Protestantism, 1865-1900.* Cambridge, Mass.: Harvard University Press, 1943; Aaron I. Abell. *American Catholicism and Social Action: A Search for Social Justice, 1865-1950.* Garden City, N.Y.: Doubleday, 1960; Charles H. Hopkins. *The Rise of the Social Gospel in American Protestantism, 1865-1915.* New Haven: Yale University Press, 1940; Henry F. May. *Protestant Churches and Industrial America.* New York: Harper, 1949; Robert D. Cross. *The Emergence of Liberal Catholicism in America.* Cambridge, Mass.: Harvard University Press, 1958.

[138] Robert D. Cross, editor. *The Church and the City, 1865-1910*. Indianapolis: Bobbs-Merrill, 1967.

[139] James F. Findlay, Jr. *Dwight L. Moody: American Evangelist, 1837-1899*. Chicago: University of Chicago Press, 1969; Jacob H. Dorn. *Washington Gladden: Prophet of the Social Gospel*. Columbus, Ohio: Ohio State University Press, 1967.

[140] Leonard L. Richards. *"Gentlemen of Property and Standing": Anti-Abolition Mobs in Jacksonian America*. New York: Oxford University Press, 1970.

[141] Kenneth T. Jackson. *The Ku Klux Klan in the City, 1915-1930*. New York: Oxford University Press, 1967.

[142] John W. Reps. *The Making of Urban America: A History of City Planning in the United States*. Princeton, N.J.: Princeton University Press, 1965.

[143] John W. Reps. *Tidewater Towns: City Planning in Colonial Virginia and Maryland*. Charlottesville, Va.: University Press of Virginia, 1971; John W. Reps. *Town Planning in Frontier America*. Princeton, N.J.: Princeton University Press, 1969; John W. Reps. *Monumental Washington: The Planning and Development of the Capital Center*. Princeton, N.J.: Princeton University Press, 1967.

[144] Mel Scott. *American City Planning Since 1890*. Berkeley, Calif.: University of California Press, 1969.

[145] Clarence S. Stein. *Toward New Towns for America*. New York: Reinhold, 1957.

[146] Seymour Toll. *Zoned American*. New York: Grossman, 1969.

[147] Christopher Tunnard and Henry Hope Reed. *American Skyline: The Growth and Form of Our Cities and Towns*. Boston: Houghton Mifflin, 1955. See also Tunnard's important book, *The City of Man*. New York: Scribner's, 1953.

[148] John Burchard and Albert Bush-Brown. *The Architecture of America: A Social and Cultural History*. Boston: Little, Brown, 1961.

[149] Wayne Andrews. *Architecture, Ambition and Americans*. New York: Harper, 1955.

[150] Carl W. Condit. *American Building: Materials and Techniques from the Beginning of the Colonial Settlements to the Present*. Chicago: University of Chicago Press, 1968; Carl W. Condit. *The Chicago School of Architecture: A History of Commercial and Public Building in the Chicago Area, 1875-1925*. Chicago: University of Chicago Press, 1964.

[151] Mel Scott. *The San Francisco Bay Area: A Metropolis in Perspective*. Berkeley, Calif.: University of California Press, 1959.

[152] Harold M. Mayer and Richard C. Wade. *Chicago: The Growth of a Metropolis*. Chicago: University of Chicago Press, 1969.

[153] Edmund H. Chapman. *Cleveland: Village to Metropolis*. Cleveland: The Western Reserve Historical Society and the Press of Western Reserve University, 1964.

[154] Walter Muir Whitehill. *Boston: A Topographical History*. Cambridge, Mass.: Harvard University Press, 1959.

[155] Harold Kirker and James Kirker. *Bulfinch's Boston, 1787-1817*. New York: Oxford University Press, 1964.

[156] William H. Wilson. *The City Beautiful Movement in Kansas City*. Columbia, Mo.: University of Missouri Press, 1964.

[157] Albert Fein, editor. *Landscape into Cityscape: Frederick Law Olmsted's Plans for a Greater New York City*. Ithaca, N.Y.: Cornell University Press, 1967; S. B. Sutton, editor., *Civilizing American Cities: A Selection of Frederick Law Olmsted's Writings on City Landscapes*. Cambridge, Mass.: The MIT Press, 1971.

[158] Stanley Buder. *Pullman: An Experiment in Industrial Order and Community Planning, 1880-1930*. New York: Oxford University Press, 1967. On an earlier industrial town, see John Coolidge. *Mill and Mansion: A Study of Architecture and Society in Lowell, Massachusetts, 1820-1865*. New York: Columbia University Press, 1942.

[159] Raymond A. Mohl and Neil Betten. "The Failure of Industrial City Planning: Gary, Indiana, 1906-1910." *Journal of the American Institute of Planners* 38: 203-215; No. 4, July 1972.

[160] Roy Lubove. *The Progressives and the Slums: Tenement House Reform in New York City, 1890-1917.* Pittsburgh: University of Pittsburgh Press, 1962.

[161] Roy Lubove. *Community Planning in the 1920's: The Contribution of the Regional Planning Association of America.* Pittsburgh: University of Pittsburgh Press, 1963. See also Roy Lubove. *The Urban Community: Housing and Planning in the Progressive Era.* Englewood Cliffs, N.J.: Prentice-Hall, 1967.

[162] Joseph L. Arnold. *The New Deal in the Suburbs: A History of the Greenbelt Town Program, 1935-1954.* Columbus, Ohio: Ohio State University Press, 1971. See also Paul K. Conkin. *Tomorrow a New World: The New Deal Community Program.* Ithaca, N.Y.: Cornell University Press, 1959.

[163] Morton and Lucia White. *The Intellectual Versus the City: From Thomas Jefferson to Frank Lloyd Wright.* Cambridge, Mass.: Harvard University Press, 1962.

[164] Robert H. Walker. "The Poet and the Rise of the City." *Mississippi Valley Historical Review* 69: 85-89; No. 1, June 1962.

[165] George A. Dunlap. *The City in the American Novel, 1789-1900.* Philadelphia: University of Pennsylvania Press, 1934; Blanche H. Gelfant. *The American City Novel.* Norman, Okla.: University of Oklahoma Press, 1954; Eugene Arden. "The Evil City in American Fiction." *New York History* 35: 259-279; No. 3, July 1954.

[166] Charles N. Glaab. "The Historian and the American Urban Tradition." *Wisconsin Magazine of History* 47: 12-25; No. 1, Autumn 1963. See also Frank Freidel. "Boosters, Intellectuals, and the American City," in Handlin and Burchard, editors. *The Historian and the City.* pp. 115-120, and Charles N. Glaab. "Historical Perspective on Urban Development Schemes," in Leo F. Schnore, editor. *Social Science and the City.* New York: Praeger, 1968. pp. 197-219.

[167] Michael H. Cowan. *City of the West: Emerson, America, and Urban Metaphor.* New Haven: Yale University Press, 1967.

[168] Peter J. Schmitt. *Back to Nature: The Arcadian Myth in Urban America.* New York: Oxford University Press, 1969.

[169] Anselm Strauss. *Images of the American City.* New York: Free Press, 1961. See also Kevin Lynch. *The Image of the City,* Cambridge, Mass.: The MIT Press, 1960, which draws upon contemporary materials and deals with perceptual problems in relation to urban forms.

[170] Don S. Kirschner. *City and Country: Rural Responses to Urbanization in the 1920's.* Westport, Conn.: Greenwood, 1970.

[171] Scott Donaldson. *The Suburban Myth.* New York: Columbia University Press, 1969. See also Charles N. Glaab. "Metropolis and Suburb: The Changing American City," in John Braeman, *et al.,* editors. *Change and Continuity in Twentieth-Century America: The 1920's.* Columbus, Ohio: Ohio State University Press, 1968. pp. 399-437.

[172] Stephan Thernstrom and Richard Sennett, editors. *Nineteenth-Century Cities: Essays in the New Urban History.* New Haven: Yale University Press, 1969. p. vii.

[173] Thernstrom. "Reflections on the New Urban History." *Daedalus* 100: 359-375; No. 2, Spring 1971.

[174] Stephan Thernstrom. *Poverty and Progress: Social Mobility in a Nineteenth-Century City.* Cambridge, Mass.: Harvard University Press, 1964. See also the following articles by Thernstrom: "Urbanization, Migration, and Social Mobility in Late Nineteenth-Century America," in Bernstein, editor. *Towards a New Past.* pp. 158-175; "Immigrants and WASPS: Ethnic Differences in Occupational Mobility in Boston, 1890-1940," in Thernstrom and Sennett, editors. *Nineteenth-Century Cities.* pp. 125-164; "Notes on the Historical Study of Social Mobility." *Comparative Studies in Society and History* 10: 162-172; No. 2, January 1968.

[175] Peter R. Knights. *The Plain People of Boston, 1830-1860: A Study in City Growth.* New York: Oxford University Press, 1971. See also Stephan Thernstrom and Peter R. Knights. "Men in Motion: Some Data and Speculations about Urban Population Mobility in Nineteenth-Century America." *Journal of Interdisciplinary History* 1: 7-35; No. 1, Autumn 1970. On eighteenth-century Boston, see James A. Henretta. "Economic Development and Social Structure in Colonial Boston." *William and Mary Quarterly* 3rd series. 22: 75-92; No. 1, January 1965.

[176] Stuart Blumin. "Mobility and Change in Ante-Bellum Philadelphia," in Thernstrom and Sennett, editors. *Nineteenth-Century Cities.* pp. 165-208; Herbert G. Gutman. "The Reality of the Rags-to-Riches 'Myth': The Case of the Paterson, New Jersey, Locomotive, Iron, and Machinery Manufacturers, 1830-1880," in *ibid.* pp. 98-124; Richard J. Hopkins. "Occupational and Geographical Mobility in Atlanta, 1870-1896." *Journal of Southern History* 34: 200-213; No. 2, May 1968; Clyde Griffen. "Making It in America: Social Mobility in Mid-Nineteenth Century Poughkeepsie." *New York History* 51: 479-499; No. 5, October 1970; Alwyn Barr. "Occupational and Geographic Mobility in San Antonio, 1870-1900." *Social Science Quarterly* 51: 396-403; No. 2, September 1970; Herman R. Lantz and Ernest K. Alix. "Occupational Mobility in a Nineteenth Century Mississippi Valley River Community." *ibid.* pp. 404-408; Paul B. Worthman. "Working Class Mobility in Birmingham, Alabama, 1880-1914," in Tamara K. Hareven, editor. *Anonymous Americans: Explorations in Nineteenth Century Social History.* Englewood Cliffs, N.J.: Prentice-Hall, 1971. pp. 172-213; William G. Robbins. "Opportunity and Persistence in the Pacific Northwest: A Quantative Study of Early Roseburg, Oregon." *Pacific Historical Review* 39: 279-296; No. 3, August 1970.

[177] Richard Sennett. *Families Against the City: Middle Class Homes of Industrial Chicago, 1872-1890.* Cambridge, Mass.: Harvard University Press, 1970.

[178] Eric E. Lampard. "American Historians and the Study of Urbanization." *American Historical Review* 67: 49-61; No. 1, October 1961; Eric E. Lampard. "Urbanization and Social Change; On Broadening the Scope and Relevance of Urban History," in Handlin and Burchard, editors. *The Historian and the City.* pp. 225-247; Eric E. Lampard. "The Dimensions of Urban History: A Footnote to the 'Urban Crisis'." *Pacific Historical Review* 39: 261-278; No. 3, August 1970. Suggestions similar to Lampard's had been made earlier in W. Stull Holt. "Some Consequences of the Urban Movement in American History." *ibid.,* 22: 337-351; No. 4, November 1953. See also the early important statistical study by Adna F. Weber. *The Growth of Cities in the Nineteenth Century.* New York: Macmillan, 1899.

[179] Roy Lubove. "The Urbanization Process: An Approach to Historical Research." *Journal of the American Institute of Planners* 33: 33-39; No. 1, January 1967.

[180] Roy Lubove. *Twentieth-Century Pittsburgh: Government, Business and Environmental Change.* New York: John Wiley, 1969.

[181] Sam Bass Warner, Jr. "If All the World Were Philadelphia: A Scaffolding for Urban History, 1774-1930." *American Historical Review* 74: 26-43; No. 1, October 1968.

[182] Sam Bass Warner, Jr. *The Private City: Philadelphia in Three Periods of Its Growth.* Philadelphia: University of Pennsylvania Press, 1968.

[183] Sam Bass Warner, Jr. *Streetcar Suburbs: The Process of Growth in Boston, 1870-1900.* Cambridge, Mass.: Harvard University Press, 1962.

[184] The following urban history readers contain much of the fundamental journal literature: Alexander B. Callow, editor. *American Urban History.* New York: Oxford University Press, 1969; Raymond A. Mohl and Neil Betten, editors. *Urban America in Historical Perspective.* New York: Weybright and Talley, 1970; Allen M. Wakstein, editor. *The Urbanization of America,* Boston: Houghton Mifflin, 1970; Kenneth T. Jackson and Stanley L. Schultz, editors. *Cities in American History.* New York: Knopf, 1972; James F. Richardson, editor. *The American*

City. Waltham, Mass.: Xerox, 1972; Paul Kramer and Frederick L. Holborn, editors. *The City in American Life.* New York: Capricorn, 1970; Jack Tager and Park Dixon Goist, editors. *The Urban Vision.* Homewood, Ill.: Dorsey, 1970. Useful documentary collections include: Charles N. Glaab, editor. *The American City: A Documentary History.* Homewood, Ill.: Dorsey, 1963; Wilson Smith, editor. *Cities of Our Past and Present.* New York: John Wiley, 1964; David R. Weimer, editor. *City and Country in America.* New York: Appleton-Century-Crofts, 1962. Combining narrative and documents are Blake McKelvey. *The City in American History.* London: George Allen and Unwin, 1969 and Christopher Tunnard. *The Modern American City.* Princeton, N.J.: Van Nostrand, 1968. A more recent study is Raymond A. Mohl and James F. Richardson. *The Urban Experience: Themes in American History.* Belmont, Calif.: Wadsworth, 1973, which serves as a topical text.

    [185] Dwight W. Hoover. *A Teacher's Guide to American Urban History.* Chicago: Quadrangle, 1971.

    [186] See, for example, Bayrd Still. *New York City: A Students' Guide to Localized History.* New York: Teacher's College Press, 1965. Other volumes have covered Cincinnati, Houston, Los Angeles, Boston, Miami, Milwaukee, San Francisco, Chicago, and Raleigh-Durham-Chapel Hill. For an example of how the city can be used as a teaching resource, see Raymond A. Mohl and Neil Betten. "Gary, Indiana: The Urban Laboratory as a Teaching Tool." *The History Teacher* 4: 5-17; No. 2, January 1971.

    [187] Blake McKelvey. "American Urban History Today." *American Historical Review* 57: 919-929; No. 4, July 1952; Charles N. Glaab. "The Historian and the American City: A Bibliographic Survey," in Hauser and Schnore, editors. *The Study of Urbanization.* pp. 53-80; and Allen F. Davis. "The American Historian vs. the City." *Social Studies* 51: 91-96, 127-135; Nos, 3, 4, March, April 1965. Articles evaluating the writing of American urban history include: Dwight W. Hoover. "The Diverging Paths of American Urban History." *American Quarterly* 20: 296-317; No. 2, Pt. 2, Summer 1968; Richard C. Wade. "An Agenda for Urban History," in Herbert J. Bass, editor. *The State of American History.* Chicago: Quadrangle, 1970. pp. 43-69; Michael H. Frisch. "L'histoire urbaine américaine: réflexions sur les tendances récentes." *Annales* 25: 880-897; No. 4, July-August 1970; Blaine A. Brownell. "American Urban History: Retrospect and Prospect." *Indiana Academy of the Social Sciences, Proceedings,* 3rd series, V, 1970. pp. 120-128; and Dana F. White. "The Underdeveloped Discipline: Interdisciplinary Directions in American Urban History." *American Studies: An International Newsletter* 9: 3-16; No. 3, Spring 1971.

    [188] See, for example, *Urban History Group Newsletter.* No. 27, April 1969. See also Bayrd Still and Diana Klebanow. "The Teaching of American Urban History." *Journal of American History* 55: 843-847; No. 4, March 1969.

· 9 ·

War: From Colonies to Vietnam

Theodore Ropp

Introduction

CLIO has been a Muse second only to Calliope of epic song as a warmonger. The appeals of what Carl von Clausewitz saw as war's "strange trinity . . . [of] violence, . . . the play of probabilities and chance, . . . [and] pure intelligence" have been enhanced for some two centuries by deliberately adding democratic and national "passions" to those of the ancient arts of the bard or seer in the village square or at the castle dinner table. Though America's end of glory in Indochina may produce more works than our marginal participation in the Great War of 1914-1918—or as many nostalgic ones as have come out of Britain since the Suez expedition of 1956—output may eventually slacken. But our mountains of war books are already so high that most of our choices must be personal ones of (1) standard histories, (2) general works on an international art and/or science to which Americans made few contributions before Alfred Thayer Mahan's *The Influence of Sea Power upon History 1660-1783* appeared in 1890, and (3) particularly well-written or well-illustrated histories or (4) well-chosen collections of readings or documents to add detail and color.[1]

Three books might be bought for school libraries. Keith L. Nelson's readings on *The Impact of War on American Life: The Twentieth Century Experience* have fine critical bibliographies on the economic, political, social, and intellectual effects of both World Wars, the Cold War, and the Warfare State, and on Conflict, Disaster, and Social Change, Non-American Wars, American Wars Generally, and American Wars before 1914. A mistitled—since it has almost nothing on the other services—*American Military History* text for Army ROTC units, in the official *Army Historical* series, also has good bibliographies and campaign and battle maps and summaries. R. Ernest and Trevor N. Dupuy's *Encyclopedia of Military History* covers the whole field, and has excellent sections on military trends at the beginning of each chronological chapter.[2] The incomplete *Wars of the United States* series edited by Louis Morton, and many illustrated weapons and battle books, may be too expensive or specialized for many libraries, but the American Heritage illustrated histories of our four major wars may be in many of them. Most of the others will be in larger libraries, in older ones which bought or were given old standbys, or in those of local military history buffs, a term derived from the leather underwear used when wearing armor. For reasons which have already been noted, teachers need not worry about creating buffs; the problem is to use their existing interests to stimulate others. Military books are also paperback and reprint publishing staples, and expensive illustrated ones may be remaindered before the next holiday buying season.[3]

European official historians have been working their documentary mountains for over a century, less for official glorification than to give vicarious experience to future commanders. Distrust of officialdom confined our historians to publishing documents and technical studies until 1945, but our soldiers began to study past wars scientifically from about the time when Stephen B. Luce—nearly two decades after hearing William T. Sherman explain why Charleston would fall to him rather than to " 'You navy fellows' "—opened the first Naval War College in 1884. Its first major product and one of the most influential works ever written by an American historian—the other was Frederick Jackson Turner's "Significance of the Frontier in American History," 1893—was Mahan's in 1890. While the Civil War book boom had begun during the war itself, the popularity of the 160 volumes of its *Official Records, 1860-1922,* the Century Company's four-volume *Battles and Leaders* collection, 1884-1888, James Ford Rhodes's seven-volume *History of the United States from the Compromise of 1850 to the Final Restoration of Home Rule in the South in 1877,* John C. Ropes's four-volume military history, 1894-1913, and the illustrated ones which preceded the Review of Reviews' ten-volume *Photographic History,* 1911, seems to have been phenomenal.[4]

One concern of these writings came from our nineteenth-century military isolation. We debated the merits of wartime volunteer or expansible regular forces long after many other powers had been forced to expand their regulars with peace-trained conscripts. The two best collections of readings on our military history happen to omit Alexis de Tocqueville's famous passages in *Democracy in America* on "Why Democratic Nations are Naturally Desirous of Peace and Democratic Armies of War," a problem area which had appeared with what Clausewitz had called "the participation of the people in this great affair of state" at the end of the eighteenth century. The Industrial Revolution reinforced that trend by making it possible to levy, arm, move, supply, and control still more Napoleonic armies, and many Americans increasingly doubted that we would ever again fight a great war with both sides starting from equal positions of unpreparedness, except for their navies.[5]

Douglas Southall Freeman's four-volume *R. E. Lee* helped to revive the Civil War boom in 1935-1936. Lee clearly appealed to that epic strain of "life *in extremis*" which had so concerned William James in 1910. By Great War standards, ours had been a costumed chess match. Freeman underplayed the appeal of machines, perhaps because he was not very interested in that military engineer who had remade the Southeast's coast defenses before taking command of the Army of Northern Virginia, perhaps because machines had helped to doom what, for many Americans, was still the last of the great Lost Causes. We are now as fearful as Montesquieu that "As soon as man enters into society he loses the sense of his weakness; equality ceases, and then commences the state of war," but biography remains one of the best approaches to a story which presents particular problems of politicians unexpectedly becoming wartime commanders and of soldiers attaining high political office after spending most of their lives in the profession of arms. And James' "Moral Equivalent of War," which "the ordinary prides and shames of social man . . . are capable of organizing," is still something more than "a question of time, of skillful propagandism, and of opinion-making men seizing historic opportunities."[6]

The Colonial and Revolutionary Wars

Our Revolution's bicentenary will be the quincentenary of Christopher Columbus's Enterprise of the Indies. Samuel Eliot Morison's *Admiral of the Ocean Sea* and *European Discovery of America,* Björn Landström's pictorial *Columbus,* Carlo M. Cipolla's *Guns, Sails, and Empires,* and J. H. Parry's *Establishment of the European Hegemony* deal with that era of "polymorphous violence" which preceded Howard H. Peckham's *Colonial Wars, 1689-1763.*[7] The Fort Caroline massacres, 1565, 1567, were our St. Bartholemew's Days. George T. Hunt shows that the *Wars of the Iroquois* were like the trade and slaving wars in Africa. Douglas E. Leach's study of King Philip's War shows settlers' reactions to one American Indian "conspiracy." John K. Mahon's *Second Seminole War*—though not in this era—is very good on logistics and tactics. And Harold L. Peterson's and Carl P. Russell's illustrated personal weapons books might be read with others on the European ships, regulars, and fortifications which helped to defend the settlers.[8]

The regularization of political, trade, land, and labor affairs in more settled areas appears in Parry's, Charles R. Boxer's, and John R. Alden's volumes on the Spanish and Dutch empires and *Pioneer America* in the *History of Human Society* series.[9] Britain took over other Europeans' colonies without, except in Acadia, much disturbance of persons, property, or religion. And the Proclamation of 1763 and the "intolerable" Quebec Act of 1774 paid her local French and Indian dividends in our Revolutionary War. All this helps to explain the uneven quality of our eighteenth-century militia—less stiffened by need and military adventurers—and the relative mildness, except on the frontier and by later popular standards, of the atrocities of our Revolutionary War.

Our military investments were relatively small. Greater technological and numerical superiority made it easier for us than for the conquistadors or Romans to regulate our primitive wards by firing when we saw the red of their skins. A half-cohort of 250 men was a big garrison for one of our legionary stockades; 1000-3500 men won the Battles of Fallen Timbers, Tippecanoe, Horseshoe Bend, and Lake Okeechobee. There were 8500 British regulars in North America in 1775; U. S. Army strength was 3813 in 1794, 16,213 in 1860, and 27,273—about a tenth that of a Roman Empire with about the same population—at the end of our frontier era in 1890. But military technological determinism comports so well with the facts of our Westward expansion, and even with a Neo-Turnerism which sees our frontier patterns as universals, that we may forget that literacy was the classical distinction between natural and civilized peoples. Because literacy provides a way of storing and replicating information, it can extend a people's reach and absorbing power over those with otherwise equal technologies, and Romans were made out of Gauls or even Jews—another People of the Book—in a few generations. And our Indians were not guerrilla warriors in the modern sense—after Napoleon's Spanish and Russian wars—of partisans supported by regulars, although the best organized Eastern tribesmen were also dependent on European metal trade goods and overt or covert support until the removal of France, Britain, and Spain from the game made their cause hopeless. But their wars are more than footnotes to American history. From King Philip's to the First Seminole War and Andrew Jackson's taking of Florida in 1818, alleged or real European-inspired Indian "uprisings" not only helped to unite Americans, but also to determine who got which of their "unoccupied" lands at the peace table.

Though Mahan saw their wars as decisive for the command of the sea and New France, King William and Queen Anne are now only British television exports. The big pictures of our next two colonial wars may be just as confusing, but those who missed their bicentenaries might read Charles P. Stacey's *Quebec 1759* and Geoffrey Marcus's *Quiberon Bay* for two "typical" eighteenth-century campaigns and battles.[10] John Shy's *Toward Lexington,* Alden's *American Revolution,* Piers Mackesy's *War for America,* and Higginbotham's *The War of American Independence* cover those events.[11] Russell F. Weigley's *Partisan War* makes sense of the *South Carolina Campaign of 1780-1782,* and Dave R. Palmer's *The River and the Rock* is a fine *History of Fortress West Point, 1775-1783.* There are many good battle and campaign books. Richard M. Ketchum's *The Battle for Bunker Hill,* Burke Davis's *The Cowpens-Guilford Courthouse Campaign,* and Harold A. Larrabee's *Decision at the Chesapeake* are among the most readable. But we still need general studies of the trade war, of those Indian Wars which partly depended on it, of foreign advisers and soldiers of fortune, of George Washington as a general, and a translation of Ernst Kipping's short *Die Truppen von Hessen-Kassel in Amerikanischen Unabhängigkeitskrieg.*[12]

American Military Institutions

Though few of our nineteenth-century Romans had read Polybius on how the old ones had concocted Cincinnatus and their other public images, we did well enough with the Anglo-Saxons—the *fyrd* still lives in *American Military History*—and Washington's sensible "Sentiments on a Peace Establishment" of 1783. "Fortunately for us," he had written, "our relative situation requires but few" professionals. We needed: (1) "A regular and standing force, for Garrisoning West Point and such other Posts" as were "necessary to awe the Indians, protect our Trade, prevent the encroachment of our Neighbours, . . . guard us . . . from surprises, and secure our Magazines"; (2) "A well organized Militia; upon a Plan that will pervade all the States, and introduce similarity in their Establishment Maneuvers, Exercise and Arms"; (3) "Arsenals of . . . Military Stores"; (4) "Academies, one or more for the Instruction of the Art Military; . . . particularly Engineering and Artillery, which are highly essential, and the knowledge of which, is most difficult to obtain. Also Manufactories of some kinds of Military Stores."[13] He did not mention the small navy which was to be refounded in 1794 to protect trade by retaliating against Barbary, French, or English violators of our maritime rights. In any case the declining threat of British and Indian wars after 1815 led to still less militia training, and each war or crisis led to a new debate over the merits of expansible regular armies and volunteer ones raised and commanded by volunteer officers.

John A. Logan's posthumous *Volunteer Soldiere of America,* 1887, came from a volunteer general and politician who felt that West Pointers had kept him from commanding the Army of the Tennessee. Emory A. Upton's *Military Policy of the United States,* circulated after his death in 1881 and published by the War Department in 1904, revived John C. Calhoun's 1820 plan for an expansible regular army.[14] The three works on these matters which are still worth reading are John M. Palmer's *America in Arms,* 1941, Walter Millis's *Arms and Men,* 1956, and Samuel P. Huntington's *The Soldier and the State,* 1957.[15] A General Staff officer whose grandfather had been a distinguished Civil War volunteer general and politician, Palmer rediscovered Washington's "Sentiments." Millis's was the first history of American military policy to deal with naval matters. Huntington's much more general and influential book is Upton by Clausewitz out of Friedrich Hegel, and sees the professional soldier as one pillar of any conservative, democratic state. But students may get the histories of the American military profession, military institutions, civil-military relations, and attitudes toward war so confused that they should begin with Weigley's or Millis's books of readings, or with Marcus P. Cunliffe's discursive *Soldiers and Civilians: The Martial Spirit in America, 1775-1865.*[16] Cunliffe sees our traditional attitudes toward war as a mixture of Southern Chevalier concepts of honor, Northern Rifleman democratic pragmatism, and Quaker hatred of war. Late nineteenth-century concepts of war as a science, Huntington notes, appealed to our technism and pragmatism, and provided a new self-image for a tiny professional soldiers' guild which no longer had to awe Indians. And there were dashes of Neo-Darwinism and Calvinism in the attitudes of Woodrow Wilson, Henry R. Luce, and John Foster Dulles.

Weigley's *History of the United State Army* is excellent. Francis P. Prucha's *Sword of the Republic: The United States Army on the Frontier, 1783-1846,* also in Morton's series, tries too hard on its peacetime utility.[17] Its early intellectual history will be considered in Thomas E. Griess's study of Dennis Hart Mahan (not yet published in 1972); its political history was one of fund-grubbing in a society whose attitudes toward war were hardly influenced by it. One-volume histories of the navy are parochial and dull; Robert D. Heinl is more parochial and livelier on the Marine Corps. Mahan set too many historians to showing that sea power was always history's most influential factor, while his own prose is so dated that the works to start with are Harold and Margaret Sprout's on naval policy, Howard I. Chapelle's, Bernard Brodie's, and William Hovgaard's on ships and weapons, and Charles O. Paullin's *History of Naval Administration, 1775-1911,* a much broader work than its title might indicate. But none of them deal, except in passing, with Mahan's "principal conditions affecting the sea power of nations," or how changes in these conditions—which were drawn from the preindustrial era—were soon to affect that *Pax Britannica* which had been one of the chief diplomatic conditions of our vanishing century of "free security" and military isolation.[18]

Barry M. Gough and Kenneth Bourne have shown how local naval forces which could be reinforced to get preponderance helped to preserve the balance of power in Northwestern North America. Neogunboatists might then study Gerald S. Graham's thirty pages on "The Illusion of 'Pax Britannica.' " It was not "the simple consequence of naval power wielded with sensible restraint by the self-appointed policeman of the world. It was the result of varied force and circumstances, the chief of which was Britain's industrial supremacy, which made possible a phenomenal commercial development . . . [and] a kind of international equality in the sharing of economic benefits" in an era when every great power, after the Napoleonic Wars, wanted to avoid major wars and did avoid a general one until 1914. So Britain could use "her navy not only as a means of conducting anything from a demonstration to a local war, but as an effective restraining force in the . . . European balance." But when other industrializing powers had to have overseas raw materials and markets and prestige weapons, and when other battle fleets, partly because of Mahan's influence, might be added to those of France and Russia, Britain's position as the world's sea power became untenable; and this became another past age of diplomatic equilibrium, though one which had permitted that "British monopoly of the seas which Mahan rightly identified with world power."[19]

The Wars of the Nineteenth Century

Our local nineteenth-century battlefields are so covered with solid scholarly works that choices of very good or readable ones must again be largely personal. Donald B. Chidsey's little *Wars in Barbary* leads into James A. Field, Jr.'s larger study of our Mediterranean naval forces; Morison is at his best on Matthew C. Perry. Anyone who thinks that we never lost a war before Vietnam might read J. Mackay Hitsman's Canadian work on the War of 1812, though the clearest losers were our Indians. Harry L. Coles has succinctly summarized the historiography of the causes of the War of 1812 and provided for the *Chicago History of Civilization* a sprightly narrative of the campaigns and naval battles. Otis A. Singletary's is still the best short account of the Mexican War. K. Jack Bauer's story of the Vera Cruz landing is the highlight of his work on its naval operations, and David S. Lavender's *Climax at*

Buena Vista again shows Zachary Taylor as a solid, lucky commander in Northeastern Mexico.[20]

It would be useful to have a new one-volume military history of the Civil War, a socio-political book about its boom and Centennial, and general studies of the naval war, infantry tactics, cavalry and horse supply, artillery and commanders' failures to group their guns when they had them for Napoleonic battles, and fortification. While the Centennial's celebrants were overkilling their audiences, Bruce Catton completed Lloyd Lewis's *Captain Sam Grant* and the late Allan Nevins carried his *War for the Union* into 1865. The detail of these and other multivolume works—or of *Samuel Frances Du Pont: A Selection from His Civil War Letters*—is a specific for that general's rating which strikes so many buffs and historians. James M. Merrill has a fine new biography of Sherman. With the growing interest in history "from the bottom up," Bell I. Wiley's two books on the common soldier, *Johnny Reb* and *Billy Yank,* should have a renewed appeal.[21] The Du Pont *Letters,* biographies of the private shipbuilder John Roach and naval engineer-in-chief Benjamin F. Isherwood, the diaries of the young naval surgeon Samuel P. Boyer, and Frank J. Merli's *Great Britain and the Confederate Navy* were among the best works on the navies.[22] Richard D. Goff's study of Confederate supply, Charles B. Dew's study of the Tredegar Iron Works, and James H. Brewer's study of Virginia's black craftsmen and laborers covered new ground. The 1911 *Photographic History,* the American Heritage volume, David Donald's *Divided We Fought,* and Francis A. Lord's *They Fought for the Union* have very fine texts with their pictures. And this war's *Official Records* are better than those on our Revolution or a huge bureaucracy's *Pentagon Papers* for getting students into documentary collections.[23]

Stewart Brooks' *Civil War Medicine* and Paul E. Steiner's *Disease in the Civil War* are complementary works. Without a scientific explanation for disease, epidemiology was in its infancy. Poor field sanitation—a chronic weakness of volunteer armies—was compounded by inadequate medical services, year-round campaigning, and heavy battle casualties. The state of medicine during the Civil War was almost as bad as that during the Crimean and Italian Wars. Yet it produced no American Florence Nightingale or Henry Dunant, perhaps because of the relative priority of medicine in Europe and in the United States or a less urbanized America had not been so shaken by great cholera epidemics during the first half of the century. Dr. Steiner deals with military and accompanying civilian casualties in eight campaigns which were as much aborted by disease as by military incompetence. Both sides later tried to avoid sickly areas or seasons; one end product may have been the magnificent disease distribution maps in that *Statistical Atlas of the United States based on the Results of the Ninth Census 1870* with which Francis A. Walker hoped "to practically inaugurate the study of political and social statistics in the colleges and higher schools of the land."[24]

Paul I. Wellman has provided a "general survey" of the Indian wars of the late nineteenth century, and Don Rickey has studied the enlisted men who fought in them. But we ought to know more about our partly foreign-manned navy. Where did its men come from, and what became of the black craftsmen described by Professor James Brewer and the Civil War sailors who found both ocean and river shipping declining? Many of them may have joined those railroad and farm machinery mechanics who were the sergeants—rather than the better known captains—of our postwar industrialization.

The Spanish-American War was, of course, a nineteenth-century one for twentieth-century purposes. Frank Freidel's and Millis's are the best one-volume accounts. Virgil Carrington Jones has a fine social and military study of those Rough Riders who inadvertently caused Theodore Roosevelt's presidential successor, once removed, to insist that no political general get a Great War command. David F. Healy and Allen R. Millett have written good books on Cuba, John Gates will have one on Philippine pacification, and a personal choice for our later Latin American small wars is Neill Macaulay's *Sandino Affair.*[25]

The Two World Wars

In 1903 the United States began to build two battleships per year. By 1923 its fleet was "second to none." By 1943 it was the strongest in the world, a reflection of American industrial might, the further mechanization of war, and two World Wars' effects on its power balances. Elting E. Morison's *Admiral Sims and the Modern American Navy,* Richard K. Morris's *John P. Holland,* and Armin Rappaport's *Navy League of the United States* deal with naval modernization; Irving B. Holley, Jr.'s work on John M. Palmer will add detail on the army. Our professional soldiers, as has been noted, combined a view of war as a science with a social role more like that of guildsmen than members of a militaristic caste. The number of officers on active peacetime duty rose from 2276 in 1860 to 7562 in 1910, or one for every 13,850 and 13,537 persons respectively. Over 30,000 active-duty German officers in 1910 each represented about 2000 persons. The numbers of ours rose to 30,745 in 1920 and 33,730 in 1940, or one for every 3842 and 4432 persons. Our 1950 figures were to be 181,465 and every 839 persons. But active-duty officers were still less numerous than physicians, 191,947, or teachers in higher educational institutions, 246,722, a group with an even higher growth rate in the next two decades.[26]

Our Great War role was decisive, but our major decisions were not military ones. The sea and land wars which we helped to win were less colorful than that in the air, which did win a following of American buffs. Canada lost six and one-half times as many men in proportion to her population, and was nearly torn apart by overseas conscription. It was hard for us—a fact which affected our later views of their ingratitude— to feel indebted to the men of the Marne or Paaschendaele, and readers might try Jack J. Roth, editor, *World War I: A Turning Point in Modern History,* before reading Edward M. Coffman's summary of our part in it. Coffman's life of Peyton C. March can go with Frederick Palmer's *John J. Pershing* until Frank E. Vandiver's new life of Pershing appears. Our war literature—despite the war's importance in the lives of particular writers—is rather thin and derivative. And the American Heritage volume, Freidel's *Over There,* or Laurence Stallings's *Doughboys* may have less impact on students than the latter's general photographic history, a warning in 1933 of another round.[27] The many works on our loss of innocence in Paris are also dated; any schoolboy now knows that it was lost somewhere between Manila and Saigon.

Interwar matters are often treated in works on World War II. Alfred F. Hurley has a fine study of *Billy Mitchell* and is writing an Air Force history for Morton's series. A collective study of those 1600 Army Air Corps officers of 1939 who were commanding 2,411,000 men by 1944 would be useful. The proportion was about the same as that in our Civil War armies. Whether more Army Air than Army or Navy officers had been in civilian life during the interwar years and whether there were more civilians in its wartime higher commands might be answered by comparative studies. Thaddeus V. Tuleja has a good short study of our Far Eastern naval policy; Harold G. Bowen discusses naval research; and *The London Journal of General Raymond E. Lee 1940-1941* is one American insider's view of Britain while we were neutral against Germany.[28]

1972 is to 1932 as 1905 was to 1865. Our four decades of sustained federal governmental activism confirmed some trends of the Progressive era, and left so many papers that most histories of these decades are official, semi-official, or private recyclings of the same first cuts into the documents. Their selling is a separate ethical question; few American leaders, in any case, had such powerful literary styles that readers need warnings about Churchillian or Gaullist historical and social poetics. Our World War II official histories, perhaps because of public skepticism or because theirs was a success story, are very honest; their weaknesses are ones of omission rather than commission. That they do not deal with personalities, except in some very obvious cases, is part of the success story of military institutions which produced commanders with, in Ferdinand Foch's words, "a common way of acting." The Army's official history is the bulkiest, but some of its authors have produced fine summaries. Kent R. Greenfield wrote the best short work on *American Strategy,* and edited one on *Command Decisions.* Charles B. MacDonald has the best history of our role in the European, or any other Theater, and Morton has the best current bibliographical surveys.[29]

The Air Force official history was written a bit too soon to treat some tactical issues. The British official historian Noble Frankland's *Bomber Offensive,* in Ballantine's *Illustrated History of World War II,* and Anthony Verrier's *Bomber Offensive* sum up campaigns in which British hopes and experiences played major roles. Holley's *Buying Aircraft,* in our Army series, follows up his *Ideas and Weapons,* but we need histories of our aircraft and air transport industries for a general history of American air power.[30] Morison's *History of United States Naval Operations in World War II* has swamped his one-volume summary and the Navy's administrative and Marine Corps histories, though not Clark G. Reynold's *Fast Carriers.*[31] Richard A. Polenberg's *War and Society* is a fine work in view of the fact that no American civil history series made systematic first cuts into the documents. There are various official histories of specialized wartime boards and agencies, but no study of *The Army and Economic Mobilization* or *The Army and Industrial Manpower* could match Richard M. Titmuss's *Problems of Social Policy* in the British civil history or some volumes in *The Economic and Social History of the World War,* edited by James T. Shotwell.[32]

Basil Collier's is a reliable general military history of World War II, but the lack of materials on some East European problems and on China make it hard to bring the whole war into focus. A. Russell Buchanan's two volumes in *The New American Nation* series are not as well focused as Gordon Wright's *Ordeal of Total War* in *The Rise of Modern Europe.* Martin Blumenson is excellent on European battles and campaigns. The interview method used so well by S. L. A. Marshall was suggested by Ardant du Picq in the 1860's.[33] Charles Bateson's *War with Japan* can be read with Ladislas Farago's story of our breaking the Japanese code, Roberta Wohlstetter's *Pearl Harbor,* Tuleja's *Climax at Midway,* the works of Stanley L. Falk and James H. and William M. Belote, Leslie Anders's *Ledo Road,* the U. S. Naval Institute's collection of Japanese accounts, and Alvin D. Coox's *Japan: The Final Agony,* in the Ballantine series.[34] These well-illustrated paperbacks cover weapons as well as campaigns and battles and are now going back to the interwar era. Many of them, as has been noted, are written by authors of official history volumes. Many of them have good bibliographies. They are generally competent, well-written, and much cheaper than competitive products for what seems to be a still growing model-maker and costume-drama market. There are no biographies or memoirs of a number of important naval and air commanders. Forrest C. Pogue's masterly *George C. Marshall* now gets into the war years. Blumenson's *Patton Papers* and D. Clayton James's *Years of MacArthur* do not; the latter should be supplemented by the Australian official historian Gavin Long's *MacArthur as Military Commander*. Barbara W. Tuchman's *Stilwell* may bring out works on such other China characters as Claire L. Chennault, or on how advisers or diplomats may go native. And the best recent works on Dwight D. Eisenhower are the Eisenhower Foundation's *D-Day* studies, John S. D. Eisenhower's *The Bitter Woods* (of the Ardennes), and Stephen E. Ambrose's *Eisenhower and Berlin*.[35]

The Contemporary Era

Louis J. Halle's and Walter LaFeber's Cold War histories are better than any of the arms race, which is best followed in such periodicals as the *Scientific American*.[36] The wars in the Near East, India, Indochina, China, and Korea—which most affected the power balance—were, except for the last two, fought in installments. After perfecting their nuclear "agents"—maximized as hydrogen bombs and miniaturized as tactical bombs, shells, mines, and depth charges—the superpowers turned to ballistic missile "delivery systems." To reach the United States, the Russians developed intercontinentals (ICBMs); the American answer was intermediate-range (IRBM) launching from nuclear-powered submarines. Ideas of "no cities" warfare and anti-ballistic missiles (ABMs) faded with the development of multiple individual-targeted reentry vehicles (MIRVs). Planes were kept airborne, submarines at sea, and missile silos hardened against a nuclear Pearl Harbor. Since the less powerful MIRVs were better for retaliatory "second" than for "first strikes," the superpowers did get on with their Strategic Arms Limitation Talks (SALT). It seemed possible for China to get that kind of retaliatory security. What others would join Britain and France in the expensive middle-power nuclear club was more arguable, since it was also argued that a non-nuclear power had more leverage on its nuclear protectors.

All this has so expanded the subject matter of contemporary military history—though this had been partly true for earlier eras of armed peace —that readers may need Mathematese and Hard and Soft Scientese as well as English. The first large study to use them all was the *United*

States Strategic Bombing Survey, which examined its effects on everything from military operations to production and morale for clues to what the Russian economist Ivan S. Bloch had studied statistically in 1898 in *The Future of War in Its Technical, Economic, and Political Relations,* a work which had helped to get Tsar Nicholas II to call the First Hague Peace Conference by predicting military deadlock, economic chaos, and political and social revolution.[37] Wartime weapons research and development and peacetime planning and opinion polling had improved Bloch's methods. Photographic and electronic fact-finding and processing devices of hitherto incredible power and speed were now applied to the military problems of who was moving what where, though those who applied them to the political problems of why they were doing something sometimes forgot that their interpretive norms came from Western and/or Marxist historical experience.

The first signs of trouble were mispredictions of the speed of Russian weapons development. Our problems of weapons costing were then compounded by financing and cost-plus procurement systems which had taken the First War's "excess" profits out of the Second. These systems had worked quite well in wartime when time was more important than money, but led to gross overruns in peacetime when results were harder to relate to increasingly speculative weapons and gross national product balance sheets, or to hot wars in which only two great powers, very early in this era, directly fought each other. The best dividing point, as has been noted, is the mid-1950's, when the bipolar world of Harry Truman and Joseph Stalin was replaced by that multipolar one which emerged when Mao Tse-tung and Charles de Gaulle became the Third World and Old World Presidents. The romanticism of their dreams is less important than the fact that—as the military balance hardened—many political systems began to grow democratic, neo-Fascist, several kinds of Marxist, Tolstoyan, and anarchist and terrorist mutants.

The shocks to American futurists began during the war. But our immediate postwar policies for economic recovery, containment, and deterrence—all firmly rooted in our immediately past experience—secured a remarkable degree of public support and were pursued with remarkable consistency. The lack of especially readable books on the immediate postwar foreign policy and military unification debates may suggest their one-sidedness. The best works are more general ones by Herbert Agar and William Appleman Williams, unless one can stomach Dean Acheson's and George F. Kennan's accounts of the Creation. MacArthur's dismissal, as seen by John W. Spanier, involved no new issues in civil-military relations. The best books on the Korean War are by David Rees, T. R. Fehrenbach, Matthew B. Ridgway, and J.

Lawton Collins, the latter being a summary of the official history and an insider's view of the role of the Joint Chiefs of Staff in MacArthur's dismissal.[38] McCarthyism was a sign of frustrated internationalist nationalism rather than one of isolationism, after the successive shocks of Russian duplicity, Mao's victory in China, and North Korean aggression.

The Eisenhower years have received less attention. "Massive retaliation" was an only too popular slogan for deterring local aggression at its presumed source, and "Engine Charlie" (Charles E.) Wilson's "more bang for a buck" promises were just as catchy. In his last word as head of the Air Force in 1946, Henry H. Arnold had seen a possible nuclear stalemate, but the speed of Russian "we try harder" catch-up might have been more widely predicted from earlier industrial races. The best military intellectual predictions of the late 1950's were Henry A. Kissinger's *Nuclear Weapons and Foreign Policy* and Brodie's *Strategy in the Missile Age*. Another set of predictions was contained in the Rockefeller Reports entitled collectively *Prospect for Change*. Titles of individual Reports were "The Mid-Century Challenge to U. S. Foreign Policy"; "International Security: The Military Aspect" (drafted by Kissinger); "Foreign Economic Policy"; "The Challenge to America: Its Economic and Social Aspects"; "The Pursuit of Excellence: Education and the Future of America"; and "The Power of the Democratic Idea." The real Eisenhower was the one who was to write in *Mandate for Change* that he had taken a university presidency in 1948 to help to set up "the American Assembly (a continuing program bringing together men of business, labor, the professions, political parties, and government for the study of major national problems), the program for the conservation of human resources, and a Chair of Peace." The shocks of Suez, Hungary, and Sputnik had led to some unease, but C. Wright Mills's 1956 *Power Elite* had been little noted and had not suggested any Establishment conspiracy. And Eisenhower's 1961 "military-industrial complex" warning probably reflected his failure to hold down defense costs and his outrage at not being informed of the U-2 flights.[39]

An alleged "missile gap" was a factor in the close Presidential election of 1960, but victory in the Cuban missile crisis of 1962 overcame the shocks of the Bay of Pigs and the Berlin Wall, and led to a new euphoria about the "flexible response" strategy worked out in the late 1950's. Robert S. McNamara's "cost effectiveness" tools were those of Bloch and the *Strategic Bombing Survey*. Alain C. Enthoven and C. Wayne Smith's *How Much Is Enough?* gives the details of McNamara's *The Essence of Security*. Since Lyndon B. Johnson's memoirs are no literary match for those of St. Augustine, Winston Churchill, or de Gaulle, the politics of the Vietnam War are better followed in the works of Ralph

K. White, Eugene Windchy, Townsend Hoopes, and Chester L. Cooper.[40] In relating military means to political ends, that war seems more like Japan's China Incident than like the Korean War. The latter had been a limited conventional war in which we had attained our original political ends. North Vietnamese threats to South Vietnam were first seen in similar terms; they came, instead, from a "modern" partisan army. This war's justification in traditional terms of prestige or resource balances rather than the newer ones of responding to any Communist aggression would have been difficult at best. The problem was then compounded by massive cost and time overruns, while official body counters and economic experts competed for attention with color films of bombing, man hunting, ambushes, war and political refugees and prisoners, and human and ecological devastation.

Our myths of popular revolts against war and taxes are as hazy as other social explosion ones—or the ideas that overpopulation, poverty, and boredom inevitably lead to increased social violence—which have grown up with the increasing participation of the people in great affairs of state. But the dangers of bogging down Western conscripts might have been foreseen. David Lloyd George, the first man of the people to become Britain's Prime Minister, had tried to "keep back the men" when his generals' victory at Paaschendaele had led them to ask for more, and the Algerian War had ended the Fourth French Republic. The Tet offensive of 1968 seems to have been directed at the South Vietnamese. Its failure strengthened them. The American generals' request for more men after this victory was denied, and Johnson decided not to enter the presidential race. His successor's efforts to end conscription left him more dependent on air and sea power to cover his ground forces' withdrawal. We can only hope that the difficulties of finding out what happened—especially on the effects of air power—with so few enemy records to exploit will not turn historians to easier Establishment conspiracy, "too little and too late," or "stab in the back" explanations.

In any case many of the traditional "practical" uses of military history will be challenged. In his 1961 pamphlet on that subject—still the best introduction to its historiography—Millis held that its future "as a useful discipline would seem to depend . . . upon the extent to which it can merge back into the general study of man and his society."[41] Some of its appeal has always been antiquarian. But with nonevents' records much scarcer and harder to interpret, peace and conflict resolution specialists might benefit from studying the misapplications of the hard and soft sciences to warfare. None of the appeals or problems of these studies have vanished. Many people still feel that studies of ways of controlling social violence in a world in which everyone has the equivalent of ten tons of TNT—however these, like other resources, are ill-distributed—and access to guns and explosives are important. And many people also fear that their world still contains others who do not wish them well and who may be willing to use force to accomplish their political or personal purposes.

FOOTNOTES

[1] Boston: Little, Brown, 1890. Hill & Wang. pb.

[2] *The Impact of War on American Life*. New York: Holt, Rinehart and Winston, 1971. pb; Maurice Matloff, editor. *American Military History*. Washington: U. S. Army, Office of the Chief of Military History, U.S.G.P.O., 1969; *Encyclopedia of Military History*. New York: Harper & Row, 1970.

[3] Bruce Lancaster. *The American Heritage Book of the Revolution*. New York: Simon and Schuster, 1958; Bruce Catton. *The American Heritage Picture History of the Civil War*. New York: Doubleday, 1960; S. L. A. Marshall. *The American Heritage History of World War I*. New York: Simon and Schuster, 1964; C. L. Sulzberger. *The American Heritage Picture History of World War II*. New York: Simon and Schuster, 1966.

[4] Clarence C. Buel and Robert U. Johnson, editors. *Battles and Leaders of the Civil War*. Reprint, intro. Roy F. Nichols, 4 vols. New York: Yoseloff, 1956; *History of the United States. . . .* New York: Macmillan, 1910; Ropes. *The Story of the Civil War*. 4 vols. New York: B. Franklin, 1894-1913; Francis T. Miller, editor. *Photographic History of the Civil War*. Reprint, 10 vols. in 5. New York: Yoseloff, 1957.

[5] For Tocqueville's and other social scientists' views use Leon Bramson and George W. Goethals, editors. *War: Studies from Psychology, Sociology, and Anthropology*. New York: Basic Books, 1964. pp. 321-338. Rev. ed. 1968. pb.

[6] *R. E. Lee*. 4 vols. New York: Scribner's, 1935-36; abr. Richard Harwell. New York: Scribner's, 1959; Bramson and Goethals. *War*. pp. 21-31.

[7] *Admiral of the Ocean Sea*. 2 vols., and abr. Boston: Little, Brown, 1942, as *Christopher Columbus: Mariner*. Mentor pb; *The European Discovery of America*. New York: Oxford, 1971; *Columbus*. New York: Macmillan, 1967; *Guns, Sails, and Empires: Technological Innovation and the Early Phases of European Expansion*. New York: Pantheon, 1965. Funk & Wagnalls pb; *The Establishment of the European Hegemony: Trade and Exploration in the Age of the Renaissance*. New ed. New York: Harper, 1961. pb; *The Colonial Wars*. Chicago: University of Chicago Press, 1964. pb.

[8] *Wars of the Iroquois: A Study in Intertribal Trade Relations*. Madison: University of Wisconsin Press, 1940. pb; Leach. *Flintlock and Tomahawk: New England in King Philip's War*. New York: Macmillan, 1958. Norton pb; *History of the Second Seminole War, 1839-1842*. Gainesville: University of Florida Press, 1967; Peterson. *Arms and Armour in Colonial America, 1526-1783*. Harrisburg: Stackpole, 1956; repr. New York: Bramhall; Russell. *Guns on the Early Frontiers: A History of Firearms from Colonial Times through the Years of the Western Fur Trade*. Berkeley: University of California Press, 1957. pb; repr. New York: Bonanza.

[9] This series is New York: Knopf; J. H. Parry. *The Spanish Seaborne Empire*. 1966; Boxer. *The Dutch Seaborne Empire, 1600-1800*. 1965; Alden. *Pioneer America*. 1966. pb.

[10] *Quebec: The Siege and the Battle*. New York: St. Martin's, 1959; *Quiberon Bay: The Campaign in Home Waters, 1759*. London: Hollis & Carter, 1960.

[11] *Toward Lexington.* Princeton: Princeton University Press, 1965. pb; *American Revolution.* New York: Harper, *New American Nation,* 1954. pb; *War for America.* Cambridge, Mass.: Harvard University Press, 1964. *The War of American Independence: Military Attitudes, Policies, and Practice, 1763-1789.* New York: Macmillan, 1971. See also Christopher Ward. *The War of the Revolution,* edited by John R. Alden. 2 vols. New York: Macmillan, 1952. On Washington as a general, see James T. Flexner. *George Washington in the American Revolution, 1775-1783.* Boston: Little, Brown, 1968; as reference works for other military leaders of the war, see the collections of articles edited by George A. Billias. *George Washington's Generals.* New York: W. Morrow, 1964, and *George Washington's Opponents: British Generals and Admirals in the American Revolution.* New York: W. Morrow, 1969.

[12] *Partisan War.* Columbia, S.C.: University of South Carolina Press, 1970; *The River and the Rock.* New York: Greenwood, 1969; *The Battle for Bunker Hill.* London: Cresset, 1963; *The Cowpens-Guilford Courthouse Campaign.* Philadelphia: Lippincott, *Great Battles of History,* 1962; *Decision at the Chesapeake.* New York: C. N. Potter, 1964; *Die Truppen. . . .* Darmstadt: Wehr und Wissen-Verlagsgesellschaft, 1965.

[13] Russell F. Weigley, editor. *The American Military: Readings in the History of the Military in American Society.* Reading, Mass.: Addison-Wesley pb, 1969. pp. 3-8.

[14] Bits of Logan and Upton are in Weigley. *American Military.* pp. 77-85, 24-31. Upton was reprinted by Greenwood (New York) in 1970.

[15] *America in Arms.* New Haven: Yale University Press, 1941; *Arms and Men: A Study in American Military History.* New York: Putnam, 1956. Mentor pb; *The Soldier and the State. The Theory and Politics of Civil-Military Relations.* Cambridge, Mass.: Harvard University Press, 1956. Vintage pb.

[16] Millis's collection is *American Military Thought.* Indianapolis: Bobbs-Merrill, 1966. pb; *Soldiers and Civilians.* Boston: Little, Brown, 1968. Another collection of readings is Raymond G. O'Connor, editor. *American Defense Policy in Perspective: From Colonial Times to the Present.* New York: John Wiley, 1965. pb; On the anti-militarist tradition use Arthur E. Ekirch, Jr. *The Civilian and the Military.* New York: Oxford, 1959. Colorado Springs, Colorado: Ralph Myles pb; or parts of Staughton Lynd, editor. *Nonviolence in America: A Documentary History.* Indianapolis: Bobbs-Merrill, 1966. pb.

[17] *History of the United States Army.* New York: Macmillan, 1967; *Sword of the Republic.* New York: Macmillan, 1969. For a different view of the more modern Army Engineers see Arthur E. Morgan. *Dams and Other Disasters: A Century of the Army Corps of Engineers in Civil Works.* Boston: Porter Sergeant, 1971.

[18] Heinl. *Soldiers of the Sea.* Annapolis: U. S. Naval Institute, 1962; Sprout and Sprout. *The Rise of American Naval Power, 1775-1918.* Princeton: Princeton University Press, 1939, 1966. pb; and *Toward a New Order of Sea Power: American Naval Policy and the World Scene, 1918-1922.* Princeton: Princeton University Press, 1940. Rev. ed. 1966. pb; Chapelle. *The History of the American Sailing Navy: The Ships and Their Development.* New York: Norton, 1949. repr. Bonanza; Brodie. *Sea Power in the Machine Age.* Princeton: Princeton University Press, 1941; Hovgaard. *Modern History of Warships.* New York: Spon and Chamberlain, 1920; Annapolis: U.S. Naval Institute, 1971; Paullin's articles date from 1905-1911; Annapolis: U.S. Naval Institute, 1968; E. B. Potter's *Naval Academy Illustrated History of the United States Navy.* New York: Thomas Y. Crowell, 1971, and *Sea Power: A Naval History,* edited by Potter and Chester W. Nimitz. Englewood Cliffs: Prentice-Hall, 1960, are fine works but are too ill-balanced to be satisfactory one-volume naval histories.

[19] Gough. *The Royal Navy and the Northwest Coast of North America, 1810-1914.* Vancouver: University of British Columbia, 1971; Bourne. *Britain and the*

Balance of Power in North America, 1815-1908. Berkeley: University of California Press, 1967; Graham. *The Politics of Naval Supremacy: Studies in British Maritime Ascendancy.* Cambridge: Cambridge University Press, 1965. pp. 118-119, 125.

[20] *Wars in Barbary. Arab Piracy and the Birth of the United States Navy.* New York: Crown, 1971; Field. *America and the Mediterranean World, 1776-1882.* Princeton: Princeton University Press, 1969; Morison. *Old Bruin.* Boston: Little, Brown, 1967; Hitsman. *The Incredible War of 1812: A Military History.* Toronto: University of Toronto Press, 1965; Coles. *The War of 1812.* Chicago: University of Chicago Press, 1965; Singletary. *The Mexican War.* Chicago: University of Chicago Press, *History of American Civilization,* 1960. pb; Bauer. *Surfboats and Horse Marineers: U. S. Naval Operations in the Mexican War, 1846-1848.* Annapolis: U. S. Naval Institute, 1969; *Climax at Buena Vista: The American Campaign in Northeastern Mexico, 1846-47.* Philadelphia: Lippincott, *Great Battles of History,* 1966.

[21] *Captain Sam Grant.* Boston: Little, Brown, 1950; Catton's volumes were *Grant Takes Command.* Boston: Little, Brown, 1969, and *Grant Moves South.* Boston: Little, Brown, 1960. Nevins' are vols. 5-8 of his *Ordeal of the Union.* 4 vols. New York: Scribner's, 1959-1971; John D. Hayes, editor. *Samuel Francis DuPont.* 3 vols. Ithaca: Cornell University Press, 1969; Merrill. *William Tecumseh Sherman.* Chicago: Rand McNally, 1971; Wiley. *The Life of Johnny Reb, the Common Soldier of the Confederacy.* Indianapolis: Bobbs-Merrill Company, 1943 and *The Life of Billy Yank, the Common Soldier of the Union.* Indianapolis: Bobbs-Merrill Company, 1952.

[22] Leonard A. Swann, Jr. *John Roach, Maritime Entrepreneur: The Years as Naval Contractor, 1862-1886.* Annapolis: U. S. Naval Institute, 1965; Edward W. Sloan III. *Benjamin Franklin Isherwood, Naval Engineer: The Years as Engineer in Chief, 1861-1869.* Annapolis: U. S. Naval Institute, 1965; Elinor and James A. Barnes, editors. *Naval Surgeon: The Diary of Dr. Samuel Pellman Boyer.* 2 vols. Bloomington: Indiana University Press, 1963; *Great Britain and the Confederate Navy.* Bloomington: Indiana University Press, 1970.

[23] Goff. *Confederate Supply.* Durham: Duke University Press, 1969; Dew. *Ironmaker to the Confederacy: Joseph R. Anderson and the Tredegar Iron Works.* New Haven: Yale University Press, 1966; Brewer. *The Confederate Negro: Virginia's Craftsmen and Military Laborers.* Durham: Duke University Press, 1969; David Donald. *Divided We Fought: A Pictorial History of the War, 1861-1965.* New York: Macmillan, 1952; *They Fought for the Union.* Harrisburg: Stackpole, 1960.

[24] *Civil War Medicine.* Springfield, Ill.: C. C. Thomas, 1966; *Disease in the Civil War.* Springfield, Ill.: C. C. Thomas, 1968; the *Atlas* was printed by Julius Bien, 1874.

[25] Wellman. *Death on Horseback: Seventy Years of War for the American West.* Philadelphia: Lippincott, 1947; Rickey. *Forty Miles a Day on Beans and Hay: The Enlisted Soldier Fighting the Indian Wars.* Norman: University of Oklahoma Press, 1963; Freidel. *The Splendid Little War.* Boston: Little, Brown, 1958. Dell pb; Millis. *The Martial Spirit: A Study of Our War with Spain.* Cambridge, Mass.: Harvard University Press, 1931; Jones. *Roosevelt's Rough Riders.* Garden City: Doubleday, 1971; Healy. *The United States in Cuba, 1898-1902: Generals, Politicians, and the Search for Policy.* Madison: University of Wisconsin Press, 1963; Millett. *The Politics of Intervention.* Columbus: Ohio State University Press, 1968; Macaulay. Chicago: Quadrangle, 1967.

[26] *Admiral Sims and the Modern Navy.* Boston: Houghton Mifflin, 1942; *John P. Holland, 1841-1914: Inventor of the Modern Submarine.* Annapolis: U. S. Naval Institute, 1966; *Navy League of the United States.* Detroit: Wayne State University Press, 1962.

[27] *World War I.* New York: Knopf, 1967. pb; Coffman. *The War to End All Wars: The American Military Experience in World War I.* New York: Oxford,

1968; Coffman. *The Hilt of the Sword—The Career of Peyton C. March.* Madison: University of Wisconsin Press, 1966; Palmer. Harrisburg: Military Service Pub. Co., 1948; *Over There.* Boston: Little, Brown, 1964; *Doughboys.* New York: Harper & Row, 1963. Popular Library pb.; Stallings. *The First World War: A Photographic History.* New York: Simon and Schuster, 1933. Repr. 1960.

[28] Hurley. *Crusader for Air Power.* New York: Franklin Watts, 1964; Tuleja. *Statesmen and Admirals: Quest for a Far Eastern Naval Policy.* New York: W. W. Norton, 1963; Bowen. *Ships, Machinery, and Mossbacks: The Autobiography of a Naval Engineer.* Princeton: Princeton University Press, 1954; James Leutze, editor. *The London Journal. . . .* Boston: Little, Brown, 1971.

[29] *American Strategy in World War II: A Reconsideration.* Baltimore: Johns Hopkins Press, 1963; *Command Decisions.* New York: Harcourt, Brace, 1959; MacDonald. *The Mighty Endeavor: American Armed Forces in the European Theater in World War II.* New York: Oxford, 1969; Morton. "Writings on World War II." Washington: Service Center for Teachers of History, American Historical Association, No. 66, 1967; "World War II: A Survey of Recent Writings." *American Historical Review,* Vol. LXXV; No. 7, Dec. 1970. pp. 1987-2008.

[30] Wesley Frank Craven and James L. Cate, editors. *The Army Air Forces in World War II.* 7 vols. Chicago: University of Chicago Press, 1948-1958; Frankland. *Bomber Offensive: The Devastation of Europe.* New York: Ballantine, 1970; Verrier. *The Bomber Offensive.* New York: Macmillan, 1968; *Buying Aircraft: Materiel Procurement for the Army Air Forces.* Washington: U.S. Army, Office of the Chief of Military History, *United States Army in World War II,* U.S.G.P.O., 1964; *Ideas and Weapons.* New Haven: Yale University Press, 1953. Reprint. Hamden, Conn.: Archon, 1971.

[31] *History of United States Naval Operations in World War II.* 15 vols. Boston: Little, Brown, 1947-1962; Morison. *The Two Ocean War.* Boston: Little, Brown, 1963; *The Fast Carriers.* New York: McGraw-Hill, 1968.

[32] *War and Society: The United States 1941-1945.* Philadelphia: Lippincott, 1972. pb; *The Army and Economic Mobilization* by R. Elberton Smith, and *The Army and Industrial Manpower* by Byron Fairchild and Johnathan Grossman are in the *U. S. Army in World War II.* Washington: Department of the Army, Office of the Chief of Military History, U.S.G.P.O., 1959, series. Titmuss's is in W. K. Hancock, editor. *United Kingdom Civil Series; History of the Second World War.* London: H.M.S.O., 1950; *Economic and Social History of the War.* 150 vols. New Haven: Yale University Press, 1921-   .

[33] Collier. *The Second World War: A Military History.* New York: William Morrow, 1967; Buchanan. *The United States and World War II.* 2 vols. New York: Harper & Row, 1964. pb; *Ordeal of Total War.* New York: Harper & Row, 1968. pb; Blumenson's works include *The Duel for France; Kasserine Pass; Bloody River: The Real Tragedy of the Rapido.* Boston: Houghton Mifflin, 1963, 1966, 1970; *Anzio.* Philadelphia: Lippincott, *Great Battles of History,* 1963; and *Sicily: Whose Victory?* New York: Ballantine, 1968. One of Marshall's best is *Night Drop: The American Airborne Invasion of Normandy.* Boston: Little, Brown, 1962. Bantam pb. Charles MacDonald. *Airborne.* New York: Ballantine, 1970. pb, is just as expert and readable.

[34] *War with Japan.* East Lansing: Michigan State University Press, 1968; Farago. *The Broken Seal: The Story of "Operation Magic" and the Pearl Harbor Disaster.* New York: Random House, 1967. Bantam pb; *Pearl Harbor: Warning and Decision.* Stanford: Stanford University Press, 1962; *Climax at Midway.* New York: W. W. Norton, 1960. Berkeley pb; Falk. *Bataan: The March of Death,* and *Decision at Leyte.* New York: W. W. Norton, 1962, 1966; Belote and Belote. *Corregidor: The Story of a Fortress,* and *Typhoon of Steel: The Battle for Okinawa.* New York: Harper & Row, 1967, 1970; *Ledo Road: General Stilwell's Highway to China.* Norman: University of Oklahoma Press, 1965; *Japanese Navy in World War II: an Anthology of Articles by Former Officers of the Imperial Japanese*

Navy and Air Defense Force. Intro. Raymond O'Connor. Annapolis: U. S. Naval Institute, 1969; *Japan: The Final Agony.* New York: Ballantine, 1970. pb; The relevant Pacific War sections of E. B. Potter and Chester W. Nimitz, *Sea Power,* were published separately as *Triumph in the Pacific: The Navy's Struggle Against Japan.* Englewood Cliffs: Prentice-Hall, 1963. pb.

[35] *George C. Marshall.* 2 vols. New York: Viking, 1963, 1966; *Papers of George S. Patton, Jr.* Houghton Mifflin, 1972; *Years of MacArthur.* Boston: Houghton Mifflin, 1970; *MacArthur as Military Commander.* Princeton: Van Nostrand, 1969; Tuchman. *Stilwell and the American Experience in China, 1941-1945.* New York: Macmillan, 1971; *D-Day: The Normandy Invasion in Retrospect.* Lawrence: University Press of Kansas, 1971; *The Bitter Woods.* New York: Putnams, 1969. Ace pb; *Eisenhower and Berlin; 1945: The Decision to Halt at the Elbe.* New York: W. W. Norton, 1967. pb.

[36] Halle. *The Cold War as History.* New York: Harper & Row, 1967. pb; LeFeber. *America, Russia, and the Cold War: 1945-1966.* New York: John Wiley, 1967. pb.

[37] *United States Strategic Bombing Survey.* 319 vols. Washington: U.S.G.P.O., 1945-   . Bloch's work was reprinted by Garland, New York, in 1971.

[38] Agar. *The Price of Power: America since 1945.* Chicago: University of Chicago Press, *History of American Civilization,* 1957. pb. Williams. *The Tragedy of American Diplomacy.* Cleveland: World, 1959. Rev. ed. 1962. Dell pb; Acheson. *Present at the Creation: My Years in the State Department.* New York: W. W. Norton, 1969; Kennan. *Memoirs: 1925-1950.* Boston: Little, Brown, 1967; Spanier. *The Truman-MacArthur Controversy and the Korean War.* Cambridge, Mass.: Harvard University Press, 1959. Norton pb; Rees. *Korea: The Limited War.* New York: St. Martin's, 1964. Penguin pb; Fehrenbach. *This Kind of War.* New York: Macmillan, 1963. Pocket Books pb; Ridgeway. *The Korean War.* Garden City: Doubleday, 1967. Popular Library pb; Collins. *War in Peacetime: The History and Lessons of Korea.* Boston: Houghton Mifflin, 1969.

[39] *Nuclear Weapons and Foreign Policy.* New York: Harper & Row, 1957. Norton pb; *Strategy in the Missile Age.* Princeton: Princeton University Press, 1959. pb; *Prospect for America.* Garden City: Doubleday, 1961; *Mandate for Change: 1953-1956.* Garden City: Doubleday, 1963. Signet pb. p. 36; *The Power Elite.* New York: Oxford, 1956. pb. The "military-industrial complex" speech is in Weigley. *American Military.* pp. 153-156.

[40] *How Much Is Enough?: Shaping the Defense Program, 1961-1969.* New York: Harper & Row, 1971. pb; *The Essence of Security: Reflections in Office.* New York: Harper & Row, 1968. pb; Johnson. *The Vantage Point: Perspectives of the Presidency, 1963-1969.* New York: Holt, 1971; White. *Nobody Wanted War: Misperception in Vietnam and Other Wars.* Garden City: Doubleday, 1968. pb; Windchy. *Tonkin Gulf.* Garden City: Doubleday, 1971; Hoopes. *The Limits of Intervention.* New York: D. McKay, 1969. pb; Cooper. *The Lost Crusade: America in Vietnam.* New York: Dodd, Mead, 1970. Other personal choices are Ralph E. Lapp. *The Weapons Culture.* New York: W. W. Norton. 1968. Penguin pb; James A. Donovan's overwritten *Militarism U.S.A.* New York: Scribner's, 1970. pb; Charles C. Moskos, Jr. *The American Enlisted Man.* New York: Russell Sage Foundation, 1970; Harry A. Marmion. *Selective Service: Conflict and Compromise.* New York: John Wiley, 1968; and Murray Polner. *No Victory Parades: The Return of the Vietnam Veteran.* New York: Holt, Rinehart and Winston, 1971. pb.

[41] "Military History." Washington: Service Center for Teachers of History, American Historical Association, No. 39, 1961. p. 18.

· 10 ·

Intellectual History

Paul K. Conkin

THE label "intellectual history," even at its best, is full of ambiguities. At its worst it has become an overused vulgarity. In the following pages I will try to remove some of the ambiguities, and possibly clarify why I increasingly do everything possible to avoid using the label at all.

In one possible sense of the label, all history is intellectual history. More exactly, all knowledge about the distinctively human past necessarily implicates human thought. Before clarifying this assertion, let me emphasize that such a broad definition of intellectual history has no discriminatory role. So used, the label only clarifies some of the distinctive attributes of all human history, or of man himself, and in no way designates a particular subdivision or field within the broad domain of historical knowledge. In this broadest sense, every historian is an intellectual historian. Such a sweeping claim, with its hint of definitional imperialism, may indeed elicit howls of outrage from historians who believe themselves unfairly slandered, or from others who rightly recognize a semantic *tour de force,* and counter with "so what?". Yet, I believe a clarification of this broadest possible meaning can be much more instructive to history teachers than my later efforts to clarify types of history.[1]

Among all the animals only man has developed a symbolic language. This is his prime tool and sets him dramatically apart from all other creatures. Other animals are conscious; other animals learn, even very complicated things. Other animals have imagination and memory, and often act rationally in the sense that they have or learn life-enhancing habits. But only man thinks. Only in him does a vast, elaborate symbolism guide the formation of habits. Other animals elaborately train their young; it is a myth that they live only by genetically determined instincts. But only in man does survival depend upon an encoded and cumulative heritage, a heritage passed on to each new generation by symbolic forms of communication. The child who does not learn to talk (or to use other parallel forms of symbolism, such as the visual signs of the deaf) remains almost helpless or, in the expressive language of the past, "dumb."

Every human child is born not only into a perceptual environment but also into a conceptual one, or to what we often loosely refer to as a cultural environment or a world of symbolic meanings. A man and a dog perceive roughly the same world; direct sense experience surely fosters almost the same perceptual images. But man alone has the ability to translate these images into an elaborate code system. In him, a carefully discriminated pattern of airwaves against an ear drum, or even the memory of such, can elicit the same image as direct sensual contact. The sound, or a phonetic and written rendition of it (a second level of coding), stands for or means the specific perception. But not perfectly. Here is the limit as well as the glory of language. We cannot name, we cannot reduce to a serviceable code, all aspects of any perception. To some extent, to name is to distort or at least to oversimplify. In fact, our most useful codes stand, not for the particularities of experience, but for the common qualities of many experiences. Proper names (John, or Fido) stand for perceived, individual objects with some continuing identity, and thus only exclude the shifting particularities that are not essential to identity (the changed clothing, or shed fur). Our much more useful class names stand for common properties in many different objects (man, dog), and thus are much more general and abstract, bypassing as they do all the particularities that bestow individual identity upon an object or person. A word, if it serves as an adequate means of communication, induces in a hearer (or reader) the exact meaning or image intended by a speaker or writer. Since many words have many meanings, the context often has as much to do with successful communication as the language used. The ambiguities of most languages do not make them any less necessary. Conceptualization is impossible without some conventional symbolism, and without the physiological equipment that sustains such symbolism. Thinking, literally, is talking to oneself.

The facile use of symbolism not only gives man a cumulative cultural heritage, but also allows him a very special relationship with the future. Animals have desires. Only man can plan. By symbolic projection, he can survey a wide range of options, some well beyond any past or any present realizable direct experience, and thus beyond the range of imagery open to other animals. Human aspirations are often self-conscious, highly discriminatory, and, most important, shared down to the smallest nuance of meaning with other persons. Symbolic communication makes a human society quite different from an animal one. The human society coheres not because of instinct (as in an ant colony), but because of shared meanings and common, projective goals. The human society alone reflects purpose. It alone is a community.

Human history is, in one sense, preëminently the history of human thought. By standing back far enough, by refusing to sort out the meanings present in his behavior, one might construct a natural history of man. Standing on a distant mountain peak, one might describe human groups as they move endlessly about on the plains below. Even without access to their symbolically expressed ideals, one might read meanings into their behavior (they obviously moved to the valley because they wanted pasture for their flock). By an imposition of one's own culturally conditioned preferences, or dubious reference to some behavior necessary to man because of his nature, one might infer intent or expectation. But we suspect that such speculation would often miss the mark. The only way to know why a group of people moved where they did is to seek out the purposes inherent in the movement, or the projective goals that are consciously present in the decision—more likely, the past thought that lies buried in the present habits of migration. To know why a human society behaves the way it does is, necessarily, to know something of the symbolic meanings that constitute its intellectual environment. In fact, human behavior that in no way reflects thought (overt and present, or implicit and past), that is in no sense purposive, rarely enters into our account of the human past. We assume all the belches and sneezes.

The lesson for historians is obvious. To understand rather than distort the human past we must decipher some of the symbolic content that is almost always present. It is easy to impose present meanings upon past behavior, to read into it the same motives that attend our own, outwardly similar behavior. (Since I always move for economic reasons, so surely did my progenitors.) It is even easier to impose present meanings upon words used by our progenitors, to assume quite foolishly that they meant what we mean by such words as democracy, property, work, or freedom. The failure to unearth subtle shifts in verbal meaning, perhaps more than anything else, makes so much of our purported American history only a caricature. This problem of word meaning is both inescapable and tremendously challenging.

Used in this broad sense, intellectual history identifies not a field but a necessary dimension in any history. Every field confronts the problem of meaning. A military historian deals with human aspirations, and often with well-calculated strategies. Even the way a general arrays his troops reflects either his own careful thought about future eventualities, or else matured habits that he developed in the past, but habits nonetheless based upon someone's strategic thinking. Even if unaware of the implications of many of his most crucial decisions, the general still reflects the conditioning influence of thought. No historian can properly understand the battle without some insight into this strategic thinking. If we cannot find the meanings present in human behavior, the purposes sought, much of it will always remain to us a baffling mystery.

Nothing is more obvious than the habitual nature of most of our action. We do not have the time to make conscious decisions in most situations, let alone think long and reflectively about them. For this reason, the vast preponderance of the human past that we can know, given a desire to know it, does not consist of man thinking, or of such unalloyed products of thought as hypotheses and beliefs. Most of man's products, most of his striving, do reflect some overt thought, some conscious planning and calculation. But these also reflect matured habits and much non-conscious behavior, and thus the living deposit of past men's thinking. Historians often allege that they have no interest in "ideas." Because of the preponderance of the habitual in their own area of investigation, they avow such other interests as political behavior, economic organization, diplomatic interchange, artistic triumphs, or patterns of social organization. In each case, however, if they are at all competent historians, they weave into their accounts the thought components—the political ideals, the conceptions of economic value, the explicit or implicit goals of foreign policy, the esthetic norms, and the preferences reflected in family or community organization. It is much more important for the production and dissemination of historical knowledge that all historians, whatever they call their speciality, deal perceptively and honestly with the meanings present in their subject area, than it is that specialists in abstraction write what they consider to be intellectual history.

Nonetheless it is possible to define a quite narrow and precise form of intellectual history, or what some historians refer to either as the history of ideas or the internal history of thought. In this perspective, intellectual history is a distinctive field, with its own special subject matter and, to an extent, its own peculiar methods. Here, as in all internal distinctions within history, selective focus is what discriminates. A historian may, if he wants, give special or even exclusive emphasis to the thought present in human events. If writing about wars, he may focus almost entirely upon strategic thinking; if about economic change, he may emphasize economic theories; if about the arts, he may focus on esthetic concepts; if about church history, he may talk only of theology. In each case he has a compelling interest in concepts and beliefs, although he may still relate these to a broader context of behavior. He may feel obligated to trace some battlefield events, or record the magnitude of changes in an economic system. But even here his emphasis is still ideational. If he could, he might prefer to eliminate all references to the battle or to the economic system. If his audience already knows about the battle, he may indulge his penchant for the exclusively conceptual. In actual fact, such "pure" intellectual history almost always departs from developed areas of historical understanding.[2] In the same way, political or military historians often assume a developed knowledge of political ideals or strategic goals, and thus write only about external events. My point here is obvious—no topically narrowed form of history exists in a vacuum. Context, purpose, and the existing state of knowledge all help guide our selective focus.

Selective interest is in no sense suspect. It is necessary if we are to write any history at all. We must select the aspects of the past that we want to know more about, and those that seem important enough to us to justify all the efforts at understanding. The danger that attends our purposeful but always in some sense arbitrary selective focus is a loss of perspective, or exaggerated claims of importance for our chosen subject. A professed intellectual historian, whatever he means by the label, may assert that "ideas," whatever he means by that elusive word, are the most determinant aspect of human behavior. Historians often debate the significance of "ideas" in human events, or contend over the relative importance of "ideas" in contrast to such equally vague entities as economic forces, irrational instincts, feelings and emotions, or social institutions. Sophomores periodically resurrect the tired old chicken-egg dilemma—which comes first, ideas or action? All such issues are bogus, based on the most irresponsible form of conceptual imprecision or on completely absurd dualities. What is an idea?—a simple concept, a perceptual image, a propositional belief, a hypothesis? Does "rational" apply to "ideas" or to behavior? What have "ideas" to do with rationality or irrationality? What are forces, or institutions, or even behavior? Are these the opposites of "ideas," or larger classes that include "ideas"? It is this semantic jungle that haunts most discussions of intellectual history.

Man not only sits, stands, and walks; he also talks. And he spends an enormous amount of time talking to himself, or thinking. This talking and thinking is a form of doing, itself a form of human behavior. For physiological reasons, a man cannot talk (or think) in complete isolation from other bodily behavior. And in his wakened hours, a man rarely does anything that does not parallel some thinking, although the two may not interact causally. Often they do. Falling down may stimulate some hard thinking about the state of one's health or the frequency of curbs on city streets. But some projective thinking, and the relishing of symbolically triggered images (of ice cream that can be purchased down the street), may well have stimulated the ill-fated walk. There is no chicken and egg. In all cases there are only interactive types of human behavior, and human behavior is distinctive only in that at times it does include some thinking behavior. Man can do things thought-fully, and that, by the way, is not the same thing as doing things rationally. Thought-full behavior includes the two possible aspects—conscious, verbal awareness and deliberation, or a configuration of habit determined in the past by such thinking, either in the actor or in his progenitors. Since almost all human behavior is, to some extent, thought-full, the domain of the specialized intellectual historian is as broad as human history itself but obviously not nearly so encompassing.

The word "idea" is terribly loose and troublesome, although it usually designates some unit of thought. In our philosophical traditions, going back as far as the Greeks, the word "idea" designated a single, distinct meaning, and particularly a class meaning or concept. In this sense, intellectual historians have to be continually concerned with ideas, for their purpose is to seek out the meanings present in past events. Often this goal leads them to the key words used by people in the past. Today, an increasing number of young intellectual historians are mainly concerned with the subtle nuances of language, and seek their specialized training in semantics or linguistic analysis. As historical critics, they demand greater precision of language from all historians, and are quick to point out the ambiguities that lurk in most conventional categories and labels (reformer, progressive, liberal, conservative, communist, racist, imperalist, isolationist). In their own historical writing they emphasize precision, endless definition, and careful distinctions. Such analytical tools, in themselves, do not constitute a subject matter or field of history. But their use does inform a growing interest in the varied meanings that people have attached to such crucial but very ambiguous words as progress, property, liberty, God, morality, science, or religion.[3] A historian with these interests will not trace a precise concept through time, but will identify the varied concepts (or images) that attach to common words. This is no easy task, requiring as it does, a meticulous concern for context and for rhetorical fashions. When well done, it is the best possible antidote for the most vicious form of presentism—the reading of present meanings into past word usage.

Arthur O. Lovejoy, the Johns Hopkins philosopher who tried to create a distinct speciality in the history of ideas, and who helped found the *Journal of the History of Ideas,* urged historians to write "biographies" of influential ideas or concepts, whatever the varying language that expressed them. He carefully distinguished his "simple" or "unit" ideas from ambiguous words (God, freedom, democracy) and from complex beliefs or ideologies (materialism, idealism, naturalism), but clearly was interested only in quite broad concepts that endured over an extended time and exerted great influence. In fact, after his careful definition of a unit idea, he selected the perfect candidate for his provocative book, *The Great Chain of Being*.[4] Lovejoy had few followers, in part because of the difficulties in his atomistic definition of ideas, in part because of the immense knowledge in several fields required to trace a single concept through many centuries and to locate it in many languages and many countries.

Most historians who describe themselves as intellectual historians in a strict sense write not about single concepts or ambiguous words but about systems of belief that include numerous related concepts, and which are often the matured product of an immense amount of human thinking. For our purposes, a belief is a proposition, valuative or descriptive, simple or complex, speculative or empirically validated, that a person is willing to accept or affirm. Many people may be unable clearly to articulate a belief, but will nonetheless enthusiastically endorse it. With Charles S. Peirce, I like to make a further distinction between mere verbal accent, which often reflects pervasive verbal fashions (everyone professes a belief in the gods), and authentic belief, which also requires a habitual propensity to act in a certain way (one who really believes that the gods respond to prayer plants his corn before the prayer meeting). When authentic beliefs cease to function at all on a verbal level, and those who hold them can only with great mental efforts verbalize their content, I refer to such implicit beliefs as "assumptions." When whole communities share such assumptions, and reflect the appropriate habits, I then use the word "institution," although the word is used in other contexts than group habits and beliefs. The lack of a clear and accepted nomenclature makes intellectual history a confusing maze of ideas, beliefs, forces, attitudes, assumptions, and images.

If human beliefs are his subject, the intellectual historian has a compelling reason to be selective in one of two directions—significance or quality. In the morass of propositions accepted by our ancestors, most were commonplace and trivial, related to proximate and ephemeral issues, or held by only a few people. Significant beliefs, to most any historian, include very basic beliefs about such subjects as reality, gods, the physical universe, man, and society; prophetic beliefs that, possibly over centuries, anticipate and then help motivate tremendous changes in man's behavior; and broadly-shared beliefs, which vitally influence the lives of a whole community. Only the historical understanding of such significant beliefs allows us to identify who we really are, to know the often unnoticed beliefs that we still reflect in our habitual behavior.

The historian's perception of what past beliefs still inhere in present institutions, his estimate of which beliefs are basic or most important, and his impression or even precise knowledge about how many people now share these beliefs, all help determine the subject of his inquiry.

Quality is a more challengeable selective criteria for the historian. Whether for good reasons or not, an intellectual historian often selects for study past beliefs that meet his own logical and esthetic criteria of excellence and writes about these even when they do not meet his criteria of significance. Thus, he writes about what he considers good theology, or good science, and ignores bad theology and bad science, even though the good had small impact and the bad was vastly influential. This selective bias parallels that of the literary historian, who may select for attention less influential works of fiction because they alone meet certain esthetic criteria. He might even define literature by these same criteria, and thus rightly insist that he could not include any fiction that did not meet his criteria and remain a literary historian. In the same way, an intellectual historian working in the history of philosophy or of some science has to use some standards to define his field. He brings the preferences of the connoisseur to his subject. He enjoys his subject and soon reflects the professional's contempt for illogical, loose, or superficial thought, or for the vulgar clichés of the intellectual marketplace. As a historian, he sees the significance of the vulgar, but he cannot sustain enough interest to explore it. He turns quickly back to the sublime, knowing that rigorous intellectual products often reveal very little about a society, since few people create these products, and some of them may never have much impact on popular thought. The intellectual historian, in such cases, disavows any interest in a whole society, or in what I would call social history.

The understandable taste for the best of human thought means that intellectual historians, in the pure sense that I now use the label, usually write about the beliefs of a narrow elite, or a small class of highly literate, original, and even brilliant men and women (and, in fact, almost exclusively so far, about men). To explore the frontiers of human thought is to find precious few frontiersmen. Intellectual historians exhaustively explore the beliefs of pioneer scientists, classic philosophers, brilliant theologians, or innovative social theorists.[5] And they do have a defense for such elitist selectivity. This defense, as a defense for any selection in history, relates to purpose, to their reasons for writing the history they do write. Over the long term, the most rigorous thinking may become widely accepted, and at that point very influential. One may write its history in order to speed the process of assimilation. Acquaintanceship with rigorous thinking may develop, in an audience, a taste for rigor and help them develop the critical tools necessary to expose the vulgar. Finally, the highly technical thought of a physicist may reveal almost nothing about his age, but it may reveal a great deal about a society a hundred years later. When Darwin first published *Origin of Species* in 1859, few people could understand or accept the idea of natural selection; today almost all literate people understand and accept it.

The thought of an elite is much more accessible than the beliefs of the masses. The beliefs of the common folk, even when they seem worthy of investigation, are still hard to decipher, particularly in the more distant past. Crude, aggregate data, subjected to statistical analysis, may reveal the outer contours of non-articulate belief. For part of our American past, we do have voting records, church attendance lists, and several intellectually revealing categories of census information. These allow broad, summary judgments about belief, particularly when we already know something about the commitments of a party or a church, and when we can reliably infer similar concerns or beliefs for those who vote or affiliate. If I know a person was a Presbyterian in 1810, I can make some highly probable guesses about his belief. But I can do this only because I already know some of the subtleties and nuances of nineteenth-century Calvinism, and I learned these, not from the artifacts left by the membership, but from careful attention to an articulate ministerial elite. My point is simple; even to interpret gross data about popular belief one needs a broad acquaintanceship with an elite, with articulate and persuasive men who helped mold the beliefs of their followers.[6]

The understanding of basic beliefs, particularly in the modern period, invites or even requires specialization and often highly technical knowledge. Few historians today attempt general histories of belief. Thus, intellectual history is a class name for common characteristics (basic beliefs in each cast) of an unending list of topical specialities—history of philosophy, of theology, of various sciences, of social thought. At great peril, a historian may try to find some configuration or coherence between contemporary but highly specialized beliefs, such as a common paradigm, a world view, or what Carl Becker metaphorically dubbed a "climate of opinion." Elusive concepts like "Enlightenment" or "romanticism" or "age of belief" often provide the ineffective glue for such efforts.[7] Some systems of thought, particularly religious and philosophical, include beliefs about almost any conceivable subject (Christianity, Marxism). Historians often write about such total systems or ideologies, but only when whole populations understand and accept them do such belief systems provide the unity for an age, or permit an intellectually unified treatment of all areas of thought. At one time, at least, we believed Calvinist Christianity was such a unifying ideology in colonial New England.[8] We now have profound doubts even about this.

Technical requirements reinforce specialization. One has to be a reasonably good theologian to understand the beliefs of any great theologian in the past, for understanding instead of oversimplification and distortion requires a grasp of all the subtleties. Without an extensive background in the physical sciences, without a grasp of key concepts, methods, hypotheses, one simply cannot understand their more recent historical development. It is even increasingly difficult for intellectual historians in highly specialized areas to communicate their finding to the layman. There is no adequate common language. Because of his interest in the continuities of thought, the intellectual historian usually emphasizes ideational causes. Among the many conditions necessary for a brilliant new hypothesis in physics, one will be the exact nature of the previously accepted hypotheses. This the historian of science will emphasize as he tells the intriguing story of the development of physical theory from the time of Newton to Einstein.[9] He may completely ignore extrinsic motives, pressures, and circumstances. It is this emphasis upon ideational causes that vindicates the distinction of "internal" history of thought from an "external" treatment, in which non-ideational factors receive equal attention.

I wish I could end my efforts at definition at this point. I wish historians in general would restrict the meaning of intellectual history to the study of past human thought, of concepts and beliefs. Needless to say, historians and non-historians alike use the label in a much more loose and broad way, as a brief scrutiny of almost any college catalogue or publisher's blurb will quickly testify. In them the label also stands for biographies of intellectuals, for the varied, often non-ideational conditions that foster thought, for the non-ideational effects of belief, for loose attempts to define and trace through time the essential character traits or perceptual habits of Americans, for the history of high and low culture, or even for types of social history. This medley of subjects still reflects the early, grab-bag courses, offered under such compound titles as "American social, cultural, and intellectual history," which first gave a place in American history curriculums for some detailed consideration of basic beliefs.

Since all original thought originates with some individual, the historian may develop as much interest in the thinker as in his beliefs. If I write a history of a belief system (a religion, a science), I can hardly disregard the contributions of individuals, of prophets and pioneers. But if my interest is in their intellectual contributions, I may have little concern for the personal reasons that led to the thinking. I am primarily interested in one "why?"—why, at that point in time, was it possible for them to think as they did? What already developed conceptual universe made their new advance possible? It is in the continuities of thought that I seek causes. But here I scarcely find the likely motives for the thinking. A motivational "why" may lead me far afield from belief, into pecuniary or status goals, into compulsive behavior, into role anxiety, or, more embracing, into some beleaguered circumstance, some crisis or conflict, which invited rationalization, not in the Freudian sense, but in the sense of long, careful, vindicating intellectual effort. In a personal biography I may even be able to suggest a broad range of reasons why Einstein developed his special theory of relativity without detailing the intellectual dilemmas that so characterized several fields of physics in the late nineteenth century. But note that some of the same selective criteria influence the intellectual biographer as well as the historian of beliefs. It was Einstein's momentous technical achievements in such areas as the special theory, and his place in the whole history of modern physics, which made him a likely prospect for a biography.[10]

In a non-biographical context, there are also many non-ideational conditions that foster and guide even the most serious forms of thinking. These include educational facilities, libraries, newspapers and journals, the electronic media, governmental and philanthropic funding, and professional organizations. A history of government support for scientific research, or of the development of graduate education in America, or of the early years of the American Economics Association obviously relates closely to the types of belief that found acceptance in America. Such institutional determinants of belief as education also reflect belief, particularly educational philosophy, but the historian of American education might well focus as much upon administration forms, financing, or political support as upon guiding ideals. Thus, most histories of education are more than histories of concepts or beliefs, and in strict terms not intellectual histories at all.[11]

Just as non-ideational factors influence thought, so human thought influences and in some small way shapes types of human activity and products of human creativity that, in their complex totality, seem anything but intellectual. A historian may begin with a carefully articulated and highly original belief, but then spend most of his time showing its subsequent dissemination, its almost inevitable popularization, and the wide range of behavioral changes that followed its acceptance.[12] If the new belief was a scientific hypothesis, he may show how acceptance of the belief allowed men to exert powerful new controls over events (technology), and then trace some of the effects of the applied knowledge. Here he conforms to an old admonition—the intellectual historian, unlike the historian of ideas, should move back and forth between formal or technical thought and the concrete consequences of such thought, between belief and action. Or, put in equally suspect terms, he should be interested not only in ideas but in their role. Unfortunately, an interest in the "role" of ideas (a historian in any field except intellectual history has to have such an interest, because his subject necessarily reflects some of the effects of thought) too often diverts attention from the exact content of specific beliefs. Almost all the Darwinisms, the theories of relativity, the various pragmatisms, and the Calvinisms that people so many of our histories are little better than vulgar caricatures. Ironically, all historians *except* the intellectual must have an interest in the non-ideational consequences of belief (in the resulting strategies of generals, the machinations of politicians, the constructions of engineers). The intellectual historian *alone* has the privilege of attending only to the precise content of past beliefs, or of analyzing one very restricted role—the influence of past beliefs upon subsequent ones.

All deliberate human creations reflect the influence of thought. But only those creations expressed in language bare their conceptual content for all to see. They are immediate products of thought; they may be direct affirmations of belief. But a newly designed engine, a musical composition, a painting may give few clues to the thought that lay behind it. Here the thought merges with the material and formal content. Even literary productions, such as a poem, contain musical and non-conceptual uses of language. In a novel the language may be largely expressive and evocative; the concepts may suggest immediate experience, support fantasy, and not reveal a great deal about the beliefs of the author. Among human creations some, by the superb skills they reflect, have gained the flattering label of *arts*. By quite arbitrary criteria, we also distinguish between practical and fine arts. When we write a history of highly instrumental arts, we write a "history of technology"; when we write of such fine arts as literature, music, or painting, we have "cultural history"; when about popular modes of expression and less talented creativity, we have a "history of popular culture." Such histories have no closer relationship to intellectual history than do political and economic history. In fact, only convention presents us from classifying a political or economic system as an object of art, and those who create or successfully administer such systems as artists. But intrinsic relationships have little to do with curriculum planning. By well-established precedents, historians often merge intellectual history and at least a history of the fine arts in both their books and their courses.[13] Personally, I find it an incompatible marriage.

Merle Curti, in his immensely influential *Growth of American Thought,*[14] wrote what he called a social history of thought. By this, he meant that he not only identified and traced influential beliefs, but that he also tried to show personal and societal influences that helped produce the beliefs. He included not only the beliefs of an intellectual elite, but also the less sophisticated beliefs of the common people. He found many of his sources in the fine and popular arts, particularly literature. This comprehensive approach forced him to treat more technical thought, particularly in theology, philosophy, and science, in quite general terms, or by a type of "external" characterization. Such a broad approach, merging as it does intellectual history, cultural history, intellectual biography, and several types of institutional history (education in particular), probably remains more useful for high school teachers than a more narrowly specialized history of basic beliefs. The most ambitious publishing effort in this area is Rand McNally's new series on *The History of American Thought and Culture,* edited by David Van Tassel.[15] The first seven volumes are uneven in quality, and generally lacking in the conceptual rigor craved by intellectual historians. But they provide a virtual encyclopedia of information.

A distinguishable type of history hardly fits any of the previous definitions. Even to link it with intellectual history is to invite all manner of confusions, but many do so identify it. This unique genre began with Henry Nash Smith's *Virgin Land: The American West as Symbol and Myth,* and ballooned in a wide range of books.[16] These historians have tried to identify prevalent images held by Americans, and have often confused the term image with such other divergent terms as myth and symbol. They have sought patterns of perception, the contours of feeling and emotion, or what they consider even more fundamental than concepts and beliefs. They believe these shared images, even when nonconscious and inarticulate, tremendously shape attitudes and behavior. Such images allow one to talk about a group mind, or to formulate theories about national character. The sources for such broad topics are as elusive and impressionistic as the themes, but more often than not these authors turn to popular and polite literature. Many are as much literary critics as historians. Their approach suffers from conceptual imprecision and from identification with now outdated theories drawn from depth psychology (Jung and Freud in particular). Their work may strike the conscientious intellectual historian as the most wanton form of speculation. Yet, what it has lacked in rigor it has balanced by speculative daring and brilliance. It still excites students by its breadth and vigor. Such a pre-conceptual level of analysis seems to explain so much, or at least tantalize so easily. Its relationship to literature, its creative potential, has insured its popularity in such fields as American Studies.

Because of an earlier coexistence in courses, intellectual and social history often remain in an increasingly coercive marriage, at least in college catalogues. This chapter cannot do full justice to social history, or give very much content to the label. It should not be considered a label parallel with, or in any sense in conflict with, intellectual history. As used here, the term intellectual history designates a selective focus upon the thought present or reflected in past human behavior. Everything in man's past relates to society. For this reason, "social" cannot designate topical discrimination. Social history is not a category comparable to economic, political, or intellectual. It labels not a distinctive aspect of human aspiration, but the scope of coverage in a history. A social historian accepts the challenge of writing about whole populations, or at least about large groupings of people. Of course he can not tell everything about the population (often he can find out very little), but the topics he does include must be as broad as the total group. He may write exclusively about beliefs (and thus also be an intellectual historian), but he tries to understand the beliefs, not of a narrow elite, but of a whole population. The same is true if he selects political or economic topics. Even the earliest self-denominated social historians reflected an interest in the life of the common people, of the masses, of the laboring class. In the thirties and forties, American social historians wrote about popular manners and fashions, about clubs and fraternities, about the family and neighborhood institutions, about nativism and immigration, and about broadly based reform movements. They often relied on testimonial data and generalized without warrant. More recent social historians have concentrated on demography, economic development, class or social structure, the working classes, and on political behavior. They have utilized broad types of data and subjected them to rigorous analysis, often with the help of computers. Since many of the newer interests parallel the concerns of social scientists, social historians often share with them both analytical tools and theoretical models.[17]

It seems to me that the major recent shift in interest among American historians has been toward social history. An increasing number of young historians want to write about a whole people, and not about powerful or persuasive or brilliant elites. Whether this turns out to be an enduring shift of interest, or an ephemeral fad, only time will tell. The growing popularity of social history reflects both a moral concern with the poor, the lowly, and the exploited, and an early and glowing fascination with new research methods. Thus, for different reasons, the field appeals to morally sensitive radicals and to technically proficient devotees of numbers, charts, and graphs, or of quantitative precision.

There is no conflict between intellectual history and social history; at times they are overlapping classes. But the interests of the two most often diverge. Intellectual historians not only write most often about elites, but feel that the thought of gifted men has more to teach us than the thought of the masses. The social historian chooses a different subject, and necessarily pursues it with different tools, presumably again because he feels that the resulting knowledge will be more beneficial for mankind. Indeed, there has been some friction, some mutual resentment and recrimination, a crossfire of depreciatory judgments, between the two so-called "fields." But the tension is unjustified. The social historian must realize that, in any comprehensive inquiry about a whole society, he has to encompass meanings and beliefs, both those articulate and, much more prevalent among the masses, those residual in habits. No more than any other historian can he ignore this universal dimension of human behavior, and no more than any other historian can he escape the obligation to treat thought with precision and rigor.

Social historians have rarely achieved the level of conceptual rigor, the concern with nuances of language, the sensitivity to doctrinal subtleties, that intellectual historians take for granted. But even as intellectual historians necessarily seek greater proficiency in semantics, logic, and linguistic analysis (or tools best acquired in philosophy courses), social historians have necessarily sought the analytical tools necessary for extracting meaning from massed data, tools that ultimately derive from mathematics. In order to tell the story of large populations, even in order to learn much about pervasive beliefs, one has to make inferences from such aggregate records as census reports, church and school records, tax and court records, birth and death reports, and employment and union records. A social historian has to count and calculate, sample, and correct sampling errors. He has to use varied types of statistical analysis to locate likely causes or to find meaningful patterns. The frequent recourse to such statistical tools gave birth to one of the many linguistic absurdities of our day—"quantitative history."

This completes a rather elaborate effort at definition. Since I am an intellectual historian, I am content. I hope I have revealed the role of thought in all areas of human history, clarified the range of specialized topics suggested by that elusive title, intellectual history, and showed the complex relationship between these topics (the history of concepts and beliefs, of intellectuals, of institutions that support intellectual endeavor, of high and low culture, of images or symbols) and social history.

If I could, I would end with a brief assessment of the recent returns in all these fields. Because of their very diversity, and the quite different developments in each, this is impossible. As a substitute for mature judgment, I can always fall back on the typical substitute. I can count. From 1960 through 1969, the *Journal of American History* reviewed almost 400 books that, after an unending series of arbitrary and difficult judgments, I decided could best fit into one of the above fields (excluding social history). In the early years of the decade these books made up approximately 20 per cent of those reviewed. By 1969 the total number of reviews had increased, but the proportion had clearly dropped to around 12 per cent, seemingly indicating a decline in interest in these types of intellectual history. It probably only reveals an increasing number of published dissertations on local political history, and a more generous review policy by the *Journal*. I also emphasize that this counting means very little. Few books neatly fit topical categories. Even so, the volume of books is staggeringly large.

In all this volume I find no dramatic new departures. Prosperity still promotes more prosperity. Puritan New England still attracts the largest volume of work in both intellectual and social history. The age of broad, sweeping surveys seems over. We will probably never have another Curti, or Ralph Gabriel, or Vernon Parrington, or even a Perry Miller. Likewise, broad interpretations, or unifying themes, are of the distant past. They all break down before rigorous analysis or reveal a distressing lack of confirming evidence. It is now clear that there has never been an American mind, or a common, distinctive American character, provided one could give a precise meaning for either concept. It even makes little sense to talk about "American thought," unless one means the varied beliefs held by Americans. Individual Americans have made dramatic contributions in almost all areas of thought, but they have contributed to an international intellectual community and have invariably drawn upon the resources of that community. National boundaries cannot confine belief, or define it. Unfortunately, much purported intellectual history still suffers from sweeping judgments, undefined terms, and flimsy evidential support. Outside a few well-developed sub-specialities, such as the history of science and of philosophy, few historians have secured the requisite technical training, or developed the compelling interest, to deal with sophisticated and specialized thinking or to place it in its intellectual environment. In fact, in the most narrow and precise sense of the term, intellectual history is still only an ungainly infant.

This deficiency may be of no great consequence to teachers, either at the high school or college level. Since I prefer total ignorance to simplistic stereotypes, I fear that any effort to introduce specialized intellectual history into high schools will do more harm than good.

By this, I mean that few teachers can or should deal with serious theology, with philosophy, or with most of the modern sciences. I have yet to find even a college-level text that does anything but distort these subjects, and thus leave students with horribly warped concepts. Darwin's conception of natural selection simply cannot be abridged into a few paragraphs, at least not in any language a beginning student could grasp. Very few present-day historians are able to grasp the rich range of meanings present in the Christian doctrine of predestination. Textbook renditions of it invariably horrify me.

What the intellectual historian does offer the high school teacher is a type of warning: be exact, be precise. Define and define and then define some more. Try, insofar as possible, to unravel the exact meanings present in the most familiar areas of the past. We can be fair to our progenitors only when we truly understand them, even as we hope that our children will be fair to us, and go to all the laborious efforts necessary to understand what we valued and what we believed. Surely high school students can at least work at understanding what John Adams meant by a "good republic," or what Abraham Lincoln might have meant by "one nation," or what Woodrow Wilson meant by "democracy." This is a very tough assignment, but a challenging one. If we ignore meanings, if we stumble over serious beliefs, we blaspheme our heritage and never come to know it. Instead, we only hurl our parochial prejudices at it. Then all our references to the past, even all our pretentious footnotes, only camouflage our historical ignorance.

FOOTNOTES

[1] The most elaborate analysis of the role of thought in all human history is in R. G. Collingwood. *The Idea of History.* New York: Oxford University Press, 1956.

[2] As a fact, almost no one writes such "pure" intellectual history. But in such technical areas as philosophy or science, the broader context may appear only in the most peripheral sense. For example, a new book by Morton G. White, *Science and Sentiment in America: Philosophical Thought from Jonathan Edwards to John Dewey,* New York: Oxford University Press, 1972, includes almost no biographical information, almost no references to the non-ideational context.

[3] The best example of such semantic history is Donald Fleming, "Attitude: The History of a Concept," in *Perspectives in American History,* I, 1967, pp. 287-365. Darrett B. Rutman, in *American Puritanism: Faith and Practice,* Philadelphia: Lippincott, 1970, is particularly concerned with definitions; the word "race" provides a focus for William Stanton's *The Leopard's Spots; Scientific Attitudes Toward Race in America, 1815-59,* Chicago: University of Chicago Press, 1960.

[4] *The Great Chain of Being: A Study of the History of an Idea.* Cambridge: Harvard University Press, 1936.

[5] We have no history of scientific theory in America. Instead we have a growing number of biographies of our best scientists. Good examples are A. Hunter Dupree.

Asa Gray, 1810-1888. Cambridge: Harvard University Press, 1959; Carl Resek. *Lewis Henry Morgan: American Scholar.* Chicago: University of Chicago Press, 1960; and Edward Lurie. *Louis Agassiz: A Life in Science.* Chicago: University of Chicago Press, 1960.

Almost all major, and most minor, American philosophers have rated biographers. Washington Square Press has sponsored a large series of intellectual biographies in its series, *The Great American Thinkers.* Loren Baritz, *City on a Hill,* New York: Wiley, 1964, and Paul K. Conkin, *Puritans and Pragmatists,* New York: Dodd, Mead, 1968, provide a broader introduction to major philosophers.

In theology, Jonathan Edwards has deservedly received the most scholarly attention; the best analysis of his theology is in Douglas J. Elwood, *The Philosophical Theology of Jonathan Edwards,* New York: Columbia University Press, 1960; less perceptive is Conrad Cherry, *The Theology of Jonathan Edwards,* Garden City: Doubleday, 1966. The only survey of American theology as a whole is by Sydney E. Ahlstrom, editor, *Theology in America; the Major Protestant Voices from Puritanism to Neo-orthodoxy,* Indianapolis: Bobbs-Merrill, 1967.

Social theory might include such diverse areas as moral philosophy, political and economic theory, the leading theories or models in the social sciences, and even utopian thought. Joseph Dorfman's *The Economic Mind in American Civilization,* 5 volumes, New York: Viking Press, 1946-1959, has no imitators in other fields. Morton G. White, *Social Thought in America; The Revolt Against Formalism,* New York: Viking Press, 1949, relates several individual thinkers around a common theme; so does R. Jackson Wilson in his *In Quest of Community: Social Philosophy in the United States, 1860-1920,* New York: Wiley, 1968.

[6] Actually, I know of no intellectual historian who has tried to derive beliefs entirely from gross data. Robert G. Pope in *The Half-Way Covenant: Church Membership in Puritan New England,* Princeton: Princeton University Press, 1969, at least relates doctrinal issues to data derived from membership lists.

[7] Daniel Boorstin's *The Lost World of Thomas Jefferson,* New York: Henry Holt, 1948, is the best possible example of an effort to find a common body of assumption relating diverse intellectuals.

[8] We have no diminution of studies on Calvinist or Puritan thought. The shadow of Perry Miller still hovers over most such efforts. Some recent contributions include: Norman Pettit. *The Heart Prepared: Grace and Conversion in Puritan Spiritual Life.* New Haven: Yale University Press, 1966; Alan Heimert. *Religion and the American Mind: From the Great Awakening to the Revolution.* Cambridge: Harvard University Press, 1966; Edmund S. Morgan. *Visible Saints: The History of a Puritan Idea.* New York: New York University Press, 1963; Robert Middlekauff. *The Mathers: Three Generations of Puritan Intellectuals, 1596-1728.* New York: Oxford University Press, 1971; T. H. Breen. *The Character of the Good Rules: A Study of Puritan Political Ideas in New England, 1630-1730.* New Haven: Yale University Press, 1970.

[9] See A. d'Abro. *The Evolution of Scientific Thought: Newton to Einstein.* 2nd ed. New York: Dover, 1950.

[10] A good example of such a biographical focus is Ola Elizabeth Winslow's highly personal biography, *Jonathan Edwards, 1703-1758,* New York: Macmillan, 1940. It seems a world removed from the run of theologically-oriented biographies. Another example is Emery Battis, *Saints and Sectaries: Anne Hutchinson and the Antinomian Controversy in the Massachusetts Bay Colony,* Chapel Hill: University of North Carolina Press, 1962, which is much more of a psychological probe than a theological analysis. But note that few biographies completely ignore extrinsic motives; few fail to encompass even subtleties of belief.

[11] As an example, Lawrence A. Cremin in *The Transformation of the School: Progressivism in American Education, 1876-1957,* New York: Knopf, 1961, ranges

from technical philosophic theories to their vulgarization and implementation. Richard B. Davis, *Intellectual Life of Jefferson's Virginia, 1790-1830,* Chapel Hill: University of North Carolina Press, 1964, illustrates the problems of relating the externals of intellectual life to a conducive environment. Thomas G. Manning, *Government in Science; The U.S. Geological Survey, 1867-1894,* Lexington: University of Kentucky Press, 1967, shows how government patronage can influence the direction and depth of scientific inquiry.

[12] The classic example of this is Bernard Bailyn's *The Ideological Origins of the American Revolution,* Cambridge: Harvard University Press, 1967.

[13] A large share of books loosely classified as "intellectual history" actually include largely cultural subjects. Some more brilliant examples are Russel B. Nye. *The Cultural Life of the New Nation, 1776-1830.* New York: Harper, 1960; Howard Mumford Jones. *O Strange New World: American Culture, the Formative Years.* New York: Viking, 1964; and Henry F. May. *The End of American Innocence: A Study of the First Years of Our Time.* New York: Knopf, 1959. I, of course, leave out a whole range of books devoted exclusively to literature, to music, and to the plastic arts.

[14] 3rd edition. New York: Harper, 1964.

[15] Chicago: Rand McNally. The largest share of books about American science and religion merge considerations of theory and doctrine with institutional development and descriptions of a larger social context. This is true of George H. Daniels, *American Science in the Age of Jackson,* New York: Columbia University Press, 1968, and Richard H. Shryock's brief survey, *Medicine and Society in America, 1660-1860,* New York: New York University Press, 1960. For the broadest possible understanding of religion (not just theology) in America, one must turn to that wonderful gift of Princeton University: James W. Smith and A. A. L. Jamison, editors, *Religion in American Life,* 4 volumes, Princeton: Princeton University Press, 1961.

[16] This unique genre began with Henry Nash Smith, *Virgin Land: The American West as Symbol and Myth,* Cambridge: Harvard University Press, 1950, and ballooned in a wide range of books, such as Richard W. B. Lewis, *The American Adam: Innocence, Tragedy, and Tradition in the Nineteenth Century,* Chicago: University of Chicago Press, 1955; Leo Marx, *The Machine in the Garden: Technology and the Pastoral Idea in America,* New York: Oxford University Press, 1964; Charles L. Sanford, *The Quest for Paradise: Europe and the American Moral Imagination,* Urbana: University of Illinois Press, 1961; Cushing Strout, *The American Image of the Old World,* New York: Harper, 1963; and William Taylor, *Cavalier and Yankee: The Old South and American National Character,* New York: Braziller, 1961.

[17] Some of the more recent and influential examples of a more traditional type of social history are: Jackson Turner Main. *The Social Structure of Revolutionary America.* Princeton: Princeton University Press, 1965; Clifford S. Griffin. *Their Brothers' Keepers; Moral Stewardship in the United States, 1800-1865.* New Brunswick: Rutgers University Press, 1960; James Harvey Young. *The Toadstool Millionaires: A Social History of Patent Medicines in America before Federal Regulation.* Princeton: Princeton University Press, 1961; and Robert H. Wiebe. *The Search for Order, 1877-1920.* New York: Hill and Wang, 1967.

The following is a representative sample of the newer interests of social historians. Note the concentration on New England and on urban phenomenon: Sumner Chilton Powell. *Puritan Village: The Formation of a New England Town.* Middletown: Wesleyan University Press, 1963; Darrett P. Rutman. *Winthrop's Boston; Portrait of a Puritan Town, 1630-1649.* Chapel Hill: University of North Carolina Press, 1965; Richard L. Bushman. *From Puritan to Yankee: Character and the Social Order in Connecticut, 1690-1765.* Cambridge: Harvard University Press, 1967; Kenneth A. Lockridge. *A New England Town: The First Hundred*

Years: Dedham, Massachusetts, 1636-1736. New York: W. W. Norton, 1970; John Demos. *A Little Commonwealth: Family Life in Plymouth Colony.* New York: Oxford University Press, 1970; Philip J. Greven, Jr. *Four Generations: Population, Land, and Family in Colonial Andover, Massachusetts.* Ithaca: Cornell University Press, 1970; Sam Bass Warner. *The Private City; Philadelphia in Three Periods of Its Growth.* Philadelphia: University of Pennsylvania Press, 1968; and Stephan Thernstrom. *Poverty and Progress: Social Mobility in a Nineteenth Century City.* Cambridge: Harvard University Press, 1964.

PART FOUR

The Reappraisal
of the American Past

· 11 ·

The Colonies to 1763

William W. Abbot

HISTORIANS of early America have tended to view the colonial period of American history in one of two general ways. Some have looked upon it as a chapter in the expansion of the West. For them, the history of early America is to be found in the story of how England created an empire in the New World, maintained it for more than 150 years, and then lost it after 1776 when the Americans took over its direction themselves. It is the saga of the Europeanization of America.

Other historians, less concerned with the European origins of America and the persistence of European or English patterns in American society, have looked for the changes the New World wrought in the life and character of transplanted Europeans. For these historians, the really important thing that happened in America before the Revolution is that a new and different society, one akin to Europe but not European, emerged and established itself. Early American history becomes the story of the Americanization of the European.

No historian, of course, has followed either approach to the exclusion of the other. The masterwork in American colonial history, Charles M. Andrews' four-volume history of the founding of the English colonies and the functioning of the old British Empire,[1] is, to be sure, an "imperial" study, but hardly exclusively so. Since the publication of Andrews' volumes in the 1930's, a number of specialized monographs on Britain's colonial policy and administration before the Revolution have appeared, and in the 1960's Lawrence H. Gipson completed his massive fifteen-volume history of the British Empire during the quarter of a century before its breakup in 1776.[2] But imperial history has hardly been the primary concern of colonial historians since the Second World War. Most have in fact been searching for patterns within colonial society itself. They have generally been less interested than imperial historians in the evolution of political institutions and more

249

interested in the formation of American society, in the creation of an "American" character and an "American" mind.

The seventeenth-century beginnings of the colonies, particularly of Massachusetts and Virginia, have attracted more attention from historians of early America than anything else except the Revolution. No time and place in American history has been studied quite so intensively and exhaustively, and perhaps so well, as Massachusetts Bay Colony (1630-1691). John Winthrop wrote his "History of New England" and William Bradford wrote "Of Plymouth Plantation" before 1650,[3] and people have been writing about New England Puritans and Puritanism ever since. In the 1930's, Samuel Eliot Morison published, among other things, a book on the intellectual life of colonial New England and three volumes on the early years of Harvard College,[4] and Perry Miller published *Orthodoxy in Massachusetts, 1630-1650: A Genetic Study* and *The New England Mind: The Seventeenth Century.*[5] Then, in the 1950's, there began the extraordinary outpouring of what seems to be an endless stream of monographs and articles on almost every conceivable aspect of life in the Bay Colony between 1630 and the 1690's. It is fair to say that the works of Morison and Miller are fathers, or grandfathers, to most of these publications.

The crucial first decade of the Puritan experiment in Massachusetts in particular has received a great amount of attention. Edmund S. Morgan's elegant little biography of John Winthrop is the best introduction to these years.[6] Morgan used Winthrop's career to reveal the connections between Puritan ideas and the steps the founders of the colony took and the procedures they followed to create and maintain the colony. Puritan thought and politics is also the theme of Darret Rutman's *Winthrop's Boston: Portrait of a Puritan Town, 1630-1649;*[7] but the great value of Rutman's book is that it provides the most circumstantial account of precisely what the builders of the Bay Colony did do to fix the pattern of settlement and create civil and religious institutions not only for Massachusetts but ultimately for all of New England as well. Perry Miller's work remains indispensable for anyone wishing to understand the Puritan experiment in Massachusetts; and his collection of essays, *Errand into the Wilderness,*[8] is admirably suited to serve as an introduction to his larger works, while in itself providing insight into the character and content of Puritan thought in New England.

Robert Middlekauff's intellectual biography of three generations of Mathers,[9] which like Miller's volumes on the New England mind carries through to the end of the seventeenth century and beyond, delineates in fresh terms and with unwonted clarity and concreteness the main currents of Puritan thought in the New World. Most of the writings on

Massachusetts spanning the period from the days of the great migration into New England in the 1630's to the troubled decades of Charles II's reign after 1660 have as their theme the gradual secularization of society and politics. In a family study very different from Middlekauff's, Richard S. Dunn traced the careers in America of three generations of Winthrops, from the arrival of John in 1630 to the death of his grandson, Wait Still, in 1717, in order to show how the Puritan of the 1630's became the Yankee of the next century.[10] Edmund Morgan, in another work dealing with seventeenth-century Massachusetts, pinpointed for analysis a crucial shift in Puritan thought and church polity coming after mid-century. His *Visible Saints: The History of a Puritan Idea*[11] is an examination of how and at what cost the Massachusetts Saints, or church members, came to terms with the alarming failure of so many of their children to experience religious conversion. The loss by the Puritans of their political monopoly in Massachusetts in the last decades of the seventeenth century was both a reason for and a consequence of the transformation of the Puritan commonwealth into the Yankee province of the eighteenth century. Bernard Bailyn's *The New England Merchants in the Seventeenth Century*[12] makes this point, and much else, clear by showing how the development of foreign trade in New England and the emergence in Boston and elsewhere of wealthy and powerful merchants put the old political arrangements of the commonwealth under great strain and ultimately forced the Puritan oligarchs to accept the new political settlement of the 1690's.

The transformation of another Puritan colony into a secular society, at a later time, is the theme of Richard L. Bushman's *From Puritan to Yankee; Character and the Social Order in Connecticut, 1690-1765.*[13] The title describes accurately what Bushman attempted to do, and has done very well. In its emphasis upon social structure and social change in Connecticut, Bushman's work is in a way closer to that of a group of scholars who have recently made intensive studies of social and family structure in certain New England communities than it is to Dunn's *Puritans and Yankees* on the one hand or to Perry Miller's *The New England Mind: From Colony to Province*[14] on the other.

Three of these studies of New England communities attracted particular attention from interested historians in the 1960's: Philip J. Greven's work on seventeenth-century Andover, Massachusetts;[15] John Demos's on Plymouth Plantation;[16] and Kenneth Lockridge's on Dedham, Massachusetts.[17] A great deal of what has been published about early America is local history, and much of it is of high quality. What sets these three studies of localities apart is that each of the historians made use of the techniques of historical demography and some of the insights of social psychology and cultural anthropology to put together his picture of a changing community in colonial America. The result is that we have new questions, and perhaps a new answer or two, about life in the first century of European settlement along the Atlantic seaboard of North America.

It seems clear that in the 1970's the most valuable additions to the historiography of early America are likely to be local histories of one kind or another, many to some extent demographic in nature. The records required to make a demographic study of a community like the one Greven has made of colonial Andover hardly exist outside New England, but Frank Craven's published lectures on the racial composition of seventeenth-century Virginia[18] and Edmund Morgan's article, "The First American Boom: Virginia 1618-1630," show what can be done with limited and seemingly unpromising evidence if the right historian does it.[19]

Professor Craven's *The Southern Colonies in the Seventeenth Century, 1607-1689*[20] remains the basic treatment of Virginia before 1700. He acknowledged his indebtedness to earlier historians like Charles M. Andrews, T. J. Wertenbaker, and P. A. Bruce; and certainly everyone who has written since the 1940's about early Virginia, particularly about the Jamestown years, owes as much or more to Craven's research and writings. By far the most influential of the post-1950 publications about seventeenth-century Virginia is Bernard Bailyn's essay, "Politics and Social Structure in Virginia."[21] Not only has it been the point of departure for a number of other studies of Virginia, published and unpublished, it has also in one sense served as inspiration, if not model, for the first demographic studies of New England towns. Sister Joan de Lourdes Leonard's analysis of Governor William Berkeley's economic program for Virginia,[22] which appeared in the *William and Mary Quarterly* in 1967, makes the events of the mid-century decades more intelligible, and the articles by Stephen S. Webb in that journal[23] help achieve the same thing for the final decades of Virginia's first century, after Bacon's Rebellion.

Bacon's Rebellion itself, usually viewed as the climactic event in the first chapter of Virginia's history, is one thing (Bacon is a patriotic hero) in Thomas Jefferson Wertenbaker's *Torchbearer of the Revolution: The Story of Bacon's Rebellion and Its Leader*[24] and another thing (Berkeley is more the hero and Bacon the villain) in Wilcomb E. Washburn's *The Governor and the Rebel: A History of Bacon's Rebellion in Virginia.*[25] Richard Lee Morton in a chapter on the Rebellion in his *Colonial Virginia*[26] tried to steer a course somewhere between these two generally contradictory treatments. Morton's two-volume history, incidentally, is a fine narrative, rich in detail and distinguished by a nice sense of place.

Most historians of seventeenth-century America—John Winthrop and Edmund Morgan, John Smith and Frank Craven—have concerned themselves with beginnings, with how things began and got going. Historians of the eighteenth century, on the other hand, have had quite different concerns. By 1700 the English settlers in North America had faced and dealt with most of the basic problems of transplanting and adapting old patterns and institutions and of devising new ones, in government, religion, economics, social arrangements, and imperial relationships. There were problems yet to be faced, of course, and solutions yet to be devised; but the problems of the eighteenth century were generally of a different sort, less elementary, more complex, more interrelated, less soluble. These differences help to explain why the eighteenth century has yielded fewer of its mysteries to intensive studies of specific localities than the seventeenth century has. Craven's treatment of seventeenth-century Jamestown is both a case study of European settlement in the New World and a chapter in the history of America as well as of Virginia; Stanley N. Katz's *Newcastle's New York*,[27] an account of factional politics in eighteenth-century New York, is a worthy contribution to the political history of colonial New York, but that is all it is.

Colonial America after 1700 became so different from what it had once been in part because of what had happened in the seventeenth century but in larger part because of the rapid and extensive growth of the colonies in the eighteenth century itself. Growth in numbers, area of settlement, productivity, trade, wealth, variety, and complexity transformed the face of America and radically altered the basic terms in which men functioned. The explosive growth of the colonies after 1700 was both cause and consequence of the maturing of colonial society, which in turn made the Revolution of 1776 possible, some would say inevitable, and did much to make it the kind of revolution it was. Every historian of the period, wittingly or not, has dealt either with growth itself or with its impact.

What Americans experienced in the eighteenth century was not simply growth in scale but growth in kind as well. For instance, not only did the colonial population increase from one to three million between 1700 and 1775 it also changed radically in its composition. Most of the increase came from non-English immigration and from native births. A question immediately arises about the effect tens of thousands of German Pietists and land-hungry Scots-Irish Presbyterians had upon colonial patterns and attitudes other than swelling the number of inhabitants. And what of the sudden majority of American-born for whom Europe was not even a dim memory? But the thing that has cried out loudest for investigation is the impact of the great number of Blacks

—by 1776 there were about 600,000 living in British continental North America—who were brought into the colonies as slaves. The consequences of the massive shift on the plantations and farms of the southern colonies from white indentured servants to African slaves beginning late in the seventeenth century were, of course, then and now, incalculably great.

The ready supply of land in America combined with infusions of British capital in the form of credit advances assured that every increase in the number of inhabitants, slave or free, would lead to an expanded area of settlement and to an increase in produce from farm and plantation and in trade on the high seas. The total wealth of the colonies rose rapidly, and in every colony disparities in incomes became wider: a disproportionate share of the wealth being generated by commercial farming and by trade flowed into the hands of those managing these enterprises, the planters and the merchants.

The eighteenth century, then, brought to America a much wider differentiation in men's wealth or condition, function, and status. There was, however, aside from slavery, no real social stratification in the European sense. In fact, because economic opportunities were far greater than in the early years of settlement, social mobility or fluidity was perhaps more pronounced in the eighteenth century than it had been in the less differentiated, and consequently in a sense more egalitarian, society of the seventeenth century. The effect of all this social and economic change upon manners and mores, living conditions, political ideas and practices, religious views and organizations, Anglo-American relations both cultural and institutional, town life, popular attitudes and aspirations—upon, in short, the character of American life and thought —has been, and will continue to be, the proper object of investigation for the historian of the first half of the eighteenth century.

The impact of social and economic change in the eighteenth century upon colonial politics has for long been summed up in the phrase, "the rise of the Assembly." The "rise" of the elective house of the colonial legislatures, in turn, may be defined as the process by which an expanding elite in eighteenth-century America gained political authority in each colony commensurate with its advancing economic and social position in the community. Jack P. Greene,[28] for example, has demonstrated how the prospering planters and lawyers in each of the southern colonies gradually won for the Assembly, and therefore for themselves, a commanding voice in colonial government. How this was achieved in South Carolina M. Eugene Sirmans spelled out in great detail in *Colonial South Carolina: A Political History, 1663-1763*;[29] and Stanley Katz's study of New York politics and Gary B. Nash's *Quakers and Politics:*

Pennsylvania, 1681-1726[30] each in its own way treats with the search for power by emerging native magnates of a different sort. In an earlier work which altered our view of eighteenth-century politics, Charles Sydnor examined the bases of the planters' political influence in Virginia, and showed how they secured and held the essential support of their constituency, the Virginia freeholders.[31] The colonial electorate, incidentally, was larger than was once thought, as Robert and Catherine Brown's studies of Massachusetts and Virginia have shown.[32]

Underlying this economic growth and the advancing political influence of native merchants and planters, especially in the southern colonies, was the expanding labor supply provided by the importation and retention of Negroes as slaves. Because slavery took root in the eighteenth century and its legacy is still so evident, historians continue to be interested in the early slave trade with Africa and the West Indies, the evolution of slavery as an institution, the conditions under which the enslaved lived and labored in the eighteenth century, and the implications of it all for whites as well as for Negroes in the eighteenth century and since. Given the incompleteness of the records, it is unlikely that anyone will be able to go much beyond what Philip D. Curtin[33] has done in identifying where the slaves in the English colonies on the continent came from and in what numbers they were imported. And people wishing to explore the implications of slavery for colonial society, and for the society of the United States, will be reading for a long time into the future *White over Black: American Attitudes toward the Negro, 1550-1812* by Winthrop D. Jordan.[34]

It is generally conceived that the material progress of the eighteenth century in British America helped loosen the hold that religion had had upon the uprooted European of the preceding century. The resurgence of religious enthusiasm and activity in the 1730's and 1740's, known as the Great Awakening, has been viewed in various lights and from a number of angles. Two important books of the 1960's, Alan E. Heimert's *Religion and the American Mind from the Great Awakening to the Revolution*[35] and Carl Bridenbaugh's *Mitre and Sceptre: Transatlantic Faiths, Ideas, Personalities, and Politics, 1689-1775,*[36] trace out in quite different ways intimate connections between the Great Awakening and the Revolution. Whatever else the implications of the religious ferment before the French and Indian War may be, it seems clear that it reinforced what immigration, geographical mobility, economic betterment, and decentralized political control were already doing to push this emerging society toward a new kind of religious pluralism. As the titles would suggest, Sidney E. Mead's "From Coercion to Persuasion: Another Look at the Rise of Religious Liberty and the

Emergence of Denominationalism"[37] and Timothy L. Smith's "Congregation, State, and Denomination: The Forming of the American Religious Structure,"[38] take one right to the heart of the matter. They also point the way to further enlightenment about the origins of American religious patterns and arrangements. A recent full and authoritative statement of the role the Baptists played in reformulating religious dogma and restructuring religious institutions and relationships in New England[39] confirms that what happened in the first half of the eighteenth century is the key to understanding what may be called the American religious settlement of the late eighteenth and early nineteenth centuries.

The most conspicuous evidence of the emergence and growth of denominationalism before the Revolution is to be found in the establishment of colleges by the Baptists, the Presbyterians, and the Dutch Reformed Church, as well as by the Anglicans and Congregationalists, primarily to provide for the training of the clergy in each denomination. It has often been asserted that the colonial colleges, founded and supported as they were by outside agencies and for specific purposes, did much to set the pattern of education generally, and higher education in particular, in the United States. Although education did not assume its central position in the American experiment until after the Revolution, many of the peculiar attributes of American education that have made it readily adaptable to the requirements of a democratic society were indeed—as Bernard Bailyn[40] has argued and Lawrence A. Cremin[41] has gone to great lengths to demonstrate—the products of the colonial experience.

Of course, it may be said with greater or lesser truth of almost any facet of American life or character that it had its beginnings in the colonial period. Histories not only of American religion and education but also of American law, agriculture, literature, journalism, technology, art, or what have you, always acknowledge the colonial origins of their subject and sometimes even deal with them.

In fact, much of the history of the colonial period has been written by historians in search of questions raised about the American Revolution, political parties, Jacksonian Democracy, sectional conflict, or about any number of other aspects of the history of the United States. To put it another way, almost any work on early American history will point forward, often explicitly, to something in the national experience of the American people. The reader of a work on colonial history even more than its author is likely to have been led back to the colonial period by his interest in the history of a later period. Once there, however, he will find himself well rewarded if he will range through some of the literature of colonial history, following his nose and letting one thing lead to another.

FOOTNOTES

[1] *The Colonial Period of American History.* 4 vols. New Haven: Yale University Press, 1934-1938.

[2] *The British Empire before the American Revolution.* 15 vols. Caldwell, Idaho: Caxton Press, and New York: Alfred A. Knopf, 1936-1970.

[3] See John Winthrop. *Winthrop's Journal "History of New England," 1630-1649,* ed. James K. Hosmer. 2 vols. New York: Scribner's Sons, 1908; and William Bradford. *Of Plymouth Plantation, 1620-1647,* ed. Samuel Eliot Morison. New York: Alfred A. Knopf, 1952.

[4] *The Intellectual Life of Colonial New England.* 2nd Edition. New York: New York University Press, 1956, originally published as *The Puritan Pronaos* (1936); *The Founding of Harvard College.* Cambridge, Mass.: Harvard University Press, 1935; *Harvard College in the Seventeenth Century.* 2 vols. Cambridge, Mass.: Harvard University Press, 1936.

[5] *Orthodoxy.* Cambridge: Harvard University Press, 1933; *The New England Mind.* New York: Macmillan, 1939.

[6] *The Puritan Dilemma: The Story of John Winthrop.* Boston: Little, Brown and Co., 1958.

[7] Chapel Hill: University of North Carolina Press, 1965.

[8] Cambridge: Harvard University Press, 1956.

[9] *The Mathers: Three Generations of Puritan Intellectuals, 1596-1728.* New York: Oxford University Press, 1971.

[10] *Puritans and Yankees: The Winthrop Dynasty of New England, 1630-1717.* Princeton: Princeton University Press, 1962.

[11] New York: New York University Press, 1963.

[12] Cambridge: Harvard University Press, 1955.

[13] Cambridge: Harvard University Press, 1967.

[14] Cambridge: Harvard Universtiy Press, 1953.

[15] "Family Structure in Seventeenth-Century Andover, Massachusetts." *William and Mary Quarterly,* 3rd ser., XXIII, April 1966, pp. 234-256; *Four Generations: Population, Land, and Family in Colonial Andover, Massachusetts.* Ithaca: Cornell University Press, 1970.

[16] "Notes on Life in Plymouth Colony." *William and Mary Quarterly,* 3rd ser., XXII, April 1965, pp. 264-286; *A Little Commonwealth: Family Life in Plymouth Colony.* New York: Oxford University Press, 1970.

[17] Kenneth A. Lockridge and Alan Kreider. "The Evolution of Massachusetts Town Government, 1640 to 1740." *William and Mary Quarterly,* 3rd ser., XXIII, Oct. 1966, pp. 549-574; Lockridge. *A New England Town: The First Hundred Years: Dedham, Massachusetts, 1636-1736.* New York: W. W. Norton & Co., 1970.

[18] Wesley Frank Craven. *White, Red and Black: The Seventeenth-Century Virginian.* Charlottesville: The University Press of Virginia, 1971.

[19] *William and Mary Quarterly,* 3rd ser., XXVIII, April 1971, pp. 169-198.

[20] Baton Rouge: Louisiana State University Press, 1949.

[21] In *Seventeenth-Century America: Essays in Colonial History,* ed. James Morton Smith. Chapel Hill: University of North Carolina Press, 1959. pp. 90-115.

[22] "Operation Checkmate: The Birth and Death of a Virginia Blueprint for Progress, 1660-1676." *William and Mary Quarterly,* 3rd ser., XXIV, Jan. 1967, pp. 44-74.

[23] See, especially, "The Strange Career of Francis Nicholson." *ibid.* XXIII, Oct. 1966, pp. 513-548.

[24] Princeton: Princeton University Press, 1940.

[25] Chapel Hill: University of North Carolina Press, 1957.

[26] 2 vols. Chapel Hill: University of North Carolina Press, 1960.

[27] Katz. *Newcastle's New York: Anglo-American Politics, 1732-1753.* Cambridge, Mass.: Harvard University Press, 1968.

[28] *The Quest for Power: The Lower Houses of Assembly in the Southern Royal Colonies, 1689-1776.* Chapel Hill: University of North Carolina Press, 1963.

[29] Chapel Hill: University of North Carolina Press, 1966.

[30] Princeton: Princeton University Press, 1968.

[31] *Gentlemen Freeholders: Political Practices in Washington's Virginia.* Chapel Hill: University of North Carolina Press, 1952. Reprinted as *American Revolutionaries in the Making* . . . New York: Free Press, 1965.

[32] *Middle-Class Democracy and the Revolution in Massachusetts, 1691-1780.* Ithaca: Cornell University Press, 1955; Robert E. and B. Katherine Brown. *Virginia, 1705-1786: Democracy or Aristocracy?* East Lansing: Michigan State University Press, 1964.

[33] *The Atlantic Slave Trade: A Census.* Madison: University of Wisconsin Press, 1969.

[34] Chapel Hill: University of North Carolina Press, 1968.

[35] Cambridge: Harvard University Press, 1966.

[36] New York: Oxford University Press, 1962.

[37] In Mead. *The Lively Experiment: The Shaping of Christianity in America.* New York: Harper and Row, Publishers, 1963.

[38] *William and Mary Quarterly,* 3rd ser., XXV, April 1968, pp. 155-176.

[39] William G. McLoughlin. *New England Dissent, 1630-1833: The Baptists and the Separation of Church and State.* 2 vols. Cambridge, Mass.: Harvard University Press, 1971.

[40] *Education in the Forming of American Society: Needs and Opportunities for Study.* Chapel Hill: University of North Carolina Press, 1960.

[41] *American Education: The Colonial Experience, 1607-1783.* New York: Harper and Row, Publishers, 1970.

· 12 ·

Revolution, Confederation, and Constitution, 1763-1787*

Jack P. Greene

BOTH because of its crucial position in modern history as the first of the great revolutions and because it gave birth to the United States of America, the American Revolution has always exercised a powerful appeal for historians. Its causes and consequences, its nature and meaning have never ceased to fascinate them, and each generation of historians has approached it anew. The result has been a welter of interpretations of why the Revolution occurred and what exactly it was. Those interpretations can be explained partly by changing intellectual styles, social, economic, and political imperatives, and psychological currents in the public world and partly by shifting conceptions of human nature and historical change within the community of historians. But they also stand as dramatic testimony to the one indisputable truth about the event itself: the American Revolution, like every other historical phenomenon of comparable magnitude, was so complex and contained so many diverse and seemingly contradictory currents that it can support a wide variety of interpretations. And yet, the extensive and intensive reappraisal of the Revolution that has occurred since World War II may have brought us closer to the perhaps impossible goal of comprehending it in full.

---

* Most of this essay was derived from the author's earlier booklet, *The Reappraisal of the American Revolution in Recent Historical Writing*. Washington, D.C.: Service Center for Teachers of History of the American Historical Association, 1967. Those portions which are taken directly from the booklet are reprinted by the permission of the American Historical Association.

Since World War II a new group of scholars has subjected the writings of older historians to critical reassessment. Reexamining the evidence at almost every major point, they have proceeded along two distinct yet complementary and overlapping lines of investigation. One line has been concerned mainly with exploring the substantive issues both in the debate with Britain and in the politics of the new nation between 1776 and 1789 and in examining the nature of internal political divisions and assessing their relationship to the dominant issues. A second line of investigation has been through the underlying assumptions of social and political behavior and has sought to explain the relationship between those assumptions and the central developments of the Revolutionary era.

Each line of investigation rests upon a conception of human nature that contrasts sharply with older interpretations. For the new group of scholars, man is not simply a pawn at the mercy of powerful, incomprehensible forces entirely beyond his control. Nor is he a creature so devoted to the pursuit of his own self-interest and so prescient as to be able to calculate ends and means. Instead, he is a limited and insecure being, attached to what he conceives to be his own interests and, often more importantly, to those principles, values, institutions, and aspirations around which he has built his life, and he responds emotionally to every contingency that seems to threaten any portion of his existence— his ideals as well as his interests. Man's limitations mean that his perceptions of the threat will rarely be accurate (indeed, he will probably see threats that do not exist), that he will be subject to self-delusion so that even his understanding of his own behavior will be distorted, and that he will rarely be able to foresee the results of his actions, though he will often try to do so. In short, he is a creature who, as A. O. Lovejoy has put it, "is forever 'rationalizing' but . . . is scarcely ever rational," a being who is at once at the mercy of history—of the larger developments within his lifetime—and, within the limits imposed by his nature and the physical and cultural environment in which he lives, free to make choices and take actions—perhaps even great creative and selfless actions—which may affect significantly the course of history. To understand the historical process, the new group of scholars assumes, one must understand the nature of broad historical forces, the behavior of individuals and groups, and the interaction between historical forces and human behavior. To understand human behavior, moreover, one must understand man's explanations of his own actions because, no matter how distorted those explanations may be, man does act upon them and they become powerful causative forces.

The new investigations have focused upon seven major problems: (1) the nature of the relationship between Britain and the colonies prior to 1763; (2) the nature of social and political life within the colonies and its relationship to the coming of the Revolution; (3) the reasons for the estrangement of the colonies from Britain between 1763 and 1776; (4) the explanations for the behavior of the British government and its supporters in the colonies between 1763 and the loss of the colonies in 1783; (5) the revolutionary consequences of the Revolution; (6) the character of the movement for the Constitution of 1787 and its relationship to the Revolution; and (7) the nature and meaning of the Revolution to the men who lived through it.

(1) Relationships Prior to 1763

In the evaluation of the causes of the Revolution, one of the central problems has been the character of the relationship between Great Britain and the colonies prior to 1763. Most earlier interpretations viewed that relationship as an unhappy one for the colonists, who resented the navigation system and chafed under the restrictions imposed upon them by the home government. This view, which was widely held in Britain and among British officials in the colonies during the eighteenth century, has been sharply challenged by several of the newer investigations. In *The Navigation Acts and the American Revolution,* Oliver M. Dickerson[1] examined the navigation system as it operated in the eighteenth century and concluded that it did not work serious hardships upon the colonies. This view was similar to the interpretations of earlier imperial historians, especially George L. Beer. But Beer and other imperial writers assumed that the widespread smuggling was symptomatic of American discontent with the navigation acts, and it was upon this point that Dickerson sharply disagreed. He denied that the colonists in the period before 1763 either regarded the system as a grievance or made any serious attempt to evade it except in the case of tea and sugar after the passage of the Molasses Act in 1733. In general, he found that the system was adequately enforced without major objections from the colonists, who appreciated the fact that its benefits far outweighed its objectionable features. These findings, Dickerson argued, indicated that the navigation acts were the "cement of empire," a positive force binding the colonies to the mother country.

This happy arrangement was upset in 1764, when the British undertook, with the Sugar Act, to substitute a policy of trade taxation for the older system of trade protection and encouragement. But "England's most fateful decision" was the establishment, in 1767 at Boston, of a separate Board of Customs for the continental colonies. Between 1768 and 1772, this Board engaged in what Dickerson, accepting at face value contemporary colonial opinion, judged was little less than "customs racketeering," as they employed legal technicalities and unscrupulous methods to plunder large amounts from colonial merchants, including such future Revolutionary leaders as John Hancock and Henry Laurens. The more blatant abuses came to an end after 1770 as the commissioners and their supporters lost influence in Britain, but the damage had been done, and it was their wholesale attack on American liberty and property, not American opposition to the old navigation system or addiction to smuggling, that caused the intense colonial hostility to the new board.

Other historians have disagreed with Dickerson about the colonial attitude toward the navigation system and the effects of the system on the colonial economy. Lawrence A. Harper[2] and Curtis P. Nettels[3] have argued that the burdens placed on the colonies by the navigation acts far exceeded the benefits. On the basis of more sophisticated and systematic analytical techniques, however, Robert Paul Thomas has indicated that Dickerson was closer to the truth than either Harper or Nettels. Finding that between 1763 and 1772 the annual per capita loss to the colonists averaged only about twenty-six cents per person or about .5 per cent of estimated per capita income, Thomas concluded that neither the navigation acts nor the new trade regulations adopted after 1763 imposed significant economic hardships upon the colonial economy.[4] Thomas' discoveries do not mean that powerful and articulate segments of the colonial population such as the New England merchants or the large Virginia planters might not have borne an unduly high proportion of the total loss and that for some such groups the navigation acts as they were enforced after 1763 might have constituted a serious grievance. Additional research will be required before these arguments can be evaluated more fully, but one point seems to have been rather firmly established: the colonists were not unhappy with the navigation system as it operated in the decades just before 1763, although their acceptance of the system may have depended largely on the fact that it was only loosely administered.

That political relations for much the same reasons were equally satisfactory to the colonists prior to 1763 was Jack P. Greene's argument in *The Quest for Power: The Lower Houses of Assembly in the Southern Royal Colonies, 1689-1776*.[5] From the last decades of the seventeenth century, colonial officials in London had envisioned a centralized empire with a uniform political system in each of the colonies and with the imperial government exercising supervision over the subordinate governments. But they had never made any systematic attempt to achieve these goals during the first half of the eighteenth century. The result, if the experience of the four southern royal colonies was typical, was the development of an arrangement that permitted colonial lower houses considerable latitude in shaping the constitutions of the colonies without requiring Crown officials to relinquish their ideals. Sporadic opposition from London officials and royal governors did not prevent the lower houses from acquiring an array of *de facto* powers and privileges and, in the process, transforming themselves from the dependent lawmaking bodies they were intended to be into miniature Houses of Commons and, in almost every colony, shifting the constitutional center of power from the executive to themselves. The growing divergence between imperial ideals and colonial reality mattered little so long as each side refrained from openly challenging the other. Severe friction in this area did not develop until after 1763 when Parliament and the Crown in its executive capacity challenged at important points the authority of the lower houses and the constitutional structures they had been forging over the previous century and a half. Then, the sanctity of the rights and privileges of the lower houses became a major issue between the home government and the colonists as imperial officials insisted upon an adherence to the old imperial ideals while colonial legislators came to demand rigid guarantees of colonial rights and eventually imperial recognition of the autonomy of the lower houses in local affairs and the equality of the lower houses with Parliament. Like the navigation system, then, which was satisfactory to the colonists largely because it was laxly enforced, political and constitutional relations were not a source of serious tension prior to 1763 largely because imperial authorities had never made any sustained attempt to make colonial practice correspond to imperial ideals.

With the profusion of British patriotism that poured from the colonies throughout the Seven Years' War and their propensity for quarreling among themselves, the absence of serious friction between the mother country and her North American possessions in either realm in 1763 made the possibility of a united revolt by the colonies against Britain seem remote indeed. As Richard Koebner has shown in *Empire,*[6] however, the patriotism and the bickering, like the absence of friction, were deceptive. An investigation of the history of the terms "empire," "imperial," and "imperialism" in the language of Western Europe from Rome to the Congress of Vienna, Koebner's study contained a section on British and colonial uses of the terms in the seventeenth and eighteenth centuries. It showed that the notion of the British Empire did not acquire a prominent place in British historical consciousness until after the Glorious Revolution and that even then it was a restricted concept that referred only to Great Britain and Ireland and not to British possessions overseas. Only after 1740 did the colonies acquire a place in the empire, and then the impetus for that development came from the colonies, not the home islands. Aware of their increasing importance to Britain and exhilarated by a vision of future greatness, Americans began to conceive of the colonies as the "British Empire in America," and out of this concept emerged the idea of the empire as a worldwide political system held together by mutual allegiance and the harmony of interests among constituent parts. This vision was, however, an American creation, and in the decade preceding the Revolution British officials had not yet come to regard the colonies as part of the empire, much less as equal partners. That British officials, with the notable exception of Massachusetts Governor Francis Bernard, did not understand that the American view of the empire included the colonies and could not, therefore, appreciate the implications of equality inherent in that concept helps to explain why they were unable to grasp assumptions behind American constitutional arguments and so thoroughly misconstrued the nature of American intentions. When they did begin in the 1760's to employ a broader concept of empire that took in the colonies, they used it as a device to bring about a more unified constitutional arrangement that would guarantee the subordination, not the equality, of the colonies. This profound divergence of thought between Great Britain and the colonies about the current and future role of the colonies in the British political community—a divergence that contributed substantially to the breakdown in communications that occurred between 1763 and 1776—helps make clear both why American leaders felt such an extraordinary sense of betrayal at the new measures adopted after 1763 and how the British national feeling they expressed in the early 1760's could be dissipated so quickly over the next decade as it became clear that the imperial government did not share their conception of the place of the colonies in the empire.[7]

The older Whig and imperial historians to the contrary notwithstanding, then, recent studies strongly suggest that the Revolution cannot be attributed either primarily or directly to colonial discontent with conditions as they operated before the 1760's.

(2) Political, Social, and Economic Divisions Within the Colonies

Other scholars have directed their attention to the study of political life within the individual colonies during the era of the Revolution, and their findings indicate that major modifications are required in the older conceptions of both early American politics and the Revolution. Investigators of Maryland, New Jersey, Connecticut, Pennsylvania, Rhode

Island, Georgia, Virginia, New Hampshire, and New York have analyzed the impact of the debate with Britain upon local politics and assessed the importance of the peculiar configuration of the economic, social, and political life of each colony in shaping its response to that debate.[8] Although these works reveal that the relative importance of the major substantive issues and the pattern of the Revolutionary movement varied from colony to colony and that there were special, and occasionally significant, local grievances against the imperial government, they also call attention to some important common features. Everywhere relations with Britain were relatively harmonious prior to 1763 and politics within the colonies was primarily elitist in nature. Public office—both appointive and elective—and political leadership were in the hands of upper-class groups, and, although there were occasional manifestations of social and economic discontent among the lower classes, that discontent never resulted in widespread demands for basic changes in the customary patterns of upper-class leadership. Political divisions, despite the contentions of earlier historians, were not along class lines and not between rival ideological groups of radicals and conservatives. Rather, they revolved around the ambitions of rival factions among the elite. The debate with Britain was in many instances the occasion for one faction to gain political predominance at the expense of its rivals, but, significantly, the faction that stood for the strongest line of resistance to British policy usually emerged victorious. Within the colonies, then, the direction of local politics and the balance of political forces were influenced, and in some cases altered profoundly, by the debate after 1763 over Parliament's authority and the extent of the Crown's prerogative in the colonies. The constitutional debate was thus not only the primary political concern within most colonies from 1763 to 1776, these studies seem to indicate, but also the most powerful agency of political change.

An even more direct challenge to the Progressive conception of the Revolution came from Robert E. and B. Katherine Brown in two studies of the relationship between politics and social structure in Massachusetts and Virginia.[9] The Browns' discoveries that in both colonies the economic structure was highly fluid, property widely distributed, and lower-class economic and social discontent minimal indicated that neither colony was so rigidly stratified as to produce the kind of social conflicts which Progressive historians thought were the stuff of colonial politics. By showing as well that the franchise was considerably wider than had previously been supposed, the Browns also demonstrated that the predominance of the upper classes in politics did not depend upon a restricted franchise, that they had to have the support of men from all classes to gain elective office.

That both of these conclusions are probably also applicable to most other colonies is indicated by the findings of several other recent independent investigations of Connecticut, New York, New Jersey, Pennsylvania, and Rhode Island.[10] All of these studies argue that the franchise in these colonies was very wide and that the vast majority of free adult males could expect to acquire enough property during their lifetime to meet suffrage requirements. Similarly, Jackson Turner Main in *The Social Structure of Revolutionary America*[11] demonstrated that, although there were great extremes in wealth and in standards and styles of living in American society during the late eighteenth century, it was relatively free from poverty and had, especially by European standards, a high rate of vertical mobility, great social and economic opportunity, and a supple class structure. This combination of economic abundance and social fluidity, Main concluded, tended "to minimize those conflicts which might have grown out of the class structure and the concentration of wealth" that was occurring in older settled areas on the eve of the Revolution.

Other studies of the underlying assumptions and modes of behavior of early American politics by J. R. Pole[12] and Richard Buel, Jr.,[13] have helped to resolve what, within the modern democratic conceptions employed by the Progressive historians and such recent writers as Robert E. Brown, was such a massive and incomprehensible paradox: why, in the words of Pole, "the great mass of the common people might actually have given their consent to concepts of government" that by "systematically" excluding them "from the more responsible positions of political power" restricted "their own participation in ways completely at variance with the principles of modern democracy." Revolutionary society, these studies have found, was essentially "a deferential society" that operated within an integrated structure of ideas fundamentally elitist in nature. That structure of ideas assumed that government should be entrusted to men of merit; that merit was very often, though by no means always, associated with wealth and social position; that men of merit were obliged to use their talents for the benefit of the public; and that deference to them was the implicit duty of the rest of society. To be sure, representative institutions provided the people with the means to check any unwarranted abuses of power by their rulers, but the power the people possessed was "not designed to facilitate the expression of their will in politics but to defend them from oppression." Both Pole and Buel concluded that, although these assumptions were undermined by the Revolution and gave way after 1790 to an expanded conception of the people's role in the polity, they continued to be the predominant elements underlying American political thought over the whole period from 1763 to 1789.

Obviously, many more specialized studies of developments within individual colonies will be required before the nature of internal political divisions and their relationship to the coming of the Revolution will be understood fully. The investigations already published do, however, suggest four tentative conclusions that flatly contradict arguments of earlier historians: the configuration of politics and the nature of social and economic divisions varied enormously from state to state; social and political opportunity was remarkably wide; class struggle and the demand for democracy on the part of unprivileged groups were not widespread and not a primary causative factor in the coming of the Revolution; and colonial political life operated within a structure of commonly-accepted values that assigned positions of leadership in the polity to members of the social and economic elite.

(3) The Estrangement of the Colonies, 1763-1776

One of the results of the discoveries that tensions between Britain and the colonies prior to 1763 were relatively mild and that political rivalries within the colonies were, in most cases, secondary in importance to the constitutional debate with Britain between 1763 and 1776 has been that historians have come to focus upon that debate in their search for an explanation for the coming of the Revolution. The guiding question in this search has been why the colonists became unhappy enough in the years after 1763 to revolt. To answer this question a number of historians have sought to identify and assess the importance of the several substantive issues between the colonies and Great Britain.

Thus Bernhard Knollenberg explored the nature and areas of American discontent during the early 1760's in *Origin of the American Revolution: 1759-1766*.[14] Although he agreed with other recent writers that Americans were generally happy with the existing relationship with Britain through the middle decades of the eighteenth century, he contended that trouble began not in 1763 but in 1759, when British military successes made it unnecessary to placate the colonies further and permitted imperial authorities to inaugurate a stricter policy. Over the next four years a wider and more intensive use of such traditional checks as the royal instructions and legislative review seriously antagonized colonial leaders in almost every colony. Discontent increased measurably, beginning in the spring of 1762, when first the Bute and then the Grenville ministries undertook a variety of general reform measures designed to tighten up the colonial system. In 1763 came a series of steps that was particularly unpopular in New England, including the decision to use the royal navy to curb smuggling and to enforce the previously laxly administered Molasses Act of 1733 and various white pines acts. Also in 1763, imperial officials decided to station a large standing army in the colonies and to limit western expansion into the region beyond the Allegheny mountains. The necessity of paying for the army led to the decision to tax the colonies and to Parliament's passage in 1764 of the Sugar Act, which provided for extensive reforms in colonial administration, and in 1765 of the Stamp Act, which touched off the colonial uprising in 1765-1766. According to Knollenberg, then, the cumulative effect of British policy over the previous six years, and not the Stamp Act alone, brought the colonies to the brink of rebellion during the Stamp Act crisis.

That the Stamp Act and the threat of parliamentary taxation which it contained were easily the most important sources of American dissatisfaction in the uprising of 1765-1766 has, however, been persuasively argued by Edmund S. Morgan and Helen M. Morgan in *The Stamp Act Crisis: Prologue to Revolution,*[15] one of the two or three most important books published on the era of the Revolution since World War II. The Morgans' study strongly suggested that American concern for and devotion to the constitutional arguments they employed were considerably greater than most scholars during the previous half century had assumed, and demonstrated the importance of political and constitutional considerations in the American case against the Sugar and Stamp Acts. As the subtitle suggested, the work argued for the decisiveness of the Stamp Act crisis in the unfolding Revolutionary drama. Not only did it raise the issue of the extent of Parliament's jurisdiction in the colonies by forcing American leaders and Parliament into a precise formulation of directly opposing views, but it also created an atmosphere of mutual suspicion that pervaded all subsequent developments and quite possibly precluded any peaceful settlement of the issue. Thereafter, Americans scrutinized every parliamentary action for possible threats to their constitutional rights, while British authorities became increasingly convinced that American opposition was simply a prelude to an eventual attempt to shake off the restraints of the navigation acts and perhaps even political dependence.

The final crisis of the pre-Revolutionary years was analyzed in detail by Benjamin Woods Labaree in *The Boston Tea Party.*[16] The tea party, he argued, was the decisive event in the chain of events that led to the outbreak of war and the Declaration of Independence. It was the tea party, he pointed out, that produced a new spirit of unity among the colonies, after more than two years of disharmony following the abandonment of the nonimportation agreements against the Townshend duties in 1770, and finally determined British officials to take a firm stand against colonial opposition to parliamentary taxation by making an example of Boston. The punitive measures they adopted posed the new question of whether the colonists had any rights at all with which to protect themselves from the power of Parliament, caused the rest of the colonies to unite behind Boston, drove patriot leaders to deny that Parliament had any authority whatever over the internal affairs of the colonies, and put both sides into an inflamed state that made war a virtual certainty. In an important modification of a long-accepted interpretation, Labaree discovered that among American smugglers of Dutch tea the fear that the Tea Act of 1773 would enable the East India Company to undersell them and so gain a monopoly of the American market was less important in stirring resistance to East India Company tea than earlier historians had suggested. Although he did not deny that the tea smugglers, who were largely confined to New York and Philadelphia, were concerned over the threat of monopoly, he found it a secondary issue among patriot leaders and the public at large. What concerned them far more was the possibility that the Tea Act was simply a ruse to inveigle them into paying the tea duty and admitting the long-contested right of Parliament to tax the colonies for revenue. By this discovery Labaree seconded the argument of other recent writers: the constitutional rights, especially Parliament's attempts to tax the colonies for revenue, were the primary issues between Britain and the colonies in the fateful years between 1763 and 1776.

Along with a number of studies of specific important issues,[17] these investigations have together made it possible to achieve a clear understanding of the importance and relative weight of the several substantive issues in the American case against the British government. Important segments of the colonists had occasionally been alarmed by such things as the Anglican effort to secure an American episcopate or the attempts by imperial officials to curtail the power of the lower houses of assembly, but the colonists were generally satisfied with their connection with Britain before imperial officials adopted stricter measures after 1760 that fundamentally challenged American rights and property. Parliament's attempts to tax the colonies for revenue were far and away the most serious of these measures. The consistency of their constitutional demands down to 1774 revealed both the commitment of the colonists to the constitutional principles on which they stood and their concern about the constitutional question. Only after 1774 did the American protest cease to be largely a series of responses to provocations by the imperial government and become an aggressive movement intent not just on securing exemption for the colonies from all parliamentary measures but also, in a striking escalation of their earlier demands, strict limitations upon the Crown's use of many of its traditional devices of royal control over the colonies. Throughout the debate the primary issues in the minds of the colonists were, then, of a political and constitutional nature involving matters of corporate rights, political power, individual liberty, security of property, and rule of law. Although, as Edmund S. Morgan has taken pains to emphasize,[18] all of these objects of concern were intimately coupled with "self-interest" and were conceived of as the necessary safeguards of the colonists' fundamental well-being—social and economic, as well as political—the opposition to Great Britain, these new studies seem to indicate, was much less directly social and economic in character than earlier historians had suggested.

These conclusions have been considerably enriched and somewhat altered by several recent explorations of the habits of thought that conditioned the American response to the substantive issues in the quarrel with Britain. These studies of what is essentially the psychology of colonial resistance have been especially concerned with the Americans' conception of human nature. At least since the early nineteenth century it has been conventional to attribute to the eighteenth century an optimistic conception of man and a belief in his ability to perfect the "good life on earth."[19] But this view, A. O. Lovejoy has insisted,[20] is a "radical historical error." Some eighteenth-century writers did subscribe to such a view of human nature, but, Lovejoy argued, the "most widely prevalent opinion about human nature" was that men were imperfect creatures who were usually actuated "by non-rational motives—by 'passions,' or arbitrary and unexamined prejudices, or vanity, or the quest for private economic advantage." This unflattering view of human nature provided the foundation for an elaborate theory of politics which, in its essential elements, was traceable as far back as antiquity and which —as Z. S. Fink,[21] J. G. A. Pocock,[22] and, especially, Caroline Robbins,[23] among others, have shown—manifested itself in several forms in seventeenth- and eighteenth-century English thought and was especially congenial to those political groups on the fringes or completely out of political power. At the heart of this theory were the convictions that man in general could not withstand the temptations of power, that power was by its very nature a corrupting and aggressive force, and that liberty was its natural victim. The protection of liberty against the malignancy of power required that each of the various elements in the polity had to be balanced against one another in such a way as to prevent any of them from gaining ascendancy over the rest. A mixed constitution was the means by which this delicate balance was to be achieved, but power was so pervasive and so ruthless that nothing was safe from it.

In *The Ideological Origins of the American Revolution*[24] Bernard Bailyn showed precisely how this theory of politics with its underlying view of human nature shaped the American response to British measures after 1763. Within the context of the ideas associated with this theory of politics, Bailyn found the succession of regulatory measures taken by the British government and royal officials in the colonies after 1763 appeared to be "evidence of a deliberate conspiracy launched by plotters against liberty both in England and in America." Far from being "mere rhetoric and propaganda," such words as slavery, corruption, and conspiracy "meant something very real to both writers and their readers" and expressed "real fears, real anxieties, a sense of real danger." Above all else, Bailyn argued, it was this reading of British behavior and "not simply an accumulation of grievances" that "in the end propelled" the colonists into rebellion. The distortions in their interpretation of the actions of the British government, Bailyn implied, mattered much less than that Americans believed it. Ideas thus played a dual role in the coming of the Revolution. They both provided a framework within which Americans could explain British and their own behavior and determined in significant and fundamental ways their responses to the developing situation.[25]

The moral and emotional dimension of the American response to British policy, touched on by Bailyn, was further emphasized in two separate articles by Edmund S. Morgan[26] and Perry Miller.[27] Both writers called attention to an important aspect of the Revolutionary experience that had largely eluded earlier historians: the extent to which the reactions of Americans to British measures had been accompanied and conditioned by an uneasy sense that it was not just British degeneracy but their own corruption that was responsible for their difficulties.[28] The crisis in imperial relations caused Americans to go through a process of intensive self-examination, to become acutely aware of the vicious tendencies within themselves and their societies, and to come to the conclusion that it was not just the degeneracy of the British government and British society that they had to fear but their own imperfect natures and evil inclinations as well. Both Morgan and Miller inferred that the Revolution was an internal fight against American corruption as well as an external war against British tyranny.[29]

These studies of the psychology of American resistance have added new dimensions to our understanding of the colonial reaction to British policy after 1763. First, they have shifted the focus from the ostensible to the underlying issues in the dispute by making explicit what, in the several investigations of substantive grievances, had been largely only implicit: that it was not only the *desire* to preserve their traditional rights and privileges against attacks by the imperial government but also the *fear* of what might happen to them once those bulwarks against arbitrary power had been removed that drove the colonists to revolt. Secondly, they have traced the origins of this fear directly to the colonists' conception of human nature with its sense of man's imperfections and of his inability to resist the corrupt influences of power. Thirdly, they have shown that that conception derived both, as Bailyn has argued, from a long philosophical tradition which came to the colonists largely through the writings of British dissenters and, as Miller and Heimert have suggested, from experiential roots. From their individual and collective experience the colonists understood how frail and potentially evil man was, and their deep-seated anxieties about the state of individual and social morality within the colonies helped to sharpen and shape their response to and was in turn heightened by the manifestations of what they took to be corruption and the corrosive effects of power on the part of the imperial government. Finally, on the basis of these conclusions it becomes much clearer why the colonists had such an exaggerated reaction to what, in retrospect, appear to have been no more than a series of justifiable and not very sinister actions by the parent state and why they so grossly misunderstood the motives and behavior of the ministry and Parliament and insisted upon interpreting every measure they found objectionable as part of a malign conspiracy of power against colonial, and ultimately all British, liberty. From the perspective of these studies, then, the Revolution has become not merely a struggle to preserve the formal safeguards of liberty against flagrant violations by the British but, in a deeper sense, a moral crusade against British corruption, a crusade made all the more compelling by the American belief that only by a manly opposition to and, after 1776, a complete separation from, that corruption could they hope to restore American virtue and save themselves from becoming similarly corrupt.

(4) The Roots of Tory and British Behavior

In their preoccupation with discovering and explaining the nature of American discontent between 1763 and 1776, most writers of the 1960's neglected to give adequate attention to the Tory and British side of the Revolutionary controversy. If, as they infer, the patriots stood for the maintenance of the *status quo* and represented the dominant drift of colonial opinion, what can be said of the Tories, the classic conservatives in the Revolutionary drama? If the British government was not trying to establish a tyranny in the colonies, as everyone now would agree, why did it continue to pursue policies that Americans found so objectionable? Both of these questions have been the subject of recent study.

That the Tories were indeed only a small minority of the total colonial population and that they were clearly out of step with the vast majority of their compatriots have been confirmed by the findings of two new works on loyalism. In *The King's Friends: The Composition and Motives of the American Loyalist Claimants,*[30] Wallace Brown concluded on the basis of a systematic analysis of the backgrounds of those loyalists who submitted claims for compensation to the British government that the total number of loyalists constituted no more than 7.6 to 18 per cent of the total white adult population. Earlier writers[31] had emphasized the upper-class character of loyalism, but Brown found that, although loyalism was "a distinctly urban and seaboard phenomenon"— except in New York and North Carolina where there were "major rural, inland pockets" of loyalists—with a clear "commercial, officeholding, and professional bias," its adherents came from all segments of society and represented a rough cross section of the colonial population. Only in Massachusetts, New York, and to a lesser degree Georgia were substantial numbers of the upper class represented, and even in those colonies the vast majority of the upper classes were clearly not loyalists. If, in terms of general social and economic background, the Tories were virtually indistinguishable from the Whigs, as Brown's investigation suggested, the question remains exactly how they were different.

This question has been taken up by William H. Nelson in *The American Tory,*[32] a penetrating study that focuses on the psychological character of the loyalists. The key to loyalism, Nelson argued, was weakness arising from the loyalists' inherent disparateness, lack of organization, unpopular political views, and marginal position in colonial society. Unlike their opponents, Tory leaders did not consult among themselves, never developed a community of feeling or a common sense of purpose, had no clear alternative to the Whig drift, and did not even know each other. Unable to cultivate public opinion, they held social and political ideas and values that could prevail in the colonies only with British assistance. Rank and file Tories were concentrated among non-English and religious minorities and among people in peripheral areas, "regions already in decline, or not yet risen to importance" such as the western frontier and the maritime region of the middle colonies, and represented a series of conscious minorities who looked to Britain for support against an external enemy like the Indians or the dominant majority. It was weakness, then, Nelson argued, along with alienation from or suspicion of the prevailing Whig majority, and not simple loyalty, that tied the Tories to Britain and, he implied, was responsible for their choice after the Declaration of Independence.

If the work on American grievances did not imply that the British politicians were in the wrong, it did suggest that they misjudged the situation in the colonies between 1763 and 1783 and that, if the preservation of the empire was one of their primary objectives, they blundered badly. If, as some earlier historians have argued, the measures of the imperial government were wise, just, and well calculated to serve the interests of the empire as a whole, imperial authorities failed utterly to persuade the colonists of the fact. How this breakdown in understanding could have occurred in a political community so celebrated for its political genius has been partially explained by Sir Lewis Namier in his exhaustive analyses of British politics during the opening years of the reign of George III[33] and by other scholars in a number of studies working out the implications of his findings.[34] A long line of earlier historians from Horace Walpole to Sir George Trevelyan had charged George III with attempting to destroy the influence of the Whig oligarchy and reestablish the supremacy of the Crown over Parliament. The King's American program, they had suggested, was part of the same pattern, and the English Whigs and the Americans were aligned against a common enemy in a common struggle against tyranny.

Namier and his followers have challenged this interpretation at every point. They have argued that there were no parties in the modern sense, only loosely organized factions and family groups; that what mattered most in politics was not ideology or the attachment to principle but the struggle for office, power, and advantage; that political issues revolved about local rather than national or imperial considerations; that the "political nation"—the people who took some active role in politics— was largely restricted to a narrow elite in the middle and upper echelons of British social structure; that all groups, as well as the King, accepted the traditional Whig principles that had evolved out of the revolutionary settlement; and that George III did not have to subvert the constitution to gain control over Parliament because, as in the case of his predecessor and grandfather, George II, his power to choose his own ministers and his control over patronage assured him of considerable influence in determining Parliament's decisions.

What these conclusions mean in terms of the misunderstanding with the colonies, though no one has worked them out in detail, is fairly clear. They reinforce the suggestions of the students of American grievances that British policy was shortsighted and inept. If British political leaders were so preoccupied by the struggle for office and so deeply involved in local matters, it is not difficult to see why they were unable to take a broader view in dealing with the colonies. The engrossment of the ministers and the leaders of Parliament in internal British politics and prior to 1770, the frequent changes in administration meant, as several recent books have shown,[35] that much of the responsibility for shaping the details of colonial policy devolved upon the bureaucracy, second-line officials in the Treasury, Board of Trade, American Department, and Law Offices who remained in office despite shifts in administration. Two books, Michael Kammen, *A Rope of Sand: The Colonial Agents, British Politics, and the American Revolution*,[36] and Jack M. Sosin, *Agents and Merchants: British Colonial Policy and the Origins of the American Revolution, 1763-1775*,[37] have demonstrated that colonial agents and merchants concerned in the colonial trade operated as a kind of rudimentary lobby to present the views of the colonists and actually managed to secure several important concessions from the government. But the agents themselves, and certainly not the merchants, did not always have accurate and up-to-date information about the situation in the colonies and, in any case, most colonial information came to the bureaucracy either from British officials in the colonies, most of whom were unsympathetic to the American cause, or from self-styled experts in both Britain and the colonies who, as John Shy has remarked, often "had some ax to grind or private interest to serve." There was, moreover, no sure way for colonial officials to obtain a clear and undistorted version of American views, and this absence of effective channels of communication could lead only to a massive breakdown in understanding in a crisis such as the one that developed after 1773.

Even more important in inhibiting effective action by imperial officials, still other studies have indicated, were their preconceptions about what colonies were and ought to be. Reinforced by the association in the official mind of the opposition in the colonies with the radical and, to many members of the British political nation, profoundly disturbing Wilkite agitation in Britain,[38] those preconceptions, according to recent investigations of four of the key figures in British politics—Townshend, Shelburne, Dartmouth, and Germain[39]—were of the utmost importance in shaping the responses of individuals of every political stripe to the imperial crisis. Similarly, Bernard Donoughue[40] has demonstrated how severely those preconceptions limited the range of choices open to the government in the critical period between the Boston Tea Party in December, 1773, and the outbreak of war in April, 1775. No one either in or out of office, Donoughue found, was able to escape from the oppressive weight of dominant ideas and habits of thinking and to grapple with the possibility that, as Americans were insisting, the empire might be preserved without totally subordinating the colonies to Parliament.

The traditional explanation for this failure has been that the men in power lacked vision, magnanimity, and statesmanship. But Donoughue's work pointed to more than a mere series of individual weaknesses. If men could not go beyond the prescribed boundaries of thought and language within which the system required them to work, then perhaps the system itself was incapable of adjustment at that time and the old British Empire may have been less the victim of the men who presided over its dissolution than they were the victims of the system of which the empire was a part. Given his commitment to the revolutionary settlement and to the supremacy of Parliament, George III could not possibly have stood apart from Parliament as a royal symbol of imperial union as the colonists desired.[41]

(5) Revolutionary Consequences

The net effect of the new studies of the coming of the Revolution has been to reestablish the image of the Revolution as a conservative protest movement against what appeared to the men of the Revolution to have been an unconstitutional and vicious assault upon American liberty and property by a tyrannical and corrupt British government. The Revolution, Daniel J. Boorstin argued in *The Genius of American Politics*,[42] had now to be understood as "a victory of constitutionalism." The major issue was "the true constitution of the British Empire," and because the leaders of the Revolution regarded it as an "affirmation of faith in ancient British institutions," the "greater part of the institutional life of the community . . . required no basic change."

Recent investigations of the concrete political and social changes that accompanied the Revolution have tended to reinforce this image. Detailed studies of the political development of three states, Maryland, New Jersey, and Delaware, after 1776 have indicated that there was virtually no change in the traditional patterns of political leadership and little identifiable interest among any segment of society in achieving a more democratic polity.[43] By contrast, as Robert J. Taylor has shown,[44] the Revolution seems to have served as a much more profound educative and democratizing force among the people of western Massachusetts. Traditionally conservative and deeply suspicious of the commercial east, the westerners were slow in joining the easterners in opposing the British, but once they had thrown in their lot with the patriot cause they took the Revolutionary doctrine of popular sovereignty very seriously. At least in that corner of the new United States the contest with Britain was accompanied by a potentially powerful revolution in the political expectations of ordinary citizens, a revolution that, to the profound disturbance of political leaders up and down the Atlantic seaboard, might ultimately spread to other regions and other states.

This revolution in expectations did not, however, proceed very far during the period of the Revolution. As Elisha Douglass showed in *Rebels and Democrats*,[45] a study of the process of constitution-making in the states, the internal political revolution that, according to the Progressive historians, had occurred in 1776 was a very modest revolution indeed. There was, Douglass found, an articulate, if not very large, group of "democrats" who viewed the Revolution not as an end in itself but as a means to rebuild society on the principles of the Declaration of Independence, and to that end they demanded "equal rights for all adult males and a government in which the will of the majority of citizens would be the ultimate authority for political decision." Ardently opposed, however, by the dominant Whig leaders, who were suspicious of democracy and wanted governments that would check majority rule and retain the traditional system of political leadership, the democrats scored only limited gains in just three states—North Carolina, Pennsylvania, and Massachusetts—and even in those states they were unable to gain permanent control. A more subtle and, ultimately, more important democratizing force was the increase in popular participation in politics described by Jackson Turner Main.[46] By opening up a large number of new political opportunities, the Revolution drew an increasingly greater number of ordinary citizens into politics with the result, Main found, that the social base of both the upper and lower houses of the legislature was much broader after 1776 than it had been in the late colonial period. This development did not, however, lead to either a wholesale turnover in political leadership or immediate repudiation of the ideals of upper-class leadership. Along with the new ideology of popular government fashioned by some of the democrats, it nevertheless did help to pave the way for the eventual breakdown of the old habits of deference, the ascendency of the belief in a more popular government, and the veneration of majority rule in the early part of the nineteenth century.

Although more work remains to be done before firm conclusions can be drawn, it also seems clear, as Frederick B. Tolles noted in 1954 in a survey of recent studies, that the concrete social changes emphasized by J. Franklin Jameson some thirty years earlier were less sweeping and less significant than he had thought.[47] Louis Hartz presented the most elaborate statement of this theme in *The Liberal Tradition in America*.[48] Taking for his text Tocqueville's observation that the great advantage of Americans lay in the fact that they did not have to "endure a democratic revolution," Hartz argued that "the outstanding thing about the American effort of 1776 was . . . not the freedom to which it led, but the established feudal structure it did not have to destroy."

The prevailing view thus came to be that the Revolution was predominantly a conservative Whiggish movement undertaken in defense of American liberty and property, preoccupied throughout with constitutional and political problems, carried on with a minimum of violence—at least when seen in the perspective of other revolutions—and with little change either in the distribution of political power or in the structure and operation of basic social institutions, and reaching its logical culmination with the Federal Constitution. Whatever democratic stirrings may have accompanied it were subordinate and incidental to the main thrust of events and to the central concerns of its leaders. As Benjamin Fletcher Wright insisted,[49] the Spirit of '76 seemed to be represented less accurately by the writings of Thomas Paine—whose ideas, as Cecelia M. Kenyon had shown,[50] were decidedly atypical of the dominant patterns of thought among American Revolutionary leaders—or even the Declaration of Independence than by the state constitutions of 1776, 1777 and 1780, constitutions which were shaped out of traditional materials and revealed the commitment of the men of the Revolution to "order and stability as well as liberty," to the ancient British concept that "liberty required constitutional order."

This stress upon the preservative character of the Revolution tended to divert attention from any revolutionary or radical implications that may have accompanied it, and not until the early 1960's did a few scholars set out to discover just what was revolutionary about the Revolution. The most systematic and thorough exploration of this theme was by Bernard Bailyn.[51] What "endowed the Revolution with its peculiar force and made of it a transforming event," Bailyn declared, was not the "overthrow of the existing order"—which nowhere occurred—but the "radical idealization and rationalization of the previous century and a half of American experience." Many of the social and political goals of the European Enlightenment, Bailyn pointed out, had already "developed naturally, spontaneously, early in the history of the American colonies, and they existed as simple matters of social and political fact on the eve of the Revolution." Because habits of mind and traditional ways of thinking lagged far behind these fundamental changes in the nature of colonial social and political life, however, there was on the eve of the Revolutionary debate a sharp "divergence between habits of mind and belief on one hand and experience and behavior on the other." By requiring a critical probing of traditional concepts and forcing the colonists to rationalize and explain their experience—"to complete, formalize, systematize, and symbolize what previously had been only partially realized, confused, and disputed matters of fact"—the Revolution helped to end this divergency. Most of the political ideas that emerged from this process—the conceptions of representative bodies as mirrors of their constituents, of human rights as existing above and limiting the law, of constitutions as ideal designs of government, and of sovereignty as divisible—were at once expressive of conditions that had long existed in the colonies and a basic reconception of the traditional notions about the "fundamentals of government and of society's relation to government." By "lifting into consciousness and endowing with high moral purpose" these "inchoate, confused elements of social and political change," the Revolutionary debate thus both released social and political forces that had long existed in the colonies and "vastly increased their power." The movement of thought quickly spilled over into other areas, and the institution of chattel slavery,[52] the principle of the establishment of religion, and even conventional assumptions about the social basis of politics and the constitutional arrangements that followed from those assumptions were called into question. Ultimately, in the decades after the Revolution, these "changes in the realm of belief and attitude" and, more especially, the defiance of traditional order and distrust of authority contained within them affected the very "essentials" of American social organization and, Bailyn pointed out, helped permanently to transform the nature of American life.

Gordon S. Wood has built upon these foundations a comprehensive analysis of the development of American political thought from the Declaration of Independence to the adoption of the Federal Constitution.[53] Like Bailyn, Wood stressed the radicalism of the spirit of '76, locating it not in the relatively minor (outside Pennsylvania) transfer of political leadership from old to new men emphasized by older historians and not in the radical reconception of politics described by Bailyn but in the American expectation that the Revolution would usher in a "new era of freedom and bliss" not only for themselves but for the whole of mankind. The strength and nature of such millennial aspirations among the evangelical clergy have recently been discussed at length by Alan Heimert,[54] but Wood has pushed the argument considerably farther. He contended that such aspirations constituted the very core of American social and political thought during the first stages of the Revolution. What lay behind these utopian impulses and what gave the "Revolution its socially radical character," according to Wood, was the confident expectation that separation from a degenerate Britain and the institution of a republican government would purge America of its moral and social impurities, altering, in the process, the very character of the American people by transforming them into virtuous citizens who would eschew the vices and luxuries of the old world in favor of the simple virtues, put aside all individual concerns for the common good, and reconstruct their societies so that the only meaningful social distinctions would be those arising from natural differences among men. Precisely because they put such extraordinarily high hopes upon the regenerative effects of republican government, the construction of the new state governments—the "building of this permanent foundation for freedom"—thus became a work of enormous importance.

That these hopes were misplaced became abundantly clear to a significant number of Americans over the following decade. A spirit of extreme localism came to pervade politics and representatives were elected not because of their virtue or talent but because of their popularity and willingness to abide by the wishes of their electors. Instead of governments devoted to the selfless pursuit of the common good, America thus seemed to have produced a series of petty, excessively mutable legislative tyrannies which provided neither stable government nor protection for the liberty and property of their citizens. Even worse, it became obvious that republican government had not brought about the change in the character of the American people that had been hoped for in 1776. "The self-sacrifice and patriotism of 1774-75 soon seemed to give way to greed and profiteering at the expense of the public good." As these tendencies were accelerated by prosperous economic conditions in the 1780's, many leaders and intellectuals came to the conclusion that Americans simply did not have the virtue "necessary to sustain republican governments." Even more than the political malfunctioning of the states, this disillusionment, the fear that the great republican hopes of 1776 would be sacrificed to the self-interest and parochialism of Americans themselves, Wood suggested in a significant new conclusion, was what made the 1780's "truly critical for American intellectuals."

If the Revolution failed to achieve the millennial visions of 1776, however, it nonetheless succeeded, Wood showed, in generating an emerging *American* conception of politics. That sovereignty resided in the people rather than in any institution of government, that constitutions were compacts established by the sovereign power of the people and were unalterable by government, that government should be divided into separate parts not because each part represented a different social constituency but simply because it would act as a check upon the others, that every part was equally representative of the people, that because all sovereignty derived from the people power could be distributed among various levels of government, that republican government might be founded on self-interest because the clashing of interests would always prevent any one from gaining the ascendancy, and that liberty involved not merely the right of the subject to participate in government but "the protection of individual rights against *all* government encroachments"— all of these ideas which we now recognize as fundamental to the "American science of politics" had been hammered out gradually and fitfully by many different individuals in response to the pressures of democratic politics between the Declaration of Independence and the Constitution. The achievement of the Federalists, the author showed far more clearly than any previous writer, was "to bring together into a comprehensive whole [those] diffuse and often rudimentary" ideas and "to make intelligible and consistent the tangles and confusions" among them.[55]

If, then, as most recent writers have indicated, the Revolution was at its center a fundamentally conservative movement concerned primarily with the preservation of American liberty and property, it also had some distinctly radical features, as the works of Bailyn and Wood make clear. Its radicalism was to be found, however, less in the relatively modest social and political changes that accompanied it than in the power of its ideas. But the full impact of the radical ideas of the Revolution, their complete expression in the institutions and values of American life, Wood and Bailyn seemed to agree, came not during the Revolution but over the next half century in the political movements associated with Thomas Jefferson and Andrew Jackson. Thus, as William H. Nelson remarked in another essay on "The Revolutionary Character of the American Revolution,"[56] even "if the American revolutionists did not fight for democracy, they contributed to its coming . . . because their individualistic concepts of government by consent and republican equality led irresistibly in a democratic direction."

(6) The Federal Constitution

The forces for and against the movement for a stronger central government in the 1780's, the nature of the divisions over the Constitution of 1787, and the relationship of the Constitution to the Revolution have also received considerable attention over the past quarter century. Much of this attention has been focused upon Charles A. Beard's economic interpretation of the Constitution,[57] and the clear consensus has been that that interpretation is seriously deficient in almost every respect.

The most ambitious analysis of the Beard thesis was presented by Forrest McDonald in *We the People: The Economic Origins of the Constitution*.[58] After doing much of the research Beard had said would be necessary to validate his interpretation, McDonald was able to state categorically that Beard's "economic interpretation of the Constitution does not work." Far from being as unrepresentative of the American electorate as Beard had inferred, the Philadelphia Convention, McDonald argued, "constituted an almost complete cross section of the geographical areas" and organized political interest groups "existing in the United States in 1787." Neither did the delegates compose a "consolidated economic group" nor did "substantial personality interests" provide the dynamic element in the movement for the Constitution, as Beard had argued. In both federal and state conventions the amount of real property in land and slaves held by the proponents of the Constitution far exceeded the value of their holdings in public securities and other forms of personal property, wealth in both personal and real property was substantially represented among both Federalists and Antifederalists, and in "no state was the Constitution ratified without the consent of the farmers and a majority of the friends of paper money." The whole story, McDonald implied, could be told without reference to class conflict and the struggle for democracy—the two themes that had received most emphasis from Beard and his followers. Not class but state, sectional, group, and individual interests and the complex interplay among them comprised the economic forces behind the Constitution. Any economic interpretation of the Constitution would therefore necessarily be pluralistic, but, McDonald indicated, the primary organizing unit would be the individual states. Not only were the activities of most interest groups circumscribed by state boundaries, but those interests that reached across state boundaries, such as the interest in the public debt, "operated under different conditions in the several states, and their attitudes toward the Constitution varied with the internal conditions in their states." The contest over the Constitution was thus "at once *a contest* and *thirteen* contests," and, McDonald suggested in his most important new general conclusion, the outcome in each state seemed to depend upon how satisfied its citizens were—how well their economic interests were being served—under the Articles of Confederation.

That McDonald had overstated his case against Beard and that his focus upon narrow and specific interests tended to obscure the larger, and presumably more significant, divisions over the Constitution was the argument of two formidable critics: Jackson Turner Main and Lee Benson. Main, who had been over much of the same material as McDonald, presented his own explanation of the fight over the Constitution in his book, *The Antifederalists: Critics of the Constitution, 1781-1788*.[59] Insisting that there were important ideological and economic differences between Federalists and Antifederalists, Main subscribed to the Beardian view that the ideological split was between advocates of aristocracy and advocates of democracy. He carefully pointed out, however, that not all Antifederalists were democrats. Most Antifederalist leaders were, in fact, well-to-do and were interested less in democracy than in local self-rule and a weak central government. These leaders, who were the chief spokesmen for antifederalism, tended to mute the democratic voices of rank-and-file Antifederalists, the small property holders who were "fundamentally anti-aristocratic" and "wanted a government dominated by the many rather than the few." Similarly, Main argued that the economic division over the Constitution was in general along class lines with small property holders opposing large property holders, debtors against creditors, and paper money advocates opposed to hard money supporters. As he carefully pointed out, however, there were so many exceptions to his general conclusion that the contest could not possibly be explained "exclusively in terms of class conflict." A far more important division, he suggested, which cut across class lines, was that between the commercial and non-commercial regions, between "the areas, or people, who depended on commerce, and those who were largely self-sufficient."

In *Turner and Beard: American Historical Writing Reconsidered*,[60] Lee Benson subjected McDonald's work to a different kind of criticism. Based upon a "crude version of economic determinism that assumes men behave primarily as members of interest groups that keep a profit-and-loss account of their feelings and calculate the cash value of their political actions," McDonald's interpretive system, Benson charged, was even more grossly distorting than Beard's. That system might conceivably be applicable to the activities of pressure groups in the normal legislative process, but it was clearly inappropriate to the study of a national "Constitutional revolution" like the one that occurred in 1787-1788. Such a revolution involved a conflict of ideology, and ideology, Benson argued, was never the "direct product of self-interest" and "always cuts across the lines of interest groups." On the assumption that "social environment and position in the American social structure mainly determined men's ideologies, and, in turn, their ideologies mainly determined their opinions on the Constitution," Benson proposed to devise a system of interpretation based not on narrow economic interest groups but upon broad symbolic social groups. The principal division in this "social interpretation of the Constitution" was between "*agrarian-minded*" men and "*commercial-minded*" men. Ostensibly, the division was over what kind of central government the United States would have, with the agrarian-minded favoring a government of strictly limited powers that was close to the people and the commercial-minded a government that could "function as a creative, powerful instrument" for realizing broad social ends.

The controversy over Beard's interpretation of the Constitution had thus generated three alternative and partially contradictory sets of hypotheses about the hard social and economic forces behind the Constitution. All three scholars were in general agreement on a number of key points: there were discernible socio-economic divisions over the Constitution; those divisions exerted a profound, and probably primary, influence in the struggle; their nature and operation were enormously more complicated than Beard had ever imagined; and whether class divisions were important or not, the contest was not a match between the haves and the have-nots. The dispute was mainly over which divisions were most important and what was the precise nature of the divisions. The possibility of achieving some synthesis between Main's "commercial" and "non-commercial" categories on one hand and Benson's "commercial-minded" and "agrarian-minded" on the other was clear enough, but McDonald's insistence that the struggle was between strong (satisfied) states and weak (dissatisfied) states and was shaped by the conflicting ambitions of a multitude of special interest groups seemed completely irreconcilable with the arguments of either Main or Benson. Clearly, as Main pointed out, an enormous amount of work would be required before these competing propositions could be evaluated.

Some of the work has subsequently been performed by E. James Ferguson and McDonald. In *The Power of the Purse: A History of American Public Finance, 1776-1790*,[61] Ferguson explored the relationship between public finance and the movement for constitutional reform. It was Ferguson's thesis that the question of how the public debts incurred during the War for Independence were to be paid, whether by the states or by Congress, was the "pivotal issue in the relations between the states and the nascent central government" during the Confederation period. On this question the alignment was broadly the same as that which Main and Benson had seen in the struggle over the Constitution: mercantile capitalists versus agrarians. The former were "nationalists" who favored sound money backed by specie, strong central financial institutions, and the absolute sanctity of contracts and property, while the latter were localists who wanted cheap paper money, state-oriented finance, and easy ways of discharging debts. Seeing in the debt a lever by which they could secure the taxing power for the Congress, the nationalists, led by Robert Morris, endeavored between 1780 and 1786 to vest the debt in Congress and give Congress the taxing power to support it. But these endeavors ran into opposition from the advocates of state-oriented finance, some states began to take care of the interest on the debt, and the nationalist movement, for all practical purposes, collapsed between 1784 and 1786. Except for the foreign debt, on which

Congress partially defaulted, the period was not critical in terms of finance, and what produced the nationalist resurgence that led to the Constitution of 1787 was not public bankruptcy and currency depreciation but the nationalists' "fear of social radicalism" following the flood of paper money emissions in 1785-1786 and Shays' Rebellion. Though it was not entirely clear from Ferguson's account whether the merchants advocated a strong central government so that they could handle the debt or, as he seemed to suggest, the debt was simply a means of achieving the anterior goal of a strong central government, Ferguson had demonstrated that the political goals of the nationalists were "interwoven with economic ends, particularly the establishment of a nationwide regime of sound money and contractural obligation."

McDonald, who presented the results of his work in a paper and a book-length essay,[62] agreed with Ferguson that the public debt and the public lands were the "material sinews of union," and served as the basis for a national economic interest which formed around Robert Morris and provided the impetus for the movement to give Congress the taxing power in the early 1780's. He also agreed that the virtual collapse of that movement in 1783-1784 did not bring economic disaster. Where he differed from Ferguson was on the nature of the major political alignments and the central issue that divided them. The debate over whether to augment the powers of Congress, as McDonald saw it, only masked a deeper and much more fundamental issue—whether the United States would be politically one nation or not; and where individuals stood on that question depended on a number of variables, including where they lived, whether their states were thriving, their economic interests, and their ideological commitments. By suggesting that "accessibility to transportation—and through it to communication— predisposed Americans to be narrow or broad in their loyalties, to oppose or favor the establishment of a national government," McDonald seemed to be adopting categories similar to those earlier used by Main and Benson. But McDonald left no doubt that in his mind this division was distinctly secondary to the interplay of competing economic interests. Although the number of separate interests was vast, the most important division, McDonald contended in an important elaboration of his central conclusion in *We the People,* was between those who thought their interests would best be served by a strong national government and those who had a vested interest in the continued primacy of the state governments. The behavior of some men, however, could not, McDonald admitted, be explained purely in terms of self-interest. Some of the Antifederalists were republican ideologues who would have opposed the Constitution no matter what their interests were. More important, the

Constitution was so impressive an achievement that the men who wrote it obviously had to have been inspired by something more than the sordid materialism that normally characterized American politics.

McDonald's admission that the behavior of the men who wrote and pushed through the Constitution, as well as that of *some* of their opponents, could not be explained entirely or even largely in terms of their economic and social interests underlined the fundamental weakness in most of the post-World War II literature on the Confederation and Constitution. In sharp contrast to recent writers on the pre-Revolutionary period, these students of the Constitution did not advance very far beyond earlier historians in explaining what the ostensible and immediate *political* issues and underlying ideology were, how men of all political hues saw and reacted to the problems of the Confederation and the issues raised by the Constitution, and how they explained their behavior to themselves, their contemporaries, and posterity, whatever social and economic considerations may have consciously or unconsciously helped to shape their behavior. There seemed to be a general agreement that the Constitution was a bold political stroke, but the exact nature of that stroke, what it represented to the people who supported and opposed it, had not been made completely clear.

A considerable amount of light has been thrown upon this problem by several other writers. In a suggestive article,[63] John P. Roche emphasized the extent to which the Constitution was at once the product of democratic political procedures and a reflection of the Founders' aspirations for the new country. The Founders, he argued, had to be understood "first and foremost" as "superb democratic politicians" who were spokesmen for "*American* nationalism," a "new and compelling credo" that emerged out of the American Revolution. Far from being an antidemocratic document, as earlier historians had claimed, Roche concluded, the Constitution was a "vivid demonstration of effective democratic political action" and a clear indication that the Founding Fathers had to operate, and were aware they had to operate, "with great delicacy and skill in a political cosmos full of enemies to achieve the one definitive goal—popular approbation."

As Main has suggested, it was precisely the extreme continental nationalism of the Federalists, and the possibility that they might have sacrificed the libertarian inheritance of the Revolution to it, that so worried their Antifederalist opponents. That the Antifederalists were correct in thinking that they smelled a conspiracy but that they seriously misunderstood its character and intent was the conclusion of Stanley Elkins and Eric McKitrick in "The Founding Fathers: Young Men of the Revolution,"[64] a perceptive analysis of the nature of both the divisions over the Constitution and the nationalistic aspirations of the Federalists. The Federalist conspiracy, Elkins and McKitrick contended, was against not liberty but "particularism and inertia," which in the mid-1780's seemed to the Federalists on the verge of robbing the young nation of its future promise. Significantly younger than their opponents, many leading Federalists, Elkins and McKitrick pointed out, had "quite literally seen their careers launched in the Revolution." What made them nationalists, then, what gave them the "dedication, the force and éclat" to attempt to overcome the "urge to rest, to drift, to turn back the clock" that was represented by the Antifederalists and seemed to have a stranglehold on the country from 1783 to 1787, was not "any 'distaste' for the Revolution . . . but rather their profound and growing involvement in it." Fundamentally, then, Elkins and McKitrick concluded, the struggle was between energy and inertia, and the Constitution was "sufficiently congenial to the underlying commitments of the whole culture—republicanism and capitalism— that" once inertia had been overcome and the basic object of discontent, the absence of a Bill of Rights, removed, opposition to the new government melted away. After a dozen years of anxiety, the men of the Revolution could be reasonably confident in 1788-1789 that "*their* Revolution had been a success." Far from trying to overturn the Revolution, the Federalists were thus trying to bring it to a favorable conclusion.

Beneath the political maneuvering described by Roche and behind the desire for a more energetic government emphasized by Elkins and McKitrick, other writers have demonstrated, were certain basic ideas that were central to the whole Revolutionary experience. As A. O. Lovejoy has shown,[65] the framers of the Constitution had not changed their mind about human nature as a result of their experience during the Revolution: they still "had few illusions about the rationality of the generality of mankind." To prevent social anarchy and to guarantee—even to save —the success of the republican experiment in America from the unhappy fate it had suffered everywhere else,[66] they were persuaded, clearly required a stable and vigorous political system that would check such popular excesses.[67] Yet, as Martin Diamond has indicated,[68] they were also deeply devoted to popular government, to the idea that political authority should be " 'derived from the great body of the society, not from . . . any favoured class of it.' " However considerable were the roles of economic interests, broad social forces, the personal and social aspirations of the Founders, or the pressures for political compromise, the interaction between these two ideas, between the pessimistic conception of human nature and the commitment to popular government, these writers have argued, exercised a profound shaping influence upon the proceedings of the Philadelphia Convention of 1787. Inspired, as Douglass Adair has shown,[69] by the possibilities that politics might be reduced to a science, they believed, in Lovejoy's words, that it was entirely possible by employing the method of counterpoise, the balancing of harmful elements against one another, "to construct an ideal political society out of bad human materials—to frame a rational scheme of government, in which the general good will be realized, without presupposing that the individuals who exercise ultimate political power will be severally actuated in their use by rational motives, or primarily solicitous about the general good."

To moderate the flightiness of the people and to prevent the formation of a majority faction that would stop at nothing, even tyranny, to secure its own interest, the Framers agreed, were their primary tasks. The first task they sought to accomplish by the creation of the Senate which, as Diamond has pointed out, was designed to protect property against popular excesses and to provide a check on the popular House of Representatives without in any respect going "beyond the limits" permitted by the " 'genuine principles of republican government.' " To prevent the formation of a majority faction, the Framers came up with an equally "republican remedy," a major intellectual breakthrough and the peculiar insight, as Adair has demonstrated, of James Madison. What would save the United States from the tyranny of a majority faction and the fate of earlier republics, Madison argued, was its enormous size and the multiplicity of factions and interests that would necessarily result from that size. With so many separate and diverse interests, Madison contended, there would be no possibility of enough of them submerging their differences and getting together to form a majority faction.

It was their inability to accept Madison's contentions, Cecelia M. Kenyon has argued,[70] that constituted the chief ideological difference between Antifederalists and Federalists. An intensive analysis of Antifederalist writings, she argued, revealed that they held the same pessimistic conception of human nature, with the distrust of the masses and fear of factions implied in that conception, as the Federalists. Far from being devoted to simple majoritarianism, as earlier writers had assumed, they were afraid of oppression from all quarters—from the people at large as well as from corrupt factions among the upper classes. In fact, they were fundamentally suspicious of any form of a truly "national" government because they were convinced both that no government with such extensive authority could be prevented from yielding to the temptations of power and because, unlike Madison, who thought republican government would work only in a large state, they thought that it would never work except in small polities where the government could be "an exact miniature of the people."

The Constitution thus came to be seen not as the repudiation of the Revolution but as the fulfillment of the aspirations and ideas of its dominant group of leaders. To the extent it was intended to check the popular excesses that had been one of the incidental, if also entirely logical, results of the Revolution, it was also mildly counterrevolutionary, an attempt to neutralize the radical tendencies of thought and behavior before they threw the young republic into a state of political and social chaos that, the Founders believed, would perforce lead to a tyranny as objectionable as that they had just fought a long and bloody war to escape. Through the Constitution and the powerful central government it created they hoped to reassert and provide the necessary institutional and constitutional framework for achieving the original goals of the opposition to and subsequent break with Britain: a stable and orderly government in which men, despite their imperfections, would be free to enjoy the blessings of liberty and the security of property that was so essential a part of those blessings.

This view has been in part challenged by Gordon S. Wood in *The Creation of the American Republic.* The disagreement over the proper remedy for the ills of the country during the 1780's, Wood argued, revealed a longstanding, though previously largely concealed, rift in American political ideology. One side—Calvinists and future Anti-federalists—clung to "moral reform and the regeneration of men's hearts" as the only effective cures, while the other—Liberal Christians and future Federalists—looked "to mechanical devices and institutional contrivances as the only lasting solution." The movement for a stronger central government culminating in the adoption of the Federal Constitution in 1788 was spearheaded by men of the latter persuasion who sought to salvage the Revolution and to restrain its many unintended excesses by constructing a national *republican* government that would neutralize the "vices" of the state governments and not be dependent, like them, on the virtue of the people for its success.

In treating the bitter struggle over the Constitution, Wood seemed to align himself with older historians in declaring that the conflict was fundamentally social, "between aristocracy and democracy," and that the Constitution was "intrinsically" an aristocratic document designed to check the democratic tendencies of the period. But his analysis seems to suggest that, no matter how contemporaries conceived of it, the debate was really over what kind of *democratic* government Americans should have. The Federalists, who believed that only virtuous and talented men—the "natural aristocracy"—were capable of providing effective republican government, stood for an elitist, nationally-oriented democracy, while the Antifederalists, who thought that such men were not sufficiently close to the people in general to be responsive to the true interests of the entire society, favored a popular, locally-based democracy.

Wood's argument that the Constitution was a repudiation of the Revolution was based upon the questionable assumption that the utopian impulses of 1776 were the central components of the spirit of 1776. But it is by no means clear that the optimism of most Revolutionary leaders in 1776 did not derive more from their confidence that they could contrive constitutions that would neutralize the viciousness of men rather than from the hope that republican government would effect a wholesale renovation in human nature.

Because of its very newness and because it did so much to reshape not simply the political ideas but the political aspirations of men both in America and elsewhere in the world, the original system of politics encapsulated by the Federalists in the Constitution, far more than the genuine but transitory millennialism of 1776, may have been not only the most lasting but also the most radical—socially as well as politically—contribution of the Revolution.

(7) The Nature of the Revolution

What lay behind the events, issues, and interests of the era of the American Revolution, what gave them shape and coherence for the men of the Revolution, scholarship over the past quarter century seems to indicate, were their preconceptions about the nature of man and the function of government. Given the intense preoccupation of American leaders, from the Stamp Act crisis to the adoption of the Constitution of 1787, with human nature and its relationship to the political process, it is now clear that they were grappling with and were fully conscious that they were grappling with the knottiest and most challenging of human problems. The central concern of the men of the American Revolution was not merely the reaffirmation of their Anglo-colonial heritage and not simply the protection of liberty and property but, as Edmund S. Morgan has put it,[71] the discovery of means "to check the inevitable operation of depravity in men who wielded power." This "great intellectual challenge," Morgan argued, engaged the "best minds of the period" as politics replaced theology as "the most challenging area of human thought and endeavor" and the intellectual leaders in America "addressed themselves to the rescue, not of souls, but of governments, from the perils of corruption." This fear of human nature, Morgan emphasized, lay behind the resistance of the colonists to Britain between 1763 and 1783 and their insistence that "the people of one region ought not to exercise dominion over those of another" unless those subject to that domination had some control over it; this same fear, Morgan noted, drove them to adopt written constitutions that would, by establishing "the superiority of the people to their government," give the people some protection against "man's tyranny over man."

The meaning of the American Revolution has thus come to be seen primarily in the constitutions it produced and the ideas that lay behind them. Hannah Arendt presented the fullest and most systematic exposition of this view in *On Revolution*,[72] a trenchant analysis of the great revolutions of the late eighteenth century and the revolutionary tradition they spawned. The most significant fact about the American Revolution, Arendt argued, was that armed uprising and the Declaration of Independence were accompanied not by chaos but by a "spontaneous outbreak of constitution-making." And, she contended, the "true culmination" of the Revolutionary process was not the struggle for liberation from Britain but the effort to establish the freedom represented by those constitutions. Fear of human nature, of the "chartless darkness of the human heart," and the conviction that, in John Adams' phrase, there could be nothing "without a constitution" were initially behind this fever of constitution-making. But it was the possibility of creating a "community, which, even though it was composed of 'sinners,' need not necessarily reflect this 'sinful' side of human nature," the exhilarating hope, as Hamilton expressed it, that men might establish "good government from reflection and choice" and not be forever dependent "for their political constitutions on accident and force," that eventually made them conceive of constitution-making as the "foremost and the noblest of all revolutionary deeds" and emboldened them to try the great experiment in federalism in 1787. To devise a national system which would, as Madison put it, "guard . . . society against the oppression of its rulers" by checking the various powers of government against one another and still have sufficient power to protect "one part of society against the injustice of the other part" was not, and the Founders never understood it to be, an easy task that could be accomplished to perfection. But they had the confidence of the public and a degree of confidence in one another present elsewhere only among conspirators, Arendt contended, and their accomplishment was notable. With the Constitution of 1787 they managed both to consolidate the power of the American Revolution and to provide a foundation for the freedom that was the ultimate concern of the Revolution.

FOOTNOTES

[1] Philadelphia: University of Pennsylvania Press, 1951.

[2] "The Effects of the Navigation Acts on the Thirteen Colonies," in *The Era of the American Revolution: Studies Inscribed to Evarts Boutell Greene.* Richard B. Morris, editor. New York: Columbia University Press, 1939. pp. 1-39; and "Mercantilism and the American Revolution." *Canadian Historical Review* 23: 1-15; No. 1, March 1942.

[3] "British Mercantilism and the Economic Development of the Thirteen Colonies." *Journal of Economic History* 12: 105-114; No. 2, Spring 1952.

[4] "A Quantitative Approach to the Study of the Effects of British Imperial Policy upon Colonial Welfare: Some Preliminary Findings." *Journal of Economic History* 25: 615-638; No. 4, December 1965.

[5] Chapel Hill: University of North Carolina Press, 1963.

[6] Cambridge, Eng.: Cambridge University Press, 1961.

[7] On the developing sense of American self-consciousness, see Lawrence A. Cremin. *American Education: The Colonial Experience.* New York: Harper, 1970; Clinton Rossiter. *Seedtime of the Republic: The Origin of the American Tradition of Political Liberty.* New York: Harcourt, 1953; Max Savelle. *Seeds of Liberty: The Genesis of the American Mind.* New York: Knopf, 1948; Richard L. Merritt. *Symbols of American Community, 1735-1775.* New Haven: Yale University Press, 1966; Michael Kraus. *Intercolonial Aspects of American Culture on the Eve of the Revolution.* New York: Columbia University Press, 1928; and Carl Bridenbaugh. *Cities in Revolt: Urban Life in America, 1743-1776.* New York: Knopf, 1955. On the colonists' continuing reliance upon Britain for normative values, see Jack P. Greene. "Search for Identity: An Interpretation of the Meaning of Selected Patterns of Social Response in Eighteenth-Century America." *Journal of Social History* 3: 189-220; No. 3, Spring 1970.

[8] Charles A. Barker. *The Background of the Revolution in Maryland.* New Haven: Yale University Press, 1940; Donald L. Kemmerer. *Path to Freedom: The Struggle for Self-Government in Colonial New Jersey, 1703-1776.* Princeton: Princeton University Press, 1940; Oscar Zeichner. *Connecticut's Years of Controversy, 1750-1776.* Chapel Hill: University of North Carolina Press, 1949; Theodore Thayer. *Pennsylvania Politics and the Growth of Democracy, 1740-1776.* Harrisburg: Pennsylvania Historical and Museum Commission, 1953; David Hawke. *In the Midst of a Revolution.* Philadelphia: University of Pennsylvania Press, 1961; David S. Lovejoy. *Rhode Island Politics and the American Revolution, 1760-1776.* Providence: Brown University Press, 1958; Kenneth Coleman. *The American Revolution in Georgia, 1763-1789.* Athens: University of Georgia Press, 1958; W. W. Abbot. *The Royal Governors of Georgia, 1754-1775.* Chapel Hill: University of North Carolina Press, 1959; Thad W. Tate. "The Coming of the Revolution in Virginia: Britain's Challenge to Virginia's Ruling Class, 1763-1776." *William and Mary Quarterly.* 3rd series. 19: 323-343; No. 3, July 1962; Jere R. Daniell. *Experiment in Republicanism: New Hampshire Politics and the American Revolution, 1741-1794.* Cambridge: Harvard University Press, 1970; and Patricia U. Bonomi. *A Factious People: Politics and Society in Colonial New York.* New York: Columbia University Press, 1971.

[9] *Middle-Class Democracy and the Revolution in Massachusetts, 1691-1780.* Ithaca: Cornell University Press, 1955; *Virginia, 1705-1786: Democracy or Aristocracy?* East Lansing: Michigan State University Press, 1964.

[10] Charles S. Grant. *Democracy in the Connecticut Frontier Town of Kent.* New York: Columbia University Press, 1961; Milton M. Klein. "Democracy and Politics in Colonial New York." *New York History* 40: 221-246; No. 3, July 1959; Richard P. McCormick. *The History of Voting in New Jersey: A Study of the Development of Election Machinery, 1664-1911.* New Brunswick: Rutgers University Press, 1953; Thayer, *Pennsylvania Politics;* and Lovejoy, *Rhode Island Politics.*

[11] Princeton: Princeton University Press, 1965.

[12] "Historians and the Problem of Early American Democracy." *American Historical Review* 67: 626-646; No. 3, April 1962.

[13] "Democracy and the American Revolution: A Frame of Reference." *William and Mary Quarterly.* 3rd series. 21: 165-190; No. 2, April 1964.

[14] New York: Macmillan, 1960.

[15] Chapel Hill: University of North Carolina Press, 1953.

[16] New York: Oxford University Press, 1964.

[17] See Thomas C. Barrow. *Trade and Empire: The British Customs Service in Colonial America, 1660-1775.* Cambridge: Harvard University Press, 1967; Carl Bridenbaugh. *Mitre and Sceptre: Transatlantic Faiths, Ideas, Personalities, and Politics, 1689-1775.* New York: Oxford University Press, 1962; Carl Ubbelohde. *The Vice-Admiralty Courts and the American Revolution.* Chapel Hill: University of North Carolina Press, 1960; and John Shy. *Toward Lexington: The Role of the British Army in the Coming of the American Revolution.* Princeton: Princeton University Press, 1965.

[18] *The Birth of the Republic, 1763-1789.* Chicago: University of Chicago Press, 1956.

[19] Carl L. Becker. *The Heavenly City of the Eighteenth-Century Philosophers.* New Haven: Yale University Press, 1932.

[20] Baltimore: Johns Hopkins Press, 1961.

[21] *The Classical Republicans: An Essay in the Recovery of a Pattern of Thought in Seventeenth-Century England.* Evanston: Northwestern University Press, 1945.

[22] "Machiavelli, Harrington, and English Political Ideologies in the Eighteenth Century." *William and Mary Quarterly.* 3rd series. 22: 549-583: No. 4, October 1965.

[23] *The Eighteenth-Century Commonwealthman: Studies in the Transmission, Development and Circumstances of English Liberal Thought from the Restoration of Charles II until the War with the Thirteen Colonies.* Cambridge: Harvard University Press, 1959.

[24] Cambridge: Harvard University Press, 1967.

[25] The place of American conceptions of the past in this framework is analyzed by H. Trevor Colbourn. *The Lamp of Experience: Whig History and the Intellectual Origins of the American Revolution.* Chapel Hill: University of North Carolina Press, 1965.

[26] "The Puritan Ethic and the American Revolution." *William and Mary Quarterly.* 3rd series. 24: 3-43; No. 1, January 1967.

[27] "From the Covenant to the Revival," in *The Shaping of American Religion.* James Ward Smith and A. Leland Jamison, editors. Princeton: Princeton University Press, 1961. pp. 322-368.

[28] Some of the possible sources of these tensions are discussed briefly in Gordon S. Wood. "Rhetoric and Reality in the American Revolution." *William and Mary Quarterly.* 3rd series. 23: 3-32; No. 1, January 1966, and Greene. "Search for Identity."

[29] Alan Heimert has explored the religious aspects of the Revolution in far greater detail in *Religion and the American Mind from the Great Awakening to the Revolution.* Cambridge: Harvard University Press, 1966.

[30] Providence: Brown University Press, 1965.

[31] Most notably, Claude H. Van Tyne. *The Loyalists in the American Revolution.* New York and London: Macmillan, 1902.

[32] Oxford: Clarendon Press, 1961.

[33] *The Structure of Politics at the Accession of George III.* London: Macmillan, 1929; *England in the Age of the American Revolution.* London: Macmillan, 1930; *Crossroads of Power: Essays on Eighteenth-Century England.* London: Macmillan, 1962.

[34] The most important among these studies are Richard Pares. *King George III and the Politicians.* Oxford: Clarendon Press, 1953, a general discussion of the politics of the reign in the light of Namier's conclusions; John Brooke. *The Chatham Administration, 1766-1768.* London: Macmillan, 1956, and Ian R. Christie. *The End of North's Ministry, 1780-1782.* London: Macmillan, 1958, two detailed studies of the structure and course of British politics during important segments of the Revolutionary years; Charles R. Ritcheson. *British Politics and the American Revolution.* Norman: University of Oklahoma Press, 1954, a narrative

of the impact of the American troubles upon British politics; and Eric Robson. *The American Revolution in Its Political and Military Aspects, 1763-1783.* London: Oxford University Press, 1955, a collection of interpretive essays.

[35] Especially Dora Mae Clark. *The Rise of the British Treasury: Colonial Administration in the Eighteenth Century.* New Haven: Yale University Press, 1960; Franklin B. Wickwire. *British Subministers and Colonial America, 1763-1783.* Princeton: Princeton University Press, 1966; Shy. *Towards Lexington;* and Jack M. Sosin. *Whitehall and the Wilderness: The Middle West in British Colonial Policy, 1760-1775.* Lincoln: University of Nebraska Press, 1961.

[36] Ithaca: Cornell University Press, 1968.

[37] Lincoln: University of Nebraska Press, 1965.

[38] The nature and impact of this agitation has recently been analyzed in Ian R. Christie. *Wilkes, Wyvill and Reform: The Parliamentary Reform Movement in British Politics, 1760-1785.* London: Macmillan, 1963; George Rudé. *Wilkes and Liberty: A Social Study of 1763 to 1774.* Oxford: Clarendon Press, 1962; and Eugene Charlton Black. *The Association: British Extraparliamentary Political Organization, 1769-1793.* Cambridge: Harvard University Press, 1963.

[39] Sir Lewis Namier and John Brooke. *Charles Townshend.* London: Macmillan, 1964; John Norris. *Shelburne and Reform.* London: Macmillan, 1963; B. D. Bargar. *Lord Dartmouth and the American Revolution.* Columbia: University of South Carolina Press, 1965; and Gerald Saxon Brown. *The American Secretary: The Colonial Policy of Lord George Germain, 1775-1778.* Ann Arbor: University of Michigan Press, 1963.

[40] *British Politics and the American Revolution: The Path to War, 1773-1775.* London: Macmillan, 1964.

[41] A more detailed and comprehensive analysis of the implications of recent writings on British politics in the eighteenth century for the understanding of the Revolution will be found in Jack P. Greene. "The Plunge of Lemmings: A Consideration of Recent Writings on British Politics and the American Revolution." *South Atlantic Quarterly* 47: 141-175; No. 1, Winter 1968.

[42] Chicago: University of Chicago Press, 1953.

[43] Philip A. Crowl. *Maryland During and After the Revolution: A Political and Economic Study.* Baltimore: Johns Hopkins Press, 1943; Richard P. McCormick. *Experiment in Independence: New Jersey in the Critical Period, 1781-1789.* New Brunswick: Rutgers University Press, 1950; John A. Munroe. *Federalist Delaware, 1775-1815.* New Brunswick: Rutgers University Press, 1954.

[44] *Western Massachusetts in the Revolution.* Providence: Brown University Press, 1954.

[45] Chapel Hill: University of North Carolina Press, 1955.

[46] "Government by the People: The American Revolution and the Democratization of the Legislatures." *William and Mary Quarterly.* 3rd series. 23: 391-407; No. 3, July 1966; and "Social Origins of a Political Elite: The Upper House in the Revolutionary Era." *Huntington Library Quarterly* 27: 147-158; No. 2, February 1964.

[47] "The American Revolution Considered as a Social Movement: A Re-Evaluation." *American Historical Review* 40: 1-12; No. 1, October 1954. J. Franklin Jameson. *The American Revolution Considered as a Social Movement.* Princeton, N.J.: Princeton University Press, 1926.

[48] New York: Harcourt, 1955.

[49] *Consensus and Continuity, 1776-1787.* Boston: Boston University Press, 1958.

[50] "Where Paine Went Wrong." *American Political Science Review* 45: 1086-1098; No. 4, December 1951.

[51] "Political Experience and Enlightenment Ideas in Eighteenth-Century America." *American Historical Review* 57: 339-351; No. 2, January 1962, and *The Ideological Origins of the American Revolution.*

[52] On the emergence of the antislavery impulse during the Revolution and the factors that stunted its development, see the superb discussion in Winthrop D. Jordan. *White over Black: American Attitudes towards the Negro, 1550-1812*. Chapel Hill: University of North Carolina Press, 1968.

[53] *The Creation of the American Republic, 1776-1787*. Chapel Hill: University of North Carolina Press, 1969.

[54] *Religion and the American Mind from the Great Awakening to the Revolution*. Cambridge: Harvard University Press, 1966.

[55] For additional discussion of the radical character of many of these ideas and their institutionalization within the broader context of Western European development, see R. R. Palmer. *The Age of Democratic Revolution.* . . . Princeton: Princeton University Press, 1959.

[56] *American Historical Review* 70: 998-1014; No. 4, July 1965.

[57] *An Economic Interpretation of the Constitution of the United States*. New York: Macmillan, 1913.

[58] Chicago: University of Chicago Press, 1958.

[59] Chapel Hill: University of North Carolina Press, 1961.

[60] Glencoe, Ill.: Free Press, 1960.

[61] Chapel Hill: University of North Carolina Press, 1961.

[62] "The Anti-Federalists, 1781-1789." *Wisconsin Magazine of History* 46: 206-214; No. 3, Spring 1963; *E Pluribus Unum: The Formation of the American Republic, 1776-1790*. Boston: Houghton Mifflin, 1965.

[63] "The Founding Fathers: A Reform Caucus in Action." *American Political Science Review* 55: 799-816; No. 4, December 1961.

[64] *Political Science Quarterly* 86: 181-216; No. 2, June 1961.

[65] *Reflections on Human Nature*.

[66] On this point see Douglass G. Adair. " 'Experience Must Be Our Only Guide': History, Democratic Theory, and the United States Constitution," in *The Reinterpretation of Early American History: Essays in Honor of John Edwin Pomfret*. San Marino: Huntington Library, 1966. pp. 129-148.

[67] Among several excellent analyses of the relation of Shays' Rebellion to the movement for stronger central government see the discussion in J. R. Pole. *Political Representation in England and the Origins of the American Republic*. London: Macmillan, 1966; New York: St. Martin's Press, 1967.

[68] "Democracy and The Federalist: A Reconsideration of the Framers' Intent." *American Political Science Review* 53: 52-68; No. 1, March 1959.

[69] " 'That Politics May Be Reduced to a Science': David Hume, James Madison, and the Tenth Federalist." *Huntington Library Quarterly* 20: 343-360; No. 4, August 1957.

[70] "Men of Little Faith: The Anti-Federalists on the Nature of Representative Government." *William and Mary Quarterly*. 3rd series. 12: 3-43; No. 1, January 1955.

[71] "The American Revolution Considered as an Intellectual Movement," in Arthur M. Schlesinger, Jr., and Morton White, editors. *Paths of American Thought*. Boston: Houghton Mifflin, 1963. pp. 11-33.

[72] New York: Viking, 1963.

· 13 ·

The Early National Period, 1789–1823

Shaw Livermore, Jr.

O NE will look in vain through the historical literature of the decade of the 1960's to find a new lens through which to view the early national period of American history. No major theme was announced around which the curious could assemble the record of American strivings to build a new society; no major historian launched upon a new reconstruction or synthesis that would direct us to place the period in a new relation with the years before or after. It would be fair to say that there seems to have been an effort to disengage our attention from the traditional battlegrounds of the Progressive historians and their critics, to clear away the fascinations of determinist schemes now hopelessly rent by the thorns of evidence, but one must call upon faith to sustain the hope that we are poised at a new takeoff stage. Scores of investigators scrambled over the landscape, but most succumbed eventually to the temptations of old quarrels, presentist allures, or the despair of baffling contradictions and meaninglessness. To bring balance, perspective, or a judicious temperament to the problem is generally the best one can summon up as a substitute for the striking and fresh.

Work went forward on familiar fronts. New volumes appeared in the only major effort to represent the collective knowledge and wisdom of the profession, *The New American Nation Series*. The diplomatic arena attracted a strong contingent, as did the realm of the biographer, with its unparalleled riches of the great and near-great to feast upon. Coupled with biography, there was impressive progress in magisterial editions of the collected papers of national leaders. Perhaps the most vital sector was the continuing inquiry into the nature, workings, and composition of political parties. This interest, which was quickened during the 1960's by outside infusions from political science, sociology, and developmental studies, should continue to evoke considerable enthusiasm. A few arresting inquiries into the nature and institutionalization of American democracy appeared during the decade, though the subject remains murky and in dispute. Contemporary concerns were probably most responsible for the considerable excitement generated by new inquiries into that most awesome, nigh unimaginable, part of the American past, slavery. Its centrality was even more insisted upon by several historians and the level of anguish was accordingly raised even higher. As could be expected, the fires of the frontier did not die out and American Indian policy was given closer attention. Last, a competent cadre continued the task of informing us about the springs of economic development.

The lack of new focus in historical studies of the period is registered in five works from *The New American Nation Series*. John Miller told us once again that the Federalist program during the 1790's has much to be said for it, that Alexander Hamilton had remarkable prophetic powers, and that however attractive Thomas Jefferson's democratic ideals it was a good thing the Federalists had their way for a time at least. These judgments may well be sound but they tell us little about why men figured things as they did, why some recognized Hamilton's "genius," and others held a different notion about the "good" society. The approach keeps us at the titillating but essentially unhistorical level of arguing over whether Hamilton or Jefferson was the more admirable fellow, a level that appears over and again as the accepted field of honor. Marshall Smelzer accepted the gauge when he told us that we have misunderstood Jefferson as a doctrinaire democrat instead of the "Whiggish moderate" that he was, and that if we accept this view we will realize that the Jeffersonians neither repudiated nor repealed their original principles and that they responded intelligently to unforeseen circumstances. In both cases the authors seemed to be groping for a statement about that hardy American animal, pragmatism. If so, we need to know how it came into existence, what its environmental circumstances have been, and the sequence of its adaptive mechanisms.[1]

As the great antagonists passed off the field, George Dangerfield introduced us to another familiar American entity, nationalism, by suggesting that there seem to have been two separate breeds, the one economic and the other democratic. The notion is promising but Dangerfield left us only with the suggestion while staying for the most part on the familiar but still mysterious broken terrain of the post-war period. Though some historians have been trying to carve out a new domain of cultural history, drawing mainly from cultural anthropology, Russel Nye's account is largely a descriptive foray into traditional areas of literature, education, religion, and science. Francis Philbrick's account of the West is largely directed toward refuting Frederick Jackson Turner's views of a half century and more ago. Each of these five books is skillfully composed, fairminded in judgment, and reasonably reflective of current scholarship, but they are only upon the rarest occasion moving.[2]

Thomas Jefferson and Alexander Hamilton remain the central figures of the age for biographers and analysts. Merrill Peterson's full-scale biography of Jefferson is probably the best one-volume account yet published. Peterson was generally friendly to Jefferson though he confessed that after years of close study Jefferson remained a mystery to him. At times the lofty idealist, at others the compromising politician, at once the man of conscience and the backslider, Jefferson is for Peterson an enormously complicated man. Beginning with the first volume in 1948, Dumas Malone published his fourth in 1970, covering the first presidential years, and we have a richly-detailed, friendly account that shows Jefferson orchestrating a highly successful first term in the White House. Malone is not so troubled by the intricacies of Jefferson's conduct, and we have him as an Olympian in good standing. That Jefferson can inspire resentment and outright hostility is abundantly apparent in Leonard Levy's savage attack upon Jefferson's record in the area of civil liberties and Lawrence Kaplan's thesis that Jefferson's continued enthrallment with France led him to distort his sense of American national interest. Jefferson's relation to slavery was scored by several writers during the decade. The best work on Hamilton is clearly Broadus Mitchell's concluding volume. Mitchell relentlessly defended Hamilton against all the familiar attacks, big and small, and oriented the whole work around Hamilton's great dream of establishing a cohesive, centrally-directed America. The mixture of admiration and suspicion that has always surrounded Hamilton is manifest in Gerald Stourzh's inquiry, which sharply displays an extraordinarily ambitious man intent upon the business of building an imposing American empire.[3]

Federalists seem generally to fare better in attracting historians than Republicans. While no full-scale biographies of John Adams appeared, two assessments were made of the change in Adams' political perspective after his ten years in Europe at the close of the Revolution. Both authors concluded that Adams became more fearful for the American experiment. The list of biographical studies of lesser Federalist leaders is impressive. We have new accounts of John Jay and Rufus King of New York, Theodore Sedgwick and Fisher Ames of Massachusetts, and Charles Cotesworth Pinckney and William Loughton Smith of South Carolina. Special mention should be made of an extensively revised edition of Samuel Eliot Morison's classic study of Harrison Gray Otis, one that gives us fascinating new glimpses of upper-class society, and a careful

new study of John Marshall's jurisprudence. Two other works have as
their special problem the process of conversion from the Federalist to
Republican faiths. Irving Brant completed his mind-boggling study of
James Madison with a sixth volume on the years after 1812. Brant sustained his impressive design to elevate Madison to the very first rank
of American statesmen. His effort was seconded by a recent one-volume
account by Ralph Ketcham and by Adrienne Koch's affectionate assessment of Madison's reflections in his last years upon constitutionalism
and governance. The serious lack of good studies of second-level
Jeffersonian politicians is somewhat alleviated by two modest portraits
of Daniel Tompkins of New York and John Breckenridge of Kentucky.[4]

The number of expensive enterprises engaged in publishing the papers
of the great men who left imprints upon the early national period is
staggering. Beyond bringing material together in printed form for researchers, the editors in many cases give us commentary and explication
that make reading them more pleasurable than an embarrassing number
of scholarly monographs. The acknowledged masters are Julian Boyd
of the Jefferson papers and Lyman Butterfield of the Adams project.
They set standards of excellence that encouraged others. The work was
slow. As of 1972 we had Jefferson's papers only to 1791, in spite of
eighteen volumes, and though all the Adams papers have been micro-
filmed for distribution to libraries, we still look ahead to a printed
chronological series. The four-volume set of the *Diary and Autobiography of John Adams* remains a gem. The Hamilton venture went forward
rapidly, the letters now complete through 1794. Seven volumes of Madison papers appeared, bringing the record only to the year 1784. For a
later generation of leaders there were three volumes of Clay papers
running to 1824 and four volumes of Calhoun papers to 1820.[5]

With foreign policy more at the center of affairs than at any time
until the middle of this century, one continues to find a large effort
directed to the search for a proper understanding of the American
national interest and toward assessments of successive efforts to effect
that interest. In a highly influential account, Felix Gilbert characterized
the essence of American foreign policy as a largely successful integration
of utopian assumptions about a new world system, assumptions that
were powerfully shaped by the Enlightenment, into considerations of
power politics as practiced in the late eighteenth century. Paul Varg
emphasized the latter half of this equation in crediting the Federalists
with a more effective grasp of the true American interest, while Arthur
Ekirch gave us a good account of the intellectual underpinnings for the
American policy of isolationism, a policy brought to fruition under
Republican auspices. An unabashed admirer of Hamilton, Gilbert

Lycan, sketched out his hero's design for opposing the expanding French Revolutionary influence, and an equally unabashed advocate for Jefferson, Julian Boyd, laid out a documentary record of Hamilton's alleged perfidy in 1790 as part of his continuing effort to keep the United States firmly within the British orbit. Jerald Combs, using the Jay Treaty imbroglio as a focus, thoughtfully showed the significant differences of outlook of Federalists and Republicans in defining a proper American national interest. Three works appeared which help to fill in the more narrowly diplomatic record of the 1790's, each of them adopting a more friendly version of British aims and practices than usually appears in secondary accounts. A thorough and persuasive account of the difficulties with France at the end of the decade gives us a view of John Adams being genuinely torn, even sometimes vacillating, and of a French government significantly conciliatory after the XYZ Affair. Peter Hill wrote a full and appreciative story of the role played by a most attractive Federalist, William Vans Murray, in bringing the French tangle to a reasonable conclusion by 1800.[6]

Clearly the most significant assessments of American foreign policy formation and diplomatic encounters during the Republican years came in two volumes by Bradford Perkins. The first volume takes us from a state of satisfactory relations with Great Britain down to the declaration of war in 1812, and the second, with a brilliant recounting of the Ghent negotiations, takes us back to establishment of a secure relation by 1823. Perkins found little to commend in the writhings of Jefferson and Madison during the slide into war, their problems being both important faults of imagination and execution. In his second volume Perkins concluded that the improvement in relations is to a great extent attributable to a peculiarly felicitous rapport between John Quincy Adams and Castlereagh. The special problem of the War of 1812 attracted further consideration, with perhaps the most compelling conclusion being that of Roger Brown when he argued that a profound concern for republican ideals and Republican Party needs was far more important than we had thought in explaining why Madison and congressional leaders acted as they did during the year before war. A specialized account of Pennsylvania is of some interest and it adds weight to the general approaches of Perkins and Brown. Another investigator would direct us once again to the maritime problem and away from the various notions announced in the last several decades that purely domestic conflicts and urges were at the root of it. Harry Coles published a particularly clear account of the war itself.[7]

Interest in work on political parties during the period was heightened by the realization that the American example prefigured the general trend toward partisan organization as a critical device in making mass participation democratic systems work in other societies. Political scientists had long been concerned with parties as organizational devices, but American historians have only recently begun to seek out the circumstances in which parties arose so dramatically during the 1790's. Two important books illustrate this trend. Roy Nichols traces the history of American parties beginning with British practices in the Middle Ages and concluding with a fully-formed pattern by the late 1840's. Where Nichols used the arresting word "invention" to describe this process, Richard Hofstadter pointed to the "idea" of a party system and he skillfully related the evolutionary steps of thought and practice that led to general acceptance of a legitimate opposition. Both men built upon earlier work. Noble Cunningham completed a two-part study of the Jeffersonian Republicans in 1963 in which his concern throughout was with the building and management of a party structure. A major conclusion of the work is that national parties did not grow out of local structures but had instead been consciously molded by party leaders in Philadelphia and Washington. The explicit concerns of political science and developmental studies are manifest in an inquiry by William Chambers, though his work is not so solidly founded in original sources as Cunningham's.[8]

The concern for structure was blended with older interests in the ideological components of parties, interest conflicts, and the calculations of ambitious party leaders. David Fischer pointed effectively to a second generation of Federalist leaders who adopted the organizational techniques of their opponents and softened, at least publicly, their elitist values. The desire for office and opportunities for maneuvering by Federalists after 1815 are major themes in another study of the developing American party system. Norman Risjord isolated a wing of the Republican Party and showed how tenaciously its members tried to use the Party to serve their conservative needs. Drawing effectively upon another concern of political science, the accumulation and exercise of power, James Young drew a striking picture of Washington society in the early decades of the century. The Republican disdain for concentrated power produced a sharply compartmentalized government in which even living patterns were affected. In Young's view the trend was increasingly dangerous for effective government until Andrew Jackson dramatically reasserted presidential power. Conflict within the Republican ranks was detailed in two other works, one using a focus of the arguments over the structure and powers of the judiciary and the other showing how many Republican leaders were deeply involved in the Yazoo land schemes.[9]

One of the most troublesome problems that has emerged from party studies is the fact that when the historian centers upon national issues and institutional trends as the coagulants of party formation he often makes a persuasive case, yet when other investigators single out individual states or regions the importance of such national matters seems to evaporate in a welter of parochial concerns and machinations. Alfred Young's careful study of the New York Republicans showed the persistence of colonial alliances and distinctive state problems, and although Carl Prince was principally concerned to reconstruct the growth of party structure in New Jersey he showed over and again that the horizons of most Republicans there seemed to be restricted to the borders of the state. Studies of each party in Massachusetts concluded that the particular social make-up, religious disputes, and political style of the state had far more to do with party alignment than policy decisions by the general government or larger ideological conflicts. Lisle Rose's picture of the Southern Federalists did include some concern for national matters, but the connection with the Northern wing of the party is far more tenuous than the grounding in peculiar Southern practices and outlooks.[10]

The developing democratic matrix within which parties formed is the subject of three challenging projects. Yehoshua Arieli considered the interrelationship between individualism and democracy in producing a distinctive American nationalism. He found that the capacity for using democratic means to adjust conflict and a continuing though often puzzling penchant for quasi-socialist schemes kept the centrifugal tendencies of individualism within bounds. A thorough investigation of the suffrage through this period produced some curious results, among them that the effective eligible electorate in the colonial period had been astonishingly broad, that there was not for the most part a passionate concern for suffrage reform, and that changes usually came from passing partisan interests rather than from larger ideological considerations. A social scientist, Sidney Aronson, considered the top-level appointees of three presidents and discovered only a modest change in their social antecedents and connections over a forty-year period, with the change between the appointees of Jefferson and Jackson being even more modest. He acknowledged that the change may well have been sharper among appointees at the lower levels. Although not directly addressed to the problem of American democracy, two other studies display interesting sidelights. The dramatic story of prison reform shows a powerful belief in the redemptive power of individualism to destroy the corrupting charms of criminal society, and a study of elementary-school textbooks shows us something of the mode of diffusing democratic norms.[11]

The curse of American democracy, slavery, prompted a number of important new books. Two works with a larger compass are valuable for an understanding of the early national period. Winthrop Jordan's inquiry into the nature of racial attitudes became very influential, as did the conclusions of David Brion Davis in investigating the early abolition movement. Donald Robinson insisted that slavery was far more fundamental in framing political disputes than has been generally understood, and Robert McColley argued that in spite of some apparently favorable trends toward emancipation, slavery was deeply imbedded in Jefferson's Virginia, with Jefferson himself abjuring an effective campaign against it. According to William Freehling, in a most persuasive account, the fear of Northern attacks upon slavery is the central explanation for the nullification movement in South Carolina. A new assessment of the Denmark Vesey episode adds substance to this argument. Thomas Abernethy's general survey of Southern history during the early national period accents the importance of the frontier, but slavery nonetheless remains as a constant counterpoint. That Northern attitudes toward slavery were deeply marked by ambivalence is amply demonstrated in Leon Litwack's account of the legal and administrative disabilities suffered by blacks in the North.[12]

Our knowledge of the frontier has been significantly expanded. Malcolm Rohrbaugh ranged over the mass of material showing the evolution of land policy and, of particular importance, the actual local administration of this policy. The central thrust of his work is the great force and effectiveness of the desire to get public lands into the hands of individuals. Father Paul Prucha showed us the comprehensive role of the army in clearing the way for distribution of land to white settlers. A forceful though not always persuasive examination of denominational activity on the Northern frontier led T. Scott Miyakawa to conclude that Protestantism acted to produce a conservative conformity rather than the usual image of innovative individualism. Another work attempts to bring some order to the confusing religious melée on the Southern frontier and suggests that by mid-century the fear of Catholicism had brought most of the Protestant sects together. Reginald Horsman incorporated much recent scholarship in a skillful general survey of frontier life.

The Indian dimension of the frontier continues to interest historians. Prior to his account of the army's activity, Father Prucha had written an excellent narrative of the government's Indian policy. His basic theme is the belief of national leaders that the only effective way to mediate the relation between the races was to vest effective power and administrative capacity in the national government. Political forces, principally centered in Congress, and the persistence of squatters and traders constantly vitiated the government's efforts. Reginald Horsman singled out Jefferson's notion of extending white civilization to the Indian for special blame in accounting for the failures of American policy. Horsman had previously given us a good biography of Matthew Elliot, who managed the British government's Indian affairs on the Northwest frontier for more than twenty years before the War of 1812. Two accounts of the anguishing process leading to removal of the Cherokees and the Choctaws give us a good view of the whole removal problem.[13]

Although there were a number of economic studies falling within the period, only a few of them attempt to integrate their findings into the whole of American development. Curtis Nettels completed an important volume for the valuable Holt, Rinehart series on American economic history. In it he stressed the factors which led to an emerging national economy in place of a localized, colonial pattern, but he may well have overemphasized the degree to which the economy was effectively national by 1815. The implications of Nathan Miller's study of New York go beyond the state's borders in detailing the increasing desire and ability of private enterprisers to be free from public direction and encouragement. The impact of the depression beginning in 1819 upon existing political and economic patterns shows up nicely in Murray Rothbard's monograph.[14]

Even so brief a survey of historical scholarship during the past several years on the early national period would indicate that materials were gathered and new directions hinted at for a general departure from the old controversies, but the work awaited a more comprehensive imagination and the touch of a new Turner or Beard.

FOOTNOTES

[1] John C. Miller. *The Federalist Era, 1789-1801.* New York: Harper & Row, 1960; Marshall Smelser. *The Democratic Republic, 1801-15.* New York: Harper & Row, 1968.

[2] George Dangerfield. *The Awakening of American Nationalism, 1815-28.* New York: Harper & Row, 1965; Russel Blaine Nye. *The Cultural Life of the New Nation, 1776-1830.* New York; Harper & Row, 1960; Francis Philbrick. *The Rise of the West, 1754-1830.* New York: Harper & Row, 1965.

[3] Merrill D. Peterson. *Thomas Jefferson and the New Nation.* New York: Oxford University Press, 1970; Dumas Malone. *Jefferson the President: First Term, 1801-05.* Boston; Little, Brown, 1970; Leonard W. Levy. *Jefferson and Civil Liberties; the Darker Side.* Cambridge: Belknap Press of Harvard University Press, 1963; Lawrence S. Kaplan. *Jefferson and France; An Essay on Politics and Political Ideas.* New Haven: Yale University Press, 1967; William Cohen. "Thomas Jefferson and the Problem of Slavery." *Journal of American History* 34: 503-526; No. 3, December 1969; Broadus Mitchell. *Alexander Hamilton: The National Adventure, 1788-1804.* New York: Macmillan, 1962; Gerald Stourzh. *Alexander Hamilton and the Idea of Republican Government.* Stanford: Stanford University Press, 1970.

[4] John R. Howe, Jr. *The Changing Political Thought of John Adams.* Princeton: Princeton University Press, 1966; Edward Handler. *America and Europe in the Political Thought of John Adams.* Cambridge: Harvard University Press, 1964; Richard B. Morris. *John Jay, The Nation and the Court.* Boston: Boston University Press, 1967; Robert Ernst. *Rufus King, American Federalist.* Chapel Hill: University of North Carolina Press, 1968; Richard E. Welch, Jr. *Theodore Sedgwick, Federalist: A Political Portrait.* Middletown: Wesleyan University Press, 1965; Winfred E. A. Bernhard. *Fisher Ames, Federalist and Statesman, 1758-1808.* Chapel Hill: University of North Carolina Press, 1965; Marvin Zahniser. *Charles Cotesworth Pinckney, Founding Father.* Chapel Hill: University of North Carolina Press, 1967; George C. Rogers, Jr. *Evolution of a Federalist: William Loughton Smith of Charleston, 1758-1812.* Columbia: University of South Carolina Press, 1962; Samuel E. Morison. *Harrison Gray Otis, 1765-1848: The Urbane Federalist.* Boston: Houghton Mifflin, 1969; Robert K. Faulkner. *The Jurisprudence of John Marshall.* Princeton: Princeton University Press, 1968; Lynn W. Turner. *William Plumer of New Hampshire, 1759-1850.* Chapel Hill: University of North Carolina Press, 1962; George Dangerfield. *Chancellor Robert R. Livingston of New York, 1746-1813.* New York: Harcourt, Brace, 1960; Irving Brant. *James Madison: Commander in Chief, 1812-1836.* Indianapolis: Bobbs-Merrill, 1961; Ralph Ketcham. *James Madison; A Biography.* New York: Macmillan, 1971; Adrienne Koch. *Madison's "Advice to My Country."* Princeton: Princeton University Press, 1966; Ray W. Irwin. *Daniel D. Tompkins: Governor of New York and Vice President of the United States.* New York: New York Historical Society, 1968; Lowell Harrison. *John Breckenridge: Jeffersonian Republican.* Louisville, Ky.: Filson Club, 1969; see also another biography of Aaron Burr, Herbert S. Parmet and Marie B. Hecht. *Aaron Burr: Portrait of an Ambitious Man.* New York: Macmillan, 1967.

[5] Julian Boyd, editor. *Papers of Thomas Jefferson.* Princeton: Princeton University Press, 1950-   ; Lyman H. Butterfield, editor. *Diary and Autobiography of John Adams.* 4 vols. Cambridge: Belknap Press of Harvard University Press, 1961; Harold C. Syrett and Jacob E. Cook, editors. *Papers of Alexander Hamilton.* New York: Columbia University Press, 1961-   ; William T. Hutchinson and William M. E. Rachal, editors. *The Papers of James Madison.* Chicago: University of Chicago Press, 1962-   ; James F. Hopkins, editor. *The Papers of Henry Clay.* Lexington: University of Kentucky Press, 1959-   ; W. Edwin Hemphill and Robert L. Meriwether, editors. *The Papers of John C. Calhoun.* Columbia: University of South Carolina Press, 1959-   .

[6] Felix Gilbert. *To the Farewell Address: Ideas of Early American Foreign Policy.* Princeton: Princeton University Press, 1961; Paul A. Varg. *Foreign Policies of the Founding Fathers.* East Lansing: Michigan State University Press, 1963; Arthur Ekirch, Jr. *Ideas, Ideals and American Diplomacy,* New York: Appleton-Century-Crofts, 1966; Gilbert L. Lycan. *Alexander Hamilton and American Foreign Policy: A Design for Greatness.* Norman: University of Oklahoma Press, 1970; Julian Boyd. *Number 7, Alexander Hamilton's Secret Attempts to Control American Foreign Policy, with Supporting Documents.* Princeton: Princeton University Press, 1964; Jerald Combs. *The Jay Treaty; Political Battleground of the Founding Fathers.* Berkeley: University of California Press, 1970; Charles R. Ritcheson. *Aftermath of Revolution; British Policy toward the United States, 1783-1795.* Dallas: Southern Methodist University Press, 1969; Jack L. Cross. *London Mission; The First Critical Years.* East Lansing: Michigan State University Press, 1968; Gerald H. Clarfield. *Timothy Pickering and American Diplomacy, 1795-1800.* Columbia: University of Missouri Press, 1969; Alexander De Conde. *The Quasi-War: The Politics and Diplomacy of the Undeclared War with France, 1797-1801.* New York: Scribner's, 1966; Peter P. Hill. *William Vans Murray, Federalist Diplomat: The Shaping of Peace with France, 1797-1801.* Syracuse: Syracuse University Press, 1971.

[7] Bradford Perkins. *Prologue to War: England and the United States, 1805-1812*. Berkeley: University of California Press, 1961. *Castlereagh and Adams: England and the United States, 1812-1823*. Berkeley: University of California Press, 1964; Roger H. Brown. *The Republic in Peril: 1812*. New York: Columbia University Press, 1964; Victor Sapio. *Pennsylvania and the War of 1812*. Lexington: University Press of Kentucky, 1970; Reginald Horsman. *The Causes of the War of 1812*. Philadelphia: University of Pennsylvania Press, 1962; Harry L. Coles. *The War of 1812*. Chicago: University of Chicago Press, 1965. See also Reginald Horsman. *The War of 1812*. New York: Knopf, 1969.

[8] Roy Franklin Nichols. *The Invention of the American Political Parties*. New York: Macmillan, 1967; Richard Hofstadter. *The Idea of a Party System: The Rise of Legitimate Opposition in the United States, 1780-1840*. Berkeley: University of California Press, 1969; Noble Cunningham. *The Jeffersonian Republicans in Power: Party Operations, 1801-09*. Chapel Hill: University of North Carolina Press, 1963; William Nisbet Chambers. *Political Parties in a New Nation*. New York: Oxford University Press, 1963.

[9] David Hackett Fischer. *The Revolution of American Conservatism: The Federalist Party in the Era of Jeffersonian Democracy*. New York: Harper & Row, 1965; Shaw Livermore, Jr. *The Twilight of Federalism*. Princeton: Princeton University Press, 1962; Norman Risjord. *The Old Republicans: Southern Conservatism in the Age of Jefferson*. New York: Columbia University Press, 1965; James Sterling Young. *The Washington Community, 1800-1828*. New York: Columbia University Press, 1966; Richard E. Ellis. *The Jeffersonian Crisis: Courts and Politics in the Young Republic*. New York: Oxford University Press, 1971; C. Peter Magrath. *Yazoo: Law and Politics in the New Republic*. Providence: Brown University Press, 1966.

[10] Alfred F. Young. *The Democratic Republicans of New York; The Origins, 1763-1797*. Chapel Hill: University of North Carolina Press, 1967; Carl E. Prince. *New Jersey's Jeffersonian Republicans: The Genesis of an Early Party Machine, 1789-1817*. Chapel Hill: University of North Carolina Press, 1967; Paul Goodman. *The Democratic-Republicans of Massachusetts: Politics in a Young Republic*. Cambridge: Harvard University Press, 1964; James M. Banner, Jr. *To the Hartford Convention: The Federalists and the Origins of Party Politics in Massachusetts, 1789-1815*. New York, Knopf, 1969; Lisle A. Rose. *Prologue to Democracy: The Federalists in the South, 1789-1800*. Lexington: University of Kentucky Press, 1968.

[11] Yehoshua Arieli. *Individualism and Nationalism in American Ideology*. Cambridge: Harvard University Press, 1964; Chilton Williamson. *American Suffrage from Property to Democracy; 1760-1860*. Princeton: Princeton University Press, 1960; Sidney H. Aronson. *Status and Kinship in the Higher Civil Service: Standards of Selection in the Administrations of John Adams, Thomas Jefferson, and Andrew Jackson*. Cambridge: Harvard University Press, 1964; W. David Lewis. *From Newgate to Dannemora: The Rise of the Penitentiary in New York, 1796-1848*. Ithaca: Cornell University Press, 1965; Ruth Miller Elson. *Guardians of Tradition: American Schoolbooks of the Nineteenth Century*. Lincoln: University of Nebraska Press, 1964.

[12] Winthrop D. Jordan. *White over Black: American Attitudes toward the Negro, 1550-1812*. Chapel Hill: University of North Carolina Press, 1968; David Brion Davis. *The Problem of Slavery in Western Culture*. Ithaca: Cornell University Press, 1966; Donald L. Robinson. *Slavery in the Structure of American Politics, 1765-1820*. New York: Harcourt, Brace, 1971; Robert McColley. *Slavery and Jeffersonian Virginia*. Urbana: University of Illinois Press, 1964; William W. Freehling. *Prelude to Civil War: The Nullification Controversy in South Carolina, 1816-1836*. New York: Harper & Row, 1966; John Lofton. *Insurrection in South Carolina: The Turbulent World of Denmark Vesey*. Yellow Springs: Antioch Press, 1964; Thomas P. Abernethy. *The South in the New Nation, 1789-1819*.

Baton Rouge: Louisiana State University Press, 1961; see also David Bertelson. *The Lazy South.* New York: Oxford University Press, 1967; Leon Litwack, *North of Slavery: The Negro in the Free States, 1790-1860.* Chicago: University of Chicago Press, 1961.

[13] Malcolm Rohrbough. *The Land Office Business: The Settlement and Administration of American Public Lands, 1789-1837.* New York: Oxford University Press, 1968; Francis Paul Prucha. *The Sword of the Republic: The United States Army on the Frontier, 1783-1846.* New York: Macmillan, 1969; T. Scott Miyakawa. *Protestants and Pioneers: Individualism and Conformity on the American Frontier.* Chicago: University of Chicago Press, 1964; Walter B. Posey. *Religious Strife on the Southern Frontier.* Baton Rouge: Louisiana State University Press, 1965; Reginald Horsman. *The Frontier in the Formative Years, 1783-1815.* New York: Holt, Rinehart & Winston, 1970; Francis Paul Prucha. *American Indian Policy in the Formative Years: The Indian Trade and Intercourse Acts, 1790-1834.* Cambridge: Harvard University Press, 1962; Reginald Horsman. *Expansion and American Indian Policy, 1783-1812.* East Lansing: Michigan State University Press, 1967, *Matthew Elliot, British Indian Agent.* Detroit: Wayne State University Press, 1964; Thurman Wilkins. *Cherokee Tragedy: The Story of the Ridge Family and the Decimation of a People.* New York: Macmillan, 1970; Arthur H. DeRosier, Jr. *The Removal of the Choctaw Indians.* Knoxville: University of Tennessee Press, 1970.

[14] Curtis P. Nettels. *The Emergence of a National Economy, 1775-1815.* New York: Holt, Rinehart & Winston, 1962; Nathan Miller. *The Enterprise of a Free People: Aspects of Economic Development in New York State during the Canal Period, 1792-1838.* Ithaca: Cornell University Press, 1962; Murray N. Rothbard. *The Panic of 1819: Reactions and Policies.* New York: Columbia University Press, 1962.

· 14 ·

The Jacksonian Era, 1824–1848

Frank Otto Gatell

ANDREW JACKSON, like any of the great figures of American history, has been the subject of intensive investigation by succeeding generations of his countrymen. American historians have argued long and heatedly over the significance of this remarkable individual, and over the importance of the Jacksonian Era. The period bears Jackson's name, and apparently no amount of historical revisionism can take it away from him. Whatever his actual role, whether as molder of events, or as mere symbol and political opportunist enjoying the benefits of a good thing, the age and the name seem permanently linked. If for no other reason, the convenience of such identification assures its continued application.

But to attach a name to an age does not explain it, and very often the simplification which accompanies such labeling does violence to the variety and richness of the bygone period. The explanation process, the attempts to find the "essence" of an age, present far more difficulties, although it is a process sufficiently important to warrant the attempts. Among other characterizations, the Jacksonian Era has been subtitled, "The Age of the Common Man"; "The Age of the Workers' Awakening"; and "The Age of Liberated Capitalism." The lure and attractiveness of Jackson have proved so potent that succeeding American generations have tried to identify their central purposes, in some way, with the supposedly central themes of the Jacksonian movement.[1]

If we leave aside the accounts of participants, Jacksonian historiography began in 1860, the year a biography of Jackson appeared written by James Parton, "The Father of Modern Biography" in the United States. This work and those following in the nineteenth century formed part of the "Whig" interpretation of history. The authors came mostly from the ranks of the conservative reformers of the late nineteenth century; they were mostly middle-class northeasterners, and have been classified as "scholarly mugwumps." Such writers as Parton, William

Graham Sumner (another Jackson biographer), and James Schouler responded negatively to the person of Andrew Jackson, whom they condemned as an illiterate barbarian.

Largely reacting to their own times, the Gilded Age of business domination, the Whig historians concentrated their reform interests on the civil service crusade, and criticized Jackson savagely on that account. Jackson emerged as the inventor of the "spoils system," under which competent men suffered exclusion from public office to make room for loyal but incompetent political hacks. Whig historians believed that men of worth in Jackson's day (like the men of worth of their own time) had been barred from office by the Democracy. James Parton concluded severely that if all of Jackson's public acts had been "perfectly wise and right, this single feature [the spoils system] of his administration would suffice to render it deplorable."[2] The Whig interpretation of the late nineteenth century demonstrated that historical treatments of Jacksonianism would be heavily tainted with present-mindedness.

In our own century, a new group of Jackson interpreters shifted the emphasis to popular democracy, especially the frontier version. The Progressive historians contended that democracy flowered during Jacksonian times, and that Jackson himself nurtured it. A new Jackson stepped out of the pages of William E. Dodd, Vernon L. Parrington, and Charles and Mary Beard. John S. Bassett, whose biography of Jackson remains, a half-century after publication, the best yet written, lauded Jackson's "brave, frank, masterly leadership of the democratic movement which then established itself in our life." And even the Democrats' record on patronage received a refurbishing, as Carl R. Fish found positive, egalitarian aspects in the Jacksonians' principle and practice of "rotation in office."[3]

Although he did not write a book specifically about Jackson, Frederick Jackson Turner became the natural leader of this new group. The renowned historian of the American frontier transformed Jackson into the focal point for those elements of democracy native to the North American continent. That democracy supposedly reached full maturity in the unsophisticated but dynamic egalitarianism produced by the frontier. In *Rise of the New West,* Turner vividly described Jackson's arrival in Congress in 1799: "the frontier, in the person of its leader, had found a place in the government. This six-foot backwoodsman, angular, lantern-jawed, and thin, with blue eyes that blazed on occasion; this choleric, impetuous, Scotch-Irish leader of men; this expert duellist and ready fighter; this embodiment of the contentious, vehement, personal west, was in politics to stay." The quotation exudes charm rather than accuracy, since Jackson, in 1799, had not yet assumed leadership of any movements, democratic or otherwise. Later in the same book, Turner noted that by 1820, Jackson "had now outgrown the uncouthness of his earlier days, and had become stately and dignified in his manner." One suspects, however, that Turner much preferred the uncouth version of '99.[4]

All of this "man-of-the-forest" hoopla served a purpose. Such identifications allowed admiring historians to slight or ignore altogether the contradictions arising from Jackson's high status as a member of the Tennessee "aristocracy," such as it was in those days. He belonged to his state's landowning, speculating elite, and he possessed considerable wealth both in real property and in slaves. Yet progressive historians dwelt on the more pleasing and harmonious image of Jackson, the successful frontiersman (still the most admired American folk-hero) who never really left the people behind, especially not the little people.

The turn-of-the-twentieth-century, frontier-Progressive interpretation, coming as it did to an America already far advanced in the unsettling processes of industrialization and urbanization, constituted as much an exercise in nostalgia as in retrospective social analysis. But it also contains an obviously retarding element, so far as its chances for surviving were concerned. Most of the frontier had been declared closed (Turner himself ruefully cited the report of the Commissioner of the Land Office which certified such a closure). Thus the genius of the frontier democracy of Jackson's time would presumably be lost to future generations in an industrialized America. To be kept alive, Jacksonian Democracy would have to be transformed or transplanted from the western, agricultural frontier to America's new frontier, the city.

This salvage operation had been suggested in the 1920's, it came to be argued during the New Deal 1930's, and it received its most effective expression in 1945, at the hands of a young historian at Harvard named Arthur M. Schlesinger, Jr.[5] Schlesinger, taking up the hypothesis suggested in the 1920's by his father (himself, another Harvard professor), argued that Jacksonian democracy had not been exclusively a frontier, or even solely an agrarian affair. To combat that view, Schlesinger devoted much of his analysis to the alleged sources of Jacksonian radicalism among urban workingmen and artisans. He came just short of claiming that Northeastern urbanism provided the only true, unspoiled source of Jacksonianism. According to Schlesinger, "it has seemed in the past that Jacksonian democracy, which had always appeared an obvious example of Western influence in American government, is not perhaps so settled a case as some have thought. Its development was shaped much more by reasoned and systematic notions about society, and many of its controlling beliefs and motives came rather from the East and South, than from the West." Schlesinger devoted much space to these Atlantic seaboard, especially Northeastern seaboard influences, and he detailed such previously neglected topics as Jacksonianism in New England and in New York City, stressing class conflict and the anti-business pronouncements of spokesman for social radicalism wherever he could find them, and whenever they could be identified with Jacksonianism. In Schlesinger's overview, Jacksonian democracy became a problem of classes, not sections.

Again we have an apparent contradiction: this time, the unlikely prospect of Eastern city workers lining up politically behind a planter from Tennessee. It might seem too incongruous, even for the highest flights of historical imagination. But the New Deal setting for this historical viewpoint explains a good deal. Andrew Jackson, as the workingmen's champion, seemed credible to Americans of the New Deal era. After all, they had just lived through the presidency of Franklin Roosevelt, a Hudson River Valley squire whose administrations resulted in a partial revolution in American life—a revolution which benefitted the urban worker enormously. In Schlesinger's pages, the Jacksonian movement became almost a forerunner of the New Deal; and Jackson's mansion outside Nashville, The Hermitage, became the architectural forerunner of the mansion at Hyde Park, Roosevelt's country estate on the Hudson River. Schlesinger's work won critical acclaim and the Pulitzer Prize; a soft-cover, abridged edition soon appeared (long before the "paperback revolution").

In the wake of triumphant reception given Schlesinger's *Age of Jackson* other pro-Jacksonian studies appeared, not all of them urban-oriented, however. William Carleton's lively discussion of class conflict during the Van Buren years (1837-1841) did uphold the Schlesinger views regarding Northeast Locofocoism, and the commitment of monied, and presumably conservative, Americans to the Whig Party. Paul Murray's monograph on the Georgia Whigs shifted the substantiating locale to a Southern and more rural state than Massachusetts or New York, but with similar results. In Georgia, argued Murray, conservative Whigs reluctantly adopted democratic forms out of expediency not conviction, and the party battles represented a clash of the numerical democracy (Democrats) versus the party of property (Whigs).[6]

By the mid-1950's, Charles Sellers rose to the fore among those scholars displaying a pro-Jacksonian bent. An article on banking and politics in Tennessee following the Panic of 1819 defends Jackson's anti-banking record during the 1820's; another article, this one on the Tennessee background of the Jackson candidacy in 1824, demonstrates that Jackson's political savvy and popularity (both in Tennessee and elsewhere) set a bandwagon in motion that the schemers of the Nashville Junto, who thought they could toy with Jackson and then dump him, failed to control. In 1957, Sellers published the first volume of his major work, a biography of James K. Polk, painting a portrait of a hardworking, dedicated (if somewhat dour) Jacksonian, actively and sincerely fighting the forces of privilege and bank monopoly. As for Jackson's opponents, Sellers described Southern Whigs as men tied or allied to the region's commercial agriculture—merchants in cities and towns, professionals serving them, and planters with close connection to staple production for distant markets. This revisionist article stresses the *nationality* of the two-party struggle, particularly during the 1840's, the fact that men from all sections could and did unite in national parties taking stands on national issues.[7]

But these refinements and extensions of previously-established views did not represent the historiographical consensus of the 1950's. No interpretation, however brilliantly conceived or however topical, can sustain itself indefinitely; and not if the subject remains sufficiently important and attractive to keep up historians' interest. Schlesinger's working class thesis came under heavy attack almost at once, and the liberated capitalism, or entrepreneurial thesis began supplanting it.[8] First, a group of historians at Columbia University directly challenged Schlesinger's account of organized labor in the Jacksonian era. Joseph Dorfman, an economic historian, type-cast many alleged labor leaders as middle-class businessmen despite their radical-sounding rhetoric, and Richard B. Morris debunked Jackson's supposed sympathy for labor by detailing his role as a "strike-breaker" who used force to quell workers rioting on a construction project. Several of Morris' students examined voting in Northeastern cities and concluded that low-income, working-class districts more often than not voted against the Democrats, and that organized Working Men's parties consistently opposed Jackson and the Democrats. Another Columbia professor, Harold C. Syrett, summed up the negative views of this group on Jackson (and Jacksonian historiography) in a compilation on Jackson's "contribution to the American tradition," an unflattering portrait which nevertheless granted Jackson's creative role in establishing the doctrine of majority rule and the practice of strong presidential leadership.[9]

One of the most influential revisionist statements on Jackson had already been made by Richard Hofstadter, again of Columbia University. In *The American Political Tradition* (1948), Hofstadter stated the entrepreneurial thesis cogently and (as it would turn out for some time) persuasively. Jacksonianism, he argued, represented not only a "phase in the expansion of democracy," but also in the "expansion of liberated capitalism." The small capitalist, the "man-on-the-make," became the quintessential Jacksonian. He attacked the ruling establishments, political and economic, in order to terminate the privileges of others and gain for himself the opportunity of rising since "democratic upsurge was closely linked to the ambitions of the small capitalist."

Thus, in place of the collisions of class conflict, most postwar historians wrote of an America of capitalist consensus. During the 1950's, the age of the organization man, the nation's rough edges, if not smoothed completely, had been sanded down to reduce scratching. Historians of that decade had little trouble in constructing yet another Jacksonian period, the age of the enterprising, middle-class businessman, the rising capitalist. The general view came out with particular clarity and polemical emphasis in the work of Louis Hartz, who contended that America had never experienced anything but a liberal capitalist existence. The feudal stage had been skipped, and basic agreement on fundamentals, not radical class struggle, shaped American history.[10]

Jacksonian democracy, as a separate entity, had thus been taken to the historiographical woodshed. Historians sought to demonstrate that many if not all of Jackson's intimates were out for the fast buck, an acquisitive instinct shared with most Americans. In addition, Jackson's attack on the Bank, previously lauded as the most exhilarating victory of the people over the monied aristocrats, itself came under attack. Fritz Redlich, in a seminal study of early American banking, defended Nicholas Biddle's financial acumen and highlighted his creative role as a nascent central banker, points which received further support in an economic study of the second national bank by Walter B. Smith. Bray Hammond then took over as the leader among those historians of Jacksonian era banking who wrote from an entrepreneurial point of view. His *Banks and Politics . . .* , the Pulitzer Prize winner for 1957, flayed the Jacksonians as both ignorant and hypocritical. They "were no less drawn by lucre than the so-called conservatives, but rather more. They had no greater concern for human rights than the people who had what they were trying to get," and their "crusade" ended in the creation of greater monopolies and vested rights than those they labored to destroy. Hammond implied that Jacksonians did this consciously, shamelessly prattling about agrarianism and popular rights.[11]

For Jackson himself, Hammond reserved the greatest scorn, dubbing him an arrogant *naif,* easily manipulated by designing lieutenants. The chief designer, in Hammond's account, was New York's Martin Van Buren, a political manipulator with an economic aim: to shift the center of financial power from Philadelphia (Chestnut Street) to New York City (Wall Street). Hammond attempted to tone down his antipathy toward the Jacksonians in sardonicism and feigned resignation, but Van Buren and the rapacious state bankers proved too hard to stomach, and Jackson emerged as an ignorant, old man. The assault on Jackson continued in another banking study, this one "non-entrepreneurial." Two years after the publication of Hammond's massive study, Nicholas Biddle found an additional champion, and, belatedly, a biographer. Although Thomas P. Govan kept Jackson center stage as instigator of the Bank War (a second divergence from the Hammond line), he felt that little more than an uninformed and vicious prejudice against bankers and capitalists had prompted Jackson's attack on Biddle and his valuable institution.[12]

The liberated capitalist theme predominated in state studies as well. Assessing Jackson's impact on North Carolina politics, William S. Hoffman denied that the Bank War could be called class war. Democrats in that state presented the conflict in personalist terms, Jackson vs. Biddle. Furthermore, Jacksonianism was not a democratic frontier movement, since most Democratic Party leaders came from the eastern part of North Carolina, districts of the heaviest concentrations of slaves and of large-scale slave-holding. In a study of the Mississippi Jacksonians, Edwin A. Miles also stressed *personality*, Jackson's strong popular appeal whatever he said or did, as a deciding political factor, as well as the support Jackson received from merchants and wealthy planters of the Natchez region. Also in 1960, Walter Hugins returned the by now one-sided debate to the Northeast. In a monograph on New York City's Working Men's parties, Hugins revived and bolstered the Columbia School's contentions, arguing that the "Workies" attacked monopolies because they wanted their share of the capitalist pie. These essentially middle-class mechanics and small businessmen led a movement including men from a broad spectrum of occupations and professions, and they did so out of a commitment to democratic capitalism and equality of opportunity.[13]

Two other books of the 1950's contributed significantly to the changing climate of opinion. John W. Ward did not attack Jackson; instead he bypassed the man in search of the symbols behind him. To his supporters (and to many of his detractors), Jackson symbolized the agrarian ideal: the rustic, nonintellectual but intuitive individual who scorned the effete sensibilities of an over-civilized and thus corrupted Europe. While categorizing the Jacksonian symbol into three controlling elements, Nature, Providence, and Will, Ward also isolated the reactionary aspects of the image. Thus abundant cheap land became a self-deluding factor in Americans' hopes for staving off the corrupt future that awaited an advanced society. And by dwelling on the images constructed around the figure of Jackson, whatever their objective merits or demerits, Ward passed over what had been so positive and so compelling in the pages of pro-Jackson writers, the flesh-and-blood Jackson. On this rarified plane of cultural history, Jackson seemed hardly to matter; what people cared to believe about him took on greater importance.[14]

Ward had noted the rapidly widening gap between the Jacksonian democratic ideal and actual state of modernizing American society. Two years later, in 1957, Marvin Meyers grappled with this very problem, seeking a resolution (at least in the Jacksonians' minds) and contributing a valuable modification of the entrepreneurial thesis. Meyers saw the Jacksonians as "two-faced." Not in the most vulgar sense of the term, but in their disjointed, ambivalent attempt to preserve the virtues of Jeffersonian republicanism (looking backwards), while they intrepidly threw themselves into the economic scramble of their own day (looking forward). Jacksonian rhetoric and Democratic policies received sustained and serious attention in Meyers' pages, but the split between older forms of agrarianism and the newer commercialism proved too much to handle. The Jacksonians became hypocritical in practice, if not consciously so in ideology. They ended trapped by visions of an unattainable and perhaps non-existent past, while the capitalistic future came on with avalanche-like force.[15]

Other fronts opened up in the war against Progressive Jacksonian historiography. One of the bloodiest of these campaigns occurred over the issue of the *origins* of Jacksonianism, the politics of the 1820's. Turner had written, almost as an act of faith, of a Jackson movement springing from the democratic forest; yet Schlesinger carefully avoided in-depth discussion of Jackson's pre-presidential years. Earlier probing expeditions which questioned or refuted Turnerian views found rough going. For example, Thomas P. Abernethy seemed intent on rolling back the tide when he denied any connection between the rise of Jackson and the rise of frontier democracy. And in 1940, Philip S. Klein published a study of the rampant factionalism of Pennsylvania politics in the 1820's, subtitled "A Game Without Rules." The Jackson bandwagon in that state groaned under the weight of many a self-serving politico who cared not a whit for Andrew Jackson's principles—if indeed he could enumerate them.[16]

These isolated views became the consensus in the 1950's. The monographs of Hoffman and Miles, which stressed the absence of ideology and commitment to party principle in North Carolina and Mississippi, have already been mentioned. In 1957, Harry R. Stevens reported that in the election of 1824 in Ohio he could find no discernible difference between the groups which supported the several presidential candidates; and another study of Pennsylvania, this one covering the years 1833-1848, has the theme of Democratic factionalism and Jackson's personal appeal. Alvin Kass in a study of New York politics, 1800-1830, uncovered much deviousness and factionalism, and opined that "parties were held together by the drive for electoral victory" and little else.[17] Writers on the 1820's also directed much attention to the extent of Jackson's appeal among ex-Federalists, coming close to claiming, and in some cases implying, that a majority of ex-Federalists supported Jackson in 1828.[18] No one has yet (as of 1972) systematically traced their careers through the 1830's, however, to see if Jacksonian ex-Federalists still alive by 1840 kept the Jacksonian faith.

Like political parties, most of the historiographical "schools" have produced a leader. The group under discussion has put major emphasis on party organization, *per se,* and sees party platforms and arguments over "issues" as mere window-dressing, serving a "cosmetic function" whereby those controlling the party machinery sought to energize and patronize the gullible faithful. Parties exist principally to elect candidates to office. The most systematic analyst of Jacksonian systems in these terms has been Richard P. McCormick. His major work, a study of party formation in the 1820's and 1830's, appropriately titled *The Second American Party System,* details state-by-state the operations of party machines. McCormick contended that competing national parties reappeared after the Era of Good Feelings in order, primarily, to battle for the presidency. McCormick gave little weight to such traditional issues as the tariff or the Bank War in effecting party formation or factional transformation. In two widely-read articles, McCormick questioned the belief in bloc-voting along class lines, and denied that Jackson won the presidency in 1828 as a result of an electoral revolution which brought the "common man" to the polls for the first time.[19]

Once the standard pro-Democratic interpretation had been undermined some historians "moved over" into the Whig camp. Most twentieth-century writers (as of 1972) have been hostile to Whiggery, so that a monograph published in the 1930's on Henry Clay and the Whig party, a work sympathetic to Clay, represents a definite exception to generally accepted views.[20] So too does the early work of Glyndon G. Van Deusen, a prolific author of "Whig Studies." Van Deusen first produced a life of Clay in 1937, and a decade later followed it up with biographies of two important New York Whig journalists, Thurlow Weed and Horace Greeley.[21] While the Turner-Schlesinger views reigned, Van Deusen remained a gentle polemicist without an audience. In the 1950's, however, he found receptive listeners. An article on Whig thought highlighted two important themes consonant with the historiographical axioms of that decade: the basic similarities in outlook existing among both Democrats and Whigs, and the Whigs' more optimistic, expansive vision of economic and social development. Van Deusen's survey of Jacksonian Era politics, though purporting to treat events "objectively," judges the Jacksonians harshly, concluding that they had no positive program for national development.[22] Leonard White's influential volume on administrative history, *The Jacksonians,* assigns the Democratic bureaucrats generally lower grades as administrators than he had given to Federalist and National Republican predecessors, or than those he gave to Whigs.[23]

Several state studies furthered the Whig rehabilitation. Articles by Grady McWhiney and Thomas B. Alexander helped counteract the effect of Charles Sellers' pro-Jacksonian writings. McWhiney argued that Alabama Whigs could not be called an upper-class party, that Whig and Democratic leaders did not differ greatly as to social and economic standing. More concerned with the Alabama electorate than Whig leadership, Alexander and his corps of researchers questioned the validity of traditional views of Southern Whiggery when applied to Black-Belt districts. No clear-cut class voting patterns emerged there, although the haves versus have-nots dichotomy seemed to obtain in Alabama's hill country.[24] Such qualifications, inevitable perhaps in monographs relying more and more on quantified political and sociological data (data which allowed for increased precision in minute particulars but mitigated against the formulation of broad generalizations), did not obscure the "pro-Whig" historians' basic contentions—namely, that Jacksonian era Americans had not divided politically along class lines, and that Whigs and Democrats had more in common than previous historians thought, or than their leaders cared to admit.

Lee Benson, a pro-Whig writer with a penchant for quantitative techniques *and* broad generalizations, called on historians to scrap the entire concept of Jacksonian Democracy.[25] Benson studied politics in New York state from the vantage points of sociological and political science theory. In *The Concept of Jacksonian Democracy,* he dismissed Jacksonian rhetoric as "claptrap" and found no differences in social status between Democratic and Whig leaders. In addition, Benson theorized that men of wealth supported either Whig or Democratic party with equal facility and frequency. Most importantly, he argued that a voter's religious affiliation and ethnocultural background acted as far more positive determinants of political behavior than economic status or rational responses to the surface issues of party politics. Though the book deals only with New York, concentrating on voting behavior in 1844,

Benson did not hesitate to claim the probability of the applicability of his theses to other states. Instead of the Age of Jackson, Benson concluded, historians should refer to the Age of Egalitarianism. Benson did indeed make sweeping revisions in previous Jacksonian historiography by standing the Dixon Ryan Fox[26] and Schlesinger accounts of New York politics on their heads, and by arguing that Whigs, as proponents of an activist, liberal state, represented the progressive element. Yet Benson's suggested catchphrase, Age of Egalitarianism, did not stray so far from the previous marks as he seemed to think, bearing a close resemblance to a previous historical caption: The Age of the Common Man. Still, Benson's toning down of economic factors, and his view of Jacksonism as a negative, anti-reformist movement, constituted so sharp a reversal that *Concept* may be regarded as the culmination of the anti-Schlesinger historiographical trend.

Consensus history remains (as of 1972) the most recent comprehensive interpretation in Jacksonian historiography, and subsequent work in the period, though increasingly chary of the consensus-entrepreneurial beliefs, has not been unified to form a substitute overview. Nevertheless, complaints and qualification regarding consensus have been voiced frequently. In 1962, John Higham warned: "The conservative frame of reference is giving us a bland history"; and recently, J. R. Pole asked us to remember that "the history we have to record is that of the United States under Jackson and Van Buren, not under Clay; yet it is permissible to think that the history of that period would have been significantly different if Clay had been elected in 1832, and that such differences would have been due to genuine differences of purpose."[27]

Similar observations by other historians add up to a growing reluctance to abandon altogether traditional interpretative roads to Jacksonianism. In 1959, Herbert J. Doherty published a study of Florida's Whigs, and two years later Arthur W. Thompson followed with a look at the Florida Democrats. Both men tried to apply the brakes on the rush to consensus history. Doherty found substantial differences between the parties, especially in the fact that the propertied and commercial classes in Florida favored Whiggery over Democracy. Thompson wrote of party battles over "real issues," and of the Democrats' battle against all types of monopolies.[28] Several years later, two additional studies of another Southern state bolstered these views. The Whig Party of Missouri, argued John V. Mering, represented the state's economic elite to a much greater extent than the Democrats, and "Missouri Whigs were simply not convincing in their professions of devotion to the common man." Robert E. Shalhope took direct issue with Richard McCormick's thesis of national party formation as a scramble primarily for the presidency. In Missouri, at least, doctrinal issues did play a central role in party formation. Shalhope rejected the McCormick approach as antiseptic and stifling, one which failed to explain the Democrats' attachment to republicanism.[29]

On the broader ground of national politics, qualifying neo-Progressives began to speak out. Robert V. Remini produced a new study of the presidential election of 1828. Although he gave great emphasis to the effects of party organization in determining the outcome, as well as to the fact that Adams had not been routed so badly as previous historians had implied, Remini clearly *liked* Andrew Jackson. His short biography of Jackson, published in 1966, makes even clearer the depth of that admiration.[30] Lynn L. Marshall argued convincingly in an article in 1963 that Amos Kendall, the Kitchen Cabinet's "radical," had acted as chief ghostwriter for Jackson's Bank Veto Message; and an article on the origins of the Whig Party (its "strange stillbirth" Marshall dubbed it) commented on the Whigs' lack of rapport with the egalitarian politics of their age, of the stuffiness and pomposity which inhibited their success in the search for votes.[31] In a series of articles, Major L. Wilson added more weight to the argument that Jacksonian politics contained some substance, and that important ideological differences existed between the parties. Such differences, according to Herbert Ershkowitz and William G. Shade, produced clear differences in voting patterns between Whig and Democratic members of state legislatures; the Democrats, for example, usually voting against bills favoring corporation and banks, the Whigs usually supporting humanitarian reform bills and (in the North) antislavery measures. The two major parties, they concluded, represented "contrasting belief systems."[32]

The Jacksonians' war against the Bank also enlisted some new recruits. Robert Remini, already a prolific writer in the Jacksonian field, added a short analysis of the Bank War which concentrates on the Jackson-Biddle confrontation of 1831-34 and which differs greatly from the Hammond or Govan versions. Several articles by Frank Otto Gatell, in Richard Hofstadter's words, "shed new light on this controversy and give some comfort to historians in the Progressive tradition."[33] Gatell attacked Hammond's entrepreneurial account of the Bank War and the claim that Van Buren had started the fracas in order to build up Wall Street, as well as Lee Benson's assignment of New York's rich men to either party in equal numbers.[34] Martin Van Buren comes in for further positive treatment in James C. Curtis' study of that ill-fated administration, an account generally favoring the President and crediting him with sincerity in demanding the "divorce" of government and banking through establishment of subtreasuries. Several students of Charles Sellers also contributed Bank War studies: James R. Sharp investigated Democratic banking policies in the states, and after the Panic of 1837. He found the Democratic majority consistently anti-banking (in all sections), though far from consistently successful. John M. McFaul, on the other hand, looked into the earlier but usually neglected period between 1834 and 1837 (from Removal to the Panic) to find consistency and the search for system on the part of Jackson's Secretaries of the Treasury, a revisionist point of view even for many pro-Jacksonian historians.[35]

The persistence and strength of present-mindedness in Jacksonian historiography has already been made abundantly, perhaps lamentably, clear. If each age has seen Jacksonism through its own spectacles (pun intended), then the state of American politics and society in the 1960's should have helped produce a confusing situation in Jacksonian studies. Though it surely did, some of the confusion's undigested but positive results may provide valuable materials for future syntheses, since many historians are now exploring (as of 1972) topics previously ignored or glossed over. Among such newly-vitalized themes are Jacksonian Indian policy, slavery, the problems of wealth and poverty, and the social basis of politics.

Needless to say, Indian Fighter Jackson has not fared well in the newer studies of Indian policy. His campaigns against the Seminoles still remain (as of 1972) mostly in the hands of military historians and Jackson buffs, but the removals of the "Civilized Tribes" in the 1830's do not. Mary E. Young's works reveal the extent of frauds that accompanied the white man's land greed in the South and Southwest, and she found little positive to say about "Jacksonian justice."[36] In-depth studies of Indian removal understandably leave Jackson and his supporters in the villains' roles, as in the cases of books on the Cherokees by Thurman Wilkins, and the Choctaws by Arthur DeRosier, and a reassessment by Joseph C. Burke of the unavailing efforts made to halt removal by appeals to the federal courts.[37] An isolated attempt by Francis P. Prucha to say good things, or at least neutral things, about Jackson and the Indians did *not* turn around the consensus.[38]

Similarly, assessments of Jacksonians and the issues of slavery and abolition are not favorable. The importance of slavery in American politics, even in decades during which it did not figure as a dominating, *surface* issue, has received more attention.[39] Richard H. Brown surveyed Jacksonian politics in the aftermath of the Missouri crisis and argued that Van Buren, in making a deal with Virginians in 1826, had virtually assured that the Jackson Party would be a proslavery party. Certainly it was an anti-abolitionist party. Gerald S. Henig demonstrated amply that Jackson & Co. had no sympathy with abolition, a movement which, whatever its moral content, offered no political mileage for the Democratic coalition. Leonard L. Richards' stimulating monograph on the riots which abolition activities provoked during the 1830's reveals the extremes to which many high-ranking Northern Democratic politicians were willing to go to put down abolitionism.[40]

Richards' study of rioting is but one of several exploratory studies on violence among a people which has always prided itself on its commitment to the rule of law. Election-days violence, though all too frequent, has not yet been studied systematically (as of 1972), but monographs are appearing on the riots provoked by depression and nativism, as well as by race. David Grimsted's pioneering overview, hopefully part of a larger work, concludes that (Jacksonian) democracy contained the "very basic tendencies and tensions" which produced rioting.[41]

The extent of poverty and maldistribution of wealth of Jacksonian times also command much more attention from historians now than previously. Raymond A. Mohl's study of poverty and "welfare" in New York deals with the early national period, stopping at 1825, but is indicative of the kind of works we can expect shortly dealing with the second quarter of the nineteenth century. The limited upward social mobility achieved by poor Americans of the period (in most cases, none at all), as analyzed by such quantifying historians as Stuart Blumin and Peter R. Knights, punches wide holes in the Jacksonian man-on-the-make thesis.[42] And at the other end of the economic spectrum, Douglas Miller and Edward Pessen debunked the myth (historical and contemporary) that middle-class Jacksonian America lacked an economic elite of extremely rich men.[43]

The historiography of Jacksonian politics had become largely a quest for clues to the social basis of politics. Organizational forms still have relevance, witness the work of Richard Hofstadter and Michael Wallace on the acceptance of the idea of political parties, and the work of James S. Chase on the rise of the nominating convention.[44] Yet the massive social structure, rather than the political superstructure alone, intrigues more and more political historians. Bertram Wyatt-Brown investigated the "evangelicals" in religion, and their abortive attempts to dominate American politics directly during the late 1820's. And Ronald P. Formisano (a Lee Benson student) has published a study of Jacksonian and antebellum politics in Michigan which gives the kind of attention to religion and ethnicity as political determinants which his mentor called for a decade before.[45]

Social history (once dismissed as "pots and pans" history), even the *new* social history, was very far from achieving a new synthesis of Jacksonian society and politics (as of 1972). Meanwhile, the debate goes on, as evidenced by two books on Jacksonianism which, as the saying goes, might have been written on different planets. Edward Pessen's *Jacksonian America,* an attempt to encompass the whole period, found little that is admirable or even consistent in the Democracy's record. It was an age of materialism and opportunism, and of a much-vaunted but illusory egalitarianism. Jackson's political "warfare was largely confined to the field of rhetoric." On the other planet, Donald B. Cole saw many traditional images applicable to New Hampshire. Though the state's Democratic party was complex, embracing city lawyers and poor farmers, "they all stood for democratic economic and political principles," and they believed "they were defending the public against private privilege."[46]

The normal difficulties of making historiographical predictions are now compounded by the tremors which have so violently shaken the United States during the last ten years. Only a person with a vision of the future much clearer than most of us possess should even make the attempt. Yet if past experience is any guide (and most historians seem to think that it is), the Jacksonian Era will not be discarded in history's dustbin, nor will the man who gave it a name be forgotten.

FOOTNOTES

[1] Jacksonian Era historiography is particularly rich. See, in particular, Charles Sellers. "Andrew Jackson versus the Historians." *Mississippi Valley Historical Review* 44: 615-634; No. 4, March 1958; Alfred A. Cave. *Jacksonian Democracy and the Historians.* Gainesville: University of Florida Press, 1964; and Edward Pessen. "The Modern Jacksonian Controversy," in Pessen. *Jacksonian America: Society, Personality and Politics.* Homewood, Ill.: Dorsey Press, 1969. pp. 384-393. I have relied heavily on the first two sources cited in discussing works published before 1950.

[2] Quoted in Sellers. "Jackson versus the Historians." p. 617.

[3] *Ibid.,* pp. 618-623; John S. Bassett. *The Life of Andrew Jackson.* Garden City: Doubleday. p. 1911.

[4] Frederick J. Turner. *Rise of the New West, 1819-1829.* New York: Harper, 1906. pp. 189, 191. See also Turner's posthumously published volume, *The United States 1830-1850: The Nation and Its Sections.* New York: Henry Holt, 1935.

[5] The works by father and son, respectively: Arthur M. Schlesinger. *New Viewpoints in American History.* New York: Macmillan, 1922. pp. 200-219; Arthur M. Schlesinger, Jr. *The Age of Jackson.* Boston: Little, Brown, 1945.

[6] William G. Carleton. "Political Aspects of the Van Buren Era." *South Atlantic Quarterly* 50: 167-185; April 1951; Paul Murray. *The Whig Party in Georgia, 1825-1853.* Chapel Hill: University of North Carolina Press, 1948.

[7] Charles Sellers. "Banking and Politics in Jackson's Tennessee, 1817-1827." *Mississippi Valley Historical Review* 41: 61-84; No. 1, June 1954; "Jackson Men With Feet of Clay." *American Historical Review* 62: 537-551; No. 3, April 1957; *James K. Polk, Jacksonian, 1795-1843.* 2 vols. Princeton: Princeton University Press, 1957; "Who Were the Southern Whigs?" *American Historical Review* 59: 335-346; No. 2, January 1954.

[8] Cave. *Jacksonian Democracy and the Historians.* ch. 3.

⁹ Joseph Dorfman. "The Jackson Wage-Earner Thesis." *American Historical Review* 54: 296-306; No. 2, January 1949; Richard B. Morris. "Andrew Jackson, Strikebreaker." *American Historical Review* 55: 54-68; No. 1, October 1949; Harold C. Syrett. *Andrew Jackson: His Contribution to the American Tradition.* Indianapolis: Bobbs-Merrill Co., 1953. For references to the articles on urban voting see Sellers. "Jackson versus the Historians." p. 627, fn. 28.

¹⁰ Richard Hofstadter. *The American Political Tradition and the Men Who Made It.* New York: Knopf, 1948. ch. 3; Louis Hartz. *The Liberal Tradition in America: An Interpretation of American Political Thought Since the Revolution.* New York: Harcourt, Brace & World, 1955. pp. 89-142.

¹¹ Fritz Redlich. *The Molding of American Banking: Men and Ideas, Part I, 1781-1840.* New York: Hafner Publishing Co., 1947; Walter B. Smith. *Economic Aspects of the Second Bank of the United States.* Cambridge: Harvard University Press, 1953; Bray Hammond. *Banks and Politics in America, from the Revolution to the Civil War.* Princeton: Princeton University Press, 1957.

¹² Thomas P. Govan. *Nicholas Biddle: Nationalist and Public Banker, 1786-1844.* Chicago: University of Chicago Press, 1959.

¹³ William S. Hoffmann. *Andrew Jackson and North Carolina Politics.* Chapel Hill: University of North Carolina Press, 1958; Edwin A. Miles. *Jacksonian Democracy in Mississippi.* Chapel Hill: University of North Carolina Press, 1960; Walter Hugins. *Jacksonian Democracy and the Working Class: A Study of the New York Workingmen's Movement, 1829-1837.* Stanford: Stanford University Press, 1960.

¹⁴ John W. Ward. *Andrew Jackson: Symbol for an Age.* New York: Oxford University Press, 1955.

¹⁵ Marvin Meyers. *The Jacksonian Persuasion: Politics and Belief.* Stanford: Stanford University Press, 1957.

¹⁶ Thomas P. Abernethy. "Andrew Jackson and the Rise of Southwestern Democracy." *American Historical Review* 49: 64-77; No. 1, October 1927; Abernethy. *From Frontier to Plantation in Tennessee: A Study in Frontier Democracy.* Chapel Hill: University of North Carolina Press, 1932; Philip S. Klein. *Pennsylvania Politics, 1817-1832: A Game Without Rules.* Philadelphia: Historical Society of Pennsylvania, 1940.

¹⁷ Harry R. Stevens. *The Early Jackson Party in Ohio.* Durham: Duke University Press, 1957; Alvin Kass. *Politics in New York State, 1800-1830.* Syracuse: Syracuse University Press, 1965.

¹⁸ For example, see Shaw Livermore, Jr. *The Twilight of Federalism: The Disintegration of the Federalist Party, 1815-1830.* Princeton: Princeton University Press, 1962; Mark H. Haller. "The Rise of the Jackson Party in Maryland, 1820-1829." *Journal of Southern History* 28: 307-326; No. 3, August 1962.

¹⁹ Richard P. McCormick. *The Second American Party System: Party Formation in the Jacksonian Era.* Chapel Hill: University of North Carolina Press, 1966; "Suffrage Classes and Party Alignments: A Study in Voting Behavior." *Mississippi Valley Historical Review* 46: 397-410; No. 3, December 1959; "New Perspectives on Jacksonian Politics." *American Historical Review* 65: 288-301; No. 2, January 1960.

²⁰ George R. Poage. *Henry Clay and the Whig Party.* Chapel Hill: University of North Carolina Press, 1936.

²¹ Glyndon G. Van Deusen. *The Life of Henry Clay.* Boston: Little, Brown, 1937; *Thurlow Weed: Wizard of the Lobby.* Boston: Little, Brown, 1947; *Horace Greeley: Nineteenth-Century Crusader.* Philadelphia: University of Pennsylvania Press, 1953. Yet another New York Whig benefitted from a sympathetic treatment in Van Deusen's *William Henry Seward.* New York: Oxford University Press, 1967.

²² Van Deusen. "Some Aspects of Whig Thought and Theory in the Jacksonian Period." *American Historical Review* 63: 305-322; No. 2, January 1958; *The Jacksonian Era, 1828-1848.* New York: Harper, 1959.

[23] Leonard D. White. *The Jacksonians: A Study in Administrative History, 1829-1861*. New York: Macmillan, 1954.

[24] Grady McWhiney. "Were the Whigs a Class Party in Alabama?" *Journal of Southern History* 23: 510-522; No. 4, November 1957; Thomas B. Alexander, et al. "Who Were the Alabama Whigs?" *Alabama Review* 16: 5-19; No. 1, January 1963.

[25] Lee Benson. *The Concept of Jacksonian Democracy: New York As a Test Case*. Princeton: Princeton University Press, 1961.

[26] Dixon Ryan Fox. *The Decline of Aristocracy in the Politics of New York, 1801-1840*. New York: Columbia University Press, 1919.

[27] John Higham. "Beyond Consensus: The Historian as Moral Critic." *American Historical Review* 67: 609-625; No. 3, April 1962. p. 616; J. R. Pole. "The American Past: Is It Still Usable?" *Journal of American Studies* 1: 63-78; No. 1, April 1967. p. 73.

[28] Herbert J. Doherty, Jr. *The Whigs of Florida 1845-1854*. Gainesville: University of Florida Press, 1959; Arthur W. Thompson. *Jacksonian Democracy on the Florida Frontier*. Gainesville: University of Florida Press, 1961.

[29] John V. Mering. *The Whig Party in Missouri*. Columbia: University of Missouri Press, 1967. p. 70; Robert E. Shalhope. "Jacksonian Politics in Missouri: A Comment on the McCormick Thesis." *Civil War History* 15: 210-225; No. 3, September 1969.

[30] Robert V. Remini. *The Election of Andrew Jackson*. Philadelphia: Lippincott, 1963; *Andrew Jackson*. New York: Twayne, 1966.

[31] Lynn L. Marshall. "The Authorship of Jackson's Bank Veto Message." *Mississippi Valley Historical Review* 50: 466-477; No. 3, December 1963; "The Strange Stillbirth of the Whig Party." *American Historical Review* 72: 445-468; No. 2, January 1967.

[32] Major L. Wilson. " 'Liberty and Union': An Analysis of Three Concepts Involved in the Nullification Controversy." *Journal of Southern History* 42: 331-355; No. 3, August 1967; and "The Concept of Time and the Political Dialogue in the United States, 1828-48." *American Quarterly* 19: 619-644; No. 4, Winter 1967; Herbert Ershkowitz and William G. Shade. "Consensus or Conflict? Political Behavior in the State Legislatures During the Jacksonian Era." *Journal of American History* 53: 591-621; No. 3, December 1971.

[33] Robert V. Remini. *Andrew Jackson and the Bank War: A Study in the Growth of Presidential Power*. New York: Norton, 1967; Richard Hofstadter. *The Progressive Historians: Turner, Beard, Parrington*. New York: Knopf, 1968. p. 496.

[34] Frank Otto Gatell. "Sober Second Thoughts on Van Buren, the Albany Regency, and the Wall Street Conspiracy." *Journal of American History* 53: 19-40; No. 1, June 1966; "Money and Party in Jacksonian America: A Quantitative Look at New York City's Men of Quality." *Political Science Quarterly* 82: 235-252; No. 2, June 1967. Robert Rich found a similar situation in Boston: " 'A Wilderness of Whigs': The Wealthy Men of Boston." *Journal of Social History* 4: 263-276; No. 3, Spring 1971.

[35] James C. Curtis. *The Fox at Bay: Martin Van Buren and the Presidency, 1837-1841*. Lexington: University Press of Kentucky, 1970; James R. Sharp. *The Jacksonians versus the Banks: Politics in the States After the Panic of 1837*. New York: Columbia University Press, 1970; John M. McFaul. *The Politics of Jacksonian Finance*. Ithaca: Cornell University Press, 1972.

[36] Mary E. Young. "Indian Removal and Land Allotment: The Civilized Tribes and Jacksonian Justice." *American Historical Review* 64: 31-45; No. 1, October 1958; "The Creek Frauds: A Study in Conscience and Corruption." *Mississippi Valley Historical Review* 42: 411-437; No. 3, December 1955.

[37] Thurman Wilkins. *Cherokee Tragedy: The Story of the Ridge Family and the Decimation of a People*. New York: Macmillan, 1970; Arthur DeRosier, Jr. *The Removal of the Choctaw Indians*. Knoxville: University of Tennessee Press, 1970;

Joseph C. Burke. "The Cherokee Cases: A Study in Law, Politics, and Morality." *Stanford Law Review* 21: 500-531; No. 3, February 1969.

[38] Francis P. Prucha. "Andrew Jackson's Indian Policy: A Reassessment." *Journal of American History* 66: 527-539; No. 3, December 1969; see also Prucha's *American Indian Policy in the Formative Years.* Cambridge: Harvard University Press, 1962. esp. ch. 9.

[39] For example, Donald L. Robinson. *Slavery in the Structure of American Politics, 1765-1820.* New York: Harcourt Brace Jovanovich, 1971; and William W. Freehling. *Prelude to Civil War: The Nullification Controversy in South Carolina, 1816-1836.* New York: Harper & Row, 1966, which sees the tariff fight as an occasion for a defense of slavery.

[40] Richard H. Brown. "The Missouri Crisis, Slavery, and the Politics of Jacksonianism." *South Atlantic Quarterly* 65: 55-72; No. 1, Winter 1966; Gerald S. Henig. "The Jacksonian Attitude Toward Abolitionism in the 1830's." *Tennessee Historical Quarterly* 28: 42-56; No. 1, Spring 1969; Leonard L. Richards. *"Gentlemen of Property and Standing": Anti-Abolition Mobs in Jacksonian America.* New York: Oxford University Press, 1970.

[41] Elizabeth M. Geffen. "Violence in Philadelphia in the 1840's and 1850's." *Pennsylvania History* 36: 381-410; No. 4, October 1969; David Grimsted. "Rioting in Its Jacksonian Setting." *American Historical Review* 77: 361-397; No. 2, April 1972.

[42] Raymond A. Mohl. *Poverty in New York, 1783-1825.* New York: Oxford University Press, 1971; Stuart Blumin. "Mobility and Change in Ante-Bellum Philadelphia," in Stephan Thernstrom and Richard Sennett, editors. *Nineteenth-Century Cities: Essays in the New Urban History.* New Haven: Yale University Press, 1969. pp. 165-208; Peter R. Knights. *The Plain People of Boston, 1830-1860.* New York: Oxford University Press, 1971.

[43] Douglas T. Miller. *Jacksonian Aristocracy: Class and Democracy in New York, 1830-1860.* New York: Oxford University Press, 1967; Edward Pessen. "The Egalitarian Myth and the American Social Reality: Wealth, Mobility, and Equality in the 'Era of the Common Man'." *American Historical Review* 76: 989-1034; No. 4, October 1971.

[44] Richard Hofstadter. *The Idea of a Party System: The Rise of Legitimate Opposition in the United States, 1780-1840.* Berkeley: University of California Press, 1969; Michael Wallace. "Changing Concepts of Party in the United States: New York, 1815-1828." *American Historical Review* 74: 453-491; No. 2, December 1968; James S. Chase. "Jacksonian Democracy and the Rise of the Nominating Convention." *Mid-America* 45: 229-249; No. 4, October 1963.

[45] Bertram Wyatt-Brown. "Prelude to Abolitionism: Sabbatarian Politics and the Rise of the Second Party System." *Journal of American History* 58: 316-341; No. 2, September 1971; Ronald P. Formisano. *The Birth of Mass Political Parties: Michigan, 1827-1861.* Princeton: Princeton University Press, 1971.

[46] Edward Pessen. *Jacksonian America: Society, Personality, and Politics.* Homewood, Ill.: Dorsey Press, 1969. p. 346; Donald B. Cole. *Jacksonian Democracy in New Hampshire, 1800-1851.* Cambridge: Harvard University Press, 1970. p. 246.

· 15 ·

Background to Conflict:
Slavery, Abolition, and Politics

Robert W. Johannsen

"SINCE 1950," wrote David Donald in 1960, "historians have written surprisingly little about the causes of the American Civil War." From a subject which had "once attracted the attention of the best brains in the historical profession," he continued regretfully, the question of Civil War causation had become simply a convenient exercise in the study of American historiography. That this should be so was symptomatic of the state of historical study in the United States. Donald suggested four reasons why scholars were no longer attracted to research on the causes of the Civil War: (1) the field had been so dominated by the giants of the profession that historians no longer felt any assurance that they could find something new that was worth saying; (2) a significant contribution to the field would require "complex, difficult, technical, and expensive research"; (3) the study of the causes of the Civil War was filled with what Donald called "semantic boobytraps"; and (4) the dominant trend in American historical study had been away from conflict and toward continuity and consensus. As he pondered the state of historical writing on the threshold of the sixties, Donald found it ironical that historians were so little interested in the causes of the Civil War at a time when the nation was preparing to commemorate the centennial of that tragic conflict.[1]

Similar conclusions could as well have been expressed for the 1960's. The nation survived a four-year-long observance of the Civil War centennial, but its energies had been focussed on the more dramatic, and hence more popular, aspects of the struggle, and little attention was given to a study of its causes. One might quarrel with the reasons which Donald suggested for the earlier neglect but the fact still remained that few historians addressed themselves to the complex problem of causation. Avery Craven, who has devoted a lifetime of research and publication to the coming of the Civil War, pointed to the magnitude of the task. "The futility of trying to understand and explain the causes of the American Civil War," he insisted, "grows on anyone who gives much time and thought to the subject. . . . The more one knows of the American people who got themselves into that war and of the tangled factors which played upon them, the less he is inclined to generalize and to offer simple answers."[2] Perhaps this more than anything else explains the reticence of historians to come to grips with the question of causes.

Interest in the causes of the Civil War, however, has never flagged. Even though little new ground has been turned, fascination with the question continues as it has for over a century. Aware that a multiplicity of complex causes and events operated during the first half of the nineteenth century to push the nation into civil conflict, historians have generally adopted an eclectic view. Older arguments and interpretations have been anthologized for the convenience of teachers and students and earlier studies of the coming of the war have been made available to a new generation of scholars in reprint editions.[3] Interest in the years preceding the Civil War has been growing but there is less emphasis on a narrow search for explanations and solutions and more emphasis on the need for understanding early nineteenth-century America.

Donald himself has suggested that the war can best be understood "as the outgrowth of social processes which affected the entire United States during the first half of the nineteenth century." He found the roots of conflict in the American character itself. The faith in progress, individualism and rejection of authority which marked the period resulted in a social atomization and an increased popular participation in government. Thus, he concluded, Americans suffered from an "excess of liberty" that made it difficult for them "to arrive at reasoned, independent judgments upon the problems which faced their society." The disorganization of society and the lack of a viable conservative tradition left them ill-prepared to cope with the political crises that shook the nation in the 1850's.[4]

Some scholars have persisted in the traditional effort to discover the terms by which the causes of the Civil War can be easily identified and reduced to the simplest level of understanding, although their methods have been anything but traditional. For example, Barrington Moore, Jr., whose brief and inadequately researched study has been called "the most successful attempt at a Marxian analysis of the South and the coming of the war," found conflict to be inevitable between the "labor-repressive agricultural system" of the South and the "competitive democratic capitalism" of the North. The causes of the war lie in the growth of different economic systems "leading to different (but still capitalist) civilizations with incompatible stands on slavery." Moore simply recast the older economic and culture-conflict interpretations in a new mold, dubbing the war "the last capitalist revolution."[5] Lee Benson was spurred by the hope that objective and scientific explanations for the war might be found, thus ending the controversy once and for all. Arguing that American historians have failed to develop a credible explanation for the causes of the war because they have not yet developed a genuinely scientific historiography, Benson has urged the utilization of "more powerful conceptual and methodological tools with which to reconstruct the behavior of men in society over time." No objective alternative to the traditional explanations, however, has as yet been advanced.[6]

Since the appearance of Allan Nevins' monumental survey of antebellum America few historians attempted to synthesize the period in terms of the conflict that climaxed it.[7] Aware of the limitations inherent in generalizing about an extremely complex period, most historians of the 1960's turned to a deeper investigation of some of the problems and issues of the early nineteenth century without trying to assess their responsibility for the coming of the war. The period from the 1820's through the 1850's has been examined more for itself, for the insights it might offer to an understanding of American thought and activity, than simply as a backdrop to the Civil War. Uncertainty about the causes of the war, Kenneth Stampp noted, forced historians back to the sources.[8] The concerns and anxieties of the years following the Second World War, especially in the field of racial relations and accommodation, have helped in no small way to shape the study of early nineteenth-century America. At the same time, the results, even though influenced by contemporary problems, have been remarkably free of the kind of moralizing that characterized earlier studies. Three areas in particular have benefited from this closer scrutiny: the character of the institution of slavery and its impact on blacks and whites; the abolitionist and antislavery movements; the political behavior of Americans during the mid-century years.

Slavery

The current study of slavery in the antebellum South owes much to the conjunction of two significant forces: the traditional view of slavery represented in the early twentieth-century writings of Ulrich B. Phillips and the new concern for America's racial problems and attitudes. Although certain elements of Phillips' interpretation of slavery had been questioned before, his generally sympathetic view of slavery as a benign and benevolent institution did not come under attack until the 1940's and after. Richard Hofstadter was one of the first to question Phillips' methodology and to emphasize the need for new studies. Kenneth Stampp, urging an end to "glib generalizing" about slavery, suggested new directions for historical inquiry that would bring historians to a more objective view of the institution. Above all, Stampp contended, slavery must be viewed through the eyes of the slave as well as through the eyes of the slaveholder. It was clear from their arguments that both historians were moved by the primacy of racial issues in their own time. "No historian of the institution [of slavery]," wrote Stampp, "can be taken seriously any longer unless he begins with the knowledge that there is no valid evidence that the Negro race is innately inferior to the white, and that there is growing evidence that both races have approximately the same potentialities."[9]

Stampp followed his own suggestions when he published his classic synthesis of southern slavery, *The Peculiar Institution,* in 1956. Others in the meantime had responded to his call, and the foundations for a reassessment of slavery were laid.[10] During the 1960's, this reassessment focussed on three important aspects of the institution. First, historians and economists carried the "perennial" question of the profitability of slavery into a new stage of sophisticated analysis. Secondly, slavery was viewed in a hemispheric and even worldwide context as historians, employing techniques of comparative history, sought common themes as well as differences in the institution as it existed in different areas and nations. Finally, the utilization of psychological and behavioral concepts resulted in new and more meaningful studies of the impact of slavery on the individuals involved in it—the slave and the slaveholder—and on the South itself.

Although the question of the profitability of slavery and the role of slavery in the southern economy had been argued since antebellum times, it was U. B. Phillips who gave it its first important scholarly treatment. Phillips maintained that slavery was no longer economically profitable to the slaveholder by the mid-nineteenth century and that it had become a burden to economic growth in the South. He added, however, that it was a burden the southern people had no option but to accept, for slavery was more than an economic institution. It had become a necessary social institution. In 1929, Charles W. Ramsdell supplemented Phillips' view when he contended that slavery had reached its natural limits of expansion before the Civil War and was a dying institution. By the 1930's, Phillips and Ramsdell were challenged by revisionists, notably Lewis C. Gray and Robert R. Russel, whose research led them to different conclusions, and the debate was continued by others in later years.[11]

Surveying the debate in 1963, Harold D. Woodman suggested that two separate issues had been confused in the effort to answer the question of profitability. Some had regarded the plantation-slavery enterprise as a business or industry while others focussed on slavery as an economic system, relating the institution to southern economic growth. Woodman called for a greater recognition of the complexities involved in these approaches and of the need for more precise definitions, and he strongly urged scholars to overcome the narrowness imposed on their inquiries by their own disciplines. "The real question is neither one of bookkeeping nor one of economic profit," Woodman wrote, but one of economic history. He questioned whether it could be studied adequately in purely economic terms that ignored the political and social characteristics of the institution.[12]

At the time that Woodman was urging a broader approach, economists were deeply involved in an elaborate study of the economics of slavery, part of a "new departure" that has been variously labelled the new economic history, econometric history or cliometrics. In 1958, two Harvard economists, Alfred H. Conrad and John R. Meyer, using quantitative evidence and elements of economic theory, challenged the traditional view that slavery was dying in 1860 and that it had discouraged southern economic growth. On the contrary, they found slavery to be an efficient form of economic organization that was profitable "to the whole South." It was not a deterrent, "from the strict economic standpoint," to the growth of the southern economy.[13] Conrad and Meyer opened an entire new line of investigation for economists, and their article, far from settling the issue, stimulated a burst of interest and activity. Some have questioned aspects of their methodology, and others have suggested refinements in data, but in general the conclusions of their original statement have been upheld. According to a recent summation of the work which economists have devoted to the question, slavery was "a vigorous economic system on the eve of the Civil War."[14]

Slavery, however, was more than an economic system in the antebellum South, as historians from Phillips to Woodman have pointed out, and any attempt to study it solely "from the strict economic standpoint" will likely lead to oversimplification and distortion. Critics of the Conrad-Meyer approach have argued effectively that slavery cannot be isolated from non-economic factors. Its role even as an economic institution was conditioned by social considerations which at times rendered the question of profits and viability irrelevant.[15] One of the most thorough replies to the work of the econometricians was in Eugene D. Genovese's brilliant and provocative study of slavery. Insisting on the term "political economy" rather than "economics" of slavery, Genovese questioned the accuracy of the data used by Conrad and Meyer and criticized their effort to view slavery narrowly as an economic institution. Returning to some of the early assumptions of U. B. Phillips, he argued that the economic role of slavery could not be studied apart from the political and social structure which slavery supported in the South. Slavery, much more than simply a form of labor, was at the root of southern civilization, providing a "distinct class structure, political community, ideology and set of psychological patterns"; the South, as a result, "increasingly grew away from the rest of the nation and from the rapidly developing sections of the world." Genovese's Marxian analysis of the antebellum South as a premodern or prebourgeois society has aroused criticism but his conclusion is clear and soundly argued—the plantation-slavery system, in its total impact, retarded southern growth and development.[16]

One significant avenue toward a greater understanding of the role of slavery, as well as of the place of the individual slave within the system, has been the comparative study of slavery. Was slavery harsher or more oppressive in some areas than in others? Slaves were human beings as well as chattels. To what extent was this dual character recognized in those areas where the institution was an integral part of social and economic organization? Historians during the past decade have sought answers to these questions, but the methods of comparative history are still so new and the research still so incomplete that the results have been mixed.[17]

In 1946, at a time when many traditional views of slavery were being challenged, Frank Tannenbaum published a brief study suggesting the fruitful possibilities of a comparative approach to the institution. The differences in race relations between the United States and Latin America, Tannebaum argued, could be traced to differences in the slave systems which each area had once supported. Slavery had been less harsh and severe in Latin America where the slave was recognized as a human being as well as a piece of property than in the United States where slavery was defined solely in terms of property. These basic differences were attributed to the presence in Latin America of two mitigating institutions, the law (an extension of Roman law) and the Catholic Church, both of which recognized the essential humanity of the Negro slave. Tannenbaum's conclusions were later reinforced by Stanley Elkins in his *Slavery: A Problem in American Institutional and Intellectual Life,* a ground-breaking and (as time would reveal) highly controversial work that has been judged the most influential study of slavery in the United States published since World War II. Elkins drew heavily on Tannenbaum's findings but added further dimension to the contrast between the United States and Latin America. Not only the absence of mitigating institutions and traditions but also the "dynamics of unopposed capitalism" (absent in Latin America) dehumanized the slave in the United States.[18]

The Tannenbaum-Elkins thesis (as it came to be called) received additional support from Herbert S. Klein's study of slavery in Virginia and Cuba. Noting that both scholars had been criticized for their emphasis on the law and on legal structures and for ignoring the differences between law and practice, Klein proposed to study the "social and economic dynamics" of slavery in the New World. His research substantiated the conclusion that Latin American slavery differed sharply from slavery in the United States. Like Tannenbaum, Klein found implications in these differences for later race relations. Slavery in Virginia reinforced a caste system based on color which eventually survived slavery to form a serious block to social integration whereas slavery in Cuba, defined in more human terms, did not discourage integration.[19]

The comparative history of slavery, although widely recognized as an important new field of inquiry, has so far exhibited certain weaknesses and critics have been quick to point them out.[20] Arnold Sio, writing in 1965, added a comparison of Roman slavery to that of the United States and Latin America and focussed his attention on the property, racial and personal components in the definition of slave status. He found greater similarities between slavery in the United States and slavery in Latin America than had been conceded by Tannenbaum and Elkins. The assumptions of the comparative historians were further examined and questioned by David Brion Davis, whose Pulitzer Prize-winning book *The Problem of Slavery in Western Culture* is a monument to recent scholarship on slavery. Davis pointed out the differences in slavery within the countries themselves and emphasized the difficulties in generalizing about the comparative severity of slave systems. There was a wide variation and flexibility in slavery, especially in the regulation of the slave's daily life and in defining his relationships with other people, that could not be revealed in a study of legal status alone. A plausible argument, he suggested, could be made that, in terms of legal protection and physical well-being, slaves in the United States were as favorably treated as any in history. Only in the difficulty of manumission was slavery in the United States unique and this, Davis believed, was not so much due to slavery as to social attitudes toward racial integration. Carl Degler also took issue with the conclusions of Tannenbaum and Elkins in his comparison of the slave systems of the United States and Brazil. While there were differences in the practice of slavery in the two countries, there was little difference either in the conception of the slave or in the legal protection of the slave's humanity.[21]

For Stanley Elkins, the comparison of slavery in the United States and Latin America formed only part of his effort to discover the total impact which the institution had on the individual slave. His conclusion that slavery in Latin America was mitigated by certain legal and religious influences in contrast to the United States led him to questions concerning the development of slave personality. American slavery, he suggested, operated as a closed system; did not such a closed system, he then asked, produce "noticeable effects upon the slave's very personality"?[22] In his answer, Elkins extended the limits of research into new and unfamiliar areas (for the historian). It is no exaggeration to say that much of the recent study of slavery has revolved about his pioneering work.[23]

Through the use of social psychology and personality theory, Elkins found support for the persistent stereotype of the typical southern plantation slave as a Sambo—"docile and irresponsible, loyal but lazy, humble but chronically given to lying and stealing; . . . full of infantile silliness," utterly dependent upon his master, to whom he felt a "childlike attachment." Explanations for this slave character based on race and on slavery in the abstract were rejected, for slavery had existed in other societies where the Sambo stereotype was noticeably absent. Sambo was a uniquely American product, he suggested, conditioned by the unique and dehumanizing quality of American slavery. All lines of authority descended from the master, and absolute power for the master meant the absolute dependency of the slave. Elkins used the analogy of the Nazi concentration camp to emphasize his point. Both were closed and repressive systems; each required a "childlike conformity." The master and the SS guard provided the only link with the "outside world" for the slave and the inmate.[24]

Predictably Elkins' study of the impact of slavery on the personality of the slave, though couched in suggestive and tentative language, aroused a wide critical response. Strong objections were raised against his acceptance of the Sambo stereotype. Slavery, it was said, was a more flexible institution, allowing the slave a wider opportunity for the development of personality than Elkins had recognized. The Sambo stereotype did not reflect the slave's real personality; it was simply that side of his personality that was presented to the whites, a mask that could be removed at will. One critic insisted that "Sambo existed wherever slavery existed," that Elkins had merely described the "slavish" personality, but that there were situations when docility became rebelliousness. The limitations of the concentration camp analogy were pointed out.[25] Summing up the controversy, Kenneth Stampp concluded that too much emphasis had been placed on Elkins' hypothesis, perhaps because of the novelty of his methodology, and not enough on gathering empirical evidence. From his wide familiarity with the sources of southern slavery he suggested an alternative hypothesis which allowed for greater variety in personality development but urged that the entire question should be subjected to renewed investigation.[26]

The study of slavery during the past decade—its profitability, its relative severity in different areas, its impact on the slave's personality—has dealt with the institution in its rural, agricultural setting. The conclusions that have been drawn are applicable primarily to the field hands on the large plantations. The household slaves, the slave drivers, the slaves on the small farms might all provide exceptions to these findings. They await investigation. There were other slaves in the antebellum South, however, who were not confined to agricultural pursuits. Richard Wade examined slavery in southern cities, where the institution was conditioned by an entirely different set of circumstances. The difficulties in maintaining discipline over the urban slave, the proximity of slaves with whites and free blacks, the very nature of the pursuits with which the urban slaves were occupied contributed to the gradual erosion of urban slavery. By 1860 slavery was disintegrating in the southern cities. The use of slave labor in southern industries was studied by Robert Starobin. While there were obvious contrasts between plantation slavery and industrial slavery, Starobin found that industrial slaves suffered from the same drudgery, unhealthiness, protest and repression that was often experienced by their brethren in the countryside.[27]

In contrast with the close study of slaves and slavery, little attention has been devoted to the southern defense of slavery, perhaps because it is puzzling to historians concerned with the quality of today's racial relations. William S. Jenkins' largely descriptive monograph on *Pro-Slavery Thought in the Old South,* published in 1935, is still (1972) the standard work. Several scholars in the 1960's, however, suggested new ways of looking at the slaveholders' defense by employing psychological arguments. According to Charles Sellers, southerners, because of their ambivalent attitude toward slavery, experienced a painful inner conflict as they recognized (at least subconsciously) the contradiction between slavery and their traditional devotion to liberalism and Christianity. Their feelings of guilt forced them to smother their convictions and to produce an increasingly dogmatic and irrational defense of slavery. This conflict of values, intensified by the attacks from outside the South, finally drove them to an extreme, belligerent and even violent resolution of their problem. In a similar vein, Ralph Morrow traced the proslavery argument to the same internal strains and psychological needs of southerners. Slavery's defenders were not trying to convince either the North or the nonslaveholders in the South of slavery's merits but sought to strengthen and confirm the convictions of the slaveholders themselves.[28] David Donald related the proslavery argument to other political and social movements in pre-Civil War America. Taking several proslavery writers as examples, he concluded that they were frustrated individuals who longed for an earlier day when men like themselves had been leaders in the South and when slavery had contributed to the unity and grace of southern life. The proslavery argument, far from being an aberration in its time, was simply part of a quest for social stability in a rapidly changing world.[29]

Slavery, as writers from Phillips to Genovese have pointed out, was central to the development of a particular set of cultural patterns in the South, and to view slavery in isolation from these patterns is to distort its meaning to the people of the South. Earlier works by such writers as Wilbur Cash and Rollin Osterweis, which emphasized romantic elements in southern thinking,[30] have been supplemented by studies which seek to identify the effects of slavery on southern culture and to view this culture in a broader national setting. Clement Eaton's important analysis of the South's defensive attitude, resulting in what he called an "intellectual blockade" against ideas that might threaten the *status quo* of slavery, appeared in a new and expanded edition in 1964. Eaton continued his study of southern culture in two valuable works, *The Growth of Southern Civilization* and *The Mind of the Old South*.[31] William W. Freehling suggested a new importance for slavery in southern political behavior in his provocative study of the nullification crisis, which he sees as a "prelude to Civil War." Finally, William R. Taylor examined the myths and legends by which the South sought to distinguish itself from the rest of the nation, building a sectional culture based on images which drew much of their force from the existence of slavery and which tended to cloud the fact that North and South were more alike than either section would admit.[32]

Never before was the institution of slavery so intensively studied, and in 1972 there were no signs that the emphasis of the past decade would diminish. While most of the writers of the 1960's were concerned with illuminating the institution in all its ramifications, there were implications in their work for the question of Civil War causation, for it is clear that all of them regarded slavery as the primary element in the developing sectional conflict.

The Abolition Movement

The same circumstances that stimulated a re-examination of slavery during the years since the Second World War also turned scholars to a re-evaluation of the critics of slavery.[33] The concern for problems of race and especially for the civil rights movement of the 1950's and 1960's provided a new framework for the study of the abolition movement and its leaders. The vicissitudes of the abolitionist image over the past century are well-known. First hailed as heroes in a great moral struggle against slavery that reached its climax in the Civil War, the abolitionists fell from grace in the twentieth century. The revisionist historians of the 1930's and 1940's viewed them as irresponsible fanatics and agitators who helped to plunge the nation into violent conflict over issues that were essentially unreal. By 1970 the wheel of historical interpretation had turned full circle. As historians returned to the moral question of slavery as a basic issue in the coming of the Civil War,[34] the abolitionists' image was refurbished and they once more enjoyed the stature that had been theirs in the late nineteenth and early twentieth centuries. There were, however, some significant differences between their earlier treatment and their treatment in the 1960's. While scholars of the 1960's viewed the abolition movement sympathetically, they were less interested in vindication and more critical and balanced in their evaluations. Also few attempts were made to regard the abolitionists solely in terms of the causes of the Civil War. It was not their role in the web of causation that gave them importance but rather their commitment to human freedom and racial equality. The fact that their concerns were also our concerns has been sufficient to provide the impetus to a full-scale study and analysis of their goals, motives and tactics.[35]

Midway through the 1960's, Martin Duberman sought to illustrate (and to encourage) the new and more sympathetic light in which abolitionists were held by gathering a series of essays from scholars whom he considered to be in the "vanguard" of the re-examination. A second purpose of his collection was to present statements of other points of view but, he confessed, he could find no one willing at the time to draw the older, unsympathetic portrait of the movement. The omission was significant. The conversion of historians had been remarkably swift and a surprising (to Duberman) consensus existed in their analysis of abolition and abolitionists.[36]

Few attempts were made in the 1960's to survey the abolition movement in its entirety. Dwight Dumond brought his long-standing concern for the movement to a peak with the publication of *Antislavery: The*

Crusade for Freedom in America, the story of "this country's greatest victory for democracy" from slavery's colonial beginnings to its abolition in the Civil War. Dumond's work, comprehensive, detailed, and of great importance for the information it amassed, resembled the less critical view of earlier days more than it did the newer scholarship of the last decade.[37] Louis Filler, selecting more modest dimensions for his study of the crusade against slavery, insisted that abolition must be considered in the context of pre-Civil War reform. Abolition, he argued, was "the central hub of reform," yet it had received only fragmented treatment; by focussing on its leaders, scholars missed the interrelationship of reform movements as well as the complexities of antislavery thought. He drew an important but often overlooked distinction between abolition and antislavery arguments and linked both with the sectional politics of the antebellum years. Filler's study anticipated the direction of subsequent research and is a necessary starting point for anyone wishing to probe the meaning of the abolition movement both to its own time and to ours.[38]

Following Filler's lead, several scholars have placed the abolition movement in a nationwide and even worldwide reform setting. Approaching abolition as a problem in intellectual history, David Brion Davis undertook a large-scale study of the movement in both British and American thought of which his *Problem of Slavery in Western Culture* was the first result. Both the British and American antislavery movements had reached a crucial turning point by 1830 as gradualism gave way to a new emphasis on immediatism, "a shift in total outlook from a detached, rationalistic perspective on human history and progress to a personal commitment to make no compromise with sin." Davis linked this shift with the rise of evangelical religion and romanticism.[39] The importance of evangelicalism in shaping the new concept of sin expressed by abolitionists in their demand for "immediate emancipation" was further revealed by Anne Loveland. John L. Thomas probed the impact of perfectionism and the idea of utopia, key doctrines of the moral reformers, on abolitionist thought in the 1840's and 1850's.[40]

In his study of *Slavery,* Stanley Elkins suggested that abolitionists were motivated by an exaggerated individualism that stemmed from an anti-institutional bias common to reformers and transcendentalists generally. In the absence of a strong institutional framework, abolitionists moved into abstraction, moral absolutism and radicalism in disregard of the channels and responsibilities of power, viewing the question of slavery uncompromisingly in terms of sin and guilt. In a society as loosely structured as was that of early nineteenth-century America their movement was all the more dangerous and, Elkins seems to suggest, regrettable. Elkins' conclusions were challenged by Aileen Kraditor in her searching analysis of the strategies and tactics adopted by abolitionists. Objecting to Elkins' identification of the entire movement with its radical wing, Kraditor emphasized the variety and conflict that existed among abolitionists. Some of them were radical in outlook, believing, like William Lloyd Garrison, that American society was fundamentally immoral and desiring a complete reconstruction of the social order. But others were conservative, reformers rather than radicals, seeking to strengthen existing society by purging it of its immoral elements. The latter, constituting the majority of abolitionists, did not share the radical rejection of institutions but preferred to work through institutions to achieve their ends. The abolition movement was divided by a conflict in theory which was manifested in a conflict in practice.[41]

The study of abolition's role in the reform movement of the early nineteenth century inevitably raised questions regarding the motivation of those who were its leaders. Why did humanitarian reform generally, and abolitionist reform in particular, appear in its new militant and immediatist garb precisely at this point in time? Why were so many individuals moved so suddenly to commit their energies to the reform of evils that were not new to American society? David Donald suggested that the best way to answer these questions was to look closely at the leadership. His study of abolitionist leaders aroused one of the more lively historical controversies in recent years. Donald analyzed one hundred and six abolitionists, "the hard core of active antislavery leadership in the 1930's," and found psychological roots for their involvement in the movement. They were young, New Englanders for the most part, descended from old and distinguished families and indifferent to the new problems of urban and industrial growth. "An elite without function, a displaced class in American society," they found in abolitionism "a chance for a reassertion of their traditional values, an opportunity for association with others of their kind, and a possibility of achieving that self-fulfillment which should traditionally have been theirs as social leaders." The crusade against slavery was "the anguished protest of an aggrieved class against a world they never made."[42]

The defenders of the abolitionists were quick to reply. When Donald extended his interpretation in his Pulitzer Prize-winning first volume on Charles Sumner, his critics vented their displeasure.[43] Others emphasized the danger involved in applying broad labels and characteristics to a group as diverse as the abolitionists. Martin Duberman upheld the use of psychological concepts in historical study but warned that there is so little information about the individual personalities and careers of the majority of abolitionists that no valid composite portrait could be drawn. "We know far too little about why men do anything—let alone why they do something so specific as joining a reform movement—to assert as confidently as historians have, the motives of whole groups of men." The key to an understanding of the abolition movement, Betty Fladeland argued, lies in the social and economic ferment of the times rather than in the peculiarities of the individual leaders. The large numbers, the myriad personalities and the "vast diversity of exigencies" which impelled them to join the movement, she insisted, rendered it impossible to categorize the abolitionists. Larry Gara suggested that it is not even easy to determine who was an abolitionist since the term was always highly subjective and carried different meanings at different times and with different groups and individuals. Historians have always used broad and simple labels in order to simplify difficult and complicated movements; with reference to the abolitionists, the consensus now seems to hold that such stereotyping tends only to distortion.[44]

Taking issue with Donald on a different level, Gerald Sorin tested what he called the "tension-reduction theory of political radicalism" (that the primary objective of radical agitation is to relieve tensions and frustrations caused by social dislocation) by studying New York State's abolitionist leadership. He drew a somewhat different portrait of the abolitionists: they were largely from urban areas, highly educated and moderately prosperous, pursuing the most influential occupations in their communities, engaged in public service, and intensely religious. Unlike Donald, he concluded that their community status was generally higher than that of their fathers and that there was little evidence that they felt insecure or frustrated because of any social or economic dislocation. They were, on the contrary, "motivated by a reawakened religious impulse, a strong sense of social justice, and the sincere belief that they were not only insuring their own freedom from guilt, but that they would affect society in such a way as to assure social justice for everyone."[45]

If abolitionists were too diverse to be easily categorized as a group and if their motivations varied with their personalities, then it became the task of historians to study them as individuals in order to discover and appreciate the many dimensions of the crusade. The call for a closer and more careful study of abolition leaders resulted in the publication of a large number of biographies during the 1960's. In fact, it might be argued that the most meaningful work on the abolitionists in those years, quantitatively and qualitatively, took the form of biographical study. Since 1960, new and generally sympathetic biographies appeared of Wendell Phillips, Lydia Maria Child, Elijah P. Lovejoy, Thomas Wentworth Higginson, the Grimké sisters, Lewis Tappan, Benjamin

Lundy, Cassius M. Clay and James Russell Lowell.[46] A new interest in those abolitionists who sought to achieve their goals through direct involvement in politics has resulted in biographies of John P. Hale, Owen Lovejoy, George W. Julian, Benjamin F. Wade and Joshua R. Giddings, in addition to Donald's now-completed study of Charles Sumner. Stephen Oates produced a long-needed and scholarly study of one of the most enigmatic abolitionists, John Brown.[47] A badly neglected area has been the study of black participation in the movement. The gap was partially filled by the superb work of Benjamin Quarles, whose biography of Frederick Douglass and work on black abolitionists generally added a significant new dimension to our understanding of the crusade. Not only were blacks participants in the struggle but also, as Quarles pointed out, they brought their own firsthand experience to bear on the movement since many of them had been slaves themselves. Quarles' work was an important beginning; much yet needs to be done to fill out the story.[48]

The focal point in the study of abolitionist leadership has always been the controversial figure of William Lloyd Garrison, and historians have been as divided on Garrison as were the abolitionists themselves.[49] Controversy still clings to Garrison, and in a period of new sympathy and understanding for the struggle against slavery he has not always been treated as kindly as many other figures in the movement. Two new and ambitious biographies of Garrison, the first full treatments in several decades, appeared in the same year, 1963; both argue Garrison's central importance to the abolition movement, a position which had been denied him by some earlier writers. To Walter M. Merrill, Garrison's essential role was that of a publicist. He was the man to whom primary credit should be given for bringing the problem of slavery to the attention of the American people. According to the more critical John L. Thomas, Garrison personified "the great strength and the equally great weakness of radical reform." "More than any other American of his time," Thomas concluded, "he was responsible for the atmosphere of moral absolutism which caused the Civil War and freed the slave."[50] The fiery editor received appreciative treatment in Kraditor's work, in Truman Nelson's selection of documents from *The Liberator* and in Wyatt-Brown's essay on Garrison as a unifying force in the abolition movement. A definitive edition of Garrison's letters is now under way, two volumes of which have already appeared.[51]

An important new aspect of abolition study was the relation between the crusade against slavery and the effort to achieve full equality for blacks in American society. Although abolition has been treated more favorably and sympathetically in recent years, there has been little inclination to gloss over the weaknesses and shortcomings of the movement and its leaders. It had long been recognized, but seldom emphasized, that many abolitionists shared the same racial prejudices that were commonly held by their contemporaries. Anxious to destroy slavery and to win freedom for southern blacks, they were often less enthusiastic over according free blacks an equal place in their own society. Even the question of black membership in abolitionist organizations was hotly debated in some quarters. The Peases, close and careful students of abolitionist attitudes and arguments, traced this problem to a fundamental ambivalence running through the antislavery movement that was due in part to the abolitionists' view of the Negro as an abstraction. Much of what was said, the Peases pointed out, revealed an implicit and often explicit belief in the racial inferiority of the Negro. They were "torn between a genuine concern for the welfare and uplift of the Negro and a paternalism which was too often merely the patronizing of a superior class."[52] Other scholars have touched the same problem. Leon Litwack exposed the widespread belief in the racial inferiority of blacks in the antebellum North as well as the dilemma on which many abolitionists were caught in their attitudes toward blacks. A significant portion of the antislavery argument, Eugene Berwanger demonstrated, was avowedly founded on convictions of racial inferiority; many northerners were antislavery precisely because they were anti-Negro.[53]

Such studies merely substantiate the conclusions of recent writers on abolition that the movement was so remarkably varied in its scope and character as to defy simple explanations and descriptions. Obviously not all abolitionists shared the ambivalent attitude toward the Negro which some historians have found; many of them raised their voices in protest and worked tirelessly against slavery in the South and racial prejudice wherever it might be found. Indeed, in the public mind (North as well as South) abolitionism was generally identified with racial equality. Abolitionists, regardless of the quality of their arguments, were lumped together in the public mind as advocates of Negro equality in every respect, including miscegenation, and because of this commonly-held stereotype they became the targets of overt hostility and violence. Looking at the opposition to the abolition movement in the 1830's, Lorman Ratner found it to be based on anti-Negro prejudice, a fear of racial equality and the belief that antislavery activity drew much of its strength from British, and therefore alien, influences. Leonard Richards studied the violence to which abolitionists were often subjected and analyzed the composition of anti-abolition mobs. Their members were drawn from the ranks of prominence and respectability, "gentlemen of property and standing," individuals who feared racial assimilation. But violent opposition to abolitionism, Richards added, cannot be explained solely in terms of the antislavery movement. Putting a new twist on Donald's thesis, Richards contended that the violent anti-abolitionists were protesting against a movement that threatened their own elite status and moral leadership and undermined the values and traditions of the older America in which they had been schooled.[54]

The relationship between the abolition movement and the struggle for racial equality is unmistakable, especially to a generation which is still wrestling with the problems left over from mid-nineteenth century. Because it fell short of achieving a full commitment to the cause of black freedom, even though the institution of slavery was abolished, Merton Dillon judged the abolition movement a failure. Slavery was destroyed by the Civil War but racial prejudice remained. The great goal of most abolitionists was not realized—"the creation of a society in which . . . men of all colors could live together in harmony and equality."[55]

Politics in the 1850's

While historians have been attracted to new studies of slavery and the abolition movement, they have been slower to investigate the impact of the resulting sectional conflict on the political life of the nation during the decade and a half following the outbreak of the Mexican War. Two reasons may account for their reluctance: first, political history, regarded as old-fashioned and less challenging than social and cultural interpretations, has not been in vogue in recent years; and secondly, the political events of the 1850's have been studied so extensively in the past that students are discouraged that anything new about them could be discovered. Yet it is in the political conflict of the 1850's that the immediate background of the Civil War lies. It was not until the disagreement over slavery entered the political stream that the masses of Americans were touched by it; politics brought the issues of sectional conflict to the level of popular discussion where they became at once more familiar and more dangerous.

The great works of synthesis that cover the politics of midcentury, the several volumes in Allan Nevins' series and Roy Nichols' classic analysis of Democratic party politics during the latter fifties,[56] remain unchallenged, and nothing comparable in scope or design has been attempted since they appeared. Historians of the period have concentrated on more specialized studies of some of the decade's political events and movements, but they have also been intrigued with the process of political change and development during this period of sectional stress. While no dramatic or controversial theses have been advanced (in contrast with slavery and the abolition movement), many new insights have been achieved.

The politics of the fifties were turbulent and fluid, marked by shifting party alignments, and it is not an easy task to follow their twisted and often confusing course. Historians have traditionally viewed the decade from the vantage point of the Civil War. An artificial pattern has often been imposed upon the decade in the attempt to isolate and identify those forces which seemed to lead to the ultimate breakdown of the Union. The result, in some cases, has been dubious history. Joel Silbey objected to the preoccupation of historians with those conditions that led to the crisis of 1860-61 and suggested that the slavery issue was never the sole or overriding issue for all members of the electorate. Disagreements over the role of the immigrant in society and over the role of government in the nation's economic life, he pointed out, vied with the sectional issue of slavery for attention (although it should be noted that even these controversies, and especially the latter, took on a distinctive sectional character and neither was totally divorced from the slavery issue). Silbey traced the "transformation of American politics" from 1840, when political behavior was characterized by strong institutional and partisan loyalties, to the mid-1850's, when issues became more important than party differences. In another context, he applied quantitative methodology to voting behavior in the lower house of Congress to demonstrate that with the rise of the slavery issue in the fifties party loyalties were supplanted by sectional allegiances. Thomas Alexander, employing the same techniques in a parallel project, concluded that voting on economic issues tended to follow party lines while alignments on issues relating to slavery revealed sectional divisions.[57]

Politically speaking, the decade of the fifties began with the discussion of slavery and territorial expansion that accompanied the outbreak of the Mexican War.[58] The territorial issue, the question whether slavery should or should not be allowed in the national territories, brought slavery into political channels where it remained, dominant and disruptive, until the Civil War. The territories assumed a symbolic importance that transcended their practical significance, and the arguments became increasingly abstract. For the North, the issue was a means for halting the expansion of southern power and for striking a first blow against slavery itself; for the South, it became a first line of defense in the effort to protect the section's institutions and social order.

Chaplain W. Morrison's study of the spark that touched off the conflagration, the Wilmot Proviso, emphasizes the impact which this effort to keep slavery out of the Mexican Cession had on Democratic party politics in the late 1840's. More a political maneuver than a genuine assault on slavery, the Proviso, in Morrison's view, was an attempt to restrict the growth of southern power as well as an opportunity to preserve the territories for free white labor. Addressing himself to the motivation behind the Proviso, Eric Foner considered the move as a defensive effort of certain northern Democrats who were concerned with the growth of antislavery sentiment among their constituents. Kinley Brauer studied the impact of the issue of slavery and expansion on Whig party politics in Massachusetts in the latter 1840's, an important examination of a local area that ought to be emulated for other parts of the country.[59]

The story of the Compromise of 1850, which attempted to resolve the issues raised by the Wilmot Proviso following four years of disruptive sectional debate, has been told by Holman Hamilton. Concerned primarily with the progress of the various compromise bills through Congress, Hamilton exposed some of the behind-the-scenes maneuvers and shifting party alignments that contributed to their passage. Usually credited to Henry Clay and the Whigs, the success of the compromise, Hamilton pointed out, was due in greater measure to Democratic leadership, especially that of Stephen A. Douglas. Still significant is Robert R. Russel's analysis of the compromise as it dealt with the territorial issue, published in 1956.[60]

The compromise was widely hailed as a final settlement of the sectional issues but it soon became obvious that its effects were only temporary. The focus of conflict shifted for a time from the territorial question to the issues raised by the Fugitive Slave Act, but in 1854 the territorial question was again thrust into national politics, this time by the passage of the Kansas-Nebraska Act. Russel discussed some of the issues involved in the passage of the act, but the legislation needs fresh study for it provided the impetus for new and significant political formulations.[61] The party system proved unable to withstand the pressures and strains that followed. The Whig party, in a state of disorder, suffered its final demise, the Democratic party developed cracks that could no longer be easily ignored and, most importantly, the Republican party emerged as a protest against the growth of southern power in the nation's politics.

In a major work on the politics of the fifties, Eric Foner examined the ideology of the Republican party during its early years, placing the movement in a perspective that not only tells much about the attitudes that held Republicans together but also casts light on the coming of the Civil War. Republicans, according to Foner, urged the superiority of the northern social system, summed up in the words "free labor," and saw in the southern, slavery-based system a threat to the free, mobile and open society which they equated with the fulfillment of national destiny. The ideology was flexible enough to encompass a wide variety of political and economic interests, but on one point Republicans were agreed: slavery must be contained. A growing number went one step further and argued that it must also be ultimately destroyed. Slavery was the major political issue of the 1850's, and the Republican party was pre-eminently an antislavery party. "The free labor assault upon slavery and southern society," Foner argued, "coupled with the idea that an aggressive Slave Power was threatening the most fundamental values and interests of the free states, hammered the slavery issue home to the northern public more emphatically than an appeal to morality alone could ever have done." Still, local issues and concerns played a large part in party development, as Michael Holt showed in his study of the formation of the Republican party in Pittsburgh. Social, ethnic, and religious factors were more important to the growth of Republican strength in this industrial city than were the slavery issue and the fear of southern power.[62]

Events in Kansas following the Kansas-Nebraska Act dramatized the issue of slavery in the territories, turned popular attention toward the slavery question, and promoted the growth of the Republican party. With only a few exceptions, historians have avoided the almost unbelievably complicated developments in that troubled territory from 1854 to 1858. One of the exceptions is James Rawley. While threading his way through the entanglements of "bleeding Kansas" he has also offered a new explanation for the coming of the war. Modifying the position advanced by the revisionists years ago, Rawley suggested that the war was the work of a generation flawed by racial prejudice. Racism permeated the period's politics, frustrated the efforts to solve the sectional issues exemplified by the Kansas struggle, and lay "at the root of the causes of the Civil War." Indeed, Rawley insisted that racial prejudice made the war inevitable.[63]

At the heart of the sectional debate were differing constitutional interpretations. Since 1846, each side sought support and justification in the United States Constitution. The disagreement over the power of Congress to legislate for or against slavery in the territories and the commitment of the South to the doctrine of states' rights, as well as the significance of constitutional issues to the crisis between the North and South, have been extensively treated in studies by Robert Russel and Arthur Bestor. In 1857, the Supreme Court formally entered the fray with its Dred Scott decision, bringing the force of the Constitution to the side of the South. The controversy aroused by the decision and the questions which historians have directed to it have been summarized in a recent collection of documents by Stanley Kutler.[64]

The year 1858 marked a turning point in the sectional politics of the decade. Kansas was lost to the South as its voters turned down the indirect referendum on the Lecompton constitution, and southerners began the search for new guarantees for their institutions. The Republican party achieved dramatic success in the elections for Congress, forcing southern leaders to reassess their role in national politics, and in that same year the issues of the conflict were highlighted in the Lincoln-Douglas debates. In the centennial year of the debates, Paul Angle published the best edition of the speeches made by the two Illinoisans, placing them in the larger context of the election campaign of which they were a part, and in the following year Harry Jaffa's ambitious analysis of the issues in the debates appeared. Don Fehrenbacher illuminated Lincoln's role in the 1858 campaign, especially in his incisive treatments of the House-Divided speech and the Freeport Question, and Richard Heckman sketched the history of the debates campaign.[65]

A plethora of biographies has appeared since 1960, and our knowledge of the politics of the 1850's has been considerably expanded by the studies of the men whose careers crossed the decade. Biographies were published of such major figures as James Buchanan, John J. Crittenden, Stephen A. Douglas, William H. Seward, Charles Sumner and Roger B. Taney,[66] but most of the biographical writing focussed on lesser individuals, whose stories perhaps reveal more clearly the varied character of political life during this crisis decade. Of the latter, studies were made of Charles Francis Adams, David R. Atchison, Robert J. Walker, William Pitt Fessenden, Edwin M. Stanton, Benjamin F. Wade, Edward Bates, Lyman Trumbull, Simon Cameron, John Letcher, Robert Toombs, Joseph Lane and David C. Broderick.[67]

Lincoln is a special case. Interest in Lincoln showed no signs of diminishing although the character of Lincoln scholarship has been shifting. The publication of his collected works in 1953, the observance of a whole series of centennials relating to Lincoln and the Civil War, and the questions raised by the civil rights struggle moved scholars to penetrate beyond the legendary figure to a more realistic portrait of the prairie politician. With the attempt to focus on the historical Lincoln has come a more critical view of his words and deeds. Civil rights reformers have found it difficult to reconcile some of Lincoln's statements with the image of the "Great Emancipator," and some have rejected the historian's quest for objectivity and truth altogether in favor of polemical denunciation. But such aberrations are few and in any case carry little weight. Lincoln studies in the recent past have, on the whole, been characterized by balance and scholarship and a new appreciation of his role in his own time has been gained.[68]

Only one full-scale biography of Lincoln has been published during the past two decades, Reinhard Luthin's *The Real Abraham Lincoln*, and it (in spite of the title) added little to what was already known. Historians have instead turned to more specialized treatments of certain aspects of his life—his childhood, his experience as a young state legislator and as a national Congressman, and his legal career.[69] Facilitated by the easy availability of his collected works, several studies of Lincoln's political thought emphasized his pragmatic outlook, his nationalism, and the astuteness with which he responded to the sectional challenges of his time. Fehrenbacher concluded that Lincoln during the 1850's was driven by political ambition, but it was "an ambition leavened by moral conviction and a deep faith in the principles upon which the republic had been built."[70]

The political conflict of the 1850's rapidly approached its climax as the decade came to an end. The story of these last years, with that of the final sectional confrontation in the election of 1860, still awaits the analysis that it needs and deserves. By 1970 no full study of the 1860 election had been published since that of Emerson Fite appeared in 1911, although limited and specialized treatments had appeared.[71] The critical months that followed the election have been more fortunate. The studies of the secession crisis by David Potter and Kenneth Stampp, while confined to the northern experience, remain authoritative. They were supplemented by a superb account of the secession movement in South Carolina by Steven Channing, in which the author emphasized the deep-seated fear which gripped southerners during the last days of the Union. Slavery, Channing insisted, was the fundamental cause of the sectional conflict and the source of southern anxiety. Fear for the future of slavery, fear of slave insurrection, and fear for the integrity of southern civilization itself achieved political expression in the mounting argument for disunion. Several scholars, taking a fresh look at the crisis, have attempted to define and answer some of the questions raised by the Republican triumph, the division of the Democratic party, the secession of the South and the decision of the Republicans to reject both compromise and secession.[72]

For well over a century, historians have been probing the events of early nineteenth-century America in a persistent effort to find explanations for the Civil War. In spite of the vast amount of publication that has resulted, one may safely assume that the probing will continue, for the coming of the Civil War is still baffling in many ways and historians have only scratched the surface. This does not mean that the modes of historical research and scholarship are, and will be, unchanging. Far from it. The study of history has profited immensely from changing ways of looking at the past, from the introduction of new methodologies and from the shifting vantage point of the historian himself. Such shifts and changes have been more apparent at some times than at others. Historical study in the 1970's is in such a period of change, and this is no more clearly demonstrated than in the study of the early nineteenth-century background to the Civil War. Historians and others may learn much from the current investigations of slavery, the abolition movement and the political developments of the 1850's for they illustrate all the dangers and pitfalls as well as the insights that are to be gained from changing fashions in historical research. Leaving the broader, less precise and ultimately frustrating questions of causation aside, scholars have concentrated on the events, institutions and beliefs of nineteenth-century America for themselves, no longer dominated by hindsight—the knowledge that the Civil War happened. Out of all this will emerge, hopefully, a better understanding of how and why Americans in those troublous years acted as they did.

FOOTNOTES

[1] David Donald. "American Historians and the Causes of the Civil War." *South Atlantic Quarterly* 59: 351-355; No. 3, Summer 1960. For recent, general discussions of the historiography of the coming of the Civil War, see Charles E. Cauthen and Lewis P. Jones. "The Coming of the Civil War," in Arthur S. Link and Rembert W. Patrick, editors. *Writing Southern History: Essays in Historiography in Honor of Fletcher M. Green.* Baton Rouge: Louisiana State University Press, 1965. pp. 224-48; and the more comprehensive and analytical essay by David M. Potter, "The Literature on the Background of the Civil War," in his *The South and the Sectional Conflict.* Baton Rouge: Louisiana State University Press, 1968. pp. 87-150.

[2] Avery Craven. *An Historian and the Civil War.* Chicago: University of Chicago Press, 1964. p. 1.

[3] Three recent anthologies devoted to the causes of the Civil War are Kenneth M. Stampp, editor. *The Causes of the Civil War.* Englewood Cliffs, N. J.: Prentice-Hall, 1965; Edwin C. Rozwenc, editor. *The Causes of the American Civil War.* Boston: D. C. Heath, 1961; and Hans L. Trefousse, editor. *The Causes of the Civil War: Institutional Failure or Human Blunder?* New York: Holt, Rinehart and Winston, 1971.

[4] David Donald. *An Excess of Democracy: The American Civil War and the Social Process.* Oxford: Clarendon Press, 1960. In a critique of Donald's thesis, A. E. Campbell has suggested that America's isolation from external threat not only affected the manner in which Americans dealt with their domestic problems but also made it more likely that serious domestic problems would arise. "An Excess of Isolation: Isolation and the American Civil War." *Journal of Southern History* 29: 161-174; No. 2, May 1963.

[5] Eugene D. Genovese. "Marxian Interpretations of the Slave South," in Barton J. Bernstein, editor. *Towards a New Past: Dissenting Essays in American History.* New York: Pantheon Books, 1968. p. 117; Barrington Moore, Jr. *Social*

Origins of Dictatorship and Democracy: Lord and Peasant in the Making of the Modern World. Boston: Beacon Press 1966. Chapter III: "The American Civil War: The Last Capitalist Revolution." Genovese modified Moore's analysis, arguing that the conflict resulted because the North was bourgeois and the South was pre-bourgeois.

[6] Lee Benson. "Causation and the American Civil War" and "Explanations of American Civil War Causation: A Critical Assessment and a Modest Proposal to Reorient and Reorganize the Social Sciences," in *Toward the Scientific Study of History: Selected Essays of Lee Benson.* Philadelphia: Lippincott, 1972. pp. 81-97, 225-340.

[7] Allan Nevins. *The Ordeal of the Union.* 2 vols., New York: Scribner's, 1947, and *The Emergence of Lincoln.* 2 vols., New York: Scribner's, 1950. Exceptions are Roy F. Nichols. *The Stakes of Power, 1845-1877,* New York: Hill and Wang, 1961; and Elbert B. Smith. *The Death of Slavery: The United States, 1837-65.* Chicago: University of Chicago Press, 1967. Both volumes are brief and cover the Civil War as well as the pre-Civil War years. Nichols' is essentially a political study while the theme of Smith's work is revealed in his title.

[8] Stampp, editor. *The Causes of the Civil War.* p. vi. For a critique of the common tendency to study the early nineteenth century in terms of the Civil War, see Joel H. Silbey. "The Civil War Synthesis in American Political History." *Civil War History* 10: 130-140; No. 2, June 1964.

[9] Richard Hofstadter. "U. B. Phillips and the Plantation Legend." *Journal of Negro History* 29: 109-124; No. 2, April 1944; Stampp. "The Historian and Southern Negro Slavery." *American Historical Review* 57: 613-624; No. 3, April 1952. p. 620.

[10] Stampp. *The Peculiar Institution: Slavery in the Ante-Bellum South.* New York: Knopf, 1956. For a convenient collection of articles illustrating the current status of research and writing on slavery, see Allen Weinstein and Frank Otto Gatell, editors. *American Negro Slavery: A Modern Reader.* New York: Oxford University Press, 1968.

[11] Ulrich B. Phillips. "The Economic Cost of Slaveholding in the Cotton Belt." *Political Science Quarterly* 20: 257-275; No. 2, June 1905; Charles W. Ramsdell. "The Natural Limits of Slavery Expansion." *Mississippi Valley Historical Review.* 16: 151-171; No. 2, September 1929; Lewis C. Gray. *History of Agriculture in the Southern United States to 1860.* 2 vols., Washington: The Carnegie Institution, 1933; Robert R. Russel. "The General Effects of Slavery Upon Southern Economic Progress." *Journal of Southern History* 4: 34-54; No. 1, February 1938.

[12] Harold D. Woodman. "The Profitability of Slavery: A Historical Perennial." *Journal of Southern History* 29: 303-325; No. 3, August 1963.

[13] Alfred H. Conrad and John R. Meyer. "The Economics of Slavery in the Ante-Bellum South." *Journal of Political Economy* 66: 95-130; No. 2, April 1958. This essay was later reprinted in Conrad and Meyer. *The Economics of Slavery and Other Studies in Econometric Study.* Chicago: Aldine, 1964.

[14] Robert William Fogel and Stanley L. Engerman. "The Economics of Slavery," in Fogel and Engerman, editors. *The Reinterpretation of American Economic History.* New York: Harper and Row, 1971. pp. 311-41. The literature on the economics of slavery has assumed voluminous proportions. Much of it has been collected in Hugh G. J. Aitken, editor. *Did Slavery Pay?* New York: Houghton Mifflin, 1971.

[15] See, for example, Douglas F. Dowd. "The Economics of Slavery in the Antebellum South: A Comment," reprinted in Aitken, editor. *Did Slavery Pay?* pp. 179-82.

[16] Eugene E. Genovese, *The Political Economy of Slavery: Studies in the Economy and Society of the Slave South.* New York: Pantheon, 1965.

[17] A good collection of recent writings on the comparative history of slavery is Laura Foner and Eugene D. Genovese, editors. *Slavery in the New World: A Reader in Comparative History.* Englewood Cliffs, N. J.: Prentice-Hall, 1969.

[18] Frank Tannenbaum. *Slave and Citizen: The Negro in the Americas.* New York: Knopf, 1946; Stanley M. Elkins. *Slavery: A Problem in American Institutional and Intellectual Life.* Chicago: University of Chicago Press, 1959. pp. 27-80.

[19] Herbert S. Klein. *Slavery in the Americas: A Comparative Study of Virginia and Cuba.* Chicago: University of Chicago Press, 1967. A by-product of the comparative study of slavery has been an investigation of the relation between slavery and racial prejudice. Was slavery the source of racial prejudice or did prejudice antedate slavery? Carl Degler has explored this question in "Slavery and the Genesis of American Race Prejudice." *Comparative Studies in Society and History* 2: 49-66; No. 1, October 1959.

[20] For example, Stampp's conclusion in a review of Klein's book: "The comparative study of slavery in the Americas . . . makes it abundantly clear that new conceptualizations and methodological innovations, valuable though they may be, are poor substitutes for research," *American Historical Review.* 73: 771; No. 3, February 1968.

[21] Arnold A. Sio. "Interpretations of Slavery: The Slave Status in the Americas." *Comparative Studies in Society and History* 7: 289-308; No. 3, April 1965; David Brion Davis. *The Problem of Slavery in Western Culture.* Ithaca, Cornell University Press, 1966. Chapter 8: "The Continuing Contradiction of Slavery: A Comparison of British America and Latin America"; Davis. "Slavery," in C. Vann Woodward, editor. *The Comparative Approach to American History.* New York: Basic Books, 1968. pp. 121-34; Carl N. Degler. "Slavery in Brazil and the United States: An Essay in Comparative History." *American Historical Review* 75: 1004-1028; No. 4, April, 1970. Genovese, in the second of his projected studies of slavery, finds both the Tannenbaum-Elkins approach and the Davis approach wanting because they proceed from the same basic concern for race relations. Slavery, Genovese argues, "must be understood primarily as a class question and only secondarily as a race or a narrowly economic question." *The World the Slaveholders Made: Two Essays in Interpretation.* New York: Pantheon Books, 1969. Part One: "The American Slave Systems in World Perspective." pp. 14-15.

[22] Elkins. *Slavery.* pp. 81-82.

[23] The importance of Elkins' work is amply demonstrated in Ann J. Lane, editor. *The Debate over Slavery: Stanley Elkins and His Critics.* Urbana, Ill.: University of Illinois Press, 1971.

[24] Elkins. *Slavery.* pp. 82-85, 128-30.

[25] See the following essays, reprinted in Lane, editor. *The Debate over Slavery.* Earle E. Thorpe. "Chattel Slavery and Concentration Camps." pp. 23-42; Eugene D. Genovese. "Rebelliousness and Docility in the Negro Slave: A Critique of the Elkins Thesis." pp. 43-74; Mary Agnes Lewis. "Slavery and Personality." pp. 75-86; and George M. Fredrickson and Christopher Lasch. "Resistance to Slavery." pp. 223-44. Genovese emphasized the inadequacy of psychological models as substitutes for empirical research and urged that scholars now solve the problems raised by Elkins "by the more orthodox procedures of historical research." pp. 73-74.

[26] Kenneth M. Stampp. "Rebels and Sambos: The Search for the Negro's Personality in Slavery." *Journal of Southern History* 37: 367-392; No. 3, August 1971.

[27] Richard C. Wade. *Slavery in the Cities: The South, 1820-1860.* New York: Oxford University Press, 1964; Robert S. Starobin. *Industrial Slavery in the Old South.* New York: Oxford University Press, 1970.

[28] William S. Jenkins. *Pro-Slavery Thought in the Old South.* Chapel Hill: University of North Carolina Press, 1935; Charles G. Sellers, Jr. "The Travail of Slavery," in Sellers, editor. *The Southerner as American.* Chapel Hill: University of North Carolina Press, 1960. pp. 40-71; Ralph E. Morrow. "The Proslavery Argument Revisited." *Mississippi Valley Historical Review.* 48: 79-94; No. 1, June 1961. The so-called "guilt thesis" has been reviewed by James M. McPherson who related the proslavery argument to the "need to soothe troubled Southern con-

sciences" but who found its basis in matters of race and the need to maintain white supremacy. "Slavery and Race." *Perspectives in American History.* III, 1969. pp. 360-73. Genovese has termed the guilt thesis "irrelevant" in his analysis of the arguments of George Fitzhugh, the South's foremost apologist for slavery. *The World the Slaveholders Made.* Part II: "The Logical Outcome of the Slaveholders' Philosophy: An Exposition, Interpretation, and Critique of the Social Thought of George Fitzhugh of Port Royal, Virginia." pp. 115-224.

[29] David Donald. "The Proslavery Argument Reconsidered," *Journal of Southern History* 37: 3-18; No. 1, February 1971.

[30] Wilbur J. Cash. *The Mind of the South.* New York: Knopf, 1941; Rollin G. Osterweis, *Romanticism and Nationalism in the Old South.* New Haven: Yale University Press, 1949.

[31] Clement Eaton. *The Freedom-of-Thought Struggle in the Old South.* Rev. ed. New York: Harper and Row, 1964; *The Growth of Southern Civilization, 1790-1860.* New York: Harper, 1961; *The Mind of the Old South.* Baton Rouge: Louisiana State University Press, 1964; rev. ed., 1967.

[32] William W. Freehling. *Prelude to Civil War: The Nullification Controversy in South Carolina, 1816-1836.* New York: Harper & Row, 1966; William R. Taylor. *Cavalier and Yankee: The Old South and American National Character.* New York: G. Braziller, 1961.

[33] Merton L. Dillon has reviewed recent scholarship on the abolitionists more thoroughly than is possible here in "The Abolitionists: A Decade of Historiography, 1959-1969." *Journal of Southern History* 35: 500-522; No. 4, November 1969.

[34] For example, in Arthur M. Schlesinger, Jr. "The Causes of the Civil War: A Note on Historical Sentimentalism." *Partisan Review* 16: 469-481; No. 10, October 1949.

[35] See Bertram Wyatt-Brown. "Abolitionism: Its Meaning for Contemporary American Reform." *Midwest Quarterly* 8: 41-55; No. 1, October 1966.

[36] Martin Duberman, editor. *The Antislavery Vanguard: New Essays on the Abolitionists.* Princeton: Princeton University Press, 1965. The revisionist view of the abolitionists has found an echo in Arnold Whitridge, *No Compromise! The Story of the Fanatics Who Paved the Way to the Civil War,* New York: Farrar, Straus and Cudahy, 1960, but such expressions are now rare. At the same time, it is not to be implied that sympathetic treatments of the abolitionists were unknown in the 1930's. Recent work owes much to the earlier studies of such scholars as Dwight L. Dumond and Gilbert H. Barnes.

[37] Dwight Lowell Dumond. *Antislavery: The Crusade for Freedom in America.* Ann Arbor: University of Michigan Press, 1961. Published at the same time was Dumond's comprehensive *A Bibliography of Antislavery in America.* Ann Arbor: University of Michigan Press, 1961.

[38] Louis Filler. *The Crusade Against Slavery, 1830-1860.* New York: Harper, 1960. A recent study of the movement which views the abolitionists as reformers rather than revolutionaries is Carleton Mabee. *Black Freedom: The Nonviolent Abolitionists from 1830 Through the Civil War.* New York: Macmillan, 1970. For a record of the movement, with few new insights, see Henry H. Simms. *Emotion at High Tide: Abolition as a Controversial Factor, 1830-1845.* Richmond: William Byrd Press, 1960. A useful documentary collection illustrating the variety of antislavery expressions, with an informative introduction, is William H. and Jane H. Pease, editors. *The Antislavery Argument.* Indianapolis: Bobbs-Merrill, 1965.

[39] David Brion Davis. "The Emergence of Immediatism in British and American Antislavery Thought." *Mississippi Valley Historical Review* 49: 209-230; No. 2, September 1962. For a discussion of this shift in reform thought generally, see John L. Thomas. "Romantic Reform in America, 1815-1865." *American Quarterly* 17: 656-681; No. 4, Winter 1965.

[40] Anne C. Loveland. "Evangelicalism and 'Immediate Emancipation' in American Antislavery Thought." *Journal of Southern History* 32: 172-188; No. 2, May

1966; John L. Thomas. "Antislavery and Utopia," in Duberman, editor. *The Anti-slavery Vanguard.* pp. 240-69.

[41] Elkins. *Slavery.* pp. 140-206; Aileen S. Kraditor. *Means and Ends in American Abolitionism: Garrison and His Critics on Strategy and Tactics, 1834-1850.* New York: Pantheon Books, 1969.

[42] David Donald. "Toward a Reconsideration of Abolitionists," in *Lincoln Reconsidered.* Vintage ed., New York: Random House, 1961. pp. 19-36 (quotations from pp. 26, 33, 35, 36). David Brion Davis has written of the abolitionists' use of the conspiracy theme, conjuring up an image of subversion and evil, as "a means of articulating individual and communal anxieties over being duped and slipping behind." *The Slave Power Conspiracy and the Paranoid Style.* Baton Rouge: Louisiana State University Press, 1969. p. 29.

[43] Donald. *Charles Sumner and the Coming of the Civil War.* New York: Knopf, 1960; Louis Ruchames. "The Pulitzer Prize Treatment of Charles Sumner." *Massachusetts Review* 2: 749-769; No. 4, Summer 1961; Paul Goodman. "David Donald's *Charles Sumner* Reconsidered." *New England Quarterly* 37: 373-387; No. 3, September 1964. The reaction to Donald's thesis presents an interesting historiographic problem. Although historians have been admonished to employ the techniques of other disciplines and to account for human motivation, the application of these techniques to the abolitionists was objected to, as Dillon has suggested, as if "to assert that abolitionists were complicated and sometimes humanly flawed was to allege that their cause was in some way unworthy"; in a time of academic activism on racial issues, to question "the motives of earlier reformers was by implication to question one's own." "The Abolitionists: A Decade of Historiography, 1959-1969." *Journal of Southern History* 35: 500-522; No. 4, November 1969. pp. 504-505, 507.

[44] Martin B. Duberman. "The Abolitionists and Psychology." *Journal of Negro History* 47: 183-191; No. 3, July 1962. p. 186; Betty Fladeland. "Who Were the Abolitionists?" *Journal of Negro History* 49: 99-115; No. 2, April 1964. Larry Gara. "Who Was an Abolitionist?" in Duberman, editor. *The Antislavery Vanguard.* pp. 32-51.

[45] Gerald Sorin. *The New York Abolitionists: A Case Study of Political Radicalism.* Westport, Conn.: Greenwood, 1971. p. 119.

[46] Irving H. Bartlett. *Wendell Phillips: Brahmin Radical.* Boston: Beacon Press, 1961; Helen G. Baer. *The Heart Is Like Heaven: The Life of Lydia Maria Child.* Philadelphia: University of Pennsylvania Press, 1964; Milton Meltzer. *Tongue of Flame: The Life of Lydia Maria Child.* New York: Crowell, 1965; Merton L. Dillon. *Elijah P. Lovejoy, Abolitionist Editor.* Urbana: University of Illinois Press, 1961; Tilden G. Edelstein. *Strange Enthusiasm: A Life of Thomas Wentworth Higginson.* New Haven: Yale University Press, 1968; Gerda Lerner. *The Grimké Sisters from South Carolina: Rebels Against Slavery.* Boston: Houghton Mifflin, 1967; Bertram Wyatt-Brown. *Lewis Tappan and the Evangelical War Against Slavery.* Cleveland: Press of Case Western Reserve University, 1969; Merton L. Dillon. *Benjamin Lundy and the Struggle for Negro Freedom.* Urbana: University of Illinois Press, 1966; David L. Smiley. *Lion of White Hall: The Life of Cassius M. Clay.* Madison: University of Wisconsin Press, 1962; Martin B. Duberman, *James Russell Lowell.* Boston: Houghton Mifflin, 1966. A series of short vignettes of New England abolitionists is in Lawrence Lader. *The Bold Brahmins: New England's War Against Slavery, 1831-1863.* New York: Dutton, 1961.

[47] Richard H. Sewell. *John P. Hale and the Politics of Abolition.* Cambridge: Harvard University Press, 1965; Edward Magdol. *Owen Lovejoy: Abolitionist in Congress.* New Brunswick: Rutgers University Press, 1967; Patrick W. Riddleberger. *George Washington Julian, Radical Republican: A Study in Nineteenth-Century Politics and Reform.* Indianapolis: Indiana Historical Bureau, 1966; Hans L. Trefousse. *Benjamin Franklin Wade: Radical Republican from Ohio.* New York: Twayne, 1963; James B. Stewart. *Joshua R. Giddings and the Tactics of Radical Politics.* Cleveland: Press of Case Western Reserve University, 1970;

Donald. *Charles Sumner and the Rights of Man.* New York: Knopf, 1971; Stephen B. Oates. *To Purge This Land With Blood: A Biography of John Brown.* New York: Harper and Row, 1970.

[48] Benjamin Quarles. *Frederick Douglass.* Washington: Associated Publishers, 1948; new ed., Englewood Cliffs, N.J., 1968. *Black Abolitionists.* New York: Oxford University Press, 1969. For an account of the odds against which black abolitionists had to struggle in a movement that was dominated by whites, see Leon F. Litwack. "The Emancipation of the Negro Abolitionist," in Duberman, editor. *The Antislavery Vanguard.* pp. 137-55.

[49] David Alan Williams. "William Lloyd Garrison, the Historians, and the Abolitionist Movement." Essex Institute, *Historical Collections* 98: 84-99; No. 2, April 1962. See also James Brewer Stewart. "Peaceful Hopes and Violent Experiences: The Evolution of Reforming and Radical Abolitionism, 1831-1837." *Civil War History* 17: 293-309; No. 4, December 1971.

[50] Walter M. Merrill. *Against Wind and Tide: A Biography of William Lloyd Garrison.* Cambridge: Harvard University Press, 1963; John L. Thomas. *The Liberator: William Lloyd Garrison, A Biography.* Boston: Little, Brown, 1963. pp. 455-56, 4. See also Louis Filler. "Garrison Again, and Again: A Review Article." *Civil War History* 11: 69-75; No. 1, March 1965.

[51] For Kraditor, see above, footnote 41; Truman J. Nelson, editor. *Documents of Upheaval: Selections from William Lloyd Garrison's "The Liberator," 1831-1865.* New York: Hill and Wang, 1966; Bertram Wyatt-Brown. "William Lloyd Garrison and Antislavery Unity: A Reappraisal." *Civil War History* 13: 5-24; No. 1, March 1967; *The Letters of William Lloyd Garrison.* Cambridge: Harvard University Press, 1971. Vol. I: *I Will Be Heard! 1822-1835,* edited by Walter M. Merrill; Vol. II: *A House Dividing Against Itself, 1836-1840,* edited by Louis Ruchames.

[52] William H. and Jane H. Pease. "Antislavery Ambivalence: Immediatism, Expediency, Race." *American Quarterly* 17: 682-695; No. 4, Winter 1965. p. 695.

[53] Leon F. Litwack. *North of Slavery: The Negro in the Free States, 1790-1860.* Chicago: University of Chicago Press, 1961, and "The Abolitionist Dilemma: The Antislavery Movement and the Northern Negro." *New England Quarterly* 34: 50-73; No. 1, March 1961; Eugene H. Berwanger. *The Frontier Against Slavery: Western Anti-Negro Prejudice and the Slavery Extension Controversy.* Urbana: University of Illinois Press, 1967. For a related study, important but more limited in scope, see Larry Gara's explosion of the myth of the underground railroad. *The Liberty Line: The Legend of the Underground Railroad.* Lexington: University of Kentucky Press, 1961.

[54] Lorman Ratner. *Powder Keg: Northern Opposition to the Antislavery Movement, 1831-1840.* New York: Basic Books, 1968; Leonard L. Richards. *"Gentlemen of Property and Standing": Anti-Abolition Mobs in Jacksonian America.* New York: Oxford University Press, 1970.

[55] Dillon. "The Failure of the American Abolitionists." *Journal of Southern History* 25: 159-177; May 1959. p. 176.

[56] Roy Franklin Nichols. *The Disruption of American Democracy.* New York: Macmillan, 1948.

[57] Joel H. Silbey, editor. *The Transformation of American Politics, 1840-1860.* Englewood Cliffs, N.J.; Prentice-Hall, 1967, and *The Shrine of Party: Congressional Voting Behavior, 1841-1852.* Pittsburgh: University of Pittsburgh Press, 1967; Thomas B. Alexander. *Sectional Stress and Party Strength: A Study of Roll-Call Voting Patterns in the United States House of Representatives, 1836-1860.* Nashville: Vanderbilt University Press, 1967.

[58] For an important interpretation of the ideas and attitudes that lay behind the dramatic national expansion of the 1840's, see Frederick Merk. *Manifest Destiny and Mission in American History: A Reinterpretation.* New York: Knopf, 1963.

See also Norman A. Graebner, editor. *Manifest Destiny*. Indianapolis: Bobbs-Merrill, 1968.

[59] Chaplain W. Morrison. *Democratic Politics and Sectionalism: The Wilmot Proviso Controversy*. Chapel Hill: University of North Carolina Press, 1967; Eric Foner. "The Wilmot Proviso Revisited." *Journal of American History* 56: 262-279; No. 2, September 1969; Kinley J. Brauer. *Cotton versus Conscience: Massachusetts Whig Politics and Southwestern Expansion, 1843-1848*. Lexington:University of Kentucky Press, 1967.

[60] Holman Hamilton. *Prologue to Conflict: The Crisis and Compromise of 1850*. Lexington: University of Kentucky Press, 1964; Robert R. Russel. "What Was the Compromise of 1850?" *Journal of Southern History* 22: 292-309; No. 3, August 1956.

[61] Robert R. Russel. "The Issues in the Congressional Struggle Over the Kansas-Nebraska Bill, 1854." *Journal of Southern History* 29: 187-210; No. 2, May 1963. For an historiographic survey of the act, see Roy F. Nichols. "The Kansas-Nebraska Act: A Century of Historiography." *Mississippi Valley Historical Review* 43: 187-212; No. 2, September 1956.

[62] Eric Foner. *Free Soil, Free Labor, Free Men: The Ideology of the Republican Party Before the Civil War*. New York: Oxford University Press, 1970. p. 309; Michael Fitzgibbon Holt. *Forging a Majority: The Formation of the Republican Party in Pittsburgh, 1848-1860*. New Haven: Yale University Press, 1969.

[63] James A. Rawley. *Race and Politics: "Bleeding Kansas" and the Coming of the Civil War*. Philadelphia: Lippincott, 1969.

[64] Robert R. Russel. "Constitutional Doctrines with Regard to Slavery in the Territories." *Journal of Southern History* 32: 466-486; No. 4, November 1966; Arthur Bestor. "State Sovereignty and Slavery: A Reinterpretation of Proslavery Constitutional Doctrine, 1846-1860." *Journal of the Illinois State Historical Society* 54: 117-180; No. 2, Summer 1961, and "The American Civil War as a Constitutional Crisis." *American Historical Review* 69: 327-352; No. 2, January 1964; Stanley I. Kutler, editor. *The Dred Scott Decision: Law or Politics?* Boston: Houghton Mifflin, 1967.

[65] Paul M. Angle, editor. *Created Equal? The Complete Lincoln-Douglas Debates of 1858*. Chicago: University of Chicago Press, 1958; Harry V. Jaffa. *Crisis of the House Divided: An Interpretation of the Issues in the Lincoln-Douglas Debates*. Garden City: Doubleday, 1959; Don E. Fehrenbacher. *Prelude to Greatness: Lincoln in the 1850's*. Stanford: Stanford University Press, 1962; Richard Allen Heckman. *Lincoln vs. Douglas: The Great Debates Campaign*. Washington: Public Affairs Press, 1967.

[66] Philip S. Klein. *President James Buchanan*. University Park, Pa.: Pennsylvania State University Press, 1962; Albert D. Kirwan. *John J. Crittenden: The Struggle for the Union*. Lexington: University of Kentucky Press, 1962; Gerald M. Capers. *Stephen A. Douglas: Defender of the Union*. Boston: Little, Brown, 1959; Damon Wells. *Stephen Douglas: The Last Years, 1857-1861*. Austin: University of Texas Press, 1971; Glyndon G. Van Deusen. *William Henry Seward*. New York: Oxford University Press, 1967; David Donald. *Charles Sumner and the Coming of the Civil War*. New York: Knopf, 1960; and Walker Lewis. *Without Fear or Favor: A Biography of Chief Justice Roger Brooke Taney*. Boston: Houghton Mifflin, 1965.

[67] Martin B. Duberman. *Charles Francis Adams, 1807-1886*. Boston: Houghton Mifflin, 1961; William E. Parrish. *David Rice Atchison of Missouri, Border Politician*. Columbia, Mo.: University of Missouri Press, 1961; James P. Shenton. *Robert John Walker: A Politician from Jackson to Lincoln*. New York: Columbia University Press, 1961; Charles A. Jellison. *Fessenden of Maine, Civil War Senator*. Syracuse: Syracuse University Press, 1962; Benjamin P. Thomas and Harold M. Hyman. *Stanton: The Life and Times of Lincoln's Secretary of War*. New

York: Knopf, 1962; Hans L. Trefousse. *Benjamin Franklin Wade, Radical Republican from Ohio.* New York: Twayne, 1963; Marvin R. Cain. *Lincoln's Attorney General, Edward Bates of Missouri.* Columbia, Mo.: University of Missouri Press, 1965; Mark M. Krug. *Lyman Trumbull, Conservative Radical.* New York: A. S. Barnes, 1965; Erwin Stanley Bradley. *Simon Cameron, Lincoln's Secretary of War.* Philadelphia: University of Pennsylvania Press, 1966; F. N. Boney. *John Letcher of Virginia.* University, Ala.: University of Alabama Press, 1966; William Y. Thompson. *Robert Toombs of Georgia.* Baton Rouge: Louisiana State University Press, 1966; James E. Hendrickson. *Joe Lane of Oregon: Machine Politics and the Sectional Crisis, 1849-1861.* New Haven: Yale University Press, 1967; and David A. Williams. *David C. Broderick, A Political Portrait.* San Marino, Calif.; Huntington Library, 1969.

[68] For discussions of Lincoln in American historiography, see David M. Potter. "The Lincoln Theme and American National Historiography," in *The South and the Sectional Conflict.* pp. 151-76; Don E. Fehrenbacher. *The Changing Image of Lincoln in American Historiography.* Oxford: Clarendon Press, 1968; and Robert W. Johannsen. "In Search of the Real Lincoln, or Lincoln at the Crossroads." *Journal of the Illinois State Historical Society* 51: 229-247; No. 3, Autumn 1968.

[69] Reinhard H. Luthin. *The Real Abraham Lincoln: A Complete One Volume History of His Life and Times.* Englewood Cliffs, N.J.: Prentice-Hall, 1960; Louis A. Warren. *Lincoln's Youth: Indiana Years, Seven to Twenty-one, 1816-1830.* New York: Appleton-Century-Crofts, 1959; Paul Simon. *Lincoln's Preparation for Greatness: The Illinois Legislative Years.* Norman, Okla.: University of Oklahoma Press, 1965; Donald W. Riddle. *Congressman Abraham Lincoln.* Urbana: University of Illinois Press, 1957; John J. Duff. *A. Lincoln: Prairie Lawyer.* New York: Rinehart, 1960; and John P. Frank. *Lincoln as a Lawyer.* Urbana: University of Illinois Press, 1961.

[70] T. Harry Williams. "Abraham Lincoln: Pragmatic Democrat," in Norman A. Graebner, editor. *The Enduring Lincoln.* Urbana: University of Illinois Press, 1959. pp. 23-46; David Donald. "Abraham Lincoln and the American Pragmatic Tradition," in *Lincoln Reconsidered.* pp. 128-43; Richard N. Current, editor. *The Political Thought of Abraham Lincoln.* Indianapolis: Bobbs-Merrill, 1967; James A. Rawley. "The Nationalism of Abraham Lincoln." *Civil War History* 9: 283-298; No. 3, September 1963; Thomas J. Pressly. "Bullets and Ballots: Lincoln and the 'Right of Revolution.'" *American Historical Review.* 67: 647-662; No. 3, April 1962; Fehrenbacher. *Prelude to Greatness.* p. 161. Current has reviewed what we do not know about Lincoln in *The Lincoln Nobody Knows.* New York: McGraw-Hill, 1958.

[71] For example, Norman A. Graebner, editor. *Politics and the Crisis of 1860.* Urbana: University of Illinois Press, 1961.

[72] David M. Potter. *Lincoln and His Party in the Secession Crisis.* New Haven: Yale University Press, 1942; new ed., 1962; Kenneth M. Stampp. *And the War Came: The North and the Secession Crisis, 1860-1861.* Baton Rouge: Louisiana State University Press, 1950; Steven A. Channing. *Crisis of Fear: Secession in South Carolina.* New York: Simon and Schuster, 1970; George Harmon Knoles, editor. *The Crisis of the Union, 1860-1861.* Baton Rouge: Louisiana State University Press, 1965.

· 16 ·

Civil War and Reconstruction, 1861–1877

Robert F. Durden

THE decade of the 1960's, with its first half filled with accelerating change in the role of black people in American life and its second with angry divisiveness produced by the war in Vietnam, brought some sharp shifts in the thinking and writing of historians of the Civil War era. While interest in and sympathy for the newly freed black men and women of a century ago grew to new heights, a novel and paradoxical element was introduced when a younger and increasingly anti-war generation began to question some of the patriotic and moral certainties of the New Nationalist historians, such as Arthur Schlesinger, Jr., Allan Nevins, and Bruce Catton, who loomed large in the years after World War II. John S. Rosenberg, for example, pointed to the influence of the issues of race and war in the continual reinterpretation of the Civil War and called for a new revisionism, "a new way of *evaluating*" the war, that would be openly presentist in arguing that, contrary to Lincoln's solemn pledge at Gettysburg, "those dead did die in vain."[1]

Such bold questioning of the war that a distinguished novelist, Robert Penn Warren, called the North's "Treasury of Virtue" (and the South's "Great Alibi") may be a harbinger of things to come. The solid, durable achievements of the decade were, nevertheless, in a more traditional vein. David Donald's updating of James G. Randall's *The Civil War and Reconstruction,* especially because of its comprehensive bibliography and extensively revised section on the postwar period, made the volume more than ever an indispensable starting point for any serious student of the era.[2] Another major achievement was the completion by Allan Nevins of his singularly ambitious, eight-volume study of the Civil War, with the last two volumes appearing in the year of his death (1971). Relying on primary sources as well as the vast secondary literature, Nevins developed in his final volumes the theme that the giant scope of the war effort forced American society to transform itself.[3] Nevins also collaborated with James I. Robertson, Jr., and Bell I. Wiley to produce a critical bibliography of some 5,000 items dealing with the Civil War.[4]

A collection of essays written by Avery Craven during a span of almost three decades enabled one to study the evolution in his thinking about the war and particularly showed his growing awareness of the centrality of the slavery question. Collections of essays by William B. Hesseltine, Frank L. Owsley, and David Potter, three outstanding scholars now deceased but whose work continues to be seminal, also appeared.[5]

Though of the older generation in age, Edmund Wilson pungently foreshadowed the new revisionism in *Patriotic Gore: Studies in the Literature of the American Civil War.*[6] Through his disaffection with the United States government and hatred of all wars, Wilson had become, according to one reviewer, a "latter-day Copperhead." But in writing of a rich array of individuals from Grant, Lincoln, and Harriet Beecher Stowe to Alexander Stephens and Mary Boykin Chesnut, Wilson revealed fascinating human and literary dimensions of the era.

The North and the War

Despite the publication of much trivia during the war's centennial years, a vast amount of more significant work appeared. A succinct introduction to the controversial subject of the war's first shot at Fort Sumter was provided by Richard N. Current, while George H. Knoles edited a useful collection of essays in which eight leading scholars presented their distilled views concerning the larger aspects of the secession crisis.[7] Climaxing a lifetime of research on Lincoln, Reinhard H. Luthin published an unusually detailed, one-volume biography that dealt extensively with the political background.[8]

First-rate biographies of Seward and Stanton, the two key members of Lincoln's cabinet, filled important gaps, and a careful editing of the diary of Gideon Welles provided the first complete version of that invaluable source.[9]

With its generally sympathetic approach to the controversial and somewhat enigmatic Stanton, the Thomas-Hyman biography mentioned above was only one of a whole array of studies that presented the Radical wing of the Republican party in a more favorable light. That development meshed with the attempts to define Radical Republicanism with greater precision and to determine just who the Radicals really were. In the second and concluding volume of his prize-winning biography of Charles Sumner, David Donald masterfully painted warts and all in his portrait of a man "great in weaknesses but greater in strength," a consistent champion first for the Negro's freedom and then for his equality. Donald also used a quantitative study of roll-call votes to argue the thesis that the Radicals came from overwhelmingly "safe" Republican districts and that they, as well as Lincoln and other Republican factions, were politicians first and foremost who were controlled by the desire to win reelection rather than by principles or prejudices.[10] Edward L. Gambill employed the technique of Guttman scalogram analysis in an attempt to determine who the Radicals were, and Glenn M. Linden employed roll-call votes to argue that the Radicals as a group did not pursue clear-cut economic policies but, like other senators, tended to vote along geographical or sectional lines.[11]

In addition to questioning the older views of such historians as Howard K. Beale and T. Harry Williams who tended to see the Radicals as more or less cohesive along economic as well as politico-racial lines, newer studies tend to minimize the conflict between President Lincoln and the Radicals. Hans L. Trefousse, for example, in a biography of Senator Ben Wade and in a collective portrait of the Radicals, argued that not only were they "protagonists of democracy" and "friends of the Negro," but that there was a basic unity of purpose and general collaboration between them and the President. Scholarly biographies of other important Republican leaders in Congress, such as William Pitt Fessenden, Lyman Trumbull, and George W. Julian, figured in the more complex and sympathetic approach to the Radicals.[12]

Although certainly not as popular as political history and biography, the economic aspect of the war received fresh attention in the 1960's. In arguing the thesis that the Civil War, contrary to the generally accepted notion, retarded rather than stimulated the North's industrial development, Thomas C. Cochran provoked much lively debate.[13] Paul W. Gates traced agricultural developments during the war; Bray Hammond emphasized the war's centralizing impact on banking and the states; James McCague dealt with a colorful, important episode in railway history; and Leonard P. Curry provided the first concise, congressionally-centered study of a host of important, nonmilitary enactments.[14]

In the realm of intellectual history, perhaps the most important study to appear was that by George M. Frederickson, who showed the impact of the war on the thinking of the anti-institutional reformers such as the Emersonians as well as on certain of their conservative contemporaries. Given the confused, dogmatic, and contradictory responses of the North's intellectual elite, one reviewer suggested that Frederickson's study supported the older thesis that secession and war were indeed the work of a blundering generation who proved unable to understand or cope with a long-simmering crisis that exploded in 1861. On the other hand, Ernest L. Tuveson emphasized the close connection between the Civil War and the widespread popular conviction that the nation had a special "redemptive mission" in the world.[15]

The importance of the Negro, both as an actor in the war and as a subject of controversy, gained increased recognition. Benjamin Quarles carefully traced the changing and sometimes ambiguous relationship of Lincoln and the blacks, while James McPherson demonstrated in one book that the abolitionists continued their crusade for equal rights throughout the war and postwar periods and in another (an unusual and useful collection of documents, well adapted for use by students) that the Negro was a vital participant in the struggle for his freedom.[16]

The Northern white racism that was entangled with the war and its results—a theme that began to receive recognition in the 1950's—received additional emphasis in studies by V. Jacque Voegeli and Forrest G. Wood. Analyzing anthropometric studies made during the war and used subsequently to support discrimination against blacks, John S. Haller pointed to the irony in the fact that the war which freed the slaves also "helped to justify racial attitudes of nineteenth century society."[17] The anti-Negro riots in New York City were described by James McCague, and Eugene C. Murdock explored the workings of the draft and the bounty system.[18]

The Middle Western and Border states have received increased attention. Frank L. Klement showed the economic, political, and racial aspects of Copperheadism and wrote an even-handed study of the war's most famous dissenter, Clement L. Vallandigham. The complex pattern of events in Missouri was examined by William E. Parrish, and Richard O. Curry performed the same task for West Virginia. Among a host of state studies inspired by the observance of the centennial, two outstanding volumes were Emma Lou Thornbrough's book on Indiana and Victor Hicken's on Illinois. Borrowing many techniques from the behavioral sciences, Paul Kleppner argued that religious and ethnic allegiance rather than economic or class ties determined elections in Ohio, Michigan, and Wisconsin.[19]

In the military area of the North at war, Bruce Catton's preëminently readable books continued to loom large and another stylistic master, Shelby Foote, who is also a novelist, published the second volume of his trilogy. Biographies of Generals Thomas (two of him, in fact), Halleck, Meade, and Butler appeared; Ezra J. Warner provided a useful compilation of short biographies of the Union generals; and two able military historians, T. Harry Williams and Warren W. Hassler, Jr., each undertook the task of assessing several Union commanders.[20]

Among individual battles, Gettysburg received significant attention. Edwin B. Coddington treated both sides in the entire campaign with balance and fairness, while Warren W. Hassler, Jr., examined the crucial first day's action in great detail. Publication of the papers of Ulysses S. Grant will enrich Civil War scholarship as will the publication of other such primary sources as the pamphlets edited by Frank Freidel.[21] Collections of stimulating, wide-ranging essays for the general reader as well as the specialists, and treating North and South as well as military and non-military subjects, were edited by David Donald and Grady McWhiney.[22]

The Confederacy

Although many non-military aspects of Confederate history continued to be neglected, historians produced a number of significant works that should help in correcting the balance. Readable, comprehensive introductions to the entire Confederate experience were provided by Charles P. Roland and Frank E. Vandiver. Written with urbanity and fairness, both volumes were useful in the classroom as well as to scholars. Arguing that the exigencies of the war forced Southerners to accept undreamed of centralization as well as other paradoxical changes, Emory M. Thomas interpreted the Confederacy as a "revolutionary experience," while Thomas B. Alexander in an influential article emphasized a certain continuity through the war and postwar periods provided by "persistent Whiggery."[23]

For the secession crisis and first shot in the war, Steven A. Channing's study of the pivotal state, South Carolina, argues convincingly that widespread fear of Republican-inspired slave insurrection or abolition was at the heart of the movement. Ralph A. Wooster used the manuscript population returns of the 1860 census to furnish significant data about the 1,859 individuals who were members of the secession conventions, and Donald E. Reynolds took a close, interpretative look at Southern newspapers in the secession crisis.[24]

Much political and administrative history of the Confederacy has yet to be done, but Wilfred Buck Yearns provided a useful study of the Confederate Congress that may be supplemented by Richard E. Beringer's statistical profile of the congressmen themselves. The writing of the provisional and permanent constitutions of the Confederacy was studied by Charles Robert Lee, Jr., while May Spencer Ringold provided an overall view of the state legislatures during the war.[25]

The trail-blazing researches of Bell I. Wiley into the history of the Negroes in the South during the war have never been adequately followed-up, but James H. Brewer carefully studied the "Confederate Negro" in Virginia with impressive, even if paradoxical, results. Another generally neglected topic has been Confederate journalism, but J. Cutler Andrews thoroughly covered the war-reporting of the Southern newspapers and provided a helpful introduction to the larger topic of the Confederate press as a whole. Hodding Carter, a readable historian and journalist himself, also dealt with the South's wartime newspapers.[26]

Economic and social studies of the Confederacy also lag far behind military works, but Charles B. Dew's solid book on the Tredegar Iron Works in Richmond filled one important gap. Just as Dew's work had larger implications concerning the nature and limitations of the Southern economy, the study of Virginia's wartime railroads by Angus J. Johnston points up the larger weaknesses in Confederate railway policy. The phenomenon of war refugees, so common in European history albeit rather rare in the American experience, was examined by Mary Elizabeth Massey, who also studied the impact of the war upon Southern women. The Civil War experience also loomed largely in Anne Firor Scott's highly interpretative analysis of the myth and reality of the Southern lady.[27]

Good biographies of Confederate leaders appeared in significant number, but the continued lack of a scholarly and balanced study of Jefferson Davis left a large hole in Confederate historiography. The concluding volume of Hudson Strode's trilogy appeared, carrying Davis from the closing phase of the war until his death in 1889; but the author's uncritical approach and failure to organize and analyze marred the ambitious undertaking. More scholarly but sympathetic brief assessments of Davis appeared in the works of Roland and Vandiver mentioned above, and William J. Cooper, Jr., also undertook a partial reassessment of the oft-maligned Confederate President. Although only the first of the projected twenty volumes of the papers of Davis was published, the project promised ultimately to be of vital significance for the overdue full-scale study that is needed. Douglass Southall Freeman painted the definitive, four-volumed military portrait of Robert E. Lee some time ago, but Lee the man continued to interest students of the war. Clifford Dowdey published a readable, one-volume biography of the elusive Virginian, and Marshall W. Fishwick concentrated on Lee in the few but significant years he lived after the war.[28]

Among the civilian leaders of the Confederacy, the North Carolina governor, Zebulon Vance, ranks high in interest and significance. Glenn Tucker wrote a popular biography of Vance and Richard E. Yates a more limited, scholarly study of Vance's complicated relationships with the Confederate government. Biographies of wartime governors of Virginia and Louisiana as well as of the Confederate postmaster general and later Texan political leader, John H. Reagan, also appeared. Joseph H. Parks analyzed in an article the stormy anti-Richmond antics of Georgia's Governor Joseph E. Brown, and Alvy L. King wrote a biography of Louis T. Wigfall, a prominent Texan fire-eater who as a Confederate senator bitterly opposed the Davis Administration.[29]

Concerning the Confederate military leaders, Ezra J. Warner's biographical dictionary of some 425 generals serves all students of the war. Among the studies of individual generals, those dealing with Albert Sidney Johnston, Leonidas Polk, Braxton Bragg, William J. Hardee, Stonewall Jackson, Daniel H. Hill, and Sterling Price are noteworthy.[30]

Thanks to the centennial, a number of studies of states and cities appeared. Monographs focused on the Civil War in Mississippi, North Carolina, Louisiana and Florida; and books dealing with life in Vicksburg, Savannah, Athens (Ga.), New Orleans, and Charleston enriched the social and civilian history of the war. Louis H. Manarin's able editing of the minutes of Richmond's city council made an important source widely available, and the late Rembert Patrick studied the fall of the Confederate capital while Emory M. Thomas wrote its wartime "biography."[31]

Military historians of the Confederacy continued the task of filling in the relatively neglected "western" parts of the picture. Archer Jones defended Jefferson Davis in an original analysis of military operations west of the Alleghenies during the middle phase of the war, and Thomas L. Connelly wrote an impressive, two-volumed study of the ill-fated Army of Tennessee. From an overall viewpoint, Ludwell H. Johnson wrote a spirited critique of some recent themes in Civil War military history; while, with a narrower focus, James I. Robertson, Jr., wrote a complete account of the famed volunteer brigade commanded by Thomas J. Jackson, and Wilbur S. Nye followed the vanguard of Lee's army in its approach to Gettysburg.[32]

Relating to the military aspect, Richard D. Goff published a study of Confederate supply and James L. Nichols of logistics in the Trans-Mississippi department. Tackling an old and sore topic of controversy, Ovid L. Futch produced what some reviewers hailed as the first objective study of Andersonville prison, and Memory F. Mitchell examined one key aspect of conscription in North Carolina. Confederate operations in Canada, the Richmond government's spies, the contraband trade, the flight of certain Confederates to Mexico, and the veterans in gray were subjects of studies that helped to make the Civil War not only the richest area of United States history but surely the most written-about war in history.[33]

Diplomacy and the Naval War

Several important works added knowledge concerning the international aspect of the war. Complementing the careful study of *Great Britain and the American Civil War* that was published by E. D. Adams in 1924, Lynn M. Case and Warren F. Spencer provided a comparable volume on Franco-American relations. Daniel B. Carroll's study of the French ambassador to Washington added another dimension, and Serge Gavronsky showed how French liberals championed the Northern cause as an indirect way of attacking Napoleon III's regime. A group of historians explored the impact of the war in France as well as in Britain, Canada, Latin America, Russia, and Central Europe, while Robin W. Winks explained the especially numerous and often exasperating repercussions in Canada.[34]

Although Joseph M. Hernon, Jr., touched on what he regarded as oversimplifications concerning English opinion, his study concentrates on the Irish response to the war. Martin B. Duberman's prize-winning biography of Charles F. Adams deals extensively with Adams' vital service as the United States' minister to Britain, and John E. Cairnes, author of an influential pro-Northern book published in 1862, was the subject of a monograph. Another and pro-Southern perspective was taken by Viscount Wolsely, while Stuart L. Bernath untangled the diplomatic and legal aspects of the prize cases.[35]

The starting point for the study of Confederate diplomacy remains Frank L. Owsley's *King Cotton Diplomacy*. Charles P. Cullop, however, analyzed the Richmond government's propaganda effort while Henry Blumenthal suggested that over-optimistic Confederates failed to appreciate the importance of foreign aid and "paid dearly for simply ignoring the possibility of non-recognition."[36]

For the naval history of the war, Bern Anderson supplied a one-volume synthesis, and Virgil Carrington Jones completed his trilogy on the subject. William N. Still, Jr., tackled the hitherto-neglected subject of shipbuilding by the Confederacy, and John D. Milligan provided a reliable account of the Union's freshwater navy.[37]

Reconstruction

A decade ago the author of the equivalent portion of a *Yearbook* suggested that "recent publications on the Reconstruction Period seem to be in short supply," but that certainly ceased to be true in the 1960's.

New and challenging studies of the postwar period were even more numerous than for the war itself, and the revisionist interpretation, with its more sympathetic approach to the Radical Republicans and their programs, triumphed in sweeping fashion.

Several revisionist syntheses appeared, with John Hope Franklin's volume leading the way in 1961; it inspired Avery Craven to remark in a review that, "Reconstruction, like death, has lost its sting." Kenneth Stampp followed with a succinct overview that afforded an excellent introduction to perhaps the most controversial topic in American history. The late Rembert W. Patrick authored a longer but balanced study, and Avery Craven, temporarily abandoning his more familiar antebellum terrain, embraced a number of revisionist viewpoints while still refusing to accept the entire canon of the 1960's.[38]

Fuller and more sympathetic treatment of the Negro characterized all of the above volumes, but Lerone Bennett, Jr., a senior editor of *Ebony* magazine, wrote an exaggerated account for a popular audience. A probing and more balanced study, well adapted for use in the classroom, was that by Robert Cruden.[39]

The struggle in the Federal government about the kind of peace that was to be made began long before the war ended. The late William B. Hesseltine tackled the task of analyzing Lincoln's ever-changing policies, and Ludwell H. Johnson closely examined two crucial aspects of the President's program. Two prize-winning studies that bridged the wartime and postwar periods are by Willie Lee Rose and Herman Belz, the former focusing on the South Carolina sea islands and the latter on Lincoln and the Congress with which he had to work.[40]

As important as Lincoln continued to be in the re-examination of Reconstruction, there were more studies that spotlighted Andrew Johnson, generally in a highly unsympathetic manner. In a widely read and influential volume, Eric L. McKitrick pointed to Johnson as bearing the central responsibility for the allegedly unfortunate direction that Reconstruction ultimately took, while LaWanda and John H. Cox also pointed to Johnson's failure to build a political coalition of moderate Republicans and Democrats, a failure they saw as rooted in Johnson's insensitivity toward civil rights and the Negro. An Englishman, W. R. Brock, reinforced the revisionist view of Andrew Johnson but also emphasized weaknesses inherent in the Constitution itself and in a government of checked-and-balanced powers that proved unequal to the crisis.[41]

The Fourteenth Amendment was carefully studied in great detail by Howard Jay Graham in a work that, among other things, should forever lay the ghost of the "conspiratorial" theory about its alleged pro-business origins. William Gillette saw the Fifteenth Amendment as primarily concerned with the politics of Republicans in the North and only secondarily with the South, although LaWanda and John H. Cox dissented from the thesis. Contrary to the prevailing view, Stanley I. Kutler argued that the Supreme Court during the period pursued an independent rather than a subservient course.[42]

A number of scholars, attacking the thesis of Charles A. Beard and his followers, questioned the interpretation of the Radicals as a cohesive faction, especially in economic matters. Robert P. Sharkey and Irwin Unger, for example, emphasized diversity and disunity among both businessmen and politicians. Walter T. K. Nugent concentrated on the complexities of the money question, a chronic albeit ever-changing issue in American history.[43]

Three groups in the South—the Negroes, carpetbaggers, and scalawags —received fresh attention, largely from revisionists. Joel Williamson's careful study of South Carolina's freedmen argued that they met and largely overcame multitudinous problems. A comparable study for Florida was made by Joe M. Richardson, while Oken Edet Uya carefully researched his biography of Robert Smalls, a prominent black leader in South Carolina. Letters written by two Quaker sisters from "contraband camps" were edited by Henry L. Swint, and Theodore B. Wilson wrote the first book-length study of the controversial black codes. Especially valuable and well documented was the massive study of the Ku Klux Klan by Allen W. Trelease.[44]

Prominent among reconsiderations of the carpetbaggers was the work of Richard N. Current, and Jack B. Scroggs gave them much of the credit for "lasting constitutional reforms of a progressive and democratic nature." The biography of Albion W. Tourgée, a novelist and leading carpetbagger in North Carolina, by Otto H. Olsen presents him in a sympathetic light. Olsen also viewed scalawags, and particularly William W. Holden of North Carolina, more favorably, while Allen W. Trelease used statistics and geography to locate the bulk of the white Republicans of the South. One prominent scalawag of Mississippi, James Lusk Alcorn, was portrayed in a scholarly fashion by Lillian A. Pereyra.[45]

Two studies of General Oliver O. Howard, head of the Freedmen's Bureau, present him in a sympathetic light, although the newer one suggests that Howard and the Bureau ultimately "failed the freedmen" largely because most white Americans failed to sympathize with the true aspirations of the Negroes. The Bureau's operation in South Carolina and in Louisiana was the subject of two monographs, and James E. Sefton studied the related but larger subject of the Army's role in Reconstruction.[46]

Well researched, revisionist studies of a number of Southern states are yet to be done, but Alan Conway and then Elizabeth Studley Nathans focused on Georgia. William C. Harris analyzed the first phase of Mississippi Reconstruction, while W. McKee Evans published two monographs that illuminated facets of Reconstruction in North Carolina. The study of Virginia's Conservatives by Jack P. Maddex, Jr., offers a challenging interpretation, but William C. Nunn reflected a now largely outmoded viewpoint in his book on Texas. Richard O. Curry edited a volume of essays that examined the fierce political battles in the Border States, while William E. Parrish concentrated on Missouri in a monograph.[47]

For the South as a whole, the perceptive articles written for the *Nation* immediately after the war by John R. Dennett afford a candid view. Nash K. Burger and John K. Bettersworth portrayed ten prominent ex-Confederate leaders in their postwar roles, while Paul M. Gaston traced the emergence of the New South creed in the years immediately following Appomatox. Despite the tub-thumping for industrialization, Clement Eaton showed that much of the South's antebellum civilization survived the war and Reconstruction. The doctrine of white supremacy, analyzed carefully by Claude H. Nolen and approached in a starkly psychological fashion by Lawrence J. Friedman, would probably have to be recognized as the Old South's primary, and most tragic, legacy to the not-so-New South.[48]

FOOTNOTES

[1] "Toward a New Civil War Revisionism." *American Scholar* 38: 250-272; No. 2, Spring 1969.

[2] Boston: D. C. Heath, 1961.

[3] *The Ordeal of the Union* (Volumes VII and VIII). *The War for the Union: The Organized War, 1863-1864,* and *The War for the Union: The Organized War to Victory, 1864-1865.* New York: Scribner's, 1971.

[4] *Civil War Books: A Critical Bibliography.* Two volumes. Baton Rouge: Louisiana State University Press, 1967, 1969.

[5] Avery Craven. *An Historian and the Civil War.* Chicago: University of Chicago Press, 1964; Richard N. Current, editor. *Sections and Politics: Selected Essays by William B. Hesseltine.* Madison: State Historical Society of Wisconsin, 1968; Harriet C. Owsley. *The South: Old and New Frontiers; Selected Essays of Frank Lawrence Owsley.* Athens: University of Georgia Press, 1969; David Potter. *The South and the Sectional Conflict.* Baton Rouge: Louisiana State University Press, 1968.

[6] New York: Oxford University, 1962.

[7] Richard N. Current. *Lincoln and the First Shot.* New York: J. B. Lippincott, 1963; George H. Knoles, editor. *The Crisis of the Union, 1860-1861.* Baton Rouge: Louisiana State University Press, 1965.

[8] *The Real Abraham Lincoln: A Complete One Volume History of His Life and Times.* Englewood Cliffs, N.J.: Prentice-Hall, 1960. Other significant books touching on Lincoln were Willard L. King, *Lincoln's Manager: David Davis.* Cam-

bridge: Harvard University Press, 1960, which treats the political and judicial career of one of Lincoln's closest advisors, and Dean Sprague, *Freedom Under Lincoln,* Boston: Houghton Mifflin, 1965, which tells how the Lincoln Administration dealt with wartime dissidents. P. J. Staudenraus edited *Mr. Lincoln's Washington: Selections from the Writings of Noah Brooks, Civil War Correspondent.* South Brunswick: Yoseloff, 1967, important newsletters by the correspondent who had the closest journalistic association with Lincoln.

[9] Glyndon G. Van Deusen. *William Henry Seward.* New York: Oxford University Press, 1967; Benjamin P. Thomas and Harold M. Hyman. *Stanton: The Life and Times of Lincoln's Secretary of War.* New York: Knopf, 1962; Howard K. Beale, editor. *Diary of Gideon Welles, Secretary of the Navy under Lincoln and Johnson,* 3 vols. New York: W. W. Norton, 1960. Biographies of two other cabinet members were Marvin R. Cain. *Lincoln's Attorney General: Edward Bates of Missouri.* Columbia: University of Missouri Press, 1965, and Erwin S. Bradley. *Simon Cameron, Lincoln's Secretary of War: A Political Biography.* Philadelphia: University of Pennsylvania Press, 1966. H. Draper Hunt published *Hannibal Hamlin of Maine: Lincoln's First Vice-President,* Syracuse: Syracuse University Press, 1969, inspiring one reviewer to comment that perhaps "historians should simply admit that an inscrutable Providence directs the selection of American Vice-Presidents."

[10] David Donald. *Charles Sumner and the Rights of Man.* New York: Knopf, 1970, and *The Politics of Reconstruction, 1863-1867.* Baton Rouge: Louisiana State University Press, 1965.

[11] Edward L. Gambill. "Who Were the Senate Radicals?" *Civil War History* 11: 237-44; No. 3, September 1965; Glenn M. Linden. " 'Radicals' and Economic Policies: The House of Representatives, 1861-1873." *Civil War History* 13: 51-65; No. 1, March 1967 and " 'Radicals' and Economic Policies: The Senate, 1861-1873." *Journal of Southern History* 32: 189-199; No. 2, May 1966.

[12] Hans L. Trefousse. *Benjamin Franklin Wade: Radical Republican from Ohio.* New York: Twayne, 1963, and *The Radical Republicans: Lincoln's Vanguard for Racial Justice.* New York: Knopf, 1969; Charles A. Jellison. *Fessenden of Maine: Civil War Senator.* Syracuse: Syracuse University Press, 1962; Mark M. Krug. *Lyman Trumbull: Conservative Radical.* New York: A. S. Barnes, 1965; and Patrick W. Riddleberger. *George Washington Julian, Radical Republican: A Study in Nineteenth-Century Politics and Reform.* Indianapolis: Indiana Historical Bureau, 1966. Other relevant biographies were Edward Magdol. *Owen Lovejoy: Abolitionist in Congress.* New Brunswick: Rutgers University Press, 1967; Sister Mary Karl George. *Zachariah Chandler: A Political Biography.* East Lansing: Michigan State University Press, 1969; LeRoy H. Fischer. *Lincoln's Gadfly: Adam Gurowski.* Norman: University of Oklahoma Press, 1964; and Richard H. Abbott. *Cobbler in Congress: The Life of Henry Wilson, 1812-1875.* Lexington: University of Kentucky Press, 1971.

[13] "Did the Civil War Retard Industrialization?" *Mississippi Valley Historical Review* 48: 197-210; No. 2, September 1961. The replies and critiques were too numerous to list here, but a convenient introduction to the debate is Harry N. Scheiber. "Economic Change in the Civil War Era: An Analysis of Recent Studies." *Civil War History* 11: 396-411; No. 4, December 1965.

[14] Paul W. Gates. *Agriculture and the Civil War.* New York: Knopf, 1965; Bray Hammond. *Sovereignty and an Empty Purse: Banks and Politics in the Civil War.* Princeton: Princeton University Press, 1970; James McCague. *Moguls and Iron Men: The Story of the First Transcontinental Railroad.* New York: Harper and Row, 1964; and Leonard P. Curry. *Blueprint for Modern America: Non-military Legislation of the First Civil War Congress.* Nashville: Vanderbilt University Press, 1968.

[15] George M. Frederickson. *The Inner Civil War: Northern Intellectuals and the Crisis of the Union.* New York: Harper and Row, 1965; Ernest L. Tuveson. *Re-*

deemer Nation: The Idea of America's Millennial Role. Chicago: University of Chicago Press, 1968. Allan Nevins, editor. George Templeton Strong. *Diary of the Civil War, 1860-1865.* New York: Macmillan, 1962; Walter Lowenfels, editor. *Walt Whitman's Civil War.* New York: Knopf, 1960; and William Hanchett. *Irish: Charles G. Halpine in Civil War America.* Syracuse: Syracuse University Press, 1970, are other books that deal with intellectual and social aspects.

[16] Benjamin Quarles. *Lincoln and the Negro.* New York: Oxford University Press, 1962; James McPherson. *The Struggle for Equality: Abolitionists and the Negro in the Civil War and Reconstruction.* Princeton: Princeton University Press, 1964, and *The Negro's Civil War: How American Negroes Felt and Acted During the War for the Union.* New York: Pantheon, 1965. John Hope Franklin commemorated the centennial with *The Emancipation Proclamation,* Garden City: Doubleday, 1963, and Tilden G. Edelstein's *Strange Enthusiasm: A Life of Thomas Wentworth Higginson,* New Haven: Yale University Press, 1968, treats a prominent abolitionist who led a Negro regiment in the war. Charles L. Wagandt studied emancipation in a key border state in *The Mighty Revolution: Negro Emancipation in Maryland, 1862-1864,* Baltimore: Johns Hopkins Press, 1964.

[17] Voegeli. *Free but Not Equal: The Midwest and the Negro during the Civil War.* Chicago: University of Chicago Press, 1967; Wood. *Black Scare: The Racist Response to Emancipation and Reconstruction.* Berkeley: University of California Press, 1968; and Haller. "Civil War Anthropometry: The Making of a Racial Ideology." *Civil War History* 16: 309-324; No. 4, December 1970. Haller's *Outcasts from Evolution: Scientific Attitudes of Racial Inferiority, 1859-1900,* Urbana: University of Illinois, 1971, had not appeared in time to be discussed here.

[18] McCague. *The Second Rebellion: The Story of the New York City Draft Riots of 1863.* New York: Dial, 1968, and Murdock. *Patriotism Limited, 1862-1865: The Civil War Draft and the Bounty System.* Kent: Kent State University Press, 1967.

[19] Klement. *The Copperheads in the Middle West.* Chicago: University of Chicago Press, 1960; *The Limits of Dissent: Clement L. Vallandigham and the Civil War.* Lexington: University of Kentucky Press, 1970, and "Midwestern Opposition to Lincoln's Emancipation Policy." *Journal of Negro History* 49: 169-183; No. 3, July 1964. Parrish. *Turbulent Partnership: Missouri and the Union, 1861-1865.* Columbia: University of Missouri, 1963; Curry. *A House Divided: A Study of Statehood Politics and the Copperhead Movement in West Virginia.* Pittsburgh: University of Pittsburgh, 1964; Thornbrough. *Indiana in the Civil War Era, 1850-1880. The History of Indiana.* Vol. III. Indianapolis: Indiana Historical Bureau, 1965; Hicken. *Illinois in the Civil War.* Urbana: University of Illinois, 1966; and Kleppner. *The Cross of Culture: A Social Analysis of Midwestern Politics, 1850-1900.* 2nd ed. New York: Free Press, 1970. A related collection of eleven articles is Frederick C. Luebke, editor. *Ethnic Voters and the Election of Lincoln.* Lincoln: University of Nebraska Press, 1971. Other pertinent biographical studies were: Kenneth W. Wheeler, editor. *For the Union: Ohio Leaders in the Civil War.* Columbus: Ohio State University Press, 1968; James P. Jones. *"Black Jack": John A. Logan and Southern Illinois in the Civil War Era.* Tallahassee: Florida State University Press, 1967; and Irving Katz. *August Belmont: A Political Biography.* New York: Columbia University Press, 1968.

[20] Catton. *Never Call Retreat* (the last of his three-volumed Centennial History). New York: Doubleday, 1965; *Grant Takes Command* (third volume of biography begun by the late Lloyd Lewis). Boston: Little, Brown, 1969; Foote. *The Civil War: A Narrative.* Volume II. *Fredericksburg to Meridian.* New York, Random House, 1963; Francis F. McKinney. *Education in Violence: The Life of George H. Thomas and the History of the Army of the Cumberland.* Detroit: Wayne State University Press, 1961; Wilbur Thomas. *General George H. Thomas, The Indomitable Warrior: A Biography.* New York: Exposition, 1964; Stephen E. Ambrose. *Halleck: Lincoln's Chief of Staff.* Baton Rouge: Louisiana State University

Press, 1962; Freeman Cleaves. *Meade of Gettysburg.* Norman: University of Oklahoma Press, 1960; Richard S. West, Jr. *Lincoln's Scapegoat General: A Life of Benjamin F. Butler, 1818-1893.* Boston: Houghton Mifflin, 1965; Warner. *Generals in Blue: Lives of the Union Commanders.* Baton Rouge: Louisiana State University Press, 1964; Williams. *McClellan, Sherman and Grant.* New Brunswick: Rutgers University Press, 1962, and Hassler. *Commanders of the Army of the Potomac.* Baton Rouge: Louisiana State University Press, 1962.

[21] Coddington. *The Gettysburg Campaign: A Study in Command.* New York: Scribner's, 1968; Hassler. *Crisis at the Crossroads: The First Day at Gettysburg.* University: University of Alabama Press, 1970; John Y. Simon, editor. *The Papers of Ulysses S. Grant.* Vol. II: *April-September 1861.* Carbondale: Southern Illinois University Press, 1969; Friedel, editor. *Union Pamphlets of the Civil War, 1861-1865.* 2 vols. Cambridge: Belknap Press of Harvard University, 1967. Other books of military interest were: T. Harry Williams. *Hayes of the Twenty-Third: The Civil War Volunteer Officer.* New York: Knopf, 1965; Paul E. Steiner. *Disease in the Civil War: Natural Biological Warfare in 1861-1865.* Springfield, Ill.: Charles C Thomas, 1968 and *Medical-Military Portraits of Union and Confederate Generals.* Philadelphia: Whitmore Publishing Co., 1968; Warren Ripley. *Artillery and Ammunition of the Civil War.* New York: Van Nostrand Reinhold, 1970; and Ray C. Colton. *The Civil War in the Western Territories: Arizona, Colorado, New Mexico, and Utah.* Norman: University of Oklahoma Press, 1959.

[22] Donald, editor. *Why the North Won the Civil War.* Baton Rouge: Louisiana State University Press, 1960; McWhiney, editor. *Grant, Lee, Lincoln and the Radicals: Essays on Civil War Leadership.* Evanston: Northwestern University Press, 1964. Another book that students might enjoy is James A. Rawley, *Turning Points of the Civil War.* Lincoln: University of Nebraska Press, 1966.

[23] Roland. *The Confederacy.* Chicago: University of Chicago Press, 1960; Vandiver. *Their Tattered Flags.* New York: Harper and Row, 1970, and also "Some Problems Involved in Writing Confederate History." *Journal of Southern History* 36: 400-410; No. 3, August 1970, for neglected areas of research; Thomas. *The Confederacy as a Revolutionary Experience.* Englewood Cliffs, N.J.: Prentice-Hall, 1971; Alexander. "Persistent Whiggery in the Confederate South, 1860-1877." *Journal of Southern History* 27: 305-329; No. 3, August 1961. Curtis A. Amlund, *Federalism in the Southern Confederacy.* Washington: Public Affairs Press, 1966, also argued that the war forced centralization on the South.

[24] Channing. *Crisis of Fear: Secession in South Carolina.* New York: Simon and Schuster, 1970; Wooster. *The Secession Conventions of the South.* Princeton: Princeton University Press, 1962; Reynolds. *Editors Make War: Southern Newspapers in the Secession Crisis.* Nashville: Vanderbilt University Press, 1970. Interesting studies of the war's beginning were Ludwell H. Johnson, "Fort Sumter and Confederate Diplomacy," *Journal of Southern History* 26: 441-477; No. 4, November 1960, and Grady McWhiney, "The Confederacy's First Shot," *Civil War History* 14: 5-14; No. 1, March 1968.

[25] Yearns. *The Confederate Congress.* Athens: University of Georgia Press, 1960; Richard E. Beringer. "A Profile of the Members of the Confederate Congress." *Journal of Southern History* 33: 518-541; No. 4, November 1967; Lee. *The Confederate Constitutions.* Chapel Hill: University of North Carolina Press, 1963; Ringold. *The Role of the State Legislatures in the Confederacy.* Athens: University of Georgia Press, 1966.

[26] Brewer. *The Confederate Negro: Virginia's Craftsmen and Military Laborers, 1861-1865.* Durham: Duke University Press, 1969; Andrews. *The South Reports the Civil War.* Princeton: Princeton University Press, 1970; Carter. *Their Words Were Bullets: The Southern Press in War, Reconstruction, and Peace.* Athens: University of Georgia Press, 1969.

[27] Dew. *Ironmaker to the Confederacy: Joseph R. Anderson and the Tredegar Iron Works.* New Haven: Yale University Press, 1966; Johnston, *Virginia Rail-*

roads in the Civil War. Chapel Hill: University of North Carolina Press, 1961; Massey. *Refugee Life in the Confederacy.* Baton Rouge: Louisiana State University Press, 1964, and *Bonnet Brigades.* New York: Knopf, 1966; Scott. *The Southern Lady: From Pedestal to Politics, 1830-1930.* Chicago: University of Chicago Press, 1970. Another work that focused on women was H. E. Sterk. *Partners in Rebellion: Alabama Women in the Civil War.* Rutherford, N. J.: Fairleigh Dickinson University Press, 1970. Willard E. Wright, "The Churches and the Confederate Cause," *Civil War History* 6: 361-373; No. 4, December 1960, is a useful introduction to a large topic, and Betsy Fleet and John D. P. Fuller, editors, *Green Mount: A Virginia Plantation Family during the Civil War; Being the Journal of Benjamin Robert Fleet and Letters of His Family,* Lexington: University of Kentucky Press, 1962, is a valuable chronicle.

²⁸ Strode. *Jefferson Davis: Tragic Hero.* New York: Harcourt, Brace, 1964; Cooper. "A Reassessment of Jefferson Davis as War Leader: The Case from Atlanta to Nashville." *Journal of Southern History* 36: 189-204; No. 2, May 1970; Haskell M. Monroe, Jr., and James T. McIntosh, editors. *The Papers of Jefferson Davis,* Vol. I, *1808-1840.* Baton Rouge: Louisiana State University Press, 1971; Dowdey. *Lee.* Boston: Little, Brown, 1965; Fishwick. *Lee After The War.* New York: Dodd, Mead, 1963. For a rare attack on Lee and the rejoinder, see Thomas L. Connelly. "Robert E. Lee and the Western Confederacy: A Criticism of Lee's Strategic Ability," *Civil War History* 15: 116-132; No. 2, June 1969, and Albert Castel. "The Historian and the General: Thomas L. Connelly versus Robert E. Lee." *ibid.,* 16: 50-63; No. 1, March 1970.

²⁹ Tucker. *Zeb Vance: Champion of Personal Freedom.* Indianapolis: Bobbs-Merrill, 1965; Yates. *The Confederacy and Zeb Vance.* Tuscaloosa: Confederate Publishing Company, 1958; F. N. Boney. *John Letcher of Virginia.* University: University of Alabama Press, 1966; Vincent H. Cassidy and Amos E. Simpson. *Henry Watkins Allen of Louisiana.* Baton Rouge: Louisiana State University Press, 1964; Ben H. Procter. *Not Without Honor: The Life of John H. Reagan.* Austin: University of Texas Press, 1962; Parks. "States Rights in a Crisis: Governor Joseph E. Brown versus President Jefferson Davis." *Journal of Southern History* 32: 3-24; No. 1, February, 1966; King. *Louis T. Wigfall: Southern Fireater.* Baton Rouge: Louisiana State University Press, 1970.

³⁰ Warner. *Generals in Gray: Lives of the Confederate Commanders.* Baton Rouge: Louisiana State University Press, 1959; Charles P. Roland. *Albert Sidney Johnston: Soldier of Three Republics.* Austin: University of Texas Press, 1964; Joseph H. Parks. *General Leonidas Polk, C.S.A.: The Fighting Bishop.* Baton Rouge: Louisiana State University Press, 1962; Grady McWhiney. *Braxton Bragg and Confederate Defeat,* Vol. I, *Field Command.* New York: Columbia University Press, 1969; Nathaniel C. Hughes. *General William J. Hardee: Old Reliable.* Baton Rouge: Louisiana State University Press, 1965; Lenoir Chambers. *Stonewall Jackson.* 2 vols.; New York: Wm. Morrow, 1959; Leonard Hal Bridges. *Lee's Maverick General: Daniel Harvey Hill.* New York: McGraw-Hill, 1961; and Albert Castel. *General Sterling Price and the Civil War in the West.* Baton Rouge: Louisiana State University Press, 1968.

³¹ John K. Bettersworth and James W. Silver, editors. *Mississippi in the Confederacy.* 2 vols. Baton Rouge: Louisiana State University Press, 1961; John G. Barrett. *The Civil War in North Carolina.* Chapel Hill: University of North Carolina Press, 1963; John D. Winters. *The Civil War in Louisiana.* Baton Rouge: Louisiana State University Press, 1963; John E. Johns. *Florida during the Civil War.* Gainesville: University of Florida Press, 1963; Peter F. Walker. *Vicksburg: A People at War, 1860-1865.* Chapel Hill: University of North Carolina Press, 1960; A. A. Hoehling, *et al. Vicksburg: Forty-Seven Days of Siege.* Englewood Cliffs, N.J.: Prentice-Hall, 1969; Alexander A. Lawrence. *A Present for Mr. Lincoln: The Story of Savannah from Secession to Sherman.* Macon, Georgia: Ardivan Press, 1961; Kenneth Coleman. *Confederate Athens.* Athens: University of

Georgia Press, 1967; Gerald M. Capers. *Occupied City: New Orleans under the Federals, 1862-1865*. Lexington: University of Kentucky Press, 1965; E. Milby Burton. *The Siege of Charleston, 1861-1865*. Columbia: University of South Carolina Press, 1970; Manarin, editor. *Richmond at War: The Minutes of the City Council, 1861-1865*. Chapel Hill: University of North Carolina Press, 1966; Patrick. *The Fall of Richmond*. Baton Rouge: Louisiana State University Press, 1960; and Thomas. *The Confederate State of Richmond: A Biography of the Capital*. Austin: University of Texas Press, 1971.

[32] Jones. *Confederate Strategy from Shiloh to Vicksburg*. Baton Rouge: Louisiana State University Press, 1961; Connelly. *Army of the Heartland: The Army of Tennessee, 1861-1862*, and *Autumn of Glory: The Army of Tennessee, 1862-1865*. Baton Rouge: Louisiana State University Press, 1967, 1971; Johnson. "Civil War Military History: A Few Revisions in Need of Revising." *Civil War History* 17: 115-130; No. 2, June 1971; Robertson. *The Stonewall Brigade*. Baton Rouge: Louisiana State University Press, 1963; Nye. *Here Come the Rebels!* Baton Rouge: Louisiana State University Press, 1965.

[33] Goff. *Confederate Supply*. Durham: Duke University Press, 1969; Nichols. *The Confederate Quartermaster in the Trans-Mississippi*. Austin: University of Texas Press, 1964; Futch. *History of Andersonville Prison*. Gainesville: University of Florida Press, 1968; Mitchell. *Legal Aspects of Conscription and Exemption in North Carolina, 1861-1865*. Chapel Hill: University of North Carolina Press, 1965; Oscar A. Kinchen. *Confederate Operations in Canada and the North*. North Quincy, Mass.: Christopher Publishing House, 1970; John Bakeless. *Spies of the Confederacy*. Philadelphia: Lippincott, 1970; Ludwell H. Johnson. "Commerce Between Northeastern Ports and the Confederacy, 1861-1865." *Journal of American History* 54: 30-42; No. 1, June 1967; Andrew F. Rolle. *The Lost Cause: The Confederate Exodus to Mexico*. Norman: University of Oklahoma Press, 1965; and William W. White. *The Confederate Veteran*. Tuscaloosa: Confederate Publishing Company, 1962.

[34] Case and Spencer. *The United States and France: Civil War Diplomacy*. Philadelphia: University of Pennsylvania Press, 1970; Carroll. *Henri Mercier and the American Civil War*. Princeton: Princeton University Press, 1971; Gavronsky. *The French Liberal Opposition and the American Civil War*. New York: Humanities Press, 1968; Harold Hyman, editor. *Heard Round the World: The Impact Abroad of the Civil War*. New York: Knopf, 1969; Winks. *Canada and the United States: The Civil War Years*. Baltimore: Johns Hopkins Press, 1960. Two works that reflected current European interest in the Civil War rather than merely in that war's international aspect were by an Italian scholar and a group of Russian historians: Raimondo Luraghi. *Storia della guerra civile americana*. Torino: G. Einaudi, 1966; Ada M. Stoflet, translator. "The Civil War—Russian Version (I): from the Soviet Encyclopedia," and Joseph A. Logsdon. "The Civil War—Russian Version (II): the Soviet Historians." *Civil War History* 8: 357-364, 365-372; No. 4, December 1962.

[35] Hernon. *Celts, Catholics and Copperheads: Ireland Views the American Civil War*. Columbus: Ohio State University Press, 1968; Duberman. *Charles Francis Adams, 1807-1886*. Boston: Houghton Mifflin, 1961; Adelaide Weinberg. *John Elliot Cairnes and the American Civil War: A Study in Anglo-American Relations*. London: Kingswood Press, 1970; James A. Rawley, editor. Field Marshal Viscount Wolseley. *The American Civil War: An English View*. Charlottesville: University of Virginia Press, 1964; Bernath. *Squall Across the Atlantic: American Civil War Prize Cases and Diplomacy*. Berkeley: University of California Press, 1970.

[36] Cullop. *Confederate Propaganda in Europe: 1861-1865*. Coral Gables: University of Miami, 1969; Blumenthal. "Confederate Diplomacy: Popular Notions and International Realities." *Journal of Southern History* 32: 151-171; No. 2, May 1966.

[37] Anderson. *By Sea and by River: The Naval History of the Civil War.* New York: Knopf, 1962; Jones. *The Civil War at Sea, July 1863-November 1865: The Final Effort.* New York: Holt, Rinehart, Winston, 1962; Still. *Confederate Shipbuilding.* Athens: University of Georgia Press, 1969; Milligan. *Gunboats Down the Mississippi.* Annapolis: U.S. Naval Institute, 1965. Other related studies were: Frank J. Merli. *Great Britain and the Confederate Navy, 1861-1865.* Bloomington: Indiana University Press, 1970; Frank L. Owsley, Jr. *The C.S.S. Florida: Her Building and Operations.* Philadelphia: University of Pennsylvania Press, 1965; Milton F. Perry. *Infernal Machines: The Story of Confederate Submarine and Mine Warfare.* Baton Rouge: Louisiana State University Press, 1965; William N. Still, Jr. *Iron Afloat: The Story of the Confederate Armorclads.* Nashville: Vanderbilt University Press, 1971; Edward W. Sloan, III. *Benjamin Franklin Isherwood, Naval Engineer: The Years as Engineer in Chief, 1861-1869.* Annapolis: U. S. Naval Institute, 1965; and James M. Merrill. *Battle Flags South: The Story of Civil War Navies on Western Waters.* Rutherford, N.J.: Fairleigh Dickinson University Press, 1970.

[38] Franklin. *Reconstruction: After the Civil War.* Chicago: University of Chicago Press, 1961; Stampp. *The Era of Reconstruction, 1865-1877.* New York: Knopf, 1965, and for a perceptive review that warned today's historians about allowing their own equalitarian ideology to warp their history, as white supremacist attitudes did that of the "Dunning school," see Thomas J. Pressly. "Racial Attitudes, Scholarship, and Reconstruction: A Review Essay." *Journal of Southern History* 32: 88-93; No. 1, February 1966; Patrick. *The Reconstruction of the Nation.* New York: Oxford University Press, 1967; Craven. *Reconstruction: The Ending of the Civil War.* New York: Holt, Rinehart, and Winston, 1969.

[39] Bennett. *Black Power, U.S.A.: The Human Side of Reconstruction, 1867-1877.* Chicago: Johnson Publishing Company, 1967; Cruden. *The Negro in Reconstruction.* Englewood Cliffs, N.J.; Prentice-Hall, 1969. Convenient collections of essays, the first two revisionist in tone and the third illustrating older viewpoints, were: Harold M. Hyman, editor. *New Frontiers of the American Reconstruction.* Urbana: University of Illinois Press, 1966; Kenneth Stampp and Leon Litwack, editors. *Reconstruction: An Anthology of Revisionist Writings.* Baton Rouge: Louisiana State University Press, 1969; and Richard N. Current, editor. *Reconstruction in Retrospect: Views from the Turn of the Century.* Baton Rouge: Louisiana State University Press, 1969. Useful historiographical essays were by Larry Kincaid, "Victims of Circumstance: An Interpretation of Changing Attitudes Toward Republican Policy Makers and Reconstruction," *Journal of American History* 57: 48-66; No. 1, June 1970, and Richard O. Curry, "The Abolitionists and Reconstruction: A Critical Appraisal," *Journal of Southern History* 34: 527-545; No. 4, November 1968. A leading spokesman for the "New Left," Staughton Lynd, commented on a number of the newer studies in "Rethinking Slavery and Reconstruction," *Journal of Negro History* 50: 198-209; No. 3, July 1965.

[40] Hesseltine. *Lincoln's Plan of Reconstruction.* Tuscaloosa: Confederate Publishing House, 1960; Johnson. "Lincoln's Solution to the Problem of Peace Terms, 1864-1865." *Journal of Southern History* 34: 576-586; No. 4, November 1968, and "Lincoln and Equal Rights: The Authenticity of the Wadsworth Letter." *Journal of Southern History* 32: 83-87; No. 1, February 1966; for Harold M. Hyman's critique of the last-mentioned article and Johnson's reply, see *Civil War History* 12: 258-266; No. 3, September 1966 and *ibid.* 13: 66-73; No. 1, March 1967; Rose. *Rehearsal for Reconstruction: The Port Royal Experiment.* Indianapolis: Bobbs-Merrill, 1964; Belz. *Reconstructing the Union: Theory and Policy during the Civil War.* Ithaca: Cornell University Press, 1969.

[41] McKitrick. *Andrew Johnson and Reconstruction.* Chicago: University of Chicago Press, 1960; Cox and Cox. *Politics, Principle, and Prejudice, 1865-1866: Dilemma of Reconstruction America.* New York: Free Press of Glencoe, 1963; Brock. *An American Crisis: Congress and Reconstruction, 1865-1867.* New York:

St. Martin's Press, 1963. Robert V. P. Steele, under the pen name of "Lately Thomas," published a readable but undocumented biography, *The First President Johnson: The Three Lives of the Seventeenth President of the United States of America.* New York: William Morrow, 1968.

[42] Graham. *Everyman's Constitution: Historical Essays on the Fourteenth Amendment, the "Conspiracy Theory," and American Constitutionalism.* Madison: State Historical Society of Wisconsin, 1968; Gillette. *The Right to Vote: Politics and the Passage of the Fifteenth Amendment.* Baltimore: Johns Hopkins Press, 1965; Cox and Cox. "Negro Suffrage and Republican Politics: The Problem of Motivation in Reconstruction Historiography." *Journal of Southern History* 33: 303-330; No. 3, August 1967; Kutler. *Judicial Power and Reconstruction Politics.* Chicago: University of Chicago Press, 1968.

[43] Sharkey. *Money, Class and Party: An Economic Study of the Civil War and Reconstruction.* Baltimore: Johns Hopkins Press, 1959; Unger. *The Greenback Era: A Social and Political History of American Finance, 1865-1879.* Princeton: Princeton University Press, 1964; Nugent. *The Money Question During Reconstruction.* New York: W. W. Norton, 1967, and *Money and American Society, 1865-1880.* New York: Free Press, 1968. Other related studies were: David Montgomery. *Beyond Equality: Labor and the Radical Republicans, 1862-1872.* New York: Knopf, 1967; Peter Kolchin. "The Business Press and Reconstruction, 1865-1868." *Journal of Southern History* 33: 183-196; No. 2, May 1967; Glenn M. Linden. " 'Radical' Political and Economic Policies: The Senate, 1873-1877." *Civil War History* 14: 240-249; No. 3, September 1968; and Matthew T. Downey. "Horace Greeley and the Politicians: The Liberal Republican Convention in 1872." *Journal of American History* 53: 727-750; No. 4, March 1967.

[44] Williamson. *After Slavery: The Negro in South Carolina During Reconstruction, 1861-1877.* Chapel Hill: University of North Carolina Press, 1965; Richardson. *The Negro in the Reconstruction of Florida, 1865-1877.* Tallahassee: Florida State University Press, 1965; Uya. *From Slavery to Public Service: Robert Smalls, 1839-1915.* New York: Oxford University Press, 1971; Swint, editor. *Dear Ones at Home: Letters from Contraband Camps.* Nashville: Vanderbilt University Press, 1966; Wilson. *The Black Codes of the South.* University: University of Alabama Press, 1965; Trelease. *White Terror: The Ku Klux Klan Conspiracy and Southern Reconstruction.* N. Y.: Harper & Row, 1971. Related studies were: August Meier. "Negroes in the First and Second Reconstructions of the South." *Civil War History* 13: 114-130; No. 2, June 1967; E. Merton Coulter. *Negro Legislators in Georgia During the Reconstruction Period.* Athens: Georgia Historical Quarterly, 1968; and John Hope Franklin, editor. *Reminiscences of An Active Life: The Autobiography of John Ray Lynch.* Chicago: University of Chicago Press, 1970.

[45] Current. "Carpetbaggers Reconsidered," in D. H. Pinkney and Theodore Ropp, editors. *A Festschrift for Frederick B. Artz.* Durham: Duke University Press, 1964, and *Three Carpetbag Governors.* Baton Rouge: Louisiana State University Press, 1967; Scroggs. "Carpetbagger Constitutional Reform in the South Atlantic, 1867-1868." *Journal of Southern History* 27: 475-493; No. 4, November 1961; Olsen. *Carpetbagger's Crusade: The Life of Albion Winegar Tourgée.* Baltimore: Johns Hopkins Press, 1965; Olsen. "Reconsidering the Scalawags." *Civil War History* 12: 304-320; No. 4, December 1966; Trelease. "Who Were the Scalawags?" *Journal of Southern History* 29: 445-468; No. 4, November 1963; Pereyra. *James Lusk Alcorn: Persistent Whig.* Baton Rouge: Louisiana State University Press, 1966.

Other biographies of the period were: Richard L. Zuber. *Jonathan Worth: A Biography of a Southern Unionist.* Chapel Hill: University of North Carolina Press, 1965; John L. Waller. *Colossal Hamilton of Texas: A Biography of Andrew Jackson Hamilton, Militant Unionist and Reconstruction Governor.* El Paso: Texas Western Press, 1968; Norma L. Peterson. *Freedom and Franchise: The Political Career of B. Gratz Brown.* Columbia: University of Missouri Press, 1965; Ross A.

Webb. *Benjamin Helm Bristow: Border State Politician.* Lexington: University of Kentucky Press, 1969; David M. Abshire. *The South Rejects a Prophet: The Life of Senator D. M. Key, 1824-1900.* New York: Praeger, 1967.

[46] John A. Carpenter. *Sword and Olive Branch: Oliver Otis Howard.* Pittsburgh: University of Pittsburgh Press, 1964; William S. McFeely. *Yankee Stepfather: General O. O. Howard and the Freedmen.* New Haven: Yale University Press, 1968; Martin Abbott. *The Freedmen's Bureau in South Carolina, 1865-1872.* Chapel Hill: University of North Carolina Press, 1967; Howard A. White. *The Freedmen's Bureau in Louisiana.* Baton Rouge: Louisiana State University Press, 1970; Sefton. *The United States Army and Reconstruction, 1865-1877.* Baton Rouge: Louisiana State University Press, 1967. Related studies were: Carol K. R. Bleser. *The Promised Land: The History of the South Carolina Land Commission, 1869-1890.* Columbia: University of South Carolina Press, 1969; Christine Bolt. *The Anti-Slavery Movement and Reconstruction: A Study in Anglo-American Cooperation, 1833-1877.* New York: Oxford University Press, 1969; John V. Bratcher, translator and editor. "A Soviet Historian Looks at Reconstruction." *Civil War History* 15: 257-264; No. 3, September 1969.

[47] Conway. *The Reconstruction of Georgia.* Minneapolis: University of Minnesota Press, 1966; Nathans. *Losing the Peace: Georgia Republicans and Reconstruction, 1865-1871.* Baton Rouge: Louisiana State University Press, 1968; Harris. *Presidential Reconstruction in Mississippi.* Baton Rouge: Louisiana State University Press, 1967; Evans. *Ballots and Fence Rails: Reconstruction on the Lower Cape Fear.* Chapel Hill: University of North Carolina Press, 1967, and *To Die Game: The Story of the Lowry Band, Indian Guerrillas of Reconstruction.* Baton Rouge: Louisiana State University Press, 1971; Maddex. *The Virginia Conservatives, 1867-1879: A Study in Reconstruction Politics.* Chapel Hill: University of North Carolina Press, 1970; Nunn. *Texas under the Carpetbaggers.* Austin: University of Texas Press, 1962; Curry, editor. *Radicalism, Racism, and Party Realignment: The Border States during Reconstruction.* Baltimore: Johns Hopkins Press, 1969; Parrish. *Missouri under Radical Rule, 1865-1870.* Columbia: University of Missouri, 1965. Among related works were: James H. Whyte. *The Uncivil War: Washington during the Reconstruction, 1865-1878.* New York: Twayne, 1958, and Louis R. Harlan. "Desegregation in New Orleans Public Schools During Reconstruction." *American Historical Review* 67: 663-675; No. 3, April 1962. Two studies of Northern states in the period were: Erwin S. Bradley. *The Triumph of Militant Republicanism: A Study of Pennsylvania and Presidential Politics, 1860-1872.* Philadelphia: University of Pennsylvania Press, 1964 and Felice A. Bonadio. *North of Reconstruction: Ohio Politics, 1865-1870.* New York: New York University Press, 1970.

[48] Henry M. Christman, editor. Dennett. *The South As It Is, 1865-1866.* New York: Viking, 1965; Burger and Bettersworth. *South of Appomatox,* New York: Harcourt, Brace, 1959; Gaston. *The New South Creed: A Study in Southern Mythmaking.* New York: Knopf, 1970; Eaton. *The Waning of the Old South Civilization, 1860's-1880's.* Athens: University of Georgia Press, 1968; Nolen. *The Negro's Image in the South: The Anatomy of White Supremacy.* Lexington: University of Kentucky Press, 1967; Friedman. *The White Savage: Racial Fantasies in the Postbellum South.* Englewood Cliffs, N.J.: Prentice-Hall, 1970.

· 17 ·

Politics
from Reconstruction to 1900

Walter T. K. Nugent

I. The Knowledge Explosion and Gilded Age History

IN HIS widely-read textbook on American diplomacy, Thomas A. Bailey dubbed the 1870's and 1880's the "nadir period" in foreign policy, a time when events were few, and almost none were memorable. The same term could be applied to domestic politics between Reconstruction and the Spanish-American War, and most non-professionals would not demur. Though the late nineteenth century was crucial to America's development into an urban, industrial, affluent society, the politics of that time has been, though gaudy and grimy, of little consequence to the present-day student. The short and often diminishing time allotted in primary and secondary schools to the search for a usable past seems better spent in considering events that were stark, epochal, and/or urgent, such as the Revolution, the Civil War, Reconstruction, industrialization, the changing position (from prone to semi-erect) of minorities. Who cares whether so-and-so was a Stalwart or a Half-Breed? Why bother to learn the pressures behind Congress' mandates to the Treasury about silver purchases in 1878, 1890, and 1893? And who needs to know about the Mugwumps other than as original exemplars of "a fellow who sits on a fence, with his mug on one side and his wump on the other"?

But before we write the obituary of late nineteenth-century politics as a topic worthy of serious concern any more, we should consider a few points. One is the need to scrutinize the oft-repeated statement of James Lord Bryce, the English commentator on American institutions who came to be regarded as the Gilded Age's answer to Tocqueville, to the effect that the difference between the Republicans and Democrats was no more than that between "Tweedledum and Tweedledee." Bryce's observations were occasionally astute, but seldom less so than in that instance. Republican and Democratic politics from the seventies through the nineties, at least prior to the Bryan-McKinley campaign of 1896, were indeed criticized even in 1972 for not coming to grips with "the real issues," meaning social and economic change. But that criticism requires the definition of the importance of issues by hindsight rather than on the period's own terms; it must assume that national issues were the key determinants of national political behavior in elections—an assumption almost certainly more true after 1930 than in 1870-1900; it must ignore late nineteenth-century Americans' obviously deep concern with party politics; and it must forget that the fundamental political act of voting was practiced among those eligible much more often in the Gilded Age than it has been since 1900, especially during the progressive era and the twenties. In short, politics in the late nineteenth century may have failed to deal with the "real issues" as we may define them, but the facts of voter participation alone show conclusively that politics and partisanship made an immense difference to the people of the time. And it is with them, not abstractions, that historians must deal.

Since 1959, historians have increasingly tried to resolve the apparent contradiction between a politics seemingly devoid of substance, and a politics of intense contemporaneous concern. To judge by the quantity of their efforts, interest in that politics has also increased substantially. A reasonably inclusive list of books and articles on late nineteenth-century politics, those dealt with in the previous survey of this kind and those published between 1959 and 1971,[1] reveals a breadth and depth of scholarship which cannot be explained simply by the greater availability of research grants and the greater affluence of scholarly publishers during the 1960's. Any list almost inevitably involves some arbitrariness, but if we attempt to include all books and articles published in that period which impinge on national parties or issues to any significant degree, omitting only items of purely local or antiquarian interest, we can arrive at a fairly clear idea of the recent concerns and findings of historians.

Quantitatively the results of such a listing are quite clear. Excluding books about Reconstruction, McKinley-era imperialism, and other foreign policy, all discussed elsewhere in this book, the list includes 31 books published prior to 1940; 18 published in 1940 through 1949; and 34 published in 1950 through 1958. Most, but by no means all, of these have been superseded in method, sources used, and findings by books published from 1959 through 1971. In those years, 74 books of significance about Gilded-Age politics and issues appeared: 20 in 1959-63, 16 in 1964-67, and a very hefty 38 in 1968-71. A roughly similar upward curve could be plotted for significant articles in scholarly journals. Some of the articles, and many of the books, which appeared after the mid-1960's have a freshness of approach, method, and results which set them off from earlier scholarship for more reasons than their mere newness; in other words, there is more to be said in 1972 about the publications of the last four or five years than there was to be said in, say, 1967 about the publications of the half-decade immediately before then.

II. General Trends, 1959-1971

Several characteristics distinguish the scholarship of the last dozen years from that which preceded it, quite aside from specific results. The following seem to be the main ones:

1. "Progressive" history is dead, and middle-class bias is dying. Unlike certain other major areas in American historiography, the Gilded Age was not visited to 1971 by the New Left; Irwin Unger's commentary in 1967 on "The 'New Left' and American History: Some Recent Trends in United States Historiography" included virtually no references to it. With two exceptions—Kolko's *Railroads and Regulation 1877-1916,* whose New Leftism is apparent in the conclusion that railroad regulation was a joint effort by the railroads and government to protect capitalist industry from "the attacks of a potentially democratic society," and Pollack's *Populist Response to Industrial America,* which attempts to find in Populism a radical critique, paralleling Marxism at points, of American industrial capitalism—historians did not find historical roots for late-1960's radicalism in Gilded Age politics. Yet the "progressive" interpretation of the period, which regarded its politics as a series of manipulations by spoilsmen and corruptionists often enleagued with growing corporate monopolies to plunder labor and farmers—or, put differently, the struggle (unsuccessful before the progressive era) of the downtrodden to end exploitation by Bourbons and bosses—no longer prevails. Perhaps the most explicit statement of the "progressive" interpretation was Merrill's *Bourbon Democracy of the Middle West* (1953); the Bourbon Democrats are defined as "a cabal of industrialist-financier entrepreneurs operating within the Democratic party . . . [whose] task was to occupy the only really vulnerable outpost in the political-economic empire of big business, the discontented agrarian Middle West," and who were defeated within the Democratic party by Bryan's nomination in 1896. Though Bryan lost the election, "In the Progressive Movement, the New Freedom, and the New Deal, liberal leaders utilized the experience of 1896 as an invaluable guide." Justice triumphed, though it took a while. Thus the progressives and New Dealish historians of the 1940's and 1950's did manage to find a "usable past" in Gilded Age politics, while one eluded the New Leftists in the 1960's.[2]

Like progressivism itself, "progressive" history came in different flavors. One of these carried a strong dash of Marxian rhetoric, especially in Matthew Josephson's *The Politicos* (1938), whose vast mine of information overflows and survives its constricting framework.[3] This kind of Old Left, "progressive" history had no scholarly descendants in the 1960's. Another kind, more in the "respectable" mainstream, magnified the importance of middle-class non-partisan reformers such as the Liberal Republicans, civil service reformers, Mugwumps, Clevelandites, and anti-imperialists, since it seemed easy and valuable to regard them as progenitors of twentieth-century liberalism.

Historians of the 1960's took pains to amputate any progressive or middle-class appendages from their work. To give a few examples: Hoogenboom's history of federal civil service reform describes the reformers as men with large axes to grind, and by no means the disinterested altruists they and their later apologists made them out. Decker's analysis of the politics of railroad land grants strenuously avoids any heroes vs. villains polarity. Even more trenchantly, Yearley's discussion of the parallels between legal public finance (i.e., taxation) and extralegal public finance (i.e., the fund-raising devices of political-party organizations) represents each as derived from the values and aims of very different people devoted to the control of government for their respective ends.[4]

2. *Economic self-interest, and "national issues" involving it, are much less often assumed to have been prime motivators in politics.* The dominant practice in American historiography, inspired by Charles A. Beard, has been to assume that political actions—lobbying, legislating, voting, or whatever—were motivated by economic self-seeking. There have been many roots, varieties, and degrees of economic interpretation, much of it fruitful and necessary, just as Beard's *An Economic Interpretation of the Constitution* was in 1913. Indeed few in the 1970's would, or should, say that economic motivation in political history can be ignored. Unfortunately, many historians have ignored any other kind of motivation, while never demonstrating empirically (which they almost certainly could not do) that economic motivation is universally valid or even exclusively valid in given cases. They have also assumed implicitly that people voted or otherwise acted politically with near-perfect perception of what their self-interest was.

Combined with this has been another unproved assumption: that people agreed that the important issues were the ones which national leaders or platforms said were important. Hence we have been told, for example, that the voters elected Harrison in 1888 because they feared the results of Cleveland's low-tariff stand, and then that the overwhelming Democratic congressional victory of 1890 resulted from dislike of the Republicans' high-protectionist McKinley tariff of that year. One cannot have it both ways. Also, the Omaha platform of 1892 has often been represented as the thinking of all Populists; it was not. All of these assumptions have now been challenged, and the likelihood raised that other motivating forces operated besides economic gain. As Garraty put it, "The safest generalization that can be made about political alignments [in the 1880's], aside from the obvious sectional division, is that party preferences were more influenced by family tradition, religion, and local issues of the moment than by the policies or pronouncements of statesmen and their organizations." And Kleppner, quantitatively and convincingly, denied that the single variable of economic class was even particularly useful in explaining voting behavior; instead, religion, ethnic group, and personal value systems consistently affected voting patterns. This finding, Kleppner wrote, "suggests that the human actors of the era did not share the later historian's evaluations of 'real' and 'non-real' issues." Recent historians of the Farmers' Alliance and Populism have continued to stress economic factors, but not without due care; and as Kleppner wisely pointed out, "Ethnic and religious conflicts do *not* at all times and places have political salience. It is of no analytical value to substitute a brand of ethnocultural determinism for the economic determinism that currently permeates American political historiography."[5]

In general, dualistic frameworks have given way to pluralistic frameworks. The demise of progressive historiography has involved discussing events as the product of a multiplicity of social and political groups, not simply exploiters vs. exploited or some such dualism, and such groups have come to include ethnic, religious, ideological, and other kinds besides economic ones.

3. Newer studies are briefer, less narrative, more social-scientific. The typical scholarly book published in the 1960's on Gilded-Age politics contained a text of around 250 pages; seldom did newer books approach the bulk of Allan Nevins' *Cleveland* or Josephson's 708 pages. While the overall organization of most of the literature was chronological rather than topical, it was not narrative, in the sense of blow-by-blow activities of leaders, as often as it was analytical, in the sense of sorting out the actions of groups. Political historians have long borrowed concepts and methods from political scientists, and historical studies involving voting analysis predate the computer, as did Roscoe Martin's book on Texas Populism (1933) or Knoles' on the 1892 election (1942). But a wholly new level of statistical sophistication began to appear in the late 1960's, notably in works by Hackney, Kleppner, Luebke, Rogin, and Jensen, involving precise correlations of multiple variables over time.[6] This trend will almost certainly grow.

4. *A wider definition and use of "primary sources" is emerging.* While most monographic studies continued to utilize traditional kinds of appropriate sources such as manuscripts, newspapers, government documents, and almanacs, some historians have looked to other kinds of past remains, certainly beyond the papers which happen to repose in the Manuscripts Division of the Library of Congress. Benson pioneered in the use of papers and proceedings of trade, labor, and farm organizations and groups; many historians, often aided by the computer's capacity to store, manipulate, and relate large masses of data, have used precinct-level voting returns, state and federal manuscript censuses, legislative roll calls, and local land and tax records; Lawrence Goodwyn reconstructed an episode in Texas Populism in large part through oral tradition.[7]

5. *Biography has become less common, state histories more common.* For decades Gilded Age historians have studied microcosms, either individuals or localized problems, with the hope of illumining large aspects of the period. Prior to the 1960's they often did so by writing the "lives and times" of nationally prominent individuals, and by a conservative count about three dozen such biographies remain part of the useful literature, published as far back as Barnes' laudable *Carlisle* (1931) or before.[8] Between 1959 and 1971, however, about half as many appeared.[9] On the other hand, perhaps 16 state or regional studies which bear significantly on national history were published prior to 1959, and upwards of twice as many between then and 1971. And the later state studies superseded earlier ones in subtlety and thoroughness in many more instances than the later biographies superseded the earlier ones.[10] This trend away from biography and toward state studies underscores the desire of recent historians to deal with groups rather than individuals, followership as well as leadership, and behavior rather than rhetoric—i.e., the search for what people did rather than what they said they were doing.

6. *A minor revival of institutional history is appearing.* American historians' concern with the development of social and political institutions began with Frederick Jackson Turner, if not before, but like so many of Turner's methodological contributions it fell into desuetude during the 1940's and 1950's. Pomeroy's pathfinding *The Territories*

and the United States 1861-1890 was one of the few to appear, and remains an excellent if too-brief examination of "the administrative conditions of the units which framed the frontier West." The best-known work in this category published in the 1950's is Leonard White's *The Republican Era 1869-1901,* valuable for its detail on the operations of most important federal agencies, but it suffers from a bloodlessness consequent on its ignoring of practical politics, its insensitivity to chronological change, and its political-scientist author's unfamiliarity with important aspects of the historical context. If histories of pressure groups are included here, one must mention Mary Dearing's rather discursive treatment of the Grand Army of the Republic(an party).[11] A reinvigoration of institutional history began in 1966 with the publication of Rothman's *Politics and Power,* which analyzes, in part by quantitative career-line analysis, the personnel and operations of the U.S. Senate. In 1970 Yearley's monumental study of the changing philosophy and practice of taxation and party finance appeared; so did Robert D. Marcus' history of the Republican National Committee and G.O.P. organization (he concluded that there was very little in 1880 and not much more in 1896, despite Mark Hanna's fame as an organizer). Three books do not make a trend, but perhaps they make the start of one.[12]

7. *Historians are increasingly attentive to the social bases of politics (or, from Rhodes to Reality in Gilded-Age surveys).* Once upon a time, history was past politics, and politics meant, rather exclusively, the comings and goings of presidents, members of Congress, other leading statesmen, and the "great national issues" they talked about. This narrowness characterized many of the otherwise impeccable biographies and monographs published before 1960, as well as general surveys from the time of Rhodes (1919) until very recently. Rhodes confined himself to past politics in the strict sense, except for a few sniffish pages on labor troubles and immigration. His Republican-manufacturer bias, perhaps understandable in a brother-in-law of Mark Hanna,[13] led him to a kind of slack-jawed admiration for Hayes' veto of Bland-Allison, a justification of the execution of the Haymarket anarchists, and such imbalances as spending 14 pages on the Republican convention of 1880, one-half page on the Democratic. Rhodes' book is valueless today, but his biases, both substantive and methodological, infected many a textbook writer and, presumably, students, until tempered by the publication of Josephson's popular *The Politicos* nearly twenty years later. Josephson had his own quite contrasting viewpoint, now obsolete and mistaken in stressing a class-sectional interpretation of politics and on such points as regarding the electorate "indifferent" to the party battles of the 1880's,

but his concern for party organization and the richness of his coverage of people and issues afford the book a degree of utility.[14]

Several general surveys of the Gilded Age or its politics have appeared since Josephson's. Some show almost no methodological innovation. The two volumes on the period in the New American Nation series are only partly devoted to politics, but despite their concerns with economics, society, and thought, they fail to integrate politics with those other areas; the book on the 1880's makes the traditional assumption that the major parties did not deal with "real issues" and left them to the later progressives. Another survey covering 1877 to 1914 devotes a chapter to "The Politics of Complacency," and though long on color, it is short on analysis.[15] A lengthy treatment of Gilded Age politics by Wayne Morgan, published in 1969, is one of the most conservative, and both in concerns and attitude is reminiscent of Rhodes.[16] Though it makes a stab at "relevance"—"Tariff protection, free silver, and civil service reform only sound archaic. As reciprocity, inflation, and bureaucracy they are very much alive"—it is foiled in that attempt by centering almost exclusively on presidents, elections, and the machinations of party leaders. It errs in regarding 1876-1896 as a Republican era (belied by the voting returns, which were closer in presidential elections than in any other period, and which favored the Democrats in 8 of 12 congressional elections); as a time when the national G.O.P. gained "coherent national form and direction" (disproved by Marcus' *Grand Old Party*); and when "Republicans learned to unify, organize, and harmonize diverse followers with issues like tariff protection, federal economic regulation, and the currency" (though local and non-economic issues and attitudes were critical in most times and places, as Kleppner and Luebke showed). Despite a mass of detail about leaders, there is little concern with patronage, organizational problems, economic or ethnic-religious groups, sectional or state peculiarities, issues such as prohibition and woman suffrage, or why voting preferences shifted; there is hardly a trace of behaviorism or quantification. Morgan's book suffers from no lack of diligence, and surely he intended it to contain and omit the things it did; but while it would have been especially valuable in 1959, its omissions made it out-of-date with newer trends in 1969, when it was published.

Two other surveys of the period, Samuel P. Hays' *The Response to Industrialism 1885-1914,* and Robert H. Wiebe's *The Search for Order 1877-1920*, deal with more than the Gilded Age and more than politics. But each of them[17] integrated the principal political trends into general social history. Wiebe's general proposition—that American society, a miscellany of discrete local communities in the 1870's, sought and failed to find cohesion by the 1890's, and fell into a profound divisive crisis solved at the expense of pervasive bureaucratization in the progressive era—and his many second-order conclusions supporting that idea are as provocative as any existing treatment. From the perspective of early 1972, it appears that if, among regional studies, Benson's *Merchants, Farmers and Railroads* (1955) was the first of a new history, and Merrill's *Bourbon Democracy of the Middle West* (1953) the last of an old, then among general surveys Morgan's is the last of the old, and Wiebe's and Hays' the first of the new.[18]

Wiebe's influence operates not only through *The Search for Order,* but also his teaching; he was *doktorvater* for the study which became Marcus' *Grand Old Party.* C. Vann Woodward and David Donald have been exceptionally influential as graduate teachers, but much of the push in the 1960's toward behaviorism, quantification, and social-political history came from Hays and Lee Benson, as teachers and as essayists, particularly in the Benson items already mentioned and in Hays' "The Social Analysis of American Political History 1880-1920."[19] Concern with the social bases of politics has appeared not only in Kleppner and Luebke, whose books are explicitly Hays-Bensonite, but in such diverse places as, notably, Degler's refreshing "American Political Parties and the Rise of the City" (1964), Moger's *Virginia: Bourbonism to Byrd 1870-1925* (1968), Hackney on Alabama, and Hair's *Bourbonism and Agrarian Protest: Louisiana Politics 1877-1900* (1971).[20]

III. Specific Issues and Events

So much for recent historians' approaches; now for their findings.

1. The Money Question, Greenbackism, and Pre-Populist Radicals. Teachers of American history have for years pulled up short when they arrived in their courses at Populism and agrarian radicalism, because they encountered in their path the bimetallic barrier of the money question. It had to be dealt with somehow, if "1896 and all that" was to be made understandable; but they could neither ignore nor circumvent nor penetrate it. In the 1960's, however, the amalgam of gold, silver, bonds, bimetallism, specie resumption, and greenbacks had been melted down. Unger's *The Greenback Era* refined the economic and political origins of the money question in the 1870's, and Nugent's *Money and American Society 1865-1880* assayed the social and ideological group involvements with monetary policy as well as the connections between monetary problems in America and western European countries. In another essay, Nugent discussed the beginnings of the money question in the late 60's through to its reemergence and resolution in the mid-90's.[21]

To these authors, the apparently quixotic concern of greenbackers and Populists—and labor, merchants, bankers, manufacturers, Northeastern editors and pundits, clergy, miners, and of course politicians—with grains of silver and numbers of circulating greenbacks lay in the close connection of money and banking with ideas and rhetoric about political economy, and therefore with public morals: the money question was always a *moral* question.

Despite recent warnings by Formisano and Shade about the imprecision of the term "agrarian radicalism," unrest did exist among Grangers, greenbackers, and other agrarians, and after all, more than half the labor force were farmers until well into the 70's. Shannon's *Farmer's Last Frontier* is still useful on the Grange and Alliance, though Buck's *Granger Movement* is not, and one is better advised to read regional studies such as Saloutos' *Farmer Movements in the South* or state studies such as Scott's *Agrarian Movement in Illinois* on Grangers, or Moger's or Pulley's histories of Virginia on the Readjuster movement of William Mahone.[22]

2. Civil Service Reform and the Three Unmemorable Presidents. From the late 60's through the Liberal Republican bubble of 1872 onward into the days of Hayes, Garfield, and Arthur, civil service reform was a lively issue. That it was not just a matter of "righteousness," as Rhodes was content to see it, but rather a matter affecting its genteel advocates, the chieftains of state and local political machines, and presumably those who held patronage jobs (a sizable group yet to be heard from), is now evident, thanks in largest measure to Ari Hoogenboom's *Outlawing the Spoils.* This book disagreed with Josephson's contention that the civil service reformers were businessmen seeking to control politicians; some of the reformers were businessmen, but more were high-status professionals. Concerning the final passage of civil service reform in the Pendleton Act of 1883, Hoogenboom recognized the impetus of Garfield's assassination, and also the Republicans' desire to freeze their cohorts into jobs they might lose, but for a civil service shelter, in the 1884 election.[23]

The other events of political note between 1877 and 1885 were the whimpering end of Reconstruction, still best told in Woodward's graceful *Reunion and Reaction;* the Bland-Allison act and specie resumption, ending the first stage of the money question as an issue, and best read of in books on that subject; and the vigorous but now virtually inconsequential political infighting between Half-Breeds and Stalwarts in 1880, adequately reflected in Taylor's *Garfield,* Jordan's *Conkling,* and (best because it draws many conclusions about Republican organization) Marcus' *Grand Old Party.* The national Republicans' dismal efforts to build a base among Southern whites (Hayes by favoring Bourbons, Garfield and Arthur by favoring Independents and Readjusters) and thus abandon the freedmen (to the dismay of the Grant-Radical-Stalwart faction, regarded by progressive historians as malodorous) were intelligently reviewed by DeSantis and Hirshson.[24]

Links did exist between the Liberal Republicans of 1872, the Half-Breeds of 1880 and after, the Mugwump bolters of 1884, and the Republican anti-imperialists of 1898-1900. These connections have been discussed in Tomsich's *A Genteel Endeavor,* Welch's *George Frisbie Hoar and the Half-Breeds,* and Beisner's *Twelve Against Empire.*[25]

3. *Cleveland, Harrison, and the Tariff.* The portrait of Grover Cleveland as an honest, decisive negativist has been reinforced by recent scholarship. Cleveland's first term, and to a slightly lesser extent Harrison's term, were preëminently responsible for earning the period its "politics of equilibrium" and "where-were-the-real-issues" reputation, and if one sticks to the non-achievements of these presidents and their congresses one can quarrel little with it. Democratic infighting has been explored by Garraty, Nevins in *Grover Cleveland,* and Barnes in *John G. Carlisle,* and more recently in Bass' biography of David B. Hill; Sievers' biography of Harrison discusses Republican vicissitudes, as does Marcus with a sharp eye on the politician-plutocrat connection. The interdependence in 1890 of the McKinley tariff, the Sherman Anti-Trust Act, the Sherman Silver Purchase Act, and the Lodge "force bill" on Negro suffrage is perhaps best read of in Morgan's *From Hayes to McKinley.* But for a convincing analysis of what gripped the voters in 1890 and 1892, see Kleppner's *Cross of Culture.*[26]

4. *Government Institutions, and the Regulation of Business.* Several institutional histories have already been mentioned (II.6 above). Because historians are increasingly discovering that many railroad and other corporate actions once charged off to villainy were really the product of flaws in administration, administrative and regulatory history are now closely intertwined. A first-rate keynote essay on why federal policy toward business was so lax and inefficient (focussing on railroad land grants but carrying general implications) is Farnham's "The Weakened Spring of Government"; Decker's *Railroads, Lands, and Politics* is another useful exploration. The Grangers' anti-monopoly battle now appears less a matter of heroic rhetoric and more one of practical interest combining not only farmers but various kinds of urban businessmen, thanks to Benson's *Merchants, Farmers and Railroads,* and Harold D. Woodman's "Chicago Businessmen and the Granger Laws." On the multiple forces behind the creation of the Interstate

Commerce Act, Purcell's "Ideas and Interests" discounts ideology and stresses self-interest (though it disagrees with Kolko that the railroads favored the Act), and Neilson's biography of Senator Shelby Cullom provides legislative history.[27]

5. *State and Regional histories: the South.* The South had more scholarly attention than any subject in this period except Populism. This focus is not surprising, given the importance and fascination of the reversal of Reconstruction, the fate of the freedmen, the creation of the Democratic "Solid South," Southern Populism, and the pimply adolescence of Jim Crow. One book, Woodward's *Origins of the New South 1877-1913,* dealt with all of this and more. Revisions of it in the twenty years since its publicity were surprisingly minor for a book of such scope. But it has been added to in significant ways, especially by state histories, of which about a dozen appeared between 1959 and 1971. Collectively they provide much new material on the Bourbon regimes (and tend to revise Woodward's *Origins* somewhat, by restoring that term), on their opponents (frequently agrarians), and on the precarious political position of Southern blacks. Outstanding among these histories are Cooper on South Carolina, especially informative on the Wade Hampton redeemers, and asserting that Tillmanism arose from sectional and factional, not class, conflicts; Bleser's study of freedman resettlement in South Carolina, also good on the Hampton-to-Tillman story; Hair's vigorous and penetrating dissection Louisiana's Byzantine politics; and Maddex's *Virginia Conservatives,* which succeeds best of all in getting inside the minds and motives of the Bourbons.[28] Several other books, notably by Barr on Texas, Moger on Virginia, Pulley on Virginia, and Hackney on Alabama, not only illumine Bourbon days but also address themselves with much success to the problem, highly significant for national politics, of Populist/progressive continuity and the pre-1900 roots of Southern progressivism. All, in varying contexts, find the two great reform movements discontinuous in most important respects.[29]

These books also deal with the political position of Negroes. On that subject the brief modern classic is Woodward's *Strange Career of Jim Crow,* showing that legal segregation and disfranchisement occurred not during the Bourbon regimes but afterwards. For an interesting "control" study of Negroes in politics, since it deals with a non-Confederate and hence non-Reconstructed state which once permitted slavery, see Calcott's *The Negro in Maryland Politics 1870-1912.*[30] Useful historical material remains in Key's *Southern Politics.* On agrarianism, Saloutos' *Farmer Movements in the South* is comprehensive, while Kirwan's *Revolt of the Rednecks* and Rogers' *The One-Gallused*

Rebellion, a book with more detail on certain points than Hackney's and a bit more sympathetic to Populist efforts among Negro voters, examine two black-belt states.[31]

6. *State and Regional Histories: the Midwest and West.* Histories of Midwestern states written between 1959 and 1971 are much scarcer than of Southern ones, and most concentrate on Populism. Of the regional histories, Nye's *Midwestern Progressive Politics* focusses on reform movements, especially after 1900, and Merrill's *Bourbon Democracy* is severely vitiated by its bluntly polar, exploiters-victims framework. But Midwestern political history is now graced by Kleppner's *Cross of Culture,* an intensive local-level study of voting patterns, which finds among many other things that ethnic-cultural issues such as prohibition, woman suffrage, Sunday closing laws, and nativist public school laws affected voters much more than "great national issues" like the McKinley tariff. Basing his research on Wisconsin, Michigan, and Ohio, and correlating voting with occupation, ethnicity, rural-urban differences, and wealth, Kleppner found that Republicans and reform parties tended to attract "pietists," i.e., the more evangelical people whether native or immigrant, and the Democrats tended to attract "ritualists." The distinction is not universal, is probably better put as a continuum than as a polarity, and needs refinement, but Kleppner's contribution to understanding the roots of political behavior is undoubtedly a major one.[32]

Farther west, Pomeroy began the intelligent study of the territories, and was followed by Lamar's excellent *Dakota Territory,* Gould's careful, clear *Wyoming* (both of which examine extensively the socioeconomic bases of politics), and Eblen's quantitative study of territorial governors. Glass on Nevada, Beckett on Washington, and Tutorow's biography of Leland Stanford are useful, while Rogin's work on California in the Populist period is methodologically elegant.[33]

7. *Other Regional, State, and Local Studies.* New England, home of genteel reformers, Stalwarts, and many immigrants, had a political history as complicated as any in the Gilded Age, and much of it still (as of 1972) needs to be written. The genteel group, however, has received capable treatment in Mann's *Yankee Reformers in an Urban Age,* from Tomsich's collective biography of the small, precious group of important opinion leaders, and in Welch's able biography of Senator Hoar.[34] Blake McKelvey's compendium of urban phenomena includes material on politics, and several older books reveal, with varying degrees of hilarity, the operations of city bosses. Two recent biographies of urban politicians, Holli's on Hazen Pingree of Detroit and Zane Miller's *Boss Cox's Cincinnati,* not only depict their "heroes" but explain how and why

machines ran, and were even, in significant ways, instruments of reform for otherwise unrepresented citizens.[35]

8. Populism. Populism's historiography has been as turbulent in its way as its history. First it was seen as a chapter in the history of liberalism, a forerunner of progressivism, an expression of frontier individualism and democracy, in the still basic *Populist Revolt* of John D. Hicks and the several state-level studies which appeared prior to 1940.[36] Then, in the 50's, as McCarthyism produced severe doubts in the minds of intellectuals about ultra-democratic movements, and questions about their historical roots, and as historians began to look at progressivism and the New Deal with glasses less rose-colored than before, Populism was suddenly portrayed as a retrograde, nativistic, provincial, anti-Semitic, even proto-fascist and hysterical episode. Several non-historians were unrestrained in expressing this viewpoint, but it also appeared, with important qualifications but thus all the more convincingly to readers, in Richard Hofstadter's *The Age of Reform: From Bryan to F.D.R.*

In another historiographic turnabout, a more realistic and essentially more favorable view began to appear, first in essays, then in scholarly books and articles.[37] Two essays critical of *The Age of Reform* appeared in 1959, a graceful one by Woodward drawing on data from Southern Populism, and a more strident one by Norman Pollack disputing Hofstadter's research design. Beginning in 1962, when Pollack's *Populist Response to Industrial America* constructed a quasi-Marxist radical ideology from scattered Midwestern Populist sources, and in 1963 when Nugent's *The Tolerant Populists* disagreed with the revisionists of the 50's and asserted that Populism in Kansas was a rational, legitimate political response to economic distress, scholarship on Populism proceeded voluminously and unanimously to reject the revisionists of the 50's. It examined what the Populists did, not just what they said, and who they were, in detail, and generally refurbished them—neither as heroes nor villains, but rather, as Hackney described the Alabama Populists, "neither backward-looking nor revolutionary [but] merely provincial."[38]

In several studies, scholars delved into the social and economic characteristics of Populists in Kansas, Nebraska, Alabama, and elsewhere, and found (1) that they were a rural lower-middle class pushed uncomfortably close to tenancy by real economic problems, especially mortgage burdens and transportation costs which were high relative to the prices they received for their produce; (2) that for reasons sometimes of humanitarianism, sometimes of political expediency, they courted (with varying success) Negro votes in the South and immigrant votes in the Midwest; (3) that they were not completely free of xenophobia, anti-Semitism, or racism, but were less infected than their non-Populist contemporaries; (4) that their rhetoric was eclectic and unoriginal; (5) that they failed in their economic objectives because accidents, divisive non-economic issues such as race, prohibition, and woman suffrage, and lack of skilled leadership kept them from political power.[39]

The role of Populism in the Bryan-McKinley campaign of 1896, explaining the decision to fuse with the Democrats, is the subject of Durden's *Climax of Populism*. Several other studies of the 1896 election, some of which also deal with why the Democrats failed to become the nation's majority party despite the favorable augury of the 1890 election, and why the Republicans did win majority status, now exist. Many other books and articles relating to Populism, together with their conclusions, could be mentioned; space limitations forbid. The subject will undoubtedly continue to attract scholarly attention.[40]

9. Negroes and Politics. Despite the limited success of Populists in seeking and getting Negro votes, the net effect of Populism on Southern Negro voting, in the opinion of recent scholars, was to frighten many white Democrats into seeking disfranchisement of Negroes (and often many poorer whites) by law or constitutional amendment. As Barr put it, regarding Texas, "The impulse toward white men's associations or white primaries became statewide in the 1890's when growing Populist strength split the white vote and made it possible for a Negro minority to swing an election"; and as Hair explained, the Louisiana Populists were never divided and dispersed by the race issue, but were simply counted out, and then the black component was disfranchised in 1896-98.[41] The story varied in detail from state to state, but the alleged corruptibility of Negro voters (still a point of departure in books such as Rice's *Negro in Texas,* and, in view of Goodwyn's "Populist Dreams and Negro Rights," yet to be proved conclusively or even probably), their dalliance with Bourbons as in the case of the Cuney Republicans in Texas or, more often, with Populism or other agrarian movements, and their general good sense in recognizing that the "white power structure" offered them few goodies, is well summarized by Hackney: "Progressives and other white Alabamians eliminated the theft of Negro votes by eliminating Negro voting."[42] Judging from the mass of newer state-level studies, Negro voters generally had a very clear view of how best to vote in their own interests, whether in post-Reconstruction Virginia with the Mahone Readjusters (see Moger), or in Louisiana at the time of the Exodusters (see Hair), or in South Carolina (see Bleser) in the 80's, or in Texas during Populist days (see Goodwyn).[43]

10. Shifting National Party Balances. The history of the national parties, as institutions, and the great change in national politics from a period of tight balance between the major parties (1874-1893) to one of Republican dominance (1894-1928) have received considerable recent comment. Marcus and Kleppner assert persuasively that the apparent issue-less-ness of the 1880's cloaked a fine realization by both major parties that (1) specific ethnic and local voting groups were attached to them, (2) if a party brought out a critical issue or a charismatic leader it would disturb such attachments and hurt itself (as indeed happened in a minor way when the Republicans nominated Blaine in 1884 and in a major way when the Democrats nominated Bryan in 1896), and (3) after 1890 neither party could count as before on its constituent voting groups, not just because of hard times, but also because of the emergence of issues affecting group sensitivity (liquor, woman suffrage, public schools) and because the national Democratic party was split first by Cleveland who was too pro-Eastern, then by Bryan who was too pro-Western.

Thus the 1890's emerge as a pivotal decade in American politics, as in society and culture. Populism thus becomes one factor among several in making it so, since it helped indirectly to produce such phenomena as disfranchisement in the South, the weakening of the Democracy in the demographically and economically dominant Northeast, and the solidification of the Republican party both as the protector of large-scale capitalism and as "the party of energy and change."[44]

11. Progressivism's Roots (or Lack of Them) in the Gilded Age. Contrary to Hicks' view that progressivism was a lineal descendant of Populism, and despite William Allen White's quip that Theodore Roosevelt caught Bryan in swimming and stole all his clothes except "the frayed underdrawers of free silver," recent scholarship claims almost unanimously that the Populists and the progressives were different people using different means to arrive at different social ends. Hackney's conclusion about Alabama could stand as the rough truth for a number of states in the South and elsewhere: "The Progressive movement . . . was a loose federation of the leadership and membership of different associations and informal groups interested in short-term reform. . . . Populism was a protest of the alienated against the established community, and the Progressives were the true spokesmen for the local community against the forces linking Alabama to the outside world: the low-down thieving Yankees and their tyrannical railroads." In the Northeast, according to recent studies, much social legislation of a progressive kind appeared in cities and states during the 90's, thanks to leaders and groups unconnected to agrarianism but rather to urban political blocs of varying status and ethnicity—sometimes immigrant groups, sometimes descendants of the Half-Breeds.[45]

The politics of the Gilded Age, then, has begun to come into its own as a subject of study, not just as a rude precursor of "modern reform," but as a set of events which transfixed millions of people for a generation. We still need to ask why and how, but if the next decade of historiography is as freshly productive as the last, we may have good answers.

FOOTNOTES

[1] Robert F. Durden. "Politics in the Gilded Age, 1877-1896." *Interpreting and Teaching American History*. Thirty-first Yearbook. Washington, D.C.: National Council for the Social Studies, 1961. pp. 180-97. The present chapter will refer to many books, but to few journal articles—not for any lack of them (there are scores) but because of (1) the abundance of books deserving comment, (2) the tendency of the significant content of articles to appear later in books, (3) the inaccessibility of many journals to teachers, and (4) the insignificant content of many articles.

[2] Unger, in *American Historical Review* 72: 1237-63; No. 4, July 1967; Gabriel Kolko. *Railroads and Regulation 1877-1916*. Princeton: Princeton University Press, 1965, esp. p. 239; Norman Pollack. *The Populist Response to Industrial America: Midwestern Populist Thought*. Cambridge: Harvard University Press, 1962; Horace S. Merrill. *Bourbon Democracy of the Middle West 1865-1896*. Baton Rouge: Louisiana State University Press, 1953, esp. pp. 2, 272-273.

[3] Matthew Josephson. *The Politicos 1865-1896*. New York: Harcourt, Brace & World, 1938; for examples of Marxian rhetoric see esp. pp. 50, 258, 479.

[4] Leslie E. Decker. *Railroads, Lands, and Politics: The Taxation of the Railroad Land Grants, 1864-1897*. American History Research Center. Providence: Brown University Press, 1964; Ari Hoogenboom. *Outlawing the Spoils: A History of the Civil Service Reform Movement 1865-1883*. Urbana: University of Illinois Press, 1961; Clifton K. Yearley. *The Money Machines: The Breakdown and Reform of Governmental and Party Finance in the North, 1860-1920*. Albany: State University of New York Press, 1970.

[5] John A. Garraty. *The New Commonwealth 1877-1890*. New York: Harper & Row, 1968, esp. p. 238; Paul Kleppner. *The Cross of Culture: A Social Analysis of Midwestern Politics 1850-1900*. New York: The Free Press, 1970, esp. pp. 34, 100-01. Other efforts to recognize non-economic motivation include two books on the origins of the money question: Walter T. K. Nugent. *Money and American Society 1865-1880*. New York: The Free Press, 1968, and Irwin Unger. *The Greenback Era: A Social and Political History of American Finance 1865-1879*. Princeton: Princeton University Press, 1964. Robert L. Beisner's *Twelve Against Empire: The Anti-Imperialists, 1898-1900*. New York: McGraw-Hill Book Company, 1968, which found the anti-imperialists' objections were "constitutional, economic, moral, racial, political, and historical," p. 216; Robert D. Marcus' *Grand Old Party: Political Structure in the Gilded Age 1880-1896*. New York: Oxford University Press, 1971, and William J. Cooper, Jr.'s *The Conservative Regime: South Carolina 1877-1890*. Baltimore: Johns Hopkins Press, 1968, which explain the events they are concerned with on grounds of sheer factional advantage; and Wallace Farnham's "The Weakened Spring of Government: A Study in Nineteenth-Century American History." *American Historical Review* 68: 662-80; No. 3, April 1963, which suggests that failures of federal regulation stemmed not from exploitation or some such thing but from an explicit commitment to *laissez faire*—what might be called a positive belief in inactivity.

[6] Allan Nevins. *Grover Cleveland: A Study in Courage.* New York: Dodd, Mead, 1933; Josephson. *op. cit.* Also, Roscoe Martin. *The People's Party in Texas: A Study in Third Party Politics.* Austin: The University of Texas Bulletin [Bureau of Research in the Social Sciences, Study no. 4], 1933; George Harmon Knoles. *The Presidential Campaign and Election of 1892.* Stanford: Stanford University Press, 1942. Lee Benson made methodological contributions of exceptional influence in his *The Concept of Jacksonian Democracy: New York as a Test Case.* Princeton: Princeton University Press, 1961; "Research Problems in American Political Historiography," in Mirra Komarovsky, editor. *Common Frontiers of the Social Sciences.* Glencoe: The Free Press, 1957. pp. 113-83, and *Merchants, Farmers and Railroads: Railroad Regulation and New York Politics 1850-1887.* Cambridge: Harvard University Press, 1955. Also, Sheldon Hackney. *Populism to Progressivism in Alabama.* Princeton: Princeton University Press, 1969, using Pearson product moment coefficients; Kleppner. *op. cit.*; Frederick C. Leubke. *Immigrants and Politics: The Germans of Nebraska 1880-1900.* Lincoln: University of Nebraska Press, 1969, using Spearman's rho. Richard Jensen. *The Winning of the Midwest: Social and Political Conflict, 1888-1896.* Chicago: University of Chicago Press, 1971, was not available to me prior to the deadline for this chapter, but it is inconceivable in view of his many other contributions (esp. Charles M. Dollar and Richard J. Jensen. *Historian's Guide to Statistics.* New York: Holt, Rinehart & Winston, 1971.) that it does not rely on quantitative methods.

[7] Benson. *Merchants, Farmers and Railroads. op. cit.*; see in particular the methodological notes and appendices in Hackney, Kleppner, and Luebke. *op. cit.* Also, Lawrence C. Goodwyn. "Populist Dreams and Negro Rights: East Texas as a Case Study." *American Historical Review* 76: 1435-56; No. 5, December 1971.

[8] These are cited in Durden's essay in the 1961 NCSS Yearbook, *loc. cit.*; they include biographies of William B. Allison (by Sage), Altgeld (Barnard, Ginger), Arthur (Howe), Bellamy (Morgan), Blaine (Muzzey), Bryan (Werner, Hibben), Carlisle (Barnes), William E. Chandler (Richardson), Cleveland (Merrill, Nevins), Debs (Ginger), Stephen B. Elkins (Lambert), Hamilton Fish and U.S. Grant (Nevins), Foraker (Wolters), Garfield (Caldwell), Henry George (Barker), A. P. Gorman (Lambert), Wade Hampton (Jarrell), Hanna (Croly), Benjamin Harrison (Sievers, vol. I), Hayes (Barnard), Abram Hewitt (Nevins), Kasson (Younger), Plunkitt (Riordan), L. L. Polk (Noblin), "Czar" Reed (Robinson), Philetus Sawyer (Current), Schurz (Fuess), Tillman (Simkins), Tom Watson (Woodward), Watterson (Wall), Whitney (Hirsch), and W. L. Wilson (Summers).

[9] These include several articles on Chester A. Arthur by Thomas C. Reeves: *Historian* 31: 573-582; No. 4, August 1969; *Political Science Quarterly* 84: 628-637; No. 4, December 1969; *Vermont History* 38: 177-188; No. 3, Summer 1970; *New-York Historical Society Quarterly* 54: 319-337; No. 4, October 1970; on William Jennings Bryan, an interesting sketch by Paul W. Glad, *The Trumpet Soundeth: William Jennings Bryan and His Democracy 1896-1912.* Lincoln: University of Nebraska Press, 1960, and the full-scale biography by Paolo E. Coletta, *William Jennings Bryan.* Lincoln: University of Nebraska Press, [3 vols.], 1964-1969; David M. Jordan. *Roscoe Conkling of New York: Voice in the Senate.* Ithaca: Cornell University Press, 1971, a lengthy and interesting treatment of the master spoilsman; David Lindsey. *"Sunset" Cox, Irrepressible Democrat.* Detroit: Wayne State University Press, 1959; James Neilson. *Shelby M. Cullom, Prairie State Republican.* Urbana: University of Illinois Press, 1962; Stanley P. Hirshson. *Grenville M. Dodge, Soldier, Politician, Railroad Pioneer.* Bloomington: Indiana University Press, 1967; Martin Ridge. *Ignatius Donnelly.* Chicago: University of Chicago Press, 1962, now a standard on Midwestern Populism; John M. Taylor. *Garfield of Ohio: The Available Man.* New York: W. W. Norton, 1970, essentially a trade book; Steven B. Cord. *Henry George: Dreamer or Realist?* Philadelphia: University of Pennsylvania Press, 1965; John A. Carpenter. *Ulysses S. Grant.* New York: Twayne Publishers, 1970, which is brief and more sympathetic than

Nevins' biography; Harry J. Sievers. *Benjamin Harrison*, vols. 2 and 3. Indianapolis: Bobbs-Merrill, 1968, which is a humane treatment of the man whom an associate said had a personality like a "dripping cave"; Herbert J. Bass. *"I Am a Democrat": The Political Career of David Bennett Hill*. Syracuse: Syracuse University Press, 1961, on the machine Democrat who almost overthrew Cleveland in his own state; Richard E. Welch, Jr. *George Frisbie Hoar and the Half-Breed Republicans*. Cambridge: Harvard University Press, 1971, which contains many asides on the half-breed and anti-imperialist predecessors of progressivism; Robert C. Cotner. *James Stephen Hogg: A Biography*. Austin: University of Texas Press, 1959, which is somewhat establishmentarian but thorough on Texas' protoprogressive; Melvin G. Holli. *Reform in Detroit: Hazen S. Pingree and Urban Politics*. New York: Oxford University Press, 1969, on an ebullient big-city reform mayor; Norman E. Tutorow. *Leland Stanford: Man of Many Careers*. Menlo Park: Pacific Coast Publishers, 1971, on California's politician-entrepreneur. No biography yet exists of John Sherman, though Jeannette P. Nichols promised one in her article on Sherman in the *Dictionary of American Biography* published some decades ago.

[10] The useful state and regional studies will be discussed in part III.

[11] Earl S. Pomeroy. *The Territories and the United States 1861-1890: Studies in Colonial Administration*. Seattle: University of Washington Press, 1969; originally published by University of Pennsylvania Press, 1947; I have used the 1969 reprint, which includes a wide-ranging new introduction by the author. Also, Leonard D. White. *The Republican Era 1869-1901: A Study in Administrative History*. New York: Macmillan, 1958; Mary R. Dearing. *Veterans in Politics: The Story of the G. A. R.* Baton Rouge: Louisiana State University Press, 1952.

[12] David J. Rothman. *Politics and Power: The United States Senate 1869-1901*. Cambridge: Harvard University Press, 1966; Yearley. *op. cit.*; Marcus. *op. cit.* A more restricted institutional history, but one executed with an eye to the general direction of institutional change and Gilded Age-progressive reform, is L. E. Fredman's *The Australian Ballot: The Story of an American Reform*. East Lansing: Michigan State University Press, 1968.

[13] Harvey Wish. *The American Historian*. New York: Oxford University Press, 1960. p. 218.

[14] James Ford Rhodes. *History of the United States, from the Compromise of 1850 to the McKinley-Bryan Campaign of 1896*. vol. 8, 1877-1896; New York: Macmillan, 1919. pp. 97, 114-28, 283, and *passim*; Josephson. *op. cit.*, pp. 287, 465 and *passim*.

[15] Garraty. *op. cit.*, chaps. 6 and 7; Harold U. Faulkner. *Politics, Reform and Expansion 1890-1900*. New York: Harper & Row, 1959; both in the New American Nation Series. Also, Ray Ginger. *Age of Excess: The United States from 1877 to 1914*. New York: Macmillan, 1965, chap. 6. In fairness it should be said that the last two appeared prior to much of the more exciting new scholarship.

[16] H. Wayne Morgan. *From Hayes to McKinley: National Party Politics 1877-1896*. Syracuse: Syracuse University Press, 1969.

[17] Samuel P. Hays. *The Response to Industrialism 1885-1914*. Chicago: University of Chicago Press, 1957, esp. chap. 7; Robert H. Wiebe. *The Search for Order 1877-1920*. New York: Hill & Wang, 1967, esp. chap. 4.

[18] Three other recent books which survey Gilded Age culture but which do not deal with politics in any direct way are Rowland Berthoff's *An Unsettled People*, New York: Harper & Row, 1971; Paul A. Carter's *The Spiritual Crisis of the Gilded Age*, De Kalb: Northern Illinois University Press, 1971; and Howard Mumford Jones' *The Age of Energy*, New York: Viking, 1971.

[19] *Political Science Quarterly* 80: 373-94; No. 3, September 1965.

[20] Carl N. Degler. "American Political Parties and the Rise of the City: An Interpretation." *Journal of American History* 51: 41-59; No. 1, June 1964; Allen W. Moger. *Virginia: Bourbonism to Byrd 1870-1925*. Charlottesville: The

University Press of Virginia, 1968; Hackney. *op. cit.*; William I. Hair. *Bourbonism and Agrarian Protest: Louisiana Politics 1877-1900.* Baton Rouge: Louisiana State University Press, 1971, esp. chap. 3. See also the 1969 introduction in Pomeroy. *op. cit.*, p. xv.

[21] Unger. *op. cit.*; Nugent. *Money and American Society 1865-1880. op. cit.* For a brief survey of the money question, with a glossary of terms, see Nugent. *The Money Question During Reconstruction.* New York: W. W. Norton, 1967. Nugent, "Money, Politics, and Society," in H. W. Morgan. *The Gilded Age.* Syracuse: Syracuse University Press, 1970. pp. 109-27.

[22] Ronald P. Formisano and William G. Shade. "The Concept of Agrarian Radicalism." *Mid-America* 52: 3-30; No. 1, January 1970; Fred A. Shannon. *The Farmer's Last Frontier: Agriculture 1860-1897.* New York: Farrar & Rinehart, Inc., 1945; Solon J. Buck. *The Granger Movement.* Cambridge: Harvard University Press, 1913; Theodore Saloutos. *Farmer Movements in the South 1865-1933.* Berkeley: University of California Press, 1960; Roy V. Scott. *The Agrarian Movement in Illinois 1880-1896.* Urbana: University of Illinois Press, 1962; Moger. *op. cit.*; Raymond H. Pulley. *Old Virginia Restored: An Interpretation of the Progressive Impulse 1870-1930.* Charlottesville: The University Press of Virginia, 1968. Dennis S. Nordin. "A Revisionist Interpretation of the Patrons of Husbandry, 1867-1900." *Historian* 32: 630-43; No. 4, August 1970, reevaluated the non-political aspects of Grangerism. The Granger laws will be discussed in section III. 4. For other radicalism, see Howard Quint. *The Forging of American Socialism.* Columbia: University of South Carolina Press, 1953; Edward McNair's fugitive book of 1959 on the Bellamy movement, *Edward Bellamy and the Nationalist Movement. . . .* Milwaukee: Fitzgerald Co., 1957; and the biographies of Henry George referred to above.

[23] For detail see also Gerald W. McFarland. "Partisan of Non-Partisanship: Dorman B. Eaton and the Genteel Reform Tradition." *Journal of American History* 54: 806-22; No. 4, March 1968, on an early civil-service administrator; Carpenter. *U.S. Grant, op. cit.*, for a view of Grant's civil service efforts revised in favor of the "presidential failure"; and Jordan. *Roscoe Conkling, op. cit.*, on the Stalwart leader's opposition to reform. On the post-1883 operation of civil service see A. Bower Sageser. *The First Two Decades of the Pendleton Act.* Lincoln: University of Nebraska Press, 1935, and White. *Republican Era. op. cit.*

[24] C. Vann Woodward. *Reunion and Reaction: The Compromise of 1877 and the End of Reconstruction.* Boston: Little, Brown, 1951; Taylor Garfield. *op. cit.*; Jordan Conkling. *op. cit.*; Marcus. *op. cit.*; Stanley P. Hirshson. *Farewell to the Bloody Shirt: Northern Republicans and the Southern Negro 1877-93.* Bloomington: Indiana University Press, 1962; Vincent P. De Santis. *Republicans Face the Southern Question: The New Departure Years, 1877-1897.* Baltimore: Johns Hopkins Press, 1959.

[25] John Tomsich. *A General Endeavor: American Culture and Politics in the Gilded Age.* Stanford: Stanford University Press, 1971; Welch. *op. cit.*; Beisner. *op. cit.* See also sections III.10 and III.11 below.

[26] Garraty. *op. cit.*; Nevins. *Cleveland. op. cit.*; Barnes. *op. cit.*; Bass. *op. cit.*; Sievers. vol. 3, *op. cit.*; Kleppner. *op. cit.*

[27] Farnham. *loc. cit.*; Decker. *op. cit.*; Benson. *Merchants, Farmers, and Railroads, op. cit.*; Harold D. Woodman. "Chicago Businessmen and the 'Granger' Laws." *Agricultural History* 36: 16-24; No. 1, January 1962; Edward A. Purcell, Jr. "Ideas and Interests: Businessmen and the Interstate Commerce Act." *Journal of American History* 54: 561-78; No. 3, December 1967; Neilson. *Shelby Cullom. op. cit.* For the kind of people who were agrarian leaders, see Gerald L. Prescott. "Wisconsin Farm Leaders in the Gilded Age." *Agricultural History* 44: 183-99; No. 2, April 1970. The subject of business regulation is of course even more central to economic history; see chapter 18.

[28] Baton Rouge: Louisiana State University Press, 1951; Cooper. *op. cit.*; Carol K. R. Bleser. *The Promised Land: The South Carolina Land Commission 1869-1890.* Columbia: University of South Carolina Press, 1969; Hair. *op. cit.*; Jack P. Maddex, Jr. *The Virginia Conservatives 1867-1897: A Study in Reconstruction Politics.* Chapel Hill: University of North Carolina Press, 1970. Maddex points out that the Bourbons provided "free public schools, however modest by twentieth-century standards, [which] were a revolutionary innovation, an important concomitant of the nascent industrial society"; were laissez-faire concerning railroads and canals; did nothing for "impoverished farmers"; and "guaranteed to freedmen a modicum of civil rights by a judicial equality that did not imperil white supremacy in government and society"; they also buried the state-rights theories of the 1850's (pp. 295 and *passim*). Hair provides another angle; of Major Burke, the state treasurer who personally appropriated $1.27 million of Louisiana funds in the 80's, he says, "No Reconstruction swindler had ever approached that figure" (p. 141).

[29] See also III.11 below. Alwyn Barr. *Reconstruction to Reform: Texas Politics 1876-1906.* Austin: University of Texas Press, 1971; Moger. *op. cit.*; Pulley. *op. cit.*; Hackney. *op. cit.* Two particularly useful biographies of key non-Populist but agrarian-based state leaders are Cotner's Hogg and Simkins' Tillman, *op. cit.*

[30] Margaret L. Callcott. *The Negro in Maryland Politics 1870-1912.* Baltimore: Johns Hopkins Press, 1969. See also section III.9.

[31] V. O. Key, Jr. *Southern Politics.* New York: Knopf, 1949; Saloutos. *Farmer Movements. op. cit.*; William Warren Rogers. *The One-Gallused Rebellion: Agrarianism in Alabama 1865-1896.* Baton Rouge: Louisiana State University Press, 1970; Albert D. Kirwan. *The Revolt of the Rednecks: Mississippi Politics 1876-1925.* Lexington: University of Kentucky Press, 1951. Rogers and Hackney have superseded political aspects of James F. Doster. *Railroads in Alabama Politics 1875-1914.* University, Alabama: University of Alabama Studies. No. 12, 1957, and Allan J. Going. *Bourbon Democracy in Alabama 1874-1890.* University, Alabama: University of Alabama Press, 1951, for the most part. See also III.8, on Populism. Woodward. *Strange Career of Jim Crow.* New York: Oxford University Press, 1955.

[32] Russell B. Nye. *Midwestern Progressive Politics: A Historical Study of its Origins and Development 1870-1950.* East Lansing: Michigan State College Press, 1951; Merrill. *op. cit.*; Kleppner. *op. cit.*

[33] Pomeroy. *op. cit.*; Howard R. Lamar. *Dakota Territory 1861-1889: A Study of Frontier Politics.* New Haven: Yale University Press, 1956; Lewis L. Gould. *Wyoming: A Political History 1868-1896.* New Haven: Yale University Press, 1968; Jack E. Eblen. "Status, Mobility, and Empire: The Territorial Governors 1869-1890." *Pacific Northwest Quarterly* 60: 145-53; No. 3, July 1969; Mary Ellen Glass. *Silver and Politics in Nevada 1892-1902.* Reno: University of Nevada Press, 1969; Paul L. Beckett. *From Wilderness to Enabling Act.* Pullman: Washington State University Press, 1968; Tutorow. *op. cit.*; Michael P. Rogin. "California Populism and the 'System of 1896.'" *Western Political Quarterly* 22: 179-96; No. 1, March 1969, largely duplicated in the first chapter of Michael P. Rogin and John L. Shover. *Political Change in California 1890-1966.* Westport, Conn.: Greenwood Publishing Corp., 1970.

[34] Arthur Mann. *Yankee Reformers in the Urban Age.* Cambridge: Harvard University Press, 1954; Tomsich. *op. cit.*; Welch. *op. cit.* Other biographies already cited deal with Northeastern political figures. Also abundant are autobiographies and memoirs, which the Half-Breeds and Mugwumps, especially, were never diffident about writing. On New York see Benson's *Merchants, Farmers and Railroads,* and Bass's *"I Am a Democrat," op. cit.,* among recent works.

[35] Blake McKelvey. *The Urbanization of America 1860-1915.* New Brunswick: Rutgers University Press, 1963, esp. part II; Walton Bean. *Boss Ruef's San Fran-*

cisco. Berkeley: University of California Press, 1952; William Riordan. *Plunkitt of Tammany Hall.* New York: Knopf, 1948; first published 1905; Lloyd Wendt and Herman Kogan. *Lords of the Levee.* Indianapolis: Bobbs-Merrill Company, 1943; M. R. Werner. *Tammany Hall.* Garden City: Doubleday, Doran, 1928; Holli. *op. cit.*; Zane Miller. *Boss Cox's Cincinnati: Urban Politics in the Progressive Era.* New York: Oxford University Press, 1968.

[36] John D. Hicks. *The Populist Revolt.* Minneapolis: University of Minnesota Press, 1931; Alex M. Arnett. *The Populist Movement in Georgia.* New York: Columbia University Press, 1922; John B. Clark. *Populism in Alabama.* Auburn: Auburn Printing Company, 1927; Roscoe Martin. *op. cit.*; Herman C. Nixon. "The Populist Movement in Iowa." *Iowa Journal of History and Politics* 24: 3-107; No. 1, January 1926; William duBose Sheldon. *Populism in the Old Dominion: Virginia Farm Politics 1885-1900.* Princeton: Princeton University Press, 1935.

[37] Richard Hofstadter. *The Age of Reform.* New York: Knopf, 1955. For a summary and critique of this and other examples of the 1950's revisionism on Populism, see: Walter T. K. Nugent. *The Tolerant Populists: Kansas Populism and Nativism.* Chicago: University of Chicago Press, 1963, Part I, and Theodore Saloutos. "The Professors and the Populists." *Agricultural History* 40: 235-54: No. 4, October 1966.

[38] C. Vann Woodward. "The Populist Heritage and the Intellectual." *American Scholar* 29: 55-72; No. 1, Winter 1959-60; Norman Pollack. "Hofstadter on Populism: A Critique of 'The Age of Reform.' " *Journal of Southern History* 26: 478-500; No. 4, November 1960; Pollack. *Populist Response. op. cit.*; Nugent. *Tolerant Populists. op. cit.*; Hackney. *op. cit.* p. 326.

[39] On the identity and socioeconomic characteristics and problems of the Populists, see especially Stanley B. Parsons. "Who Were the Nebraska Populists?" *Nebraska History* 44: 83-99; No. 2, June 1963; Walter T. K. Nugent. "Some Parameters of Populism." *Agricultural History* 40: 255-70; No. 4, October 1966; Robert Higgs. "Railroad Rates and the Populist Uprising." *Agricultural History* 44: 291-97; No. 3, July 1970; Hackney. *op. cit., chap.* 1; the striking reconstruction of a Populist confrontation by Goodwyn. *loc. cit.*; O. Gene Clanton. *Kansas Populism: Ideas and Men.* Lawrence: University Press of Kansas, 1969, a valuable leadership study. Also, on Negro and immigrant relations, and the role of the Farmers' Alliance, see William H. Chafe. "The Negro and Populism: A Kansas Case Study." *Journal of Southern History* 34: 402-19; No. 3, August 1968; David Stephens Trask. "Formation and Failure: The Populist Party in Seward County, 1890-1892." *Nebraska History* 51: 281-301; No. 3, Fall 1970; D. Jerome Tweton. "The Midwestern Immigrant and Politics: A Case Study." *Mid-America* 41: 104-13; No. 2, April 1959; Frederick C. Luebke. "Main Street and the Countryside: Patterns of Voting in Nebraska during the Populist Era." *Nebraska History* 50: 257-75; No. 3, Fall 1969; Peter H. Argersinger. "Road to a Republican Waterloo: The Farmers' Alliance and the Election of 1890 in Kansas." *Kansas Historical Quarterly* 33: 443-69; No. 4, Winter 1967; Karel D. Bicha. "A Further Reconsideration of American Populism." *Mid-America* 53: 3-11, No. 1, January 1971; Herbert Shapiro. "The Populists and the Negro: a Reconsideration," in August Meier and Elliott Rudwick, editors. *The Making of Black America.* Vol. II. New York: Atheneum, 1969. pp. 27-36; Robert Saunders. "Southern Populists and the Negro, 1893-1895." *Journal of Negro History* 54: 240-61; No. 3, July 1969, and "The Transformation of Tom Watson, 1894-1895." *Georgia Historical Quarterly* 54: 339-56; No. 3, Fall 1970; Frederick A. Bode. "Religion and Class Hegemony: A Populist Critique in North Carolina." *Journal of Southern History* 37: 417-38; No. 3, August 1971; David B. Griffiths. "Far-western Populist Thought: A Comparative Study of John R. Rogers and Davis H. Waite." *Pacific Northwest Quarterly* 60: 183-92; No. 4, October 1969; and parts of Rogers, Glass, and other state studies mentioned earlier.

[40] On the election of 1896, see Durden. *op. cit.*; Kleppner. *op. cit.*, chaps. 7 and 8; Luebke. *Immigrants and Politics. op. cit.*; Rogin. "California Populism." *loc. cit.*; Paul W. Glad. *McKinley, Bryan, and the People.* Philadelphia: J. B. Lippincott Co., 1964; J. Rogers Hollingsworth. *The Whirligig of Politics: The Democracy of Cleveland and Bryan.* Chicago: University of Chicago Press, 1963; Stanley L. Jones. *The Presidential Election of 1896.* Madison: University of Wisconsin Press, 1964; Gilbert C. Fite. "William Jennings Bryan and the Campaign of 1896: Some Views and Problems." *Nebraska History* 47: 247-64; No. 3, September 1966, and "Republican Strategy and the Farm Vote in the Presidential Campaign of 1896." *American Historical Review* 65: 787-806; No. 4, July 1960. Relevant biographies include, in addition to those mentioned on Bryan, Donnelly, Polk, and Watson, O. Gene Clanton. "Intolerant Populist? The Disaffection of Mary Elizabeth Lease." *Kansas Historical Quarterly* 34: 189-200; No. 2, Summer 1968; Chester McA. Destler, *Henry Demarest Lloyd and the Empire of Reform.* Philadelphia: University of Pennsylvania Press, 1963; H. Wayne Morgan. *William McKinley and His America.* Syracuse: Syracuse University Press, 1963; Karel Bicha. "Jerry Simpson: Populist without Principles." *Journal of American History* 54: 291-306; No. 2, September 1967. On Tom Watson, see the Saunders article cited in the previous note, and Charles Crowe. "Tom Watson, Populists, and Blacks Reconsidered." *Journal of Negro History* 55: 99-116; No. 2, April 1970.

[41] Barr. *op. cit.*, p. 199; Hair. *op. cit.*, chap. 11; Goodwyn. *loc. cit.*

[42] Lawrence D. Rice. *The Negro in Texas 1874-1900.* Baton Rouge: Louisiana State University Press, 1971; Hackney. *op. cit.*, p. 146.

[43] Moger, Hair, Bleser, and Goodwyn. *op. cit.* (this listing is not exhaustive). The decline of Negro suffrage was surveyed in Paul Lewinson. *Race, Class and Party: A History of Negro Suffrage and White Politics in the South.* New York: Oxford University Press, 1932, now largely superseded by state studies but quite unbiased for its time. Unacceptably paternalistic, but still informative, is Samuel D. Smith. *The Negro in Congress 1870-1901.* Port Washington, N.Y.: Kennikat Press, Inc., 1966; originally published 1940. Recent books on the state level, besides Callcott. *op. cit.*, include Frenise A. Logan. *The Negro in North Carolina 1876-1894.* Chapel Hill: University of North Carolina Press, 1964, and Charles Wynes. *Race Relations in Virginia 1870-1902.* Charlottesville: University of Virginia Press, 1961.

[44] Marcus. *op. cit.*; Kleppner. *op. cit.* See also Hollingsworth. *op. cit.*, on the Cleveland-Bryan split in the Democracy; Robert Kelley. *The Transatlantic Persuasion: The Liberal-Democratic Mind in the Age of Gladstone.* New York: Knopf, 1969, for correspondences in Anglo-Canadian-American political thought and action (one of the too few ventures into comparative history). The quotation is from Degler. *loc. cit.* p. 44. For two brief, balanced essays on the makeup and changes of the major parties, see Lewis L. Gould. "The Republican Search for a National Majority," in Morgan. *Gilded Age. op. cit.* pp. 171-87, and R. Hal Williams. "'Dry Bones and Dead Language': The Democratic Party." *ibid.* pp. 129-48.

[45] Hackney. *op. cit.* p. 324; see also relevant passages in Barr, Blodgett, Bode, Doster, Holli, Moger, Pulley, and Tomsich. *op. cit.* The Gilded-Age roots of progressivism have also been explored by David P. Thelen. "Social Tensions and the Origins of Progressivism." *Journal of American History* 56: 323-41; No. 2, September 1969, and in various works concentrating on progressivism by Arthur Mann (*Yankee Reformers. op. cit.*); J. Joseph Huthmacher, esp. "Urban Liberalism and the Age of Reform." *Mississippi Valley Historical Review* 49: 231-41; No. 2, September 1962; Richard Abrams. *Conservatism in a Progressive Era: Massachusetts Politics, 1900-1912.* Cambridge: Harvard University Press, 1964, and others.

· 18 ·

The Transformation
of the American Economy,
1877–1900

J. Carroll Moody

Introduction

"A REVOLUTION is taking place in economic history in the United States." This dramatic statement came from the pen of an economist in 1963, and it spoke for a growing number of economic historians who were "both skeptical of traditional interpretations of U.S. economic history and convinced that a new economic history must be firmly grounded in sound statistical data."[1] During the years that have followed, the econometricians or Cliometricians, as the practitioners of the "new economic history" are often called, turned out several books and many articles reassessing various questions that had engaged historians for decades. They also filled the pages of scholarly journals with articles explaining their new approaches to investigating our economic past, criticizing traditional economic history, and defending themselves against the inevitable counterattacks.

How did this "revolution" begin? It can best be explained by the emergence after World War II of an almost consuming passion for the study of economic growth and development. There is little doubt that this phenomenon resulted from worldwide concern with promoting economic development in the "underdeveloped" nations. Many economic historians turned their attention to studying how the relatively prosperous, industrialized nations of the world had reached their stage of development. So great was this preoccupation that it led one scholar to conclude that "the discussion of economic development has provoked an outpouring of analytical and empirical literature which probably exceeds the quantity of writing devoted to any other economic problem in the course of the last two centuries."[2]

Studies in economic development, not surprisingly, led to considerations of political, social and intellectual milieus within which economic growth took place, but considerably more emphasis was placed upon what was measurable. The absence of data series for most of United States history, however, led to major efforts to try to seek out new statistics and, where they could not be found, to estimate them, using sophisticated statistical techniques and modern data processing equipment. Even with the resulting accumulation of "hard" data—as distinguished from the random sampling of the past or the reliance upon traditional, "literary" sources—a means had to be found whereby such figures could be utilized to explain economic growth. The means adopted was economic theory—input-output analysis, capital and location theory, and other tools of the economists' trade. Economic growth historians applied their data and tools to "developed" countries, compared those countries with each other, and investigated what "backward" countries lacked to explain their underdeveloped economic state.

Probably the most noted and controversial theory of economic development came from W. W. Rostow, *The Stages of Economic Growth: A Non-Communist Manifesto*.[3] Rostow, like most traditional economic historians, tended to view economic growth and industrialization as synonymous. It followed, therefore, that prime consideration should be given to investigating preindustrial societies and the reasons for their transition to an industrialized society. Rostow defined two preindustrial stages as "traditional society" and "preconditions for take-off." These two stages were followed by a "take-off into self-sustained economic growth" that had occurred in the United States between 1843 and 1860.

While Rostow's theories of the beginnings of industrialization and self-sustained economic growth found their way into numerous scholarly writings, criticisms of his model soon emerged.[4] Other economists and historians already had begun their attempts to reconstruct and interpret the statistical record of the performance of the American economy, and their findings cast doubt on Rostow's contention that a "spurt" in growth occurred in the decade and a half prior to the Civil War.[5] At the same time, Thomas C. Cochran launched a direct attack on the older Beard-Hacker thesis that the Civil War era had promoted industrial growth.[6] In place of theories of discontinuities and dramatic watersheds, the new statistical evidence suggested a steadier long-term rate of economic growth.

The availability of more reliable statistics and the growing body of useful theory prompted a number of economists to turn to the writing of economic history. The works they produced, however, implicitly and explicitly rejected the statistical and theoretical groundings of older interpretations. The creed of this "new economic history" was first formally presented in 1957 by John R. Meyer and Alfred H. Conrad in an essay titled "Economic Theory, Statistical Inference and Economic History."[7] The following year these same authors applied their methods to an old controversy concerning the profitability of slavery in the antebellum South.[8] Within a surprisingly short time, the prestige of econometric history was convincingly demonstrated by the attention it received in the *Journal of Economic History* and other scholarly publications.[9]

A major example of the unusual methodology utilized by the new economic history is Robert Fogel's *Railroads and American Economic Growth: Essays in Econometric History*.[10] Fogel dealt directly with the traditional, widely-held contention that railroads provided the indispensable element for economic growth during much of the nineteenth century. In order to determine if this were the case, he projected a nation in which railroads did not exist, or what he termed a "counterfactual conditional." As a substitute he hypothesized the extension of roadways and water routes to provide for increasing transportation needs. He then asked the question: What social savings were provided by the railroads in comparison to savings which could have been effected by this imaginary water and road network? His answer, provided by statistical data and economic theory, was that railroads provided some social savings, but not nearly what most historians had assumed. In any case, Fogel concluded, railroads were not indispensable for economic growth.

Fogel's study of the railroads provoked a large amount of interpretative and methodological controversy, which has not (as of 1972) ended.[11] At a minimum, critics asserted that to apply the adjective "new" to the use of statistics and theory in writing economic history is to ignore many earlier works in the field. More direct criticism, however, centered upon the questions of the reliability of reconstructed data, the use of questionable economic theory, and the posing of counterfactual conditions (which, as distinguished from hypotheses to be proved, are "figments" of the imagination).

The defenders of the new economic history replied that all historians use counterfactual *assumptions* in their work, but they do not make them explicit so that the reader can judge for himself how those assumptions have been dealt with. The traditional historians, they argued, not only assume "as-if" questions, but in solving them they use only fragmentary data, traditional literary sources, and a few crude theoretical constructs. And so the debate continued.

There is little doubt, however, that historians using more traditional methods also continue to enrich our knowledge of the past. Business and entrepreneurial history, although utilizing theory drawn from economics, sociology, and social psychology, supplement in crucial ways the macroeconomic approach of the econometricians.[12] Whatever methods help us to understand such a crucial facet of our past should be welcomed, and one hopes that economists and historians of all types would agree with Gunnar Myrdal that "the distinction between factors that are 'economic' and those that are 'non-economic' is, indeed, a useless and nonsensical device from the point of view of logic, and should be replaced by a distinction between 'relevant' and 'irrelevant' factors, or 'more relevant' and 'less relevant.' "[13] A survey of the literature dealing with the economic history of the United States in the period from the 1870's to the turn of the twentieth century reveals that while the Cliometricians have contributed much to understanding the process of economic growth, traditional historians continue to make valuable contributions as well.

General Works

Despite the heightened criticism of traditional economic and business histories as being narrow in conception and outlook and telling us little about the overall reasons for economic development, few attempts were made to produce syntheses of the newer research in economic history. Douglass C. North led the way, however, in attempting to reorient economic history around theory and quantative data in order that history might "be something more than a subjective reordering of the facts of the past as man's perspective changes with each generation. . . ." Besides a body of very creative scholarship of his own, he provided us with *Growth and Welfare in the American Past: A New Economic History*.[14] This brief, nontechnical synthesis of the findings of several Cliometricians covers American history from the Colonial period to the mid-1960's. North discussed traditional explanations regarding economic development and its effects on farmers and workers, but he found most of them wanting. He concluded, for example, that statistical evidence lends no proof to Rostow's assertion that during our "take-off" period there was a substantial rise in capital formation and that the railroads provided a leading sector with a high rate of growth. He also questioned the usual assertions that the government played a major role in economic development, that farmers' grievances resulted from the predatory practices of the railroads, and that monopolies prevented workers from enjoying increasing real wages. Overall, North's *Growth and Welfare* is an excellent book for the non-specialist to read as a starting place for understanding how the new economic history interprets the past.

A few textbooks written for college classroom use embody theoretical and quantitive approaches to explain economic history during the later nineteenth century. Certainly the most interesting is *Ascent to Affluence: A History of American Economic Development,* written by Charles H. Hession and Hyman Sardy.[15] They employed brief expositions of the theories of such disparate scholars as Max Weber, Karl Marx, Thorstein Veblen, Joseph A. Schumpeter and John Maynard Keynes to analyze various periods of American economic history. Hession and Sardy then use recent qualitative and quantitative data to determine to what extent these theories coincide with "historical reality."

One might suspect that the traditional, non-econometric historians would not dare to offer a general synthesis in the face of such quantified and theoretical works. Louis M. Hacker accepted the challenge, however, in publishing *The World of Andrew Carnegie: 1865-1901*[16] which he claimed is "a continuation and amplification" of his noted book published in 1940, *The Triumph of American Capitalism.* But whereas Hacker used categories of Marxist analysis in the latter work, the former uses William Graham Sumner's theory of *mores* and Joseph A. Schumpeter's theory of entrepreneurship to explain how an underdeveloped nation could become the "mightiest industrial power in the world" in less than four decades. Like Edward Kirkland before him,[17] Hacker used the statements of nineteenth-century elites to discover America's *mores,* or those "rules of conduct which determine right and wrong." Hacker concluded that most Americans gave eager assent to "acquisition, unequal wealth, the competitiveness and ruthlessness of the period's entrepreneurs, or innovators." And those innovators, according to Hacker, were the main wellsprings of economic change during the latter part of the nineteenth century. Some will no doubt conclude that Hacker's earlier works came closer to explaining economic development than his *World of Andrew Carnegie.* They might also hope that we will soon have a genuine and sophisticated Marxian history of this crucial period.

The West and Economic Development

Historians continued to devote major attention to the Trans-Mississippi West, although emphasis shifted somewhat from the traditional "cowboys and Indians" stories to investigations of political, social and economic aspects of frontier development. The West, after all, provided food and raw materials for the older, urban and industrial sections, as well as an extensive market for eastern manufactured goods and capital investment. A new generation of historians, in short, studied the West as an underdeveloped region.

Nowhere was this new focus better illustrated than in studies dealing with capital investment in the West, frontier entrepreneurship, and the exploitation of the region's vast natural resources. Since the publication forty years ago of Edward Everett Dale's *The Range Cattle Industry: Ranching on the Great Plains from 1865 to 1925*,[18] a number of historians turned their attention to specialized studies of that important western industry. Gene M. Gressley provided a valuable study of eastern investment in the cattle-ranching enterprises of the West and the management activities of cattlemen in making those investments profitable.[19] The period of greatest investment encompassed the years 1882-1886; thereafter, when the Great Plains Bubble burst, a group of cattlemen and eastern capitalists attempted to salvage their operations by forming the American Cattle Trust. When that experiment failed three years later, the investors began selling their land to farmers, reinvesting in local banks, or putting their money into distant and unrelated enterprises. William M. Pearce,[20] Lester Fields Sheffy,[21] and William C. Holden[22] studied individual land and cattle companies, concentrating on the English, Scottish, and eastern American investors and their relationship with their rancher-managers.[23]

English and Scottish investors contributed capital to many other Western economic activities, as Clark C. Spence so admirably demonstrated in regard to British investment in the mining frontier.[24] His study was supplemented by W. Turrentine Jackson, *The Enterprising Scot: Investors in the American West After 1873*.[25] Jackson challenged the assumption that British investments were immensely profitable, but he acknowledged that such foreign funds aided in developing the region by expanding the railroads, allowing the introduction of new technology in mining, and facilitating improved livestock breeding and marketing. The most lucrative field for investments was in mortgages and securities, especially in railroads, but mining investments generally failed to produce good returns. In general, Scottish capitalists failed when they invested in land, timber, colonization, agriculture and manufacturing, partly because of American nationalistic reactions. Congress restricted alien land ownership and various legislative and judicial restrictions were placed on business activities by foreigners. Jackson nevertheless concluded that "Scottish contribution to the total capital investment in the United States was certainly impressive," especially in the West.

There is little doubt that foreign or domestic investors would not have been so willing to commit their capital to economic activities in an underdeveloped region without the aid and advice of scientists who explored and charted the vast natural resources of the West. Clark C. Spence's *Mining Engineers and the American West: The Lace-Boot Brigade, 1849-1933*[26] sets out to "view the engineer for what he was, picture him against the background of his work, describe his actual professional role and accomplishments, delineate the problems he faced and the life he led, and assess the imprint that he made on western environment during the years from the California gold rush down to the years of the Great Depression." Spence characterized the mining engineer as a central figure of the industrial era because he advanced and stabilized the mining industry, while at the same time he publicized the region's resources. The mining engineers in the West were mainly initiators and adapters and they were strongly motivated toward economic success. Geologists also aided in the exploitation of the West's natural resources and were often sent into the region by eastern investors who were anxious that their investments would produce profits. Thurman Wilkins told the story of the brilliant young geologist Clarence King, who conducted geological surveys of the West while remaining contemptuous of the materialism of the times.[27] Another scientist, who aided in the development of the Pennsylvania and then the California oil industry, was Benjamin Silliman, Jr., who began his career as a chemistry professor at Yale. Gerald T. White chronicled Silliman's scientific work in California on behalf of eastern entrepreneurs and the controversies between him and William D. Whitney, head of the California Geological Survey, who considered Silliman as having "sold out" to his backers.[28]

One of the results of this scientific exploration was the development of the California oil industry, the origin and early development of which was told by Gerald White in *Formative Years in the Far West: A History of Standard Oil Company of California and Predecessors through 1919*.[29] White sketched the background of that industry, beginning with the 1850's when geologists searched for petroleum and entrepreneurs acquired land, drilled wells, built small refineries and began marketing operations. Eastern capitalists and Pennsylvania oilmen joined California investors in developing this emerging industry, and in 1878 Standard Oil of Ohio opened a branch office in San Francisco and increasingly became an important factor in the California oil industry.

The importance of western mining to the economic development of the United States is well established, and two historians produced new studies of that subject. Rodman W. Paul grouped western mining frontiers into four stages: the decade from 1848 to 1858 when the California gold rush not only produced fortunes, but also aided in peopling other areas of the West with prospectors and miners who went "bust"; a second decade from 1858 to 1868 when new mining innovations were applied to silver and lead mining in various parts of the West and the Comstock Lode had its beginnings; the decade beginning in 1879 when placer mining declined and eastern and European capital was introduced into the industry; and the era following 1879 when Colorado became the preëminent mining region, engineers and scientists made it possible and profitable to utilize the West's vast store of minerals, and western mining became increasingly integrated into the national economy.[30] William S. Greever wrote a more traditional account of the mining rushes from 1848 to 1900, but he emphasized the social, economic, political and cultural life of the times. He reached the conclusion that these mining rushes hastened the settlement of the West and brought "geographical patterns quite different from those which would have developed out of a steady, orderly pushing of the frontier line westward. . . ."[31]

The Agricultural Sector of the Economy

Until late in the nineteenth century the American economy depended primarily upon its agriculture. A majority of people lived and worked in nonurban places, and the "sons of the soil" were idealized as the steady, hard-working, independent citizenry upon whom the continued health of the nation depended. Contemporary farmers and their spokesmen charged that advancing industrialization and urbanization threatened to injure seriously or destroy the sturdy yeoman. Railroads discriminated against farmers in setting freight charges; the government disposed of public lands to benefit speculators and special interests; manufacturers engaged in monopolistic conspiracies to raise the prices of products the farmers needed to buy; and money lenders cheated farmers by charging exorbitant interest rates and quickly foreclosing on mortgages when borrowers could not pay. Farmers tried to reverse their declining position by organizing as Grangers, Greenbackers or Populists, but their efforts were largely unavailing against the forces of the consolidated power of the urban-industrial complex.

The preceding was the main theme of the work produced by historians of American agriculture, most of whom wrote from a rural perspective. These historians concentrated on the more prosaic aspects of rural life, they detailed the man-made and natural calamities visited on the farmer, and they gave heavy attention to the efforts of agrarians to solve their problems through political organization. Recently, however, there has been a noticeable trend toward critically evaluating the rhetoric of nineteenth-century agrarian spokesmen and investigating agriculture in the same fashion as other sectors of the economy.[32] Some historians have concluded that farmers were victims of traditional myths that surrounded them, and that farmers were not especially victimized by declining price levels, discriminatory railroad freight rates, depredations of land speculators, hard money, and unfair mortgage interest rates.

In spite of the new directions and conclusions of these studies, a scholar concluded in 1961 that "agricultural history does not rank high in American historiography today."[33] Less attention has been paid to the study of agricultural history, considering its great importance to our history as a whole, than to many other aspects of American life. Gilbert C. Fite's *The Farmers' Frontier, 1865-1900*[34] (as of 1971) is the only broad history of late nineteenth-century agriculture published since the excellent and comprehensive treatment written by Fred A. Shannon[35] over a quarter of a century ago. Fite's work is essentially an economic history of the farmers' frontier. He gave attention to land sales and acquisitions, human and livestock population statistics, costs of acquiring machinery and farm buildings, figures on acreage under cultivation and the value of farm crops, and the general business practices and conditions of rural families during the period.

Most historians of agriculture view the years following the Civil War as "revolutionary" because of the vast amounts of land opened to cultivation, the application of science and technology to farming, and the increased yield of products resulting from both these extensive and intensive developments. Clarence H. Danhof pointed out, however, that one should not accept simplistically the notion that it was not until those changes took place that farmers shifted from subsistence or semi-subsistence farming to commercial farming.[36] He dated that transition as having taken place in the years between 1820 and 1870, as more and more farmer-businessmen produced surpluses for sale to the growing populations in urban areas. Moreover, American farmers were long involved in a worldwide market. This meant that farmers needed the same quality of information about market conditions and the same quality of managerial skills as their fellow-businessmen in the cities. It appears, however, that farmers generally lacked both, which was part of their problem.

Allan G. Bogue discussed the shift from general to specialized farming, along with its problems, in *From Prairie to Corn Belt: Farming on the Illinois and Iowa Prairies in the Nineteenth Century*.[37] He showed that the ultimate specialization of the "corn belt" in a basic crop, along with the raising of hogs and feeder cattle, was accomplished by rational and intelligent responses of the region's farmers, although he concluded that entrepreneurial abilities did not measure up to those available to manufacturers. Eric E. Lampard told a similar story in *The Rise of the Dairy Industry in Wisconsin: A Study in Agricultural Change, 1820-1920*.[38] In Wisconsin attempts to substitute other crops for wheat proved unsuccessful, and after the 1860's specialization in milk and cheese production called for vast improvements in livestock breeds and diets, manufacturing techniques, and marketing practices. Lacking any central authority to mandate those improvements, the alternative was educating the thousands of farmers involved in dairying. Fortunately, cooperative organization supplanted individualistic practices, and practical business attitudes gave Wisconsin dairymen a special place in distant markets.

The South presented a different pattern from that of other agricultural regions of the country, because it had long specialized in a cash crop for a commercial market. Two studies examine the relationship of the southern cotton grower with his market. George Ruble Woolfolk adopted a Beardian framework to explain that northern and western merchants forged a political alliance following the Civil War to dominate the Southern market and were successful because southerners failed to reserve their own market to themselves.[39] In a more illuminating work, Harold D. Woodman provided an institutional study of the financing and marketing of cotton from the beginning of the nineteenth century to the mid-1920's.[40] Devoting the major part of his study to brokers and factors, he concluded that by the 1880's improved transportation diverted the cotton trade away from the coastal markets to interior markets. The factor was, in turn, supplanted by storekeepers, who became agents for American and European cotton buyers. These storekeepers, who were oftentimes landlords as well, provided goods on credit in return for cotton. Thus, an interdependency between storekeeper and cotton grower was established, although Woodman was convinced that the South remained a dependent colonial region throughout the nineteenth century. Moreover, although the postbellum changes in cotton marketing led to a larger and wealthier middle-class of town merchants and bankers, economic diversification of the South was deterred in particular by a limited supply of liquid capital.

Despite the high quality of recent works in American agricultural history, there is need for more regional and state studies, as well as studies of individual crops, technological and scientific developments, and business and marketing practices.[41] Reynold M. Wik's book on the use of steam power on the farm needs to be joined by other studies of the introduction and use of technology in agriculture.[42] The contention that farmers were victims of predatory money lenders should be investigated beyond the limits established by Allan G. Bogue.[43] Finally, we need to know much more about the capital market and about agriculture's role in international trade than is supplied by two brief, although excellent, articles.[44]

Railroads and Economic Growth

Historians continue to give great attention to the financing, construction and operation of American railroads. Their interest can be explained, in part, by the romance attached to the "iron trails," but probably more important is the long-held assumption that railroads provided the main impetus to economic expansion, especially industrialization, during much of the nineteenth century. Two of the "new" economic historians used their econometric tools to analyze such claims. In investigating antebellum railroads, Albert Fishlow concluded that returns on investments during the years from 1830 to 1860 probably provided as good returns as alternative uses of capital, and that the "social rate of return" proved railroads beneficial to the economy as a whole. While denying Rostow's designation of railroads as the leading factor in spurring industrial growth in the 1840's, Fishlow concluded that they gave impetus to important technological innovations in the iron industry, induced migration which in turn stimulated agriculture, and contributed to the construction boom of the 1850's.[45] As noted earlier, Robert Fogel denied that railroads were "indispensable" to economic growth and argued that alternative forms of transportation would have resulted in only slightly diminished social savings.[46]

Two other studies of railroads take issue with conventional interpretations. Fogel's *The Union Pacific Railroad: A Casebook in Premature Enterprise*[47] contends that Congress avoided serious debate about the merits of public versus private ownership in voting massive aid to constructing the first transcontinental railroad, and simply yielded to public demand that such aid be given. Even at that, Fogel concluded that the enterprise was "premature" because of the unwillingness of private enterprise to undertake the project. He also viewed the Credit Mobilier as offering the possibility of large enough profits to induce promoters to invest in what appeared to be a risky venture. Julius Grodinsky followed up his rather favorable treatment of Jay Gould[48] with *Transcontinental Railroad Strategy, 1869-1893: A Study of Businessmen.*[49] He discussed the strategies of the familiar speculators and entrepreneurs, such as Gould, Hill, Harriman, Villard and Huntington, in fighting nature and each other so as to create and control railroad systems outside the east, as well as their abilities in raising capital to secure their positions. He concluded that these promoters were ambitious, bold and imaginative, and that they accomplished "one of the greatest industrial feats in the world's history" by creating a transportation system that brought vast natural resources into the national economy.

Other historians have continued to make contributions to understanding the development and role of railroads in American life of a more traditional kind.[50] John F. Stover filled a great need for a general history of railroads with his clearly-written and concise synthesis, *American Railroads*.[51] Richard C. Overton, on the other hand, concentrated on one railroad line, emphasizing the firm and its management. He did an outstanding job, however, in relating the Burlington line to general railroad history.[52] Both Stover and Overton differed from Fogel in believing that railroads were highly important to the nation's economic development.

Business and Industry

BUSINESS LEADERSHIP

Interest in the lives and careers of businessmen has shown no sign of diminution in recent years. A majority of the numerous biographical studies appearing in the past decade, however, tend to be concerned with entrepreneurs who are not so well-known as the Rockefellers, the Goulds, and the J. P. Morgans.[53] It is clear that the dominant characterization of Gilded Age business and industrial leaders as "robber barons" who plundered the nation of its natural resources, corrupted democratic institutions, and oppressed farmers and workers, all for their own self-interest, continues to give way to a moral relativism that guides scholars to view businessmen by the standards of the society in which they lived and worked. Entrepreneurial historians view their subjects as creative agents in economic change, and they argue that the long-run material gains for society far outweighed the immediate antisocial and self-serving activities of nineteenth-century business leaders.[54]

The best of the biographical studies present a balanced portrait, carefully assessing the contributions of their subjects but not omitting or explaining away their shortcomings as entrepreneurs or human beings. The most ambitious and, in some ways, the most successful of recent biographies of business leaders is Joseph Frazier Wall's *Andrew Carnegie*,[55] a massive and fascinating book. Wall carefully reviewed Carnegie's exposure and ties to Chartism in his native Scotland and explained how he adapted his views to conditions and events in his adopted America. The story of Carnegie's rise from a telegraph messenger boy to the world's best-known steelmaker is retold, but with verve and new explanations. Carnegie did embody the Horatio Alger legend, but he benefited greatly from being in the right place at the right time and from the aid of powerful and highly-placed friends. Wall gave credit to Carnegie as an innovator when he deserved it, but he did not hesitate to be critical when Carnegie was shortsighted. Some of the most interesting discussion centers on Carnegie's success in accumulating capital (in his case, not in saving pennies from a weekly paycheck), and Wall laid to rest Carnegie's public assertion that he had succeeded by giving all his attention to steel production ("put all your eggs in one basket and then watch that basket"). The other familiar aspects of Carnegie's life are well covered: his supposed adherence to Social Darwinism and his formulation of the Gospel of Wealth; his negotiations with J. P. Morgan that led to the formation of U. S. Steel; and his philanthropy and peace activities. In all, this is a thoroughly enjoyable and illuminating biography of one of the leading figures of industrial America.

Three other biographies of prominent business figures deserve special mention. Edward C. Kirkland continued his distinguished scholarly career with a biography of one of the most paradoxical members on the American business scene, Charles Francis Adams, Jr.[56] Kirkland discussed Adams' important role in the Massachusetts Railroad Commission and his career as president of the Union Pacific Railroad. He portrayed a man who never attained the eminence of his illustrious ancestors or brothers, who was drawn to reform movements, and who, in spite of amassing a considerable amount of money, was highly critical of workers, politicians, and fellow-businessmen. Chester M. Destler traced the career of the attorney who represented independent oil producers of western Pennsylvania in their struggles against monopolistic practices of railroads, pipelines, and Standard Oil Company, in *Roger Sherman and the Independent Oil Men.*[57] Finally, John A. Garraty provided an interesting account of the early business career of George W. Perkins, who later became a partner in J. P. Morgan and Co.[58] Garraty's account includes some very useful information about business methods in insurance enterprises before the twentieth century.

BUSINESS AND INDUSTRIAL HISTORY AND TECHNOLOGY

Few noteworthy studies of entire industries have appeared in the 1960's, although there are two exceptions. Harold F. Williamson and Arnold R. Daum provide a broad and outstanding treatment of the petroleum industry during its formative years in *The American Petro-*

leum Industry: The Age of Illumination, 1859-1899.[59] The volume is particularly useful for its discussions of technological innovations in the production, refining, and transportation of petroleum products, and for its excellent section on the industry's foreign markets. About half the volume is devoted to the quarter-century after 1874 when Standard Oil dominated the industry. The authors concluded that this contemporary symbol of monopoly benefited from preferential railroad treatment, but Standard was efficient and consumers probably would not have gained much from more competition.

Peter Temin's *Iron and Steel in Nineteenth-Century America: An Economic Inquiry* is the first major attempt to chronicle and analyze the development of that most important industry.[60] Using economic analysis, Temin dealt with the market for and production of steel, the application of technology to production, price movements, and the organization of production. He concluded that the story of the industry from 1830 to 1900 resulted from the "increasing sophistication in the use of heat and a growing demand for iron and steel," while in the short-run the "growth of the economy produced a demand for rails which led to the exploitation of the Bessemer process."

America's eldest manufacturing industry still commands attention from historians. Paul F. McGouldrick, in his *New England Textiles in the Nineteenth Century: Profits and Investments,* dealt with the period from about 1835 to the late 1880's in analyzing profit rates, dividend policy, and investment behavior.[61] The shift of textile manufacturing from New England to the South is the subject of Jack Blicksilver's *Cotton Manufacturing in the Southeast: An Historical Analysis.*[62] The story told is one of initial hasty construction of small, uneconomic, and poorly-managed mills that were unable to compete with their northern rivals. Many of these enterprises failed, but slowly and through trial-and-error others survived and by the turn of the century were competing with northern firms. A case study of one of the survivors is Robert Sidney Smith's *Mill on the Dan: A History of Dan River Mills, 1882-1950.*[63]

A few historians continued to explore regional economic development by concentrating on business firms and industrial developments that benefited from the location's natural advantages. Woolen textile manufacturing in the Middle West contributed to that region's growth and development from the time of the Civil War until the turn of the century, according to Norman L. Crockett.[64] Because of the area's geographic isolation from the East, and in spite of shortages of capital and skilled labor, high interest rates, and retarded technology, the midwestern woolen industry operated at a profit by producing coarse and medium-grade woolens to meet local needs. Improved transportation and technology gradually ended this particular enterprise. Water power created by the Fox River caused a number of Wisconsin towns to concentrate first on flour milling and eventually on paper manufacturing, which is the subject of Charles N. Glaab and Lawrence H. Larsen, *Factories in the Valley: Neenah-Menasha, 1870-1915*.[65] An excellent study of entrepreneurial activity in relationship to environment, technology, and marketing has been provided by Ralph W. Hidy, Frank Ernest Hill, and Allan Nevins in *Timber and Men: The Weyerhaeuser Story*.[66] These authors show how a family firm in Illinois evolved into the central force in lumbering operations in Wisconsin and Minnesota, and then into a southern and western empire producing a wide range of forest products for an international market.

Whatever the contributions to the economy made by regional specialization, the factors causing the nationalization of the American market offered new challenges to entrepreneurs and their firms to rationalize their operations in order to take advantage of an expanded market. Important and imaginative work was done by Alfred D. Chandler, Jr. in analyzing how American business met this challenge. His article, "The Beginnings of 'Big Business' in American Industry," shows that by 1893 producers of consumers' goods developed integrated operations, both vertical and horizontal, to secure raw materials, manufacture, distribute and finance their business. Soon thereafter manufacturers of producers' goods followed suit. Chandler concluded that "*the* major innovation in the American economy between the 1880's and the turn of the century was the creation of the great corporations in American industry."[67]

The great merger movements beginning in the 1890's received new statistical analysis in Ralph L. Nelson's *Merger Movements in American Industry, 1895-1956*.[68] The study concludes that the development of the capital market was the most important factor in causing combinations during the first wave occurring from 1895 to 1904 and that, not surprisingly, there was no important impact on the movement by the antitrust laws. He also found that merger activity was at least 20 per cent greater than earlier estimates have shown. Dealing with the sugar refining industry, Alfred S. Eichner traced the evolution from small-scale competitive firms to large-scale noncompetitive trusts and finally to oligopolistic structure.[69] Eichner concluded that the move toward consolidation was prompted by the smaller, less efficient producers in an effort to stabilize prices and regulate production.

Turning from the corporate efforts to organize themselves to better serve a large national market, Mira Wilkins has produced a pioneering study titled *The Emergence of Multinational Enterprise: American*

Business Abroad from the Colonial Era to 1914.[70] According to the author: "The conclusion is obvious, yet no single historian has previously documented it: by the start of the 1890's, leading American inventors, manufacturers, and marketers of sewing machines, harvesters, typewriters, elevators, printing presses, boilers, electrical apparatus, drugs, explosives, film, petroleum, and insurance already had investments outside the United States." This expansion was primarily a continuation of domestic growth, which followed three steps: first, the establishment of overseas marketing agencies, primarily in the more urbanized and technologically advanced areas of Europe and Canada; second, the creation of manufacturing plants to avoid costly tariffs, patent restrictions, and other nationalistic business regulations; and third, investment in overseas sources of raw materials, which came mainly after the business consolidations of the 1890's.

Entrepreneurial activity and business organization alone do not, of course, account for the rapid economic development in the later nineteenth century. Historians have long ascribed a major role in that regard to the development and dissemination of technology. Jacob Schmookler studied inventions in the paper, agricultural equipment, petroleum refining, and railroad industries and concluded that such inventions seldom resulted from scientific discoveries but rather from "the recognition of a costly problem to be solved or a potentially profitable opportunity to be seized; in short, a technical problem or opportunity evaluated in economic terms."[71] Those problems, according to H. J. Habakkuk, were labor scarcity and increasing wage rates, causing a substitution of machines for men.[72] Some historians insisted, as well, that more attention must be given to investment in human capital, particularly in the training of scientists and engineers and educating a labor force capable of making efficient use of new technology.[73]

BANKING, SECURITIES MARKETING, AND LIFE INSURANCE ENTERPRISES

Several studies appeared in the 1960's that deal with the development of financial intermediaries and their role in facilitating economic growth. An overall view of American financial policies and institutions is provided by Margaret G. Myers's *A Financial History of the United States.*[74] This concise, nontechnical work focuses mainly on the evolution of the money market and it is set in broad economic and social contexts. Three other notable works deal with different types of banking institutions. Paul B. Trescott's *Financing American Enterprise: The Story of Commercial Banking* relates the development of commercial banks to the general economic development of the country from the late eighteenth to just after the middle of the twentieth century.[75] He concluded that commercial banks were the main institutional sources of capital, having been outranked in importance only by reinvested business income and the personal savings of wealthy individuals. A less important capital-supplying role was played by mutual savings banks, according to Weldon Welfling's *Mutual Savings Banks: The Evolution of a Financial Intermediary,* although in New York and the New England states their deposits usually exceeded those of commercial banks.[76] Some material on investment banks in the pre-twentieth century era is presented by Vincent P. Carosso's *Investment Banking in America;* however most of the book deals with developments after the turn of the century.[77]

Historians have long recognized the important economic role played by capital investments of both British and eastern American investors. Dorothy R. Adler discussed the evolution of the market for American securities in London, from a primitive state in the 1840's when British ironmakers accepted railroad bonds as payment for rail purchases to more sophisticated approaches in the decades after 1850 when the volume of securities increased markedly.[78] She concluded that although British investments in American railroads reached a market value of $1,500,000,000 by 1890, British capitalists seldom attempted to manage an American railroad. Instead, they established bondholder protection committees whose physical and moral presence was felt on Wall Street. Arthur M. Johnson and Barry E. Supple in *Boston Capitalists and Western Railroads: A Study in the Nineteenth-Century Railroad Investment Process* showed how several groups of Boston capitalists invested profits earned from commerce in the developing railroad network west of the Alleghenies.[79] Unlike British investors, they did take an active role in the selection of management, at least until investment banking and more professional management became important in the 1890's.

As of 1970, there is no adequate study of the securities market, although Lance Davis and Thomas R. Navin and Marian V. Sears provided brief treatments of important aspects of its development and operation.[80] A noteworthy attempt to tell the story of the most important securities exchange is Robert Sobel's *The Big Board: A History of the New York Stock Market.*[81] Somewhat less useful for the late nineteenth century and written with a different purpose is Cedric B. Cowing's *Populists, Plungers, and Progressives: A Social History of Stock and Commodity Speculation, 1890-1936.*[82]

Those who are interested in the capital formation role and the investment activities of life insurance companies will be disappointed that there still (as of 1970) are few studies on the subject. In many ways the best introduction is still Douglass North, "Capital Accumulation in Life Insurance Between the Civil War and the Investigation of 1905,"[83] although Morton Keller's *The Life Insurance Enterprise, 1885-1910:*

A Study in the Limits of Corporate Power adds more detailed information.[84] Keller concentrated on the five largest insurance companies to show how internal rivalries and external pressures caused entrepreneurs to alter their business practices and policies. One of the most interesting developments was the evolution of investment practices that led to the close relationship between insurance companies and the New York financial community.

Conclusion

It should be apparent that the decade of the 1960's has seen a rich variety of economic and historical studies that have greatly enhanced our knowledge of economic growth and development. Both "traditional" and "new" scholars broadened our understanding of the past, and we would be the poorer if either had relegated economic history exclusively to the other. We must have adequate statistical data to support our generalizations, and theory provided by economists, sociologists, and other social scientists can be utilized to explain economic change and bring order to masses of data. However, the tools of the economists can seldom explain human motivations, aspirations, or reactions, and the records of humans—letters, diaries, and other "literary" remains—are just as valuable in economic history as in any other branch of history. Moreover, if economic history is to be useful and esthetically pleasurable to a wide audience, it must not become so technical and esoteric that only one practitioner can speak to another.

The Cliometricians, in spite of their often exaggerated claims of having revolutionized the field of economic history, have thus far made only limited contributions and those have been rather narrowly focused. Two leading new economic historians evaluated quantitative economic history in 1971 and acknowledged that it had been "too narrowly focused in space and time." They also concluded that "compared to the attention given to problems of growth and efficiency there has been a neglect of the problems of distribution and equity."[85] Finally, and this is perhaps the major failing of the new versus the old, they recognized that "the greatest challenge to econometric historians is the determination of interaction among economic, political and social factors in the establishment of the institutions through which economic activities are carried on."[86] Cliometricians have been able to measure economic activity and to apply sophisticated models to their statistics, but the so-called traditionalists, with their literary sources, continued to assess the institutional, social and political framework within which economic development took place. One can only hope that the debate over method will not preclude the sharing of the insights of both groups.

FOOTNOTES

[1] Douglass North. "Quantative Research in American Economic History." *American Economic Review* 53: 128-130; No. 1, Pt. 1, March 1963.

[2] Barry E. Supple, editor, in "Introduction" to *The Experience of Economic Growth: Case Studies in Economic History*. New York: Random House, 1963. p. 3. This volume contains a selection of writings about economic development in several countries and provides a good introduction to the subject. A useful selection of articles pertaining to economic development in the United States is Ralph L. Andreano, editor. *New Views on American Economic Development: A Selective Anthology of Recent Works*. Cambridge: Schenkman Publishing Co., 1965.

[3] Cambridge University Press, 1960.

[4] See especially Henry Rosovsky. "The Take-Off into Sustained Controversy." *Journal of Economic History* 25: 271-275; No. 2, June 1965; and Albert Fishlow. "Empty Economic Stages." *Economic Journal* 75: 112-125; No. 297, March 1965.

[5] The two most noted volumes of compilations, reconstructions, and analyses of national income and product accounting data are William N. Parker, editor. *Trends in the American Economy in the Nineteenth Century*. National Bureau of Economic Research Studies in Income and Wealth. XXIV. Princeton: Princeton University Press, 1960; and Dorothy S. Brady, editor. *Output, Employment, and Productivity in the United States After 1800*. National Bureau of Economic Research Studies in Income and Wealth. XXX. New York: National Bureau of Economic Research, 1966.

[6] "Did the Civil War Retard Industrialization?" *Mississippi Valley Historical Review* 48: 197-210; No. 2, September 1961. Cochran's analysis and his affirmative reply led to criticism from Stephen Salsbury. "The Effect of the Civil War on American Industrial Development." *The Economic Impact of the American Civil War,* edited by Ralph Andreano. Cambridge: Schenkman Publishing Co., 1962. pp. 161-168; Harry N. Scheiber. "Economic Change in the Civil War Era: An Analysis of Recent Studies." *Civil War History* 11: 396-411; No. 4, December 1965; and Pershing Vartanian. "The Cochran Thesis: A Critique in Statistical Analysis." *Journal of American History* 51: 77-89; No. 1, June 1964.

[7] *Journal of Economic History* 17: 522-544; No. 4, December 1957.

[8] "The Economics of Slavery in the Ante Bellum South." *Journal of Political Economy* 66: 95-130; No. 2, April 1958.

[9] Numerous articles by Cliometricians explaining their methodologies and findings have appeared during the previous decade. Ralph L. Andreano, editor. *The New Economic History: Recent Papers on Methodology*. New York: Wiley, 1970, contains several of those essays that originally appeared in *Explorations in Entrepreneurial History, Second Series*. See also Robert W. Fogel. "The New Economic History, Its Findings and Methods." *Economic History Review*. Second Series. 19: 642-656; No. 3, December 1966; and Albert Fishlow and Robert W. Fogel. "Quantative Economic History: An Interim Evaluation, Past Trends and Present Tendencies." *Journal of Economic History* 31: 15-42; No. 1, March 1971.

[10] Baltimore: Johns Hopkins Press, 1964.

[11] For critiques dealing directly with issues raised by Fogel, see Peter D. McClelland. "Railroads, American Growth, and the New Economic History: A Critique." *Journal of Economic History* 28: 102-123; No. 1, March 1968; and Marc Nerlove. "Railroads and American Economic Growth." *ibid.* 26: 107-115; No. 1, March 1966. Generally critical of the claims made by the Cliometricians are Fritz Redlich. "'New' and Traditional Approaches to Economic History and Their Interdependence." *Journal of Economic History* 25: 480-495; No. 4, December 1965; and Harry N. Scheiber. "On the New Economic History—and Its Limitations: A Review Essay." *Agricultural History* 41: 383-395; No. 4, October 1967.

[12] Three useful discussions of the trends in business and entrepreneurial history are Hugh G. J. Aitken, editor. *Explorations in Enterprise*. Cambridge: Harvard

University Press, 1965; Harold F. Williamson. "Business History and Economic History." *Journal of Economic History* 26: 407-417; No. 4, December 1966; and Ralph W. Hidy. "Business History: Present Status and Future Needs." *Business History Review* 44: 483-497; No. 4, Winter 1970.

[13] *Economic Theory and Under-Developed Regions.* London: Gerald Duckworth and Co., 1957. p. 10.

[14] Englewood Cliffs: Prentice-Hall, 1966. A similar work has recently been published by North's colleague, Robert Higgs. *The Transformation of the American Economy, 1865-1914: An Essay in Interpretation.* New York: Wiley, 1971.

[15] Boston: Allyn and Bacon, 1969. See also Lance E. Davis, Jonathan R. T. Hughes and Duncan M. McDougall. *American Economic History: The Development of a National Economy.* 3rd ed. Homewood, Ill.: Richard D. Irwin, 1969; and John M. Peterson and Ralph Gray. *Economic Development of the United States.* Homewood, Ill.: Richard D. Irwin, 1969.

[16] Philadelphia: Lippincott, 1968. In addition, Hacker recently published a general history that not only vigorously challenges many of the conclusions reached by the Cliometricians but also some of his own earlier interpretations. *The Course of American Economic Growth and Development.* New York: Wiley, 1970.

[17] Kirkland's *Industry Comes of Age: Business, Labor and Public Policy, 1860-1897,* New York: Holt, Rinehart and Winston, 1961, is a well-written and valuable survey of the period, although it takes the point of view of successful 19th-century business and professional elites.

[18] Norman: University of Oklahoma Press, 1960. This reprint of the 1930 edition now makes this scarce work available to many more individuals and libraries.

[19] *Bankers and Cattlemen: The Stocks-and-Bonds, Havana-Cigar, Mahogany-and-Leather Side of the Cowboy Era: Politics, Investors, and Operators from 1870 to 1900.* New York: Knopf, 1966.

[20] *The Matador Land and Cattle Company.* Norman: The University of Oklahoma Press, 1964.

[21] *The Francklyn Land & Cattle Company: A Panhandle Enterprise, 1882-1957.* Austin: The University of Texas Press, 1963.

[22] *The Espuela Land and Cattle Company: A Study of A Foreign-Owned Ranch in Texas.* Austin: Texas State Historical Association, 1970. This revised edition of the author's *The Spur Ranch,* published in 1934, uses new evidence to produce new interpretations.

[23] See also Wilbur Coe. *Ranch on the Ruidoso: The Story of A Pioneer Family in New Mexico, 1871-1968.* New York: Knopf, 1968; Robert H. Fletcher. *Free Grass to Fences.* New York: University Publishers, 1960, a rather poor account of the Montana cattle industry; and J. Orin Oliphant. *On the Cattle Ranges of the Oregon Country.* Seattle: University of Washington Press, 1968, primarily an economic study that provides a good comparison with the Great Plains cattle industry. A significant contribution to frontier urban history is made by Robert R. Dykstra's *The Cattle Towns,* New York: Knopf, 1968, which shows how businessmen and town promoters in several Kansas towns took advantage of the economic opportunities afforded by the cattle trade.

[24] *British Investments and the American Mining Frontier, 1860-1901.* Ithaca: Cornell University Press, 1958.

[25] Chicago: Aldine Publishing Co., 1968.

[26] New Haven: Yale University Press, 1970.

[27] *Clarence King, A Biography.* New York: Macmillan, 1958.

[28] *Scientists in Conflict: The Beginnings of the Oil Industry in California.* San Marino: The Huntington Library, 1969. An interesting account of the relationship between science, technology and economic growth is found in Walter K. Ferguson. *Geology and Politics in Frontier Texas, 1845-1909.* Austin: The University of Texas Press, 1969.

[29] New York: Appleton-Century-Crofts, 1962.

[30] *Mining Frontiers of the Far West, 1848-1880.* New York: Holt, Rinehart and Winston, 1963.

[31] *The Bonanza West: The Story of Western Mining Rushes, 1848-1900.* Norman: The University of Oklahoma Press, 1963. A Utah copper mine that pioneered in opencut mining and other mechanical and mass-production innovations is the subject of Leonard J. Arrington and Gary B. Hansen. *"The Richest Hole on Earth": A History of the Bingham Copper Mine.* Logan: Utah State University Press, 1963. The current interest in ecology makes for great interest in Robert L. Kelley's *Gold vs. Gain: The Hydraulic Mining Controversy in California's Sacramento Valley.* Glendale: Arthur H. Clark Co., 1959. A very interesting compilation of drawings and photographs of mining activities of all types is Howard N. and Lucille L. Sloane. *A Pictorial History of American Mining: The Adventure and Drama of Finding and Extracting Nature's Wealth from the Earth, From Pre-Columbian Times to the Present.* New York: Crown Publishers, 1970.

[32] As examples, see Douglass C. North. *Growth and Welfare in the American Past.* pp. 137-148; and Robert Higgs. *The Transformation of the American Economy.* pp. 79-106.

[33] Gilbert C. Fite. "Expanded Frontiers in Agricultural History." *Agricultural History* 35: 175-181; No. 4, October 1961. p. 176.

[34] New York: Holt, Rinehart and Winston, 1966.

[35] *The Farmer's Last Frontier.* New York: Farrar and Rinehart, 1945.

[36] *Change in Agriculture: The Northern United States, 1820-1870.* Cambridge: Harvard University Press, 1969.

[37] Chicago: University of Chicago Press, 1963. An important companion volume that traces the characteristics and changes in land use and ownership during that transitional period is Margaret Beattie Bogue. *Patterns from the Sod: Land Use and Tenure in the Grand Prairie, 1850-1900.* Springfield, Ill.: Illinois State Historical Library, 1959.

[38] Madison: The State Historical Society of Wisconsin, 1963.

[39] *The Cotton Regency: The Northern Merchants and Reconstruction, 1865-1880.* New York: Bookman Associates, 1958.

[40] *King Cotton and His Retainers: Financing and Marketing the Cotton Crop of the South, 1800-1925.* Lexington: University of Kentucky Press, 1968.

[41] A model study is C. Vann Woodward. *Origins of the New South, 1877-1913.* Baton Rouge: Louisiana State University Press, 1951. See also Carol K. Rothrock Bleser. *The Promised Land: The History of the South Carolina Land Commission, 1869-1890.* Columbia: University of South Carolina Press, 1969; and Robert L. Brandfon. *Cotton Kingdom of the New South: A History of the Yazoo Mississippi Delta from Reconstruction to the Twentieth Century.* Cambridge: Harvard University Press, 1967. Earl W. Hayter has collected and revised several of his previously published articles, as well as contributing some new ones, about barbed wire, veterinary medicine, and swindlers of farmers in *The Troubled Farmer, 1850-1900: Rural Adjustment to Industrialism.* DeKalb: Northern Illinois University Press, 1968. An important study of the dissemination of information to farmers is provided by Roy V. Scott. *The Reluctant Farmer: The Rise of Agricultural Extension to 1914.* Urbana: The University of Illinois Press, 1970.

[42] *Steam Power on the American Farm.* Philadelphia: University of Pennsylvania Press, 1953. See also Wayne D. Rasmussen. "The Impact of Technological Change on American Agriculture." *Journal of Economic History* 22: 578-591; No. 4, December 1962.

[43] *Money at Interest: The Farm Mortgage on the Middle Border.* Ithaca: Cornell University Press, 1955. A recent study in the Bogue tradition concludes that money invested in frontier Iowa land from 1840-1890 yielded more than the best average yields from stocks and bonds and that non-resident investors "served a useful and often beneficial function." See Robert P. Swierenga. *Pioneers and Profits: Land Speculation on the Iowa Frontier.* Ames: Iowa State University Press. 1968.

[44] Lance E. Davis. "The Investment Market, 1870-1914: The Evolution of a National Market." *Journal of Economic History* 25: 355-399; No. 3, September 1965; and Morton Rothstein. "America in the International Rivalry for the British Wheat Market." *Mississippi Valley Historical Review* 47: 401-418; No. 3, December 1960.

[45] *American Railroads and the Transformation of the Ante Bellum Economy.* Cambridge: Harvard University Press, 1965.

[46] *Railroads and American Economic Growth.*

[47] Baltimore: The Johns Hopkins Press, 1960.

[48] *Jay Gould: His Business Career, 1867-1892.* Philadelphia: University of Pennsylvania Press, 1957.

[49] Philadelphia: University of Pennsylvania Press, 1962.

[50] Two studies of the transcontinental railroad are Wesley S. Griswold. *A Work of Giants: Building the First Transcontinental Railroad.* New York: McGraw-Hill, 1962; and Robert W. Howard. *The Great Iron Trail: The Story of the First Transcontinental Railroad.* New York: G. P. Putnam's Sons, 1962. Lesser known railroad lines are treated by Robert G. Athearn. *Rebel of the Rockies: A History of the Denver and Western Rio Grande Railroad.* New Haven: Yale University Press, 1962; Mildred H. Smith. *Early History of the Long Island Railroad, 1834-1900.* Uniondale, Long Island: Salisbury Printers, 1958; and James R. Fair, Jr. *The North Arkansas Line: The Story of the Missouri and North Arkansas Railroad.* Berkeley, Calif.: Howell-North Books, 1969. A study of railroads in a single state, although written for general readers, is Willis F. Dunbar. *All Aboard: A History of Railroads in Michigan.* Grand Rapids: Eerdmans Publishing Co., 1969. Charles N. Glaab's *Kansas City and the Railroads: Community Policy in the Growth of a Regional Metropolis.* Madison: The State Historical Society of Wisconsin, 1962, is a model study of the relationship between community development and railroad development. An unusual study of the competitive practices of railroads is provided by William L. Taylor. *A Productive Monopoly: The Effect of Railroad Control on New England Coastal Steamship Lines, 1870-1916.* Providence: Brown University Press, 1970.

[51] Chicago: University of Chicago Press, 1961.

[52] *Burlington Route: A History of the Burlington Lines.* New York: Knopf, 1965.

[53] Recent attention has been given to western entrepreneurs and their contributions to the region's economy: Norman E. Tutorow. *Leland Stanford: Man of Many Careers.* Menlo Park, Calif.: Pacific Coast Publishers, 1971; Gordon B. Dodds. *The Salmon King of Oregon: R. D. Hume and the Pacific Fisheries.* Chapel Hill: The University of North Carolina Press, 1963; John Fahey. *Inland Empire: D. C. Corbin and Spokane.* Seattle: University of Washington Press, 1965; and Harry E. Kelsey, Jr. *Frontier Capitalist: The Life of John Evans, Jr.* Boulder: Pruett Publishing and State Historical Society of Colorado, 1969; and Stanley P. Hirshson. *Grenville M. Dodge: Soldier, Politician, Railroad Pioneer.* Bloomington: Indiana University Press, 1967. Studies of eastern entrepreneurs include Richard O'Connor. *Gould's Millions.* Garden City: Doubleday, 1962, a popular account; Paul Sarnoff. *Russell Sage: The Money King.* New York: Ivan Obolensky, Inc., 1965; Anita Shafer Goodstein. *Biography of A Businessman: Henry W. Sage, 1814-1897.* Ithaca: Cornell University Press, 1962, which provides a good case study of the transition from mercantile to industrial capitalism; and Leonard A. Swann, Jr. *John Roach. Maritime Entrepreneur: The Years As Naval Contractor, 1862-1886.* Annapolis: U.S. Naval Institute, 1965. Two recent works chronicle the careers of American businessmen whose successes were primarily outside the country: Jacob Adler. *Claus Spreckels: The Sugar King in Hawaii.* Honolulu: University of Hawaii Press, 1966; and Watt Stewart. *Keith and Costa Rica: A Biographical Study of Minor Cooper Keith.* Albuquerque: University of New Mexico Press, 1964. We are also fortunate to have an updated version of Fritz

Redlich's *The Molding of American Banking: Men and Ideas.* New York: Johnson Reprint Corp., 1968.

[54] Of the recent reviews of the "robber baron" controversy, see John Tipple. "The Anatomy of Prejudice: Origins of the Robber Baron Legend." *Business History Review* 33: 510-524; No. 4, Winter 1959; and "The Robber Baron in the Gilded Age: Entrepreneur or Iconoclast?", in H. Wayne Morgan, editor. *The Gilded Age: A Reappraisal.* Syracuse: Syracuse University Press, 1963. pp. 14-37. Different points of view are offered by Allan Solganick. "The Robber Baron Concept and Its Revisionists." *Science and Society* 29: 257-269; No. 3, Summer 1965; and Gabriel Kolko. "The Premises of Business Revisionism." *Business History Review* 33: 330-344; No. 3, Autumn 1959.

[55] New York: Oxford University Press, 1970.

[56] *Charles Francis Adams, Jr., 1835-1915: The Patrician At Bay.* Cambridge: Harvard University Press, 1965.

[57] Ithaca: Cornell University Press, 1967.

[58] *Right-Hand Man: The Life of George W. Perkins.* New York: Harper & Brothers, 1960.

[59] Evanston: Northwestern University Press, 1959.

[60] Cambridge: The M.I.T. Press, 1964. Albert H. Z. Carr's *John D. Rockefeller's Secret Weapon.* New York: McGraw-Hill Book Co., 1962, is the story of Standard Oil's Union Tank Car Company.

[61] Cambridge: Harvard University Press, 1968.

[62] Atlanta: Bureau of Business and Economic Research, School of Business Administration, Georgia State College of Business Administration. Bulletin No. 5, 1959.

[63] Durham: Duke University Press, 1960.

[64] *The Woolen Industry of the Midwest.* Lexington: University of Kentucky Press, 1970.

[65] Madison: The State Historical Society of Wisconsin, 1969. See also Nollie Hickman. *Mississippi Harvest: Lumbering in the Longleaf Pine Belt, 1840-1915.* University, Miss.: The University of Mississippi Press for the Forest History Society, 1962; and Powell A. Moore. *The Calumet Region: Indiana's Last Frontier.* Indianapolis: Indiana Historical Bureau, 1959.

[66] New York: Macmillan, 1963. For a discussion of another type of enterprise, see Joseph G. Knapp. *The Rise of American Cooperative Enterprise, 1620-1920.* Danville, Ill.: Interstate Printers and Publishers, 1968, although it concentrates mainly upon agricultural cooperatives.

[67] *Business History Review* 33: 1-31; No. 1, Spring 1959. Chandler has extended this study into the 20th century in *Strategy and Structure: Chapters in the History of the Industrial Enterprise.* Cambridge: The M.I.T. Press, 1962. A brief, popularized history of business that tells us little that is new is John Chamberlain's *The Enterprising Americans: A Business History of the United States.* New York: Harper & Row, 1963.

[68] National Bureau of Economic Research, General Series No. 66, Princeton: Princeton University Press, 1959. The economic setting within which business consolidations increased is the subject of Charles Hoffmann's *The Depression of the Nineties: An Economic History.* Westport, Conn.: Greenwood Publishing Corp., 1970.

[69] *The Emergence of Oligopoly: Sugar Refining as a Case Study.* Baltimore: The Johns Hopkins Press, 1969.

[70] Cambridge: Harvard University Press, 1970.

[71] *Invention and Economic Growth.* Cambridge: Harvard University Press, 1966.

[72] *American and British Technology in the Nineteenth Century: The Search for Labour-Saving Inventions.* Cambridge University Press, 1962.

[73] See, for example, Douglass C. North. *Growth and Welfare in the American Past.* pp. 6-7. Two excellent studies deal with the development of engineering as a profession: Raymond H. Merritt. *Engineering in American Society, 1850-1875.*

Lexington: The University Press of Kentucky, 1969; and Monte A. Calvert. *The Mechanical Engineer in America, 1830-1910: Professional Cultures in Conflict.* Baltimore: The Johns Hopkins Press, 1967.

[74] New York: Columbia University Press, 1970.

[75] New York: Harper & Row, 1963.

[76] Cleveland: Press of Case Western Reserve University, 1968.

[77] Cambridge: Harvard University Press, 1970. See also John A. Kouwenhoven. *Partners in Banking: An Historical Portrait of a Great Private Bank, Brown Brothers Harriman & Co., 1818-1968.* Garden City: Doubleday, 1968; and David Cole. *The Development of Banking in the District of Columbia.* New York: William-Frederick Press, 1959. Although it deserves more treatment than a footnote reference, Milton Friedman and Anna Jacobson Schwartz, *A Monetary History of the United States, 1867-1960,* Princeton: Princeton University Press, 1963, is a major contribution to understanding the money supply, although it may prove to be difficult reading for the non-specialist.

[78] *British Investment in American Railways, 1834-1898.* Edited by Muriel E. Hidy. Charlottesville, Va.: University Press of Virginia, 1970.

[79] Cambridge: Harvard University Press, 1967.

[80] Lance Davis. "The Investment Market, 1870-1914: The Evolution of a National Market." *Journal of Economic History* 25: 355-399; No. 3, September 1965; "Capital Immobilities and Finance Capitalism: A Study of Economic Evolution in the United States, 1820-1920." *Explorations in Entrepreneurial History,* Second Series. 1: 88-105; No. 1, Fall 1963; Thomas R. Navin and Marian V. Sears. "The Rise of the Market for Industrial Securities." *Business History Review* 19: 105-138; No. 2, June 1955.

[81] New York: The Free Press, 1965.

[82] Princeton: Princeton University Press, 1965. See also George W. Bishop. *Charles H. Dow and the Dow Theory.* New York: Appleton-Century-Crofts, 1960.

[83] In William Miller, editor. *Men in Business: Essays on the Historical Role of the Entrepreneur.* New York: Harper Torchbooks, 1962. pp. 238-253.

[84] Cambridge: Harvard University Press, 1963. Another useful study is R. Carlyle Buley. *The Equitable Life Assurance Society of the United States, 1859-1964.* 2 Vols. New York: Appleton-Century-Crofts, 1967.

[85] Albert Fishlow and Robert Fogel. "Quantitive Economic History: An Interim Evaluation, Past Trends and Present Tendencies." *loc cit.* p. 31.

[86] *Ibid.* p. 39. There have been, for example, many excellent works dealing with government-business relations. On the subject of government regulation see Gabriel Kolko. *Railroads and Regulation, 1877-1916.* Princeton: Princeton University Press, 1965; Robert W. Harbeson. "Railroads and Regulation, 1877-1916: Conspiracy or Public Interest?" *Journal of Economic History* 27: 230-242; No. 2, June 1967; Paul W. MacAvoy. *The Economic Effects of Regulation. The Trunk-Line Railroad Cartels and the Interstate Commerce Commission Before 1900.* Cambridge: The M.I.T. Press, 1965; and Jordan Jay Hillman. *Competition and Railroad Price Discrimination: Legal Precedent and Economic Policy.* Evanston: Transportation Center at Northwestern University, 1968. The legal, promotional and regulatory activities of state and federal governments are the subjects of Robert S. Hunt. *Law and Locomotives: The Impact of the Railroad on Wisconsin Law in the Nineteenth Century.* Madison: The State Historical Society of Wisconsin, 1958; James Willard Hurst. *Law and Economic Growth: The Legal History of the Lumber Industry in Wisconsin, 1836-1915.* Cambridge: Harvard University Press, 1964; Gerald D. Nash. *State Government and Economic Development: A History of Administrative Politics in California, 1849-1933.* Berkeley: Institute of Governmental Studies, University of California, 1964; Carter Goodrich. *Government Promotion of American Canals and Railroads, 1800-1890.* New York: Columbia University Press, 1960; and Arnold M. Paul. *Conservative Crisis and the Rule of Law: Attitudes of Bar and Bench, 1887-1895.* Ithaca: Cornell Univ. Press, 1960.

· 19 ·

The Progressive Years, 1900–1917

Robert H. Wiebe

Introduction

THE fundamental issue at stake in the history of the progressive period is modernization, and around this issue a profound change in scholarship is occurring. Once historians concentrated upon the impressive range of reforms that marked those years: the regulation of business through such agencies as the Federal Trade Commission, a Federal Reserve System, and a strengthened Interstate Commerce Commission; the dedication of settlement and social workers, educators and philanthropists, to humanize the city and protect its poorer citizens; the attacks upon venality in government and the demands for closer ties between voters and officeholders; and the recognition of a public interest in such matters as the dangers of factory work, the waste of natural resources, and the adulteration of food. Ultimately it was the men and women behind the reforms—the progressives—who dominated these studies. The era belonged to its stars: the flamboyant Theodore Roosevelt and the impassioned Woodrow Wilson, fighting Bob LaFollette and patient Jane Addams, the muckrakers and the insurgents. People saw problems and led movements to correct them.

Now the subject has grown less personal, more abstract. Biographies are no longer common. Reformers appear less important in their own right and more significant as parts of a larger pattern, as clues to a general social puzzle. Historians increasingly concern themselves with social change and social control, with the distribution of power and its uses, with the ways people thought and how the ways they thought affected the ways they acted. In sum, the current student of the progressive years wants to know how American society was put together and how it functioned. Behind these investigations is a compelling sense that something big was abroad in the land around 1900, that some fundamental shift was underway during the progressive years, and it is this feeling which has elevated modernization—the term that best captures its essence—to the place of primacy.

As elusive as it is important, *modern* is a conceptual expression of our present, an attempt to abstract from our society those critical characteristics that distinguish not merely today from yesterday or the United States from Ghana but one way of life, one quality of culture, from some other. Modernization is the process creating this present. What saves modernization from becoming everyman's intellectual plaything—one more excuse to claim universality for one's own experience—is the model, or ideal-type, that transcends any single society and describes the basic elements of something we might call urban-industrial society, wherever it is found. Honest people differ over the model. Nevertheless, there is approximate agreement that its components are found somewhere in these categories: the mechanization of production and distribution; the impersonality of social relations, including large bureaucratic organizations and centralized power; the development of mass communication with increasing uniformity of attitudes; and the secularization of popular thought, accompanied by a greater discipline to the clock and calendar and by a rising faith in scientific solution to human problems. Some people believe America is now passing beyond or turning away from the society these categories suggest. We hear more and more terms like "post-industrial" and "post-modern" or simply "the new society." But the very difficulties of finding a satisfactory vocabulary underline the tentativeness of the changes it describes. Modern, in the sense of this paragraph, still dominates our national life.

No historian claims that the whole of America pivoted at some time between 1900 and 1917. All scholars recognize that complex social processes unfold awkwardly, unevenly, with consequences that require decades to develop. Nevertheless, because so many historians have designated this era as peculiarly critical to a major transition and have defined the transition as one from a decentralized, agrarian-minded, nineteenth-century America to an increasingly integrated, urban-oriented, twentieth-century society, we are asked to see the shape of our time, however rough, emerging around these years. The issues of what made American society modern, what effects such a profound change had upon the lives of those who experienced it, and what problems the early stages of modernization left to later generations have reoriented the scholarly quest.

What has happened to the history of the progressive era, therefore, is far more than an alteration in priorities, deemphasizing one problem in order to emphasize another. The cast of our picture is so different we can no longer say it contains more of this, less of that, in comparison with an older view. The subjects that exercised an earlier generation of historians are being transformed to serve very different purposes. While the works of these scholars provide an indispensable accumulation of information and a pattern of questions and answers no one wishes to ignore, recent historians have tried to see all of this through another lens, to begin again in their search for the proper angle of historical vision.

Overview

Like the participants in the progressive movement, the earliest historians of these years agreed that something special had transpired early in the twentieth century. How they demonstrated the era's importance tells us a good deal about what message they wanted us to receive. In 1931, Harold Underwood Faulkner[1] could argue that the very concentration of so much reform activity in so few years was itself sufficient reason to study them. This had been the focus of the reformers themselves, and its logical consequence was an evaluation of the period's significance in terms also familiar to the progressives: Did these reforms succeed or fail? Faulkner judged them favorably. So did Russel B. Nye's *Midwestern Progressive Politics*,[2] which traced the reforms of the progressive movement into the New Deal and assigned progressive leaders a major part in a reform tradition that, in the main, had achieved its objectives. John Chamberlain,[3] on the other hand, argued that because none of the leading progressives had had the courage to pursue America's problems to their core—to the dominance of finance capitalists—their flimsy efforts had collapsed by the 1920's. Louis Filler similarly lamented the failure of substantial reform in *Crusaders for American Liberalism*,[4] a sympathetic study of the muckrakers that ended with their defeat at the hands of scheming big businessmen. If in a hypothetical debate Chamberlain and Filler could have convinced Faulkner and Nye that indeed the reforms had failed, Faulkner and Nye could no longer have justified their books. Both sides judged the era according to the efficacy of its reforms. If the reforms succeeded, the era was important; if they did not, it was not.

Now historians assert that changes so basic, so irrevocable, were occurring around the progressive years that the meaning of the future depends upon them, not their meaning upon the future. Questions of success and failure are at best subsidiary, at worst irrelevant. If something fundamental happened, importance is a self-evident proposition. Historians may consider it a turn for the better or for the worse, but they no longer debate its significance. The problem now is to define the general process of change: to locate its sources, to examine its implications in various areas of society, and, for historians of the progressive era, to specify the place of what happened between 1900 and 1917 in the broader story of modernization.

Here as in so many other realms Richard Hofstadter's *Age of Reform*[5] set an early standard against which historians continue to test their ideas. Hofstadter viewed modern social change in America as a number of distinct steps rather than as a steady development. Progressivism was separated from Populism on one side and the New Deal on the other as a particular attempt by well-to-do but uneasy Americans to square an organized, impersonal society with an older individualistic ethic—an effort, in other words, to reconcile incompatibles. However quixotic, progressivism shifted the initiative from rural to urban America and located problems that in a quite different way the New Deal would also meet.

Three other general interpretations have since appeared. Samuel P. Hays in *The Response to Industrialism: 1885-1914*[6] smoothed Hofstadter's peaks and troughs into a gradual line of change. Beginning in the late nineteenth century, increasingly tough-minded interest groups discarded an earlier utopian style and demanded immediate economic advantages appropriate to an urban-industrial society, a pattern of adaptation that after 1900 produced the reforms we associate with progressivism. In a later article[7] Hays placed these changes in a theoretical framework. As the United States moved from the nineteenth into the twentieth century, it altered from a society resting upon personal community life and values into an impersonal, integrated, and cosmopolitan society. Along this continuum we can trace the movement toward modern America. Robert H. Wiebe in *The Search for Order: 1877-1920*[8] also emphasized the change from a society of island communities to one of impersonality and bureaucracy, but unlike Hays he found a sharp break around 1900, a collapse of nineteenth-century society followed by the gradual emergence of a new twentieth-century system. Finally, Ray Ginger's *Age of Excess*[9] located the progressive years in a phase of capitalist development that was characterized by an inability to absorb the surpluses of its industrial plant. These were tense, raw years, Ginger told us, with harsh oppression of the working class and imperialistic drives for markets abroad. Only a world war saved the system from its flaws.

There are salient differences among these four interpretations. Hofstadter, supplemented by Otis L. Graham's account[10] of bewildered progressives facing the New Deal, stresses the limited, ambivalent nature of the changes of the early twentieth century, while Ginger, Hays, and Wiebe judge them both more sweeping and more intimately linked to developments later in the century. Ginger and Hays assign greater determining power to economic forces and business organization and describe a steady flow of change; whereas Hofstadter and Wiebe find greater significance in the distinctive ways people perceive and attempt to master their world and, in addition, discover a signal discontinuity between the nineteenth and twentieth centuries. However, what characterizes these four above all is their common emphasis upon major social changes that subordinate reforms and reformers to the process of America's modernization.

Thought and Values

One of the critical indicators of modernity, as the works of Hofstadter, Graham, and Wiebe illustrate, is the manner in which people think. A number of excellent studies explore that subject, and each reveals a basic shift in or near the progressive years toward styles we can recognize as similar, perhaps fundamental, to our own. The most important of these studies is still Morton G. White's *Social Thought in America*,[11] an analysis of the innovative roles of John Dewey, Thorstein Veblen, Oliver Wendell Holmes, Jr., Charles Beard, and James Harvey Robinson. Their radical turn around 1900 to relativism, a revolt against the timeless abstractions that dominated nineteenth-century thought, was designed to coordinate ideas with social and scientific process and prepare Americans to manage the particular conditions in which they lived. Eric F. Goldman in *Rendezvous with Destiny*[12] recasts the same approach and spreads it more gradually over time. The transformation that he describes centered about the pace of change and man's power to control it. By the progressive years, Goldman writes, American intellectuals were proclaiming society's capacity to determine its own destiny, to master the world through disciplined intelligence. Like White, Goldman places a socially-conscious relativism at the heart of this revolution in American thought. While both men accuse the relativists of confusing means and ends and evading the need for precise values, both consider the change profound, one that would dominate much of twentieth-century America.

The optimism of the new faith in social engineering is captured in Samuel Haber's *Efficiency and Uplift*,[13] an examination of the ways in which Frederick Taylor's program for scientific management came to be viewed as a mechanism for harnessing human energies to an endless, rational progress. In *Prohibition and the Progressive Movement 1900-1920*,[14] James H. Timberlake describes the hopes that reformers invested in prohibition as one scheme of social engineering. Charles Forcey, *The Crossroads of Liberalism*,[15] traces the failure of three spokesmen of progressivism—Herbert Croly, Walter Weyl, and Walter Lippmann—to penetrate the surface of a comparable optimism about American democracy's capacity for limitless improvement and the consequent collapse of liberalism soon after the progressive era as a vehicle for effective reform.

Henry F. May[16] attacks the problem of a transition to modernity in another fashion. It was the importation of a certain cluster of ideas about man, art, and society, May declares, ideas associated with such Europeans as Nietzsche and Freud, that converted a small circle of intellectuals around the First World War and prepared America for a dramatic change from the simple certainties of small-town life to the mysteries of irrationality and contingency that infuse the modern mind. While Christopher Lasch[17] pushed the transition back to the turn of the century and concerns himself more with the psychic state of his subjects, he too stresses the significance of new ideas about sex, combined with new urges for personal expression, as basic components of a newly self-conscious intellectual community. The path of modern dissent, he believes, was set early in the 1900's.

Among those who have written major works on the intellectual history of the progressive years, only David W. Noble offers a sharply different picture. In *The Paradox of Progressive Thought*,[18] Noble characterizes the intellectuals of the era as utopians trapped by intellectual contradictions that paralyzed them in the face of an unanticipated catastrophe, the First World War. Dreams of an irresistible progress and a dawning day of man's mastery over his environment dissolved in the holocaust, and nothing was salvaged. Contrary to the usual view, Noble discovered not building blocks for the future but only the rubble of failure.

Two books that deal more with popular than with systematic thought offer parallel views of the movement into modern times. In *From the Depths*,[19] Robert H. Bremner details a broadening social awareness around the turn of the century to the human implications of an urban-industrial society and early efforts to ameliorate the lot of those who were cramped and defeated by the new order. John Higham turns over the coin. *Strangers in the Land*[20] analyzes the fears and hates that grew early in the century toward European immigrants and the repressive policies that tried to preserve an older, more homogeneous America.

With the exception of Noble, these intellectual and social historians have a common objective: the delineation of crucial changes marking the emergence of modern America. Theirs are almost uniformly critical studies, ones that emphasize the vagueness of the new relativism, the deficiencies of the new liberalism or the new radicalism, the failure to solve problems of poverty and ethnic conflict. Whether or not these qualities are attractive or even utilitarian, historians tell us that they represent the modern mind, that these patterns of thinking are the precursors of our time. In general, agreement upon the destruction of old certainties and the arrival of new faiths links these studies with the works of Hofstadter, Hays, and Wiebe.

Groups and Institutions

Another avenue into the progressive era explores changes in group and institutional behavior. Probably more scholarly energy in recent years has been devoted to this area than to any other. The subjects are highly visible, indeed very inviting. A labor union, a public school system, an organization of articulate reformers welcomes the scholar with a clearly defined subject and a ready set of data. Yet historians are now taking such visibility more as a clue than as a convenience. Why at approximately the same time did so many groups become so prominent? Why at approximately the same time did a wide range of institutions acquire new toughness and purpose? These questions, which underpin the works of Hofstadter, Hays, and Wiebe, serve also as a foundation for the studies of particular groups and institutions.

REFORMERS

The first group to attract scholars were the progressives themselves. While reforms preoccupied the historian, it was appropriate to concentrate upon the men and women who sponsored them, and a decade ago the most debated scholarly question was: Who were the progressives? Once again Hofstadter sketched the most provocative answer. The progressives, he said, were substantial citizens whose sense of importance rested upon traditional ways and values and whose reforms tried to preserve their positions of leadership against such new agglomerations of power as large corporations, city machines, and organized labor. In two books[21] George E. Mowry expanded and modified that description to include the reformers' faith in progress and the goodness of man and their dedication to gradualism and democracy. Although a number of historians have since taken issue with Hofstadter and Mowry, the peak of involvement with that particular question has clearly passed. Reform has so blended with larger issues of social change that Peter G. Filene[22] declares we should discard such terms as "progressive" and "progressive movement" as imprecise and misleading. When someone returns to the problem, as Sheldon Hackney does in *Populism to Progressivism in Alabama,*[23] he poses it for different reasons. Hackney's interest in defining Alabama progressives is to distinguish them from the Populists and thereby establish a major social break in that state at the turn of the century.

As historians less often ask who did or did not participate in reform, they have turned to subtler issues of quality in group and institutional behavior. In effect, historians now need to know what the actions of this group or that institution reveal about the changing nature of American society early in the twentieth century. In the process, new questions have invested many older studies with a fresh importance.

ECONOMIC GROUPS AND INSTITUTIONS

Histories of economic groups and institutions present what is by now a familiar picture. Although they vary in matters of timing, location, and explanation, almost all of them describe major changes occurring between 1900 and 1917. Two studies of big business, written far apart in time and in perspective, suggest an interim stage of modernization roughly analogous to the one Hofstadter outlines in the realm of progressive values. In Frederick Lewis Allen's *The Lords of Creation,*[24] J. Pierpont Morgan, drawing early in the twentieth century upon his massive financial resources and his even more overpowering reputation, exercised for the first time in American history a central control over the New York money market, itself a dominant institution in a new sense by 1900. Thirty years after Allen's book, Alfred D. Chandler, Jr., *Strategy and Structure,*[25] finds in the first two decades of the twentieth century many large corporations beginning to systematize control over sprawling enterprises that had grown so rapidly and raggedly during the late nineteenth century. Like Allen, Chandler describes a rather simple centralization, one that by the 1920's would give way to considerably more complex and diffuse patterns of power in both high finance and corporate structure. Both of these men, in other words, identify a significant but limited transition, a bridge between the chaotic late nineteenth century and a sophisticated modernization later in the twentieth.

Other studies of business locate more lasting changes during the progressive era. Allan Nevins' and Frank E. Hill's *Ford*[26] discusses the development before the First World War of modern mass production for a mass market in durable consumer goods. Morton Keller in *The Life Insurance Enterprise, 1885-1910*[27] and John A. Garraty in *Right-Hand*

Man[28] both described the emergence of the life insurance industry in approximately modern form, with Keller placing more emphasis upon controls that arose inside the corporations and Garraty more emphasis upon public pressures for responsible leadership. Parallelling these changes, Marguerite Green, *The National Civic Federation and the American Labor Movement, 1900-1925*,[29] examines an organization that reflected a new concern among certain big businessmen for broad public policy.

Farmers, Grant McConnell tells us in *The Decline of Agrarian Democracy*,[30] experienced equally basic changes in organization early in the twentieth century, changes that broke with the loose democratic tradition of the previous century and led to the establishment of elitist pressure groups, specifically the American Farm Bureau Federation. Social divisions in the countryside widened, and prosperous farmers increasingly allied themselves with business. Here the shift is radical, permanent, and essentially complete by the First World War. Bernard Mandel tells a similar story from a similar perspective in *Samuel Gompers*.[31] Around 1900 the American Federation of Labor, by then a sturdy organization of craft unions, turned from broad reform and humane concerns under Gompers' leadership toward the prejudiced self-interest of a wage-earning elite. Philip Taft[32] discusses these institutional developments with much greater sympathy for Gompers' difficulties and accomplishments.

SOCIAL GROUPS AND INSTITUTIONS

Groups and institutions that, for lack of a more precise term we may call social, extend the story of modernization with their own variations in timing and emphasis. In a manner reminiscent of White's "Revolt against Formalism," Lawrence A. Cremin's *The Transformation of the School*[33] describes how public education had acquired a new functional, socially-conscious definition by the early twentieth century, preparing the way for more formal changes in the 1920's. Echoing Haber's study of the efficiency passion and McConnell's account of institutional antidemocracy, Raymond E. Callahan's *Education and the Cult of Efficiency*[34] analyzes the dehumanizing, cost-accounting qualities of scientific management in the field of school administration. Laurence R. Veysey's *The Emergence of the American University*[35] offers a smoother account of the institutional transition in higher education. Competing concepts of liberal, utilitarian, and scientific education that had vied for dominance since the Civil War were blended—or blurred—in managerial compromises around 1900, giving the major universities the mixed, flexible forms that mark them as another institution of the modern era.

Among the new professions and specializations that proliferated during the progressive years, settlement and social work has received particular attention. Allen F. Davis in *Spearheads for Reform*[36] describes the mobilization of reform energies by settlement workers and their liberal allies in a number of systematic, effective drives to change both public consciousness and public policies. In *The Professional Altruist*,[37] Roy Lubove analyzes the process of professionalization rather than group action, and his account indicates that as the field of social work matured, it, like school administration as Callahan depicts it, was guided more and more by efficiency and detached rationality at the sacrifice of a certain exuberant humaneness.

Women, who played critical roles in settlement and social work and public education, were simultaneously demanding more general privileges in a modernizing society. While suffrage received most of the publicity, the special needs of female wage-earners, expanded services and protection for mothers and children, and movements to improve the morals of the nation, especially with regard to prostitution and liquor, also attracted many recruits. William L. O'Neill surveys this growing activity in *Everyone Was Brave*[38] and concludes on a note of failure. The women's movement, he writes, lacked an adequate framework for comprehending the position of women in American society. Suffrage, which came to dominate the movement, merely blinded women to the deeper issues of their subjection. By implication, Aileen Kraditor's *The Ideas of the Woman Suffrage Movement, 1890-1920*[39] supports this interpretation by delineating the narrow social vision of those who led the campaign for the vote. Women, the judgment runs in summary, contributed to the general process of modernization without significantly improving their position within that society.

Government and Politics

Because so many programs required government support, a fundamental part of modernization during the progressive era involved new relations between citizens and government. Historians have specified three areas of basic change: the ways citizens influenced government, the renovation of governments at all levels to accommodate new needs, and a new dynamic between government and citizens, a pattern of continuous interaction that separates the progressive years from the nineteenth century and points toward modern political behavior.

The classic study of citizen organization is Peter Odegard's *Pressure Politics*,[40] an account of single-minded, persistent leverage by a disciplined minority, the Anti-Saloon League, to achieve one goal, prohibition. What Odegard, a political scientist, offers as a timeless lesson in tactics, such studies as McConnell's of the Farm Bureau Federation and Davis's of the settlement workers root in the early twentieth century when pressure groups were first acquiring a modern cast. So also do Lubove's *The Progressives and the Slums*[41] and Wiebe's *Businessmen and Reform.*[42] Although Lubove judges the housing reformers of New York City too negative, too obsessed with ending evils, he describes systematic organization under the leadership of experts. These professional reformers ensured continuity to the activities of their groups and applied specialized knowledge to their campaigns. A new faith in facts and statistics, in scientific argumentation, also influenced such areas as the law, as Alpheus T. Mason mentioned in his biography of Louis D. Brandeis,[43] the reform of city finances,[44] and opposition to child labor.[45] While reform-minded businessmen relied in a strikingly new way upon the expert, their primary contribution to the new politics, as Wiebe's book illustrates, was nationwide organization not merely to sponsor legislation but even more to demand continuing regulation of the economy by the national government.

Oddly we have much less information about the modernization of political parties. Theodore J. Lowi's *At the Pleasure of the Mayor*[46] analyzes new uses of the patronage, and Zane L. Miller's *Boss Cox's Cincinnati*[47] examines the responses of an urban chieftain to a city newly integrated by transportation. Otherwise, we view changes in party behavior obliquely. David A. Shannon's discussion[48] of the Socialist Party, for example, tells by implication of the coordination of sectarian fragments in a reasonably stable, nationwide party that placed a degree of cooperation above the doctrines of any one group.

As governments at all levels extended their responsibilities, new values of systematic procedure and a new importance for effective administration gave them modern qualities. The best studies of this subject concern the national government. The sum of information about the progressive years in A. Hunter Dupree's *Science in the Federal Government*[49] provides an excellent picture of the government's range—its new roles in administering, coordinating, and encouraging activities that had previously been local, often private matters, and its new dependence upon a variety of highly trained specialists. From a very different vantage point, William Preston, Jr., in *Aliens and Dissenters,*[50] describes the expanding capacity of the federal government for surveillance and suppression even before the First World War. The clearest account of the new dynamic between government and citizens that progressive politics produced appears in Hays, *Conservation and the Gospel of Efficiency.*[51] Businessmen and experts, reformers and bureaucrats, interacted in pioneering attempts to manage the use of natural resources from a new center of power in Washington. Such continuing flows of force between citizens and government, between constituents and officials, capture the essence of truly modern politics.

Power

The final aspect of modernization, while intimately related to matters of groups and government, involves its own distinctive set of questions. Who holds power in American society? How has that power been exercised? Questions that lie close to the heart of today's examination of the adequacy of American democracy and the morality of its policies at home and abroad are equally basic to an understanding of the progressive years. Indeed, to the extent modern American society emerged before the First World War—that is, to the extent the progressive period can best be comprehended as early modernization—yesterday's problems of power merge with today's. The new shape of power relations in the first two decades of the twentieth century establishes the contours for later years, and issues won or lost in the progressive era limit the options available to us in the 1970's.

Until recently the standard discussions of power in public affairs concentrated upon major political figures. These discussions rested primarily on the assumption that officials with the legal rights to act did in fact make policy decisions and should be held responsible for them. The best presentations of that approach are Mowry's *The Era of Theodore Roosevelt,* and Arthur S. Link's *Woodrow Wilson and the Progressive Era, 1910-1917.*[52] Together they describe the transformation of the Presidency from a largely passive, often peripheral office late in the nineteenth century to a place at the center of national life in the early twentieth. Roosevelt and Wilson expanded its scope to include not only an array of new prerogatives but also a guiding role in the formation of public opinion. Concomitantly, the President assumed the initiative in formulating public policy, setting an agenda for Congress and prodding it to action. As national politics assumed greater and greater significance in national life, the President acquired radically greater authority in national politics. Because Roosevelt's Presidency marks the dramatic shift from the nineteenth century, he has received special attention. John Morton Blum's *The Republican Roosevelt,*[53] which frames many of the issues about Presidential power that other historians have developed, analyzes Roosevelt's attitudes toward power as well as his techniques for employing it. William H. Harbaugh's *Power and Responsibility,*[54] and G. Wallace Chessman's *Theodore Roosevelt and the Politics of Power*[55] elaborate the story along similar lines.

The transformation in government and politics bears an obvious affinity to changes that Chandler outlines for corporations, Wiebe for business groups, Taft for the AFL, and McConnell for the Farm Bureau Federation: the nationalization of scope, the centralization of authority, the appearance of a directing elite or individual, and the continuity of policies. It is logical, in other words, to see these revolutions in power as a single social process, as common institutional expressions of modernization. Because roughly comparable processes of centralization were also occurring within states and cities and because historians have found a smaller compass more manageable, most scholars have chosen to explore the implications of these new patterns of power on a limited scale. Two such studies emphasize the uncertain influence of these new mechanisms. Irwin Yellowitz in *Labor and the Progressive Movement in New York State, 1897-1916*[56] contrasts the relative incapacity of middle-class reform organizations and labor unions to marshal popular support with the relative strength of another means of mobilizing power, the mass-circulation daily paper. It was William Randolph Hearst, not the progressives and their allies, Yellowitz concludes, who found a sympathetic response from New York's wage-earners. J. Joseph Huthmacher[57] analyzes the dependence of middle-class progressives upon the cooperation of Tammany Hall in passing and implementing reform legislation in New York.

Other scholars have examined the distribution of benefits under the new system of power. Two studies, one classic and one recent, illustrate these inquiries. C. Vann Woodward's *Origins of the New South, 1877-1913*[58] sketches a pattern of state reform in the South similar to that in the North. But along with the usual reforms, Woodward tells us, came the systematic segregation of blacks. Progressivism was "For Whites Only." The same general techniques behind reform, in other words, applied equally well to suppression, a theme that again suggests changes in American society transcending any particular set of reforms. In *Conservatism in a Progressive Era*,[59] Richard M. Abrams finds that the new political order served the opponents of reform as readily as its advocates. Massachusetts, which had pioneered in reform legislation before 1900, remained after 1900 under the control of men who used the new system to maintain prerogatives they already held.

By far the most exciting analyses of power have come from Gabriel Kolko in *The Triumph of Conservatism*[60] and James Weinstein in *The Corporate Ideal in the Liberal State: 1900-1918*,[61] two studies that have deeply impressed a younger generation of scholars. Both focus on the relationship between newly mobilized business power and modern government.

Both find business the master of government, and both see that mastery as fundamental to progressivism, indeed to modernization. Kolko examines the origins and meaning of national legislation that governed the conduct of corporations, including banks. Because corporate consolidations around 1900 did not bring the tight, predictable control over the economy that big businessmen sought, Kolko states, magnates turned to the federal government for supplementary authority. Corporate leaders, in effect, dictated the major economic legislation of the progressive era to complete a dominance they had not been able to secure by private means. Modernization meant the coordination of corporations and government in the service of a capitalist elite, the harnessing of government for the coming decades to broad national interests as business leaders defined them. Weinstein employs the same interpretive framework in analyzing both national reforms and such state and local reforms as workmen's compensation and efficiency systems in city government. Also depicting government as essentially the puppet of corporations, he emphasizes the overtly antidemocratic purposes behind much of progressivism.

These studies draw the outlines of a corporate state with systematic power at all levels of government that business magnates could use as they chose. It is this systematic quality that distinguishes the interpretation of Kolko and Weinstein from that of Matthew Josephson in *The President Makers,*[62] an earlier account of big businessmen defeating such democratic reformers as Robert La Follette and Amos Pinchot. Where Josephson traced the power of a business elite, particularly Wall Street financiers, in both the Republican and Democratic parties, Kolko and Weinstein sketch a far broader range of corporate power throughout the political system. Where Josephson created the impression of endless skirmishes and dramatic encounters, Kolko and Weinstein picture the steady, irresistible working of an elite's will through all agencies of government. The one told a political story, the others described a governing process. If Josephson wrote about modern times, Kolko and Weinstein write about modernization, a system of power rather than its occasional exercise.[63]

Transition

These many studies modify but do not fundamentally alter the four general pictures of the progressive era: Hofstadter's of an uncertain step by an anxious middle class toward a modern society that the New Deal greatly advances, Hays' of a society gradually transforming from a community to a cosmopolitan base and adapting its institutions as it changes,

Ginger's of a society dominated by capitalists who struggle to solve economic problems they are generating, and Wiebe's of a new system emerging from the ruins of an old, fragmented society. The total effect of scholarship on the progressive era, therefore, is to confirm a critical transition, with historians debating the sources and timing of change but not the overarching framework of modernization.

Overwhelmingly historians have concentrated upon visible institutions and articulate citizens. Each of the four views of the progressive era is drawn from such prominent materials—the actions of parties and Presidents, of intellectuals and professionals, of businessmen and labor leaders. We are only now beginning to learn something about those who lived beneath these prominences. We know, for example, that comfortable Americans discovered poverty around the turn of the century, but we know almost nothing about the lives of the poor. We know that whites established an elaborate system of Jim Crow for blacks, but we know very little about the black experience inside segregation. We know that some women demanded the suffrage, but we have scarcely touched the lives of those who would soon gain the vote. We know that successful farmers organized during these years, but we have little aside from statistical charts to tell us about the far more numerous farmers who did not organize. We know that the AFL came to stay, but we have only glimpses of the large majority of wage-earners who remained outside its unions.

A few studies help. David Brody's re-creation[64] of social patterns among unorganized steelworkers is as ingenious as it is invaluable. Melvyn Dubofsky discusses the Industrial Workers of the World in *We Shall Be All*[65] with a sensitive eye to its members. Humbert S. Nelli's *Italians in Chicago 1880-1930*[66] and Moses Rischin's *The Promised City*[67] look beneath a leadership to its constituents. Hints about newly arrived immigrant groups also appear in John M. Allswang's statistical analysis of political behavior, *A House for All Peoples*.[68] However useful, these few books merely underline the extent of our ignorance. What modernization meant to the less articulate, whether or not modernization even captures the meaning of their lives, stands as the major challenge for another wave of historians.

FOOTNOTES

[1] *The Quest for Social Justice, 1898-1914. A History of American Life.* New York: Macmillan, 1931.

[2] *Midwestern Progressive Politics: A Historical Study of Its Origins and Development, 1870-1950.* East Lansing, Mich.: Michigan State College Press, 1951.

[3] *Farewell to Reform: The Rise, Life, and Decay of the Progressive Mind in America.* New York: John Day, 1932.

[4] New York: Harcourt, Brace, 1939.

[5] *The Age of Reform: From Bryan to F. D. R.* New York: Alfred A. Knopf, 1956.

[6] *The Chicago History of American Civilization.* Chicago: University of Chicago Press, 1957.

[7] "Political Parties and the Community-Society Continuum." *The American Party Systems: Stages of Political Development.* Edited by William Nisbet Chambers and Walter Dean Burnham. New York: Oxford University Press, 1967. pp. 152-81.

[8] *The Making of America.* New York: Hill and Wang, 1967.

[9] *Age of Excess: The United States from 1877 to 1914.* New York: Macmillan, 1965.

[10] *An Encore for Reform: The Old Progressives and the New Deal.* New York: Oxford University Press, 1967.

[11] *Social Thought in America: The Revolt against Formalism.* New York: Viking, 1949.

[12] *Rendezvous with Destiny: A History of Modern American Reform.* New York: Alfred A. Knopf, 1952.

[13] *Efficiency and Uplift: Scientific Management in the Progressive Era.* Chicago: University of Chicago Press, 1964.

[14] Cambridge, Mass.: Harvard University Press, 1963.

[15] *The Crossroads of Liberalism: Croly, Weyl, Lippmann, and the Progressive Era, 1900-1925.* New York: Oxford University Press, 1961.

[16] *The End of American Innocence: A Study of the First Years of Our Own Time, 1912-1917.* New York: Alfred A. Knopf, 1959.

[17] *The New Radicalism in America [1889-1963]: The Intellectual as a Social Type.* New York: Alfred A. Knopf, 1965.

[18] Minneapolis: University of Minnesota, 1958.

[19] *From the Depths: The Discovery of Poverty in the United States.* New York: New York University Press, 1956.

[20] *Strangers in the Land: Patterns of American Nativism 1860-1925.* New Brunswick, N. J.: Rutgers University Press, 1955.

[21] *The California Progressives.* Berkeley: University of California Press, 1951. *The Era of Theodore Roosevelt, 1900-1912.* The New American Nation Series. New York: Harper, 1958.

[22] "An Obituary for 'The Progressive Movement.' " *American Quarterly* 22: 20-34; No. 1, Spring 1970.

[23] Princeton, N. J.: Princeton University Press, 1969.

[24] New York: Harper, 1935.

[25] *Strategy and Structure: Chapters in the History of Industrial Enterprise.* Cambridge, Mass.: The M. I. T. Press, 1962.

[26] Allan Nevins, with the collaboration of Frank E. Hill. *Ford: The Times, the Man, the Company, 1865-1915.* New York: Scribner's, 1954.

[27] *The Life Insurance Enterprise, 1885-1910: A Study in the Limits of Corporate Power.* Cambridge, Mass.: Belknap Press of Harvard University Press, 1963.

[28] *Right-Hand Man: The Life of George W. Perkins.* New York: Harper, 1960.

[29] Washington, D. C.: The Catholic University of America, 1956.

[30] Berkeley: University of California Press, 1953.

[31] *Samuel Gompers: A Biography.* Yellow Springs, O.: Antioch Press, 1963.

[32] *The A. F. of L. in the Time of Gompers.* New York: Harper, 1957.

[33] *The Transformation of the School: Progressivism in American Education, 1876-1957.* New York: Alfred A. Knopf, 1961.

[34] *Education and the Cult of Efficiency: A Study of the Social Forces That Have Shaped the Administration of the Public Schools.* Chicago: University of Chicago Press, 1962.

[35] Chicago: University of Chicago Press, 1965.

[36] *Spearheads for Reform: The Social Settlements and the Progressive Movement, 1890-1914.* New York: Oxford University Press, 1967.

[37] *The Professional Altruist: The Emergence of Social Work as a Career, 1880-1930.* Cambridge, Mass.: Harvard University Press, 1965.

[38] *Everyone Was Brave: The Rise and Fall of Feminism in America.* Chicago: Quadrangle Books, 1969.

[39] New York: Columbia University Press, 1965.

[40] *Pressure Politics: The Story of the Anti-Saloon League.* New York: Columbia University Press, 1928.

[41] *The Progressives and the Slums: Tenement House Reform in New York City, 1890-1917.* Pittsburgh: University of Pittsburgh Press, 1963.

[42] *Businessmen and Reform: A Study of the Progressive Movement.* Cambridge, Mass.: Harvard University Press, 1962.

[43] *Brandeis: A Free Man's Life.* New York: Viking, 1946.

[44] C. K. Yearley. *The Money Machines: The Breakdown and Reform of Governmental and Party Finance in the North, 1860-1920.* Albany, N. Y.: State University of New York Press, 1970.

[45] Walter I. Trattner. *Crusade for the Children: A History of the National Child Labor Committee and Child Labor Reform in America.* Chicago: Quadrangle Books, 1970.

[46] *At the Pleasure of the Mayor: Patronage and Power in New York City, 1898-1958.* New York: Free Press of Glencoe, 1964.

[47] *Boss Cox's Cincinnati: Urban Politics in the Progressive Era.* New York: Oxford University Press, 1968.

[48] *The Socialist Party of America: A History.* New York: Macmillan, 1955.

[49] *Science in the Federal Government: A History of Policies and Activities.* Cambridge, Mass.: Harvard University Press, 1957.

[50] *Aliens and Dissenters: Federal Suppression of Radicals: 1903-1933.* Cambridge, Mass.: Harvard University Press, 1963.

[51] *Conservation and the Gospel of Efficiency: The Progressive Conservation Movement, 1890-1920.* Harvard Historical Monographs. Cambridge, Mass.: Harvard University Press, 1959.

[52] *The New American Nation Series.* New York: Harper, 1954. See also Link. *Wilson.* 5 vols to date. Princeton, N. J.: Princeton University Press, 1947.

[53] Cambridge, Mass.: Harvard University Press, 1954.

[54] *Power and Responsibility: The Life and Times of Theodore Roosevelt.* New York: Farrar, Straus and Cudahy, 1961.

[55] *The Library of American Biography.* Boston: Little, Brown, 1969.

[56] Ithaca, N. Y.: Cornell University Press, 1965.

[57] "Urban Liberalism and the Age of Reform." *Mississippi Valley Historical Review* 49: 231-41; No. 2, September 1962.

[58] *A History of the South.* Baton Rouge, La.: Louisiana State University Press and the Littlefield Fund for Southern History of the University of Texas, 1951.

[59] *Conservatism in a Progressive Era: Massachusetts Politics, 1900-1912.* Cambridge, Mass.: Harvard University Press, 1964.

[60] *The Triumph of Conservatism: A Reinterpretation of American History, 1900-1916.* New York: Free Press of Glencoe, 1963. See also Kolko. *Railroads and Regulation, 1877-1916.* Princeton, N. J.: Princeton University Press, 1965.

[61] Boston: Beacon Press, 1968.

[62] *The President Makers: The Culture of Politics and Leadership in an Age of Enlightenment, 1896-1919.* New York: Harcourt, Brace, 1940.

[63] For additional information on that system of power, see William Appleman Williams. *The Contours of American History.* Cleveland: World, 1961.

[64] *Steelworkers in America: The Nonunion Era.* Harvard Historical Monographs. Cambridge, Mass.: Harvard University Press, 1960.

[65] *We Shall Be All: A History of the Industrial Workers of the World.* Chicago: Quadrangle Books, 1969.

[66] *Italians in Chicago 1880-1930: A Study in Ethnic Mobility.* New York: Oxford University Press, 1970.

[67] *The Promised City: New York's Jews 1870-1914.* Cambridge, Mass.: Harvard University Press, 1962.

[68] *A House for All Peoples: Ethnic Politics in Chicago 1890-1936.* Lexington, Ky.: University Press of Kentucky, 1971.

· 20 ·

Rise to Great World Power, 1865–1918

Daniel M. Smith

IN THE second half of the nineteenth century, the United States emerged as one of the world's foremost economic and potentially military powers. With a vast internal market, a multiplying population, and an amazingly productive agricultural and industrial system, the new world colossus rapidly eclipsed its European competitors in the sinews of power. Economic growth stimulated interest in foreign markets, and the State Department acted with increasing energy to encourage overseas trade and to keep markets open. A heightened sense of national pride and destiny accompanied these economic changes, resulting in the building of the New Navy in the 1880's and 1890's and an expansionist foreign policy. The spectacular war with Spain in 1898 merely dramatized America's status as a great world power in fact as well as in potential.[1]

Marked changes in approach and method characterize recent diplomatic historiography.[2] Whereas earlier scholars relied primarily upon official documents and concentrated upon formal diplomatic relations, today's specialists utilize multinational viewpoints and integrate social, economic, and intellectual materials into their diplomatic studies. Historians especially are concerned with climates of opinion and the role of pressure groups and opinion elites in shaping foreign policy. Three rather distinct interpretive "schools" of diplomatic historians seem to exist today (as of 1971), although of course the work of many scholars defies neat categorization. These are the Liberal Internationalists, the Realists, and the New Left.

The Liberal Internationalist viewpoint is well illustrated in the work of Dexter Perkins, an esteemed senior in the profession.[3] Perkins took a generally favorable and optimistic view of America's role and record in world affairs. The United States, in his judgment, consistently manifested its democratic culture and values in its foreign policies. Contrary to those critics who would label the United States imperialistic from birth, Perkins carefully distinguished between expansionism into adjacent territory, that resulted in full incorporation of these areas into our national life, and that brief spasm of overseas imperialism at the end of the nineteenth century. Even then, American imperialism was benevolent, colonial areas soon being permitted a measure of local rule and eventually either freed or granted commonwealth status. He doubted that economic factors *per se* explain the Spanish-American War or intervention in World War I, or that they adequately account for our so-called dollar diplomacy in Latin America and the Far East.

Realist critiques of American foreign policy began to affect diplomatic historians in the years after 1945. The intellectual godfathers of the Realist school were not professional diplomatic historians: Walter Lippmann, journalist and commentator; Hans J. Morgenthau, political scientist; and George F. Kennan, diplomat turned historian. Kennan perhaps had the greatest impact. In a brief volume of lectures, *American Diplomacy, 1900-1950,* he analyzed the American approach to foreign affairs as "legalistic-moralistic," and questioned the nation's capacity to devise and pursue coherent and sound policies free from the distortions imposed in the past by a sovereign democratic public opinion.[4] Too often Americans have projected their moral standards and aspirations upon the world scene as criteria for judging others, he wrote, and too optimistically have sought panaceas for international conflicts in illusory schemes of world law, world courts, and leagues of nations. We failed to understand our own interests and the interests of others clearly, and did not see the necessary correlation between policy and the power to achieve it. Our wars, therefore, especially 1898, 1917, and 1941, became not wars for clearly discerned national interests and realistic goals, but crusades for justice and perpetual peace.

In the 1960's, another school of thought emerged, the New Left. Mostly young scholars and many professedly radically inclined, and deeply disturbed by America's domestic shortcomings and interventionist Cold War policies, these writers searched America's past for keys to its present predicament. They drew inspiration particularly from Charles A. Beard and the "Old Left" progressives, a group of early twentieth-century historians who adopted an economic interpretive approach and insisted upon making history relevant to the needs of the present. More immediately, the New Left is indebted to the work of William Appleman Williams, a leading figure in the so-called Wisconsin school of diplomatic historians. Williams in studies such as *The Tragedy of American Diplomacy* and *The Roots of the Modern American Empire*[5] depicted the United States as embarked upon a path of economic imperialism or "open-door" informal empire, directed at acquiring and dominating foreign markets and resources rather than territory and colonies. This overseas thrust began early in our history as an agricultural expansionism; it was taken over by the business community, the "metropolitans," particularly after the Panic of 1893 and the depression which followed, as the easiest solution to the domestic problem of industrial overproduction and cycles of depression and social unrest. If overseas outlets could be obtained for our surplus manufactures and capital, domestic prosperity and tranquillity seemed assured without the necessity of any fundamental changes in the social-economic system. Thus Williams sought to understand American foreign relations in terms of our domestic history. The inevitable result of our global open-door expansionism, in his view and that of the New Left generally, unfortunately was a steadily accelerating cycle of penetration, domination, interventionism, and wars. The end result was America's Cold War role as world policeman to suppress reformist and radical nationalist revolutions threatening the status quo and America's global economic predominance. While some New Left studies have been carefully done and have raised significant questions or advanced stimulating new insights, this school on the whole is seriously marred by monolithic economic interpretations, to the neglect of other motivating forces in history, and by sweeping moral judgments.[6]

1. America Looks Outward, 1865-1889

The post-Civil War era in American foreign relations, long dismissed as the "nadir of American diplomacy," underwent a "rediscovery" by historians during the 1960's. Far from a period of quiescence, recent accounts depict 1865-1889 as years of revolutionary economic changes at home and the beginning of a dynamic foreign policy abroad, directed at expanding overseas markets for the products of American farms and factories. One of the first of these studies, *The Awkward Years* by David M. Pletcher, examined the Garfield-Arthur administrations, 1881-1885, and found a little-noted transition in foreign affairs between the introspective Reconstruction era and the tempestuous diplomacy of the 1890's.[7] Reflecting a new mood of national power and prestige, and increasing interest in foreign markets for surplus goods and capital, the Congress and the State Department manifested greater awareness and energy in foreign relations.

Walter La Feber's *The New Empire*[8] is unquestionably the most influential reappraisal of these years, and is usually regarded as the soundest work to emerge from the so-called Wisconsin school of diplomatic historians. La Feber emphasized the all-pervasive influence of economics in American foreign policy after 1865. The dream of continental empire had been fulfilled; the quest for a "new empire" of trade, not territory or colonies, had begun. Commerce might, of course, require some naval bases and coaling stations. Rapid industrial growth and recurrent economic depressions, as in 1873 and 1893, convinced many observers that the only remedy lay in obtaining adequate overseas markets for surplus production. A maturing economy otherwise would outproduce domestic consumption, with the inevitable consequences of domestic unemployment and social unrest. La Feber analyzed these economic developments and their influence on foreign policy from the time of William H. Seward,[9] whom he termed our greatest Secretary of State since J. Q. Adams, to the 1898 war with Spain. Long before the "watershed" of the 1890's, American officials and their business supporters marked out a course of informal commercial empire for the United States as vital to its domestic prosperity and tranquillity.

Attesting to the impact of *The New Empire,* a recent historical convention devoted a session to a reappraisal of the study. According to a survey of diplomatic historians, about two-thirds of the respondents acknowledged that they had been greatly to moderately affected by La Feber's volume, although few had changed the chronological structures of their courses as a result.[10] But not all historians accepted his interpretation. Paul S. Holbo at this convention criticized La Feber's study as provocative but unsatisfactory in analysis and research.[11] Earlier, Holbo evaluated the New Left economic interpretation of the 1865-1895 era and found it, in his opinion, greatly oversimplified and unsupportable by the historical facts. In their attempts to erect a monolithic economic theory, those scholars had ignored anti-expansionist groups and forces in America. Advocates of tariff protectionism, for example, polar opposites of an open-door free trade empire, were powerful in Congress and within the dominant Republican Party—and they were concerned about the domestic market, with little interest in overseas outlets. Not even the hard times of the 1880's, writes Holbo, inspired economic expansionism abroad, while Democratic President Grover Cleveland revealed little interest in foreign markets during his two administrations, even after the Panic of 1893. The expansionism that did take place, in his view, was more accidental than planned or sought.[12] *Politics, Strategy and American Diplomacy,*[13] by John A. S. Grenville and George Berkeley Young, tends to substantiate Holbo's criticisms of the La Feber approach. Where La Feber stresses the Cleveland administration's concern with economic interests—he explains Cleveland's rather bellicose policy in the Venezuelan Crisis of 1895 as less the result of domestic politics and popular Anglophobia than concern about Latin American markets and foreign threats—Grenville and Young emphasize domestic political maneuvering and gullibility to Venezuelan propaganda.

Probably a majority of American diplomatic historians fall somewhat in between these two points of view. Important economic changes between 1865 and 1889 surely affected foreign policy, explaining at least in part the exuberant nationalism and imperialism of the 1890's. Yet to describe this entire span of years as internationalist rather than isolationist, and to see economic factors as the only or the primary explanation of events seems oversimplified and unsound. Foreign policy during this long era followed no consistent pattern nor manifested any overriding interest. That the State Department from time to time paid attention to overseas commerce was hardly new; our government, and indeed most governments, always had shown an interest in trade. A persuasive account that takes into account a variety of impulses toward expansionism is Milton Plesur's *America's Outward Thrust*.[14] Plesur discussed cultural ties with Europe and its imperialistic example, the missionary impulse, Social Darwinism, and a growing sense of national power and prestige. Although he tended to emphasize the role of economics, he pointed out that businessmen generally were oblivious or nearly so to the lure of foreign markets until the 1890's. The author acknowledged that there is much evidence for the traditional interpretation of this era as one of isolation and neglect of foreign affairs, but he saw it as one of transition toward the activism of the 1890's.

2. America Comes of Age, 1889-1901

One basic question has preoccupied those who have studied the 1890's: did the United States acquire an empire more or less accidentally, or was it the logical culmination of powerful economic forces and consciously adopted policy? The "Old Left" or Beardian progressive historians long ago saw the answer in economic imperialism. As for the war with Spain over Cuba, Charles A. Beard wrote that the damages suffered by American traders and investors in Cuba provided "abundant fuel for the moral fire kindled by the sensational press in the United States. . . ."[15] In *Expansionists of 1898,* Julius W. Pratt carefully analyzed the business press in the United States and concluded that the evidence did not support Beard's thesis.[16] The business world, just recovering from the Panic of 1893, opposed intervention in Cuba lest war disturb the economy. Even many investors in Cuba opposed intervention, preferring continued Spanish control to native independence and possible misrule. Other scholars concurred with Pratt that the American causes of the 1898 war are to be found in an aroused popular jingoism or martial temper, whipped up by the sensationalist press and perhaps seeking psychological relief from domestic tensions and frustrations in a glorious crusade to liberate Cuba. A war to free Cuba ironically brought unforeseen and unplanned opportunities (save perhaps for a few, such as Theodore Roosevelt or Henry Cabot Lodge) to acquire an empire.[17] Economic interests helped explain the decision to acquire the Philippines, after victory brought them within America's grasp, but did not explain the original decision to intervene in Cuba.

Professor La Feber in *The New Empire* returned to the Old Left's economic interpretation of the 1890's but in a more scholarly and sophisticated way. He quoted the declaration by President Cleveland that American interest in Cuba was "by no means of a wholly sentimental or philanthropic character," for the civil war threatened to ruin the "industrial value" of the island.[18] American intervention cannot be adequately explained primarily in terms of the yellow press and popular passions overwhelming politicians such as President William McKinley. Although the business community at first opposed the idea of intervention, it finally decided that even war with all its hazards was preferable to a continual state of uncertainty and alarms that threatened to undermine business confidence and economic recovery from the 1893 depression. McKinley responded to this mood of the business community, as well as to his own sense of America's economic and humanitarian stake in Cuba. Another recent study written from the New Left point of view but well-balanced and researched, David Healy's *US Expansionism: The Imperialist Urge,* generally concurs with La Feber's interpretation that expansionism and war flowed from the economic thrust for overseas markets for America's surplus production and capital.[19] The basic question for our age, declared Healy, is how important are overseas business activities to our domestic economy.

Probably most historians have found more intellectually satisfying broader-based accounts that range beyond a concentration upon economic factors in explaining the causes of war and expansionism in the 1890's. Ernest R. May in 1961 published *Imperial Democracy,* an important study that utilized multi-archival research and examined the coming of the Spanish-American War from a multinational point of view.[20] He saw McKinley as a man of peace earnestly trying to resolve an intractable problem in Cuba without resorting to force. Humanitarianism as well as economic losses and the burdens of trying to enforce neutrality convinced him that the civil war must soon be ended. The President deliberately sought time for diplomacy by distracting the jingoes in Congress and the American public. All his initiatives failed, for Spain would neither sell Cuba (for the United States to free) nor grant it true autonomy or independence, and yet manifestly it was unable to suppress the rebellion. Finally, despairing of realism in Madrid, fearful of possible European complications, and fully aware of the domestic political costs of continued neutrality, McKinley gave Spain a virtual ultimatum in March 1898: end reconcentration, proclaim an armistice, and, if terms could not be reached with the rebels, accept American mediation which obviously would mean Cuban independence. The evidence indicates, May concluded, and contrary to the usual view, that the Spanish government would not and could not accept McKinley's last demand even if it had been allowed more time. Faced with the terrible choice of a war that he did not want or the defying of an aroused public and probable political unpopularity and defeats, McKinley chose war: "When public emotion reached the point of hysteria, he succumbed."[21]

Was McKinley a weak chief executive yielding his own best judgment to the passions of public opinion, as May suggested? H. Wayne Morgan in two books, *William McKinley and His America* and *America's Road to Empire,* denied that McKinley capitulated to the war hysteria and the jingoistic yellow press.[22] Far from weak and indecisive as usually depicted, McKinley was portrayed by Morgan as an able and independent-minded executive and political leader. He decided upon armed intervention only after he had exhausted other alternatives for ending a civil war he believed could not and should not be permitted to drag on indefinitely. His principal defect lay not in the war decision but in failing earlier to try to calm public opinion. Grenville and Young in *Politics, Strategy, and American Diplomacy* agreed that McKinley was far· abler than usually granted. Why, then, has his reputation suffered at the hands of historians? In part because of McKinley's reticence in expressing his own views, his habit of always seeming to agree with those to whom he talked or who offered him advice, and his political tactic of presenting his actions as merely responses to the public will when in fact such often was not the case. Equally or even more important in explaining McKinley's reputation as a weak president, however, was the revulsion against imperialism that many Americans experienced soon after 1898 and which historians have reflected. Critics saw Cleveland as the courageous chief executive who had held off the jingoes at great political costs, in contrast to his allegedly weak successor capitulating to popular passions. Grenville and Young also refuted the old story that Theodore Roosevelt, then Assistant Secretary of the Navy, and a handful of other avowed imperialists were responsible for events that culminated in acquisition of the Philippines. The Navy Department long had planned a naval assault on the Philippines as a strategic action in case of war, and it had the approval of President McKinley. As for the eventual decision to take all of the Philippines, the authors concurred with Morgan in giving credit primarily to McKinley. Important economic, missionary and *realpolitik* reasons explained his decision, and not merely public opinion which in fact he helped to mould in a favorable direction.[23]

Several recent accounts enlarge our understanding of international politics and the anti-imperialist movement in the United States after 1898. *Twelve Against Empire,* by Robert L. Beisner, probes the genesis and the causes of the failure of the anti-imperialist campaign against acquisition of the Philippines and other colonies.[24] Beisner saw the anti-imperialist movement as reflecting a conservative dismay at changes at home and abroad affecting the United States. Already alarmed at the disruptions to traditional American values and mores inflicted by rapid industrialization and urbanization, and the influx annually of hordes of "undesirable" immigrants from eastern and southern Europe, conservative anti-imperialists viewed colonialism as the final blow to the American dream and destiny. Their failure to roll back the imperialist tide, in Beisner's judgment, resulted from disunity among the anti-imperialists, their inability to understand that few if any practical alternatives existed after Dewey smashed Spanish power in the Philippines, and above all that they urged a negative course of abstention or withdrawal upon a highly nationalistic public and Congress. A brief comparison of opposition to the war and imperialism of 1898 with opposition in the War of 1812 and the Mexican War is by Samuel Eliot Morison, Frederick Merk, and Frank Freidel.[25] Two studies of improving Anglo-American relations during this period, *Great Britain and United States Expansion* by R. G. Neale and *The Great Rapprochement* by Bradford Perkins, supplement the account by Charles S. Campbell, Jr., *Anglo-American Understanding.*[26]

3. Statesmanship and Great World Power, 1901-1919

A good overview is provided by Julius W. Pratt's *Challenge and Rejection.*[27] Howard K. Beale in *Theodore Roosevelt and the Rise of America to World Power* examined the development of Roosevelt's thought about foreign affairs and the major policies of his administration.[28] Beale portrayed TR as a realistic statesman with a firm grasp of the relationship between national policy and power. Perceiving the interest of the United States in a stable world balance, Roosevelt threw his diplomatic weight behind the Anglo-French entente and skillfully used diplomacy to avert a general war in the Moroccan crisis. Increasingly he saw imperial Germany as the principal threat to Europe's peace and a potential menace to the United States. In East Asia, he viewed Russia as the chief danger to the Open Door and China, and Japan as her natural checkweight. Roosevelt realistically appreciated that both American interests and power in the Far East were quite limited. He relied upon Japan to curb Russian expansionism and sought to promote Japanese-American friendship, meanwhile prepared to retreat from the Open Door as necessary. Despite Beale's criticism of TR for reliance upon old-fashioned imperialistic methods, especially in dealing with China, his portrait of Roosevelt is generally favorable. That is also true of a more recent study, *Theodore Roosevelt and the International Rivalries* by Raymond A. Esthus.[29] Traversing familiar terrain, Esthus generally confirmed Beale's findings. A practical diplomatist, TR worked to preserve international stability as conducive to the best interests of the United States. His attention largely focused upon Europe, where lay the greatest danger to world peace, especially after he had helped end the Russo-Japanese War at Portsmouth.[30]

The origins and evolution of the Open Door policy in East Asia continue to attract scholarly attention. Historians during the 1950's, while strongly affected by George F. Kennan's criticism in *American Diplomacy* of Hay's notes as born in ignorance and impractical idealism, nevertheless realized that some actual economic interests and even more hope also underlay the Open Door policy.[31] In the 1960's, New Left scholars continued to develop the economic theme, as noted before, following the lead of William Appleman Williams. Thomas J. McCormick in *China Market: America's Quest for Informal Empire* agreed with Williams and La Feber that the United States pursued a global Open Door policy as best suited for American economic prosperity and preeminence.[32] By 1898, he wrote, a consensus had developed among American conservative businessmen, politicians, and journalists that overseas markets were the only acceptable solutions to the problem of domestic overproduction and cycles of depression. Foreign outlets would provide the key marginal difference between domestic stagnation and prosperity, and the national government under Cleveland and McKinley reflected this conviction and translated it into foreign policy. Insular imperialism was one result, seeking bases and entrepôts for foreign markets rather than territory for its own sake, while the Open Door notes of Hay were another facet of the same thrust. He depicted Hay's notes as far from unrealistic or quixotic; the notes expressed a realistic and well-planned attempt to promote an "informal empire" of trade without the burdens of old-fashioned colonialism. Hay hoped to utilize the existing balance of power in the Far East and growing fear of a major world war to achieve his goal of an Open Door deemed most favorable to American interests. Yet while the Open Door policy protected China against further dismemberment, it denied her the right to modify or close her markets to promote her own industrial development.

Critics of the New Left, while acknowledging that economic factors had a role in the Open Door policy, charge an overemphasis to the virtual exclusion of other motivating forces, such as the religious missionary impulse, nationalistic pride, and domestic politics. Marilyn Blatt Young, in a trenchant essay "American Expansion, 1870-1900" and in *The Rhetoric of Empire,* pointed out the need to distinguish between a rhetoric that spoke of vast potential markets in China and of America's alleged need of such outlets versus the actuality that the United States had little concrete economic interests in East Asia nor need for them.[33] Moreover, in her view the historian ought to differentiate between those few Americans like Henry Cabot Lodge who desired to expand American power and wealth abroad, and the larger group that merely sought peaceful extensions of trade—it adds little to our understanding to label all who favored trade as imperialists. Finally, she questioned the practical results of Hay's notes. The greatest deterrent to Chinese partition, in her opinion, came not from Hay's policy but from the fact that no nation stood to gain much from China's dismemberment and all preferred less costly spheres of influence. Paul A. Varg, in *The Making of a Myth,* analyzed the popular rhetoric about a vast market of four hundred million potential customers for American goods in China, and concluded that the Open Door policy was ineffective and a delusion.[34] American trade with China scarcely exceeded 3 per cent of our total foreign trade at any time, owing to China's primitive economy and its resistance to Western values and goods. Moreover, rhetoric aside, American businessmen and investors showed little actual interest in China, finding more attractive "pastures" at or nearer home. Yet the myth of the market persisted, and along with it another, that China was making rapid strides toward modernization and political development.[35]

Professor Esthus has contributed greatly to our thinking about the evolution of the Open Door policy. In an influential article, "The Changing Concept of the Open Door," he noted that Secretary Hay soon retreated from the broader implications of his notes, falling back upon simply an insistence upon equality of treatment for American commerce within the spheres of influence other powers had acquired in China.[36] Roosevelt, never attaching much importance to the Open Door or American economic interests in China, continued Hay's approach. Two American officials, however, Willard Straight and F. M. Huntington Wilson, conceived the Open Door as signifying not merely commercial equality of opportunity in China for Americans but equal investment opportunities also and a vigorous defense of Chinese political and territorial integrity. They were to help persuade William H. Taft, Roosevelt's successor in the White House, to adopt a strongly anti-Japanese policy and "dollar diplomacy" in a futile attempt to increase American influence and strengthen the Open Door in Manchuria. The legacy of the Straight-Huntington-Taft policy lingered on to affect the Wilson administration and its successors.

In his study of *Theodore Roosevelt and Japan,* Esthus rejected the older interpretations of the Taft-Katsura Agreed Memorandum of 1905 and the Root-Takahira Agreement of 1908 as Rooseveltian *realpolitik* "bargains" with Japan, conceding her a free hand in Korea and Manchuria in exchange for reassurances about the safety of the Philippines and Japanese moderation in China.[37] Esthus viewed these agreements as merely air-clearing exchanges of views aimed at improving Japanese-American relations during a period of great tension in Asian affairs. Another Rooseveltian scholar, Charles E. Neu in *An Uncertain Friendship,* covered a shorter period of TR's diplomacy in the Far East.[38] Neu concluded that Roosevelt was far more interested in conciliating Japan and retaining her friendship than he was in maintaining a genuine balance of power in the Far East by playing off Japan and Russia. On the whole TR met success; he cannot be blamed for his successors' new departures and blunders in East Asia.

In *The Foreign Policies of the Taft Administration,* Walter and Marie Scholes utilized multi-archival research in tracing Taftian diplomacy toward the Far East and Latin America.[39] Taft showed much less interest in Europe and the international balance of power than had TR. He and his Secretary of State, lawyer Philander C. Knox, did not think of policy in terms of power and balance, but emphasized commercial connections and saw international controversies as soluble by legal techniques and arbitration. Knox approached diplomacy as almost a form of litigation where he represented his client, the United States, in adversary relations with other states. Taft and Knox believed that the United States needed outlets for its surplus production and capital. Therefore they adopted a vigorous course to defend the Open Door policy in China and to advance American political and financial predominance in the Caribbean. The authors saw economic motives as largely explaining Taft-Knox "dollar diplomacy" in Asia and Latin America, although those two officials sincerely believed that their policies not only benefited

America but also aided developing nations to modernize and achieve progress. Their policies achieved meager and most unfortunate results: estrangement of Japan and mounting anti-Yankee sentiment in Latin America.

The most recent general appraisal of Woodrow Wilson's major foreign policies is by Arthur S. Link in *Wilson the Diplomatist.*[40] In that brief collection of essays, and in his multi-volume biography, Link saw Wilson as an idealist and practitioner of uplift or "missionary diplomacy" who nevertheless was often more practical and far-visioned than his critics have granted. Alexander and Juliette George, *Woodrow Wilson and Colonel House,* have written a sound and persuasive psychological study; less satisfactory is the prejudiced effort by Sigmund Freud and William C. Bullitt.[41] *Woodrow Wilson and World Politics* by N. Gordon Levin, Jr., presents a sophisticated reinterpretation of the intellectual thrust of Wilsonian diplomacy. According to Levin, Wilson's ultimate goal was "the attainment of a peaceful liberal capitalist world order under international law, safe from both traditional imperialism and revolutionary socialism, within whose stable confines a missionary American could find moral and economic pre-eminence."[42] Although he emphasized Wilson's concern with expanding American economic interests abroad, Levin avoided the dogmatism of many New Left historians who have tended to dismiss Wilsonian idealism as a rhetorical facade for economic imperialism. Wilson genuinely believed that a democratic and freer trading world would serve both America's and the world's best interests. Eventually he set his face against not only German imperialism but that of Japan as well, as Burton F. Beers pointed out in *Vain Endeavor,* a study of the contrast between Secretary of State Robert Lansing's realistic readiness to bargain with Japan and Wilson's idealistic resolve to halt her expansionism by ending all spheres of influence in China.[43] Dana G. Munro in *Intervention and Dollar Diplomacy in the Caribbean* examined dollar diplomacy-missionary diplomacy in that area and concluded that considerations of security (Panama Canal) and humanitarian motives, rather than profit seeking, explain American policy.[44]

4. The Great Departure, 1914-1918

If the 1890's marked a watershed in American foreign relations, the First World War wrought an even greater departure for the United States. Despite the heady wine of victorious war and empire in the Nineties and Roosevelt's constructive leadership in the early 1900's, most Americans retained the isolationist psychology of a bygone era. The global war that erupted in 1914 rudely disturbed American assumptions of disinterestedness, neutrality, and relatively costless security. The Great War affected American emotions and interests in numerous and painful ways, demonstrating at least to the perceptive that isolation was an illusion and impartial neutrality unattainable. Great economic and potential military power inevitably demanded a new world role of the United States.

The delayed sense of shock following America's involvement in World War I—the great departure from traditional neutrality and non-entanglement, underscored by the sending of an American army to fight on the continent of Europe—probably ensured a subsequent great debate about the causes of intervention. Historians during the Twenties and especially the Thirties sought not merely the truth about the events of 1914-1917 but hoped to influence the current and future foreign policies of the United States.[45] Disillusioned liberals, blaming the demise of progressivism and the postwar triumph of political conservatism on American participation in the recent war, resolved that foreign crusades should not again abort domestic reform. "Revisionist" historians attacked the official or wartime explanation of the 1917 intervention as forced upon a peaceful and genuinely neutral America by Germany's ruthless submarine assaults on American lives and rights. Instead they attributed the war to the patently pro-Allied sympathies of President Wilson and his key advisers, the one-sided war trade and financial ties with the Allies, and the administration's so-called neutrality policies that in fact favored the Allies and enraged Germany. Some scholars, of course, rose to the defense of Wilson and intervention.[46] After the Second World War, the focus of the debate shifted. Probably influenced by the obvious implications of that recent struggle for America's security, scholars began to ask different questions about the World War I era: had Wilson and his advisers any concept of endangered national security in 1914-1917, or were their thoughts and policies largely idealistic and hence impractical?[47] Most historians concede that war with Germany probably would not have come except for the submarine, but Wilson and his advisers at least theoretically could have chosen other policies than strict accountability. Why did they choose the course of strict accountability? And why did Germany persist in the U-boat campaign at the risk of hostilities with America?

Realist scholars such as Kennan and Osgood recognized that some high American officials during the neutrality period had concluded that a German victory in Europe would endanger the security and the economic interests of the United States. President Wilson and most Americans, however, did not think in terms of national interests and

power but of rights and ideals. When the nation entered the war, therefore, it was as a legalistic and moralistic reaction to the outrage of
Germany's underseas warfare. Edward H. Buehrig in *Woodrow Wilson
and the Balance of Power* attacked that thesis in a subtle study that
detected realistic balance of power and national interest concepts
in Wilsonian thinking and policy as well as a more idealistic concern about neutral rights and international morality.[48] The President
finally led his people into war in pursuit of a lasting peace that
would serve American interests and ideals. Arthur S. Link, whose
studies of Wilson have been cited earlier, and Ernest R. May in *The
World War and American Isolation*[49] essentially concurred with
Buehrig. The President's chief advisers, Colonel E. M. House and
Robert Lansing, exerted much influence on American policy and Wilson
himself shared to some degree their realistic appraisals of America's
interest in preserving a favorable balance of power and Germany's
potential threat to this nation's security and institutions. American
neutrality policies in fact did favor the Allies though unintentionally.
Yet Germany did not launch unrestricted submarine warfare simply out
of anger at the United States or merely to sever the war trade; its goals
were to starve Britain into submission and thereby end the stalemate on
the Western Front in a sweeping victory. Even if Washington had
treated the belligerent camps more evenly, Link and May contended,
Germany probably still would have resorted to the full use of its most
promising weapon—the findings of a European scholar, Karl E. Birnbaum, however, suggested the opposite possibility.[50] Why did Wilson
choose to hold Germany strictly accountable for use of the submarine,
even to the point of entering the war against her? Apparently he did so
because of a mixture of moral outrage, concern with international law and
neutral rights, and legitimate American economic interests. The nation's
prestige as a great and proud power, and its capacity to influence world
affairs for good, comprised another and interconnected reason. Yet
Wilson clung to neutrality as long as he deemed possible, convinced that
it was best for America and for the world. He finally decided upon
intervention, and his fellow citizens accepted it, only when the renewed
submarine campaign made clear that Germany endangered America's
rights and interests and was the chief barrier to world peace. Thus a
combination of practical and idealistic factors underlay Wilson's policies
and his decision to enter the war, with the idealistic elements probably
predominating.

The Great Departure,[51] by the author of this essay, synthesizes these
findings of recent scholarship. Simplistic explanations of intervention that
emphasize exclusively one or another factor, whether the submarine or

one-sided neutrality or endangered security, do not suffice to explain that complex event. Germany's leaders brushed aside the likelihood of war with America because it already seemed to be aiding Germany's enemies as fully as it could, and above all because the underseas weapon held out the prospect of a sweeping triumph over the Allies. The American government opposed ruthless and unrestricted U-boat warfare as inhumane and wanton, violative of neutral rights and lives, disruptive of trade, and damaging to American prestige as a great and responsible world power. Wilsonian policies thus embodied practical as well as moral and idealistic considerations. Wilson accepted war in 1917 because Germany's actions and his past policies left little other choice, and because he had come to view Germany as a ruthless militaristic power and a menace to the kind of world order the President believed must be established with the peace. New Left historians disagree with the above, choosing to emphasize Wilson's alleged quest for an economic open-door world that the United States could dominate.[52] The recent study by N. Gordon Levin, however, essentially supports the Buehrig-Link-May approach. In *Wilson and World Politics,* Levin does not belittle economic motives but sees Wilson as sincerely combining them with liberal ideology. The United States intervened in 1917 because Germany appeared to endanger the nation and its hoped-for "peaceful liberal capitalist world order," an order that intermeshed America's economic interests and security with its moral democratic political aspirations.

Although relatively neglected compared to the neutrality or peace conference periods, America's role as a belligerent in World War I is beginning to receive more scholarly attention. The most recent general accounts are found in three previously mentioned works, Smith's *The Great Departure,* Pratt's *Challenge and Rejection* and Levin's *Wilson and World Politics.* Smith and Levin agreed that Wilson's wartime goals, viewed by realists as the quintessence of naive utopianism, in fact merged idealistic with practical considerations. It is true that the President and most of his fellow citizens thought of their nation's goals as noble and disinterested, in striking contrast to the territorial and financial designs of the Allies that were beginning to be revealed. Yet Wilsonian aims if realized would have served both American ideals and enlightened self-interests. The United States, satisfied with its existing boundaries and the world's foremost industrial and financial power, obviously could have no interest in the spoils of war. It did require, however, a stable international order within which it could enjoy security and prosperity, and of course such an order would benefit the entire world. That new order, in accordance with the tenets of Western liberal thought, would be just and more permanent if founded upon universal political democracy and liberal capitalism. Sublime idealism from one point of view, Wilsonian internationalism, as Levin points out, also can be defined as enlightened realism and self-interest. Lawrence W. Martin in *Peace Without Victory* and Arno J. Mayer in *Political Origins of the New Diplomacy* explored the political and intellectual aspects of Wilsonian liberalism and war goals. Carl P. Parrini's *Heir to Empire* presents a "New Leftist" view that the Wilson administration cooperated with business leaders during the war to supplant British dominance with American leadership of an open-door global economy.[53]

Aspects of coalition diplomacy are handled by Arthur Willert's *The Road to Safety, A Study in Anglo-American Relations,* and by W. B. Fowler's *British-American Relations,* that concentrates upon Sir William Wiseman's role as liaison agent to the American government.[54] David F. Trask in *The United States in the Supreme War Council* discussed Wilson's unwillingness to allow that body to intrude into political decisions affecting American war aims.[55] Wilson's role in encouraging the emergence of new and hopefully democratic states in Europe was examined by Louis L. Gerson in *Woodrow Wilson and the Rebirth of Poland,* and by Victor S. Mamatey in *The United States and East Central Europe.*[56] Mamatey concluded that the "Balkanization" of Europe that followed the war, often criticized by the realists, did not result from the Fourteen Points. Wilsonian liberalism perhaps speeded up the process, but the new states arose primarily because of the nationalistic aspirations of their peoples and the disintegration of the Austro-Hungarian and Russian empires during the war. *The Inquiry* by Lawrence E. Gelfand analyzes the organization, functions and influence of a group of scholars assembled by Colonel House to aid Wilson in preparing for the peace conference.[57] Wilson's turning to a group of academicians to give him, in his words, a "guaranteed position" at the peace negotiations attested to the liberal faith in human rationality, objective scholarship, and social planning. The experts of the Inquiry prepared nearly 2000 reports, of varying quality, and were to have a considerable impact upon the Paris Peace Conference. In general, the Inquiry and its work supports the argument that Wilson was far more practical in diplomacy than often thought.

American participation in the Siberian intervention continues to arouse scholarly interest. As Peter G. Filene comments in *Americans and the Soviet Experiment,* the unexpected Bolshevik revolution in November 1917, overthrowing the apparently promising provisional government, rudely shocked the American public and government.[58]

Most Americans and their leaders regarded the Bolsheviks as traitors to the Russian people and the March 1917 liberal revolution. Lenin's undemocratic and fanatically impractical regime had betrayed the Allies by withdrawing from the war and inciting revolution and class conflict everywhere. Conversely, some American liberals regarded the new experiment in Russia with a measure of tolerance and sympathy, and condemned armed intervention against it. Three principal explanations of American intervention in Siberia in mid-1918 have been offered: Betty Miller Unterberger's *America's Siberian Expedition* views intervention as undertaken to curb unilateral Japanese action and expansionism; the New Left, represented by William Appleman Williams in *American-Russian Relations,* attributed the intervention to a desire to snuff out the Bolshevist heresy at birth; and George F. Kennan in *Soviet-American Relations* concluded that military reasons—to protect the "trapped" Czech legion in Russia, to guard military supplies previously shipped to Vladivostak, and to prevent the allegedly advancing Germans from overrunning the entire country—explain Wilson's reluctant decision to intervene.[59] Kennan's interpretation seems most compatible with the evidence. Thus an army was dispatched to cooperate with the Allies against largely imaginary threats—in fact, German penetration proved grossly exaggerated, while the Czech legion was more than capable of defending itself against the Bolsheviks. What explains the frenzied climate that led to Wilson's decision? Christopher Lasch, in an historiographical essay on intervention,[60] agreed with Kennan that the answer lies in wartime strains and hysteria within the United States and the Allied countries, Allied anxieties to restore the eastern front against the Central Powers, and the general tendency to depict Germany as an incredibly sinister super foe. Since these fears later seemed clearly absurd, Lasch comments, scholars were driven to discover more rational explanations such as opposing Japanese imperialism or suppressing Bolshevism.

Domestic politics during the belligerency years presented a fitting prelude to the politics of peacemaking. Seward W. Livermore's *Politics Is Adjourned* recounts the intense maneuvering for partisan advantage behind the facade of patriotic support of the war effort by both major political parties in the United States.[61] Despite Wilson's declaration that "politics is adjourned," politics persisted throughout the war years and the ensuing peacemaking. Democrats tried to benefit from the war effort, while Republicans exploited every real or imagined defect of mobilization. Republican victory in the elections of 1918 heralded the political fight over the forthcoming treaty of peace.

5. Conclusion

In retrospect, after the American Senate rejected the Versailles Treaty and Wilson's League of Nations that embodied the goal of a stable liberal democratic and capitalist world order, it seemed that the United States had failed the challenge of world leadership that it had taken up in 1917. Yet it proved impossible in the Twenties to withdraw from all the burdens and responsibilities of great world power, and crises in the Thirties were to compel the nation once more to face the challenge that Wilson had tried to meet during the First World War. A forthcoming study by Robert A. Skotheim and Daniel M. Smith, "Authoritarianism and American Foreign Policy: Policy-Makers and Intellectuals, 1914-1948," reveals a continuous theme or interwoven connection in American thought and policy in the two world wars and the Cold War of this century. American policymakers and a majority of intellectuals during the First World War formed a consensus that the nation's democratic values and its material interests were menaced by statist authoritarianism or Prussianism. The "War against Autocracy" combined both idealistic concepts and national interests, and the threat was envisaged as coming not only from the Kaiser's Germany but to a lesser degree from imperialist Japan and Bolshevik Russia as well. President Wilson, for example, informed the American people in 1919 that Communist Russia was as reprehensible a form of autocracy as czarism had been. These stereotypes were to be revived during the Thirties and Forties as the menace of totalitarianism—Nazi Germany, Fascist Italy, militaristic Japan, and Communist Russia. The First World War formed a link in thought and policy with the Second World War and the Cold War.

FOOTNOTES

[1] For texts that survey American foreign relations and embody recent scholarly findings, see Thomas A. Bailey. *A Diplomatic History of the American People.* 8th edition. New York: Appleton-Century-Crofts, 1969; Samuel Flagg Bemis. *A Diplomatic History of the United States.* 5th edition. New York: Holt, Rinehart & Winston, 1965; Nelson Manfred Blake and Oscar Theodore Barck, Jr. *The United States in Its World Relations.* New York: McGraw-Hill, 1960; Wayne S. Cole. *An Interpretive History of American Foreign Relations.* Homewood, Ill.: Dorsey Press, 1968; Alexander De Conde. *A History of American Foreign Policy.* 2nd edition. New York: Scribner's, 1971; Robert H. Ferrell. *American Diplomacy, A History.* Rev. and expanded edition. New York: W. W. Norton, 1969; Richard W. Leopold. *The Growth of American Foreign Policy: A History.* New York: Alfred A. Knopf, 1962; and Julius W. Pratt. *A History of United States Foreign Policy.* 2nd edition. Englewood Cliffs, N. J.: Prentice-Hall, 1965. Daniel M. Smith, *The American Diplomatic Experience,* Boston: Houghton Mifflin, 1972, is a short interpretive account; see also Ruhl J. Bartlett. *Policy and Power: Two Centuries of American Foreign Relations.* New York: Hill and Wang, 1963.

[2] See the essays by Charles E. Neu. "The Changing Interpretive Structure of American Foreign Policy," and by David F. Trask. "Writings on American Foreign Relations: 1957 to the Present," in John Braeman *et al.* editors. *Twentieth-Century American Foreign Policy*. Columbus: Ohio State University Press, 1971. pp. 1-57, 58-118.

[3] Dexter Perkins. *The American Approach to Foreign Policy*. Cambridge: Harvard University Press, 1951, 1953. Revised edition by Atheneum, 1968; Frederick Merk, *Manifest Destiny and Mission in American History,* New York: Knopf, 1963, is another good example of this school.

[4] George F. Kennan. *American Diplomacy, 1900-1950.* Chicago: University of Chicago Press, 1951. Also see Hans J. Morgenthau. *In Defense of the National Interest; A Critical Examination of American Foreign Policy.* New York: Alfred A. Knopf, 1951; and Robert E. Osgood. *Ideals and Self-Interest in America's Foreign Relations: The Great Transformation of the Twentieth Century.* Chicago: University of Chicago Press, 1953.

[5] William Appleman Williams. *The Tragedy of American Diplomacy.* Cleveland & New York: World Publishing Co., 1959. Revised edition. New York: Dell, 1962; and *The Roots of the Modern American Empire: A Study of the Growth and Shaping of Social Consciousness in a Marketplace Society.* New York: Random House, 1969.

[6] Critiques of New Left historiography are by Irwin Unger. "The 'New Left' and American History—Some Recent Trends in United States Historiography." *American Historical Review* 72: 1237-1263; No. 4, July 1967; William W. MacDonald. "The Revisionist Cold War Historians." *Midwest Quarterly* 11: 37-49; No. 1, October 1969; and Daniel M. Smith. "The New Left and the Cold War," a review essay in *The Denver Quarterly* 4: 78-88; No. 4, Winter 1970.

[7] David M. Pletcher. *The Awkward Years: American Foreign Policy under Garfield and Arthur.* Columbia: University of Missouri Press, 1962.

[8] Walter La Feber. *The New Empire: An Interpretation of American Expansion, 1860-1898.* Ithaca: Cornell University Press, 1963.

[9] For a good reappraisal of Seward, see the biography by G. G. Van Deusen. *William Henry Seward.* New York: Oxford University Press, 1967.

[10] Professor Robert Beisner's survey, presented at the 1971 convention of the Organization of American Historians.

[11] Paul S. Holbo. "A View of *The New Empire*." A paper delivered at a meeting of the Organization of American Historians on April 16, 1971.

[12] Paul S. Holbo. "Economics, Emotion, and Expansion: An Emerging Foreign Policy," in *The Gilded Age,* edited by H. Wayne Morgan. 2nd edition. Syracuse: Syracuse University Press, 1970. pp. 199-221.

[13] John A. S. Grenville and George Berkeley Young. *Politics, Strategy, and American Diplomacy: Studies in Foreign Policy, 1873-1917.* New Haven: Yale University Press, 1966.

[14] Milton Plesur. *America's Outward Thrust: Approaches to Foreign Affairs, 1865-1890.* De Kalb: Northern Illinois University Press, 1971.

[15] Charles A. and Mary R. Beard. *The Rise of American Civilization.* New York: Macmillan, 1927 and 1930. 2 vols. II. p. 369.

[16] Julius W. Pratt. *Expansionists of 1898: The Acquisition of Hawaii and the Spanish Islands.* Baltimore: Johns Hopkins Press, 1936.

[17] Joseph E. Wisan. *The Cuban Crisis as Reflected in the New York Press, 1895-1898.* New York: Columbia University Press, 1934; Richard Hofstadter. "Manifest Destiny and the Philippines," in Daniel Aaron, editor. *America in Crisis.* New York: Knopf, 1952. pp. 173-200; Foster Rhea Dulles. *The Imperial Years.* New York: Crowell, 1956; and Howard K. Beale. *Theodore Roosevelt and the Rise of America to World Power.* Baltimore: Johns Hopkins Press, 1956.

[18] La Feber. *The New Empire.* pp. 295-296.

[19] David Healy. *U S Expansionism: The Imperialist Urge in the 1890s.* Madison: University of Wisconsin Press, 1970.

[20] Ernest R. May. *Imperial Democracy: The Emergence of America as a Great Power.* New York: Harcourt, Brace & World, 1961.

[21] *Ibid.* p. 268.

[22] H. Wayne Morgan. *William McKinley and His America.* Syracuse: Syracuse University Press, 1963; and *America's Road to Empire: The War with Spain and Overseas Expansion.* New York: Wiley, 1965.

[23] See, too, Margaret Leech. *In the Days of McKinley.* New York: Harper, 1959. Paul S. Holbo in "Presidential Leadership in Foreign Affairs: William McKinley and the Turpie-Foraker Amendment," *American Historical Review* 72: 1321-1335; No. 4, July 1967, also argues persuasively the case for McKinley as a strong chief executive. See his article, "The Convergence of Moods and the Cuban-Bond 'Conspiracy' of 1898," *Journal of American History* 55: 54-72; No. 1, June 1968, for an absorbing account of political paranoia and the Teller Amendment forswearing annexation of Cuba.

[24] Robert L. Beisner. *Twelve Against Empire: The Anti-Imperialists, 1898-1900.* New York: McGraw-Hill, 1968.

[25] Samuel Eliot Morison, Frederick Merk, and Frank Freidel. *Dissent in Three American Wars.* Cambridge: Harvard University Press, 1970.

[26] R. G. Neale. *Great Britain and United States Expansion, 1898-1900.* East Lansing: Michigan State University Press, 1966; Bradford Perkins. *The Great Rapprochement: England and the United States, 1895-1914.* New York: Atheneum, 1968; Charles S. Campbell, Jr. *Anglo-American Understanding, 1898-1903.* Baltimore: Johns Hopkins Press, 1957.

[27] Julius W. Pratt. *Challenge and Rejection: The United States and World Leadership, 1900-1921.* New York: Macmillan, 1967.

[28] Howard K. Beale. *Theodore Roosevelt and the Rise of America to World Power.* Baltimore: Johns Hopkins Press, 1956.

[29] Raymond A. Esthus. *Theodore Roosevelt and the International Rivalries.* Waltham: Ginn-Blaisdell, 1970. Also see David H. Burton's *Theodore Roosevelt: Confident Imperialist.* Philadelphia: University of Pennsylvania Press, 1968.

[30] Eugene P. Trani in *The Treaty of Portsmouth: An Adventure in American Diplomacy.* Lexington: University of Kentucky Press, 1969, concurred with the praise Roosevelt's biographers accord TR for his vision and role in this settlement. William L. Neumann's *America Encounters Japan: From Perry to MacArthur,* Baltimore: Johns Hopkins Press, 1963, also credits Roosevelt with a clear grasp of power realities in the Far East. For a more critical view of Roosevelt's methods, consult Paul S. Holbo, "Perilous Obscurity: Public Diplomacy and the Press in the Venezuelan Crisis, 1902-1903." *Historian* 32: 428-448; No. 3, May 1970.

[31] Paul A. Varg. *Open Door Diplomat: The Life of W. W. Rockhill.* Urbana: University of Illinois Press, 1952; and Charles S. Campbell, Jr. *Special Business Interests and the Open Door Policy.* New Haven: Yale University Press, 1951.

[32] Thomas J. McCormick. *China Market: America's Quest for Informal Empire, 1893-1901.* Chicago: Quadrangle Books, 1967.

[33] Marilyn Blatt Young. "American Expansion, 1870-1900: The Far East," in *Towards A New Past: Dissenting Essays in American History,* edited by Barton J. Bernstein. New York: Pantheon Books, 1968. pp. 176-201; and *The Rhetoric of Empire: American China Policy, 1895-1901.* Cambridge: Harvard University Press, 1968.

[34] Paul A. Varg. "The Myth of the China Market, 1890-1914." *American Historical Review* 73: 742-758; No. 3, February 1968; and *The Making of a Myth: The United States and China, 1897-1912.* East Lansing: Michigan State University Press, 1968.

[35] Jerry Israel pointed out the interreaction between American business, religious, and reform interests in China and denied that the Open Door was a heartless ex-

ploitative policy. " 'For God, for China and for Yale'—The Open Door in Action." *American Historical Review* 75: 796-807; No. 3, February 1970; and *Progressivism and the Open Door: America and China, 1905-1921.* Pittsburgh: University of Pittsburgh Press, 1971.

[36] Raymond A. Esthus. "The Changing Concept of the Open Door, 1899-1910." *Mississippi Valley Historical Review* 46: 435-454; No. 3, December 1959.

[37] Raymond A. Esthus. *Theodore Roosevelt and Japan.* Seattle: University of Washington Press, 1966.

[38] Charles E. Neu. *An Uncertain Friendship: Theodore Roosevelt and Japan, 1906-1909.* Cambridge: Harvard University Press, 1967.

[39] Walter V. and Marie V. Scholes. *The Foreign Policies of the Taft Administration.* Columbia: University of Missouri Press, 1970.

[40] Arthur S. Link. *Wilson the Diplomatist: A Look at His Major Foreign Policies.* Baltimore: Johns Hopkins Press, 1957; *Wilson.* 5 volumes to date. Princeton: Princeton University Press, 1947-1965. Also see Link. *Woodrow Wilson and the Progressive Era: 1910-1917.* New York: Harper, 1954.

[41] Alexander L. and Juliette L. George. *Woodrow Wilson and Colonel House: A Personality Study.* New York: John Day, 1956; Sigmund Freud and William C. Bullitt. *Thomas Woodrow Wilson, A Psychological Study.* Boston: Houghton Mifflin, 1967.

[42] N. Gordon Levin, Jr. *Woodrow Wilson and World Politics: America's Response to War and Revolution.* New York: Oxford University Press, 1968. p. vii.

[43] Burton F. Beers. *Vain Endeavor: Robert Lansing's Attempts to End the American-Japanese Rivalry.* Durham: Duke University Press, 1962.

[44] Dana G. Munro. *Intervention and Dollar Diplomacy in the Caribbean, 1900-1921.* Princeton: Princeton University Press, 1964. In reference to Asia and Latin America, also see Warren I. Cohen. "From Contempt to Containment: Cycles in American Attitudes toward China," in *Twentieth-Century American Foreign Policy,* edited by John Braeman *et al.* Columbus: Ohio State University Press, 1971. pp. 502-559; Robert E. Quirk. *An Affair of Honor: Woodrow Wilson and the Occupation of Veracruz.* Lexington: University of Kentucky Press, 1962; and Kenneth J. Grieb. *The United States and Huerta.* Lincoln: University of Nebraska Press, 1969.

[45] As Warren I. Cohen points out in *The American Revisionists: The Lessons of Intervention in World War I.* Chicago: University of Chicago Press, 1967.

[46] An excellent historiographical guide to the first phase of the scholarly debate over World War I is by Richard W. Leopold. "The Problem of American Intervention, 1917: An Historical Retrospect." *World Politics* 2: 405-425; No. 3, April 1950. Also see Richard L. Watson, Jr. "Woodrow Wilson and His Interpreters, 1947-1957." *Mississippi Valley Historical Review* 44: 207-236; No. 2, September 1957.

[47] Daniel M. Smith. "National Interest and American Intervention, 1917: An Historiographical Appraisal." *Journal of American History* 52: 5-24; No. 1, June 1965.

[48] Edward H. Buehrig. *Woodrow Wilson and the Balance of Power.* Bloomington: Indiana University Press, 1955.

[49] Ernest R. May. *The World War and American Isolation, 1914-1917.* Cambridge: Harvard University Press, 1959.

[50] Karl E. Birnbaum. *Peace Moves and U-Boat Warfare: . . . .* Stockholm: Almquist and Wiksell, 1958.

[51] Daniel M. Smith. *The Great Departure: The United States and World War I, 1914-1917.* New York: Wiley, 1965.

[52] See Lloyd C. Gardiner. "American Foreign Policy, 1900-1921: A Second Look at the Realist Critique of American Diplomacy," in Bernstein, editor. *Towards a New Past.* New York: Pantheon, 1968. pp. 202-231.

[53] Laurence W. Martin. *Peace Without Victory: Woodrow Wilson and the British Liberals.* New Haven: Yale University Press, 1958; Arno J. Mayer. *Political Origins of the New Diplomacy, 1917-1918.* New Haven: Yale University Press, 1959 —and paperback edition entitled *Wilson vs. Lenin.* Cleveland: World, 1964; and Carl P. Parrini. *Heir to Empire: United States Economic Diplomacy, 1916-1923.* Pittsburgh: University of Pittsburgh Press, 1969.

[54] Arthur Willert. *The Road to Safety, A Study in Anglo-American Relations.* London: D. Verschoyle, 1952, and New York: Praeger, 1953; W. B. Fowler. *British-American Relations 1917-1918: The Role of Sir William Wiseman.* Princeton: Princeton University Press, 1969.

[55] David F. Trask. *The United States in the Supreme War Council: American War Aims and Inter-Allied Strategy, 1917-1918.* Middleton, Conn.: Wesleyan University Press, 1961.

[56] Louis L. Gerson. *Woodrow Wilson and the Rebirth of Poland, 1914-1920.* New Haven: Yale University Press, 1953; Victor S. Mamatey. *The United States and East Central Europe, 1914-1918.* Princeton: Princeton University Press, 1957. For the domestic role of pressure groups, see Joseph P. O'Grady, editor. *The Immigrant's Influence on Wilson's Peace Policies.* Lexington: University of Kentucky Press, 1967.

[57] Lawrence E. Gelfand. *The Inquiry: American Preparations for Peace, 1917-1919.* New Haven: Yale University Press, 1963.

[58] Peter G. Filene. *Americans and the Soviet Experiment, 1917-1933.* Cambridge: Harvard University Press, 1967.

[59] Betty Miller Unterberger. *America's Siberian Expedition: 1918-1920.* Durham: Duke University Press, 1956; William Appleman Williams. *American-Russian Relations, 1781-1947.* New York: Rinehart, 1952; George F. Kennan. *Soviet-American Relations, 1917-1920.* Princeton: Princeton University Press, 1956, 1958. 2 vols. of a planned 3.

[60] Christopher Lasch. "American Intervention in Siberia: A Reinterpretation." *Political Science Quarterly* 77: 205-223; No. 2, June 1962.

[61] Seward W. Livermore. *Politics Is Adjourned: Woodrow Wilson and the War Congress, 1916-1918.* Middletown, Conn.: Wesleyan University Press, 1966.

· 21 ·

Configurations of the Twenties

Burl Noggle

THE most durable notion about the period, 1919-1929, is that it is indeed a period, with a style, content, and mood all its own.[1] A gestalt, a configuration of men and events related to one another in time and space that adds up to a patterned totality of things labeled "the Twenties" —this, derived from the historical literature, is common enough.[2] But insofar as historiography is a cumulative matter, whereby historians pile up more and more fresh evidence about a subject and thus continue to change its historical image, the picture of the Twenties changed some in the decade of the 1960's. The latest word is not necessarily the best word; still, historiography of the Sixties altered the focus on the Twenties here, blurred an outline there, and even erased some elements or created some new ones in the composite picture, though the total gestalt retains much of its traditional structure.

To begin at a crucial point, one may first examine the presidency and then work outward and downward (or perhaps it is upward), surveying the total society within which the presidency functions, covering all the standard topics and a few emerging new ones that make up the history of the Twenties. In the process, some subjects, such as the Klan and Fundamentalism, may relate to one another, while others may stand alone, but all of them, if taken together, can add up to a unifying view of the decade.

Harding was not the first president during the Twenties. Wilson held office until March, 1921; more to the point, his administration after the Armistice laid the basis for much that characterizes the Harding-Coolidge years. Wilson's failure (along with Congress) to create and direct a reconstruction program after the war was both cause and effect of that familiar "disillusionment" with World War I that historians have chronicled for a generation and that conditioned life in the Twenties.[3] Too, though the Twenties expressed an abundance of "100% Americanism," it was Wilson's attorney general, A. Mitchell Palmer, who in

1919 gave official sanction to government repression of "Reds" which, despite the cessation of the Palmer raids, left a residue of animosities and hysteria that would plague the Twenties.[4] In foreign affairs, moreover, Harding inherited a thicket of troubles left over from the Wilson intervention in Russia, the domestic quarrel over the League of Nations, and the economic conundrum of war debts, reparations, and related issues.[5]

Keeping in mind this Wilsonian postwar period as a necessary prelude and setting, one may begin a survey of the Twenties with a look at genial Warren G. Harding, which means appraisal of Robert K. Murray's hefty 1969 biography, *The Harding Era: Warren G. Harding and His Administration*.[6] This was probably the major revisionist study of the Twenties to appear in the past decade. Murray, while never minimizing Harding's extramarital adventures and his taste for the bottle and shoddy associates, portrayed a president of considerable force, ability, and political skill. Copious in detail and based upon trustworthy sources, the book is a thorough survey of the Harding administration, touching all the standard topics from taxes and tariffs to foreign policy, Congressional behavior, and electioneering. Wherever he places in the perennial rating game that historians play with the presidents' reputations, Harding, as Murray presented him, deserves better than the mark of "failure" he has commonly received.[7]

Coolidge is a trickier matter—a fact no one would enjoy more than the puckish little man from Plymouth Notch, Vermont. One hardly thinks of Calvin Coolidge in superlatives. A Coolidge Day dinner, for example, would be ludicrously inappropriate. Still, he has never been denigrated quite as much as Harding; in fact, just before World War II, Claude Fuess and William Allen White wrote biographies of him that skirted close to downright admiration. But not until 1967 did a full-bodied professional biography appear, Donald McCoy's *Calvin Coolidge: The Quiet President*.[8] If Murray tried to challenge the traditional image of Harding, McCoy tended to substantiate the convention that Coolidge was a mediocrity, though for those who care to note it, there was much that is admirable and virtuous in the Coolidge career. Despite his definite limitations, Coolidge was in many ways a man of perseverance, ability, and complexity,[9] and any history of the Twenties should not, as is often done, merely dismiss him with a joke or view him solely as symbol of a jaded nation's search for simple, bucolic virtue in the presidency following the departure of the Harding crowd.

To say that neither Harding nor Coolidge was a mere political cipher during his administration is to raise the subject of national politics in the Twenties—elections, factions, issues, legislation, and the larger society ostensibly reflected by Congress and the things it did in Washington. Studies of the election of 1920 continue for the most part to ask some questions raised long ago: Was it a referendum on the League? What happened to the Wilsonian coalition after 1916, so that it was mauled by Harding in 1920? Did the new woman suffrage amendment affect the outcome? The League, it is clear, was not the great and solemn referendum Wilson had hoped for. Both parties hedged on the subject, both Harding and Cox vacillated, and the League never emerged as a sharp issue itself or as one dividing the two candidates.[10] David Burner, in a series of articles, appraised all three presidential elections in the Twenties, much of his material turning up again in 1968 in his book, *The Politics of Provincialism: The Democratic Party in Transition, 1918-1922*. Burner's analysis of 1920 stresses Wilson's loss of control over domestic affairs after the Armistice; labor dissatisfaction over defeat of the Plumb Plan for railroads; high food prices; and the immigrant vote clustered in the East, which defected from the Democrats in large numbers.[11]

Studies of 1924 have lately focused on the conflict between Al Smith and William G. McAdoo over the Democratic presidential nomination, and this, in turn, leads to examination of the Klan, prohibition, and the rising urban vote and other forces shaping that fratricidal brawl in the Democratic convention. If it does nothing else, a study of the convention induces an appreciation for this relationship of party convention and party factions to the society out of which convention delegates came— a society of Klansmen and anti-Klansmen, Wets and Drys, Fundamentalists and Modernists, and urban-rural animosities rocking American life in a supposed period of frivolity and prosperity.[12]

The same is true of 1928, though the tensions and conflicts of that election year find personification in Smith and Hoover rather than Smith and McAdoo. There were other differences, of course, in that election, not the least of which was that Smith, after winning the nomination, ran up against a Republican who was probably impossible to beat. In 1960, on the eve of John F. Kennedy's nomination by the Democrats, Richard Hofstadter offered a provocative analysis of the election of 1928 and suggested that "there was not a Democrat alive, Protestant or Catholic, who could have beaten Hoover in 1928." The religious issue worked both ways: Smith lost votes as a Catholic, but he gained votes, too. The Republican party was united—at least more than the Democratic, which was still suffering from its fracture of 1924. Above all, the Democrats were faced with the overwhelming fact of (apparent) prosperity and the "immense prestige" of Herbert Hoover.[13]

Hofstadter drew in part upon the work of Samuel Lubell, who in an influential book of 1952, *The Future of American Politics,* first popularized the idea that Smith, even in defeat, drew a large bloc of voters into the Democratic Party, particularly northeastern urban, hyphenated, Catholic labor. These people, children of that great wave of migration from south-central Europe of the 1880's and 1890's, presumably identified with Smith, who attracted them to the party and thereby, so ran the Lubell thesis, began to build the Roosevelt coalition of the 1930's. This and other themes of the election of 1928 historians pursued all through the Sixties. Most studies were refinements on the Hofstadter-Lubell analysis or warnings of the need to keep other matters in mind, such as personality conflicts peculiar to a given state, or tactical blunders of the Democratic party organization.[14] Then in 1969, Jerome Clubb and Howard Allen published an important study, "The Cities and the Election of 1928: Partisan Realignment?"[15] Other historians have begun making gestures toward quantitative analysis of politics in the 1920's. But Clubb and Allen have developed this technique into a science if not an art, and they have seriously undermined the Lubell version of the Smith-to-Roosevelt bequest. Clubb and Allen studied election returns in some twenty metropolitan areas, 1920 to 1936 (in some cases 1922 to 1934), noting the trends in off-year and presidential-year Congressional elections, as well as the presidential vote. They simply did not find the steady drift toward the Democratic Party during the years that Lubell's more limited figures had indicated. There was evidently a Smith vote in 1928; the man did indeed exercise a magnetic appeal. But this was a personal, one-shot phenomenon. The vote for Smith was not matched by a vote for other Democrats in other offices between the early Twenties and the early Thirties. Clubb and Allen found no support for the view that an "Al Smith Revolution" of 1928 preceded the "Roosevelt Revolution" of the 1930's. Their conclusions may mean that we are back to the Depression as the primary explanation for Roosevelt's victory in 1932, though this should not obscure the significant urbanization, the traumas of urban life, and the shift of votes into the Democratic Party that were, in fact, occurring in the Twenties.

However elected, what did the presidents, congressmen, and senators of the Twenties accomplish, and what did their legislative hassles reveal about American life in the decade? One may simply consider, item by item and in isolation, hardy perennials of politics in the decade, such as tariffs, taxes, farm prices, electric power, and immigration restriction. But any one of several other approaches may be more feasible and provide better integration of material. For example, politics in the decade can be appraised by comparing legislation and political leadership of the

Twenties to the Progressive Era before the war and the New Deal of the Thirties. In 1959, Arthur S. Link provided a springboard for this kind of conceptualizing when he raised the question, "What Happened to the Progressive Movement in the 1920's?"[16] In pursuit of an answer, Link examined the standard subjects, such as Secretary of the Treasury Andrew Mellon's tax program, or the Congressional debates over Muscle Shoals, and judged them in light of the "progressivism" they revealed. Obviously, the first and abiding difficulty here is in defining and working with the concept of progressivism. As a term applied to such diverse individuals as Theodore Roosevelt, George Perkins, Jane Addams, and John Dewey, the very label "progressive movement" is ambiguous and one at the moment subject to considerable challenge.[17] Semantics aside, Link's tactic serves to raise the useful question: How did politicians and public policy in the Twenties relate to the years preceding and following the Twenties? Such an approach minimizes the danger of unduly isolating the decade from the past that fed into it and the future that lay ahead.

In 1959, Link found that during the Twenties progressivism sputtered and lost much of its drive but still survived in various forms, such as the fight by George Norris and his supporters in Congress which kept Muscle Shoals out of private hands and saved the site as a nucleus for the TVA of the 1930's.[18] Other studies have found comparable evidence of progressivism's survival. Even that old bugaboo the Teapot Dome scandal, forever cited as evidence of governmental irresponsibility, spawned behavior by its critics—both Democrats and Republicans—that can, by definition, be labeled progressive.[19] On a related issue, Donald C. Swain showed that conservation policy in the Twenties was notable in its own right but also for inaugurating programs later credited to the New Deal.[20] A study of the Sheppard-Towner Act reveals that this maternity and infancy care act of 1921 "was a link in a chain of ideas and actions from Roosevelt to Roosevelt."[21] A major book on this theme of "welfare" legislation in the Twenties is Clark Chambers' *Seedtime of Reform*.[22] Chambers revealed a powerful current of reform at work in the Twenties, with progressive women contributing probably more than men to the growth of social welfare work and movements to abolish child labor, eliminate slums, and provide social security.

If historians traditionally have found little reform, progressive or otherwise, in the Twenties, it may be that they have looked in the wrong places or not looked at all. It is possible that the pre-war reform movement, however labeled, simply changed emphasis in the Twenties (sometimes for the worse, as Prohibition) and gained new adherents from unexpected quarters. Anne Scott discovered a "decided growth" among

Southerners in the Twenties "of the conception of state responsibility for public welfare . . . in the newer sense of ameliorating the underlying conditions that created human problems." And equally to the point, she learned that "to the growth of this idea and its application in law, Southern women made a considerable contribution."[23]

Progressivism endured in the West, too. Richard Ruetten, in an essay that ranges far beyond the limits suggested by its title, studied the ideas and behavior of a group of Western senators in the Twenties. Burton K. Wheeler (Montana), Smith W. Brookhart (Iowa), Henrik Shipstead (Minnesota), Lynn J. Frazier (North Dakota), and others continually agitated against the Republican administrations in Washington. Non-interventionists in foreign affairs, trustbusters at home, sympathetic to labor, advocates of the McNary-Haugen farm bill, and with a "deep respect for civil liberties," these "Western senatorial insurgents of the Twenties preserved a spark of reform during an uncongenial age and paved the way for the New Deal"—though once that program developed, they would often take alarm at its direction.[24]

No one has tried to depict the Supreme Court as a bastion of progressivism in the Twenties; and in fact it was, by any standard, a conservative body.[25] Yet the Chief Justice from 1921 to 1930 was William Howard Taft, an old Progressive (of a sort), and some of his interpretations would later provide a justification for the broad construction of Federal power that the Court expressed after 1937, when it began to uphold the New Deal.[26] On the other hand, students of the New Deal, if not students of the Twenties, have tended to call attention to the conservatism of the Taft court and to note the appointments by Harding of men who, come the Thirties, would try to nullify the New Deal.[27]

Studies of the Twenties that take the Progressive period, the New Deal, or both as reference points are concerned with continuity (or alteration) in an ongoing series of reforms. Men and events of the Twenties are thereby sandwiched between Progressives and New Dealers and usually portrayed in varying degrees of unfavorable contrast to these two groups. One may concentrate, however, not on this dichotomy or pendulum swing of reaction-reform but on the decade itself, with or without reference to earlier or later times, and the conflict between "rural" and "urban" cultures that permeated society then. Such a view encompasses a great deal of the political, economic, social, and intellectual life of the Twenties. To some critics, this is just the difficulty with the terms "rural" and "urban." As do many terms first exploited by social scientists and then picked up by historians, they tend to lose exactness of meaning and become umbrellas under which some historians can shelter almost anything. Yet this reflects more upon the historian than upon the validity of his terms, which can in fact refer to rather specific and even measurable things—like distribution of population. The census of 1920 was the first to reveal that a majority of Americans lived in "urban" areas (incorporated communities of 2,500 or more). This revelation, long expected but awaited with some apprehension, generated profound discussion in the Twenties and has served continually since then to illustrate the fact that urbanization, or simply "the city" in more common parlance, was a central feature, perhaps the most crucial one, in American life during the Twenties.[28] Urban historians, who made striking changes in method during the 1960's, have brought to the Twenties their fresh perspectives in writing urban history and are discussing things all but undreamed of by earlier historians of the decade: techniques of zoning that developed during the Twenties; low-cost housing programs; or the planning and construction of Shaker Heights and other "suburbs," the latter itself a major new residential pattern that developed in the period.[29]

Meanwhile, older approaches recognizing the role of the city continued to find expression. The Klan, the Church, the bottle, and other durables of the decade have long been appraised in the context of a rural-urban culture conflict. Popular tradition shows the Klansman of the Twenties as a rural (or small-town) bigot, primitive if not Fundamentalist in his Protestant faith, full of hatred for Negro, Catholic, and Jew, and suspicious of the city and its secular, sinful ways. Studies in the 1960's sometimes reinforced this image but more often qualified it and occasionally challenged part of it head-on.

One fact now seems obvious: the Klan of the Twenties differed from the Klan of Reconstruction and from the motley array of Klans and White Citizens' Councils that sprang up in the 1950's.[30] Though numbers alone do not distinguish it from the others, the Klan of the Twenties enrolled some three to five million members. As Carl Degler has pointed out, "a movement that enlisted such enthusiasm cannot be written off as composed of 'crackpots' or 'fanatics' or even of evil people."[31] Or as Robert Miller, in a brilliant essay on the Klan, stated: "The citizens of the Invisible Empire were deeply anxious men, but they were not, save for the psychotic few, moral monsters,"[32] What, then, did motivate these millions? Their very numbers, if nothing else, indicate diversity. The Klan was, noted Miller, a "many-splintered thing." These Knights were all "troubled souls," though each had his own particular enemy, be it bootlegger, gambler, evolutionist, Negro, Catholic, Jew, or any other of a myriad number of (to him) evil agents of change threatening his psychic equilibrium.

Several studies, especially Charles Alexander's *The Ku Klux Klan in the Southwest*,[33] have demonstrated that much of the Klan's violence focused upon fellow WASP's and not upon the presumed enemy in another race or church or moral clime. Though for awhile it had real political clout, the Klan was primarily a moral censor, even if its own "morality" was often an obscene and militant travesty on Protestantism and an equation of morality with a witless chauvinism, racism, and anti-intellectualism. To many a Klansman, the city was the enemy citadel, though Kenneth Jackson's recent study shows that Klansmen were prominent in cities as well as rural areas, in North and West as well as South.[34] The Dallas Klavern in one year collected $98,000 in klectokens (initiation fees) and dues. In Chicago's heterogenous ethnic and class mixture, the Klan claimed 100,000 members in the central city, and 100,000 more in the suburbs. Yet the very characteristics that Jackson found among these "urban" Klansmen are strikingly similar to those that students of the Klan usually include under the term "rural," such as religious fundamentalism, near-illiteracy, antipathy toward minority groups, and a preoccupation with "100% Americanism" and an older moral code. Klansmen, whether in city or country, were a rearguard element, bucking the new world rising around them.[35]

This is not to say that every Fundamentalist was a Klansman, though the reverse may be close to the truth. Even so, to call a Klansman a Fundamentalist hardly sharpens his identity. Much of the recent historiography on Fundamentalism has been a search for definition, for deciding just what a Fundamentalist was (and is), and where his creed began and how it has fared to the present. Ernest R. Sandeen, for example, found Fundamentalist roots deep in the nineteenth century and challenged the notion that, even in the Twenties, Fundamentalism was exclusively a parochial, rural phenomenon.[36] Another tendency has been to place the Fundamentalists somewhere along the Left-Right spectrum on political and social issues, and usually far to the right.[37] And finally, the Fundamentalist has been fitted into the rural-urban axis, where he snaps his galluses, picks his teeth, clutches his Bible (King James version) in his work-gnarled hand, and points a reproachful finger at the cosmopolites of the scarlet city.[38] This imagery has some validity, but, as Paul Carter has pointed out, "Fundamentalism in the 1920's claimed many a strategic city pulpit."[39] Conversely, country boys sometimes became liberals in their theology, and not necessarily by leaving the farm. Traditionally the Scopes Trial in Dayton, Tennessee, with William Jennings Bryan defending the Rock of Ages and the true church against liberal freethinking Clarence Darrow from Chicago, has served to exemplify the dichotomy of rural ignorance vs. urban enlightenment. Recent studies have hardly reversed the alignment, but they have shown more sympathy for Bryan than H. L. Mencken ever did, and have demonstrated the inadequacy of the simple "Science or Religion" formula applied to the controversy in the Twenties.[40]

If Klansmen have been associated with Fundamentalists, both, and especially the latter, have been linked with the Prohibitionists. Certainly the Drys tended to be strong in their Protestant faith, and the proclivity of Catholics for wine, if only in church, and the abundance of saloons, speakeasies, and rum-running gangsters in the city reinforced the rural moralists' fear of urban living. In a history of the Prohibition movement, Andrew Sinclair voiced such an interpretation in 1962. Prohibition, claimed Sinclair, "was the final victory of the defenders of the American past. On the rock of the Eighteenth Amendment, village America made its last stand." When the rock crumbled with repeal, so did "rural morality" as the "old order of the country gave way to the new order of the cities."[41] This association of Drys with rural, Anglo, Protestant traditionalists, in contrast to Wet, urban Catholics, requires some qualification. Joseph Gusfeld argued that the urban middle-class, as well as rural voters, produced that momentary Dry supremacy of the Twenties labeled Prohibition.[42] Many occupational social groups of Americans supported the experiment: social workers who thought it could alleviate the deep-seated poverty in industrial areas; professional and small businessmen who saw the drinking immigrant as a threat to sober and disciplined ways of life; old progressives who thought the end of drinking might help to end political corruption. Drys often cited not Scripture but scientific and medical data to bolster their claim that alcohol was debilitating; employers concerned with safety in their plants and mines cited drunkenness as a major cause of accidents. Nevertheless, Gusfeld found that "national prohibition sentiment" was highest "where the populations were Protestant, rural, and nativist."[43]

Did Prohibition, then, mark the temporary victory, as Sinclair would put it, of a Protestant "rural morality," and Repeal an "urban victory"? The United States was a heavy-drinking society before World War I. Despite folklore and television melodrama to the contrary, Prohibition cut consumption to perhaps one-half the prewar rate. But the rate of decrease came largely from diminished beer-drinking and not from less consumption of the harder stuff. Workers who normally drank beer drank a lot less in the Twenties. Professional and salaried classes drank as much if not more than they did before the Twenties. They could afford the bootlegged variety pouring in from Cuba, Canada, and elsewhere.[44] After repeal, alcoholic consumption did not rise appreciably; in fact a "long run trend toward moderation" set in.[45]

The total rate of consumption did soon exceed that of the 1911-15 level. Yet statistics are one thing and cultural symbols another. While it lasted, Prohibition and the searing debate that it engendered did demonstrate a conflict of cultures. The old dichotomies of urban-rural, Catholic-Protestant, working class-middle class, and immigrant-nativist gained an added alignment: Wet-Dry. And if Bryan at Dayton, Tennessee, came to personify the bone-dry, old-stock American fighting for his version of God and country, then Al Smith in 1928 if not in 1924 came to represent the challenge. But Smith lost in 1928, and the powerful coalition that Franklin D. Roosevelt put together in the 1930's contained too many diverse elements, such as countless old Dry, Anglo, rural Protestants, for it to represent an absolute victory of "urban" over "rural" America. And to the degree that abstinence is linked to Fundamentalism, abstainers are still around in force, for Fundamentalism, as Paul Carter pointed out, is hardly a spent or dying force. Assemblies of God, Soul-Saving Stations, and Billy Graham, who in the 70's had a friend in the White House, bear witness to the endurance of that old rural morality that supposedly died in the Twenties.[46]

To talk of rural and urban cultures in conflict is to follow a lead established by Walter Lippmann and other social commentators in the Twenties. But historians of the Twenties did not begin to stress such terms until the 1950's. In an illuminating essay in 1966, Don Kirschner nicely distinguished some older interpretations of the 1920's, such as Charles Beard's that used largely "rational" economic interpretations, from more recent ones that stressed "irrational" or cultural motivations to explain human behavior in the Twenties.[47] In 1955 Richard Hofstadter, in his *The Age of Reform,* became one of the first to stress "culture conflict" in appraising the Twenties and to assign more importance to loss of status than to loss of income. As he portrayed the period, economic differences between competing groups were less significant than were cultural differences. But as Kirschner suggested, some Protestants were more nativist than others, and often there was more conflict among Protestants than between them and Catholics. In the city, Poles could be as anti-Semitic as any rural Fundamentalist. And was it possible that some farmers in the Twenties were trying not just to hold onto a certain "status" in the culture but to feed their families? In any case, what connection, if any, existed between a man's economic and his cultural status?

In *City and Country: Rural Responses to Urbanization in the 1920's,*[48] Kirschner tried to grapple with such questions, though he restricted himself to Iowa and Indiana for his data, and the city to which farmers in these states "responded" was often the particular, and perhaps unique, city of Chicago. Kirschner's argument, stripped of all its subtleties and qualifications, is this: Farmers during the Twenties were in economic trouble. And even though they were beginning to use techniques and items taken from the city, such as cost accounting and radio, they also felt challenged by an alien style of life that emanated from the city, a style they contrasted sharply with their own presumably superior one. In case after case, rural legislators from districts voted one way, those from urban districts another, on such "cultural" matters as Prohibition, legalized boxing, and horse racing. On economic issues, such as salaries for state officials, regulation of hours for labor, or tax assessments on property, rural districts voted according to their economic interest, as they interpreted that interest. Thus, the farmer in the Twenties (at least in two states) felt both cultural and economic pressures and sought to protect his interest in each category. He was no more irrational over defending his culture, his status, than he was over pursuing his economic goals. Nevertheless, the rural-urban culture conflict began to dim in the decade, because the farmer, however agonizing it was, began to accept the enemy. "Farmers were finding a new place for themselves in the fast-changing world of the 1920's, and it was a place in the new world of the cities."[49]

A focus on the "culture" of the Twenties, then, should not obscure the "economy" of the decade. The old idea that agriculture was in economic trouble in the period is still worth emphasizing. The annual per capita income of people who lived on the farm in 1929 averaged $273; the national average was $750. Declining prices and high operating costs in the Twenties placed the farmer in "exactly the opposite position from that in the prewar years."[50] Production outran demand, partly because of wartime expansion but also from the farmer's increased efficiency. Yet if farmers could better their production they could not, as industry could, limit it to their price advantage. Efforts to cope with the farm problem finally centered on the McNary-Haugen bill, which passed Congress twice only to receive a Coolidge veto each time. Gilbert Fite has clearly explained these developments. Little of the story he tells is in particular dispute among historians, if only because Fite himself has done so much to delineate agricultural history of the Twenties. With agriculture, however, one is back to the theme of the Twenties as prelude to the New Deal—in this case the McNary-Haugen plan ostensibly preparing the way for the AAA.[51] But if the early AAA was "conservative" in the sense that it benefited the more prosperous and larger landowners at the expense of the sharecropper, and thereby offered no challenge to the existing agricultural system, George Peek and other advocates of McNary-Haugenism in the Twenties were equally conservative. Evaluating the plan's backers, Fite noted that "much of the argument in favor of doing something for agriculture was based on the belief that prosperous, land-owning farmers were the main bulwark against radicalism and socialism."[52]

Labor leaders in the Twenties were just as conservative, at least those in the American Federation of Labor.[53] When Samuel Gompers died in 1924, AFL leadership passed to William Green, who equaled Gompers in his concern for respectability and moderation in the AFL and his opposition to Communism. Yet if farm leaders were fearful that agricultural discontent might produce "radicalism," Green should have been terrified. As Irving Bernstein's history of labor in the Twenties so starkly reveals, living and working conditions were often appalling. Unemployment was so severe that "social workers, burdened with the misery that followed in its wake, became alarmed."[54] Even those workers with jobs often suffered. In 1929, nearly six million families (over 21 per cent of the nation's total) received less than $1,000 a year; another six million received less than $1,500; another eight million drew in less than $2,500. Thus, 20 million families, or 71 per cent of all American families, took in less than $2,500 a year. "The combined incomes of 0.1 per cent of the families at the top of the scale were as great as those of the 42 per cent at the bottom."[55] And yet historians continue to label the Twenties a "prosperity decade." Perhaps this is because, despite these gross inequities, labor generated little overt protest or violence in the Twenties; and few social critics came forward to lament labor's condition. To explain the lack of unionization, Bernstein stressed the gradual rise in living standards for labor during the decade, and the materialism, individualism, and conservatism of labor itself. Too, the heterogeneity of the labor force encouraged internal factionalism more than it did unity and union growth.[56] As for Gompers and Green and other union leaders, they seemed, Bernstein judges, "bereft of ideas . . . ideological prisoners of the past." Even John L. Lewis, whose United Mine Workers union was the largest and most powerful voice in America labor during the decade, was "a warm if occasionally inconsistent proponent of economic orthodoxy."[57]

All blame for union weaknesses in the Twenties, then, should not fall on antiunion employers. But that opposition was there, and it was sometimes vicious. From the steel strike of 1919, with its ominous outcome, to the textile strikes in Gastonia and other Southern towns in 1929, where labor folk heroes were born but where the opposition was often primitive in its cunning, labor faced an entrenched adversary in the Twenties.[58] So did those workers and ideologists leaning far enough left to be labeled Socialist, Wobbly, or Communist, though each of these groups suffered varying fates. The Wobblies all but disappeared, destroyed by the war and the Red Scare.[59] In the conventional view, the Socialists—meaning particularly the Socialist Party of America—reached their zenith in 1912, then trailed off, torn by internal dissension, especially over World War I.[60] In partial refutation of this, James Weinstein charted the course of a viable Socialist Party, one with mass support at the polls, enduring up to about 1920. After that, as he portrays it, the party "lost its organizational cohesion and a sense of direction."[61] But in one form or another the socialist movement extended with some force well into the Twenties. As Socialist and Communist organizations splintered in 1921 and 1922, the Farmer-Labor Party tried to "bring together all the radical forces in the United States committed to the development of an independent third party of workers and farmers." A maze of groups, varying in ideology from far left to moderate, appeared for a moment and went under. The election of 1924, in which La Follette running on his Progressive ticket was a key figure, marked the effective end of any radical unity. "Debs' death in 1926 symbolized the fate of the Party," though for another two decades the party "would continue to go through the motions."[62] The Communist movement, fractured by the Palmer raids and internal dissent, had by the mid-Twenties become isolated and would not return to prominence in American politics until the early Thirties.[63]

Meanwhile, the Republican party and its major spokesmen such as Herbert Hoover claimed full credit unto themselves and American capitalism for the relative lack of labor militancy and the relative prosperity that much of labor enjoyed. Hoover, an influential figure in this story, as he was in much of the decade's political and economic history, recognized the need for labor unions, if only as a means for more efficient organization and production of manpower.[64] Nor was Hoover's Republican party a monolithic bloc opposing the rights of labor in the Twenties;[65] neither were all businessmen opposed to various forms of "welfare" programs. In fact, as a few recent studies have shown, "business thought" during the Twenties encompassed any number of welfare programs that paternalistic corporation leaders—mostly from large and prosperous firms—sought to design for their employees, perhaps to some degree out of humanity but also in order to increase efficiency, to undercut more radical programs, and to retain control over the labor force.[66] But as politicians or as capitalists, men such as Hoover were, in fact, trying to sustain and rationalize a system they were comfortable in and one that they considered the best of all possible worlds. Ellis Hawley depicted Secretary of Commerce Hoover as a transitional figure in the Twenties, one who worked for efficient production, technological innovation, and the elimination of waste, while at the same time he sought to hold onto old mythologies and images of competitive individualism. He wanted a world of "cooperative individualists" and "competitive cooperation," in which the "American system," as he called it, would flourish above all others.[67] Even after the Great Crash, Hoover continued to keep the faith, refusing to see internal weaknesses in the system, though he, too, along with other business observers, had been troubled by the speculative mania that raged through the nation's stock exchanges in the final years of the decade.[68] The depression gave Hoover a bad name, but, as Hawley pointed out, in the Twenties his ideas seemed enlightened when set alongside those of Coolidge and Andrew Mellon.

Hoover's ambitions for the American system did not stop at the water's edge. In fact, to him the endurance of that system demanded that it extend its investments and influence out into the alien world. Hoover's ideas and his role as Secretary of Commerce in two administrations make him one of the central figures in the shaping of American diplomacy in the Twenties. He was even more crucial just beyond the decade, when in 1931 Japanese troops struck in Manchuria, and Hoover, now President, overrode Henry Stimson's impulse to move against Japan.[69] If the Manchurian episode initiated a sequence of steps leading to World War II (and this is a traditional view), Wilson at Versailles twelve years earlier at the beginning of the decade closed out World War I and, for better or worse, guided American diplomacy into the Twenties. American foreign policy in the decade may be viewed as moving between these two points and posing a question: How did the nation emerge from one war, in Europe, and thirteen years later find itself troubled with the nation, this time Asian, that it finally fought in another war? However that be answered, at Versailles in 1919 Wilson was the crucial figure. Understandably his role in the peacemaking and his fight with the U.S. Senate over ratification of the treaty and League membership have caught historians' attention—and often their deep emotions—for half a century. Among recent studies, one of the most important and certainly the heaviest is Arno Mayer's *Politics and Diplomacy of Peacemaking: Containment and Counterrevolution at Versailles, 1918-1919*.[70] Surveying affairs in all the major European countries as well as in the United States, Mayer tried to show how Wilson and the other "peacemakers" worked to stabilize governments throughout Europe, somewhere between a left and right extreme, and at the same time to contain, if not destroy, the Russian Revolution. That is, in Mayer's analysis, Russia replaces Germany as Wilson's (and the Allies') chief preoccupation. This fear of revolution, especially the Bolshevik version, animated not only Wilson and Lansing but also policy makers in the Twenties.[71]

Mayer's book illustrates a significant recent shift in diplomatic historiography of the Twenties. Once upon a time, it was common to
speak of America's retreat to isolation after World War I, of her
renunciation of responsibilities in the world. That view has now been all
but turned around. William Appleman Williams' work in the 1950's was
of great importance in this development, and much of the work done in
the 1960's reflects his thinking.[72] From the Allied intervention in Russia
in the summer of 1918,[73] to the Hoover-Stimson policies of 1931, American diplomacy in the Twenties has of late raised the question not of
"isolation," but of how much intervention and with what ramifications.
To expand and protect American markets and sources of raw materials,
to find more fields for capital investment, to check the rise of political
systems supposedly inimical to American interests, American diplomats
and policy makers in the Twenties, as now pictured, carried out a program of American expansion and influence in the world of the Twenties.[74] There are, of course, notable exceptions—historians dealing with
a more restricted theme or reiterating the older view of American retreat
from responsibility in the Twenties. The latter, either implicitly or
explicitly, often regret this "retreat" but no more than the recent scholars
seem to regret the nation's attempt to poke around in the world and to
intrude upon other peoples' lives.

Whether they are interventionists (to some degree) regretting a
retreat, or isolationists (of a sort) regretting undue intervention, or a
tertium quid falling between or remaining above the dichotomy, diplomatic historians of the Twenties in the decade of the 1960's re-examined
the old subjects and occasionally found some new ones: Wilson's fight
for ratification and League membership;[75] relations with Mexico and
Central America, forever on the brink of intervention or war;[76] concern
over American security and trade in the Far East, in the face of a
revolution in China and a burgeoning power in Japan;[77] Communist
Russia, unrecognized by the protocols of diplomacy but awesome,
feared, and frequently on Washington's mind;[78] the complex of European
debts and reparations, as well as European fields for trade and investment, along with African rubber plantations and Near Eastern oil
wells.[79] Even with all this expansion, involvement, and commitment to
world power, there were factions and individuals preoccupied with maintaining peace, whether it be by isolation or by joining the League.[80]
Others simply wanted to close the gates.[81] Some wanted to recognize the
reality and even the legitimacy of revolutionary change in Russia,
Mexico, and China. Others tried to block or to deny changes in societies
around the world.[82] Foreign policy in the Twenties was many policies,
as varied in motivation, goals, and results as the Americans who shaped
it and the rest of the world that felt its impact.[83] But if historiography

in the 1960's has demonstrated anything more than this, it showed how the American government and its people were deeply preoccupied with the world outside the United States in the Twenties.

In popular mythology, a small element of Americans, usually labeled "intellectuals," were less troubled by the outside world than by life in the United States, and so fled to Paris or other cultural meccas of Europe in the Twenties. Whatever they were, and however motivated, these American "expatriates" have always been the central element in the intellectual history of the Twenties. Associated with them, even synonymous with them, is the memorable term attributed to Gertrude Stein: "the lost generation."[84]

There was indeed an outflow of Americans to Paris and other European meccas in the Twenties, among them thousands of tourists, American businessmen and diplomats, and ex-doughboys looking up familiar battlefield sights. But the alienated artist, the fledgling writer, or the rebellious painter was in a distinct minority. Warren Susman estimated that among all the Americans settled in Paris at any one time in the Twenties, no more than one-tenth to one-fifth of them were those celebrated figures commonly called expatriates. And even these were not always spiritual exiles; rather, as Cushing Strout said, Paris in the Twenties was "the center for the artistically adventurous of every country." Many Americans just chose to live in Paris—the city was exciting, the rent was cheap, they had a grant—while writing about America.[85] So when the intellectual or literary historian focuses on the American expatriate (Hemingway's characters from *The Sun Also Rises* are the classic models.), he is dealing with a tiny if admittedly creative minority.

Intellectual history, more broadly conceived, would encompass many "levels" of American thought. Source materials would range from *The Reader's Digest,* established in 1922; to the *New Yorker* (1925); to other evidence of mass culture such as the Book-of-the-Month Club (1926); to popular outlines of knowledge that appeared in the Twenties, such as *The Story of Philosophy* or *The Outline of History*;[86] to the research and publications by physicists and other scholars in American laboratories and universities;[87] to higher realms of thought found in the sermons of Reinhold Niebuhr.[88] Faced with the formidable chore of writing a brief history of ideas in the Twenties, Roderick Nash executed it admirably by focusing on the "lost generation" theme, but then, by touching on numerous levels and varieties of American thought, demolishing (one hopes) once and for all the idea that a generation of expatriates, nihilists, bohemians, and other Hemingway characters summed up the life of the mind in the American Twenties.[89] As Nash surveyed it, the decade produced many kinds of intellectuals: chauvinistic racists (Madison Grant), novelists and poets who celebrated

America past and present (Carl Sandburg, Stephen Vincent Benet), Southern agrarians nostalgic for a dying agrarian world (Donald Davidson),[90] champions of wilderness preservation (Aldo Leopold), humanists defending the "genteel tradition" (Paul Elmer More), moral relativists seeking new standards (Walter Lippmann), and any number of others to go along with the incipient existentialists and famous artists-in-exile who did appear.[91] And finally, ultimately, there were Heroes, such as Lindbergh, Babe Ruth, and Henry Ford. If the Sacco-Vanzetti case provided a cause and a symbol of despair for certain intellectuals in the Twenties,[92] then Lucky Lindy, the Bambino, and the man from Detroit were, each in an individual way, reassuring culture figures to a nation of middle brows fearful about losing their individual distinctiveness and prowess in an urbanizing, automating, homogenizing society.[93]

Perhaps a historical configuration of the Twenties should itself strive for homogeneity, fitting all things, however trivial or transitory, into the pattern. Even though all things do not necessarily relate or even belong in a historical narrative, historians of the Twenties are remiss when they totally neglect such fundamentals as radio, jazz, Hollywood, and that melange that the Frederick Lewis Allen imitators always cite to conjure up the Twenties: crossword puzzles, flagpole sitters, raccoon coats, Mah Jong, lipstick, and *True Confession* magazines. Some of these deserve discussion and in fact have their history.[94] The rest must, at least in the present stage of historiography, find their place in broader discussions of style, taste, or morality.

Meanwhile, two fashions in American historiography have displayed opposite attitudes toward the Twenties and shown thereby how the decade serves varying purposes to those who study it. Historians of Black America have begun to probe around in the Twenties with notable results,[95] whereas the New Left has all but ignored the decade.[96] Perhaps the Black Americans (and their white colleagues in the field) are searching for historical roots, aware that the Twenties may contain as many as any other period, whereas the New Left seems preoccupied with exorcising the liberal historiography of their predecessors and with re-examining old liberal heroes, few of whom exist in the historical mythology of the Twenties. And the mythology dies hard. The picture histories with their *Life*-like captions, the Sunday supplement approach to the decade, continues to find outlet. For those who want to hold onto the Jazz Age, with its bohemians, its raccoon coats, and its petting parties, there are authors and publishers ready to serve that need. Those who want another configuration of the decade may find it by reading the material cited in this essay.[97]

FOOTNOTES

[1] I have briefly discussed the origins of this historiography in "The Twenties: A New Historiographical Frontier." *The Journal of American History* 53: 299-314; No. 2, September 1966.

[2] On configurations and *gestalts* in historiography, a clear, concise statement is John T. Marcus. "The Changing Consciousness of History." *South Atlantic Quarterly* 60: 217-225; Spring 1961.

[3] Little has been written on the general subject of reconstruction and reconversion after World War I, but see David Burner, "1919: Prelude to Normalcy," in *Change and Continuity in Twentieth-Century America: The 1920's,* edited by John Braeman, *et al.,* Columbus: Ohio State University Press, 1968, pp. 3-31, for a general view of the 1919-20 period.

[4] William Preston, Jr., *Aliens and Dissenters: Federal Suppression of Radicals, 1903-1933,* Cambridge: Harvard University Press, 1963, shows the continuity of anti-radical activity after the war. Stanley Coben, "A Study in Nativism: The American Red Scare of 1919-20," *Political Science Quarterly* 79: 52-75; No. 1, March 1964, is an outstanding essay that draws on anthropology and psychology to delineate the state of mind that Americans displayed at the beginning of the Twenties and that contributed to the growth of the Klan, to immigration restriction, and to a search for control over education in the name of "Americanism." A learned essay is Woodrow C. Whitten. *Criminal Syndicalism and the Law in California, 1919-1927.* Transactions of the American Philosophical Society, New Series, LIX, Part 2. Philadelphia: The Society, March, 1969. On "Americanism" and other forms of intolerance in the Twenties, see Paul L. Murphy. "Normalcy, Intolerance, and the American Character." *Virginia Quarterly Review* XL: 445-459; No. 3, Summer 1964, and "Sources and Nature of Intolerance in the 1920's." *Journal of American History* 51: 60-76; No. 1, June 1964.

[5] On foreign policy, see pp. 478-480 in this chapter.

[6] Minneapolis: University of Minnesota Press, 1969.

[7] David H. Stratton, "The Shadow of Blooming Grove," *Pacific Northwest Quarterly* 61: 46-49; No. 1, January 1970, is full of wit and information on the unearthing and use in the 1960's of some Harding papers in Ohio. Stratton also comments on two other recent Harding biographies: Andrew Sinclair. *The Available Man: The Life Behind the Masks of Warren Gamaliel Harding.* New York: Macmillan 1965; and Francis Russell. *The Shadow of Blooming Grove: Warren G. Harding in His Times.* New York: McGraw-Hill, 1968. Recent evidence of Harding's continued low reputation among historians is Gary M. Maranell, "The Evaluation of Presidents: An Extension of the Schlesinger Polls," *Journal of American History* 57: 104-113; No. 1, June 1970. On the other hand, Randolph Downes, along with Murray, continues to challenge this embedded distaste for Harding. Over the past two decades or so, Downes has published numerous articles on Harding, the tenor of which may be inferred from one title, "The Harding Muckfest: Warren G. Harding—Chief Victim of the Muck-for-Muck's-Sake Writers and Readers," *Northwest Ohio Quarterly* 39: 5-37; No. 3, Summer 1967. Downes has recently published the first volume of a two-volume biography, *The Rise of Warren Gamaliel Harding, 1865-1920.* Columbus: Ohio State University Press, 1970.

[8] New York: Macmillan, 1967.

[9] Two other recent titles of note are *Your Son, Calvin Coolidge: A Selection of Letters from Calvin Coolidge to His Father,* edited by Edward C. Lathem. Montpelier: Vermont Historical Society, 1968; and *The Talkative President: The Off-the-Record Press Conferences of Calvin Coolidge,* edited by Howard H. Quint and Robert H. Ferrell. Amherst: University of Massachusetts Press, 1964. For those unaware of the Coolidge warmth and shrewdness, these volumes may be a revelation.

[10] Richard L. Merritt. "Woodrow Wilson and the 'Great and Solemn Referendum,' 1920." *Review of Politics* 27: 78-104; No. 1, January 1965. For further comment on the League issue in 1920, see pp. 478-480 in this chapter. Other recent titles on 1920 include Wesley M. Bagby. *The Road to Normalcy: The Presidential Campaign and Election of 1920*. Baltimore: The Johns Hopkins Press, 1962; Gary W. Reichard. "The Aberration of 1920: An Analysis of Harding's Victory in Tennessee." *Journal of Southern History* 36: 33-49; No. 1, February 1970; and Kurt Wimer. "Woodrow Wilson and a Third Nomination." *Pennsylvania History* 29: 193-211; No. 2, April 1962.

[11] David Burner. "The Breakup of the Wilson Coalition of 1916." *Mid-America* 45: 18-35; No. 1, January 1963.

[12] On 1924, see Lee N. Allen. "The Underwood Presidential Movement of 1924." *Alabama Review* 15: 83-89; No. 2, April 1962; Allen. "The McAdoo Campaign for the Presidential Nomination in 1924." *Journal of Southern History* 29: 211-228; No. 2, May 1963; David H. Stratton. "Splattered with Oil: William G. McAdoo and the 1924 Presidential Nomination." *Southwestern Social Science Quarterly* 44: 62-75; No. 1, June 1963; and especially David B. Burner. "The Democratic Party in the Election of 1924." *Mid-America* 46: 92-113; No. 2, April 1964.

[13] Hofstadter. "Could a Protestant Have Beaten Hoover in 1928?" *The Reporter*. March 17, 1960. pp. 31-33.

[14] On historiography to the early Sixties, see Paul A. Carter. "The Campaign of 1928 Re-Examined: A Study in Political Folklore." *Wisconsin Magazine of History* 46: 263-272; No. 4, Summer 1963. On later work, see Richard L. Watson, Jr. "Some Recent Interpretations of the Election of 1928." *High School Journal* 50: 428-448; May 1967.

[15] *American Historical Review* 74: 1205-1220; No. 4, April 1969.

[16] *Ibid.* 64: 833-851; No. 4, July 1959.

[17] Peter G. Filene. "An Obituary for 'The Progressive Movement.'" *American Quarterly* 22: 20-34; No. 1, Spring 1970. In a 1963 survey, "Recent Opinion on the Decline of the Progressive Movement," *Mid-America* 45: 250-268; No. 4, October 1963, Herbert Margulies quite rightly found that "historians seem to be generally agreed that the Progressive movement was over by 1920." But even then Margulies cited Link as an exception, and now one must note that in the Sixties, as the material below indicates, Link gained much support.

[18] The basic book on this subject is Preston J. Hubbard. *Origins of the TVA: The Muscle Shoals Controversy, 1920-1932*. Nashville: Vanderbilt University Press, 1961.

[19] Burl Noggle. "Oil and Politics," in *The 1920's*, edited by Braeman, *et al*. pp. 33-65. A fuller account of the Teapot Dome affair is Noggle. *Teapot Dome: Oil and Politics in the 1920's*. Baton Rouge: Louisiana State University Press, 1962. J. Leonard Bates, *The Origins of Teapot Dome: Progressives, Parties, and Petroleum, 1909-1921*, Urbana: University of Illinois Press, 1963, closely examines a decade of struggle over oil policy that preceded the Teapot Dome affair.

[20] Swain. *Federal Conservation Policy, 1921-1933*. Berkeley and Los Angeles: University of California Press, 1963.

[21] J. Stanley Lemons. "The Sheppard-Towner Act: Progressivism in the 1920's." *Journal of American History* 55: 776-786; No. 4, March 1969.

[22] Minneapolis: University of Minnesota Press, 1963.

[23] Anne Firor Scott. "After Suffrage: Southern Women in the Twenties." *Journal of Southern History* 30: 298-318; No. 3, August 1964. On progressivism generally in the South during the Twenties, see George Brown Tindall's monumental survey, *The Emergence of the New South, 1913-1945*. Baton Rouge: Louisiana State University Press, 1967. pp. 219 ff.

[24] Richard T. Ruetten. "Senator Burton K. Wheeler and Insurgency in the 1920's," in *The American West: A Reorientation,* edited by Gene M. Gressley. Laramie: Uni-

versity of Wyoming Press, 1966. pp. 111-131, and 164-72. See also Jackson K. Putnam. "The Persistence of Progressivism in the 1920's: The Case of California." *Pacific Historical Review* 35: 395-41; No. 4, November 1966. Ruetten's Senators out of the Twenties compare in background and outlook to those old Progressives that Otis Graham, in *An Encore for Reform: The Old Progressives and the New Deal,* New York: Oxford University Press, 1967, shows opposing the New Deal during the 1930's. Ruetten's essay connects Graham's two periods and reveals what happened during the Twenties to that element of Progressivism that Graham found turning against the New Deal in the 1930's.

²⁵ See Alpheus T. Mason. *William Howard Taft: Chief Justice.* New York: Simon and Schuster, 1965; David J. Danelski. *A Supreme Court Justice Is Appointed.* New York: Random House, 1964; and William F. Swindler. *Court and Constitution in the Twentieth Century: Vol. 1. The Old Legality, 1889-1932.* Indianapolis & New York: Bobbs-Merrill, 1969.

²⁶ Stanley I. Kutler. "Chief Justice Taft, National Regulation, and the Commerce Power." *Journal of American History* 51: 651-668; No. 4, March 1965.

²⁷ Arthur M. Schlesinger, Jr., for example, says that "the Court of 1935 had been created basically by Warren G. Harding." Two of his appointees—Sutherland and Butler—were still on the bench in 1935; his nominee Taft, even though he died in 1930, "had done most to give this Court its distinctive character." *The Politics of Upheaval.* Boston: Houghton Mifflin, 1960. pp. 454-455.

²⁸ A six-volume history of the United States, published in the 1960's, offered as its final work in the series George E. Mowry's *The Urban Nation, 1920-1960.* New York: Hill and Wang, 1965. As his title suggests, Mowry emphasizes the "urban tilt" that shaped American society in the Twenties and that made the period far more "recognizable" to today than is any era before then. American history since 1920 is more or less a coherent (and urbanized) unit.

²⁹ Among other titles, see Blake McKelvey. *The Emergence of Metropolitan America, 1915-1966.* New Brunswick: Rutgers University, 1968; Charles N. Glaab. "Metropolis and Suburb: The Changing American City," in *The 1920's.* Edited by Braeman, *et al.* pp. 399-437; and Roy Lubove. *Community Planning in the 1920's.* Pittsburgh: University of Pittsburgh Press, 1963. On urban sociologists, who began to formulate their field before and then during the Twenties, and are now themselves both sources and subject for study, see Maurice R. Stein. *The Eclipse of Community.* Princeton: Princeton University Press, 1960; and Park Dixon Goist. "City and 'Community': The Urban Theory of Robert Park." *American Quarterly* 23: 46-59; No. 1, Spring 1971.

³⁰ One study of the 1960's that tends to blur any clear distinction between these Klans is David M. Chalmers. *Hooded Americanism: The First Century of the Ku Klux Klan, 1865-1965.* New York: Doubleday, 1965.

³¹ Carl N. Degler. "A Century of the Klans: A Review Article." *The Journal of Southern History* 31: 435-443; No. 4, November 1965.

³² Robert Moats Miller. "The Ku Klux Klan," in *The 1920's.* Edited by Braeman, *et al.* p. 215.

³³ Lexington: University of Kentucky Press, 1965.

³⁴ Jackson. *The Ku Klux Klan in the City, 1915-1930.* New York: Oxford University Press, 1967.

³⁵ Occasionally the Klan's activities took an odd turn, as in Oregon where the Knights became ardent defenders of the public school system out of fear that private, and especially Catholic, schools were not instilling the young with sufficient faith in "Kristianity" and patriotism. See David B. Tyack. "The Perils of Pluralism: The Background of the Pierce Case." *American Historical Review* 74: 74-98; No. 1, October 1968; and M. Paul Holsinger. "The Oregon School Bill Controversy, 1922-1925." *Pacific Historical Review* 37: 327-341; No. 3, August 1968.

[36] See Ernest R. Sandeen. "Toward a Historical Interpretation of the Origins of Fundamentalism." *Church History* 36: 66-83; No. 1, March 1967; LeRoy Moore, Jr. "Another Look at Fundamentalism: A Response to Ernest R. Sandeen." *ibid.* 37: 195-202; No. 2, June 1968; Sandeen. *The Roots of Fundamentalism: British and American Millenarianism, 1800-1930.* Chicago: University of Chicago Press, 1970; Louis Gasper. *The Fundamentalist Movement.* The Hague: Mouton, 1963.

[37] Paul A. Carter, "The Fundamentalist Defense of the Faith," in *The 1920's,* edited by Braeman, *et al.,* pp. 179-214, discusses this (and criticizes the tactic) in an essay full of fresh thought and insights on the entire subject of Fundamentalism.

[38] Some of these traits do seem evident among the Fundamentalists, but an anthology edited by Willard B. Gatewood, Jr., *Controversy in the Twenties: Fundamentalism, Modernism, and Evolution,* Nashville: Vanderbilt University Press, 1969, shows that not all virtue and light issued from the other side in the great conflict of Fundamentalism vs. Modernism.

[39] Carter. "The Fundamentalist Defense of the Faith." p. 204.

[40] Lawrence W. Levine, *Defender of the Faith: William Jennings Bryan, The Last Decade, 1915-1925,* New York: Oxford University Press, 1965, gives full attention to Bryan's political activities and also has much to say on Bryan and Fundamentalism. See also Paolo E. Coletta. *William Jennings Bryan,* vol. III: *Political Puritan, 1915-1925.* Lincoln: University of Nebraska Press, 1970. Virginia Gray, "Anti-Evolution Sentiment and Behavior: The Case of Arkansas," *Journal of American History* 57: 352-366; No. 2, September 1970, is a close study of the correlation between Fundamentalism and anti-evolutionist thinking. On the evolution controversy generally, and on the Scopes trial, see introduction and bibliography in Gatewood, *Controversy in the Twenties.*

[41] Andrew Sinclair. *Prohibition: The Era of Excess.* Boston: Little, Brown, 1962. p. 5.

[42] Joseph R. Gusfeld. "Prohibition: The Impact of Political Utopianism," in *The 1920's.* Edited by Braeman, *et al.* pp. 257-308.

[43] *Ibid.;* see also Gusfeld's monograph, *Symbolic Crusade: Status Politics and the American Temperance Movement.* Urbana: University of Illinois Press, 1963; James Timberlake. *Prohibition and the Progressive Movement.* Cambridge: Harvard University Press, 1963; and Norman Clark. *The Dry Years: Prohibition and Social Change in Washington.* Seattle: University of Washington Press, 1965.

[44] Gusfeld. "Prohibition"; and Malcolm F. Willoughby. *Rum War at Sea.* U.S. Coast Guard. Washington: Government Printing Office, 1964. Whether or not prohibition caused the crime and corruption that Al Capone and Chicago have long symbolized is still a wide open question. One good close study is Mark H. Haller. "Urban Crime and Criminal Justice: The Chicago Case." *Journal of American History* 57: 619-635; No. 3, December 1970.

[45] Gusfeld. "Prohibition." p. 283.

[46] Discussion of morality invites comment on what Frederick Lewis Allen in *Only Yesterday* called the "revolution in manners and morals" that, by his account, occurred in the Twenties. This is an enormous and elusive subject, perhaps no more so than any other, but one that has produced little reliable documentation. A recent survey of the subject is Gilman M. Ostrander. "The Revolution in Morals," in *The 1920's.* Edited by Braeman, *et al.* pp. 323-50. Two interesting essays on more or less half the population are James R. McGovern, "The American Woman's Pre-World War I Freedom in Manners and Morals," *Journals of American History* 55: 315-333; No. 2, September 1968, which accepts the notion of a revolution but pushes it back to pre-war days; and Kenneth A. Yellis, "Prosperity's Child: Some Thoughts on the Flapper," *American Quarterly* 21: 44-64; No. 1, Spring 1969, which contrasts the flapper of the Twenties and the Gibson Girl of the 1890's.

[47] Don S. Kirschner. "Conflicts and Politics in the 1920's: Historiography and Prospects." *Mid-America* 48: 219-233; October 1966.

[48] Westport, Connecticut: Greenwood, 1970.

[49] Kirschner. *City and Country.* p. 256.

[50] Gilbert C. Fite. "The Farmers' Dilemma, 1919-1929," in *The 1920's.* Edited by Braeman, *et al.* pp. 67-102.

[51] The New Deal's AAA is another story, but the connection with McNary-Haugenism is seen in some detail in Van Perkins. *Crisis in Agriculture: The Agricultural Adjustment Administration and the New Deal, 1933.* Berkeley: University of California Press, 1969.

[52] Fite. "Farmers' Dilemma." p. 99.

[53] Irving Bernstein, *The Lean Years: A History of the American Worker, 1920-1933,* Boston: Houghton Mifflin, 1960, is by far the best general account of labor in the Twenties, though the subject is gaining increasing attention, and the bibliography is becoming rich and varied. In addition to titles subsequently discussed or cited in the text, see recent issues of *Labor History* for pertinent articles.

[54] Bernstein. *Lean Years.* p. 59.

[55] *Ibid.* p. 63.

[56] Mark Perlman, "Labor in Eclipse," in *The 1920's,* Braeman, *et al.* pp. 103-45, contains figures on union decline and an extended discussion of the subject.

[57] Bernstein. *Lean Years.* pp. 90, 126.

[58] As Allen M. Wakstein expresses it, "In the decade following World War I the relationship between employees and employers ran a gamut from complete employer domination to collective ownership by the workers," but it was "employer-inspired ideas" that continued to dominate; and it was the open shop (meaning anti-union shop) that gained the widest support of all. See Wakstein. "The Origins of the Open Shop Movement, 1919-20." *Journal of American History* 51: 460-475; No. 3, December 1964. p. 460. For studies of particular conflicts, see David Brody. *Labor in Crisis: The Steel Strike of 1919.* Philadelphia and New York: J. B. Lippincott, 1965; Charles J. Bayard. "The 1927-28 Colorado Coal Strike." *Pacific Historical Review* 32: 235-250; No. 3, August 1963; James A. Hodges. "Challenge to the New South: The Great Textile Strike in Elizabethton, Tennessee, 1929." *Tennessee Historical Quarterly* 23: 343-357; No. 4, December 1964; and Robert Zieger. "Pennsylvania Coal and Politics: The Anthracite Strike of 1925-1926." *Pennsylvania Magazine of History & Biography* 93: 244-262; No. 2, April 1969.

[59] Preston. *Aliens and Dissenters;* Melvyn Dubofsky. *We Shall Be All: A History of the Industrial Workers of the World.* Chicago: Quadrangle, 1969.

[60] Sally M. Miller. "Socialist Party Decline and World War I: Bibliography and Interpretation." *Science and Society* 34: 398-411; No. 4, Winter 1970.

[61] James Weinstein. *The Decline of Socialism in America, 1912-1925.* New York and London: Monthly Review, 1967. p. x.

[62] Weinstein. *Decline.* pp. 272, 326. See also Weinstein. "Radicalism in the Midst of Normalcy." *Journal of American History* 52: 773-790; No. 4, March 1966. D. H. Leon, "Whatever Happened to an American Socialist Party? A Critical Survey of the Spectrum of Interpretations," *American Quarterly* 23: 236-258; No. 2, May 1971, is an extensive review of the historiography on Socialism and Communism in America.

[63] The standard reference is still Theodore Draper. *The Roots of American Communism.* New York: Viking, 1957; and Draper. *American Communism and Soviet Russia.* New York: Viking, 1960. But see Joel Seidman, *Communism in the United States—A Bibliography,* Ithaca: Cornell University Press, 1970, for additional titles.

[64] Hoover has been reappraised, sometimes drastically, in the past decade. An influential voice from the left has been that of William Appleman Williams, who in his *Contours of American History,* Cleveland and New York: World, 1961,

pp. 426-30, wrote appreciatively of Hoover, a "class-conscious corporation leader" with the ability to draw up a sophisticated analysis of the corporation system to which he belonged and to recognize its potential dangers and work to overcome them. On Hoover as Secretary of Commerce, see Joseph Brandes. *Herbert Hoover and Economic Diplomacy: Department of Commerce Policy, 1921-1928.* Pittsburgh: University of Pittsburgh Press, 1962. Also useful, even though they concentrate on Hoover's presidency, are Barry D. Karl. "Presidential Planning and Social Science Research: Mr. Hoover's Experts." *Perspectives in American History.* III. Cambridge: Charles Warren Center for Studies in American History, Harvard University, 1969. pp. 347-409; and Carl N. Degler. "The Ordeal of Herbert Hoover." *Yale Review* 52: 564-583; No. 4, Summer 1963. See also Joseph S. Davis. "Herbert Hoover, 1874-1964: Another Appraisal." *South Atlantic Quarterly* 68: 295-318; No. 3, Summer 1969.

[65] Robert H. Zieger. *Republicans and Labor, 1919-1929.* Lexington: University of Kentucky Press, 1969.

[66] Morrell Heald. "Business Thought in the Twenties: Social Responsibility." *American Quarterly* 13: 126-139; No. 2, Pt. 1, Summer 1961; Heald. *The Social Responsibilities of Business: Company and Community, 1900-1960.* Cleveland: Press of Case Western Reserve University, 1970; David Brody. "The Rise and Decline of Welfare Capitalism," in *The 1920's.* Edited by Braeman, et al. pp. 147-78. On a related matter, the attempt of business to tell its version of things, see Alan R. Raucher. *Public Relations and Business, 1900-1929.* Baltimore: Johns Hopkins Press, 1968.

[67] Ellis W. Hawley. "Secretary Hoover and the Bituminous Coal Problem, 1921-1928." *Business History Review* 42: 247-270: No. 3, Autumn 1968. Trade associations were important agencies in the system that Hoover envisioned, and he encouraged their formation in the Twenties. Yet this kind of business institution, and this alliance of business and government, had begun earlier and would continue past the Twenties. Hoover merely gave the matter unusual attention during the decade. The Cotton Textile Institute, for example, took form in the nineteenth century and grew through the Twenties but became even more important in the New Deal Thirties. See Louis Galambos. *Competition and Cooperation: The Emergence of a National Trade Association.* Baltimore: Johns Hopkins Press, 1966. Preceding Hoover as a "pioneer" in the Commerce Department's promotion of trade associations and other cooperative practices by business was William Redfield, Wilson's Secretary of Commerce. See Robert F. Himmelberg. "Business, Antitrust Policy, and the Industrial Board of the Department of Commerce, 1919." *Business History Review* 42: 1-23; No. 1, Spring 1968.

[68] On one of the perennial issues of the crash—the role of the Federal Reserve Board in the late Twenties—see Elmus R. Wicker. *Federal Reserve Monetary Policy, 1917-1933.* New York: Random House, 1966; and Milton Friedman and Anna Jacobson Schwartz. *A Monetary History of the United States, 1867-1960.* Princeton: Princeton University Press, 1963. Each of these studies criticizes the Fed for being too lax to discourage the Bull Market but too tight to encourage a more orderly expansion. These two books are often hard going. Much easier reading is Robert Sobel. *The Great Bull Market: Wall Street in the 1920's.* New York: W. W. Norton, 1968. A major biography that demonstrates the corporate and speculative excesses of the Twenties, as well as much more about the economy, is Forrest McDonald. *Insull.* Chicago: University of Chicago Press, 1962.

[69] Elting E. Morison. *Turmoil and Tradition: A Study of the Life and Times of Henry L. Stimson.* Boston: Houghton Mifflin, 1960; Armin Rappaport. *Henry L. Stimson and Japan, 1931-1933.* Chicago: University of Chicago Press, 1963.

[70] New York: Alfred A. Knopf, 1967.

[71] On Wilson, see also N. Gordon Levin, Jr. *Woodrow Wilson and World Politics: America's Response to War and Revolution.* New York: Oxford University Press, 1968. On Allied policy toward Bolshevism, see John M. Thompson. *Russia, Bolshevism and the Versailles Peace.* Princeton: Princeton University Press, 1966.

[72] Williams' titles on the Twenties are "The Legend of Isolationism in the 1920's." *Science and Society* 18: 1-20; No. 4, Winter 1954; "Latin America: Laboratory of American Foreign Policy in the Nineteen-Twenties." *Inter-American Economic Affairs* 11: 3-30; No. 2, Autumn 1957; and "China and Japan: A Challenge and a Choice of the Nineteen-Twenties." *Pacific Historical Review* 26: 259-279; No. 3, August 1957. See also the relevant material in his *The Tragedy of American Diplomacy*. Cleveland & New York: World 1959; and *The Shaping of American Diplomacy*. Chicago: Rand McNally, 1956. For a rejoinder to Williams see Robert J. Maddox. "Another Look at the Legend of Isolationism in the 1920's." *Mid-America* 53: 35-43. No. 1, January 1971.

[73] The most exhaustive work on American intervention is George F. Kennan. *Soviet-American Relations, 1917-20*. 2 vols.: *Russia Leaves the War*. Princeton: Princeton University Press, 1956; and *The Decision to Intervene*. Princeton: Princeton University Press, 1958. Of equal importance is his *Russia and the West Under Lenin and Stalin*. Boston: Little, Brown, 1960. Though he criticizes U.S. diplomacy in the 1917-1919 period, Kennan does not see any large policy, consciously directed toward a particular goal, emerging after the war; rather, as he portrays it, American diplomacy was a day-to-day matter often turning on the contingent and the unforeseen. In contrast, see William Appleman Williams. "American Intervention in Russia, 1917-1920." *Studies on the Left*. 3: 24-48; No. 4, Fall 1963; and 4: 39-57; No. 1, Winter 1964. Cf. Christopher Lasch. "American Intervention in Siberia: A Reinterpretation." *Political Science Quarterly* 77: 205-223; No. 2, June 1962.

[74] A survey that spells out this picture is Robert Freeman Smith. "American Foreign Relations, 1920-1942," in *Towards a New Past*. Edited by Barton J. Bernstein. New York: Random House, 1967. pp. 232-262.

[75] Ralph Stone. *The Irreconcilables: The Fight Against the League of Nations*. Lexington: University of Kentucky Press, 1970; Warren F. Kuehl. *Seeking World Order: The United States and International Organization to 1920*. Nashville: Vanderbilt University Press, 1969. For some intriguing comments on how Wilson's illness influenced his behavior in 1919, see Edwin A. Weinstein. "Woodrow Wilson's Neurological Illness." *Journal of American History* 57: 324-351; No. 2, September 1970.

[76] Daniel M. Smith. *Aftermath of War: Bainbridge Colby and Wilsonian Diplomacy, 1920-1921*. Philadelphia: American Philosophical Society, 1970; Clifford W. Trow. "Woodrow Wilson and the Mexican Interventionist Movement of 1919." *Journal of American History* 58: 46-72; No. 1, June 1971; Robert F. Smith. *The United States and Cuba: Business and Diplomacy, 1917-1960*. New Haven: College and University Press, 1962; Neill Macaulay. *The Sandino Affair*. Chicago: Quadrangle, 1967.

[77] See especially Akira Iriye. *After Imperialism: The Search for a New Order in the Far East, 1921-1931*. Cambridge: Harvard University Press, 1965. Surveying all the major powers concerned with the Far East in the Twenties, and showing their impact upon one another as well as the influence upon them of internal developments, Iriye demonstrates Ernest May's contention that the older diplomatic history is giving way to a new kind of "international history." See May. "The Decline of Diplomatic History," in George Athan Billias and Gerald N. Grob, editors. *American History: Retrospect and Prospect*. New York: Free Press, 1971. pp. 399-430.

[78] Peter G. Filene. *Americans and the Soviet Experiment, 1917-1933*. Cambridge: Harvard University Press, 1967; Denna F. Fleming. *The Cold War and Its Origins, 1917-1960*. Garden City: Doubleday, 1961. On the recent appearance of Cold War revisionists, some of whom find the origins of this conflict in the World War I period and U.S. policy of the Twenties, see Charles S. Maier, "Revisionism and the Interpretation of Cold War Origins," in *Perspectives in Amer-*

ican History, IV. Cambridge: Charles Warren Center for Studies in American History, Harvard University, 1970. pp. 313-47.

[79] Carl P. Parrini. *Heir to Empire: United States Economic Diplomacy, 1916-1923*. Pittsburgh: University of Pittsburgh Press, 1969; Joan Hoff Wilson. *American Business and Foreign Policy, 1920-1933*. Lexington: University of Kentucky Press, 1968; Richard H. Meyer. *Bankers' Diplomacy: Monetary Stabilization in the Twenties*. New York: Columbia University Press, 1970. Benjamin D. Rhones. "Reassessing 'Uncle Shylock': The United States and the French War Debt, 1917-1929." *Journal of American History* 55: 787-803; No. 4, March 1969.

[80] John K. Nelson. *The Peace Prophets: American Pacifist Thought, 1919-1941*. Chapel Hill: University of North Carolina Press, 1967; Robert James Maddox. "William E. Borah and the Crusade to Outlaw War." *Historian* 29: 200-220; No. 2, February 1967.

[81] Robert Divine. *American Immigration Policy, 1924-1952*. New Haven: Yale University Press, 1957.

[82] Cf. the positions of three crucial figures in Betty Glad. *Charles Evans Hughes and the Illusions of Innocence: A Study in American Diplomacy*. Urbana: University of Illinois Press, 1967; L. Ethan Ellis. *Frank B. Kellogg and American Foreign Relations: 1925-1929*. New Brunswick: Rutgers University Press, 1961; and Robert James Maddox. *William E. Borah and American Foreign Policy*. Baton Rouge: Louisiana State University Press, 1969.

[83] L. Ethan Ellis, *Republican Foreign Policy, 1921-1933*, New Brunswick: Rutgers University Press, 1968, is a recent attempt by a veteran scholar to survey the subject.

[84] For various interpretations of the origin and meaning of this expression, see John Malcolm Brinnin. *The Third Rose: Gertrude Stein and Her World*. Boston & Toronto: Little, Brown, 1959; Arthur Mizener. "The 'Lost Generation,'" in Robert E. Spiller, editor. *A Time of Harvest*. New York: Hill and Wang, 1962; Matthew Josephson. *Life Among the Surrealists*. New York: Holt, Rinehart, Winston, 1962. pp. 6ff.

[85] Warren Susman. "Pilgrimage to Paris: The Backgrounds of American Expatriates, 1920-1934." Ann Arbor: University Microfilms, 1958. 58-833; and Cushing Strout. *The American Image of the Old World*. New York: Harper & Row, 1963. p. 185.

[86] James Steel Smith. "The Day of the Popularizers: The 1920's." *South Atlantic Quarterly* 62: 297-309; No. 2, Spring 1963; Frank Luther Mott. *A History of American Magazines*. vol. V: *Sketches of 21 Magazines, 1905-1930*. Cambridge: Harvard University Press, 1968.

[87] Stanley Coben. "The Scientific Establishment and the Transmission of Quantum Mechanics to the United States, 1919-32." *American Historical Review* 76: 442-466; No. 2, April 1971; Robert E. L. Faris. *Chicago Sociology, 1920-1932*. San Francisco: Chandler Publication Co., 1967; John Higham, *et al. History*. Englewood Cliffs: Prentice-Hall, 1965. pp. 183ff.

[88] William Lee Miller. "The Rise of Neo-Orthodoxy." *Paths of American Thought*. Edited by Arthur M. Schlesinger, Jr. and Morton White. Boston: Houghton Mifflin, 1963. pp. 326ff.

[89] Roderick Nash. *The Nervous Generation: American Thought, 1917-1930*. Chicago; Rand McNally, 1970.

[90] But cf. Lewis P. Simpson. "The Southern Writer and the Great Literary Secession." *Georgia Review* 24: 393-412; No. 4, Winter 1970. On Southern literary and scholarly life in the decade, see Tindall. *Emergence of the New South*. pp. 285-317 and 575ff.; and Dewey W. Grantham, Jr. "The Regional Imagination: Social Scientists and the American South." *Journal of Southern History* 34: 3-32; No. 1, February 1968. On a critical view of things Southern, see George B. Tindall. "The Benighted South: Origins of a Modern Image." *Virginia Quarterly Review* 50: 281-294; Spring 1964.

[91] Biographies of literary figures were abundant in the 1960's, among them Andrew Turnbull. *Scott Fitzgerald.* New York: Scribner's, 1962; Nancy Milford. *Zelda.* New York: Harper & Row, 1970; Carlos Baker. *Ernest Hemingway: A Life Story.* New York: Scribner's, 1969; Mark Schorer. *Sinclair Lewis.* New York: McGraw Hill, 1961; and Carl Bode. *Mencken.* Carbondale: Southern Illinois University Press, 1969.

[92] G. Louis Joughin and Edmund M. Morgan, *The Legacy of Sacco & Vanzetti,* New York: Harcourt, Brace, 1948, remains the indispensable book on the subject. A more recent study, Herbert B. Ehrmann, *The Case That Will Not Die,* Boston: Little, Brown, 1969, demonstrates the validity of its title. David Felix, *Protest: Sacco-Vanzetti and the Intellectuals,* Bloomington: Indiana University Press, 1965, attempts to build a case against the two men and to criticize intellectuals for upholding them. An intriguing essay is James Grossman, "The Sacco-Vanzetti Case Reconsidered," *Commentary* 33: 31-44; No. 1, January 1962.

[93] Nash. *Nervous Generation.* pp. 126-63; John W. Ward. "The Meaning of Lindbergh's Flight." *American Quarterly* 10: 3-16; No. 1, Spring 1958; Walter Ross. *The Last Hero: Charles A. Lindbergh.* New York: Harper & Row, 1968; Harold Seymour. *Baseball.* vol. 2. *The Golden Age.* New York: Oxford University Press, 1971.

[94] Erick Barnouw. *A Tower in Babel.* vol. I. *A History of Broadcasting in the United States to 1933.* New York: Oxford University Press, 1966; Gunther Schuller. *Early Jazz: Its Roots and Musical Development.* New York: Oxford University Press, 1968; Peter A. Soderbergh. *"Aux Armes!*: The Rise of the Hollywood War Film, 1916-1930." *South Atlantic Quarterly* 55: 509-522; No. 4, Autumn 1966.

[95] A brilliant but difficult book with much on the Twenties is Harold Cruse. *The Crisis of the Negro Intellectual.* New York: William Morrow, 1967. On Harlem and on the "Harlem Renaissance" of the Twenties, see Gilbert Osofsky. *Harlem: The Making of a Ghetto.* New York: Harper & Row, 1966; and S. P. Fullinwider. "Jean Toomer: Lost Generation or Negro Renaissance?" *Phylon* 27: 396-403; No. 4, Winter 1966. On the race riots of 1919, see Arthur I. Waskow. *From Race Riot to Sit-In.* Garden City: Doubleday, 1966; and William M. Tuttle, Jr. *Race Riot: Chicago in the Red Summer of 1919.* New York: Atheneum, 1970. Recent studies of Marcus Garvey that reflect the tensions of the Sixties are Theodore G. Vincent. *Black Power and the Garvey Movement.* Berkeley: Ramparts, 1971; and Amy Jacques Garvey. *Garvey and Garveyism.* New York: Macmillan, 1970. See also David M. Tucker. "Black Pride and Negro Business in the 1920's; George Washington Lee of Memphis." *Business History Review* 43: 435-451; No. 4, Winter 1969; and Pete Daniel. "Black Power in the 1920's: The Case of Tuskegee Veterans Hospital." *Journal of Southern History* 36: 368-388; No. 3, August 1970.

[96] *Towards a New Past,* edited by Barton J. Bernstein, a book commonly associated with this elusive category, contains only one essay on the Twenties, Robert Smith's "American Foreign Relations, 1920-1942." For a new anthology, *Beyond Liberalism: The New Left Views American History,* Waltham, Mass.: Xerox College Publishing Co., 1971, editor Irwin Unger found nothing to include on the Twenties.

[97] William E. Leuchtenburg, *The Perils of Prosperity, 1914-32,* Chicago: University of Chicago Press, 1958, is a fast-paced narrative incorporating much post-1929 research, though still sounding like *Only Yesterday.* David A. Shannon, *Between the Wars: America, 1919-1941,* Boston: Houghton Mifflin, 1965, contains 100 pages of lucid and professional commentary on the decade. Paul Carter, *The Twenties in America,* New York: Thomas Y. Crowell, 1968, is an odd and disjointed essay but one full of ideas, ironic observations, and outspoken judgments.

· 22 ·

The Age of the Great Depression, 1929–1940

Otis L. Graham, Jr.

IT HAS been just over a decade since Frank Freidel surveyed the literature on the era of the Great Depression, and there has been a great outpouring of scholarly writing in the interim. "The harvest is at hand," wrote Paul Conkin in 1967, as scholars filled in many gaps in the history of the 1930's and profoundly altered the interpretation of the era. In this essay I shall reserve the interpretive questions until last, and turn first to a chronological and topical survey of the literature.[1]

As Freidel's essay revealed, the taste of historians of the 1930's runs to studies of politics, public policy, and ideas. In recent years there has been an increasing interest in "social" history, in studies of ethnic and religious minorities, social and economic institutions, science, recreation, and the like. But for the most part historians still regard the 1930's as the era of FDR and the New Deal. This bibliographical essay will reflect the continuing domination of issues of public policy, political personalities, political and social thought, while not ignoring the slow rise of interest in the private sector, in the thought and behavior of more representative Americans outside of Washington, D.C.

Probably the causes of the depression of 1929-1940 will never be enumerated to the satisfaction of all scholars, but in the last decade the intellectual dominance of the Keynesian, or "structuralists," school has loosened somewhat. Most historians probably continue to believe that the depression resulted from serious structural flaws in the American economy—a maldistribution of income, monopolistic pricing, inadequate regulation of banking, an overexpanded agriculture. Little original work has appeared in the 1960's to reinforce that view, but the rival or "monetary" theory received support in the writing of Milton Friedman, Clark Warburton, Phillip Cagan, and Elmus Wicker.[2] If the monetarists are right, the depression was really a mild business recession, magnified into catastrophe by errors in monetary management by the officials of the Federal Reserve. To achieve recovery, the nation required not structural reforms but wiser monetary policy (Friedman believed that no monetary management at all would have been preferable to the clumsy policies pursued by the Fed).[3] This view was enlarged into a critique of New Deal economic policy in Murray Rothbard, *America's Great Depression*.[4] On the other hand, Douglass North, in his influential *Growth and Welfare in the American Past*,[5] adhered to a basically structuralist view. With the strong emergence of the monetary school, historians are no nearer a consensus on the sources of the depression than in the 1930's.

As for the effects of the depression, no one has seriously challenged the accounts we have of the impact of joblessness and economic slump upon individual lives and social institutions. There has been little new work on the depression's effect upon the family, national health, education, recreation, suicide rates and other vital statistics. Several popular accounts of the social history of the nation during the Great Depression have appeared: Caroline Bird's *The Invisible Scar*,[6] Robert Bendiner's *Just Around the Corner*,[7] Don Congdon's anthology *The Thirties*,[8] and Cabell Phillips' *From the Crash to the Blitz, 1929-1939*.[9] These histories are readable and lively, but are based largely upon newspapers, periodicals, and secondary work published prior to 1960. A fascinating piece of social history built around oral history interviews is Studs Terkel, *Hard Times*.[10]

Surprisingly, the public policies of the years 1929-1933 have not received extensive treatment since 1959. Several studies of President Hoover and his administration are reported underway now that his papers are open to scholars. Albert Romasco's *The Poverty of Abundance: Hoover, the Nation, and the Depression*,[11] although written without access to the Hoover manuscripts, is a sounder and somewhat more critical book than Harris G. Warren's *Herbert Hoover and the Great Depression*.[12] Herbert Stein, in *The Fiscal Revolution in America*,[13] managed to make Hoover's economic policies not only consistent but reasonable. David Burner's *The Politics of Provincialism: The Democratic Party in Transition, 1918-1932*[14] is broader than its title might suggest, and provides a good review of the politics of the depression years to the election of 1932. The campaign of 1932, at least the Democratic side of it, has been re-examined in Rexford G. Tugwell's *The Brains Trust*.[15] For the "interregnum" we await the next volume of Frank Freidel's ongoing biography of Roosevelt.

The literature on the New Deal has increased almost geometrically. In surveying the list of memoirs published since 1959, one marvels at the longevity of the New Dealers, and wonders how anyone ever wrote the history of the New Deal without these accounts: Dean Acheson, *Morning and Noon;*[16] Thurman Arnold, *Fair Fights and Foul;*[17] Francis Biddle, *In Brief Authority;*[18] John M. Blum's memoir-histories based on the Morgenthau diaries, *From the Morgenthau Diaries: Years of Crisis, 1928-1938*[19] and *From the Morgenthau Diaries: Years of Urgency, 1938-1941;*[20] David E. Lilienthal, *The Journals of David E. Lilienthal: The TVA Years, 1939-1945,* Vol. I;[21] and Raymond Moley, *The First New Deal.*[22] Other contemporaries outside policymaking circles have now published their recollections. Two prominent literary figures who expressed strong political views are Alfred Kazin, *Starting Out in the Thirties,*[23] and Matthew Josephson, *Infidel in the Temple.*[24] In Rita Simon, editor, *As We Saw the Thirties,*[25] there are essays by Gerald L. K. Smith, Granville Hicks, Norman Thomas, Burton K. Wheeler, and others.

The harvest of biographies has been abundant, as well. Franklin Roosevelt received no full-length study after 1959 (James M. Burns' *Roosevelt: Soldier of Freedom*[26] covered the war years), but Alfred Rollins' *Roosevelt and Howe*[27] sheds considerable light on Roosevelt in the 1920's and early 1930's. The President's health problems are clarified in Dr. Howard Bruenn's article published in a medical journal in 1970.[28] Paul Conkin's *The New Deal*[29] opens with a trenchant criticism of F.D.R. Two leading scholars, John M. Blum and Clarke Chambers, wrote essays reaffirming Roosevelt's greatness,[30] but historians in general seem to have come to a slightly more critical appraisal of F.D.R., judging from the poll reported in an article by Gary Maranell.[31] During the past decade we have probably learned more about Eleanor than about Franklin. In 1968, Tamara Hareven published *Eleanor Roosevelt,*[32] followed in the same year by James Kearney's *Anna Eleanor Roosevelt.*[33] Then, in 1971, Joseph Lash, an organizer of the American Student Union in the 1930's and lifetime friend of Mrs. Roosevelt, published *Eleanor and Franklin,*[34] a moving account of Eleanor's growth into one of the most active and compassionate figures of our era.

In addition to portraits of the Roosevelts, there are good biographical studies of Will Alexander,[35] Josephus Daniels,[36] Joseph P. Kennedy,[37] William Lemke,[38] Maury Maverick,[39] Vito Marcantonio,[40] Frank Murphy,[41] John A. Ryan,[42] Donald Richberg,[43] Key Pittman,[44] Rexford G. Tugwell,[45] Henry Wallace,[46] Edwin E. Witte,[47] and two biographies of Norman Thomas.[48] Perhaps the two most important biographies of the 1960's, given the importance of their subjects and the skill of their biographers, were J. Joseph Huthmacher's *Senator Robert F. Wagner and the Rise of Urban Liberalism,*[49] and T. Harry Williams' *Huey Long.*[50]

The shelf of published monographs was also much augmented by the work of the 1960's. New Deal relief programs were reasonably well covered in earlier books, but William McDonald added a study of the arts projects as a whole,[51] and Jane D. Mathews wrote a fine account of the federal theatre project.[52] John Salmond's *The Civilian Conservation Corps, 1933-1942*[53] is a model monograph. There is still no complete study of NRA, but Louis Galambos surveyed the experience of the cotton textile industry in his *Competition and Cooperation;*[54] and Sidney Fine provided a lucid account of the auto industry in *The Automobile Under the Blue Eagle.*[55] A brilliant general view of New Deal approaches to economic planning, in which NRA was an important part, is Ellis Hawley's *The New Deal and the Problem of Monopoly.*[56] Another early New Deal initiative, the TVA, was the subject of studies by Wilmon Droze,[57] Victor Hobday,[58] and Thomas McGraw.[59]

The labor movement drew scholarly attention from the very beginning, but solid contributions continue to be made. The most important recent study is Irving Bernstein, *Turbulent Years: A History of the American Worker, 1933-1941,*[60] the second volume in a very fine but somewhat mistitled history of the labor movement between the wars. David Brody's essay, "The Emergence of Mass-Production Unionism," published in 1964, is perhaps the best short summary of labor developments during the depression.[61] Brody stressed the importance of war mobilization in solidifying the tenuous gains of the 1930's. Two absorbing monographs are Sidney Fine, *Sit-Down,*[62] and Daniel J. Leab, *A Union of Individuals: The Formation of the American Newspaper Guild, 1933-1936.*[63]

The continuing urbanization of the country has not perceptibly deflected scholarly interest away from agricultural problems of the 1930's. The past decade has produced first-rate studies of the impact of the New Deal (and the depression) upon tenant farmers, most notably David E. Conrad's *The Forgotten Farmers*[64] and Donald Grubbs' *Cry from the Cotton: The Southern Tenant Farmers' Union and the New Deal.*[65] While Grubbs was concerned with organizing efforts by lower-class farmers, John L. Shover, in *Cornbelt Rebellion: The Farmers' Holiday Association,*[66] examined similar efforts among relatively well-to-do farmers in the midwest. A spontaneous non-violent protest toward the end of the 1930's is the subject of Louis Cantor, *A Prologue to the Protest Movement.*[67] Sidney Baldwin's *Poverty and Politics*[68] is a masterful and long-needed study of the Farm Security Administration. The political influence of the Farm Bureau Federation is traced in Christiana M. Campbell's *The Farm Bureau and the New Deal.*[69] The role of intellectuals in the formulation of farm policy is clarified in Richard Kirkendall's *Social Scientists and Farm Politics in the Age of Roosevelt.*[70]

The origins of the Social Security Act are analyzed in Roy Lubove's *The Struggle for Social Security, 1900-1935,*[71] and Daniel Nelson's *Unemployment Insurance: The American Experience, 1915-1935.*[72] The administration of the act in its early years is a more interesting story than might be thought, and is told in Arthur J. Altmeyer's memoir, *The Formative Years of Social Security,*[73] and Edwin E. Witte, *The Development of the Social Security Act.*[74] The fiscal effects of the act, in particular the regressive impact of social security taxes, were outlined by Joseph Pechman *et al.* in *Social Security: Perspectives for Reform.*[75]

The past decade has also added greatly to our knowledge of the political life of the 1930's. In 1960, Arthur M. Schlesinger, Jr., published *The Politics of Upheaval,*[76] a synthesis which, like the earlier two volumes in his "The Age of Roosevelt," was Roosevelt-centered, sympathetic to the liberals, approving of the New Deal, and brilliantly written. The book contains a lively if partisan discussion of Democratic party politics through the election of 1936. Otis Graham, in an article in 1963,[77] saw in Schlesinger's book an important new utilization of the idea that there was a shift to a "second New Deal" in 1935, but William Wilson found that contemporaries did not clearly discern such a shift,[78] and William Leuchtenburg persuasively argued that the pattern was barely discernible.[79]

The New Deal's opponents have also received considerable attention. George Mayer's *The Republican Party, 1854-1964*[80] necessarily covers the 1930's in somewhat less detail than one might wish, and may be supplemented with Donald McCoy's *Landon,*[81] a very sound and sympathetic portrait of a man who was more progressive than has been thought. The uncompromising anti-New Dealers are examined in George Wolfskill, *The Revolt of the Conservatives: A History of the American Liberty League,*[82] and in Wolfskill and George Hudson's fascinating collection of the words of frightened conservatives, *All But the People.*[83] While these opponents gave FDR little difficulty, a more pragmatic and resourceful opposition grew up after the 1936 election, based in the Congress, and was able by 1938 to bring the New Deal to a halt. James T. Patterson's *Congressional Conservatism and the New Deal*[84] is an indispensable study of this development and may be supplemented by Richard Polenberg, *Reorganizing Roosevelt's Government: The Controversy Over Executive Reorganization, 1936-1939.*[85] The effect of the

New Deal on the American party system is examined in Angus Campbell *et al., Elections and the Political Order,*[86] where an important morphology of American elections is offered. Walter D. Burnham, in *Critical Elections and the Mainsprings of American Politics,*[87] found that the New Deal only briefly halted the long-term decline in voter participation in American politics.

Scholars have also been busy illuminating the turbulent "radical" sectors of American political life in the 1930's. T. Harry Williams' *Huey Long* was somewhat more sympathetic to Long than most earlier accounts, and underlined his potential as a leader of the forces of lower-middle class dissent. Abraham Holtzman's *The Townsend Movement*[88] is a fair but uninspired treatment of an important pressure group. Father Coughlin's complicated career was surveyed by Charles J. Tull, in *Father Coughlin and the New Deal.*[89] On the relation between liberals and communists in the 1930's, Eugene Lyons' inaccurate *The Red Decade* has been supplanted by Frank Warren's *Liberals and Communism,*[90] and Earl Latham's *The Communist Controversy in Washington: From the New Deal to McCarthy.*[91]

No satisfactory intellectual history of the 1930's has ever been written, although many of the studies listed above have added to our knowledge of ideas as well as action. Arthur A. Ekirch's *Ideologies and Utopias: The Impact of the New Deal on American Thought*[92] is a competent survey, but adds little new information or interpretation. Charles Alexander's *Nationalism in American Thought, 1930-1945*[93] is selective in coverage but very perceptive. Warren Susman's "The Thirties," an essay published in 1970,[94] is a brilliant study of cultural and intellectual themes. R. Alan Lawson's *The Failure of Independent Liberalism: 1930-1941*[95] is a perceptive analysis of the political and social views of an important diverse group of intellectuals who did not think the New Deal went far enough. Otis Graham's *The Old Progressives and the New Deal*[96] finds most surviving progressives quite uneasy with the New Deal, and supports the view that the two reform movements were rather different. The contribution of a talented handful of European immigrants who came to America during the 1930's is assessed in Laura Fermi's *Illustrious Immigrants: The Intellectual Migration from Europe, 1930-1941.*[97]

The 1960's were a time when historians became more sensitive to the history of non-white groups in the American population. Scholars of the 1930's filled in several gaps in the history of the Negro and the Indian, especially. An article by Leslie Fishel in 1964 describes how the New Deal, through relief appropriations, the sympathetic activities of Eleanor Roosevelt and Harold Ickes, and through Roosevelt's own warmth and concern for forgotten people, produced a major shift in black political alignments.[98] Yet the New Deal frequently failed to fight very hard for Negro rights, as we learn from articles by Robert Zangrando[99] and John Salmond,[100] and in Raymond Wolters' *Negroes and the Great Depression*,[101] a study of blacks under the NRA and AAA programs and the response of the NAACP. Roosevelt's unwillingness to give strong support to an anti-lynching law and poll tax repeal is explained, but not excused, in Frank Freidel's *F.D.R. and the South*.[102] Bernard Sternsher's *The Negro in Depression and War*[103] is a useful collection of essays with a good bibliography. What is needed, in addition to more studies of the relation between American blacks and their government, is extensive investigation of black social and intellectual history. One could wish, for example, for more studies of black contact with white-dominated legal systems, such as Dan Carter's brilliant monograph, *Scottsboro*.[104] The same may be said of the history of American Indians in the 1930's. Recent work has concentrated upon Indian policy, a useful but by no means the only approach to this minority. Three new surveys of Indian history appeared in the 1960's, each with a discussion of the New Deal's efforts at reform of policy: Angie Debo's *A History of the Indians of the United States*;[105] *Indians and Other Americans*[106] by Harold Fey and D'Arcy McNickle; and William Hagan's *American Indians*.[107] A very useful monograph is Lawrence Kelly's *The Navajo Indians and Federal Indian Policy, 1900-1935*.[108] Yet while the literature on blacks and Indians is inadequate, it is at least growing rapidly. There are even greater gaps, and less progress, in the history of other minorities. Abraham Hoffman's dissertation, "The Repatriation of Mexican Nationals from the United States During the Great Depression,"[109] not yet published in 1971, conveys much vital information about the demography of the Mexican emigrants in the United States and the forced repatriations of the early 1930's. Carey McWilliams' pioneering *North from Mexico*,[110] originally published in 1949, has been reissued.

In addition to these clusters of historical literature, there have appeared a number of important monographs which have illuminated various aspects of the 1930's. In *Labor and Liberty*,[111] Jerold Auerbach relates the history of the La Follette Civil Liberties Committee, and in the process told us much about the methods used by industrial and agricultural employers to fight unionization. The New Deal's failure to enact medical insurance is described in Daniel Hirshfield, *The Lost Reform*.[112] The Court "Packing" episode is better understood as a result of two essays by William E. Leuchtenburg.[113] At the same time that Congress stalled the Court plan it was also balking on Roosevelt's request to reorganize the executive branch. The fanatical opposition to the President's modest proposal sheds considerable light on the New Deal's loss of momentum in 1938; the story is explored in Barry D. Karl's *Executive Reorganization and Reform in the New Deal*,[114] and Richard Polenberg's *Reorganizing Roosevelt's Government*.[115] The New Deal's experimental temper and planning impulse led to various efforts at community planning, brilliantly recaptured in Paul Conkin's *Tomorrow a New World: The New Deal Community Program*.[116] Perhaps the New Deal's most discreditable experiment, undertaken almost entirely because of a powerful economic lobby and pursued without regard for its domestic and international costs, was the silver purchase program. The complex details are analyzed in John A. Brennan, *Silver and the First New Deal*.[117]

The above may be considered a selective and partial shopping list of the leading studies of the 1930's which have been published since 1959. What are the seminal works, and crucial areas, in which fundamental interpretations and perspectives are being altered? Certainly the most striking development has been the rise of a critical school with strong reformist sympathies, a "New Left" perspective upon the New Deal. Through the 1950's it was generally assumed that the New Deal had been an important break with the American past. To speak only of its leading achievements, it had made important structural reforms in the economy, among them a redistribution of income toward more egalitarianism, a shift of power from private to public hands, and the facilitation of the rise of organized labor as a force to discipline business; had democratized the political system; and had underwritten economic security through unemployment insurance, old age pensions, and federal relief. Today this perspective is sharply disputed. In the view of scholars such as Barton J. Bernstein, Paul Conkin, and Howard Zinn, the New Deal not only was no social revolution, but was quite conservative. In their view, the New Deal had no success at bringing recovery, did not provide adequate relief of poverty, did not redistribute income or wealth, did not curb the power of large corporations, did not fight racial injustice, indeed did not make any significant changes in American society. The liberal mission was to save capitalism, and, according to the new critics, at this it succeeded in a time of widespread social turbulence.[118]

What is the basis for such an interpretive shift? This sort of perspective is of course quite old, having been expressed in the 1930's, but it had no significant scholarly acceptance. The reasons for its recent influence seem to be a combination of new evidence, in the form of monographs published chiefly in the 1960's, and the impact of contemporary events upon the perspectives of younger historians. Let us turn first to the new evidence. Several recent studies have contended that there was no significant redistribution of income as a result of Roosevelt's reforms.[119] And strong labor unions, upon which the New Deal pinned much of its hope for a different balance of power in the American economy, apparently do not exert an important redistributive influence.[120] Another area of considerable scholarly activity since 1959 has been the study of economic regulation by the state, and here again the institutional reforms of the New Deal appear to have had a generally conservative resultant. In books such as those of Robert Engler and Gerald B. Nash on the oil industry,[121] Donald Whitnah and William A. Jordan on aviation,[122] Harmon Zeigler on small business,[123] Vincent P. Carosso on investment banking,[124] Michael Parrish on securities markets,[125] and above all in Ellis Hawley's brilliant *The New Deal and the Problem of Monopoly*,[126] one learns how much of the regulatory activity entered into by the government in the 1930's was done at the urgent request of the affected industry which often preferred the haven of regulated status to the rigors of competition in a slack market. Amid a general disillusionment with the experience of business regulation in the twentieth century—as one finds expressed in Louis Kohlmeier's *The Regulators*[127] or the growing shelf of reports by Ralph Nader's young associates—the New Deal's vigorous expansion of the regulatory functions of government appears at best a forlorn experiment and at worst the premeditated capture of governmental power by capitalistic interests to shore up crumbling monopoly structures. The story of regulation is vastly complex, but the expansion of federal control during the 1930's, affecting public utility holding companies, banking, securities markets, coal and oil, aviation, truck transportation, natural gas, and sectors of retail trade, seems often to have been reform by, of and for the regulated industries themselves. The actual policy outcomes of public regulation are only now becoming clear, and New Deal policy outcomes are permanently obscured by the war and subsequent developments. But in the history of business regulation in the 1930's there is much raw material for revisionist interpretations of the overall significance of Roosevelt's epoch. Today, as we consider the New Deal, we must take into account, along with the familiar landmarks such as NRA, AAA, relief, TVA, and the like, a number of measures which for various reasons had been pushed to the background: securities and banking regulation, the lending activities of the RFC, the Connally "Hot Oil" Act, the Communications Act of 1934, the Motor Carrier Act of 1935, Federal Power Act of 1935, the Guffey Coal Act, the Robinson-Patman and Miller-Tydings

Acts, the Natural Gas Act of 1938, the Civil Aeronautics Act of 1938, the Transportation Act of 1940. These, too, were aspects of public policy under a liberal government.

Yet it seems clear that a revised view of the New Deal, one which stresses the limits of its reforms, has not been simply the product of a few new studies of income distribution, the economics of the labor movement, or the politics of business regulation in the 1930's. B. J. Bernstein's extensive bibliography, one notices, cites many studies published in the 1930's, 1940's, and 1950's. It has long been understood that the social security system excluded too many workers and was regressively financed; that New Deal relief efforts never reached as many as half those in need; that the AAA displaced tenants and the FSA never had the money to aid more than a fraction of those in desperate rural poverty; that the New Deal never brought full recovery. These shortcomings had been pointed out before, but most historians until the 1960's had been more impressed with the New Deal's achievements: a significant measure of recovery and relief, the shouldering of responsibility for economic management, the expansion of public authority into chaotic areas from agriculture to industry to resource management; the realignment of American politics; the illumination of national problems; the quickening of faith in the nation's future. Surely a vital ingredient in leading some historians in the 1960's to be more impressed with New Deal failures than successes, when evidences of both had long been a part of our operative knowledge, was the nature of the 1960's themselves. In a decade jammed with social problems, when Americans were shocked to discover the persistence of desperate poverty, racism, and the tenacious economic and political power of capitalist elites, it might have been expected that at least some historians would be deeply skeptical of the claims of progress which had been made for the American past. The New Deal was the subject of an unusually vigorous critical revisionism, since liberal historians had for so long held it up as a model of successful social action.

Some have argued that the new interpretations are not permanently valid insights but the distortions produced when scholars allow contemporary events and personal ideologies to dictate their questions and their answers. There is some validity in this criticism of the new radical historians. But, as I have argued elsewhere,[128] whatever the influences operating upon the new revisionists, their impact upon those who reject their conclusions has been in important respects salutary. For too long historians tended toward an uncritical acceptance of the ends, means, and accomplishments of liberal political leaders. Our scrutiny of the historical record did not often enough penetrate relentlessly beneath political rhetoric and the facade of legislation to the actual policy outcomes measured in terms of power and money and tested empirically in the daily lives of the millions outside Washington, D.C.

Judging from the scholarly works here reviewed, this observation is yearly becoming less valid. The drift of scholarly opinion seems to be toward a consensus that the New Deal was no "social revolution," and that terms, suggesting deep and rapid social change, are not appropriate in describing the 1930's. Beyond this, of course, there is still room for vigorous controversy over the extent of social change which took place during the Great Depression, both because of public policy and despite it. The language of historians is imprecise, and surely a leading objective for the future is the more accurate measurement of social change and a refined lexicon for conveying our findings. Scholars who attempt to grasp the totality of change during that decade will probably take up positions ranging from that of William Leuchtenburg, who in a brilliant one-volume survey in 1963 described the New Deal as a "half-way revolution," to those on the critical end of the discussion who find American society in 1940 pretty much where it was in 1930. But the range of the argument, nevertheless, has narrowed, and this is a considerable achievement. At the risk of predicting the unpredictable movements of historiography, one is not likely to hear again the argument, ably expressed by Herbert Hoover for the unsympathetic or by Mario Einaudi for the sympathetic, that the New Deal was a social revolution.

An equally challenging task, in addition to the careful measurement of social change, remains the determination of the significance of our findings. Here, historians appear to divide into those who seek to apportion credit/blame, and those of a perhaps more behavioral orientation and less passionate temper of mind who seek to illuminate the social processes at work.

As to the first, this includes both those who give Roosevelt and the liberals the credit for whatever social improvements careful analysis may detect, as well as those (such as Bernstein and Zinn) who find in liberal leadership and ideas the reason that traditional social irrationalities and injustices were so little disturbed. For those who believe that men have choices, and that it is both philosophically justifiable and fruitful to be critical of bad choices, the testing of political leadership in the 1930's is a vital inquiry. One may hope that, in the future, conclusions about this matter will be reached only after the most exhaustive examination of the balance between pressures for change and the many institutional and attitudinal barriers which always bestride the path. In this connection, a lasting appraisal of the performance of Americans in the 1930's, both of their leaders and of the total society, must rest firmly upon a broad base of local, social, and comparative history. We have come very far in the study of national politics. But the interplay between dynamic social forces and barriers to change cannot be understood without observation of life in the nation in all its vastness and complexity, encompassing 127 million people (as of 1935), 48 states, over 3,000 counties, and 116,000 governmental units about which we know more than we did in 1960, but too little.[129]

Our need for local and regional history is not merely a need for more "political" history, but for social history in the broadest sense, the study of ideas both philosophic and vulgar, of economic institutions and opportunities, of science and technology, of judicial systems, of land and its use, of primary institutions, of communications, of leisure, of education. For those scholars who wish to arrive at judgments upon political leaders and movements, there cannot be good political history without knowledge of the full social setting within which men attempted social management. Finally, our standards for measuring achievement will be arrived at largely with reference to our own personal ideals and experiences, but they must also be disciplined and informed by the knowledge of what people in other nations and cultures have achieved under circumstances both similar and different. Studies of other industrial societies during the 1930's have multiplied in recent years, and the student of the Great Depression era in America must take them into account.[130] While one may not generalize freely about the complicated landscape of foreign comparative experiences, one comes away from reading in this area with a great respect for the enormity of the problem of international depression and a painful appreciation of the stubbornness of social irrationalities.

Another equally promising approach to the 1930's, and one which rests on somewhat different philosophical assumptions, is to eschew the effort to judge leaders, policies, or entire societies as they grappled with problems, and instead to attempt to lay bare the fundamental social processes at work within and between societies. Such an approach to synthesis would differ from earlier efforts, one supposes, in being less emotionally and normatively engaged, analytical rather than narrative, interdisciplinary and eclectic rather than primarily political. Here the first step has been taken by Louis Galambos, in a recent article.[131] While Galambos was not talking primarily about the 1930's, he suggested that historians attempt a synthesis based upon the thrust toward group organization and the rationalization of social processes. Robert Wiebe employed just such an approach in his *The Search for Order: 1877-*

1920,[132] and it appears to offer a useful conceptual framework with which to explore the 1930's. We know there was a striking acceleration, in the public sector, of the trend toward centralization, interrelatedness, the expansion of zones of deliberate social management to replace random and haphazard development. This same process, involving bureaucratization, rationalization, increasing organization along functional lines, the expansion of data-gathering and efforts at planning, went forward in the private sector during the depression just as it did in government. It is time to explore this dimension of American development in the 1930's, to trace its outlines, to locate its crucial social elites, to discern its technological, economic and intellectual origins, to map its advance, to assess its impact. In such a synthesis, public and private sectors lose their distinctiveness, as they are jointly caught in a common process of modernization. Scholars have already explored with some thoroughness the tendency, especially pronounced during and after the New Deal, for the zones of public and private to merge, and for private interests to capture sectors of public regulatory power in their search for stability and control.[133] These studies of the private domination of sectors of public authority have been seen as important critical sallies against the liberal Welfare State, as they are. But they should also be seen as examples of the vital insights to be gained when one turns from the traditional categories, public *vs.* private or political *vs.* social history, and explores the basic process of bureaucratic modernization which increasingly unites, blends, and some would say entraps Americans as the twentieth century advances.

FOOTNOTES

[1] For other recent surveys of the literature, see Richard S. Kirkendall. "The New Deal as Watershed: The Recent Literature." *Journal of American History* 54: 839-852; No. 4, March 1968; William J. Stewart. *The Era of Roosevelt: A Selected Bibliography* . . . . Hyde Park: Franklin D. Roosevelt Library, 1967.

[2] Milton Friedman and Anna Schwartz. *A Monetary History of the United States, 1867-1960.* Princeton: Princeton University Press, 1963; Clark Warburton. *Depression, Inflation, and Monetary Policy: Selected Papers, 1945-1953.* Baltimore: Johns Hopkins Press, 1966; Philip Cagan. *Determinants and Effects of Changes in the Stock of Money, 1875-1960.* New York: Columbia University Press, 1965; Elmus Wicker. *Federal Reserve Monetary Policy, 1917-1933.* New York: Random House, 1966.

[3] See Milton Friedman. *Capitalism and Freedom.* Chicago: University of Chicago Press, 1962.

[4] Princeton: Van Nostrand, 1963.

[5] Englewood Cliffs, N.J.: Prentice-Hall, 1966.

[6] New York: David McKay, 1966.

[7] New York: Harper and Row, 1967.

[8] New York: Simon and Schuster, 1962.

[9] New York: Macmillan and Co., 1969.

[10] New York: Pantheon, 1970.

[11] New York: Oxford University Press, 1965.

[12] New York: Oxford University Press, 1959.

[13] Chicago: University of Chicago Press, 1969.

[14] New York: Alfred A. Knopf, 1968.

[15] New York: Viking Press, 1968. A recent monograph which illuminates the critical last months of the Hoover administration is Roger Daniels, *The Bonus March,* Westport: Greenwood Publishing Co., 1971.

[16] Boston: Houghton Mifflin, 1965.

[17] New York: Harcourt, Brace and World, 1965.

[18] Garden City: Doubleday, 1962.

[19] Boston: Houghton Mifflin, 1959.

[20] Boston: Houghton Mifflin, 1965.

[21] New York: Harper and Row, 1964.

[22] New York: Harcourt, Brace and World, 1966. Since this essay was written, the author has been reminded of the importance of John Collier's *From Every Zenith,* Denver: Sage Books, 1963, indispensable for New Deal Indian policy.

[23] Boston: Little, Brown, 1965.

[24] New York: Alfred A. Knopf, 1967.

[25] Urbana: University of Illinois Press, 1967.

[26] New York: Harcourt, Brace and World, 1970. After this essay was prepared there appeared Kenneth S. Davis' *FDR: The Beckoning of Destiny, 1882-1928,* New York: G. P. Putnam, 1972, and Bernard Asbell's *The FDR Memoirs,* Garden City: Doubleday and Company, 1973, a "ghosted" memoir of Roosevelt with Asbell's supplementary notes on the President's personality and background. Both of these books shed some light on FDR's romantic involvement with Lucy Mercer Rutherfurd and Marguerite LeHand. The first relationship came to the attention of the reading public with the publication of Jonathan Daniels' *Washington Quadrille,* Garden City: Doubleday and Company, 1968.

[27] New York: Alfred A. Knopf, 1962.

[28] "Clinical Notes on the Illness and Death of President Franklin D. Roosevelt." *Annals of Internal Medicine* 72: 579-591; No. 4, April 1970.

[29] New York: T. Y. Crowell, 1967.

[30] John M. Blum. "That Kind of Liberal: Franklin D. Roosevelt After Twenty-Five Years." *Yale Review* 60: 14-23; No. 1, Autumn 1970; Clarke A. Chambers. "F.D.R., Pragmatist-Idealist: An Essay in Historiography." *Pacific Northwest Quarterly* 52: 50-55; No. 2, April 1961.

[31] "The Evaluation of Presidents: An Extension of the Schlesinger Polls." *Journal of American History* 57: 104-113; No. 1, June 1970.

[32] Chicago: Quadrangle, 1968.

[33] Boston: Houghton Mifflin, 1968.

[34] New York: W. W. Norton, 1971.

[35] Wilma Dykeman and James Stokely. *Seeds of Southern Change: The Life of Will Alexander.* Chicago: University of Chicago Press, 1962.

[36] Joseph L. Morrison. *Josephus Daniels.* Chapel Hill: University of North Carolina Press, 1966.

[37] Richard J. Whalen. *The Founding Father.* New York: New American Library, 1964.

[38] Edward Blackorby. *Prairie Rebel.* Lincoln: University of Nebraska Press, 1963.

[39] Richard B. Henderson. *Maury Maverick.* Austin: University of Texas Press, 1970.

[40] Alan Schaeffer. *Vito Marcantonio.* Syracuse: Syracuse University Press, 1966.

[41] J. Woodford Howard, Jr. *Mr. Justice Murphy.* Princeton: Princeton University Press, 1968.

[42] Francis L. Broderick. *Right Reverend New Dealer: John A. Ryan.* New York: Macmillan, 1963.

[43] Thomas E. Vadney. *The Wayward Liberal.* Lexington: University Press of Kentucky, 1970.

[44] Fred L. Israel. *Nevada's Key Pittman.* Lincoln: University of Nebraska, 1963.

[45] Bernard Sternsher. *Rexford Tugwell and the New Deal.* New Brunswick: Rutgers University Press, 1964.

[46] Edward L. and Frederick H. Schapsmeier. *Henry A. Wallace of Iowa: The Agrarian Years, 1910-1940.* Ames: Iowa State University Press, 1968.

[47] Theron F. Schlabach. *Edwin E. Witte.* Madison: State Historical Society of Wisconsin, 1969.

[48] Murray Seidler. *Norman Thomas: Respectable Rebel.* Syracuse: Syracuse University Press, 1961; Harry Fleischman. *Norman Thomas.* New York: W. W. Norton, 1964, 1969 rev.

[49] New York: Atheneum, 1968.

[50] New York: Alfred A. Knopf, 1970.

[51] William F. McDonald. *Federal Relief Administration and the Arts.* Columbus: Ohio State University Press, 1969. This study was completed in 1946, published twenty-three years later.

[52] *The Federal Theatre, 1935-1939.* Princeton: Princeton University Press, 1967.

[53] Durham: Duke University Press, 1967.

[54] Baltimore: Johns Hopkins Press, 1966.

[55] Ann Arbor: University of Michigan Press, 1963.

[56] Princeton: Princeton University Press, 1966.

[57] *High Dams and Slack Waters: TVA Rebuilds a River.* Baton Rouge: Louisiana State University Press, 1965.

[58] *Sparks at the Grassroots: Municipal Distribution of TVA Electricity in Tennessee.* Knoxville: University of Tennessee Press, 1970.

[59] *TVA and the Power Fight, 1933-1939.* Philadelphia: Lippincott, 1971.

[60] Boston: Houghton Mifflin, 1970.

[61] In John Braeman *et al.*, editors. *Change and Continuity in Twentieth Century America.* Columbus: Ohio State University Press, 1964. pp. 221-262.

[62] Ann Arbor: University of Michigan Press, 1969.

[63] New York: Columbia University Press, 1970.

[64] Urbana: University of Illinois Press, 1965.

[65] Chapel Hill: University of North Carolina Press, 1971.

[66] Urbana: University of Illinois Press, 1965.

[67] Durham: Duke University Press, 1970.

[68] Chapel Hill: University of North Carolina Press, 1968.

[69] Urbana: University of Illinois Press, 1962.

[70] Columbus: University of Missouri Press, 1966.

[71] Cambridge: Harvard University Press, 1968.

[72] Madison: University of Wisconsin Press, 1969.

[73] Madison: University of Wisconsin Press, 1966.

[74] Madison: University of Wisconsin Press, 1963.

[75] Washington: The Brookings Institution, 1969.

[76] Boston: Houghton Mifflin, 1960.

[77] "Historians and the Two New Deals, 1944-1960." *Social Studies* 54: 133-140; April 1963.

[78] "The Two New Deals: A Valid Concept?" *Historian* 28: 268-288; No. 2, February 1966.

[79] In *Franklin D. Roosevelt and the New Deal, 1932-1940.* New York: Harper and Row, 1963.

[80] New York: Oxford University Press, 1964.

[81] Lincoln: University of Nebraska Press, 1966.

[82] New York: Houghton Mifflin, 1962.

[83] New York: Macmillan, 1969.

[84] Lexington: University of Kentucky Press, 1967.

[85] Cambridge: Harvard University Press, 1966.

[86] New York: John Wiley and Sons, 1966.

[87] New York: W. W. Norton, 1970.

[88] New York: Bookman, 1963.

[89] Syracuse: Syracuse University Press, 1965.

[90] Bloomington: University of Indiana Press, 1966.

[91] Cambridge: Harvard University Press, 1966. After this essay went to press, the author's attention was called to David H. Bennett's fine study, *Demagogues in the Depression,* New Brunswick: Rutgers University Press, 1968, which tells the story of the effort to unite the followings of Long, Coughlin and Townsend in the Union Party of 1936. For interesting observations on depression-era student radicalism, see S. M. Lipset and E. C. Ladd, "College Generations—From the 1930s to the 1960s," *The Public Interest,* 25: 50-69; Fall, 1971.

[92] Chicago: Quadrangle, 1969.

[93] Chicago: Rand McNally, 1969.

[94] In Stanley Coben and Lorman Ratner, editors. *The Development of an American Culture.* Englewood Cliffs: Prentice-Hall, 1970. pp. 179-218. Two studies which break new ground in the analysis of popular culture in the 1930's are: Andrew Bergman. *We're in the Money: Depression America and Its Films.* New York: New York University Press, 1971; and R. Serge Denisoff. *Great Day Coming: Folk Music and the American Left.* Urbana: University of Illinois Press, 1971.

[95] New York: G. P. Putnam's Sons, 1971.

[96] New York: Oxford University Press, 1967.

[97] Chicago: University of Chicago Press, 1968.

[98] "The Negro in the New Deal Era." *Wisconsin Magazine of History* 48: 111-126; No. 2, Winter 1964-65.

[99] "The NAACP and a Federal Antilynching Bill, 1934-1940." *Journal of Negro History* 50: 106-117; No. 2, April 1965.

[100] "The Civilian Conservation Corps and the Negro." *Journal of American History* 52: 75-88; No. 1, June 1965.

[101] Westport, Conn.: Greenwood Publishing Co., 1970.

[102] Baton Rouge: Louisiana State University Press, 1965.

[103] Chicago: Quadrangle, 1970.

[104] Baton Rouge: Louisiana State University Press, 1969.

[105] Norman, Oklahoma: University of Oklahoma Press, 1970.

[106] New York: Harper and Row, 1959.

[107] Chicago: University of Chicago Press, 1961.

[108] Tucson: University of Arizona, 1968.

[109] Ph.D. dissertation, University of California, Los Angeles, 1970.

[110] Westport, Conn.: Greenwood, 1969. A very important study of another "oppressed group" was published after this essay went to press: see William Chafe. *The American Woman: Her Changing Social, Economic and Political Roles, 1920-1970.* New York: Oxford University Press, 1971.

[111] Indianapolis: Bobbs-Merrill, 1967.

[112] Cambridge: Harvard University Press, 1970.

[113] "The Origins of Franklin D. Roosevelt's 'Court Packing' Plan," in Philip B. Kurland, editor. *The Supreme Court Review.* Chicago: University of Chicago Press, 1966. pp. 347-400, and "Franklin D. Roosevelt's Supreme Court 'Packing Plan'," in Harold M. Hollingsworth and William F. Holmes, editors. *Essays on the New Deal.* Austin: University of Texas Press, 1969.

[114] Cambridge: Harvard University Press, 1963.

[115] Cambridge: Harvard University Press, 1966.

[116] Ithaca: Cornell University Press, 1959.

[117] Reno: University of Nevada Press, 1969.

[118] See Barton J. Bernstein. "The New Deal: The Conservative Achievements of Liberal Reform," in Bernstein, editor. *Towards a New Past.* New York: Pantheon, 1968. pp. 263-288; Paul Conkin. *The New Deal.* New York: T. Y. Crowell, 1967; Howard Zinn, editor. "Introduction" to *New Deal Thought.* Indianapolis: Bobbs-Merrill, 1966; and G. William Domhoff. "How the Power Elite Shape Social Legislation," in his *The Higher Circles.* New York: Random House, 1970. pp. 156-249. The new critics are appraised in Irwin Unger. "The 'New Left' and American History." *American Historical Review* 72: 1237-1263; No. 4, July 1967; Jerold Auerbach. "New Deal, Old Deal, or Raw Deal: Some Thoughts on New Left Historiography." *Journal of Southern History* 35: 18-30; No. 1, February 1969; and Otis L. Graham. "New Deal Historiography: Retrospect and Prospect," in Graham, editor. *The New Deal.* Boston: Little, Brown, 1971. pp. 171-179.

[119] See for example Gabriel Kolko. *Wealth and Power in America.* New York: Praeger, 1962; Herman P. Miller. *Rich Man, Poor Man.* New York: T. Y. Crowell, 1964; and Robert Lampman. *The Share of Top Wealth Holders in National Wealth, 1922-1956.* Princeton: Princeton University Press, 1961. Wartime changes in the tax structure make it difficult, of course, to assess the New Deal's impact upon income distribution. Both Miller and Lampman make somewhat more of New Deal redistributional effects than Kolko, but none finds anything resembling a social revolution.

[120] See Clark Kerr. *The Impacts of Unions on the Level of Wages.* Berkeley: University of California Press, 1960; H. G. Lewis. *Unionism and Relative Wages in the United States.* Chicago: University of Chicago Press, 1966; and George H. Hildebrand. "The Economic Effects of Unionism," in Neil W. Chamberlain *et al.,* editor. *A Decade of Industrial Relations Research, 1946-1956.* New York: Harper and Bros., 1958. pp. 98-145.

[121] Robert Engler. *The Politics of Oil.* New York: Macmillan, 1961, and Gerald D. Nash. *United States Oil Policy, 1890-1964.* Pittsburgh: University of Pittsburgh Press, 1968.

[122] Donald Whitnah. *Safer Skyways: Federal Control of Aviation, 1926-1966.* Ames, Iowa: Iowa State University Press, 1966, and William A. Jordan. *Airline Regulation in America.* Baltimore: Johns Hopkins Press, 1970.

[123] *The Politics of Small Business.* Washington: Public Affairs Press, 1961.

[124] *Investment Banking in America.* Cambridge: Harvard University Press, 1970.

[125] *Securities Regulation and the New Deal.* New Haven: Yale University Press, 1970.

[126] Princeton: Princeton University Press, 1966. The New Deal expanded federal efforts in the area of conservation, and recent studies of two of its programs affecting land use reveal the influential role of private interests in shaping regulation to serve their purposes: see Wesley Calef. *Private Grazing and Public Lands.* Chicago: University of Chicago Press, 1960; and Robert J. Morgan. *Governing Soil Conservation: Thirty Years of the New Decentralization.* Baltimore: Johns Hopkins University Press, 1966.

[127] New York: Harper and Row, 1969.

[128] See Graham. *op. cit.*

[129] The leading studies of state and local history in the 1930's include James T. Patterson's indispensable *The New Deal and the States.* Princeton: Princeton University Press, 1969; George B. Tindall's *The Emergence of the New South, 1913-1945.* Baton Rouge: Louisiana State University Press, 1967; the August 1969 issue of *Pacific Historical Review,* a symposium on the New Deal and the western states; Bernard Sternsher, editor. *Hitting Home.* Chicago: Quadrangle, 1970; Michael P. Rogin and John L. Shover. *Political Change in California: Critical Elections and Social Movements, 1890-1966.* Westport, Conn.: Greenwood, 1970; Gilman Ostrander. *Nevada: The Great Rotten Borough, 1859-1964.* New York:

Knopf, 1966; Michael Malone. *C. Ben Ross and the New Deal in Idaho.* Seattle: University of Washington Press, 1970; William H. Chafe. "Flint and the Great Depression." *Michigan History* 53: 225-239; No. 3, Fall 1969; Raymond L. Koch. "Politics and Relief in Minneapolis During the 1930s." *Minnesota History* 41: 153-170; No. 4, Winter 1968; Bruce M. Stave. *The New Deal and the Last Hurrah.* Pittsburgh: University of Pittsburgh Press, 1970.

[130] Direct comparisons of national efforts to handle recovery are few, and include Andrew Shonfield. *Modern Capitalism.* New York: Oxford University Press, 1966; William E. Leuchtenburg. "The Great Depression," in C. Vann Woodward, editor. *The Comparative Approach to American History.* New York: Basic Books, 1968. pp. 296-314; Margaret S. Gordon. *The Economics of Welfare Politics.* New York: Columbia University Press, 1963; Erik Lundberg. *Instability and Economic Growth.* New Haven: Yale University Press, 1968; Samuel Mencher. *Poor Law to Poverty Program: Economic Security Policy in Britain and the United States.* Pittsburgh: University of Pittsburgh Press, 1967; and James T. Patterson. "Federalism in Crisis: A Comparative Study of Canada and the United States in the Depression of the 1930s," in Victor Hoar, editor. *The Great Depression.* Vancouver: C. Clark, 1969. pp. 1-30. Good studies of individual nations are: Derek Aldcroft. *The Inter-War Economy: Britain, 1919-1939.* New York: Columbia University Press, 1970; the chapter on "The Exercise of Power: The Blum Experiment," in Joel Colton. *Leon Blum.* New York: Alfred A. Knopf, 1966. pp. 160-197; Bentley B. Gilbert. *British Social Policy, 1914-1939.* Ithaca: Cornell University Press, 1970; Bentley B. Gilbert. *The Evolution of National Insurance in Great Britain.* London: Michael Joseph, 1966; H. Blair Neatby. "The Liberal Way: Fiscal and Monetary Policy in the 1930's" (Canada), in Victor Hoar, editor. *The Great Depression.* pp. 84-114; A. J. P. Taylor. *English History 1914-1945.* New York: Oxford University Press, 1965; and Stephen S. Cohen. *Modern Capitalist Planning: The French Model.* Cambridge: Harvard University Press, 1970. An interesting perspective is presented in Nicholas Halasz. *Roosevelt Through Foreign Eyes.* Princeton: Van Nostrand, 1961.

[131] "The Emerging Organizational Synthesis in Modern American History." *Business History Review* 44: 279-290; No. 3, Autumn 1970.

[132] New York: Hill and Wang, 1967.

[133] The New Deal, after its early and unpleasant experience with central planning, shifted gradually, haphazardly and without much sense of clear direction toward a pluralistic system in which policy would be set by the interplay of many interest groups. Liberals thought the resultant system an improvement over the logrolling of the past, since they had aided "underdog" groups, such as farmers and labor, to gain the organizational power required to influence policy. John Kenneth Galbraith was to call this "countervailing power" in his *American Capitalism,* Boston: Houghton Mifflin, 1952, and John Chamberlain dubbed the government which maneuvered toward its ends among these interest groups "the Broker State," in his *The American Stakes,* New York: Carrick and Evans, 1940. In the 1960's, several powerful studies have documented the inherent conservatism and indeed irrationality of this system, as the most powerful business groups continue to dominate public policy as they had in the 1920's. See Henry Kariel. *The Decline of American Pluralism.* Stanford: Stanford University Press, 1961; Grant McConnell. *Private Power and American Democracy.* New York: Alfred A. Knopf, 1966; Theodore Lowi. *The End of Liberalism.* New York: W. W. Norton, 1969; and Robert P. Wolff. *The Poverty of Liberalism.* Boston: Beacon Press, 1968.

· 23 ·

Foreign Policy, 1929–1941

Robert H. Ferrell

THE bleak era of American foreign policy from the beginning of the
Great Depression until the nation's entrance into the Second World War
is an era of failure, and the period's literature reflects that fact. Through
the books about the years from 1929 to 1941 there constantly appears
the question of Why? The narrow issue of the Pearl Harbor attack—
who was guilty? why were the conniving Japanese so appallingly successful?—has been of much less interest in recent years, and it is remarkable
that during the 1960's only two books worthy of notice appeared on the
debacle of December 7, 1941, compared to the flood of volumes published in the late 1940's and early 1950's. Historians rather are looking
to the more general failures of the 1929-1941 period, or events that
were less military, less spectacular perhaps but in the long processes of
history meant much more. For individuals willing to read "in depth,"
as an expression of our own time has it, there is a good deal of new
writing now available, perhaps half a hundred titles of importance having
appeared since publication of *Interpreting and Teaching American
History* in 1961. These titles examine carefully their subjects, and are
rewarding in the extreme for anyone wishing to take the time to read
them.

The question of Why?, it is interesting to relate, is not nearly as
insistent as it was some years ago, for the country's foreign problems
during the Cold War and after have become so pressing that to many
Americans the difficulties and troubles of earlier years are rapidly taking
on the quality of an antique era, something like the pre-1914 period
seemed a quarter of a century ago. For a not inconsiderable number of
students of the 1970's the patina of age has long since covered everything before the Cold War; one might as well talk about ancient Greece
and Rome as about the Great Depression and the rise of Hitler and the
Japanese warlords. Even so, for individuals who wish to move behind

509

the superficialities of the present into the roots of the present, there is no more instructive era than the dozen years from the Wall Street crash to the resounding explosions at Pearl Harbor.

The eminent diplomatic historian, Dexter Perkins, has described in passing in his memoirs how the preoccupation of his generation, the basic international idea of scholars who came to adulthood at the time of the First World War and were in their prime during the interwar period, was collective security, and how that Wilsonian concept has proved an illusion because of the unwillingness of leaders of modern-day nations, especially democratic nations, to support each other's policies through thick and thin.[1] It is therefore not for nothing that scholars of the 1960's have done little more with the Wilsonian view of the world, as that view flourished for a while and then languished during the 1930's and died at the beginning of the Cold War. The only book of the 1960's on that significant subject, surely a subject of failure, is by Roland N. Stromberg, an able analysis, which passed largely unnoticed by American scholars when it appeared in 1963.[2] Stromberg draws the importance of the Wilsonian dream, of how Americans sought to support collective security not merely for their Hemisphere but for Europe and the world. The failure of the League of Nations without American membership became increasingly evident in the 1930's.

General books on American foreign relations during the interwar years continued to come out, and a notable volume, if only because it was written by a Frenchman, is by Jean-Baptiste Duroselle.[3] The author showed the connection between Wilson and Roosevelt, which not merely was a connection of political party and of domestic economic views but of foreign policy. Unlike many French scholars who for reasons best known to themselves have found American history altogether uninteresting, and who if they write about the United States do so from the least research they can perform, and manage to misspell a large proportion of the authors and titles they profess to have used, Duroselle knew American historical scholarship, and his volume is not merely reliable but benefits from its author's easy perspective of the European context of American diplomacy in the interwar period.

American authors have produced surveys, of which the diplomatic biography of Cordell Hull by Julius W. Pratt is outstanding.[4] Volumes 12 and 13 in the eighteen-volume series entitled *The American Secretaries of State and Their Diplomacy,* Pratt's work looks critically but in general favorably on Hull's accomplishments, with the benefit of not merely the printed literature but available manuscript and archival sources. His masterful biography was followed in 1965 with surveys by Selig Adler and Robert A. Divine.[5] The adjectives in the titles of these two

authors show their themes—Adler's *The Uncertain Giant* deals with
the entire interwar era, going back to the inauguration of Harding, and
Divine's *The Reluctant Belligerent* considers the 1930's with emphasis
on events and forces that brought President Roosevelt around to
advocating the nation's entrance into the Second World War. The books
both are contributions to series, Adler writing for the *American Diplomatic History* series edited by Armin Rappaport, a survey of the nation's
foreign relations from beginning to the present according to historical
eras, and Divine's book belonging to the *America in Crisis* series, edited
by Divine, dealing with involvement in wars from the Revolution to the
Second World War.

The three other general titles are worth mentioning at the outset of the
present chapter. One, a remarkable memoir by the diplomat-historian
George F. Kennan, covers the first part of his diplomatic career from
entrance into the Foreign Service in 1925, when the diplomacy of the
United States was more a matter of watching what other nations did
than a matter of innovation or participation, to his temporary exit from the
Department of State to Princeton's Institute for Advanced Study in 1950
after having served continuously in Europe, notably in Moscow, and
then as director of the Department's Policy Planning Staff when the
latter was organized in 1947.[6] Kennan saw from firsthand much of the
downward movement of European democratic diplomacy, the increasing
successes and then the seeming triumph of the new autocracy, and his
keen qualities of observation, tinged with his undue pessimism, make
his judgments of the moment and in retrospect a fascinating analysis.
To Kennan's memoirs the inquiring student should add the reading of a
small interpretive account of the 1930's by John E. Wiltz which has a
considerable bibliographic commentary, together with the opening chapters from the second volume of James M. Burns's now-complete biography, a veritable life and times, rather than a narrow personal narrative, of
President Franklin D. Roosevelt.[7] Burns put his themes in his volume
titles. He created almost a school of interpretation when in 1956 he published his *Roosevelt: The Lion and the Fox.* His new volume, *Roosevelt:
The Soldier of Freedom,* makes no effort to hide the fox-like qualities of
the late President, but sets everything in perspective by showing Roosevelt
the war leader, the worldwide representative of freedom, the latter-day
evangel, albeit without the tendency to high rhetoric of his Democratic
predecessor of another era.

The foreign policy of the first President of the period 1929-1941,
Herbert Hoover, had two interpretations in the 1960's. The author of
the present chapter published volume 11 in *The American Secretaries*
series, on Secretaries of State Frank B. Kellogg and Henry L. Stimson,

and made use of materials that became available after publication of his preceding books on those Secretaries.[8] His general interpretation remains a somewhat critical view of Stimson as Secretary of State, a belief that Stimson belonged more to the time of Theodore Roosevelt than to the post-1918 period, and that Stimson was not a good administrator of the Department. Still, the author maintained that Stimson's concern for peace was genuine and that as Secretary he did his best, which was to maintain the appearance of American concern when in fact the Great Depression made any serious American policy for the ensuring of world peace almost impossible. L. Ethan Ellis enlarged a study of the diplomacy of Kellogg into a survey of what he aptly described as Republican—as opposed to that of the Democratic Roosevelt—foreign policy, from Harding through Hoover, a dozen presidential years of mistakes and missed opportunities.[9] Ellis writes brightly, and based his conclusions upon massive investigation of manuscript and archival sources, and if he sometimes seems hard on the Republicans then the reader must admit that, so far as concerned the workings of the federal government, domestic and foreign, the era was not the GOP's finest hour.

The diplomacy of naval limitation remained of importance during Hoover's presidency and Stimson's secretaryship, and the first scholarly study of the London Naval Conference of 1930, by Raymond G. O'Connor, sets out the details of that assemblage of, now, so long ago.[10] O'Connor was justly critical of the conference, which because it dealt only in naval limitation, failing to accompany diplomacy with political arrangements, was much less successful than the Washington Conference of 1921-1922. He described the result in his title, *Perilous Equilibrium*. The reason for peril was the confrontation at London of two enthusiasms, the desire of American naval officers to avoid any serious reduction of their service arm, and the desire of Japanese naval officers to increase their fleet. Armin Rappaport in a small volume showed the importance of the Navy League in American naval opinion.[11] Gerald E. Wheeler employed another good title, *Prelude to Pearl Harbor,* to describe American naval policy in the Far East during the 1920's and down to the outbreak of war in Manchuria in 1931; he delineated the increasing rivalry as American naval power, secure in the Atlantic after the defeat of Germany during the World War, began to be ever more a threat to Japan.[12] To be sure, the problem went back to the antediluvian year 1898 when Commodore George Dewey sank a decrepit Spanish squadron in Manila Bay and by this victory, in which Dewey believed himself to be guided by the hand of God, propelled his country into ownership of an archipelago nearly five thousand miles removed from the Hawaiian Islands, not to mention the distance to the American West Coast. Long before the United States government in the 1930's undertook to get rid of the Philippines, the islands had become in Theodore Roosevelt's words an Achilles' heel. By the 1930's American naval prestige had been mortgaged—if one may use another figure—to the Philippines, a very insecure piece of real estate, considering Japanese power after the London Naval Conference. Theodore Friend's book about Filipino-American relations from 1929 until independence in 1946, aptly titled *Between Two Empires,* sets out the wide gaps between American foreign policy, naval strength, and imperial possessions.[13]

The present author published a book in the latter 1950's concerning, in part, American policy during the Far Eastern Crisis of 1931-1933. Armin Rappaport a few years later looked solely to Stimson's Far Eastern policy and discovered an interesting State Department document, printed in full as an appendix to his volume, showing the inner workings of the Lytton Commission of 1931-1932.[14] Neither of these books used much Japanese archival material, the captured records which after the war were first employed in the war crimes trials in Tokyo and then opened to Japanese and any other scholars able to use them. Some of the prewar records were burned in American air raids, others destroyed by the Japanese even as General MacArthur's occupying troops were entering Tokyo, but to destroy the documentary narrative of Japanese imperialism proved impossible, and after a perhaps undue period of waiting there now are some remarkable books based upon it, such as the volumes by Takehiko Yoshihashi and Sadako N. Ogata.[15] Akira Iriye of the University of Chicago showed extraordinary enterprise in reconstructing the Far Eastern past, and his *After Imperialism: The Search for a New Order in the Far East, 1921-1931,* admittedly only going to the beginning of the Manchurian crisis, is evidence of what multilingual, multiarchival scholarship can be.[16] In that volume and in more general writings Iriye has shown how complex, how variegated Japanese imperialism was—how the outward movement of the Japanese nation was no simple military-inspired, mad-dog excursion into Chinese and other territory, but a development from the forces and factors of Japanese history in the nineteenth century, since the opening of the country in the 1850's and the Meiji Restoration of 1868.[16a]

When the Roosevelt administration took over from the bitterly disappointed, the profoundly pessimistic Hoover, the first years of the new President were devoted to domestic economic recovery, and at the outset it was only on issues of foreign policy that looked toward recovery that Roosevelt showed interest. One of these was recognition of Russia. While Rooseveltian purposes for recognition were surely mixed—the exhilaration of negotiating in the White House with a real, live communist, the need to show a departure from the bankrupt Republican policy of nonrecognition, concern over the breakdown of peace in the Far East which might require cooperation between the United States government and the regime of the Bolsheviks—there seems little question but that hope for increased trade with Russia was among Roosevelt's reasons for recognition. The negotiation with Foreign Commissar Maxim Litvinov was highly personal, in the course of which the President asked "Max" what he, Max, anticipated when he died. It was therefore not unexpected that the President's first ambassador to the Soviet Union should be an individual of controversial background who would approach diplomacy in a personal way. Beatrice Farnsworth has drawn the portrait of Ambassador William C. Bullitt, from the envoy's youthful connection with diplomacy at the end of the First World War when he was present at the Paris Peace Conference and undertook a personal mission to Russia to see the new Bolsheviks, to the period 1934-1936 when Bullitt tried to exert a personal influence on Stalin and lost: it availed nothing for the ambassador to equip some Moscow citizens with baseball bats and gloves, or to organize flamboyant parties, or manage pleasant conversations; these acts were not enough to impel the calculating Stalin in the direction of the democracies rather than toward a *rapprochement* with Germany which would have the purpose of protecting Russia's European territories while the German dictator turned upon the more westerly nations.[17]

For a while during the 1930's the notion prevailed that better economic policy might save American diplomacy as well as the American pocketbook, and Joan Hoff Wilson examined the 1920's, down to 1933, for connections between American business and foreign policy.[18] Lloyd C. Gardner began his much-noticed volume, *Economic Aspects of New Deal Diplomacy,* where Miss Wilson left off.[19] The one-time Economic Adviser to the Department of State, who after retirement published a dozen or more books, Herbert Feis, recalled the ill-fated London Economic Conference of 1933, among other Rooseveltian first steps or missteps, in a volume somewhat opaquely entitled *1933: Characters in Crisis.*[20] Feis related some of the antics of the American delegates to the London Conference, such stories as how a distinguished member of the Senate chased him along a corridor in Claridge's Hotel brandishing a hunter's knife. The senator was celebrating his presence in a country where alcohol was openly for sale.

If foreign policy during the early Roosevelt years was incidental to domestic recovery, or personal opportunities to purchase liquor, in Latin American policy there was some accomplishment, and Bryce Wood investigated it in detail in his book about the Good Neighbor Policy.[21] As the years pass, nearly half a century since policy changed in the Western Hemisphere, the change seems ever less impressive; the interventions at the beginning of the twentieth century were the real changes in policy; the Good Neighbor Policy was less a change than a return to the old neighborliness. Policy fortunately changed in time to afford protection against the machinations of Nazi Germany. Alton Frye investigated the possibility of a Hitlerian invasion of the New World. He related that the Nazis were interested in and sometimes fascinated by the large numbers of German nationals and German-descended citizens of the Western Hemisphere but that there never was a plan by Hitler to occupy territory in the New World.[22] As Frye pointed out, this is not to say that the Nazis would not have gone west rather than east in 1940-1941. Hitler in July 1940 began to think of the invasion of Russia, before the Battle of Britain had been decided against Germany. He was accustomed to act upon personal perceptions. In July 1940 there was no German plan to invade Russia; had anyone looked in the German archives for a record of what the Fuehrer would do within the next year, there would have been not the slightest trace. Historians and others who argue that Hitler had no plans to invade the New World and therefore would not, are right in their evidence but the conclusion is shaky.

The last of American interventions in Central America and the Caribbean, the Nicaraguan intervention beginning in 1925, came to an end in 1933, and William Kamman has drawn that episode from archival and other sources as a small affair but symbolic of both the hopes and disappointments of the American government in seeking to teach the Latin Americans to elect good men, as President Wilson put the issue in regard to Mexico.[23] Historians have not looked closely at the relations of the United States toward Latin America in the 1930's, as well they might, for the seeds of dictatorships in Nicaragua, the Dominican Republic, Haiti, and Cuba were planted by the withdrawals during the 1930's, the relinquishment of protectorates. The result would be three interventions, one of them of a most serious sort, in the 1950's and 1960's.[23a]

The basis of American foreign policy during the dismal decade under review was isolation, an impossible policy—an illusion, as Robert A. Divine described the Neutrality Acts of the latter 1930's.[24] The acts of 1935-1941 came out of the temper of the time. Unfortunately they were themselves no illusion, for as Divine showed they testified in the most undiplomatic manner to the nation's desire to stay out of the combinations and collisions, ordinary or extraordinary, of European politics.

Wayne S. Cole published a book describing one of the movers and shakers of the decade, a senator from North Dakota, Gerald P. Nye, who when he arrived in Washington to take his Senate seat in the late 1920's had never set foot in the national capital before.[25] Nye made an undistinguished record in the Upper House, and might have left the Senate to become baseball commissioner, replacing Judge Kenesaw Mountain Landis, but stayed on and at last was chosen by Senator George Norris and an enthusiastic champion of world peace, Miss Dorothy Detzer, to head a special Senate committee investigating connections between businessmen (then in ill repute because of the Depression) and armaments. A generation before President Dwight D. Eisenhower's speechwriter, Malcolm Moos, in 1961 coined the phrase "military-industrial complex," Nye came into prominence over such an issue. The rapid approach of the Second World War, and a turning of public interest into the Neutrality Acts, blunted his investigation, although it was debatable—considering the country's then minuscule military establishment—if he would have found much, even if he had looked harder. John E. Wiltz in a volume published in 1963, a year after Cole's diplomatic biography of Nye, examined the Nye investigation and came to the conclusion that it was not altogether important, a symbol of the public mood rather than a lever or catalyst or inspiration for a new foreign policy.[26] Wiltz, even more than Cole, showed the senator's sophomoric approach to the great problems of war and peace, armaments and neutrality. It was likewise symbolic of the period, one should add, that the knife-wielding, hard-drinking senator of the London Economic Conference of 1933, the Honorable Key Pittman (D., Nev.), was chairman of the Foreign Relations Committee from 1933 until 1940, when the Demon Rum finished him off.[27]

Scholars of the 1960's, perhaps anticipating the neo-isolationism that emerged by the end of that later decade when the Vietnam War diminished the enthusiasms of so many idealistic Americans, looked carefully—much more carefully than in preceding years—at the isolationism during the 1930's. Manfred Jonas considered the isolationists from 1935 to 1941, showing how until the very eve, virtually the evening, of Pearl Harbor, isolationism maintained a hold on the country's foreign policy.[28] Warren I. Cohen remarked the importance of analogy in the philosophy of isolationism, of how the public men of the 1930's believed they were protecting the nation against a repetition of the errors of policy during the First World War, and for that matter against the errors of European governments of that earlier time, mistakes so apparent in the years after the war when the Continent's archives were opened for great documentary publications.[29] Cohen showed how the supposed circumstances of American entrance into the First World War, the lessons drawn by historians and publicists who did not look closely enough at the record (and for that matter, could not look closely enough; the American and European archives were closed to private research during the 1930's), oppressed and restrained American policy on the eve of entrance into the Second World War.

The turning of the Hitler regime toward aggression, and the slow response of the American government which as late as September 1939 did little more than declare neutrality upon the opening of the Second World War, has continued to intrigue historians. The Spanish Civil War may or may not have been a turning point, but it was a focal point of sentiment and of individual determination to stand against aggression or, as in the case of some American churchmen of the Catholic faith, to opt in favor of aggression if it meant protection of Catholicism, and Richard P. Traina described the mixed feelings of religionists, businessmen, and diplomats as the Civil War dragged on for three years to its dreary end.[30]

As for the principal figure of the German government of the 1930's, what he thought of the United States, two books appeared in 1967 which sought to examine that mystery. James V. Compton's *Swastika and the Eagle* is more thoroughly researched than Saul Friedlaender's *Prelude to Downfall*.[31] Both authors showed the German leader's momentous miscalculation but were unsure of why Hitler—in possession of the prime historical lesson of the First World War, namely, that after the German government in 1917 virtually invited American entrance into the war it discovered a year later that the Americans had put two million fresh troops into France and could break the German lines and end the war—in view of this lesson of 1917-1918 should have made the same mistake. Compton quoted Hitler's one-time friend Ernst (Putzi) Hanfstaengl as remembering that Hitler in conversation asked what the United States was except movie queens, Hollywood, and stupid records. It is true that Hitler in prewar years refused to visit the United States, and during the ill-fated years of the Second World War was wont to speak of "that melting pot" and to wonder why the more purely bred British had chosen to worship the melting pot rather than the shrine of Aryanism. The mystery of the Fuehrer's miscalculation remains.

For a while the American government during the Depression years sought to preserve decent relations with the Third Reich, but it was an ill-fated effort that does not look well in retrospect. In 1933, President Roosevelt, without large calculation and after failing in other choices, appointed a Southern Democrat and distinguished historian of the Old South then resident at the University of Chicago, William E. Dodd, as ambassador to Germany, and Dodd in letters to the President did not hesitate to point out the criminal character of the Nazi regime. This remarkable diplomat, a tragic choice because his moralism virtually overwhelmed him and eventually made him *persona non grata* with the regime, is the subject of a biography justly entitled *Democrat and Diplomat,* by Robert Dallek.[32] If Dallek's book does not testify to the importance of historians in American politics, it testifies to the *Angst,* the anxiety, of a sensitive man representing his country to a criminal government. The year after Dallek's book appeared, Arnold A. Offner in 1969 brought out *American Appeasement* in which he contended that the German policy of President Roosevelt was not much better than that of Neville Chamberlain, and considering that the United States was so much farther removed from the scene was perhaps worse.[33] Offner did not subtract much from the Roosevelt record in foreign affairs prior to 1940, as historians have drawn that era; there is not a great deal to subtract. He admittedly was an admirer of Roosevelt's war leadership. But he took the manuscript and archival sources at their own testimony. It is not without interest that Offner's book was published by the Belknap Press of Harvard University.

In the catalog of Rooseveltian mistakes, and of those of Americans in general, nothing proved as disquieting to readers of the 1960's as the story of how the Roosevelt administration failed to face up to the refugee crisis of 1938-1941. The concentration camps did not become death camps until somewhat later, but information coming out of Germany was so unmistakable, the future for the Jews and other *Untermenschen* of the Continent so dire, that the lackadaisical attitude of Americans now, in retrospect of thirty years and more, seems deplorable. Early in the 1960's accusations began to appear against Pope Pius XII, who died in 1958. A popular play in West Germany, translated and produced on Broadway, by Rolf Hochhuth, attributed to Pius a moral obtuseness that made theatergoers shudder. Arthur D. Morse published a sensational volume, *While Six Million Died: A Chronicle of American Apathy,* based (so Morse said; State Department officials claimed that he was grossly unfair) on American archival records.[34] The truth perhaps was more prosaic, less personal, not attributable to Pius XII or President Roosevelt or some Assistant Secretary of State, but as David S. Wyman showed in his *Paper Walls,* and Henry Feingold in *The Politics of Rescue,* to the unbelief of citizens of the Western democracies that governments in the twentieth century would wipe out whole groups of their citizenry.[35] The American government took a bureaucratic approach to the problem, erected paper walls as Wyman writes, and did a fraction of the rescue work that it might have done.

If scholarship has looked to the mistakes of the Depression decade and the months of neutrality in 1939-1941, it also looked to the successes, the bursts of idealism of which the American government and people always have been capable. Warren F. Kimball made a detailed study of the Lend-Lease Act of 1941 and traced the gradual conversion of President Roosevelt and his advisers to the belief that the British needed an enormous line of credit that would in fact be a gift, not a loan as in 1917-1919.[36] Kimball proved that contrary to belief at the time and by some historians, Lend-Lease did not spring full-blown from the mind of the President, but that the idea germinated slowly. For a long time Roosevelt resisted it, choosing, as Kimball related, to believe in the myth of British opulence. It is interesting that one of the supposed lessons of American participation in the First World War was that the British in early 1917 had feigned a great financial crisis and virtually frightened the Wilson administration into the war, so as to back up, via the United States Treasury, the bonds which the Allies, mostly Britain and France, had sold to American investors. Americans in the 1930's tended to believe that the British in 1917 had had a good deal more money than they let on. Kimball showed how FDR held to this belief, and could not understand Britain's virtual bankruptcy, until after British diplomats did some plain talking. Ambassador Lord Lothian landed at LaGuardia airport in November 1940 and said to reporters, "Well boys, Britain's broke; it's your money we want." When the Lend-Lease Act passed, Churchill rightly appraised this American assistance as "the most unsordid act in the history of any nation."

Another indication of American idealism was the first summit conference of the Second World War, the meeting of Roosevelt and Churchill at Placentia Bay off Newfoundland in mid-August 1941, set out in all its pageantry and melancholy (Churchill's ship, the *Prince of Wales,* was sunk by the Japanese in December) by Theodore A. Wilson.[37]

In the last months of 1941 the Germans did not declare war, despite an undeclared war in the Atlantic between the American navy and German submarines seeking to sink convoys laden with Lend-Lease goods. The attack came in the Pacific. Historians of the 1960's, as mentioned, were less concerned with the "back door to war" theory than were their predecessors of the late 1940's and early 1950's, and instead sought to analyze how American-Japanese relations went awry during the years before Pearl Harbor. They recalled that ever since the beginning of the Russo-Japanese War of 1904-1905 American officials were worried that Japanese power might turn against the United States.

The occupation of Manchuria in 1931-1933 had been an alarming affair. But whatever the developing contentions between the two great nations, in view of the rise of German power in the 1930's it has seemed to historians in retrospect increasingly unwary—one uses the word advisedly—of the Roosevelt administration to have allowed problems of the Pacific to lead to war at the same time that a conflict was coming in the Atlantic. Was war in the Pacific avoidable? Dorothy Borg, a dispassionate student who has spent years of research into the clashing interests of the two peoples, Americans and Japanese, during the interwar years, published *The United States and the Far Eastern Crisis of 1933-1938,* in which, like Akira Iriye, she showed the almost glacial movement of the two countries toward war—the depth of feeling, the impersonal nature of the forces.[38] Her title properly takes the phrase given currency by Secretary of State Stimson for the occupation of Manchuria in 1931-1933 and applies it to 1933-1938 where it had even more meaning.

Thereafter the die was cast, the forces were arrayed for war, though not inevitably, as there is no inevitability in history. David J. Lu described the importance of China policy—Japan's China policy, America's China policy—during those final years of American peace, from 1937 to 1941.[39] Waldo H. Heinrichs saw the breakdown of peace through the increasingly difficult negotiations of the American ambassador in Tokyo, Joseph C. Grew, who at last came to believe that his diplomacy had been done in by the impatience of the authorities in Washington, their unwillingness to negotiate with the Japanese even at some harm to the American diplomatic position in support of the Nationalist Chinese under Chiang Kai-shek.[40] Robert J. C. Butow considered the diplomacy of Grew's opponent in Tokyo, the leader of the government during the last weeks before the Pearl Harbor disaster, General Hideki Tojo, and indicated how Tojo's willingness to gamble led to war.[41]

In the dozen years since 1960 only two books considered the problem of Pearl Harbor, and one was a well-written general account that adds little to the literary flood of preceding years.[42] The other, by Roberta Wohlstetter, undertook to recreate the "signals" of American intelligence in the months before the disaster, to see why the officials, military and political, so misestimated Japanese intentions. Her conclusion made the Pearl Harbor attack more understandable; she believed that the signals were so confusing, so overlaid with mechanical and intellectual uncertainty, that almost the only certainty became Pearl Harbor.[43]

What future historians will make of the years 1929-1941 is difficult to say, and the once-distant year 2000, now only a generation removed from the 1970's, may see such changed views of the period as to make present-day historians appear to have looked upon the recent past with as undiscerning eyes as the writers of, say, the 1870's looked on the American Civil War. Almost the only observation which an observer of the early 1970's may be sure of is that historians are making the years 1929-1941 much more full, more detailed, and that whatever new books are to come they will have much less room to speculate, to veer off into historical error, than did the books of the past.

FOOTNOTES

[1] Dexter Perkins. *Yield of the Years.* Boston: Little, Brown, 1969.

[2] Roland N. Stromberg. *Collective Security and American Foreign Policy From the League of Nations to NATO.* New York: Praeger, 1963.

[3] Jean-Baptiste Duroselle. *From Wilson to Roosevelt.* Cambridge: Harvard University Press: 1963. Available in paperback.

[4] Julius W. Pratt. *Cordell Hull.* 2 vols. New York: Cooper Square Publishers, 1964.

[5] Selig Adler. *The Uncertain Giant: 1921-1941.* New York: Macmillan: 1965; Robert A. Divine. *The Reluctant Belligerent: American Entry into World War II.* New York: Wiley, 1965. Available in paperback.

[6] George F. Kennan. *Memoirs: 1925-1950.* Boston: Little, Brown, 1967. Available in paperback.

[7] John E. Wiltz. *From Isolation to War: 1931-1941.* New York: Crowell, 1968. Available in paperback; James M. Burns. *Roosevelt: The Lion and the Fox.* New York: Harcourt, Brace, 1956. Available in paperback; *The Soldier of Freedom.* New York: Harcourt Brace Jovanovich, 1970. For a review article on Burns see Robert Dallek, "Franklin Roosevelt as World Leader," *American Historical Review* 76: 1503-1513; No. 5, December 1971.

[8] Robert H. Ferrell. *Frank B. Kellogg and Henry L. Stimson.* New York: Cooper Square Publishers, 1963.

[9] L. Ethan Ellis. *Republican Foreign Policy: 1921-1933.* New Brunswick, N.J.: Rutgers University Press, 1968.

[10] Raymond G. O'Connor. *Perilous Equilibrium: The United States and the London Naval Conference of 1930.* Lawrence: University of Kansas Press, 1962.

[11] Armin Rappaport. *The Navy League of the United States.* Detroit, Mich.: Wayne State University Press, 1962.

[12] Gerald E. Wheeler. *Prelude to Pearl Harbor: The United States Navy and the Far East, 1921-1931.* Columbia: University of Missouri Press, 1963.

[13] Theodore Friend. *Between Two Empires: The Ordeal of the Philippines, 1929-1946.* New Haven: Yale University Press, 1965.

[14] Armin Rappaport. *Henry L. Stimson and Japan.* Chicago: University of Chicago Press, 1963.

[15] Takehiko Yoshihashi. *Conspiracy at Mukden: The Rise of the Japanese Military.* New Haven: Yale University Press, 1963; Sadako N. Ogata. *Defiance in Manchuria: The Making of Japanese Foreign Policy, 1931-1932.* Berkeley: University of California Press, 1964.

[16] Akira Iriye. *After Imperialism: The Search for a New Order in the Far East, 1921-1931.* Cambridge: Harvard University Press, 1965.

[16a] The British Foreign Office records provided the basis for a new interpretation by Christopher Thorne. *The Limits of Foreign Policy: The West, the League and the Far Eastern Crisis of 1931-1933.* London: Hamish Hamilton, 1973.

[17] Beatrice Farnsworth. *William C. Bullitt and the Soviet Union.* Bloomington: Indiana University Press, 1967; Peter G. Filene, *Americans and the Soviet Experiment: 1917-1933.* Cambridge: Harvard University Press, 1967, deals with public opinion.

[18] Joan Hoff Wilson. *American Business and Foreign Policy: 1920-1933.* Lexington: University of Kentucky Press, 1971.

[19] Lloyd C. Gardner. *Economic Aspects of New Deal Diplomacy.* Madison: University of Wisconsin Press, 1964. Available in paperback.

[20] Herbert Feis. *1933: Characters in Crisis.* Boston: Little, Brown, 1966.

[21] Bryce Wood. *The Making of the Good Neighbor Policy.* New York: Columbia University Press, 1961. Available in paperback.

[22] Alton Frye. *Nazi Germany and the American Hemisphere: 1933-1941.* New Haven: Yale University Press, 1967.

[23] William Kamman. *A Search for Stability: United States Diplomacy toward Nicaragua, 1925-1933.* Notre Dame, Ind.: University of Notre Dame Press, 1968.

[23a] The Cuban revolution received serious attention at one of its crucial points in the volume by Luis E. Agiular. *Cuba: 1933.* Ithaca: Cornell University Press, 1972.

[24] Robert A. Divine. *The Illusion of Neutrality.* Chicago: University of Chicago Press, 1962.

[25] Wayne S. Cole. *Senator Gerald P. Nye and American Foreign Relations.* Minneapolis: University of Minnesota Press, 1962.

[26] John E. Wiltz. *In Search of Peace: The Senate Munitions Inquiry, 1934-1936.* Baton Rouge: Louisiana State University Press, 1963.

[27] Fred L. Israel. *Nevada's Key Pittman.* Lincoln: University of Nebraska Press, 1963.

[28] Manfred Jonas. *Isolationism in America: 1935-1941.* Ithaca: Cornell University Press, 1966. C. David Tompkins, *Senator Arthur H. Vandenberg: The Evolution of a Modern Republican, 1884-1945,* East Lansing: Michigan State University Press, 1970, considers the first stage of the career of an eminent isolationist.

[29] Warren I. Cohen. *The American Revisionists: The Lessons of Intervention in World War I.* Chicago: University of Chicago Press, 1967.

[30] Richard P. Traina. *American Diplomacy and the Spanish Civil War.* Bloomington: Indiana University Press, 1968.

[31] James V. Compton. *The Swastika and the Eagle: Hitler, the United States, and the Origins of World War II.* Boston: Houghton Mifflin, 1967; Saul Friedlaender. *Prelude to Downfall: Hitler and the United States, 1939-1941.* New York: Knopf, 1967.

[32] Robert Dallek. *Democrat and Diplomat: The Life of William E. Dodd.* New York: Oxford University Press, 1968.

[33] Arnold A. Offner. *American Appeasement.* Cambridge: Harvard University Press, 1969.

[34] Arthur D. Morse. *While Six Million Died: A Chronicle of American Apathy.* New York: Random House, 1968.

[35] David S. Wyman. *Paper Walls: America and the Refugee Crisis, 1938-1941.* Amherst: University of Massachusetts Press, 1968; Henry Feingold. *The Politics of Rescue.* New Brunswick, N.J.: Rutgers University Press, 1970.

[36] Warren F. Kimball. *The Most Unsordid Act: Lend-Lease, 1939-1941.* Baltimore: Johns Hopkins Press, 1969. See also Robert H. Jones. *The Roads to Russia: United States Lend-Lease to the Soviet Union.* Norman: University of Oklahoma Press, 1969, and John McVickar Haight, Jr. *American Aid to France: 1938-1940.* New York: Atheneum, 1970. For the story of the Century Group, interventionists, see Mark Lincoln Chadwin. *The Hawks of World War II.* Chapel Hill: University of North Carolina Press, 1968. Available in paperback.

[37] Theodore A. Wilson. *The First Summit.* Boston: Houghton Mifflin, 1969.

[38] Dorothy Borg. *The United States and the Far Eastern Crisis of 1933-1938.* Cambridge: Harvard University Press, 1964.

[39] David J. Lu. *From the Marco Polo Bridge to Pearl Harbor.* Washington: Public Affairs Press, 1961. For its special subject, the American ambassador to China, see Russell D. Buhite. *Nelson T. Johnson and American Policy toward China: 1925-1941.* East Lansing: Michigan State University Press, 1968.

[40] Waldo H. Heinrichs. *American Ambassador: Joseph C. Grew and the Development of the United States Diplomatic Tradition.* Boston: Little, Brown, 1966.

[41] Robert J. C. Butow. *Tojo and the Coming of the War.* Princeton, N.J.: Princeton University Press, 1961. Available in paperback.

[42] Leonard Baker. *Roosevelt and Pearl Harbor.* New York: Macmillan, 1970.

[43] Roberta Wohlstetter. *Pearl Harbor: Warning and Decision.* Stanford: Stanford University Press, 1962. Available in paperback.

· 24 ·

The Domestic Life
of a Global Power, 1945–1970

Richard S. Kirkendall*

AMERICAN life between 1945 and 1970 has been dominated by the nation's giant role in world affairs; but significant developments have taken place at home, and historians have begun to pay attention to them. In the late 1950's, when Hugh G. Cleland surveyed the subject, he needed only two pages and called attention to only seventeen books. Since then, however, historical works have been published in large numbers. Although historical research on the period remains in an early stage, much significant work has been done by professional historians and by others with a historical bent. Their work suggests that as more sources become available the period will attract many scholars for historians are interested in the description, measurement, and explanation of change in human affairs, and America since the end of World War II has been a dynamic place, featuring both movement and resistance to it.

Recent Americans have been examined in a variety of ways. Although a worldly people, their religious life has been studied, chiefly in works that begin much earlier and include a section on the years since 1945. They demonstrate that religion remained an important part of American life, if no longer as important as it once was, and that the nation, once predominantly Protestant, was now pluralistic. They also suggest that for many Americans religious affiliation had replaced national origin as the basis of group identity.[1]

* I wish to thank Dean Armon F. Yanders of the College of Arts and Science, University of Missouri, Columbia, and Michael J. Cassity, a doctoral student in history, for their aid and assistance.

Education and the professions, important and rapidly expanding parts of American life in the recent period, received attention. Historical studies explored the sharp conflicts over philosophies of education, the attack upon and the decline of progressive education, efforts to raise standards, and the development of different types of educational institutions.[2] Examining the medical profession, scholars discussed recent medical progress, provided a profile of the American physician in the middle of the twentieth century, and explored medical licensing and quackery, which continued to be a large part of American life in spite of efforts to suppress it. There is also a study of the profession's pressure group, the American Medical Association, and its battle against Truman's proposal for national health insurance.[3]

The economic boom has attracted even more attention. Harold Vatter's rigorous, critical, and demanding history of the economy in the 1950's is especially important. He drew upon economic theory, focused upon economic growth, recognized accomplishments, such as the avoidance of depression and mass unemployment, and also called attention to weaknesses, especially the slow rate of growth and "structural unemployment."[4]

Most studies in economic history dealt with specific aspects of the economy, including business, which was dynamic and respectable once again in the new era of prosperity. Some Americans were still influenced by the "myth of success" and sought success in the business world.[5] Although a few authors explored small business, which remained numerous and important,[6] most examined the large firms, studying the creation of a multi-divisional, decentralized structure overseen by a large general office staffed by non-operating executives,[7] the recruitment of social scientists to help officials solve personnel problems,[8] the enlargement of management's view of its obligations to the public,[9] and the building of branches throughout the world as the giants became "multinational" corporations.[10]

Specific parts as well as broad themes were investigated. The list of industries included sugar beets, machine tools, and construction. It also included southern textiles, which was plagued by competition from abroad and from synthetic fibers; natural gas and petroleum, industries that enjoyed very rapid growth; and beer, an industry producing a very popular product.[11] And the world of finance—the stock market, life insurance, and banking—attracted historians.[12] Studies have also been made of the declining railroad industry, which was plagued with labor troubles and competition and sought to regain strength through mergers and other moves;[13] of one of the railroad's major competitors, the automobile industry, a major participant in the economic boom;[14] and of the rapidly developing aircraft and aerospace industries.[15] Radio and television, two tremendously influential industries that helped to extend the reach of others and experienced spectacular developments after 1945, have been examined in great detail,[16] and the history of one of their features, country music, has also been written. It became a big business in the period.[17]

Although many firms were large and dynamic, American business did not monopolize power in the economic system. Unions were also important in the postwar years. Studies in this field ranged from the broad survey[18] to explorations of individual unions and labor leaders.[19] The studies present a picture of a strong but troubled giant, capable of exerting a large influence on wages,[20] weakened by corruption, racial discrimination, and automation, growing but doing so more slowly than it had from 1935 to 1945.[21] The movement's pro-capitalist orientation persisted. In fact, the CIO expelled eleven unions in 1949-50 because of their links with communism,[22] and unions even began to endorse profit-sharing plans.[23] Labor-management relations did not become perfectly harmonious, as a study of the six-year Kohler strike reveals in exaggerated form,[24] but even a company with a strong anti-union tradition could learn to live with a union when forced to do so.[25] Labor participated actively in politics, although not always successfully, maintained close and important ties with the Democratic party,[26] and made partially successful efforts, led by George Meany, to root out the corruption that weakened the movement.[27]

Farming also changed significantly, becoming much more efficient and productive while the farm population declined rapidly. Historians paid some attention to these developments. Most studies of the agricultural history of this period, however, emphasized farm politics and farm policy, reflecting the large role of government in agriculture in the post-New Deal period as well as the large interest in political history.[28]

The government's role in economic affairs was one of the largest interests of students of the post-war period. They have explored government efforts to affect the behavior of both corporations and unions.[29] In a major contribution focusing on the oil industry, Gerald Nash argued that cooperation rather than conflict had become the chief characteristic of government-business relations. The leaders of two power blocs—big government and big business—had concluded that their interests, although not identical, could be served by cooperation with one another.[30] This study and others indicate that business power remained substantial. If it had been reduced, it had not been destroyed by the New Deal.[31]

The monetary and fiscal policies of the federal government have been very important forces in recent years, and their story was examined impressively. Friedman and Schwartz stressed the economic importance of the quantity of money, taking issue with those who emphasized government taxing and spending policies,[32] but the latter received even more attention. Several valuable studies explored a "fiscal revolution" involving growing confidence in the ability of fiscal policy to influence economic behavior,[33] and historians began to examine the very large impact of defense spending.[34]

With government so very important, political history could not be ignored, and political history flourished in the decade of the 60's. Much of it was written by political scientists, who made some very valuable suggestions, including the late V.O. Key's challenge to the theory that the voters are controlled by social forces or subconscious urges that propagandists manipulate. Analyzing elections between 1936 and 1960, he concluded that voters make choices and make them rationally.[35]

Political historians have developed little more than restrained enthusiasm for the postwar Presidents. Harry S Truman tops the list. Arthur M. Schlesinger, Sr. reported early in the 1960's that a group of seventy-five leading scholars placed Truman in the top ten among American presidents and rated him "near great," but Schlesinger did not point to Truman's domestic record to justify the ranking.[36] And the literature already contained some dissenting views. Thus, Walter Johnson, in a valuable survey of the presidents from Hoover to Eisenhower, criticized Truman's lack of "artistry in public relations," referred to him as a "willful, bumptious partisan, given to rash outbursts," and found no "great decisions" in domestic policy,[37] while Charles Madison insisted that Truman had not been big enough for his very demanding job.[38] Furthermore, a prominent historian, Thomas A. Bailey, challenged the poll, arguing that it had a liberal Democratic bias and that Truman, whose "remarkable record in foreign affairs" was balanced by a "rather barren record in domestic affairs," was "no better than an average President."[39]

poll, arguing that it had a liberal Democratic bias and that Truman, as one of the better Presidents. A poll of nearly six hundred members of the Organization of American Historians in 1968 ranked him in seventh place and indicated that he was regarded as strong, active, practical, and flexible and as a President of substantial accomplishments.[40]

By 1968, research on the domestic side of the Truman administration was developing rapidly, helped by the increasing availability of sources in the Truman Library.[41] Before the end of the decade, two books on labor policy appeared that provided only slim evidence in support of the view that he was a man of great accomplishments. He did use the labor issue effectively in the 1948 campaign, but he failed to obtain the labor policies that he advocated, although in part at least because of the toughness of the situation that he faced.[42] A study of farm politics and policies found some significant accomplishments, recognized obstacles, but called attention to defects in the administration, including a timid approach to many problems.[43] A study of housing policy placed heavier emphasis on Truman's opposition as a limiting factor and on his accomplishments, although the study concluded that his major victory on public housing in 1949 did not have very significant consequences.[44] A skillful examination of Truman's relations with the Eightieth Congress found "a combination of external circumstances and ineffective presidential leadership" responsible for the "unsatisfactory record" in domestic legislation in 1947-48 and also concluded that Truman was very successful where he most wanted to be: in foreign policy and in the 1948 election.[45] Still other studies called attention to weaknesses in the liberal movement that created difficulties for Truman,[46] praised one of his top advisers, John R. Steelman,[47] described and analyzed Truman's most famous victory, his reelection in 1948,[48] and investigated his often-criticized appointments to the Supreme Court.[49]

Truman's civil rights record has attracted scholars and become a focal point of controversy. In an important book on the desegregation of the armed forces, Richard M. Dalfiume stressed the strength of Truman's commitment in the area, the importance of the opposition in the South and the Army, and the size of his accomplishment.[50] In a broad survey of the civil rights issue, William C. Berman was more critical. In explaining Truman's action, he emphasized political considerations and played down humanitarian concerns, and in appraising Truman's contributions, the author maintained that although Truman "did much to shape and advance the civil rights struggle" and "helped to move the issue of civil rights into the forefront of American life," blacks made only "token gains" during the Truman years. Furthermore, Berman suggested that the President could and should have accomplished much more.[51]

Berman represented the rise of a "revisionist" interpretation of Truman's domestic record that challenges very vigorously his claim to greatness as a President. The most prolific proponent of this brand of revisionism is Barton J. Bernstein. He stressed Truman's weaknesses, including poor appointments, lack of boldness, strength, and strong commitments, and failure to present proposals as vigorously and consistently as was desirable, and he saw those weaknesses, rather than the difficulties in the situation, as chiefly responsible for Truman's problems and failures at home and as a source of later domestic crisis. Bernstein assumed that Truman was free to behave very differently and that other ways of behaving would have had much better results.[52]

Bernstein and other revisionists showed a strong interest in the civil liberties record of the Truman administration. The broader question of civil liberties in the entire postwar era produced a substantial literature and some controversy. While some interpretations stress loyalty programs, the House Un-American Activities Committee, and McCarthyism and suggest that declining liberty was an important theme in the period, others maintain that it featured growing, active, and effective concern for civil liberties.[53] Focusing on Truman, Alan Harper argued that the President was devoted to civil liberties and demonstrated that devotion by trying to safeguard security without damaging individual rights, by vetoing legislative products of the "Red Scare," and by battling against Senator Joseph R. McCarthy. Domestic pressures and the Communist threat largely explained his failure to achieve a better record.[54] Others, however, especially Athan Theoharis, argued that Truman, rather than merely the foe and victim of McCarthyism, actually helped to create it with his anti-Communist activities and his rhetoric about the dangers of communism. Truman helped to create a political climate that McCarthy exploited effectively.[55]

Other interpretations of McCarthyism emphasize forces and people outside the Truman administration and imply that Truman was not significantly responsible. By the early 1960's, the sociological and psychological interpretation developed by Richard Hofstadter and others was very influential. It stresses concerns about status, views McCarthyism as a form of mass politics, and suggests that it had roots in Midwestern Populism and Progressivism.[56] Later, however, this view was challenged by interpretations, developed most fully by Earl Latham, Michael Paul Rogin, and Robert Griffith, that emphasize political factors. These scholars rejected the suggestion that McCarthyism had roots in agrarian protest, maintained that it was supported by an elite rather than by the masses, and insisted that it was chiefly an effort by conservative Republicans to gain power.[57]

The Presidents since Truman can be discussed very briefly for historical writing on their careers had barely begun by 1970. Eisenhower was regarded, according to the 1968 poll, as no better than an average President and as weak, passive, idealistic, flexible, and a leader of small accomplishments, even though Walter Johnson and others argued that he did unify the nation after the bitter late Truman years and preserve the accomplishments of the New and Fair Deals. Episodes involving conflict and apparent conflict of interest, such as the Dixon-Yates and the Sherman Adams affairs and the many gifts to Eisenhower himself, constitute a large part of the small list of publications on the General and his administration.[58] His unpopular farm policy was also examined.[59] While not uncritical, scholars had greater admiration for Kennedy, viewing him as strong, active, and idealistic, yet flexible. They were inclined to praise his departure from Eisenhower's style and such specific features of his presidency as his endorsement of the new economics and his call for broad civil rights legislation, to blame conservatism in Congress and the bureaucracy and the shortage of time available to him for the small size of his list of concrete accomplishments, and to give him some of the credit for Johnson's domestic victories.[60] And that President is not highly regarded by historians even though most regard him as strong and active and his achievements as rather substantial. He remained a puzzle, a strange combination of practicality and inflexibility. Needless to say, by 1970 research on his administration had only begun.[61]

Although Congress was studied, chiefly by political scientists,[62] the recent performance of the Supreme Court attracted even more attention. Especially during Earl Warren's years as Chief Justice, it became a major promoter of change in civil rights, civil liberties, and political representation. The institution, its cases, methods, voting patterns, decisions, and personnel were examined, as was the opposition that it aroused.[63]

Areas of change, as well as promoters of it, were explored. These include the cities,[64] the suburbs,[65] and the West,[66] each moving at a rapid pace. No part of American life, however, generated more scholarly interest than the South. The importance of tradition, the persistence of old patterns and attitudes, and the opposition to change were not ignored,[67] but change received even more attention in the writings of Thomas D. Clark, Dewey W. Grantham, Jr., and others. They stressed the diversification and modernization of southern agriculture, rural electrification, rapid industrialization and urbanization, population movements, improvements in public health, highways and schools, the enlargement of the electorate, the growth of the Republican party, the collapse of the Byrd machine in Virginia, and other features of the dynamic South in the recent period.[68]

The most prominent part of this is the story of change in relations between whites and blacks. That story is also the major illustration of the decline in the influence of racist ideas, a development that was stimulated in part by the nation's role in the world.[69] Many aspects of race relations were explored,[70] including the integration of the armed forces,[71] the desegregation of the schools,[72] and the enfranchisement of southern Negroes.[73] The forces of change that have been examined include the Southern Conference on Human Welfare,[74] the National Association for the Advancement of Colored People and other liberal pressure groups,[75] the Civil Rights Commission,[76] the Justice Department,[77] the sit-ins,[78] and black leaders, especially Martin Luther King, Jr.[79] The studies of resistance range from examinations of racist attitudes in the Catholic Church to the development of "scientific racism."[80] Also included are impressive analyses of "massive resistance" to school integration in Virginia, Arkansas, and other parts of the South in the middle and late 1950's, a campaign that dominated for a time but ultimately failed.[81] There are also studies of Tennessee's "moderate" approach, which enabled the state to avoid large-scale violence and disruption of education but also blocked rapid desegregation and left most students in segregated schools a decade after the Brown case;[82] of the James Meredith episode at the University of Mississippi in 1962, which involved intervention by federal forces to overcome the resistance of the "never, never boys";[83] and of growing conservatism in Georgia, which was expressed in support for Republicans and for George Wallace and involved hostility toward government intervention and belief in white supremacy.[84] As a group, the studies demonstrate that significant changes took place even though not all elements of segregation and discrimination were destroyed in the South.

Increasingly, attention shifted to race relations in the North and West, and historians of the recent period have supplied some help for our efforts to understand them. Subjects studied include the migration out of the South;[85] race relations in California;[86] segregation, discrimination, and poverty in Washington, D.C. and New York City;[87] the limited political influence of black Americans,[88] and the relations between blacks and Jews.[89] Studies of attempts to change the lot of urban blacks extend from the rather cautious efforts of the Chicago Urban League[90] to the riots of the middle and late 1960's[91] and the demands of the "New Left" and "Black Power,"[92] two expressions of intense impatience with the pace of change that developed in the second half of the 1960's. Significantly related work explores the use of police forces and soldiers to manage law and order and quell civil disturbances.[93] Scholars did not ignore the calls for "relevance."

Clearly, the period between 1945 and 1970 has been attracting historians to it. It supplies the historical mind with suitable problems. Life moved at an often bewildering pace, but the story was not one of change alone. Resistance to change and the continuation of old ways have also been features of American life. Historians are excited by the opportunity to sort out the elements of change and the threads of continuity and to explain the combination that they discover.

Recent history has its shortcomings, especially the limited perspective and the obstacles blocking access to sources, but it has its virtues as well. Two pioneers in the study of recent history, Charles A. Beard and James Harvey Robinson, suggested that one of its purposes is to help the student read his daily newspaper. It is designed, in other words, to help him understand the situation in which he finds himself and thus to define the roles that he should play. It helps him to see the forces of change and of resistance that surround him.

FOOTNOTES

[1] Thomas T. McAvoy. *Roman Catholicism and the American Way of Life* and *A History of the Catholic Church in the United States.* Notre Dame: University of Notre Dame Press, 1960, 1969; James Ward Smith and A. Leland Jamison, editors. *Religion in American Life.* Princeton: Princeton University Press, 1961; Edwin Scott Gaustad. *A Religious History of America.* New York: Harper & Row, 1966; Martin E. Marty. *Righteous Empire: The Protestant Experience in America.* New York: Dial, 1970; Charles H. Anderson. *White Protestant Americans: From National Origins to Religious Group.* Englewood Cliffs: Prentice-Hall, 1970.

[2] Willis Rudy. *Schools in an Age of Mass Culture.* Englewood Cliffs: Prentice-Hall, 1965; Lawrence A. Cremin. *The Transformation of the School: Progressivism in American Education, 1876-1957.* New York: Knopf, 1961; Patricia Albjerg Graham. *Progressive Education: From Arcady to Academe, A History of the Progressive Education Association, 1919-1955.* New York: Teachers College Press, 1967; Louis Geiger. *Voluntary Accreditation: A History of the North Central Association, 1945-1970.* Menasha, Wis.: North Central Association of Colleges and Secondary Schools, 1970; Berenice M. Fisher. *Industrial Education: American Ideals and Institutions.* Madison: University of Wisconsin Press, 1967; Donald W. Disbrow. *Schools for an Urban Society.* Lansing: Michigan Historical Commission, 1968; Robert S. Morison, editor. *The Contemporary University.* Boston: Houghton Mifflin, 1966; Burton R. Clark. *The Distinctive College: Antioch, Reed & Swarthmore.* Chicago: Aldine, 1970; and George Knepper. *New Lamps for Old: One Hundred Years of Urban Higher Education at the University of Akron.* Akron: University of Akron Press, 1970.

[3] Corinne Lathrop Gilb. *Hidden Hierarchies: The Professions and Government.* New York: Harper & Row, 1966; George Martin. *Causes and Conflicts: The Centennial History of the Association of the Bar of the City of New York, 1870-1970.* Boston: Houghton Mifflin, 1970; Richard Harrison Shryock. *Medicine in America: Historical Essays* and *Medical Licensing in America, 1650-1965.* Baltimore: Johns Hopkins Press, 1966, 1967; James Harvey Young. *The Medical Messiahs: A Social History of Health Quackery in Twentieth Century America.* Princeton: Princeton University Press, 1967; Donald Meyer. *The Positive Thinkers: A Study of the American Quest for Health, Wealth and Personal Power from Mary Baker Eddy to Norman Vincent Peale.* Garden City: Doubleday, 1965; James G. Burrow. *AMA: Voice of American Medicine.* Baltimore: Johns Hopkins Press, 1963.

[4] *The U. S. Economy in the 1950's: An Economic History.* New York: Norton, 1963.

[5] John G. Cawelti. *Apostles of the Self-Made Man.* Chicago: University of Chicago Press, 1965; Richard Weiss. *The American Myth of Success: From Horatio Alger to Norman Vincent Peale.* New York: Basic Books, 1969.

[6] Harold F. Bennett. *Precision Power: The First Half Century of Bodine Electric Company.* New York: Appleton-Century-Crofts, 1959; Joseph L. Massie.

Blazer and Ashland Oil: A Study in Management. Lexington: University of Kentucky Press, 1960; William J. Parish. *The Charles Ilfeld Company: A Study of the Rise and Decline of Mercantile Capitalism in New Mexico.* Cambridge: Harvard University Press, 1961; James D. Norris. *AZn: A History of the American Zinc Company.* Madison: State Historical Society of Wisconsin, 1968; Maren Lockwood Carden. *Oneida: Utopian Community to Modern Corporation.* Baltimore: Johns Hopkins Press, 1969.

[7] Alfred D. Chandler. *Strategy and Structure: Chapters in the History of the Industrial Enterprise.* Cambridge: M.I.T. Press, 1962; "The Large Industrial Corporation and the Making of the Modern American Economy," Chandler in Stephen E. Ambrose, editor. *Institutions in Modern America: Innovation in Structure and Process.* Baltimore: Johns Hopkins Press, 1967. pp. 71-101.

[8] Loren Baritz. *The Servants of Power: A History of the Use of Social Science in American Industry.* Middletown: Wesleyan University Press, 1960.

[9] Morrell Heald. *The Social Responsibilities of Business: Company and Community, 1900-1960.* Cleveland: Press of Case Western Reserve University, 1970.

[10] Mira Wilkins and Frank Ernest Hill. *American Business Abroad: Ford on Six Continents.* Detroit: Wayne State University Press, 1964; Charles J. Kennedy, editor. *Papers of the Sixteenth Business History Conference.* Lincoln: College of Business Administration, 1969.

[11] Leonard J. Arrington. *Beet Sugar in the West: A History of the Utah-Idaho Sugar Company, 1891-1966.* Seattle: University of Washington Press, 1966; Harless D. Wagoner. *The U. S. Machine Tool Industry from 1900 to 1950.* Cambridge: M.I.T. Press, 1968; Carl W. Condit. *American Building: Materials and Techniques from the First Colonial Settlements to the Present.* Chicago: University of Chicago Press, 1968; Jack Bicksilver. *Cotton Manufacturing in the Southeast: An Historical Analysis.* Atlanta: Georgia State College of Business Administration, 1959; Robert Sidney Smith. *Mill on the Dan: A History of the Dan River Mills, 1882-1950.* Durham: Duke University Press, 1960; Henrietta M. Larson and Kenneth Wiggins Porter. *History of Humble Oil & Refining Company.* New York: Harper, 1959; John L. Loos. *Oil on Stream: A History of the Interstate Oil Pipe Line Company, 1909-1959.* Baton Rouge: Louisiana State University Press, 1959; Harold F. Williamson *et al. The American Petroleum Industry: The Age of Energy 1899-1959.* Vol. II. Evanston: Northwestern University Press, 1963; Alfred M. Leeston *et al. The Dynamic Natural Gas Industry.* Norman: University of Oklahoma Press, 1963; Gilbert C. Fite. *Farm to Factory: A History of the Consumers Cooperative Association.* Columbia: University of Missouri Press, 1965; Stanley Baron. *Brewed in America: A History of Beer and Ale in the United States.* Boston: Little, Brown, 1962.

[12] Robert Sobel. *The Big Board: A History of the New York Stock Market.* New York: Free Press, 1965; Sobel. *Panic on Wall Street: A History of America's Financial Disasters.* New York: Macmillan, 1968; R. Carlyle Buley. *The Equitable Life Assurance Society of the United States, 1859-1964.* 2 vols. New York: Appleton-Century-Crofts, 1967; Robert C. Puth. "Supreme Life: The History of a Negro Life Insurance Company, 1919-1962." *Business History Review* 43: 1-20; No. 1, Spring 1969; John A. Kouwenhoven. *Partners in Banking: An Historical Portrait of a Great Private Bank, Brown Brothers, Harriman & Co., 1818-1968.* Garden City: Doubleday, 1968; Margaret G. Myers. *A Financial History of the United States.* New York: Columbia University Press, 1970; Vincent P. Carosso. *Investment Banking in America: A History.* Cambridge: Harvard University Press, 1970.

[13] John F. Stover. *The Life and Decline of the American Railroad.* New York: Oxford University Press, 1970; Richard C. Overton. *Burlington Route: A History of the Burlington Lines.* New York: Knopf, 1965; Willis Frederick Dunbar. *All Aboard: A History of Railroads in Michigan.* Grand Rapids: Eerdmans, 1969.

[14] Allan Nevins and Frank Ernest Hill. *Ford: Decline and Rebirth, 1933-1962.* New York: Scribner's, 1963; John B. Rae. *The American Automobile: A Brief History.* Chicago: University of Chicago Press, 1965.

[15] Lee Scamerhorn in Robert G. Ferris, editor. *The American West: An Appraisal.* Santa Fe: Museum of New Mexico Press, 1963. pp. 70-80; John B. Rae. *Climb to Greatness: The American Aircraft Industry, 1920-1960.* Cambridge: M.I.T. Press, 1968; G. R. Simonson. "Missiles and Creative Destruction in the American Aircraft Industry, 1956-1961." *Business History Review* 38: 302-314; No. 2, Summer 1964; Loyd S. Swenson, Jr. *et al. This New Ocean: A History of Project Mercury.* Washington: Government Printing Office, 1966; Swenson. "The 'Megamachine' Behind the Mercury Spacecraft." *American Quarterly* 21: 210-227; No. 2, Pt. 1, Summer 1969; see the related study by Donald R. Whitnah. *A History of the United States Weather Bureau.* Urbana: University of Illinois Press, 1961.

[16] Erik Barnouw. *The Golden Web* and *The Image Empire.* New York: Oxford University Press, 1968, 1970.

[17] Bill C. Malone. *Country Music USA: A Fifty-Year History.* Austin: University of Texas Press, 1968.

[18] Philip Taft. *Organized Labor in American History.* New York: Harper & Row, 1964.

[19] Reed C. Richardson. *The Locomotive Engineer, 1863-1963: A Century of Railway Labor Relations and Work Rules.* Ann Arbor: Bureau of Industrial Relations, Graduate School of Business Administration, University of Michigan, 1963; David Brody. *The Butcher Workmen: A Study of Unionization.* Cambridge: Harvard University Press, 1964; Jack Barbash, editor. "David Dubinsky, the ILGWU, and the American Labor Movement: Essays in Honor of David Dubinsky." *Labor History* 9: 3-126; Special Supplement, Spring 1968.

[20] Robert Ozanne. *Wages in Practice and Theory: McCormick and International Harvester, 1860-1960.* Madison: University of Wisconsin Press, 1968.

[21] Irving Bernstein. "The Growth of American Unions, 1945-1960." *Labor History* 2: 131-157; No. 1, Spring 1961; F. Ray Marshall. *Labor in the South.* Cambridge: Harvard University Press, 1967; Albert A. Blum. "Why Unions Grow." *Labor History* 9: 39-72; No. 1, Winter 1968; Joseph Krislov. "Organizing, Union Growth, and the Cycle, 1949-1966." *ibid.* 11: 212-222; No. 2, Spring 1970.

[22] F. S. O'Brien. "The 'Communist-Dominated' Unions in the United States since 1950." *ibid.* 9: 184-209; No. 2, Spring 1968.

[23] I. B. Helburn. "Trade Union Response to Profit-Sharing Plans: 1886-1966." *ibid.* 12: 68-80; No. 1, Winter 1971.

[24] Walter H. Uphoff. *Kohler on Strike: Thirty Years of Conflict.* Boston: Beacon, 1966.

[25] Robert Ozanne. *A Century of Labor-Management Relations at McCormick and International Harvester.* Madison: University of Wisconsin Press, 1967.

[26] Philip Taft. *Labor Politics American Style: The California State Federation of Labor.* Cambridge: Harvard University Press, 1968; J. David Greenstone. *Labor in American Politics.* New York: Knopf, 1969; Gerald Pomper. "Labor Legislation: the Revision of Taft-Hartley in 1953-1954." *Labor History* 6: 143-158; No. 2, Spring 1965; James C. Foster. "1954: A CIO Victory?" *ibid.* 12: 392-408; No. 3, Summer 1971.

[27] John Hutchinson. *The Imperfect Union: A History of Corruption in American Trade Unions.* New York: Dutton, 1970.

[28] Wayne D. Rasmussen. "The Impact of Technological Change on American Agriculture, 1862-1962." *Journal of Economic History* 22: 578-591, No. 4, December 1962; Terry G. Summons. "Animal Feed Additives, 1940-1966." *Agricultural History* 47: 305-313; No. 4, October 1968; John T. Schlebecker. *Cattle Raising on the Plains, 1900-1961.* Lincoln: University of Nebraska Press, 1963;

William J. Block. *The Separation of the Farm Bureau and the Extension Service.* Urbana: University of Illinois Press, 1960; Gladys L. Baker, *et al. Century of Service: The First 100 Years of the United States Department of Agriculture.* Washington: USDA, 1963; Robert L. Tontz. "Memberships of General Farmers' Organizations, United States, 1874-1960." *Agricultural History* 38: 143-156; No. 3, July 1964; Robert J. Morgan. *Governing Soil Conservation: Thirty Years of the New Decentralization.* Baltimore: Johns Hopkins Press, 1966; Vernon W. Ruttan *et al.,* editors. *Agricultural Policy in an Affluent Society.* New York: Norton, 1969.

[29] David Dale Martin. *Mergers and the Clayton Act.* Berkeley: University of California Press, 1959; Donald R. Whitnah. *Safer Skyways: Federal Control of Aviation, 1926-1966.* Ames: Iowa State University Press, 1966; Arthur M. Johnson. *Petroleum Pipelines and Public Policy, 1906-1959.* Cambridge: Harvard University Press, 1967; James Willard Hurst. *The Legitimacy of the Business Corporation in the Law of the United States, 1780-1970.* Charlottesville: University Press of Virginia, 1970; John L. Blackman, Jr. *Presidential Seizure in Labor Disputes.* Cambridge: Harvard University Press, 1967; Bruno Stein. "Wage Stabilization in the Korean War Period: The Role of the Subsidiary Wage Boards." *Labor History* 4: 161-177; No. 2, Spring 1963.

[30] *United States Oil Policy 1890-1964: Business and Government in Twentieth Century America.* Pittsburgh: University of Pittsburgh Press, 1968; see also Herbert H. Lang. "Uranium Mining and the AEC: The Birth Pangs of a New Industry." *Business History Review* 36: 325-333; No. 3, Autumn 1962; Alfred D. Chandler. "The Structure of American Industry in the Twentieth Century: A Historical Overview." *ibid.* 43: 255-281; No. 3, Autumn 1969.

[31] Arthur Selwyn Miller. *The Supreme Court and American Capitalism.* New York: Free Press, 1968; Roy Lubove. *Twentieth-Century Pittsburgh: Government, Business, and Environmental Change.* New York: Wiley, 1969.

[32] Milton Friedman and Anna Jacobson Schwartz. *A Monetary History of the United States, 1867-1960.* Princeton: Princeton University Press, 1963.

[33] Edward S. Flash, Jr. *Economic Advice and Presidential Leadership: The Council of Economic Advisers.* New York: Columbia University Press, 1965; Robert Lekachman. *The Age of Keynes.* New York: Random House, 1966; Herbert Stein. *The Fiscal Revolution in America.* Chicago: University of Chicago Press, 1969.

[34] James L. Clayton. "The Impact of the Cold War on the Economies of California and Utah, 1946-1965." *Pacific Historical Review* 36: 449-473; No. 4, November 1967; Clayton. "An Unhallowed Gathering: The Impact of Defense Spending on Utah's Population Growth, 1940-1964." *Utah Historical Quarterly* 34: 227-242; No. 3, Summer 1966.

[35] *The Responsible Electorate: Rationality in Presidential Voting, 1936-1960.* Cambridge: Harvard University Press, 1966; see also George H. Mayer. *The Republican Party, 1854-1964.* New York: Oxford University Press, 1964; Carl Degler. "American Political Parties and the Rise of the City: An Interpretation." *Journal of American History* 51: 41-59; No. 1, June 1964; Edgar Litt. *The Political Cultures of Massachusetts.* Cambridge: M.I.T. Press, 1965.

[36] *Paths to the Present.* Boston: Houghton Mifflin, 1964. pp. 105, 106.

[37] *1600 Pennsylvania Avenue: Presidents and the People since 1929.* Boston: Little, Brown, 1960, 1963. Books 5-6.

[38] *Leaders and Liberals in 20th Century America.* New York: Ungar, 1961.

[39] *Presidential Greatness: The Image and the Man from George Washington to the Present.* New York: Appleton-Century-Crofts, 1966. Chap. 4 and p. 325.

[40] Gary Maranell. "The Evaluation of Presidents: An Extension of the Schlesinger Polls." *Journal of American History* 57: 104-113, No. 1, June 1970; see also Cabell Phillips. *The Truman Presidency: The History of a Triumphant Succession.* New York: Macmillan, 1966; and Kirkendall. "Harry S. Truman," in

Morton Borden, editor. *America's Eleven Greatest Presidents.* Chicago: Rand McNally, 1971.

[41] Kirkendall, editor. *The Truman Period as a Research Field.* Columbia: University of Missouri Press, 1967.

[42] R. Alton Lee. *Truman and Taft-Hartley: A Question of Mandate.* Lexington: University of Kentucky Press, 1966; Arthur F. McClure. *The Truman Administration and the Problems of Postwar Labor, 1945-1948.* Rutherford: Fairleigh Dickinson University Press, 1969.

[43] Allen J. Matusow. *Farm Policies and Politics in the Truman Years.* Cambridge: Harvard University Press, 1967.

[44] Richard O. Davies. *Housing Reform During the Truman Administration.* Columbia: University of Missouri Press, 1966; see also Davies. "Social Welfare Policies," in Kirkendall. *Truman Period.*

[45] Susan M. Hartmann. *Truman and the Eightieth Congress.* Columbia: University of Missouri Press, 1971.

[46] Alonzo L. Hamby. "The Liberals, Truman, and FDR as Symbol and Myth." *Journal of American History* 56: 859-867; No. 4, March 1970; see also Clifton Brock. *Americans for Democratic Action: Its Role in National Politics.* Washington: Public Affairs, 1962.

[47] William O. Wagnon. "John Roy Steelman: Native Son to Presidential Advisor." *Arkansas Historical Quarterly* 27: 205-225, No. 3, Autumn 1968.

[48] Irwin Ross. *The Loneliest Campaign: The Truman Victory of 1948.* New York: New American Library, 1968; Kirkendall. "Election of 1948," in Arthur M. Schlesinger, Jr. and Fred L. Israel, editors. *History of American Presidential Elections 1789-1968.* 4 vols.; New York: Chelsea House, 1971. pp. 3099-3145.

[49] Kirkendall. "Harold Burton," "Fred M. Vinson," "Tom C. Clark," "Sherman Minton," in Leon Friedman and Fred L. Israel, editors. *The Justices of the United States Supreme Court 1789-1969.* New York: Chelsea House, 1969. Vol. 4. pp. 2615-2718.

[50] *Desegregation of the U. S. Armed Forces: Fighting on Two Fronts, 1939-1953.* Columbia: University of Missouri Press, 1969; see also Monroe Billington. "Freedom to Serve: the President's Committee on Equality of Treatment and Opportunity in the Armed Forces, 1949-1950." *Journal of Negro History* 51: 262-274; No. 4, October 1966.

[51] *The Politics of Civil Rights in the Truman Administration.* Columbus: Ohio State University Press, 1970; see also Berman. "Civil Rights and Civil Liberties," in Kirkendall. *Truman Period*; Harvard Sitkoff. "Harry Truman and the Election of 1948: The Coming of Age of Civil Rights in American Politics." *Journal of Southern History* 37: 597-616; No. 4, November 1971; Robert A. Garson. "The Alienation of the South: A Crisis for Harry S. Truman and the Democratic Party, 1945-1948." *Missouri Historical Review* 64: 448-471; No. 4, July 1970; Richard D. Chesteen. " 'Mississippi Is Gone Home!' A Study of the 1948 Mississippi States' Rights Bolt." *Journal of Mississippi History* 32: 43-59; No. 1, February 1970.

[52] "The Postwar Famine and Price Control, 1946." *Agricultural History* 38: 235-240; No. 4, October 1964; "The Removal of War Production Board Controls on Business, 1944-1946." *Business History Review* 39: 243-260; No. 2, Summer 1965; "Walter Reuther and the General Motors Strike of 1945-1946." *Michigan History* 49: 260-277; No. 3, September 1965; "The Truman Administration and Its Reconversion Wage Policy." *Labor History* 6: 214-231; No. 2, Spring 1965; "The Truman Administration and the Steel Strike of 1946." *Journal of American History* 52: 791-803; No. 4, March 1966; with Allen J. Matusow, editors. *The Truman Administration: A Documentary History.* New York: Harper & Row, 1966; "Reluctance and Resistance: Wilson Wyatt and Veterans' Housing in the Truman Administration." *Register of the Kentucky Historical Society* 65: 47-66; No. 1, January 1967; "Economic Policies," in Kirkendall. *Truman Period*; "Charting a Course Between Inflation and Depression: Secretary of the Treasury Fred

Vinson and the Truman Administration's Tax Bill." *Register of the Kentucky Historical Society* 66: 53-64; No. 1, January 1968; "America in War and Peace: The Test of Liberalism," in Bernstein, editor. *Towards a New Past.* New York: Pantheon, 1968. pp. 289-321; "The Ambiguous Legacy: The Truman Administration and Civil Rights," in Bernstein, editor. *Politics and Policies of the Truman Administration.* Chicago: Quadrangle, 1970. pp. 269-314; "Election of 1952," in Schlesinger and Israel. *Presidential Elections.*

[53] Harold Hyman. *To Try Men's Souls: Loyalty Tests in American History.* Berkeley: University of California Press, 1959; John W. Caughey. *Their Majesties the Mob.* Chicago: University of Chicago Press, 1960; David P. Gardner. *The California Oath Controversy.* Berkeley: University of California Press, 1967; Rodney G. Minott. *Peerless Patriots: Organized Veterans and the Spirit of Americanism.* Washington: Public Affairs, 1962; John P. Roche. *The Quest for the Dream: The Development of Civil Rights and Human Relations in Modern America.* New York: Macmillan, 1963; Milton R. Konvitz. *Expanding Liberties: Freedom's Gains in Postwar America.* New York: Viking, 1966; Thomas C. Reeves. *Freedom and the Foundation: The Fund for the Republic in the Era of McCarthyism.* New York: Knopf, 1969.

[54] *The Politics of Loyalty: The White House and the Communist Issue, 1946-1952.* Westport: Greenwood, 1969.

[55] "The Rhetoric of Politics; Foreign Policy, Internal Security, and Domestic Politics in the Truman Era, 1945-1950," and "The Escalation of the Loyalty Program," in Bernstein. *Truman Administration.* pp. 196-268; "The Threat to Civil Liberties: A Study of Selected Criticisms of the Truman Administration's Loyalty Procedures," in Thomas G. Paterson, editor. *Cold War Critics.* Chicago: Quadrangle, 1971. pp. 266-298; *The Yalta Myths: An Issue in U. S. Politics, 1945-1955.* Columbia: University of Missouri Press, 1970; *Seeds of Repression: Harry S Truman and the Origins of McCarthyism.* Chicago: Quadrangle, 1971.

[56] Hofstadter. *The Paranoid Style in American Politics and Other Essays.* New York: Knopf, 1965; Seymour Martin Lipset and Earl Raab. *The Politics of Unreason: Right-Wing Extremism in America, 1790-1970.* New York: Harper & Row, 1970.

[57] Latham. *The Communist Controversy in Washington: From the New Deal to McCarthy.* Cambridge: Harvard University Press, 1966; *The Intellectuals and McCarthy: The Radical Specter.* Cambridge: M.I.T. Press, 1967; Griffith. *The Politics of Fear: Joseph R. McCarthy and the Senate.* Lexington: University Press of Kentucky, 1970; Griffith. "The Political Context of McCarthyism." *Review of Politics* 33: 24-35; No. 1, January 1971; see also David A. Shannon. "Was McCarthy a Political Heir of LaFollette?" *Wisconsin Magazine of History* 45: 3-9; No. 1, Autumn 1961; Vincent P. De Santis. "American Catholics and McCarthyism." *Catholic Historical Review* 51: 1-30; No. 1, April 1965; David P. and Esther S. Thelen. "Joe Must Go: The Movement to Recall Senator Joseph R. McCarthy." *Wisconsin Magazine of History* 49: 185-209; No. 3, Spring 1966; Allan Nevins. *Herbert H. Lehman and His Era.* New York: Scribner's, 1963; Donald J. Kemper. *Decade of Fear: Senator Hennings and Civil Liberties.* Columbia: University of Missouri Press, 1965; Marvin E. Stormer. *The Making of a Political Leader: Kenneth S. Wherry and the United States Senate.* Lincoln: University of Nebraska Press, 1969.

[58] Louis W. Koenig. *The Invisible Presidency.* New York: Rinehart, 1960; Aaron Wildavsky. *Dixon-Yates: A Study in Power Politics.* New Haven: Yale University Press, 1962; David A. Frier. *Conflict of Interest in the Eisenhower Administration.* Ames: Iowa State University Press, 1969.

[59] Edward L. and Frederick H. Schapsmeier. "Eisenhower and Ezra Taft Benson: Farm Policy in the 1950's." *Agricultural History* 44: 369-378; No. 4, October 1970.

[60] Arthur M. Schlesinger, Jr. *A Thousand Days: John F. Kennedy in the White House.* Boston: Houghton Mifflin, 1965; Aida DiPace Donald, editor. *John F. Kennedy and the New Frontier.* New York: Hill & Wang, 1966; James Tracy Crown. *The Kennedy Literature: A Bibliographical Essay on John F. Kennedy.* New York: New York University Press, 1968; Richard E. Neustadt. *Presidential Power: The Politics of Leadership.* New York: Wiley, 1969; Jim F. Heath. *John F. Kennedy and the Business Community.* Chicago: University of Chicago Press, 1969.

[61] Examples of what has been done are James L. Sundquist. *Politics and Policy: The Eisenhower, Kennedy, and Johnson Years.* Washington: Brookings, 1968; Don F. Hadwiger. "The Freeman Administration and the Poor." *Agricultural History* 45: 21-32; No. 1, January 1971. On other national figures of the 1950's and 1960's see Bert Cochran. *Adlai Stevenson: Patrician Among the Politicians.* New York: Funk and Wagnalls, 1969, and Joseph Bruce Gorman. *Kefauver: A Political Biography.* New York: Oxford University Press, 1971.

[62] For some important examples, see Neil MacNeil. *Forge of Democracy: The House of Representatives.* New York: McKay, 1963; Curtis Arthur Amlund. "Executive-Legislative Imbalance: Truman to Kennedy?" *Western Political Quarterly* 18: 640-645; No. 3, September 1965; Gerald Marwell. "Party, Region and the Dimensions of Conflict in the House of Representatives, 1949-1954." *American Political Science Review* 61: 380-399; No. 2, June 1967; John F. Manley. "Wilbur D. Mills: A Study in Congressional Influence." *American Political Science Review* 63: 442-464; No. 2, June 1969; Randall B. Ripley. *Majority Party Leadership in Congress.* Boston: Little, Brown, 1969.

[63] For examples see Robert J. Harris. *The Quest for Equality: The Constitution, Congress and the Supreme Court.* Baton Rouge: Louisiana State University Press, 1960; Walter F. Murphy. *Congress and the Court.* Chicago: University of Chicago Press, 1962; John D. Weaver. *Warren: The Man, The Court, The Era.* Boston: Little, Brown, 1967; Leo Katcher. *Earl Warren: A Political Biography.* New York: McGraw-Hill, 1967; John D. Sprague. *Voting Patterns of the United States Supreme Court . . . 1889-1959.* Indianapolis: Bobbs-Merrill, 1968; Leon Friedman and Fred L. Israel, editors. *The Justices of the United States Supreme Court, 1789-1969.* New York: Chelsea House, 1969; Richard C. Cortner. *The Apportionment Cases.* Knoxville: University of Tennessee Press, 1970.

[64] Blake McKelvey. *The Emergence of Metropolitan America.* New Brunswick: Rutgers University Press, 1968.

[65] Scott Donaldson. *The Suburban Myth.* New York: Columbia University Press, 1969.

[66] Earl Pomeroy. *The Pacific Slope: A History of California, Oregon, Washington, Idaho, Utah and Nevada.* New York: Knopf, 1965; W. Eugene Hollon. *The Great American Desert Then and Now.* New York: Oxford University Press, 1966; Walton Bean. *California: An Interpretive History.* New York: McGraw-Hill, 1968; Michael Paul Rogin and John L. Shover. *Political Change in California: Critical Elections and Social Movements, 1890-1966.* Westport: Greenwood, 1970.

[67] William H. Nicholls. *Southern Tradition and Regional Progress.* Chapel Hill: University of North Carolina Press, 1960; Kenneth K. Bailey. *Southern White Protestantism in the Twentieth Century.* New York: Harper & Row, 1964; Howard Zinn. *The Southern Mystique.* New York: Knopf, 1964; H. Frank Way, Jr. "Survey Research on Judicial Decisions: The Prayer and Bible Reading Cases." *Western Political Quarterly* 21: 189-205; No. 2, June 1968; Sheldon Hackney. "Southern Violence." *American Historical Review* 74: 906-925; No. 3, February 1969.

[68] Clark. *The Emerging South.* New York: Oxford University Press, 1961; Clark and Albert D. Kirwan. *The South Since Appomattox: A Century of Re-*

gional Change. New York: Oxford University Press, 1967; Grantham. *The Democratic South.* Athens: University of Georgia Press, 1963; Grantham. "The South and the Reconstruction of American Politics." *Journal of American History* 53: 227-246; No. 2, September 1966; Paul Casdorph. *A History of the Republican Party in Texas, 1865-1965.* Austin: Pemberton, 1965; J. Harvie Wilkinson III. *Harry Byrd and the Changing Face of Virginia Politics, 1945-1966.* Charlottesville: University of Virginia Press, 1968; George Brown Tindall. *The Disruption of the Solid South.* Athens: University of Georgia Press, 1971.

[69] Thomas F. Gossett. *Race: The History of an Idea in America.* Dallas: Southern Methodist University Press, 1963.

[70] For overviews see August Meier and Elliott M. Rudwick. *From Plantation to Ghetto: An Interpretive History of American Negroes.* New York: Hill & Wang, 1966; and C. Vann Woodward. *The Strange Career of Jim Crow.* 2nd rev. ed. New York: Oxford University Press, 1966.

[71] In addition to Dalfiume and Billington see Richard J. Stillman, II. *Integration of the Negro in the U. S. Armed Forces.* New York: Praeger, 1968.

[72] Sam P. Wiggins. *The Desegregation Era in Higher Education.* Berkeley: McCutchan, 1966; Henry Allen Bullock. *A History of Negro Education in the South: From 1619 to the Present.* Cambridge: Harvard University Press, 1967; Gary Orfield. *The Reconstruction of Southern Education: The Schools and the 1964 Civil Rights Act.* New York: Wiley-Interscience, 1969.

[73] Andrew Buni. *The Negro in Virginia Politics, 1902-1965.* Charlottesville: University of Virginia Press, 1967.

[74] Thomas A. Krueger. *And Promises to Keep: The Southern Conference for Human Welfare, 1938-1948.* Nashville: Vanderbilt University Press, 1967.

[75] Wilson Record. *Race and Radicalism: The NAACP and the Communist Party in Conflict.* Ithaca: Cornell University Press, 1964; Loren Miller. *The Petitioners: The Story of the Supreme Court of the United States and the Negro.* New York: Pantheon, 1966; Robert Zangrando. "The Organized Negro: The National Association for the Advancement of Colored People and Civil Rights," in James C. Curtis and Lewis L. Gould. editors. *The Black Experience in America.* Austin: University of Texas Press, 1970. pp. 145-171; Clifford M. Lytle. "The History of the Civil Rights Bill of 1964." *Journal of Negro History* 51: 275-296; No. 4, October 1966.

[76] Foster Rhea Dulles. *The Civil Rights Commission: 1957-1965.* East Lansing: Michigan State University Press, 1968.

[77] Allan Lichtman. "The Federal Assault Against Voting Discrimination in the Deep South, 1957-1967." *Journal of Negro History* 54: 346-367; No. 4, October 1969.

[78] Arthur I. Waskow. *From Race Riot to Sit-In, 1919 and the 1960's: A Study in the Connections between Conflict and Violence.* Garden City: Doubleday, 1966.

[79] John W. Rathbun. "Martin Luther King: The Theology of Social Action." *American Quarterly* 20: 38-53; No. 1, Spring 1968; Marcus H. Boulware. *The Oratory of Negro Leaders: 1900-1968.* Westport: Negro Universities Press, 1969; S. P. Fullinwider. *The Mind and Mood of Black Americans: 20th Century Thought.* Homewood: Dorsey, 1969; David L. Lewis. *King: A Critical Biography.* New York: Praeger, 1970.

[80] William A. Osborne. *The Segregated Covenant: Race Relations and American Catholics.* New York: Herder, 1967; Monroe Billington. "Public School Integration in Oklahoma, 1954-1963." *Historian* 26: 521-537; No. 4, August 1964; R. Ray McCain. "Reaction to the United States Supreme Court Segregation Decision of 1954." *Georgia Historical Quarterly* 52: 371-385; No. 4, December 1968; I. A. Newby. *Challenge to the Court: Social Scientists and the Defense of Segregation, 1954-1966.* Baton Rouge: Louisiana State University Press, 1967.

[81] Bob Smith. *They Closed Their Schools: Prince Edward County, Virginia, 1951-1964.* Chapel Hill: University of North Carolina Press, 1965; Numan V.

Bartley. *The Rise of Massive Resistance: Race and Politics in the South During the 1950's.* Baton Rouge: Louisiana State University Press, 1969.
[82] Hugh Davis Graham. *Crisis in Print: Desegregation and the Press in Tennessee.* Nashville: Vanderbilt University Press, 1967.
[83] James W. Silver. *Mississippi: The Closed Society.* New York: Harcourt, Brace and World, 1964, 1966; Russell H. Barrett. *Integration at Ole Miss.* Chicago: Quadrangle, 1965.
[84] Numan V. Bartley. *From Thurmond to Wallace: Political Tendencies in Georgia, 1948-1968.* Baltimore: Johns Hopkins Press, 1970.
[85] T. Lynn Smith. "The Redistribution of the Negro Population of the United States, 1910-1960." *Journal of Negro History* 51: 155-173; No. 3, July 1966; Rudolph J. Vecoli. *The People of New Jersey.* Princeton: Van Nostrand, 1965.
[86] Roger Daniels and Harry H. L. Kitano. *American Racism: Exploration of the Nature of Racism.* Englewood Cliffs: Prentice-Hall, 1970.
[87] Oscar Handlin. *The Newcomers: Negroes and Puerto Ricans in a Changing Metropolis.* Cambridge: Harvard University Press, 1959; Nathan Glazer and Daniel Patrick Moynihan. *Beyond the Melting Pot: The Negroes, Puerto Ricans, Jews, Italians and Irish of New York City.* Cambridge: M.I.T. and Harvard University Press, 1963; Constance McLaughlin Green. *The Secret City: A History of Race Relations in the Nation's Capital.* Princeton: Princeton University Press, 1967; Gilbert Osofsky. "The Enduring Ghetto." *Journal of American History* 55: 243-255; No. 2, September 1968; Herman D. Bloch. *The Circle of Discrimination: An Economic and Social Study of the Black Man in New York.* New York: New York University Press, 1969.
[88] Harold L. Wolman and Norman C. Thomas. "Black Interests, Black Groups, and Black Influence in the Federal Policy Process: The Cases of Housing and Education." *Journal of Politics* 32: 875-897; No. 4, November 1970; John Adrian Strayer. "The American Policy Process and the Problems of Poverty and the Ghetto." *Western Political Quarterly* 24: 45-51; No. 1, March 1971.
[89] Robert G. Weisbord and Arthur Stein. *Bittersweet Encounter: The Afro-American and the American Jew.* Westport: Negro Universities, 1970; see also Charles Herbert Stember *et al. Jews in the Mind of America.* New York: Basic Books, 1966; Max Vorspan and Lloyd P. Gartner. *History of the Jews of Los Angeles.* San Marino: Huntington Library, 1970; on other groups see S. W. Kung. *Chinese in American Life: Some Aspects of Their History, Status, Problems, and Contributions.* Seattle: University of Washington Press, 1962; Betty Lee Sung. *Mountain of Gold: The Story of the Chinese in America.* New York: Macmillan, 1967; Theodore Saloutos. *The Greeks in the United States.* Cambridge: Harvard University Press, 1964; Angie Debo. *A History of the Indians of the United States.* Norman: University of Oklahoma Press, 1970.
[90] Arvarh E. Strickland. *History of the Chicago Urban League.* Urbana: University of Illinois Press, 1966.
[91] Robert M. Fogelson. "From Resentment to Confrontation: The Police, the Negroes, and the Outbreak of the Nineteen-Sixties Riots." *Political Science Quarterly* 83: 217-247; No. 2, June 1968; Robert H. Connery, editor. "Urban Riots: Violence and Social Change." *Proceedings of the Academy of Political Science* 29: 1-190; 1968; Joseph Boskin. "The Revolt of the Urban Ghettos, 1964-1967." *The Annals of the American Academy of Political and Social Science* 382: 1-14; March 1969; Hugh Davis Graham and Ted Robert Gurr. *Violence in America.* Washington: Government Printing Office, 1969; Richard Hofstadter and Michael Wallace, editors. *American Violence: A Documentary History.* New York: Knopf, 1970.
[92] Truman Nelson. *The Right of Revolution.* Boston: Beacon Press, 1968; Ronald Berman. *America in the Sixties: An Intellectual History.* New York: Free Press, 1968; Christopher Lasch. *The Agony of the American Left.* New York: Knopf, 1969; Allen J. Matusow. "From Civil Rights to Black Power: The Case

of SNCC, 1960-1966," in Bernstein and Matusow, editors. *Twentieth Century America: Recent Interpretations.* New York: Harcourt, Brace & World, 1969. On the declining years of the "Old Left" see David A. Shannon. *The Decline of American Communism: A History of the Communist Party of the United States since 1945.* New York: Harcourt, Brace, 1959; David J. Saposs. *Communism in American Politics.* Washington: Public Affairs, 1960; Karl M. Schmidt. *Henry A. Wallace: Quixotic Crusade, 1948.* Syracuse: Syracuse University Press, 1960; William C. Pratt. "Glen H. Taylor: Public Image and Reality." *Pacific Northwest Quarterly* 60: 10-16; No. 1, January 1969; F. Ross Peterson. "Fighting the Drift Toward War: Glen H. Taylor, the 1948 Progressives, and the Draft." *ibid.,* 61: 41-45; No. 1, January 1970; Edward L. and Frederick H. Schapsmeier. *Prophet in Politics: Henry A. Wallace and the War Years, 1940-1965.* Ames: Iowa State University Press, 1970; Alan Schaffer. *Vito Marcantonio, Radical in Congress.* Syracuse: Syracuse University Press, 1966; Lawrence S. Wittner. *Rebels Against War: The American Peace Movement, 1941-1960.* New York: Columbia University Press, 1969.

[93] James Q. Wilson. *Varieties of Police Behavior: The Management of Law and Order in Eight Communities.* Cambridge: Harvard University Press, 1968; Robin Higham, editor. *Bayonets in the Streets: The Use of Troops in Civil Disturbances.* Lawrence: University Press of Kansas, 1969.

· 25 ·

The United States
in World Affairs Since 1945

Gaddis Smith

THE historian dealing with the history of American foreign relations since the end of the Second World War confronts three special problems: first, the size and complexity of the subject; second, the diversity, immensity, and partial inaccessibility of sources; and third, the distorting impact of the Vietnam war on the perceptions of both the interpreter of the past and his students.[1]

Man's understanding of history is always shaped by influences arising in the present. There is no such thing as absolute historical objectivity, only the necessity to seek it. But in no realm of historical discussion is that search more difficult than in contemporary diplomatic history. Because of the searing impact of the nation's involvement in Vietnam in the 1960's and early 1970's the search for objectivity, difficult enough in the most placid times, became extraordinary and often charged with emotion.[2]

The New Scope of Diplomatic History

Diplomatic history was never quite so narrow as some of its critics have charged. Although the most unimaginative diplomatic historians may have confined themselves to paraphrasing the formal exchange of diplomatic documents, telling the reader what one clerk wrote to another clerk, the best strove to demonstrate how a nation's foreign policy was both a product of domestic political, economic, social, and intellectual currents, and a reaction to the foreign policies of other nations. "Multi-archival research" was the maxim of the most diplomatic historians. Their goal was to analyze what happened within all of the governments whose interactions were the substance of international affairs.

543

Nevertheless, the events in diplomatic history were relatively simple until the Second World War, and so was the task of the diplomatic historian. The Secretary of State was almost always the only principal adviser to the President on foreign affairs and the chief diplomatic negotiator. The Department of State had no institutional rivals. American diplomatic representatives abroad were few in number and they carried important responsibilities. The large core of diplomacy dealt with Anglo-American relations. What remained—occasional concern with the Far East, condescending relations with Latin America, sporadic interchange with other European nations—was peripheral. The subject matter of diplomacy was limited, traditional, and easily understood by historians: maritime rights, boundaries, debt settlement, and treaties of peace and commerce. It was quite possible for one historian to write a definitive account of any of the important episodes of early American diplomatic history or even a reasonably adequate survey of policy toward an entire region over decades.[3] The job required studying the diplomatic correspondence of the participating nations, the private papers of the small number of easily identifiable main actors, a few newspapers to get a grasp of public opinion, and the legislative record where appropriate. Not easy, but manageable. Occasionally the records of a department other than State—e.g., War, Navy, Treasury—had to be looked at, or the role of non-governmental institutions such as banks, exporters, trade associations, peace societies, or missionaries had to be noted. But those occasions were rare.

The Second World War introduced a revolution for the practitioner and the historian of American diplomacy. The geographical area of American concern expanded to cover the globe while relations with Great Britain were no longer of central importance. New agencies and instruments became an essential part of foreign relations.[4] Now the historian had to understand foreign aid, the complexities of international trade and monetary arrangements, intelligence gathering and evaluation, undercover activities, propaganda (or euphemistically "information") transmission, the United Nations and its subsidiary organizations, arms control and weapons technology, and, above all, military planning and operations. The State Department, once an office no bigger than a country bank, acquired thousands of employees and supervised more than a hundred and fifty overseas embassies—while losing its dominant role in the conduct of foreign policy. The Defense Department developed an international affairs component parallel to and often more influential than the State Department. After the death of John Foster Dulles in 1959, the Secretary of State ceased to be an officer of first importance for the conduct of foreign affairs.[5] He and his Department were over-shadowed by special advisers to the President for national security affairs and their staffs in the White House—McGeorge Bundy for President John F. Kennedy, Walt W. Rostow for Lyndon B. Johnson, and Henry Kissinger for Richard M. Nixon.[6] The role of public opinion in shaping foreign policy or in being manipulated to advance foreign policy objectives became more complex and controversial.[7] In short, the boundaries between foreign and domestic affairs, never sharp even in the simplest of eras, disappeared altogether after 1945.

Primary Source Material

Before the Second World War the diplomatic historian could rely heavily on the extensive documents published by the Department of of State as *Foreign Relations of the United States: Diplomatic Papers.*[8] This monumental series first appeared in 1862. Recently the volumes, seven or eight a year, appear about twenty-five years after the events they document. Thus, in 1973 the volumes for 1947 and 1948 were being published. The *Foreign Relations* volumes contain a rich selection of cables exchanged between the State Department and American em-bassies abroad, memoranda written within the Department, some cor-respondence between the Department and other Government agencies, and records of international conferences. Most of the documents were originally secret or top secret. The selection process and editing for publication are objective and accurate. This is excellent material—pro-vided that (a) the historian and teacher are willing to wait twenty-five years or more; and (b) that the Department of State remained at the center of events. Neither proviso is likely to be true.

If the average individual becomes aware of world affairs, even on the most superficial level, about the age of twelve and before that age acquires no really usable memories of complicated national and inter-national events, then the high school student at sixteen or the college student at twenty requires an historical introduction to events only four to eight years old. That means that the Presidency of Lyndon Johnson could be as remote as that of Andrew Johnson as far as a teenage student in the mid-1970's is concerned. Unfortunately, as the pace and complexity of events increase so does the time lag between the events and publication of the first thoroughly documented histories. Reliable histories of the entry of the United States into the Second World War appeared about a decade after the event. Twenty-five years later we were only beginning to get a good inside look at the diplomacy and decision-making of the late 1940's, the crucial years when the Cold War began.[9]

The State Department at least is beginning to open up some materials for the late 1940's. But scholars as yet have no access to records of the National Security Council,[10] the Joint Chiefs of Staff after 1945, the Central Intelligence Agency, or highly classified materials in the files of the Presidents. Under the Freedom of Information Act, government records are supposed to be open to examination unless they are classified for reasons of national security. In the realm of foreign affairs, virtually all papers less than twenty-five years old are classified.[11]

What then is the historian to do? He can turn to special collections of material the Government chooses to release, such as the famous *China White Paper* of 1949,[12] but he must realize that papers compiled and released for a special purpose must be used with caution. He can turn for the subject of Vietnam to the huge collection compiled within the Department of Defense, popularly known as *The Pentagon Papers,* and published over the Government's objections.[13] He can read the memoirs of the leaders and their aides, men able to use and profit from classified material in their possession not available to independent researchers.[14] He can wade through Congressional hearings and share the frustration of Congressmen at the increasing reticence and secrecy of officials.[15] Finally, he can rely on newspapers in the hope that nothing important can remain secret for very long.

The Distorting Impact of Vietnam

Historians, like all thinking members of a society, engage in a search for mistakes of the past which can be identified as causes of problems in the present. As problems change, perceptions of the past change with them. This is one cause of the phenomenon of "revisionism" by which old interpretations are challenged and even overthrown—until replaced in turn by newer revisions.[16]

The Vietnam war has challenged the basic consensual framework within which a generation of students was taught to view the past. This framework, which might be called "the Great Cycle Theory," was founded on the old belief in the exceptional moral character of the United States. This country, alone among the great powers, was conceived in liberty and dedicated to justice. Furthermore, the physical power and the intellectual talent of the United States were so great that, if it could only be properly linked to moral purpose, there was nothing in the world which the United States could not achieve and no tragedies which it could not prevent.

The theory as applied to the international behavior of the United States in the twentieth century is implicit in virtually every textbook written between 1945 and 1960. It cropped up in newspaper editorials, speeches by Presidents, and commencement addresses. It is filled with a sense of idealism and responsibility. It goes something like this: The United States delayed too long its intervention in the First World War, because the anachronistic influence of isolationism blinded Americans to their vital interest in world order. Fortunately, under the inspiring leadership of Woodrow Wilson, the United States emerged from isolation, brought the war to an end, and shaped a new world order designed to make the world safe for democracy. Then came the first catastrophic downturn in the cycle. The Senate rejected the Versailles Treaty and concomitant American membership in the League of Nations. The nation returned to partial isolationism rejecting responsibility for preserving world peace.

American abdication of leadership in the 1920's and 1930's—so the theory goes—was a major contributing cause to the unchecked rise of totalitarianism and aggression in Europe and Asia and to the outbreak of the Second World War. Between 1939 and 1941 the cycle turned again. The United States resumed its proper role, entered the Second World War following the Japanese attack on Pearl Harbor, and led the coalition which defeated the Axis—only to confront a continuing threat, bearing many of the attributes of Nazi Germany, in the shape of Stalinist Russia and the world Communist movement that marched to Stalin's orders. Would the United States relapse yet again into isolation and irresponsibility, stand aside in the face of threatened aggression, and by failing to act in time contribute to an inevitable Third World War? The theory answers that question with a resounding "No."

Rather than stand aside, the United States took up the "second chance" seldom offered to an individual and much less to a nation. The second chance had three aspects: political, military, and economic. Politically the United States became the principal organizer and most powerful member of the United Nations, thus redeeming the formerly repudiated vision of Woodrow Wilson.[17] And when Soviet recalcitrance limited the effectiveness of the United Nations, we organized the North Atlantic Treaty Organization and a network of other security pacts around the world.[18] Economically, we supported the reconstruction of Europe through the Marshall Plan and led in the creation of a multilateral world monetary and trading system designed to prevent the narrow nationalism that had restricted trade, increased unemployment, and indirectly contributed to aggression between the First and Second World Wars.[19] Militarily, after a brief indulgence in excessive cutbacks, we maintained the force necessary to back our diplomacy and deter aggression.[20]

The theory gives a particularly self-congratulatory picture of the years 1945-1953 when President Harry S. Truman and such advisers as Secretaries of State George C. Marshall and Dean Acheson made the United States the defender of the Free World—proclaiming the Truman Doctrine in 1947 to defend nations against internal subversion or external aggression (the beginning of "Containment");[21] saving Western Europe from economic and political collapse with the Marshall Plan also proclaimed in 1947; creating NATO; rearming Europe; bringing West Germany into the defense system of the West;[22] converting Japan from a ruined enemy to a valued ally;[23] and, above all, courageously meeting Communist aggression in Korea.[24] This was the heroic age, according to the theory, when the United States abandoned isolationism forever, when Congress and the President worked together, when the American people learned and shouldered the cost of leadership.

The heroic age was followed, according to the theory, by an unimaginative holding operation during the eight years of the presidency of Dwight D. Eisenhower—no retreat into irresponsibility, but no acceptance of further responsibility either.[25] Then in 1961 came the inauguration of President John F. Kennedy. In the romantic view of Kennedy and those who shared his view of the world, and that included many writers of contemporary history, the United States began to move again. Mistakes were made and admitted (the Bay of Pigs). But the dangerous confrontation with the Soviet Union over missiles in Cuba was masterfully handled, making way for Soviet-American recognition that each could destroy the other. With the Test Ban Treaty in the summer of 1963, the Cold War seemed to be over.[26]

Then everything seemed to go wrong. President Kennedy was killed by an assassin's bullet. Under President Johnson, the small, almost unnoticed commitment in Vietnam grew into the longest, third largest, and domestically the most disruptive war in American history.[27] Why Vietnam? The question was essentially historical and involved the nation, whether everyone realized it or not, in a debate over the meaning of recent history.

Three Versions of Vietnam

There were three basic historical interpretative positions which divided the country over Vietnam. First, was the official justification which linked Vietnam to the cycle theory. Vietnam represented another challenge of Communist aggression to the Free World and to the determination of the United States. Vietnam was another Korea. To allow Vietnam to fall would cause small nations everywhere to lose faith in the United States.

To accept a Communist victory at the negotiating table would be akin to the betrayal of Czechoslovakia by France and Britain at Munich in 1938 —and, by extension, might be the prelude to the Third World War.[28]

But the official version lost credibility as the war and its horrors continued year after year. Perhaps the United States had made a mistake. Vietnam was not like Korea. We should have known better. Instead, with the best of intentions we became mired in an unwinnable conflict against a population that wanted above all to see Europeans (the French fought the same war from 1946 to 1954 when they tried and failed to recreate their colonial empire in Indochina) and Americans out of their country. The Vietcong and the North Vietnamese were not mere tools of Moscow and/or Peking, but tough and independent people fighting for their own purposes, purposes which did not threaten the national security of the United States. This view of the Vietnam war might be termed Establishment dissent. It did not question the basic validity of American foreign policy since 1945. It simply argued that Vietnam did not fit the pattern, that our involvement was an honest, if tragic, error.[29]

The third way of relating Vietnam to history was to say that American involvement involved no mistake at all, but rather was a deliberate continuation of policies in force at least since 1945. This is the left revisionist argument. It sees American foreign policy as the inevitable result of the structure of the American economy and social system. The drive to secure expanding markets and adequate supplies of raw materials, so the argument goes, leads the United States to oppose revolution everywhere, to organize allies and client states and to give protection to their reactionary governments, and to maintain an expensive military-industrial complex both as an instrument of foreign policy and as a profitable activity for the economy. Whereas the official justification of the war in Vietnam equated and thus glorified the war with earlier triumphs, the left revisionist explained and condemned the past by seeing it as a consequence of the same forces that produced Vietnam.[30]

All three ways of interpreting the Vietnam war partake of a characteristic American arrogance. The official version urges the United States to assume responsibility for developments that are really beyond the power of the United States to control. The Establishment dissenters also see American actions—in this case honest mistakes—as the prime causes of international events. The left revisionists in their way are the greatest believers in the myth of American omnipotence. The world they see is shaped almost entirely by the American counter-revolution. All three versions pay little attention to the behavior and nature of other people and nations—either in arguing for policies or writing history. The books which show a sensitive awareness of the other side of the equation, of, for example, Vietnamese politics and culture, were rare indeed.[31]

The Nixon-Kissinger Era

Richard M. Nixon was inaugurated as President in January 1969. The student of history who at that point attempted to predict the new President's policies on the basis of his previous behavior would have been led astray. During his first term, the President and his principal adviser for foreign affairs accomplished the most significant shift in foreign policy since 1945. They abandoned, in effect, the cycle theory.[32]

President Johnson had withdrawn as a candidate for re-election in 1968 because he doubted his ability to govern the country in the face of divisive domestic opposition to the Vietnam war. Johnson's error was to remain a captive of the cycle theory, to believe that the Vietnam war was like the Korean war and that American military operations in both determined whether the Free World would retain the power and credibility to resist Communist aggression.

Johnson was also partially in thrall to the "zero sum game" approach to foreign policy so characteristic of the Cold War. A zero sum game is a contest in which player A loses to the extent player B wins. For example, if two players roll dice against each other and A loses $9, then B wins $9. The zero sum game approach to foreign policy viewed every gain to the Soviet Union as a loss for the United States and *vice versa*. The greatest exemplar of this approach was Secretary of State Dean Acheson in the Truman administration, but the intellectual disciples and descendants of Acheson lingered into the late 1960's.

A third attribute of American policy and perception in the Cold War was also still present in the Johnson presidency. James Forrestal, Secretry of Defense under Truman, once observed that the principal export of the Soviet Union was chaos. The unstated corollary was that wherever any chaos existed it must be a Soviet export, and must also be intended as a threat to the United States. This attitude blinded Americans to the reality that the world is full of natural, locally produced chaos which arises and runs its course quite independent of deliberate policy by the Soviet Union or any great power.

In terms of his previous ideological hardline against Communism and his denunciations of the idea of opening relations with Communist China, one would have expected Richard Nixon to have continued the attitudes of the Cold War and perhaps even reverted to the rigid rhetoric of the 1940's and 1950's. Instead he adopted the theories of former Harvard Professor Kissinger that the postwar era of bilateral confrontation was over. A multipolar world had emerged with the United States, the Soviet Union, China, Japan, and Western Europe as the five centers of power. The relative power of the United States had declined in the process. The

Nixon-Kissinger strategy was based on seeking accommodation with Russia and China within this fluid five-power system. Thus, the President's startling visit to Peking in 1972, his subsequent visit to Moscow (both firsts in American history), progress on Strategic Arms Limitation Talks (SALT), a high level of trade with the Soviet Union, and virtual establishment of diplomatic relations with China. Simultaneously, and partly as a result of lessened tension with Russia and China, the United States withdrew all ground forces from Vietnam and in January 1973 negotiated a precarious cease-fire in that conflict. The weight of scholarly opinion in 1973 was that a new phase of foreign policy had been entered and the transition in assumptions was as significant as that which occurred, for example, between 1914 and 1917.[33]

FOOTNOTES

[1] This essay deals mainly with books published since 1961. The quickest way to get an overview of the immense literature is by consulting the reviews in the quarterly *Foreign Affairs*, a publication of the Council on Foreign Relations, New York. See the ten-year bibliographies published by the Council. The volume for 1962-72 will appear in 1974, edited by Janis A. Kreslins. Henry L. Roberts compiled the 1952-62 volume. New York: R. R. Bowker [for the Council on Foreign Relations], 1964. Consult these bibliographies for literature on geographical regions, such as Latin America or the Middle East, excluded from this essay.

[2] A good survey of the entire period is Walter LaFeber. *America, Russia, and the Cold War, 1945-1971*. 2nd edition. New York: Wiley, 1972. See also Seyom Brown. *The Faces of Power: Constancy and Change in United States Foreign Policy from Truman to Johnson*. New York: Columbia University Press, 1968.

[3] Three examples of traditional diplomatic history are: Samuel Flagg Bemis. *The Diplomacy of the American Revolution* [first published by the American Historical Association]. Reissued Bloomington: Indiana University Press, 1957; A. Whitney Griswold. *The Far Eastern Policy of the United States*. New York: Harcourt, 1938; New Haven: Yale University Press, 1962; and Dexter Perkins. *The Monroe Doctrine, 1823-1826*. Cambridge: Harvard University Press, 1927; Gloucester: Peter Smith, 1965.

[4] Valuable books on new agencies, instruments and issues are: Harry Howe Ransom. *The Intelligence Establishment*. Cambridge: Harvard University Press, 1970; John D. Montgomery. *The Politics of Foreign Aid: American Experience in Southeast Asia*. New York: Praeger [for the Council on Foreign Relations], 1962; Edward S. Mason. *Foreign Aid and Foreign Policy*. New York: Harper and Row [for the Council on Foreign Relations], 1964; Richard N. Gardner. *Sterling-Dollar Diplomacy: The Origins and the Prospects of our International Economic Order*. New York: McGraw-Hill, 1969; Paul Y. Hammond. *Organizing for Defense: The American Military Establishment in the Twentieth Century*. Princeton: Princeton University Press, 1961; Warner R. Schilling and others. *Strategy, Politics, and Defense Budgets*. New York: Columbia University Press, 1962; Harold A. Hovey. *United States Military Assistance: A Study of Policies and Practices*. New York: Praeger, 1965; Ruth B. Russell. *The United Nations and United States Security Policy*. Washington: Brookings Institution, 1968; Lincoln P. Bloomfield. *The United Nations and U. S. Foreign Policy: A New Look at the National Interest*. Boston: Little, Brown, 1967; Eugene B. Skolnikoff. *Science, Technology and*

American Foreign Policy. Cambridge: M.I.T. Press, 1967; Richard G. Hewlett and Francis Duncan. *Atomic Shield, 1947-1952,* Vol. II in the official *History of the United States Atomic Energy Commission.* University Park: Pennsylvania State University Press, 1970; Alice Kimball Smith. *A Peril and a Hope: The Scientists' Movement in America, 1945-1947.* Chicago: University of Chicago Press, 1965; Bernhard G. Bechhoefer. *Postwar Negotiations for Arms Control.* Washington: Brookings Institution, 1961; Harold Karan Jacobson and Eric Stein. *Diplomats, Scientists, and Politicians: The United States and the Nuclear Test Ban Negotiations.* Ann Arbor: University of Michigan Press, 1966; Robert G. Carey. *The Peace Corps.* New York: Praeger, 1970; Lester R. Brown. *Seeds of Change: The Green Revolution and Development in the 1970's.* New York: Praeger [for the Overseas Development Council], 1970.

[5] Books on or by the two most powerful Secretaries of State are: Dean Acheson. *Present at the Creation: My Years in the State Department.* New York: Norton, 1969; Michael A. Guhin. *John Foster Dulles: A Statesman and His Times.* New York: Columbia University Press, 1972; Gaddis Smith. *Dean Acheson.* New York: Cooper Square Publishers, 1972.

[6] For the role of special advisers and broad insight into the Kennedy and Johnson administrations see Arthur M. Schlesinger, Jr. *A Thousand Days: John F. Kennedy in the White House.* Boston: Houghton Mifflin, 1965; Walt W. Rostow. *The Diffusion of Power: An Essay in Recent History.* New York: Macmillan, 1972; David Halberstam. *The Best and the Brightest.* New York: Random House, 1972. On Kissinger see footnote 32.

[7] This complex subject is introduced in James N. Rosenau, editor. *Domestic Sources of Foreign Policy.* New York: Free Press [for the Princeton Center of International Studies], 1967.

[8] Washington: U. S. Government Printing Office.

[9] Compare Herbert Feis, *The Road to Pearl Harbor: The Coming of the War Between the United States and Japan,* Princeton: Princeton University Press, 1950, with the absence of a comprehensive account based on access to archives, for example, the crisis over the Soviet delay in withdrawing from Iran in 1946.

[10] The most famous document of the National Security Council, NSC-68—an appraisal of defense requirements worldwide in the struggle with the Soviet Union—was prepared in 1950 but in 1973 remained classified and inaccessible.

[11] For a broad discussion of the political implications see David Wise. *The Politics of Lying: Government Deception, Secrecy, and Power.* New York: Random House, 1973; the problem as it affects scholars is examined in Carol M. Barker and Matthew H. Fox. *Classified Files: The Yellowing Pages: A Report on Scholars' Access to Government Documents.* New York: Twentieth Century Fund, 1972.

[12] U.S. Department of State. *United States Relations with China with Special Reference to the Period 1944-1949.* Washington: U.S. Government Printing Office, 1949. Reissued with an introduction by Lyman P. Van Slyke as *The China White Paper,* August, 1949. Cloth in one volume, paper in two. Stanford: Stanford University Press, 1964.

[13] The facsimile, censored, official edition is U.S. Department of Defense. *United States-Vietnam Relations, 1945-1967,* 12 vols. Washington: U.S. Government Printing Office, 1971. The so-called Senator Gravel edition, *The Pentagon Papers,* 4 vols., Boston: Beacon Press, 1971, with supplemental volume, 1972, contains material censored in the official volumes. For a one-volume selection see the New York Times. *The Pentagon Papers.* New York: Quadrangle Books, 1971.

[14] A notable example of privileged use of classified material is Lyndon Baines Johnson. *The Vantage Point: Perspectives of the Presidency, 1963-1969.* New York: Holt, Rinehart and Winston, 1971. Other important memoirs published since 1961 are: Beatrice Bishop Berle and Travis Beal Jacobs, editors. *Navigating*

the Rapids, 1918-1971: From the Papers of Adolph A. Berle. New York: Harcourt Brace Jovanovich, 1973; Charles E. Bohlen. *Witness to History, 1929-1969.* New York: Norton, 1973; Chester Bowles. *Promises to Keep: My Years in Public Life, 1941-1969.* New York: Harper and Row, 1971; Dwight D. Eisenhower. *The White House Years: Mandate for Change, 1953-1956.* Garden City: Doubleday, 1963, and *Waging Peace, 1956-1961* (1965); John Kenneth Galbraith. *Ambassador's Journal: A Personal Account of the Kennedy Years.* Boston: Houghton Mifflin, 1969; Roger Hilsman. *To Move a Nation: The Politics of Foreign Policy in the Administration of John F. Kennedy.* Garden City: Doubleday, 1967; George F. Kennan. *Memoirs: 1925-1950.* Boston: Little, Brown, 1967, and *Memoirs: 1950-1963* (1972); Robert Murphy. *Diplomat Among Warriors.* Garden City: Doubleday, 1964.

[15] The one exception to the generally barren nature of public hearings are the so-called MacArthur Hearings, or more correctly, Senate Armed Services and Foreign Relations Committees, *The Military Situation in the Far East,* 5 vols. Washington: U.S. Government Printing Office, 1951.

[16] On the phenomenon of Cold War revisionism and its burgeoning literature see Thomas G. Paterson, editor. *The Origins of the Cold War.* Lexington: D. C. Heath, 1970; Robert W. Tucker. *The Radical Left and American Foreign Policy.* Baltimore: Johns Hopkins Press [for the Washington Center of Foreign Policy Research, School of Advanced International Studies, Johns Hopkins University], 1971; Robert James Maddox. *The New Left and the Origins of the Cold War.* Princeton: Princeton University Press, 1973. The seminal revisionist study is William Appleman Williams. *The Tragedy of American Diplomacy.* Rev. ed. New York: Dell, 1962. The most important studies of the Cold War are: D. F. Fleming. *The Cold War and Its Origins, 1917-1960.* Garden City: Doubleday, 1961; Louis J. Halle. *The Cold War as History.* New York: Harper and Row, 1967; Adam Ulam. *Containment and Co-Existence.* New York: Praeger, 1967; Herbert Feis. *From Trust to Terror: The Onset of the Cold War, 1945-1950.* New York: Norton, 1970; Lloyd C. Gardner. *Architects of Illusion: Men and Ideas in American Foreign Policy, 1941-1949.* Chicago: Quadrangle Books, 1970; Joyce and Gabriel Kolko. *The Limits of Power: The World and United States Foreign Policy 1945-1954.* New York: Harper and Row, 1972; John Lewis Gaddis. *The United States and the Origins of the Cold War, 1941-1947.* New York: Columbia University Press, 1972.

[17] For initial American policy and attitudes toward the United Nations see: Robert A. Divine. *Second Chance: The Triumph of Internationalism in America During World War II.* New York: Atheneum, 1967; and Ruth B. Russell. *A History of the United Nations Charter: The Role of the United States, 1940-1945.* Washington: Brookings Institution, 1958.

[18] The literature on NATO is enormous and often of ephemeral value. The following have some lasting value: Richard E. Neustadt. *Alliance Politics.* New York: Columbia University Press, 1970; Henry A. Kissinger. *The Troubled Partnership: A Re-appraisal of the Atlantic Alliance.* New York: McGraw-Hill [for the Council on Foreign Relations], 1965.

[19] Richard N. Gardner. *In Pursuit of World Order: U.S. Foreign Policy and International Organizations.* Rev. ed. New York: Praeger, 1966.

[20] In addition to items in Footnote 4, see Samuel P. Huntington. *The Common Defense; Strategic Programs in National Politics.* New York: Columbia University Press, 1961; Harold Stein, editor. *American Civil-Military Decisions: A Book of Case Studies.* University; University of Alabama Press [in cooperation with the Inter-University Case Program], 1963.

[21] For a critique of the standard version of the Truman Doctrine and its spreading application around the world see Richard J. Barnet. *Intervention and Revolution: The United States in the Third World.* New York: World, 1968.

[22] Eugene Davidson. *The Death and Life of Germany: An Account of the American Occupation.* New York: Knopf, 1959; John Gimbel. *The American Occupation of Germany: Politics and the Military, 1945-1949.* Stanford: Stanford University Press, 1968.

[23] Frederick S. Dunn. *Peace-Making and the Settlement with Japan.* Princeton: Princeton University Press, 1963.

[24] The best studies of the Korean War are John Spanier. *The Truman-Mac-Arthur Controversy and the Korean War.* Rev. ed. New York: Norton, 1965; Allen Whiting. *China Crosses the Yalu; The Decision to Enter the Korean War.* New York: Macmillan, 1960; David Rees. *Korea: The Limited War.* New York: St. Martin's Press, 1964; Glenn D. Paige. *The Korean Decision: June 24-30, 1950.* New York: Free Press, 1968.

[25] Herbert S. Parmet. *Eisenhower and the American Crusades.* New York: Macmillan, 1972.

[26] The most recent accounts, both challenges to the earlier almost worshipful volumes, are: Richard J. Walton. *Cold War and Counter-revolution: The Foreign Policy of John F. Kennedy.* New York: Viking, 1972; and Henry Fairlie. *The Kennedy Promise: The Politics of Expectation.* Garden City: Doubleday, 1973.

[27] One of the best studies of policymaking in the Johnson administration is Townsend Hoopes. *The Limits of Intervention; An Inside Account of How the Johnson Policy of Escalation in Vietnam Was Reversed.* New York: McKay, 1969.

[28] For memoir-history based on this assumption see Rostow. *The Diffusion of Power.* Footnote 6.

[29] In this category see the best account of the diplomacy of the Vietnam war written by an American participant, Chester L. Cooper. *The Lost Crusade: America in Vietnam.* New York: Dodd, Mead, 1970.

[30] Two examples are: Noam Chomsky. *American Power and the New Mandarins.* New York: Pantheon Books, 1969; and Richard J. Barnet. *Roots of War.* New York: Atheneum, 1972.

[31] Frances Fitzgerald, *Fire in the Lake: The Vietnamese and the Americans in Vietnam,* Boston: Little, Brown, 1972, stands out.

[32] Garry Wills. *Nixon Agonistes: The Crisis of the Self-Made Man,* Boston: Houghton Mifflin, 1970, is a perceptive analysis. The best history of foreign policy during the first term is Henry Brandon. *The Retreat of American Power.* Garden City: Doubleday, 1973. Also see: David Landau. *Kissinger: The Uses of Power.* Boston: Houghton Mifflin, 1972; and Stephen R. Graubard. *Kissinger: Portrait of a Mind.* New York: Norton, 1973.

[33] See the interesting essays in Henry Owen, editor. *The Next Phase in Foreign Policy.* Washington: Brookings Institution, 1973.

BOOK DESIGN AND PRODUCTION by *Willadene Price*